Different Nationalisms

Different Nationalisms

Bengal, 1905–1947

SEMANTI GHOSH

OXFORD
UNIVERSITY PRESS

OXFORD
UNIVERSITY PRESS

Oxford University Press is a department of the University of Oxford.
It furthers the University's objective of excellence in research, scholarship,
and education by publishing worldwide. Oxford is a registered trademark of
Oxford University Press in the UK and in certain other countries.

Published in India by
Oxford University Press
YMCA Library Building, 1 Jai Singh Road, New Delhi 110 001, India

ISBN-13: 978-0-19-946823-2
ISBN-10: 0-19-946823-0

Typeset in Adobe Garamond Pro 10.5/12.5
by The Graphics Solution, New Delhi 110 092
Printed in India by Replika Press Pvt. Ltd

To My Parents

Contents

Abbreviations

AICC   All India Congress Committee
AIML   All India Muslim League
BLAP   Bengal Legislative Assembly Proceedings
BLCP   Bengal Legislative Council Proceedings
BPCC   Bengal Provincial Congress Committee
BPML   Bengal Provincial Muslim League
CPI   Communist Party of India
IOL   India Office Library
IOR   India Office Records
KPP   Krishak Praja Party
NAI   National Archives of India
WBSA   West Bengal State Archives

Acknowledgements

This book first took shape as a doctoral thesis presented to Tufts University (Medford, Massachusetts, USA) in 1999. Evidently, it has been a long journey. I have incurred so many debts of gratitude during this journey that to thank everyone adequately seems to be a challenging task.

The greatest debt, of course, has been to Sugata Bose, my supervisor at Tufts University during 1995–9. He has been supporting the project since it was launched. His scholarly insight has guided me in shaping the arguments of this book in a vital way. Also, while writing the book, he provided me with help and encouragement of the kind that went beyond the usual call of duty. Ayesha Jalal has been another pillar of support during all these years. Her appreciation of my work will remain a source of inspiration to me.

The research that has gone into this book was funded by a dissertation grant (1996–7) awarded by the South Asia Programme, Social Science Research Council (SSRC), New York. I am grateful to SSRC and the Ford Foundation for offering me the support to conduct research in

Bangladesh and West Bengal, India. I was also fortunate to receive a generously funded write-up fellowship from Tufts University in 1998–9. I had the opportunity of presenting parts of the thesis at the SSRC conference in Bangladesh in 1996, and at a number of conferences organized by the Center for South Asian and Indian Ocean Studies at Tufts University between 1997 and 1999.

Working in the archives and libraries in search of source materials was not always a fun experience. I remember with deep gratitude the patient assistance provided by the librarians and staff at the following institutions: in London, UK, at the India Office Library (now part of the Oriental and India Office Collections at the British Library); in New Delhi, at the National Archives of India; in Kolkata, at the West Bengal State Archives, the National Library, and the Bangiya Sahitya Parishat Library; in Bangladesh, at the Bangladesh National Archives, Bangla Academy, and Dhaka University Library in Dhaka, the Barendra Museum in Rajshahi, the Chittagong University Library and Museum in Chittagong, and the Mymensingh Public Library in Mymensingh. I was particularly fortunate in receiving short-term affiliations from the Asiatic Society of Bangladesh and Bangla Academy in Dhaka. During my stay in Bangladesh, I benefited greatly from the long discussion sessions with insightful scholars and writers such as the late Salahuddin Ahmed, Anisuzzaman, Mustafa Nurul Islam, Abul Momen, Jamil Chaudhuri, Mofidul Haque, and Shamsuzzaman Khan. My research assistants, Hasan and Apu in Dhaka, and Mohua in Kolkata, were staunchly by my side during the frantic times spent in the archives and libraries.

Outside the libraries, the endless critical engagements with Maitreesh Ghatak were helpful in shaping my arguments. I fondly remember how the time spent with Chitralekha Zutshi, Prachi Deshpande, and Neeti Nair, three young historians-in-the-making at Tufts in the late 1990s, stimulated new ideas and helped to make old ones clearer. My thanks to Modhumita Roy, who teaches English Literature at Tufts yet possesses an enviable grip on Bengali culture and literature, for taking an interest in this work. I am grateful to David Ludden for his generous comments when I 'defended' my dissertation in 1999.

No words of gratitude can be enough for the wonderfully generous Nahas Khalil, Rupa Sayef, and Saif-ud-daula who opened their home to me in Dhaka and made me a part of their extended family ever since. During the last stage of my doctoral research, Sumita and Somnath Basu offered a sort of lavish hospitality which one can never repay.

While processing the book more than a decade after the PhD chapter, I have received invaluable help from Swapan Majumdar, Indrajit Chaudhury, Rushati Sen, Biswajit Ray, Jayanta Sengupta, Kumar Rana, and Arun Bandyopadhyay in Kolkata, Pias Majid and Arun Basu in Dhaka, and Mou Banerjee in Cambridge, USA. Indrajit Chaudhury, in particular, has been absolutely tireless in lending me books from his own collection. Saktidas Ray, who is in charge of the Anandabazar Patrika library and archives, has been a great support. The late Asoke Sen read through parts of an early draft and gave me precious advice. His wish to see this book in print had to remain unfulfilled, but various parts of this book indeed bear marks of his engagement. I am grateful to Sekhar Bandyopadhyay for writing a very encouraging review of my previous book comprising Bengali articles (2012) based on this research. My special thanks to Rudrangshu Mukherjee, a caring friend who never refuses to be a mentor when I need one. Dipesh Chakrabarty and Rochona Majumdar have provided support in many more ways than they would give themselves credit for. I am especially indebted to Anirban Bandyopadhyay who has taken a great deal of time off his own work to help me out on numerous instances. Madhuparna Banerjee proofread an earlier version of the manuscript and helped me improve the text.

My sincere gratitude goes to the editorial team of Oxford University Press, New Delhi, for their endless patience and care for this project. The book has benefited substantially from the generous yet critical comments made by two anonymous reviewers.

This book would simply not have been possible without the support of Anirban Chattopadhyay, the editor of *Anandabazar Patrika* and the head of its Editorial Department, where I have been working for the past one and a half decades. It is he who gave me his encouragement unsparingly and provided me with the space to pursue my dream.

Friends have always been a very important part of my life as well as this book, which has seen its making through various phases in Boston, Chicago, London, Dhaka, and Kolkata. Shreemantee Chaudhury, Sreeroopa Sarkar, Abanti Ghosh, Bidisha Ghosh Biswas, Bidisha Mukherjee, Ranjini Lahiri, Paromita Ghosh Majumdar, Rajashi Mukhopadhyay, Niaz Majumdar, Damayanti Datta, Tuli Banerjee, Aveek Majumdar, Pratik Chakrabarti, Indrajit Ray, Bhaswati Chatterjee, Srobona Bose Dutta, Madhumita Nag, Amitava Gupta, Siladitya Sen, Rangan Chakravarty, Paromita Chakrabarti, Sunandan Chakraborty, Sreemoti Mukherjee-Roy, Ananda Roy, Tisa Biswas, Sahana Ghosh, and Swachchashila Basu all had unflagging faith in me. The support and affection of my sister, Sravanti Bhowmik, brother-in-law, Someswar Bhowmik, and the family of my sister-in-law, Ditipriya Sarkar, have always provided me with cherished shelter. Srotaswini, my niece, never failed to be a source of joy and pride.

Disha Manaswini and Dariya Tarangini have now spent almost all of their lives hearing about this book being in the making. While both of them patiently shared their mother with this book, I cannot imagine writing it without having them as my most adorable distraction on a daily basis. Tridibesh Bandyopadhyay knows how much I owe him. His unshakeable support and quiet nudging made this book possible.

Since when I was a little girl, my parents, Sankha Ghosh and Pratima Ghosh, have been teaching me the value of respecting difference in every sphere of life. My interest in the social and cultural history of pre-partition Bengal was also aroused by their own lively interest in the subject. Their faith in me has been an abiding source of strength throughout. I dedicate this book to them.

Kolkata
30 June 2016

Introduction

This book is about the scope and possibilities of nationalism in Bengal between 1905 and 1947. The period between the partition of the province in 1905 and the great Partition dividing the province as well as the country in 1947 was witness to a unique experience of imagining 'nations' in Bengal. I use the term in plural deliberately. There indeed emerged *many* contested visions of nationhood and alternative frameworks for its realization, producing a richly nuanced discourse. This book explores the process by which an overarching concept of a grand, unifying nation came to be haunted and challenged by various 'other' nationalisms, based on 'other identities', or 'other kinds' of ideological formulations. The lynchpin for all these contesting nationalisms was the notion of 'difference', which emerges within any perceived nation and counters the ambitious claims from within any conceivable nation. These alternative imaginings of the nation could hardly be deemed 'anti-national' even if the dominant discourse on the nation-state might wish to label them as such.

Although nationalism has been an over-explored problematic in the historiography of South Asia in general, and colonial Bengal in particular, the multiple perspectives on nation were often glossed over. The terms 'nation' and 'nationalism' have usually been considered in a one-dimensional way. The central problematic of this book is to question this customary assumption. It intends to break up this one-dimensional or un-problematized category of nationalism to unravel its myriad internal imaginaries. When I read about the relationships between colonialism, anti-colonial nationalism, and the assertions of cultural difference, I often found myself in deep discomfort as it seemed impossible for me to overlook the very fundamental dissimilarities in the ways these relationships had been perceived by the Bengali nationalists. They were nationalists, no doubt, but their nations appeared so very different from each other. I wanted to probe deeper into the matter of whether these nations only appeared so, or if in reality too they denoted different qualifiers. At the same time, when I read about the competing definitions of identity, and the so-called oppositional connection between these identities and the claims to nationhood, I felt somewhat perplexed by not being able to analyse many Bengali politicians and ideologues who combined their nations with the claims of identity rather deliberately. This sense of bewilderment has motivated me in pursuing this study of the contesting and contending voices of Bengali nationalism, both its Hindu and Muslim variants. In the course of my study, I could appreciate what Sumit Sarkar indicated a few years ago to be the most valuable legacy of nationalism: 'self-criticism, debate, internal dissent'.[1] Also, the study revealed that there existed certain patterns amidst the dissenting voices, as well as certain alternative structures of national politics and ideology. It suggested that the historiographical neglect of these variations has not, perhaps, helped us to assess the value of 'difference'. The point is not that differences have so far been ignored or overlooked, but that they might have been overemphasized as difference *alone*. I have tried to show that it is possible to think and write about multiple nationalisms in Bengal, some of which, instead of dismissing difference, often accepted them and sought to forge a space for negotiating with them.

By questioning the singularity of nationalism, my book also aims to address a few historical assumptions related to this. Some of these questions have already proved to be particularly vexing in the historiography of South Asia. My study of Bengali nationalism once again confronts the supreme urgency of these questions, the first one being the nature of communities. That it is rather uncharitable to relegate all references to community as 'communal' ideology, and dismiss them as antithetical to nationalism, is now a well-heard argument.[2] Ayesha Jalal argues, 'The problem of difference in South Asia ... cannot begin to be addressed without forsaking the dichotomies between "secular" and "religious" as well as "nationalism" and "communalism".'[3] By taking up this important question once again, this book gestures towards very distinct and powerful imaginations of 'nation' by Bengal Muslims, in which community relates to nation in ways far from antithetical. In constituting this imaginary of the community, premised, among other things, on 'religious–cultural' markers, the Bengali Muslims did not rule out the possibilities of negotiating with 'regional' or broader 'national' identities. This book claims that community consciousness is neither definitionally closed to nationalist consciousness, nor must it be collapsed into it. The ties between nation and community were variously conceived by different strands *within* the community. These internal differences within a community generated multiple articulations of nationalism.

It is, therefore, counterproductive to envisage communal ideology as the exclusive site where notions of community and religion manifest themselves. The community as a whole never constituted *an* alternative nation. On the contrary, it is crucially important to reclaim the alternative, often mutually conflicting, imaginaries of the possible nation from within the folds of the community. Indeed a major objective of this work is to explore the varied ways in which 'difference' was problematized, to move beyond the unwarrantedly essentialized form in which it is commonly understood or, worse still, dismissed out of the domain of engaged historical scholarship.

The second question this study finds critical in this context is the relationship between the 'nation' and the 'region', as well as the practicality and worth of the 'region–nation', if any. This book finds that regional, that is, 'Bengali' identity indeed formed the axis around which a number of these nationalist articulations revolved. Among both the Bengali Hindu and the Bengali Muslim strands of national imaginings, 'region' remained a critical constituent, with all its linguistic and cultural particularities, primarily as a space for common national belonging for different communities. Such was the potency of the linguistic–regional nation imaginary that it could, and arguably did, offer eminently possible solutions to the complex challenges of the supra-regional nation.

Yet it would be a mistake to assume that there was *one* particular strand of regional nationalism as such which pitted itself against any supra-regional nationalism. 'Bengali nationalism' was hardly ever consciously and coherently styled as *the* competing ground against Indian nationalism. Various diverse strands of nationalism, each foregrounding and espousing the regional identity, negotiated between themselves. The regional identity itself was thus distributed across multiple articulations, resulting in a number of parallel nationalistic perspectives, which were eventually appropriated by the all-India singular nationalism in its urge to co-opt and then mobilize the abundant energy of the linguistic–national spirit.

All this makes clear that the 'other' identities like region and religion did not always necessarily impede the cause of nationalism in an absolutely antagonistic manner. In fact, they often assisted the realized experience of the nation at key moments of its articulation. There is no dispute that the eventual failure of these alternative formulations is a historical fact. But it is also important not to overemphasize this failure. It remains an important task for the postcolonial historian to recover the salience of the difference in the different, as this book will argue. In pursuing the task, this book aims to be more than yet another review of Bengali Muslim history, or an apology for the religiously informed cultural identities. At the same time, in spite of its exploration of the concept of regional nation in Bengal, this study does not intend to make a case for a Bengali nationalism as constitutively antagonistic to Indian nationalism. The purpose here is to highlight the immense, and immensely rich, possibilities of anti-colonial nationalism, and show a trajectory by which the creed of an overarching singular nationalism eventually eclipsed these 'other' nations. Of course, the inscrutabilities of Indian postcolonial experiences are well worth the exercise of revisiting these alternative 'national' possibilities working themselves out during the colonial period.[4]

Exploding Nationalism[5]

The notion of the colonial state had once brought with it strong ideas of singularity by its conception of the nation-state. That import of singular significance was responded to with a counter-ideology called 'nationalism' through subsequent mediations of various processes of incremental and qualified reception. Not unnaturally, this counter-ideology in its turn foregrounded an analogous spirit of oneness in its social and political aspirations. However, within and outside this imported creed of the singular nation, the material reality of colonial India did not match the elevated conceit of 'one nationalism' in its projected uniform march towards 'progress' or 'equality' or 'empowerment'. This process of engaged reception was, therefore, characterized throughout by multiple ideologies and made for irreversible manifestations of multiple national-isms in its course. Therein lay the paradox, right at the crossroads of the conflicting impulses of grand, uni-centric nationalism and smaller nationalisms within the contradictions of singularity and plurality.

Confronted with this paradox, most of the Indian experiences before and after 1947 have been apologetic about their 'deviations' from this singularity as 'anti-nation' or 'communal'. The persistent pre-occupation with 'oneness' led to the labelling of all present and past visions of nation as deviant, that is, as somehow not fully subscribing to the cherished ideal of 'oneness'. While the story of the intolerant, non-engaging 'two-nation' politics had been in constant focus during the late colonial period in India, the overwhelming domination of the 'one-nation' nationalism has been less attended to. But, curiously, both were rather similar, often a mirror-image of each other, in terms of their homogenizing impulse and the consequent drive of overruling any internal variations or identities within themselves. Just as the proponents of the infamous 'two-nation' theory' were completely averse to admit any other interests or identities within their perceived boundaries of two mutually exclusive nations, the protagonists of the 'one-nation vision' were equally dismissive of any rights or claims emerging from within their projectedly self-defining and centralizing imaginary. The first part of the story is already rectified, as it were, by nuanced historiographical interventions. Regarding the Muslim identity in South Asia, historians have already found it much too complex and marked by too many internal variations to be neatly termed as 'communalism', readily preparing the ground of the eventual Partition.[6] However, the latter part of the story is, at best, only half-heartedly hinted at. The task of exploding the much glorified, and vilified, singular category of 'nationalism' must now be addressed in order to recover the claims of difference from within the folds of nationalism itself.

Even the less conventional explanations of colonial nationalism, offered, for instance, by the Subaltern Studies Collective[7] against the classical historiography of a glorified 'nation', fall short of this task. When the 'fragment' of the nation discards the concept of 'modular nationalism' drawn from the Western models of nation-making exercises,[8] recovering the autonomy of the inner, spiritual domain of colonial nationalism,[9] it perhaps invests an excessive dose of autonomy within the fragment, effectively undermining its overlaps with larger imaginings of the nation and projecting them into possible nations in themselves.[10] The community as a challenge to the larger, and presumably restrictive, claims of the 'nation' then emerges as the 'other' nation by itself, which 'can give to [itself] a historically valid justification only by claiming an alternative nationhood with rights to an alternative state'.[11] Thus Partha Chatterjee's 'fragments' can be read to lead to alternative monoliths, which resist the further problematization of their own internal dissensions.[12] The internal dynamics of power and exploitation within the fragments tend to be blurred, and complex realities of tension, dissension, and contestation obfuscated. We are almost persuaded into wishing away that 'fragments' are imagined communities too, that their boundaries too are likewise arbitrary and shifting.[13] We are tempted to overlook the fact that the boundaries of these communities or 'fragments' are not impermeable, but organically tied with other communities based on other identities. This book aligns itself with the view that a shared religiosity does not by itself provide the Muslims of India an exclusive cognitive identity or an exclusive political positioning vis-à-vis other communities. A careful meandering through the internal configuration of contestations within a community is most critical for locating alternative, and complexly empowering, nationalist perspectives.

As a matter of fact, the much-professed aim of exploring the layered and shared identities can be meaningful only when it addresses how, and through which trajectories of dialogic negotiation, an individual or a collective of individuals within a community takes on a variety of forms to imagine and prioritize their multiple identities.[14] The Bengali Muslim community, for example, represented a reasonably well-formulated regional–religious identity within the broader category of the Indian Muslims, but at the same time betrayed a number of trends within itself in terms of their equation with the larger nation and approached the problem of difference in a widely varying manner. There indeed was a trend of Islamic exclusivism in Bengal during the 1940s. In reality, this trend was not characteristically tied to this decade only. Even in the 1910s, we have heard cries of 'Islam in danger', or desperately angry statements like the Bengal Muslims should 'cut off all connections with' the Muslim League if it associated itself with the 'Hindu politics of Congress'.[15] In short, this trend of ultra-conservative Islamic nationalism was not a new import in Bengal. But the existence of this trend by itself does not imply that Bengali Muslim discourse was wholly represented by it, or that the latter was devoid of any 'national' interest other than its 'Muslim' interest. What I would like to point out is that while the notions of nation and its structure were being experimented with, the primary impulse of negotiating differences for a larger cause never disappeared. There must be a critical distinction between the communitarian identity mobilizations and struggles in which 'religion played an important organizational role', or negotiations and communal identities where 'religion played the role of deeper cognitive exclusion' or separation.[16] The distinction implied here is that while the unwarranted conflation of any religiously informed cultural or political position as being 'communal' needs to be avoided, it is also critical to note the ideological or political challenge hidden in such positions around the emphasis on their difference.

The primary focus of this book lies here. Indeed this argument runs through the entire scope of this work. It notes that, during and after the swadeshi movement, many Bengali Muslims relentlessly emphasized their differences with the projected swadeshi nation and at the same time asserted their own agency and role in the newly emerging nation. This is why leaders like Maniruzzaman Islamabadi of eastern Bengal sought to promote a *swajati andolana*, akin to the swadeshi model in its 'national' objectives and agenda, but carefully distinguished from the Hindu cultural accents and urban elite preoccupations of swadeshi. This trend continued through the following three decades to reveal its full potential in the ideal of 'Pakistan' or 'Purba Pakistan' (East Pakistan) in the 1940s. The strong regional component of the Pakistan movement as it developed in Bengal must be studied as an inheritance of this consistent cultural and political positioning of extensive sections of Bengali Muslim society in the earlier decades.[17] This Bengal version of Pakistan represented a different nationalism, struggling its way through the quagmires of colonial politics. I would point out that right since the Bengali Muslim nation during the swadeshi era up to the Pakistan politics as it developed in Bengal, there was a very strong critique and an emphatic rejection of Congress nationalism. The typically Congress claims of representing 'all' communities and classes in India was potently challenged in these 'other' nationalisms. The argument heard all over was that in a country with very diverse identities and interests, no 'all-India' organization could speak for all, or at least for the very specific case of theirs. If a separate state of Pakistan was one of the alternative structures that emerged in the course of such opposition, there was also another, perhaps more persistent and more cherished, imagery of nation, essentially federal in nature, conceding the space for substantial regional autonomy.

It is by now a more or less forgotten fact of history that this idea of a 'federal' nation was an extremely powerful vision in colonial Bengal.

Many Bengali Hindu and Bengali Muslim leaders have consistently underlined its absolute naturalness and strong merits in the Indian context. In fact, the explorations of a federal nation is another major theme that runs through this book, only to point out that there was nothing called *the* Hindu nation or Hindu nationalism.[18] Especially in the case of Bengal, the imaginations of nation and political experiments with nation were only too variegated to be lumped together as a 'Hindu' discourse. Instead of equating the whole experience of nationalism with the brand of nationalism espoused by the Indian National Congress, and thereby forcing on it a complicity with Hindu majoritarianism, I would like to re-examine its internal shades. I would try to understand nationalist thought at large and its Congress version in particular separately but in a constant frame of association. In a way, then, I would like to rescue nationalism from its monolithic characterization by arguing that nationalism in Bengal indeed displayed a remarkable insight and alacrity to handle 'difference'. Even when it entailed a process of 'otherization', it did not immediately imply that combining with the 'others' was impossible or undesirable. These variegated experiments of nation must be remembered, decoded, and highlighted, as they contained within themselves remarkable possibilities of pluralist existence against the backdrop of identity politics.

Difference, Representation, and the Criticality of the Region

What does 'difference' mean in this context? Difference, a conceptual tool to be employed against the essentialization of categories used in an aspirational or practical context, usually plays a crucial role in distinguishing structural complexities of nationalist constructs. Theorists often describe difference as 'alternative fears', as an inevitable offshoot of 'the imagination as a social practice'.[19] With nations and nationalisms, these alternative spaces for imagining one's own belongings had a particularly close relationship. Moreover, in colonial societies, difference becomes an unavoidable counter-category, since it is on the basis of such disjuncture that national rights have to be asserted. In some ways, these contending rights open the floodgates of contesting claims for sovereignty from within the domain of an aspiring nation.

A number of constitutive dilemmas for the colonial modern subject surfaces here.[20] One among these was about the idea of difference itself. On the one hand, difference from the colonial rulers as an ideological construct has to be evoked to raise claims of self-assertion and self-rule.

On the other, an erasure of difference also emerges as a necessary condition within the internal realms of nationalism, without which the projected emergence of a modern nation simply fails to materialize. The colonial subject is therefore condemned to struggle for his or her right as a unified collective against the colonial ruler, and at the same time, to resolve the reality of fragmented identities within his or her own society. Faced with this dilemma, perceptions of the 'self' and the 'other' reveal striking quirks of imagination in unavoidable engagements with perceived and experienced contradictions in articulation.

Once the claims of difference emerge, an urge for representation follows inescapably.[21] Representing one's own identity and difference appears to be a cultural process to begin with, and then a political struggle in the course of time. Such politicization follows in order to institutionalize the individual and collective identities as an established practice to be performed by the rules and protocols of an emerging representative democracy, albeit in a limited form. This process is not accidental. Rather, it can be mapped in history. The process of representing identity carries a profoundly symbolic charge as possible clues to existential questions of identity: Who am I? What could I be? Who do I want to be? Discourses and systems of representation thus build spaces where individuals imagine themselves as inhabiting a collective, from where they launch themselves outward and speak to imagined interlocutors likewise situated. The contestations around the axes of an imagined Bengali nation in the first few decades of the twentieth century offer an important case study with which to explore the process of ideological constructions of difference, to be followed immediately by the emergence of a politics of difference, mediated in unanticipated and unpredictable directions by the burgeoning demands of representation of the self and the collective.[22]

The 'self' in this context does indeed assume different forms at different times, often without any implied conflict between its potential forms. Sometimes it is the communitarian self, sometimes it is the regional self, at other times it might well signal a supra-regional self. Identities and the layers of the self coexist simultaneously, side by side, manifesting themselves in varying contexts and negotiating among themselves the pressing needs of anti-colonial nationalism. The swadeshi movement in early twentieth-century Bengal is especially remarkable for the very first visible change in the numerous articulations of this self in the nationalist discourses of various shades. Not only did the number of tracts or journals or articles suddenly soar, the kinds and degrees of articulation around themes of identity too reached an unprecedented height and stretched to an unanticipated width at the same time. The claims to belonging to a collectivity of any sort as well as the claims of an assertive individuality were brought forth for the first time with so much clarity and force. This book begins with some such resilient articulations of the swadeshi era.[23]

The relentless shift back and forth from the individual to the collective remains an important characteristic of the national narratives of Bengal. In this study I seek to map the shifting focus on the self and on the collective in nationalist imagination. A continuous attention, therefore, is devoted to tracts and articles written during this time by individual authors, not professedly speaking for a clearly projected community. Beyond the customary doubts about who or what passes for a proper and rightful representation, I find such a strategy particularly helpful to address the complex processes of identity formation in a fluid climate of multiple ideological formulations. Jalal had once emphasized in the context of Muslim discourse on the need of 'keeping a balance between the individual and the community, [which] steers the analysis away from an essentialization of Muslim identity and politics'.[24] This strategy remains arguably valid for all kinds of discursive history that hopes to discern the kernel of the self-in-the-making from within messy processes of identity formulation.

Difference was not merely a 'Muslim' anxiety in colonial India. There were other identities too, fashioning their own distinct claims vis-à-vis the grand narratives of the nation. The caste discourse of Bengal was equally mediated by an analogous charge.[25] This book refers to caste discourses in the course of its arguments, although it does not dwell upon caste politics at length. With the focus firmly on religious and regional identities, this study underlines its principal argument that the problematic of difference must be seen as an unavoidable by-product of the fundamental premises of anti-colonial nationalism itself, which aims to institutionalize a cultural performance of sovereignty overwriting all underlying particularities. In doing this, the nationalists faced a curious predicament in colonial Indian society, where politics of representation, and thereby politics of enumeration, was gradually unfolding itself. On the one hand, the urgency of reorganizing the nation's base through greater popular mobilization was felt more acutely in the context of the new discourse of adult suffrage. On the other, the nation's emphasis on the indivisibility and uniformity was rendered more and more unfit for this new context due to the countless claims of diversity and difference within the larger Indian society. Consequently, the more the nation felt the urge to broaden its base, the more it was pushed to a quandary on the issue of difference.

It being so, an exploration of the problematic of difference can never be strictly confined to marginal or non-hegemonic discourses. It was just as manifestly constitutive to mainstream or hegemonic strands of nationalism, albeit informed by a distinct set of conceptual specificities. While deriving links between nation and its differences from the swadeshi days to the turbulent years of the 1940s, I argue that the proposed schemes for managing the problem of difference in ideology and politics of the so-called Hindu nationalists were varied and often mutually conflicting.[26] The engagements between these differences or marginalities on the one hand and the anxiety for a nation-to-be-realized on the other, therefore, call for some careful untangling. A major task before the nationalist project of the Bengali Hindu was to address the challenge of difference as the most vexing 'problem'. The hegemonic nationalism discourse often had to work out and recommend an urgent and modular 'cure' for this 'problem'. Again, for some, this was a 'problem' beyond any 'cure', so it was mandatory to negotiate with it. Some of them responded to the newly emerging claims of other identities with an urge to assimilate and subsume this difference within the contingently larger sign of the nation. Some, on the contrary, spoke for an alternative model of the nation with sufficient space for 'other' identities to proclaim themselves, that is, unprefaced by an overdetermining assimilation under all circumstances.[27] The latter were not the most devoted subscribers of the conventional nationalist tenets, and often found themselves consigned to the margins of history. I contend that these 'other' cultural or political formulations on the nation were formidable enough not to be written off as mere deviations.

Thus, the responses of Hindu-nationalist thinkers to the question of difference ranged from a broad universalism to inclusivism, not excluding assimilationism or a combinational nationalism. The long-term appeal of the universalist nation of Rabindranath Tagore could not be overestimated: his deep and relentless engagements with the problematic of difference earn him a central place in my narrative. There are also some relatively unfamiliar figures who deserve serious mention because of the sincerity of their engagement with the problematic of difference. For example, the swadeshi ventures of Aswinikumar Dutta in Barisal represented a creed of inclusionary secular nationalism. However, it was practically and discursively distinct from the 'composite nationalism' of Bepinchandra Pal or Aurobindo Ghose, which portrayed India as a 'federation of faiths' though with a definitive emphasis on the primacy of Hindu religious–cultural traditions. Yet another 'different' combinational approach was to be found in the new nationalism of Chittaranjan Das in the mid-1920s. His Bengal Pact might have remained incomplete as an administrative project and controversial as a conceptual proposition, but it indubitably promised an alternative stratagem of politics and a potentially rich paradigm of national(izing) ideology. Read intertextually as projections of strategic gestures towards realizations of the nation, these 'other' histories may tell us a more nuanced and much more poignant story about discursive practices in political and ideological nation-making in colonial Bengal.

Das believed that any accommodative project of nationalist politics and culture was not conceivable without powerful projections of the 'region–nation'. He was not exceptional in this regard. Nationalist ideologues or politicians of early twentieth-century Bengal very often turned the focus on regional expressions and linguistic culture, precisely because the bridging of the self and the community in Bengali national imagination seemed more readily realizable through the mediation of a linguistic–regional identity. The spatial–emotional construct of the region, performed and renewed through the universally accessible entitlement of a popular language, here provided a common platform for a people otherwise diverse in racial constitution and historical background. As a Bengali author has pithily written: '[W]ho would not accept that the southeastern part of Bengal populated by the descendants of Mongolian tribe, the south-western Bengalis largely coming from Dravidian lineage, and the traditional Brahmins directly descending from the north Indian Aryan tribes and the Bengali Mussalmans had nothing in common other than the language?'[28] Language and region thus provided an immediate location of, and hence a contesting ground for, collective belonging as compared to the remoteness of the vision of a grandly unitary Indian nation. Following the model of the Bangiya Sahitya Parishat of Calcutta (present-day Kolkata), founded in 1897 with an aim to promote studies of Bengali language and literature, a group of Muslim intellectuals introduced a literary association called the Bangiya Mussalman Sahitya Samiti in 1918. This was a direct cultural challenge, and also a not-so-pronounced project of fashioning a region–nation with a legitimacy provided for the religious identity. Significantly, before such challenges, the limits of Hindu nationalisms, even of the accommodative versions, were often exposed. When direct claims of the 'folk', the 'local', or the

Islamic forms of language were forcefully foregrounded, major literary stalwarts, including liberals like Rabindranath Tagore, could not but resist.[29] Nevertheless, the range of contending perspectives on managing linguistic difference was not exhausted by them. There were yet some others who openly enough acknowledged the need for 'a number of Bengali languages, rather than one standard Bengali',[30] and emphasized the need for the language to have a life and maturity of its own, especially during the process of nation-making. These attempts of reforming the liberal views from within before the problematic of difference appear to be of great significance from the nation's perspective.[31]

The political expressions and cultural debates on nation also present some 'other moments' of nationalist politics in Bengal. These moments were more inclusionary or accommodative in nature. The Bengal Pact (1924) of Chittaranjan Das mentioned earlier, the inter-community administration of Fazlul Huq in the early 1940s, or the propositions of an inter-community provincial administration in September 1946 or those of the 'United, Sovereign Bengal' of Suhrawardy, Abul Hashim, and Sarat Bose (June 1947) were some such moments.[32] I have noted that even when the political representation in the nation was accepted in general, there was a huge ground of contestation over the principles of that representation, as well as over the fundamental philosophical basis of those principles. The deep dissensions running through the region would make region in the end a significant dimension in nationalist imagining, but not a legitimate alternative nation.

Nevertheless, these dissensions made the region–nation full of potentials, but finally also diminished its critical political charge. This being so, despite the constant attempt of the Bengali leaders on both sides of the religious divide to resist the singularity projected both by the Congress and the Muslim League from the top, all the projects of regional nation finally had to surrender before the all-India 'national' bodies at the time of the Partition. The larger political contradictions of this 'national' story at the centre, embedded in the complicated majority–minority questions within and outside Bengal, emerged victorious in the end.

The 'Climax' of Partition?

In recent years, few other areas of academic scholarship in South Asian history have matured faster than Partition studies. While the focus of these new studies is on the social, cultural, economic, and psychological impact of the Bengal partition, political history of the Partition of India

too is breaking new ground.[33] However, there is something disconcert-
ing in the historiographical approaches to Partition, and it can be called
the 'inevitability narrative' for want of a better term. Much like the classical nationalist studies, the revisionist historiography of Partition also
suffers from a tendency of drawing a straight line of causality between
the pre-1947 events and the Partition of the province and the country
in 1947.[34] It is argued that 'communalism' was gradually rising in the
earlier decades, only to climax in the last years of colonial rule. Since
inter-community relations in the province were steadily and inevitably
deteriorating, the 'difference' had to be resolved only through an institutionalized separation of political domains. This view may be seen as the
ultimate *telos* of sub-continental history, starting at the climax and then
working backwards, only to narrativize a linear trajectory of communal
antagonism leading irreversibly to the final rupture. This makes for a
ready-made collapse of all references to religious identity, or possibly any
identity other than what is defined as 'national', with bigoted antagonism, and by extension, with a creed of separation.

Since the national and communal binary is denounced in this study
at the outset, I find this much-treaded historiographical path, a favourite
construction of this binary-driven narrative paradigm, particularly unacceptable. Such a narrative has no patience for the Hindus and Muslims
of Bengal who were keen to uphold their own religious–cultural identities, and yet opposed to partition of any kind, or who evoked an ardent
desire for framing a new 'federalized' nation with or without partition.
Most importantly, it does not wait to understand, explain, or analyse
the consistent and widespread efforts of individuals and communities
at 'normalization' of social realities working themselves out even amid
a backdrop of violence, or their frantic disbelief till the last moment at
the particular solution the politicians finally agreed upon. It is, therefore,
hard to be persuaded by the suggestion of the parochial and inward
Bengali bhadralok classes.[35] Such a suggested paradigm does not pay
enough attention to complicated discursive and imaginary potentialities
being worked out all the time until it became impossible not to accept
the fait accompli, without unacceptably high and intense personal and
collective unsettlements.[36] In an attempt to underline the enormity of
this gap, this book points towards the range of options Bengali society
had been struggling with, and the implied hope and resilience that they
embodied and projected, both inwards and outwards.[37]

Since these trends of regional accommodation finally gave in to the
demands of extra-regional pressures, partition should be seen as an

unfortunate deviation, an anticlimax of the history of Bengal nationalism. Rather than marking communalism or separatism as its overwhelming backdrop, I look for its clues in this particular disjunction. Partition in Bengal was more of a structural impasse resulting out of the contradictions of the politics of a Hindu-majority country and a Muslim-majority region than the unavoidable trajectories of communal animosities unfolding themselves within the region.[38]

Structuring the Narratives

This book is arranged in a chronological rather than a thematic order, presumably against current trends within the discipline. The reason is two-fold. First, the gradual unfolding of the dilemma underlying the national imaginings in Bengal is best studied as a continuous story running through real historical time. Second, the ideas of belonging and representation have been integrally made and remade in engagement with evolving political contexts. These political contexts were powerful enough to influence and change the imagined and lived meanings of terms such as 'identity', 'community', 'belonging', or 'representation'. In exploring the interdependence of ideology and politics, it is useful to track the evolving historical contexts over these few eventful decades. However, while the chapters are broadly arranged in a chronological way, within the chapters I break up the narrative into a number of themes for convenience of analysis.

The first chapter opens with the partition of Bengal in 1905 and ends in 1911 with the revocation of that partition. Contrary to what is widely believed, the discontent and jubilations after the announcement of the partition were not exactly identifiable respectively with the Hindus and Muslims of the region. The responses were far too complex for such a neat, water-tight identification. The Bengal Muslims were deeply divided on the project of 'nation', and on the possible compromises between their regional and religious identities. The Hindu ideologues and politicians also engaged with the problem of difference with an unprecedented intensity. Nowhere in India during this time were identity issues so fiercely debated by the highest rungs of intelligentsia and by the common people alike than in Bengal. The nature of the discourse shows that the support for the partitioned province must not be seen as anti-nationalism, but differently positioned nationalisms charged by a multi-dimensional Bengali identity. The swadeshi movement, however nationalist it may have seemed at the outset, unfortunately missed this important opportunity of acknowledging the claims of difference from within a nation. Swadeshi Bengal thus provides a unique case with such early expositions of identity discourse in the aftermath of a provincial partition. Controversies on social and cultural identities gradually led to the debates on its political representation.

The second chapter explores the debates on constitutional representation, the new grounds of 'cultural politics' during 1912–25. The imperative of deriving political rewards on the basis of social or cultural identity began to dominate the discourse of difference. Bengali Muslims claimed a greater share of representation within the province, but at the same time characteristically upheld the 'Bengal Line' in the all-India Muslim politics. The question of cultural representation generated fierce debates on the forms of Bengali language. The Bengali Hindus also elevated the discourse of difference to a higher level, taking the vital cue from the limitations of the swadeshi experience. The more broad-based trends of accommodative and combinational nationalisms emerged in turn, as did a model of the federalized nation with the twin objectives of bringing the masses within its fold and addressing different identities with greater persuasion. If we may term these new approaches as 'new nationalism', Tagore and Das should be seen as the two most insightful protagonists.

The failure of Das's new nationalist politics set the tone of the third and fourth decades of twentieth-century Bengal, argues the third chapter. A resurgence of the unitary nation was matched by the hardening of the oppositional forces of difference. The opposing viewpoints on community clashed between themselves with an unprecedented ferocity. The political contestations took a bitter shape on the questions of separate representation. In political as well as in cultural realms, 'communal' mentality began to gain its strength vis-à-vis the 'communitarian' sensibilities. The latter, however, kept itself alive enough to represent a discernible trend, and based itself critically on the regional identity. The Bengali Muslim voices of the *Shikha–Saogat* groups and the Buddhir Mukti activists[39] were a case in point. In this context, the new phase of provincial elections opened up new possibilities of linking up the less extreme trends of the region. The rise of the Krishak Praja Party (KPP), coupled with the reorientation of the Congress and the Muslim League, brought about a fresh charge in popular politics in Bengal. The forces of inter-community negotiation survived the social and political disharmony in the end, and even made new inroads into the political realms.

One of the focal points of the fourth chapter (1937–45) is the KPP, a Muslim middle-class organization with a dual emphasis on Bengali identity and the agrarian interests of cultivator (*praja*) classes. The electoral coalition of interests in the provincial administration opened up new horizons for the region–nation. While forming such coalitions, Bengal witnessed certain significant moments of failure. The non-realization of the Congress–KPP alliance was the first moment of failure because it failed to bring forth a broad-based provincial agenda. The KPP agenda being soon hijacked and appropriated by the All India Muslim League (AIML) signified the second lost opportunity. The third moment of failure came when Fazlul Huq, the most accepted and charismatic leader of the region, joined hands with the Hindu Mahasabha and consequently lost his grip over a huge regional following. Chances of the region–nation were, nevertheless, sustained in various imaginative ways, the most interesting of which, albeit a bit counter-intuitive, was to be found in the project of 'Pakistan', or, more correctly, in the regional twist given to the idea of Pakistan.

The fifth chapter deals with the last two years of colonial Bengal, 1946–7, generally considered as a moment of climax of 'communalism' in Bengal. I question both the notions of 'climax' and 'communalism'. First, the enormously rich and complex discourse of difference of the earlier decades cannot pass as merely 'communal' in my analysis. Although there is no denying that a steady trend of communal politics made itself pronounced in Bengal throughout, especially in the late 1940s, but to illustrate this trend as *the* defining characteristic of Bengali Muslim society would be grossly misleading. The 'other' trends show how fluid the Bengali society was even in the trying times of late colonial Bengal. The final 'breach' in fact appeared due to the built-in contradictions between various levels of politics, and the people were finally forced to take sides on the abruptly devised solutions of a long-drawn sociopolitical problem. Second, unlike the earlier decades, the political developments of the last couple of years of colonial Bengal could no more hope to be 'regional' in nature, and had to succumb before the pressures of trans-regional forces. Bengal thus experienced an 'anticlimax' or a deviation from its earlier histories of dialogic engagement with the problem of difference. All these previous trends of dialogue were finally sidelined by an over-decisive and centrally orchestrated process of decolonization. The creed of unitary nation was made victorious, in the end, by defeating the alternative nations of the Bengali imagination and by reducing the rich discourse of difference, henceforth, to a mere footnote in the narrative of nation.

The over-deterministic historicity of the Partition of 1947 and the 'inevitability narrative' associated with it have left their distinct mark on both the history of divided Bengal and that of the new nation-state of India. Several scholarly studies as well as journalistic works[40] have indeed noted that the dual inheritors of Bengali identity, the Indian state of West Bengal and East Pakistan, later to become Bangladesh, bear a double-edged connection, one of a linguistic–cultural commonness, and the other of a lineage of disruption and distrust. This book joins with them in locating the source, intensity, and potential of the postcolonial conflicts in the colonial history of Bengal, and traces these connections in the reality of the contesting nationalisms of that era. The decisive assertion of a Bengali Muslim identity in the Language Movement of East Pakistan (1952) and Mukti-juddha or War of Liberation (1971), therefore, does not appear an essentially postcolonial development, 'a new linguistic nationalism',[41] or 'the rise of Bengali nationalism'[42] after 1947. It can be seen as the logical extension of the pre-1947 trends of Bengali Muslim nationalism conceived and realized through cultural contestations and political negotiations, impossible to be written off as a hazy and uncertain backdrop of a communally defined Partition of blinding importance.

Similarly, the impractical and precarious obsessions of the present Indian nation-state with a unifying national spirit or a singular perspective of national sovereignty, or with fetishizing a centralized model of governance over the states, cannot call for greater urgency for historians to trace the contested pasts of such concerns. The resilience of identity politics and demands of greater federalization, or even of secessionist politics in some places, inexorably point towards a counter-force lurking right beneath the surface of national society and its politics, steadily if stealthily making its way, about to trump the menacing trend of disregarding difference for the sake of a hyper-celebrated oneness. If analysed from the point of view of 'difference' and its continuous challenge against any overarching 'nation' in the pre-1947 era, this counter-force appears only familiar and natural. The post-1947 nation-state was not the best solution, but was only a step towards deeper confusion and greater impatience around the question of multiple identities.

This book is the culmination of my doctoral dissertation ('Nationalism and the Problem of Difference, Bengal 1905–47', Tufts University, Massachusetts, USA) completed in 1999. However, I believe its relevance is still compelling. Many of these postcolonial concerns and inadequacies are best understood if seen through the optic of the nation's tensive engagements with 'difference', the principal problematic of the book. On a more personal note, my experience in the world of Indian journalism in the intervening years has served well to reinforce my interest and deepen my own engagement with this problematic. A closer look at the contemporary politics and society of India has alerted me on a regular basis to the intransigence and intractability of the problem of difference, and has translated my presumably distant academic engagement into an everyday practice of conscious experience.

A final clarification is due here. The book concludes that the Partition of 1947 came more as an anticlimax than as the logical conclusion of the events preceding it. The purpose behind this claim is not to stir up a nostalgia for 'Bengali unity', delve into a retrospective search of possible ways to avert a calamitous Partition, or to offer a normative view on the 'right' or 'wrong' nations. The purpose and objective of exploring the backdrop of the non-obvious outcome of Partition is to underscore both the cognitive and functional challenges against the concept of nation in Bengal, and finally, to understand 'difference' not as deviation, but as an inescapable part of the order in every sphere of life, to be attended to by sustained and sincere engagement.

Notes

1. Sumit Sarkar, 'Preface', in *The Swadeshi Movement in Bengal, 1903–8* (new edition, Delhi: Permanent Black, 2010), p. xxiii.
2. This was heard emphatically from Ayesha Jalal in 'Exploding Communalism: The Politics of Muslim Identity in South Asia', in *Nationalism, Democracy and Development: State and Politics in India*, edited by Sugata Bose and Ayesha Jalal (Delhi: Oxford University Press, 1997), pp. 76–103; and *Self and Sovereignty: Individual and Community in South Asian Islam Since 1850* (Delhi: Oxford University Press, 2001). The argument is also made forcefully by Sugata Bose in 'Between Monolith and Fragment: A Note on the Historiography of Nationalism in Bengal', in *Bengal: Rethinking History, Essays in Historiography*, edited by Sekhar Bandyopadhyay (Delhi: Manohar, 2001). For the construction of a false notion of 'communal consciousness' in colonial India, see Farzana Sheikh, *Community and Consensus in Islam: Muslim Representation in Colonial India, 1860–1947* (Cambridge: Cambridge University Press, 1989). For the negation of the existence of difference within the Muslim community in order to define a 'Muslim' identity in India, see Faisal Devji, *Muslim Zion: Pakistan as a Political Idea* (London: Hurst & Company, 2013).
3. Jalal, 'Exploding Communalism', p. 102.
4. In this context, however, it is important to remember that there is a fundamental difference between colonial and postcolonial national experiences of India. Between the nation as espoused by the anti-colonial nationalism

in the pre-1947 era and the nation-state that emerged in 1947, there is a vast conceptual distance. Amartya Sen has cautioned us on the need to maintain this distinction between the idea of a nation and the discipline of a nation-state: 'The concept of "nation"... is made to take on whatever abuse of power and of violence that may be attributable to the *nation-state*.' See Amartya Sen, 'On Interpreting India's Past', in *Nationalism, Democracy and Development*, p. 25. In my view, the dual formulation of nation must be taken note of in its historical analysis. In one formulation, especially in its classical nationalist use, its aspirations of arriving at a sense of political identity which can be shared by many, and its consequent conceptual flexibility must be noted. Such flexibility is woefully absent in the structures of power the nation-state represents. The second formulation of nation, ideologically wedded to the concept of the modern nation-state, expresses the latter's preoccupation with 'oneness', and thus intends to remove all traces of heterogeneity within itself.

5. I have borrowed this phrase partially from Ayesha Jalal's 'Exploding Communalism', pp. 76–103. In this article she propounds that the multiple articulation of difference by the South Asian anti-colonial Muslims cannot be categorized as 'religious communalism' and needed to be 'exploded'.

6. Jalal, 'Exploding Communalism', and *Self and Sovereignty.*

7. The *Subaltern Studies* series, which started its journey in 1982, developed a postcolonial project of writing the history of India. It discarded traditional studies of nationalism, considering them trapped in the 'modular' forms of the national society propagated by the modern West. As a corrective measure, the subaltern histories, through various contexts and approaches, attempted to revive autonomous forms of imagination of the community as against the nation.

8. Benedict Anderson, *Imagined Communities: Reflections on the Origin and Spread of Nationalism* (London: Verso, 1983). Foregrounding the independence of colonial experiences of nationalism, a famous response to Anderson's influential work came from Partha Chatterjee, *The Nation and Its Fragments: Colonial and Post-colonial Histories* (Princeton: Princeton University Press, 1993).

9. P. Chatterjee, *Nation and Its Fragments*, p. 6.

10. Sugata Bose points out that the fragment of nation, that is, community, becomes troublingly singular in this analysis, and attains a legitimacy which, if posed against the grand narrative of nation, seems to present an alternative homogenizing category. See Sugata Bose, 'Between Monolith and Fragment'.

11. P. Chatterjee, *Nation and Its Fragments*, p. 238.

12. Chatterjee's 'fragments' in this respect reminds us of Guha's famous formulation of autonomous domains of politics, namely the elite and the subaltern. See Ranajit Guha, 'On Some Aspects of the Historiography of Colonial India', in *Subaltern Studies*, vol. 1, edited by Ranajit Guha (Delhi:

Oxford University Press, 1982). The autonomous domain of the subaltern subject in the 'fragment' has also been located in Gyanendra Pandey's work on the Partition. See his *Remembering Partition: Violence, Nationalism and History of India* (Cambridge: Cambridge University Press, 2001).

13. The cue may be taken from Benedict Anderson who warns us against Ernst Gellner's assertion that since national identity is fabricated, it must be inherently false. Gellner thereby appeared to suggest that 'true' communities do exist to which the nation can be juxtaposed. Anderson points out that 'communities are to be distinguished, not by their falsity/genuineness, but by the style in which they are imagined' (Anderson, *Imagined Communities*, p. 6). Gellner's argument that 'nationalism is primarily a political principle, which holds that the political and the national unit should be congruent', and hence it is a theory of political legitimacy can be found in his *Nations and Nationalism* (Oxford: Basil Blackwell, 1983).

14. It is indeed important to step beyond the cognitive monolith of the community if Chatterjee's point is to be accepted that 'people, living in different, contextually defined, communities, can coexist peacefully, productively and creatively within large political units' (Chatterjee, *Nation and Its Fragments*, p. 238).

15. *Muslim Hitaishi*, December 29, Report on Native Papers in Bengal (henceforth RNP), no. 1 of 1917, referred to in Chapter 2.

16. Sugata Bose, 'Between Monolith and Fragment', p. 288.

17. Whereas the Bengali Muslim identity has been well-explored so far, there is still room for recovering its multiple constructs through difference and for deciphering the negotiations between these constructs and the nation. Some important studies in this context are Harun-or-Rashid, *Foreshadowing Bangladesh: Bengal Muslim League and Muslim Politics, 1936–1947* (Dhaka: Asiatic Society of Bangladesh, 1987); Shila Sen, *Muslim Politics in Bengal, 1937–1947* (New Delhi: Impex, 1977); Taj-ul-Hashmi, *Pakistan as a Peasant Utopia: The Communalization of Class Politics in East Bengal, 1920–1947* (New York: Boulders, Co., 1992); Tazeen Murshid, *The Sacred and the Secular: Bengal Muslim Discourses, 1871–1977* (Calcutta: Oxford University Press, 1995); Neilesh Bose, *Recasting the Region: Language, Culture and Islam in Colonial Bengal* (New Delhi: Oxford University Press, 2014). An important contribution on Bengal Muslims in late-nineteenth-century Bengal is Rafiuddin Ahmed, *The Bengali Muslims, 1871–1906* (second edition, New York: Oxford University Press, 1988). Also see Asim Pada Chakrabarti, *Muslim Identity and Community Consciousness: Bengal Legislative Politics, 1912–1936* (Calcutta: Minerva, 1995); Chandiprasad Sarkar, *The Bengali Muslims: A Study in Their Politicization, 1912–1929* (Calcutta: K.P. Bagchi & Co., 1991).

18. Starting from the Cambridge School of historians, neo-Cambridge historians to the subaltern historians all share this view on nationalism. See Gordon Johnson, C.A. Bayly, and John F. Richards (gen. eds), *New*

Cambridge History of India (Cambridge: Cambridge University Press, 1987); John A. Gallagher, *The Decline, Revival and Fall of the British Empire* (Cambridge: Cambridge University Press, 1982). The most noteworthy contribution in this respect has been Joya Chatterji, *Bengal Divided: Hindu Communalism and Partition, 1932–1947* (Cambridge: Cambridge University Press, 1994). Also Bidyut Chakrabarty, *The Partition of Bengal and Assam, 1932–1947* (London: Routledge, 2004). The historians of Bengal Muslim politics also have corroborated this from the other end; see Neilesh Bose, *Recasting the Region*.

19. Arjun Appadurai, 'Disjuncture and Difference in the Global Cultural Economy', in *Modernity at Large: Cultural Dimensions of Globalization* (Minneapolis: University of Minnesota Press, 1996), p. 28.

20. A remarkable insight on the dilemma of colonial modernity was offered by Partha Chatterjee in *Nationalist Thought in the Colonial World: A Derivative Discourse?* (London: Zed Books, 1986), followed by his *Nation and Its Fragments*. For the extremely rich theoretical perspectives on 'difference' in the context of Indian history, see Ranajit Guha, 'On Some Aspects of the Historiography of Colonial India', in *Subaltern Studies*, vol. 1; Homi Bhabha (ed.), *Nation and Narration* (London: Routledge, 1990); Dipesh Chakrabarty, *Provincializing Europe and the Postcolonial Thought and Historical Difference: Potential and Pitfalls of (Non-) Western Approaches to History* (Princeton: Princeton University Press, 2000); Dipesh Chakrabarty, *Habitations of Modernity: Essays in the Wake of Subaltern Studies* (Chicago: University of Chicago Press, 2002); Sudipta Kaviraj, *The Invention of Private Life: Literature and Ideas* (New York: Columbia University Press, 2015).

21. As Partha Chatterjee reminded us, 'Even if we dismiss the sociological view that declares India to be a mere collection of discrete communities as a peculiarly colonial construct, we are apparently still left with a brand of postcolonial politics whose discursive forms are by no means free of that construct' (*Nation and Its Fragments*, p. 224). The present work is indebted to a great extent to this particular insight of Chatterjee.

22. The most intriguing study of the utterly complex connects between the self and the collective in colonial India, especially in its Muslim representations, is Jalal, *Self and Sovereignty*.

23. In his classic study of the swadeshi movement, Sumit Sarkar showed how to track the cultural traditions along with the political movements of a particular time. However, one may now feel the need for a better understanding of the range of cultural variations the Bengali nation had produced. See Sumit Sarkar, *Swadeshi Movement in Bengal*. The first chapter of this book captures the spectrum of these debates and dissents during the swadeshi period.

24. Jalal, 'Preface', *Self and Sovereignty*, p. xiv.

25. Sekhar Bandyopadhyay, *Caste, Protest, and Identity in Colonial India: The Namasudras of Bengal, 1872–1947* (second edition, Oxford: Oxford University Press, 2011); Dwaipayan Sen, '"No Matter How, Jogendranath Had to Be Defeated": Scheduled Caste Federation and the Making of Partition in Bengal, 1945–47', *Indian Economic and Social History Review* 49, no. 3 (2012): 321–64; Anirban Bandyopadhyay, 'Orchestrating a Signal Victory: Ambedkar, Mandal and the 1946 Constituent Assembly Election', in *Invoking Ambedkar: Contributions, Receptions, Legacies*, edited by Biswamoy Pati (Delhi: Primus Books, 2014), pp. 33–58.

26. There were certain important disagreements on the visualization of nation between the Bengali ideologues like Rabindranath Tagore and Abanindranath Tagore, both belonging to the same family and same socio-cultural traditions. This is particularly significant as Rabindranath showed a distinct lack of enthusiasm about the Bengal School of Art, a national-ist cultural project started by his nephew Abanindranath. The divergence was not accidental but essentially stemming from their different outlooks and priorities of nationalism. A recent study on both these ideologues is Ananya Vajpeyi, *Righteous Republic: The Political Foundations of Modern India* (Cambridge, MA: Harvard University Press, 2012).

27. In studying Bengal Muslim history, it is often forgotten that the Hindu Bengali discourse did not display a linear trend of 'otherization' of the Bengali Muslims, neither did it speak with one voice on the need of addressing the problem of difference. Such a reverse homogenization of the Bengali Hindu discourse may be found in R. Ahmed, *The Bengali Muslims, 1871–1906*; and Neilesh Bose, *Recasting the Region*, p. 26.

28. Sashibhushan Basu, 'Bangala Nationality', speech read in Rajshahi Sahitya Sammilan and published in *Prabasi* 10, part 2, no. 2 (January 1911 [Agrahayan 1317 BS]), pp. 119–27; no. 3 (February 1911 [Poush 1317 BS]), pp. 326–36; no. 4 (March 1911 [Magh 1317 BS]), pp. 415–20.

29. Rabindranath Tagore, 'Bhashar Katha', *Bangla Sabda-tattwa* (1935; reprint, Calcutta: Visva-Bharati, 1984), pp. 9–10. All citations refer to the 1984 edition.

30. Nareshchandra Sengupta, 'Bhashar Akar o Bikar', *Sammilan* 6, nos 5–6 (1916), p. 167.

31. Some of the recent contributions in this trend of regional history of nation are: Neeti Nair, *Changing Homelands: Hindu Politics and Partition of India* (Delhi: Permanent Black, 2011); Neilesh Bose, *Recasting the Region*; Prachi Deshpande, *Creative Pasts: Historical Memory and Identity in Western India, 1700–1960* (Delhi: Permanent Black, 2007); and Chitralekha Zutshi, *Languages of Belonging: Islam, Regional Identity and the Making of Kashmir* (Delhi: Orient Blackswan, 2003). However, while most of these studies focus on the interrelations between region and the nation as such, this book, by claiming region to be an altogether different dimension in conceiving

the nation itself, comes closer to another study by Swarupa Gupta, which discussed 'Bengal's negotiation of the region and the nation in conceptualizations of nationhood'. See Swarupa Gupta, *Notions of Nationhood in Bengal, Perspectives on Samaj, 1867–1905* (Leiden: Brill, 2009), p. 17.

32. This usually forgotten historical fact is mentioned in Leonard A. Gordon, 'Divided Bengal: Problems of Nationalism and Identity in the 1947 Partition', *Journal of Commonwealth and Comparative Politics* 16, no. 2 (1978): 136–68.

33. From the vast body of historical literature on Bengal partition, mention must be made of Gordon, 'Divided Bengal'; Suranjan Das, *Communal Riots in Bengal, 1905–1947* (New Delhi: Oxford University Press, 1991); Ayesha Jalal, *The Sole Spokesman: Jinnah, the Muslim League and the Demand for Pakistan* (Cambridge: Cambridge University Press, 1985); Partha Chatterjee, 'The Second Partition of Bengal', in *The Present History of West Bengal: Essays in Political Criticism* (Delhi: Oxford University Press, 1997); Chatterji, *Bengal Divided*; and Bidyut Chakrabarty, *The Partition of Bengal and Assam, 1932–1947* (London: Routledge, 2004). The more recent works include Haimanti Roy, *Partitioned Lives: Migrants, Refugees, Citizens in India and Pakistan, 1947–1965* (New Delhi: Oxford University Press, 2012); Sabyasachi Bhattacharya, *The Defining Moments in Bengal 1920–1947* (New Delhi: Oxford University Press, 2014); and Debjani Sengupta, *The Partition of Bengal: Fragile Borders and New Identities* (Cambridge: Cambridge University Press, 2016).

34. The revisionist history of Partition wants to shift the focus away from the 'smoke-filled rooms and the negotiating tables where the men at the top played with the destinies of millions' and 'bring it into the towns and countryside of people'. By describing in these words her own project of re-examining the Bengal partition, Joya Chatterji portrays Hindu communalism as the principal driving force behind it. Almost by a tautological argument that the communalists brought about a communally motivated partition, she diminishes the scope of exploring variations of Hindu nationalist imagination to a deplorable emptiness. See Chatterji, *Bengal Divided*, p. 267. Similar view is presented by another study of the Bengal partition which holds that '[t]he period between 1832 and 1947 sharply shows the mutation in the formation of Hindus and Muslims as communities opposed to each other in the political arena ... what was distinctive about this period was the growth of the communities as political units in a permanent adversarial relationship', and identifies Muslim communalism as a fact of grassroots politics to be the most instrumental behind the partition. See B. Chakrabarty, *The Partition of Bengal and Assam*, pp. 1–3. Noticeably, he also asserts that 'the future of India was decided not only by those who remained decisive in "high politics", but also by those actors at the grassroots who translated the idioms of divisive politics in terms of

concrete plans and programmes'. The force of divisive politics is thereby considered so total and uncompromising that any possibility of negotiation or dialogue is either fully ruled out or reduced to a caricature. In study-ing the history of Punjab, David Gilmartin also drew a linear connection between 'communal ideology' and 'the emergence of an independent state' (that is, Pakistan) in *Empire and Islam: Punjab and the Making of Pakistan* (Berkeley: University of California Press, 1988). In the context of north India, the same argument is to be found in Mushirul Hasan, *Nationalism and Communal Politics in India 1885–1930* (Delhi: Manohar, 1991); Ian Talbot, *Provincial Politics and the Pakistan Movement: The Growth of the Muslim League in North-West and North-East India, 1937–47* (Karachi: Oxford University Press, 1988); and Sandria Freitag, *Collective Action and Community: Public Arenas and the Emergence of Communalism in North India* (Berkeley: University of California Press, 1989).

35. Chatterji, *Bengal Divided*, p. 267.
36. Important insights may be gathered from a number of works that cover the range of social experiences in late colonial Bengal. See Tapan Raychaudhri, *Perceptions, Emotions, Sensibilities: Essays on India's Colonial and Post-Colonial Experiences* (Delhi: Oxford University Press, 1999); Rajat Kanta Ray, *The Felt Community: Commonality and Mentality before the Emergence of Indian Nationalism* (Delhi: Oxford University Press, 2003); Sabyasachi Bhattacharya, *Defining Moments in Bengal*.
37. An insightful study of the political options in the late colonial Bengali society is to be found in Haimanti Roy, 'A Partition of Contingency? Public Discourse in Bengal 1946–47', *Modern Asian Studies* 43, no. 6 (2009): 1355–84. To give one option the most leverage was essentially a political move taken by the higher levels of political leadership. The political nature of the partition deliberations is underlined in Gordon, 'Divided Bengal', and S. Das, *Communal Riots in Bengal*. Also see Sabyasachi Bhattacharya, *Defining Moments in Bengal*, pp. 315–18.
38. The political contradictions of the Muslim-majority and Muslim-minority provinces were first shown by Ayesha Jalal in *Sole Spokesman*. Recently, Neeti Nair's work has also drawn attention to this argument in the context of Punjab. See Nair, *Changing Homelands*.
39. *Shikha* and *Saogat* were two journals published by the Bengali Muslim intel-ligentsia in Dacca (also known as Dhaka) in the middle of the 1920s and the early 1930s. Both the journals maintained an open-minded rational outlook with a firm focus on Bengali culture and identity as well as on the problems before 'modern' Islam in the context of Bengal. The thoughts and activi-ties of these free-thinking Bengali Muslim intellectuals, also represented by a literary group called the Muslim Sahitya Samaj, claimed for themselves the title of a rationalist-cum-humanist 'movement', which is named the Emancipation of the Intellect movement ('Buddhir Mukti Andolan').

40. See Chatterji, *Bengal Divided*; Joya Chatterji, *Spoils of Partition: Bengal and India, 1947–1967* (Cambridge: Cambridge University Press, 2007); Partha Chatterjee, 'The Second Partition of Bengal'; Asoke Mitra, '*Ei Abiswas Itihas-er Uttaradhikar*', *Anandabazar Patrika*, 20 August 2014.

41. Partha Chatterjee, 'The Second Partition of Bengal', p. 44.

42. H. Roy, *Partitioned Lives*, p. 221.

1 Unity and Difference in a Divided Homeland

1905–11

Amidst the frantic calls for 'national unity' during the swadeshi movement in early twentieth-century Bengal, a Bengali Muslim writer published a thin pamphlet called *Bangiya Mussalman* (the Bengal Muslims). In this pamphlet, the writer, Nur Ahmed, argued that all such big talk about 'national unity' was in the end superficial, with no real bearing on the deep sectarian disconnects within the so-called one and unified Bengali society being projected by the elusive word 'nation'. He was writing at a time when the colonial rulers of India were desperate to divide the province of Bengal into two parts and the idea of 'nation' was spreading fast beyond the closed circles of political and intellectual elites, with the emotionally charged calls for Hindu–Muslim unity resonating through various levels of 'nationalist' discourse.[1] Evidently, Ahmed was one of those critics who found the rhetoric of 'nation' and 'national unity' quite vacuous and the calls for an urgent Hindu–Muslim unification rather facile, though not necessarily undesirable. He presented the case persuasively:

> *Jatiya Aikya*: the national unity. A well-meaning idea, no doubt. But, most unfortunately, it is rather an implausible one. In Bengal the Hindus still refer to the Muslims as *mlechchha, javan, nede, patinede*, the Muslims retort to them by saying *kafer, malaun, mardood*. The solution lies in the self-strengthening of the Muslim *sampraday* in Bengal [italics added].[2]

As opposed to national unity, the writer wanted to play the word 'sampraday', best translated as 'community' but which, in other contexts, even becomes a contender for the expanded and glorified connotations of 'nation'. What strikes us here is that the question raised by the author against the overarching calls for a 'nation' did not lead him to use the word 'sampraday' in an oppositional way, but only as an internal qualifier. He wanted to assert that the high-spirited optimism of swadeshi nationalism must not aim for an obliteration of its component communities, that the communities were parts of this nation rather than certain stumbling blocks to be removed from its path. For him, it was important to highlight that, as a collectivity within the perceived contours of a homeland of Bengal, the Muslims had some distinctive problems and disadvantages which had to be addressed, and ideally redressed, in order to inspire them to participate in the nation-building festivals. He would offer a 'different' solution therefore: strengthening of his own community first, and then approaching the 'well-meaning idea' of unity. As early as in 1905, Nur Ahmed thus threw light on an important fault line within the fast-growing concept of a larger, unified political entity denoted by the term 'nation', without however, rejecting or disowning it.

By the time of the swadeshi movement, 'nation' had emerged as a regular political idiom in Bengal. A self-styled and prominent 'nationalist' leadership already mustered considerable political importance to be reckoned by their colonial rulers. The self-consciously modern and progressive Bengali literati began to articulate and disseminate the notions of nation (*jati*) right from the 1860s, often exploiting the pre-existing, pre-modern social traditions of shared values and ideals, as has already been analysed by scholars.[3] Yet the experience of partition signified a disjuncture in the narrative of nation in the province.[4] Initially designed in 1903, finally announced in July 1905, and put into effect in October

1905, the partition was purely a move taken from the top by the colonial government. It immediately sparked off a fear of losing the prospect of mobility as well as unity within the province, and threatened to curb the political and cultural centrality of Calcutta, the capital of British India and the prize metropolis for the whole province of Bengal. No wonder intense reactions against partition were first triggered off in Calcutta, followed by the smaller towns or mofussils. The rapidity with which the movement spread after July 1905 took the colonial administration by surprise. Even contemporaries sensed that they were living through an exceptional moment: 'One of the most memorable in the history of Bengal ... an epoch-making year, leaving a profound and far-reaching influence on the public life of Bengal and the future of the country...'[5]

However, this initial enthusiasm waned, and the political movement did not spread as widely as the leadership had wished. Sporadic boycotting of British goods and institutions could not pose a truly serious threat to the Raj. But the agitation showed its real strength in its intensity, if not in its extent. Calcutta (the colonial capital of that time), Dacca (the second-largest city in Bengal, also known as Dhaka), and the mofussil areas of Faridpur, Pabna, Dinajpur, Rangpur, and Jalpaiguri saw spates of political demonstrations by the middle-class bhadralok and the student communities, albeit in a dissipated way.[6] There is no denying that the movement served well to bridge certain gaps between disparate levels of political society in Bengal rather unexpectedly. This is most evident in the political discourse of the time. Earlier, most of the political writings could be associated with the Bengali Hindu circles, primarily based in Calcutta. The partition, on the contrary, stirred up the political imagination and ambitions of Bengali Muslims in such an effective way that they now began to address a whole new range of social, economic, and political concerns and spread those thoughts to various parts of the province. Passionately political comments for or against the partition were now to be found even in the far-lying districts of the province, which were earlier considered to be outside the margins of the political society. The internal and spatial frontiers of the Bengali political society thus began to expand quickly. Bringing various levels of society into the fold of political discourse, the early years of anti-partition agitation fashioned as swadeshi *andolan* indeed marked the first moment of glory in the career of an aspiring Bengali 'nation'.

As the rhetoric of unity was quickly spreading, it also began to elicit grave challenges. Rarely before had a single administrative policy raised the questions of social unity and disunity so effectively and aroused so many conflicting emotions. Suddenly the abstract themes of unity and disunity were offered a very tangible political content to be placed as a platform for their self-experimentations. Experiments were indeed made. While earlier, arguments about 'nation' and the 'Muslim interest' used to revolve primarily around the prospect of joining the national associations including the Congress, partition with all its tangible physical implications promptly changed the connotations of the uncertain term 'Muslim interest' and redefined it with reference to a geographically specified community, characterized by certain newly configured social–economic and cultural markers. The project of 'redefining' the interest against the thematic backdrop of the 'nation' indeed took various curious turns and twists within its own formulations. To unravel these dissensions around the newly defined Muslim interest in Bengal, therefore, constitutes the focal point of this chapter.

At the same time, I will also argue in this chapter that, as the unity–difference binary began to be employed in the Muslim discourse, the Bengali Hindus also manoeuvred variously with the symbol of *swadesh* or their 'own nation' in the context of the challenges of 'difference'. Contrary to common perception, the swadeshi Hindus often enough acknowledged difference as an inescapable 'limit' of the emergent nation, and started engaging with it rather sincerely.[7] The wide variations in the Hindu imaginative manoeuvres against this newly formulated problematic of difference belied the depiction of the swadeshi discourse as unilinear or even uni-dimensional. In the context of both Bengali Hindu and Bengali Muslim societies, therefore, internal divergences and resultant contestations on 'nation' and its problem of 'difference' indeed stood out as the most lasting legacy of swadeshi Bengal. [8]

Very significantly, despite many variations, the emerging discourse of 'otherness' was often marked by an unmistakably strong 'Bengali-ness'. Looking at the claims of 'other'-hood during the swadeshi era, one thing that cannot escape our attention is the persistence of certain parallel territorial–cultural claims. These two sets of claims were mingled, overlapping, and mutually fortifying in a way such that they would even seem inseparable at times. Even when Bengali Hindus claimed that social and cultural divergences must recede to give way to a united nation of Bengal, and marked as 'divergence' anything that deviated from their own prescribed identity-markers, the Muslims of Bengal would seldom doubt the strength of their own regional–cultural identity, but, with a remarkable self-confident resilience, would only attempt to negotiate the place of this identity within the projected visions of 'unity'. These negotiations will be charted out in the section that follows. While doing so, it will suggest that in the Bengali Muslim discourse of swadeshi Bengal, the use of the dubious term 'jati' seemed to be attractive not because of its inherent vagueness, but because of its essential fluidity and inter-changeability. The fluid expression this word entailed could alone capture their multiple but very real and intertwined identities, manifest in their debates and dissensions on their nation and national interest.

We may recall the case made by Nur Ahmed at the beginning of this chapter. His critique of the nation and his anxieties over it did not dislodge his belonging to the nation. He only wanted his own place designated in that nation with dignity as well as a recognition of that dignity. The following section will find that many like Nur Ahmed, while voicing their anxiety over similar questions, foregrounded a very strong claim for the 'Bengali Muslim' community.

Swadeshi Nation and the Bengali Muslim Identity

The historiography on Bengali nationalism has often traced the steady rise of Muslim communalism in the province leading to Muslim separatism and the eventual Partition of 1947 as a logical result of the late-nineteenth-century developments of colonial India. It is thought that, just as 'nationalism' was born out of the political conditions of colonial modernity, the 'Muslim communalism' also followed the cue of new trends of self-awareness, and blended it with the Islamic revivalist movements.[9] Bengali Muslims who actively supported the partition of Bengal in 1905 and believed that it would be beneficial to them were thus shown to be the children of this 'revivalist Islam'.[10] The antagonistic reactions to the swadeshi movement are seen merely as a logical step in the uninterrupted growth of Muslim 'communalism' or 'separatism', which over the next few decades would gradually develop into a potent counter-discourse of Indian nationalism.

In my view, the host of widely varying political and social anxieties behind either the Muslim support for partition or their opposition to swadeshi movement must not necessarily be read in terms of a 'Muslim community versus Bengali nation' schema. First, no such clear terms of contradiction can be established in the Bengali Muslim discourse. Rather, it reveals the reality of the enmeshed multiple identities growing parallelly in the context of anti-colonial nationalism. Second, as a consequence of the previous point, taking a stand for or against swadeshi appeared to be more of a strategic choice rather than a decisive mandate on one or the other set of identities or loyalties.

In the world of urban, educated Bengali Muslims during the swadeshi period, formulations of the political, social, and economic views of the community may reveal three broad trends. The most under-explored trend must be taken as the first: even if limited in number, many Muslims denounced the partition and actively supported swadeshi activities. Second, while a sizeable population, mainly rural, still remained inert, large numbers of relatively urbanized Bengali Muslims slowly stood in favour of partition. For them, the prospect of community advancements in the new province seemed particularly promising. Third, certain groups of Bengal Muslims, significantly different in their spirit and rhetoric from the second group, saw a distinct scope for furthering Islamic revivalism through this new political development. While for the second strand, regional affinities remained real and robust, for the champions of Islamic identities regional sentiments played a less significant role in their enthusiasm for a new, separate province. Any analysis of Bengali Muslim discourse must take into account the essential positional particularities of these groups, instead of lumping them together in an unwarranted haste to establish the 'nation versus community' dichotomy.

Contrary to common notions, the swadeshi movement was successful in bringing into its fold a considerable number of Muslim followers who comprised the first group discussed previously.[11] From the apparently conflicting information available on Maniruzzaman Islamabadi, the most prominent leader of Chittagong of the time, it seems that in 1905 he was an active participant in the agitation against Curzon's partition move. As the movement broke out, he joined the 'swadeshi-wallahs', and became closely affiliated with *Soltan*, the Muslim journal famous for taking a critical stand on partition.[12] However, eventually, when the province was nonetheless partitioned and functioned for a few years as a Muslim-dominated province, Islamabadi gradually changed his position. This very popular leader was joined by Ismail Hossain Siraji, another self-professed Congress leader of eastern Bengal in his early swadeshi endeavours. Allegedly, Islamabadi was so actively involved in the movement that he even made himself a target of the opposing group, and was beaten up by the pro-partition agitators on one occasion in October 1906. He continued to write swadeshi verses and taking part in swadeshi activities even after this assault.[13] However, both Islamabadi and Siraji would become advocates of the new province by 1907, as 'it would further the interests of the backward community of Bengal Muslims'.[14]

The questions that arise then are: Why did they fail to see the merit of this administrative reform earlier? Did they underplay the potential benefits likely to be derived from this reform? Or, were they oblivious to the needs of their community (sampraday) earlier? The fiery swadeshi writings of Islamabadi do not answer these adequately, but point to the fact that his initial reaction to this administrative measure was one of staunch rejection. Evidently, he failed to see any obvious merit of this sudden and drastic disruption in the life of the province. One of his fellow writers wrote in amused bewilderment: 'As if our life in Bengal had been too hard to suffer and as if we had asked help from the most esteemed Lord Curzon!'[15] It was only after the career of the new province began unfolding that the protagonists like Islamabadi discovered some serious benefits arising out of the new arrangement. In other words, it was the fait accompli that eventually changed the political and ideological alignments of these leaders. The sequence itself suggests that these leaders were not pre-inclined to the idea of a separate province for Bengali Muslims.

The unhesitating support of these leaders for the swadeshi cause cannot be seen in isolation. Reports of mass prayers held in Mymensingh (December 1904), Barisal, and Serampore (August 1905) against partition came through, only to give some credence to the previous writer's claim that 'Muslims all over Bengal stand to oppose this new provincial arrangement'.[16] In Kishoregunj, Bogra, Madaripur, Banoripara, and Tangail, locally influential Muslim leaders presided over the anti-partition meetings held in swift succession after the announcement in July 1905.[17] The Muslims of Calcutta organized a swadeshi reception on 16 February 1906 at the Albert Hall and in the contiguous premises of College Square, where 4,000 Muslims were allegedly present.[18] The Bengal Provincial Conference at Barisal in 1906, presided over by the eminent Muslim politician Abdul Rasul,[19] witnessed the presence of many mid-level Muslim leaders such as Haji Muhammad Ismail Chowdhury, Hedayet Bux, Din Muhammad, Abdur Hossain, Motahar Hossain, and Liakat Hossain. Aswinikumar Dutta, a major proponent of swadeshi ideology, was particularly successful in mobilizing local Muslim leaders during 1905–7. Encouraged by him were the relatively lesser-known poets and composers of *jatra-pala* (local theatres) or *jari-gaan* (folk songs), who spread the swadeshi spirit by their own creative channels of mass contact. The singer camp of swadeshi included Muslims like Mafizuddin Bayati as well as their better-known Hindu counterparts Mukunda Das and Hemchandra Kabiratna.[20] Although these swadeshi Muslims used to belong to the middle-class semi-urban or rural segments of society, for example, teachers, writers, or students, they also included a few zamindars like Nawab Abdur Sobhan Chaudhury of Bogra or Samimullah's brother Khwaja Atikullah. The latter moved the anti-partition resolution at the Calcutta session of Congress in 1906 and the former participated in petitioning or in *rakhi bandhan* (tying of friendship knots) ceremonies in Bogra.[21] However, speaking about landlords, just as Atikullah was no match for his more prominent brother Salimullah, the nawab of Dacca, these elite leaders were outnumbered by their pro-partition counterparts, clearly enthusiastic about the windfall gains of the partition reform.

Before assessing what the pro-partition Muslims—the second group, so to speak—considered as 'gains', it may be useful to emphasize the complex nuances of the word 'swadeshi'. During this period, the movement was integrally linked with the agenda of boycotting British goods, and therefore was resisted extensively at the local levels. First, boycotting necessarily meant endangering the interests of the less resourceful classes in the countryside, who consequently had to face tremendous hardships in marketing their own produce as well as acquiring daily provisions at more competitive prices due to the boycott of relatively cheaper British goods. One of Tagore's novels, *Ghare Baire*, written in 1916 in his post-swadeshi phase of disillusionment, brilliantly captured the nature of local tensions and the conflicted class interests around the swadeshi agenda of economic boycott. Muslim writers during this time routinely pointed out the same hardships of the village population caused by swadeshi activism.[22] In a lopsided demographic reality with the majority of rural population being Muslims, swadeshi and boycott often directly collided with the interests of their daily survival. Second, as Sumit Sarkar points out, the 'anti-landlord demagogy' of the Bengal countryside was dangerously mixed with the issue of partition. In a situation with 'many districts where no large zamindar is a Mohamedan, and in which even petty landowners of the Mohamedan persuasion are but a small minority',[23] swadeshi agitation was seen as an upper-class ploy to maintain the status quo and the partitioning of the province, a rare chance to revolt against the extortions of landlords, paving the way for future representation in local organizations.

Surely the prospect of representation was alluring enough for the relatively wealthier urban Muslim professionals also. The prospect of hard material gains definitely succeeded in extracting a strategic support for the partition. An anonymous article in a journal called *Moslem Pratibha* analysed why the Muslims should oppose the anti-partition agitation.[24] Swaraj or self-rule would bring a more direct Hindu domination in the administration, since the Hindus had long been enjoying a clear advantage in socio-economic status. Muslims, therefore, should be loyal to the Raj, and hope for the redressal of the prevailing unfairness. Partitioning the province would give them a chance to look after their own interests. Journalists like Mozammel Huq and Reyazuddin Ahmed supported partition considering its efficacy in furthering Muslim interests. Reyazuddin Ahmed was reluctant to see in the initial official move for partition anything more than an administrative arrangement or a reshuffling of the power and resources for the preservation of official interests. But 'if what the Hindu Press said was true, the Muslims stood to gain from it'.[25] For Maniruzzaman Islamabadi and Ismail Hossain Siraji in the later part of their career, after shifting their stand to support partition, the day-to-day living in the new province could eventually provide enough space for nurturing their nationalist predilections as well as hoping for a better future for their own immediate community. How seriously they engaged themselves with the advancement of their own regional community may be appreciated if one remembers that Islamabadi, once well known for an anti-partition stance and later revising his own position to become a pro-partition proponent, introduced in a number of southeast Bengal districts a *swajati andolana*, a Muslim counterpart of the movement for self-assertion, or a Muslim equivalent to that of swadeshi.[26] With an agenda bearing striking similarities to swadeshi, Islamabadi sought to generate a spirit of local reconstruction in a number of villages in Chittagong. The movement sustained its popular appeal for a few months, and brought in a good number of people as supporters.[27]

Examples of Islamabadi or Siraji prove that, even for the politically aware Muslim leaders, it was hardly clear in the beginning what would be gained by whom due to the administrative separation of the two provinces. Many Muslims failed to see in partition anything more than the removal of some obstacles in the path of their advancement. The previously mentioned pamphlet by Golam Hossain expressed utter surprise at the 'Hindu over-reaction' on the matter of the partition.[28] Hossain thought that the partition should not be made an important issue in the nationalist movement because that would alienate the pro-partition Muslims from the broader anti-colonial struggle of the nation. Once the ground was secured for the 'downtrodden Muslims', he argued, the Bengali Muslims could willingly join hands with the Hindus to attain the rightful 'national' claim for self-government. The new province proved that the Muslims were able to run and govern a province: 'So why do you not give them a chance?… As Hindus and Muslims of India have earned their right in conducting administrative matters, and acquired the necessary level of education, why should the British Raj deprive them from their political right of self-government?'[29] Many Bengali Muslims regarded the 'political right of self-government' as a natural claim during the first decade of this century. The yearning of self-government was, however, typical of a political society developing a new perception of the 'self'. This political society provided the individual a distinct voice and bridged him/her with the community in many tangible ways. As we will explore in a later section in this chapter, the redefining of the 'self' at an individual or collective level made the project of the 'nation' more meaningful on the political and the cultural domains during swadeshi.

This is exactly where they differed from the third group of the Bengali Muslims who were essentially revivalist and espoused the cause of partition only to recreate the glorious political control of the past Muslim rulers. Nawab Salimullah of Dacca and the group of Muslims gathered round the journal *Mihir o Sudhakar* reiterated the importance of 'going back to the past glories' and bringing to the fore the Muslims of 'social position and dignity'.[30] A careful examination of the pro-partition Muslim discourse thus reveals differing trends of mindset, the first essentially forward-looking in its self-assertion, and the other relatively more feudal and regressive in its political claims and social content.

Viewed thus, it is eminently possible to argue that the large number of dedicated but lesser-known social reformers (primarily the second group of pro-partition Bengali Muslims) who took up the project of Muslim self-assertion and the task of awakening and integrating the rural Muslims were equally betraying a different kind of 'nationalist' predilection. They were, however, often in agreement with the political and social agenda laid down by the first group, that is, the swadeshi Muslim leaders. At the local levels, the pro-swadeshi leaders like Maniruzzaman Islamabadi of Chittagong and the anti-swadeshi leaders like Sheikh Jamiruddin of Nadia or Sheikh Munshi Mohammad Mehraullah of Jessore[31] pursued similar kinds of local regeneration activities, like spreading education or enhancing direct participation in political life. All of them concentrated on the material and ideological 'emptiness' in Muslim peasant societies. Leaders like Munshi Mohammad Reyazuddin Ahmad and Sheikh Abdur Rahim, who either opposed swadeshi or, at the best, like the former, had a vacillating stance towards swadeshi activism, considered alike that a higher level of education, primarily through the vernacular medium, was urgently called for in the villages of Bengal. For them, only a greater attachment to one's own cultural and linguistic heritage would pave the way to ensure the self-confidence necessary for any material advancement. Their painstaking efforts to establish madrassas in villages and small towns throughout Bengal revealed the depth of their commitment.[32] Discordant voices were also heard from the ranks of Muslim social workers. It was 'too early' for the Muslims to aim 'self-rule', considered Mehraullah, although he believed in the self-awakening of the Muslims. A pro-partition advocate himself, he was somewhat apologetic about the political bearings of his own anti-swadeshi stance: 'Just as it is enormously difficult to walk with one broken leg, it does not seem to be a good idea for the Mussalmans to either blindly follow or to imitate the Hindus in the sphere of politics, until we become their equal in terms of education and experience.'[33]

The choice of political route to the cherished goal of Muslim self-assertion differed among leaders. Yet their shared goal of local self-strengthening was heard loud and clear. The early Maniruzzaman Islamabadi of Congress and the self-professedly apolitical Munshi Mehraullah did not have any agreement over the question of partition or the 'Muslim' political interest in general, but their local activities were remarkably similar. Both of them thought religious studies were important in educating Muslims. The pro-Congress Islamabadi, therefore, never ceased to rely on 'religious' studies as the foundation of a modern 'national' education. The political distance of these leaders was more of a result of perceptional difference on the ways to further Muslim interests, than of fundamental ideological differences on religion. It is enormously difficult to designate who was more 'liberal' or less 'religious' or 'communal' than the other. Since the previous century, religiously informed cultural identities formed the bedrock of national sentiment. Therefore, it is urgent for us to recognize that evocation of the past glories of Islam was not necessarily connected in a linear way with the opposition to swadeshi nationalism, or apprehensions about Hindu domination, or supporting the Muslim League. All this could be seen as resulting from a religious–cultural anxiety instead of an overt sense of religious obscurantism. The anxiety was prevalent among the Muslims even in early twentieth-century Bengal where the power of demographic composition was clearly overshadowed by the sociocultural and economic preponderance of the numerically smaller section of the upper-caste Hindus. It is only through the prism of this anxiety that one can hope to disentangle the complex and varied responses of the

Bengali Muslims. Only then one might appreciate why taking a stand for or against partition or focusing on the immediate needs of one's own social community was a political choice than a question of being more or less Islamic.

It would be an interesting exercise to note what religious affinity meant in an era of spreading rhetoric of nation. Even those idealizing 'Muslim' advancement often did not stand for religious obscurantism traceable to the desert sands of the Arabian peninsula but spoke of certain redefined religious ties in new and fresh ways. Maulavi Mohammad Hedayetullah wrote extensively on this issue. Hedayetullah, himself a devout Maulavi, was a regular columnist of *Nabanur*, the prominent 'syncretist' journal of the era. In an article written during the thick of political turmoil in 1905, he explained how the Indian territories transformed the two neighbouring religious communities in a profound way.[34] In the specific 'Indian' condition, he commented, the Islamic collectivity could only be termed as 'Indian Muslim'. How did then one explain the growing distrust and acrimony between these communities? Hedayetullah thought that the British watchword of 'divide and rule' had been successful in setting apart the communities. Lack of proper 'political education', largely unavailable in colonial society, only guaranteed this split.

Hedayetullah would also point out that the 'transformed' Indian Islam was also indirectly recognized by those who resented the 'Indianization' of their community. Their repeated references to the West Asian Islam or the constant agony of territorial displacement indicated a commitment to the Bengali Muslim community in a back-handed way.[35] A whole body of non-Indian myths and histories was, therefore, being imported into the Bengali Muslim discourse. Laments about 'Indian Islam' became a common theme of literary and historical works of this time.[36] Sometimes the sense of present moral degradation was sought to be linked with the process of Indianization:

> We were a different race, and lo,
> Quite different habits, rites, we had—
> Neither a social bond with you
> Nor a bond of life with you we had.[37]

Sometimes a tone of loss was mixed with the premonitions of a bleak future:

> Wealth and riches, science and wisdom,
> Which were not there at a Muslim door?

What was a Muslim and what is he now
In the nearest future what more in store![38]

The self-professedly Islamic trend of thought has obviously received more than its fair share of historiographical attention, abundantly documented in scholarly studies, only to assert the steady growth of Muslim revivalism leading to the final dissection of the country in 1947. It is argued that lack of any regional allegiance resulted in a supra-regional religious spirit. For example, Kazi Imdadul Huq, an early twentieth-century Bengali columnist, found comfort in the extraterritorial ties of Islam by saying that '… unlike the Hindus, the Muslims have much to look beyond the handful of their members left in India'.[39] Anisuzzaman, the noted historian, would quote this passage to argue a case that Muslims in Bengal saw themselves belonging to a supra-territorial, supra-regional Islamic entity.[40] As a result, historical or mythological claims confirming the extra-regional, hence 'different', attachments were critically important for the 'separate' political claims. Rafiuddin Ahmed also observed that the late nineteenth and early twentieth centuries saw the development of 'an identity that was Muslim and not Bengali'.[41] The census figures of the time indeed report a craze for 'Muslim' identity, pointing to the social aspirations of the underprivileged.[42]

Such interpretations seem to trouble us if we begin to ask questions such as: Did such laments about a glorious past and a decadent present necessarily entail a representation of an extra-territorial belongingness? Did the past glory of the Mussalmans depicted by Kazi Imdadul Huq contain an inherent negation of the present locational ties? Did it also not offer an evocative portrayal of the bright future possibilities based on the past achievements before a downtrodden, insecure, and anxious community? If resorting to historical reference and allusions did not necessarily imply that the nationalism of the Hindu thinkers was primarily and essentially 'Hindu', similarly, suggestions of past Muslim glory by Muslim thinkers should not automatically be held as representing an uncompromising 'Islamic'-ness. The complexities of literary and cultural allusions in the imagining and constructing the ties of nation and the community, or the discourse of jati in general, must be considered in their larger referential context instead of their narrow textual translation.

Turning from texts to the larger context might thus enable us to see how the trend of Ashrafization, explored in detail by historians like Rafiuddin Ahmed, was only limited to the upper sections of the society; failed to generate much impact on the middle-class, professional Bengali Muslims of mofussils, small towns, and villages of Bengal; and could never weaken their immediate locational ties. If these lamenting poets looked back to the West Asian traditions, they also remained, in an indirect way, well aware of their own idiosyncracies, a long-earned regional character, and sought to infuse their immediate community with the glorious spirit of the mythical Islam. For the majority of the educated urban Muslims, strong assertions of their 'Bengali'-ness went hand in hand with their cherished Islamic virtues.

We may argue therefore, that instead of a pervasive tendency of Islamic purification through a negation of regional ties, there emerged a spirited dialogue between the adherents of various ideological positions on the following question: where to strike the compromise between religious–cultural and regional–cultural identities. Evocative passages like the following are widely identifiable in Bengali Muslim discourse of this time:

> The Bengali Muslims have to rise on their own strength, just as others are doing; they have to produce, nurture and fulfil their *national life* just as others are doing; they have to grow strong and prosperous through their own enterprise, just as the Hindus are doing; never ever should we indulge in the passive expectation that the British or the Hindus would actually salvage us from our all-round degradation [emphasis added].[43]

Here, the idea of the 'national', as in most of such utterances in the early twentieth-century Muslim discourse, can be defined as *Bangiya Mussalman*. A local Muslim poet, Munshi Mozammel Huq, would turn out to be rather eloquent in one of his verses:

> To read Persian
> In Bostan—Gulestan,
> One looks for the Moktab
> As he passes nursery—
> Come lifeless Bengali who would like this to see!
>
> And after the Moktab
> One goes to suburb,
> Reading at the Madrassa
> A Maulavi he would be—
> Come lifeless Bengali who would like this to see!
>
> 'Anjuman-e-Islamia'
> 'Anjuman-e-Khairatia'
> Here and there these titles,

And who will not agree?
Come lifeless Bengali who would like this to see![44]

The sarcasm directed to the craving for a section indifferent to the 'Bengali-ness' of the regional Muslims can be found extensively in journals like *Mohammadi, Soltan*, and *Mihir o Sudhakar*, not particularly known for any pro-Hindu bias. Prominent Muslim poets like Kaikobad and the writer-turned-activist Mohammad Reyazuddin Ahmad would discuss at length the importance of the call evoked by Munshi Mozammel Huq: 'Come lifeless Bengali [that is, Bengali Muslim] who would like this to see!' These Bengali Muslims indeed arrived at the idea of a multi-tiered identity in those early years of the twentieth century, however difficult the idea might seem in retrospect.

One article deserves special mention here. Published in one of the leading pro-swadeshi journals, *Nabanur*, a strongly worded article by Syed Abul Mohammad Ismail Hossain pleaded for developing a self-conscious nation, jati.[45] In the course of his appeal, he would not forget to underline the importance of the larger commitments for and obligations towards India. India, he thought, constituted a country (*desh*), which had the unique privilege of nourishing many nations (jatis). This was a highly articulate exposition of the desh–jati dichotomy, implicitly suggested by many Muslim writers of this era.

If the ties and belongings with the larger country had to be addressed, the task of embarking on a political organization of the immediate community, nation, or jati seemed mandatory for Bengali Muslims who began to find their institutional representation at the level of high politics during this time. Although setting its first foot in Bengal, the AIML (1906) was clearly under the control of the Muslim leaders outside Bengal, and the anxiety about defending the Bengali Muslim interest was as old as the League itself.[46] For example, when partition of Bengal remained one of the main concerns of the League leadership in eastern Bengal and Assam, the Muslim League extended to them only a negligible amount of support. In the presidential address at the inaugural session of the League in 1906, Nawab Viqar-ul-Mulk of northern India made no reference to partition at all.[47] Aga Khan, the permanent president of the League until 1912, was personally against the partition of Bengal. However, at the time of the Simla Deputation (October 1906), Nawab Salimullah and Syed Nawab Ali Chowdhury earnestly insisted that the deputationists seek an assurance from the viceroy for the permanence of partition. But the demand was ultimately not incorporated into the League memorial. For the opponents of Curzonite partition, it still remained at best a 'controversial issue'.[48] As early as in the first decade of the twentieth century, there were serious fissures within the 'all-India Muslim' interest. Specific regional interests began to foreground the demands for specific policies and particularly targeted treatment by the colonial state as well as the anti-colonial 'national' associations, for which the League leadership had little time or patience. Over the next few decades, this distance between the regional Muslim interest and the all-India Muslim policies would only grow and turn into a wide crevasse.

The Bengali Muslim 'national' sentiment relied mainly on its linguistic commonality, an important vehicle for any nationalist doctrine to thrive on. However, Bengali as the primary language of this particular jati had always suffered challenges from Urdu. Not unexpectedly, at the All-India Mohammedan Educational Conference in Dacca in 1906, which preceded the birth of the All India Muslim League (December 1906), a heated controversy took place over the language issue, or the medium of instruction for Mohammedan education in Bengal. Maulavi Abdul Karim, a Muslim school inspector from Chittagong, also a delegate from the eastern Bengal and Assam province, strongly pleaded: 'The Muslims of eastern Bengal cannot do without Bengali, the vernacular of the province,... They could do without the other two languages (Urdu and Persian) though. This must be seen as a policy of self-preservation.'[49] As we shall see in the next section, this impulse of self-preservation through the linguistic–cultural medium would begin to haunt the Bengali Muslims during this time, an impulse that would push them to raise a new battle for themselves in the next half century.

Differences, therefore, were manifold: differences with the regional Hindu community as well as differences with the supra-regional Muslim community. In the wake of the early twentieth-century nationalism, the majority of the politically conscious Bengali Muslims were thus already confronted with a two-pronged struggle. They were neither comfortable with the swadeshi discourse considered to be complacent and unresponsive nor in synchrony with the overarching category of an all-India 'Muslim interest'.

Identity and the Language of Belonging

The plea above by a Muslim educationist called Maulavi Abdul Karim points to one of the most important sites of controversy around nation and its difference.[50] The question of language and culture, a vital expression of the 'nation', spawned strongly opposed viewpoints about the nature of nation to belong. In an age when cultural ties, both horizontal and vertical, were constantly forged and renewed, imagining one's *own* nation and interlinking different kinds of communities in the interest of the nation became critical.

Rafiuddin Ahmed argued that Bengali Muslims were averse to Bengali which, he thought, was evident from the practice of infusing Bengali prose with Arabic or Persian words.[51] He would even infer a 'Muslim exclusiveness', a perceptible trend in late-nineteenth-century Bengal, from such choice of language. As the Muslim masses were driven closer to the *ashraf*s (elites), the elite influence hardened the attitude of religious absolutism. A closer examination of Bengali Muslim discourse of the swadeshi era, however, would suggest otherwise.

By the onset of the twentieth century, the demand for Arabic and Persian as the lingua franca of Bengal Muslims in the interest of global Islam was more than adequately counterbalanced by the parallel demands for acknowledging Bengali as their own national language (*jatiya bhasha*). Abdul Karim Sahityabisharad asked Bengali Muslims to note similar endeavours undertaken by other such regionalized Muslim communities.[52] He cited the example of the Persians in the province of Bombay (present Mumbai) where they had made sincere efforts to cultivate Gujarati as their mother tongue, although in a modified form. Why then would Bengali Muslims not recognize Bengali as the principal medium of self-expression, he would ask, or not acknowledge their cultural distinctiveness? 'Bengal is the true home for the regional Muslim culture, and care must be taken to make the new home flourish.'[53] To his mind, discomfort about language was ungrounded and the following debate a little empty, because proficiency in 'religiously' identified languages like Urdu or Arabic could not have any fundamental contradiction with Bengali, the language of their everyday use.

The Urdu–Bengali controversy divided Bengali Muslims deeply at the turn of the century, although Urdu had little chance of success in the battle. Even Rafiuddin Ahmed, who thought that during this time they were more Muslim than Bengali, pointed out, 'To most of them, Urdu was at least as much a foreign language as Sanskrit was to the generality of the Bengali Hindus.'[54] Contemporaries also maintained that the language of the 'World Islam' was transformed by Bengali Muslims. Slowly there emerged a case for the script only, without its linguistic content, an argument that Bengali Muslims must uphold the 'Muslim version' of Bengali. 'It would be far wiser to adopt the Arabic script for Bengali following the pattern of Urdu language to make it legible to the Muslims of other parts of the world,' commented a writer.[55] However, it is important to note that just like the revivalist Muslims, Muslims of strong regional identity also often strongly favoured the use of Urdu and Arabic: nowhere was the line more blurred between the regional culture and the supra-regional religious culture than on the question of language and script.

Much of this overt preference for Urdu or Persian, nevertheless, had to do with the rebellion against the overly Sansikritizing tendencies of the Bengali literati. The clear supremacy of the Sanskritized and finely cured language of Calcutta, widely recognized as the 'real' and only version of Bengali, was duly resented by the users and takers of the many local versions of Bengali. The official Bengali language used to bear an essential mark of the Hindu-bhadralok Calcutta culture, far removed from the local dialects as well as the colloquial Bengali in and around the metropolis. For the middle-class Muslims, stretching their own dialects to match the bhadralok version of Bengali was strenuous, just as it was equally difficult for them to have a working knowledge of Urdu, Arabic, or Persian. This is why even some Muslims with strong regional–cultural identities had qualms about the widespread use of Bengali, at least its standard version.

If the form was the cause of serious resentment, the content proved to be more so. The abundant anti-Muslim words, expressions, myths, and histories were so apparent and unabashed in the standard Bengali parlance that even those who considered themselves Bangiya Mussalman could not but be left with a great deal of pain. As a result, even those who chose Bengali as their principal language of belonging were not always in agreement about the nature of the language of use. Two distinct trends may be identified here. The first group would be comfortably predisposed towards the accepted versions of the oral and written language, while the second voiced the need for a 'reformed' or more Islamic version of Bengali language and literature, better suited and more comfortable for Bengali Muslims. The 'Bengali of the Hindu *pathsalas* (traditional primary schools)' must change, many of them demanded. *Soltan*, the journal with a favourable, or at least an ambivalent stance about swadeshi movement, published numerous articles to point out how the Muslims were marginalized and demonized in the Bengali literature. The 'anti-Muslim bigotry' of Bankimchandra was virulently criticized during this period.[56] With a direct strike on the 'immersed in anti-Islamic bias' of his language and literature, the swadeshi plans for holding an anniversary celebration for Bankimchandra was opposed.[57] The critique of the Shivaji Utsav also rested itself on similar argument that the deliberate neglect of Muslim emotions would not be rewarding for the swadeshi nationalists.[58]

The choice of words and expressions was debated as well, and no less vigorously. An argument was heard among the Bengali Muslim literati that the iron-chain put by Iswarchandra Vidyasagar on the language in an attempt at its codification and purification should finally be overturned. The local/communitarian variations should be brought back, and an Islamic version of the language should be introduced as if to adorn it with a garland of roses (*gulab*).[59] More Arabic, Persian, and Urdu words would only make it richer, they argued.[60] Was it an order of the day to change the language with a free hand? These writers would consider so.

Some would, however, disagree. They would even propose that it a preposterous idea to overhaul the structure of the language as a self-aware cultural project. The language, a mobile entity, should be allowed to evolve on its own, develop its own forms if the Muslims started using Bengali more frequently and in an unselfconscious manner. Not through any revengeful project of Urduization, but the language could really be enriched by a delicate balance where its Sanskritized basis would be maintained alongside the infusion of new Islamic additions.[61] These conflicting visions of 'Mussalmani Bangla' were extensively visible throughout the Bengali Muslim discourse in swadeshi times. Scholars like Abdul Latif wanted a Bengali language to be 'created' specifically for the Mussalmans, 'as Urduized as was the language of the court', while Mir Mosharraf Hossain, a leading literary figure of the day, would denounce any such attempt towards conscious Urduization.[62] According to Mir Mosharraf and his followers, a standardized form of Bengali should be the vehicle for official and literary purposes, and local dialects should continue to exist with their own particularities.[63] It was only some years later that Mohammed Shahidullah, an able and prominent scholar and linguist, would argue at length about the most desired way the language should develop itself. The Bengali language, he thought, had multiple and varied localized forms over and above its two distinct forms divided along the line of religious rift. Selection of the 'standardized' form could, however, be made on the basis of the 'survival of the fittest' principle. The surest test for that was to find out which one had produced the largest literary opus.[64]

Interestingly, such energetic contestations were often missed by historians. The 'pro-Urdu' protagonists are often lumped together with the champions of 'Bengali with an Islamic character' into an oversimplified category of 'revivalist'. I emphasize here that these debates on the nature of Bengali strengthen the thesis of a regionally charged cultural identity of the Bengali Muslim community. The claims for negotiating cultural differences from within the structures of the regional inheritance must therefore be acknowledged. As the project of nationalism made a gradual advance, the print language inherited the built-in contestations of colloquial Bengali, which had long been in vogue in the local dialects.

No wonder, then, that such an undifferentiated representation often led to the conclusion that Bengali was defeated by the forces of pan-Islamism by the early twentieth century. The trend, according to Ahmed, was one of becoming anti-Bengali from pro-Bengali. Hence, his observations that the common practice of Bengali was evident even in the earlier decades, that only a very insignificant number of Muslim boys had ever attended the maulavi's classes in the 1870s and that the popularity of the madrassas only increased with time.[65] Referring to the post-1947 struggle for Bengali language (leading to the Language Movement of 1952) in East Pakistan, he would conclude: 'It took more than half-a-century for the Bengali Muslims to realize that their Muslim identity was in no way inconsistent with their Bengali origins.'[66] These arguments become untenable if it is taken into account that the spread of education among Bengali Muslims increased in the early years of the twentieth century, and so did the absolute numbers of madrassa-attending students.[67] To argue that the Muslims of Bengal had to wait till the 1950s to 'realize' the immediate relevance of their regional (Bengali) origin would therefore be grossly wrong and would mean a gross undermining of the complexly interwoven identities of Bengali Muslims.[68]

The question on 'national language' and on the form of national language was taken up just as urgently by Bengali Hindus, specifically by some prominent swadeshi leaders who launched and promoted a 'national education' movement. This movement, organized by leaders such as Rabindranath Tagore, Brahmabandhav Upadhyay, Satishchandra Mukherji, and Aswinikumar Dutta, spread in various parts of Bengal and showed its potential albeit in a dormant manner. Outside the intellectual stronghold of Calcutta, it flourished in districts where the swadeshi trend was strong, like Hooghly, Nadia, Barisal, Faridpur, as well as in the more remote areas like Rangpur, Dinajpur, and Mymensingh. The idea was to create the trend of 'national' vernacular education as opposed to the existing structure of colonial education, and thereby to promote an acceptable 'standard' body of knowledge and a standardized teaching of language(s) in which this knowledge was to be imparted. Although in theory there was much scope for cultural and linguistic negotiation, the aspiration of spreading into the 'local' was not matched by a corresponding intention of representing the local variations. Not surprisingly, the proponents of national education practically paid little attention to the multiplicity of claims over the Bengali language.

In a number of essays written during this period, Tagore emphasized the urgency of the need to decentralize the educational system and rescue it from the colonial order, and highlighted the value of the old Indian tradition of private enterprises for public education.[69] Education 'on national lines and under national control' became the dominant slogan of the movement.[70] Indian society had always retained local autonomy in respect of education from the legislative and administrative arenas of the state above it. 'And this notion of private educational system did not only produce *tol*s [traditional school for teaching Sanskrit] and *pathshala*s, but also a whole range of world-class institutions like Nalanda, Takshashila, Kashi, Mithila, Nabadwip, and so on [italics original].'[71] All these premier institutions survived and functioned without a hint of state funding. Along with the whole array of tols and pathshalas, Tagore wanted to promote larger institutions of worldly studies to generate a self-sustaining educational system. The idea of combining various layers of education for the elites and the masses alike was repeatedly stressed in his articles, the most insightful of which was 'Swadeshi Samaj', written in 1904.

It is one thing to agree on the broader principles, and quite another when the principles needed to be implemented. Leaders often disagreed on the focus and priorities of the movement, and on the relative merits of mass education campaign vis-à-vis the agenda of focusing on higher education or creating 'national' universities. As a result, the movement soon started to lose its direction and strength. While Tagore attempted to combine both these purposes in the ingenious idea of Visva-Bharati, a 'world university' so to speak, the proponents of mass education like Ramendrasundar Trivedi and Lalitkumar Bandopadhyay were eventually marginalized by the supporters of 'higher education policy', primarily Satishchandra Mukherji. In the heat of the debate, however, the most important issue—catering to the local needs—was lost, although the movement attained a modest degree of success in creating national schools in some districts. Aswinikumar Dutta, nevertheless, single-handedly turned the district of Barisal into a model case, by establishing some 200 primary schools by Swadesh Bandhab Samiti. But as the epithet 'national' in its narrow swadeshi sense suggested, the education imparted in those schools was typically streamlined and modelled after their Calcutta counterparts, designed to disseminate only a homogenized notion of the language and literature.

Reactions must have been gathering strength against such tendencies. During 1905, the same year when Tagore wrote the above-mentioned article 'The Education Movement' (Shikshar Andolana), the well-known journal *Nabanur* published an article by a Bengali Muslim author containing a sharp tone of indignation: '... why should these Hindu stalwarts of culture not pay even a little attention toward these differences (*baishamyo*) pervading the country?... They would even shrink at the suggestion of legitimizing local dialects or even the Muslim dialect, all of which have long been in vogue across the length and breadth of Bengal.'[72] During the early days of the swadeshi movement, the pull of traditionalism was too strong even for Tagore to allow him to step outside the old Upanishadic ashrama model of education environment. His choice of Brahmabandhab Upadhyay or the more orthodox Gurudas Banerji as leaders of his project made it amply clear why catering to such suggestions would have been difficult for him, even if he was made aware of those.

No doubt, many Bengali Muslims of the swadeshi era reached out in various ways for negotiating an alternative form of language and education, and bringing to the fore the context of multiplicity of cultural identities. The dominant swadeshi perspective, nevertheless, continued to insist on an integrational nationalism rather than a combinational one. The acknowledgement of the problem of difference in the realm of language was still devoid of a solution, or even an adequate measure of engagement.

Difference and the Confounded Concept of Swadesh

'Why should these Hindu cultural stalwarts not pay a little attention towards these differences pervading our own country?' Ekinuddin Ahmad pondered.[73] He was not a solitary figure. The imperatives of 'national unity' in a multicultural society needed an urgent response from the nationalist protagonists, and those on the other end of the scale of difference, waited impatiently for that response. Bengali Muslim discourse was in fact bursting with similar allegations during this time; yet the space for negotiation with 'others' of that nation was deplorably minimal. Nevertheless, one must note the dissonance in the awareness of swadeshi leaders and activists about this difference. There was indeed a range of reactions to this problem, mostly overlooked so far, thereby resulting in an oversimplified characterization of swadeshi discourse as unabashedly Hindu. A most important reason for revisiting the discourse of swadeshi nationalism is to correct its essentialized depiction as a 'Hindu' discourse and balance its much-abused Hindu overtones with the other more complex and far richer strands of thoughts and actions. Difference is a problematic that intrigued the Hindu ideologues and politicians no less than the Bengali Muslims of the same period. They identified the vexing problems within the project of national unity, apprehended many of its impending failures, and suggested a host of solutions, most of which often went unheeded. At the same time, these 'other' Hindu voices must not be overly glorified; their limits and short-comings must also be critically examined. Even for such an assessment, they must not be erased from history altogether. Indeed, most of these voices of reason and of prudence came from high politics or high society, yet their reverberations in larger Bengali society were not negligible, as the later chapters of this book will show. A new history of swadeshi, therefore, must take the 'different' Hindu voices into account and enable us to trace the roots of subsequent trends of liberal Hindu nationalisms in Bengal to the early years of nationalist movements.

Coming out of the general stereotype of the Bengali Hindu discourse, an exploration is therefore called for to unravel the anxieties and disagreements over the problematic of difference. Such an exploration is urgent in order to appreciate the opportunities of rapprochement, if any, and the eventual failure to do so. Surely, for the early twentieth-century Bengali nation, any discursive or political negotiations over the issue of difference seemed exceedingly difficult due to its overdependence on religious as well as historical myths. The discourse of nation constantly employed rather undifferentiated histories of a 'golden past', that is, of 'Hindu' India.[74] The event of partition intensified the process of nationalist myth-making and brought it into the realm of practical politics. Along with the typically swadeshi style of spreading the message of unity by organizing rakhi bandhan (tying bands of brotherhood) and holding 'nationalist dinners' or joint functions during Eid, leaders in their urge towards people to unite started 'historical' festivals like Shivaji Utsav or Pratapaditya Utsav, and engaged themselves in invoking past accounts of solidarity, either historical or mythical.

Confronted by urgent needs, the swadeshi response was threefold in general. The first trend was one of a cautious and careful approach towards cultural and political activities which, ironically, could never present any practical agenda of bridging the gaping social differences. The second trend was to dismiss the need for caution as such and offer a hurriedly drawn-out political programme only to pressurize the colonial rulers into reckoning a 'national' awakening. The third trend attempted to maintain distance from both the above trends, on the grounds of political alienation of the first group and social shortsightedness in case of the second. Instead, this trend of swadeshi nationalism envisaged an ambitiously composite 'nation' to be sought through the painstaking and long-winding path of mass regeneration.

As for the first section, there were those ideologues who styled themselves as Moderates within the Congress, and idealized an inclusive/composite nation. However lofty their principles might sound, their real task proved ever-elusive. The social positioning of these elite leaders without much people-contact inherently limited the scope of realizing their ultimate objective into the realms of practical politics. Surendranath Banerjea or Bhupendranath Bose repeatedly talked about 'national reconstruction' or 'national integration', but none of them addressed either the troubling issues of community identities or the facts of social–economic inequalities in the process. The announcement of the Bengal partition brought the first opportunity to mobilize people in the name of the 'Mother nation'. Perhaps the initial enthusiasm so blinded the front-running Congress leaders like Surendranath Banerjea as not to appreciate the terribly divisive character of the resultant creeds of swadeshi. He rather naively thought that partition and swadeshi 'could awaken Hindus and Mahomedans alike'.[75]

It is curious to see how these Moderate politicians in their over-anxiousness to collaborate with the administration and reliance on the covert methods of prayer and petition were placed in a quandary regarding the ground-level socioeconomic or political discord. Such uneasiness points towards the fact that despite best intentions, the lack of social exposure of these leaders and activists led to an unquestioning acceptance of the myth of communal harmony, thereby rendering the real challenges of everyday politics extremely bewildering. An article in *Nabya Bharat* by Nagendranath Chattopadhyay, a major scholar, linguist, and theologian of this time, represented the dilemma while addressing difference from both a general and specifically Indian perspective.[76] Truth has many sides; differences are indeed natural. But, according to him, the need for uniformity and the gradual elimination of differences could also not be overestimated. He wrote:

[Consequently] ... the urge to be divided into various communities is not only natural but quite healthy. Ancient India has long believed in a principle that no good can be done without any grouping; groups secure us with mutual support and cooperation.... These days, wise men in Europe and in India are directly discouraging and denigrating community ties as such, which makes man constricted and limited by nature. The question is: how to strike the right balance between difference and universality?... the answer perhaps is possible to get when we remember that ... differences in opinion (*mata-bhed*) should not necessarily bring about differences in heart (*hriday-bhed*) [italics original].[77]

'How to strike the right balance between difference and universality?' Significantly, the answer would point to an eventual non-acceptance of the fact of difference, at least any expression of difference in the practical realms. It might appear anathema to the reader, or perhaps to the author himself, how one should hope for an erasure of 'differences in heart' in case serious 'differences in opinion' arose. Sashibhushan Basu, an author of early twentieth-century Bengal, also wrote on the problem of difference and arrived at a similarly agnostic position:

Differences along the lines of religion are not unnatural, nor unparalleled in history.... But recently we are faced with a severe dilemma. We now know that it is an absolute imperative in the interest of the 'nation' to 'unite'. Again, we cannot do without our age-old social and religious idiosyncrasies.... By the merit of our education, we get the sense of the extreme dilemma we are caught in, but we hardly know what to do.[78]

Basu explained the problem by referring to Tocqueville's *Democracy in America*:[79]

Epochs sometimes occur, in the course of the existence of a nation, at which the ancient customs of a people are changed, religious beliefs disturbed, and the spell of tradition broken.... They are emancipated from prejudice, without having acknowledged the empire of reason; they are animated neither by instinctive patriotism nor by thinking patriotism but they have stopped half way between the two in the midst of confusion and distress.

Following this wisdom, Basu would argue: 'Differences around the issues of religion, regional lifestyle, and caste are pulling us back when forming a nation. But it is not wrong to belong to one's own small groups determined by such ties, as long as we can preserve some "common interest" in certain other matters.'[80] Basu found it possible to maintain and foster certain 'common interests' and thereby create a scope for building a broad-based 'nation', in spite of its basic internal differences. The two above-mentioned intellectuals never belonged to any particular political group or association, yet their expositions deserve special mention due to their remarkable agnosticism, or at best, the ever-optimism that the Congress ideologues like Banerjea held on to.

Nevertheless, for the second group comprising a large number of swadeshi ideologues and activists, addressing the challenge of difference was nothing but sheer waste of time, leaving the direct struggle against colonial rulers woefully pending. National traditions had to be based on history, myths, and symbols, which had inevitably to be infused with a sense of religious culture, namely, the Hindu spirit. It was more so, because, even for those who felt the need for the bridging of different identities and interests of society for the sake of 'unity', the imagined national community could not but be conceived in hegemonic terms. Such hegemonic notions started from the physical visions of the nation, or the way it was conceptualized. The large number of artistic portraits of the nation, and the nation evoked in swadeshi songs, poems, and idioms, gave rise to a distinct cult of Bangajanani, Mother Bengal.[81] The image of Mother Bengal soon became linked to the image of the nation suggested in the final verse of Bankimchandra's song 'Bande Mataram', a key national hymn by this time.

To the protagonists of more active resistance to colonial authority, the need to promulgate and popularize these notions and visions of Mother Bengal was only too urgent. If in the process of such political–cultural exercise some 'others' felt neglected or offended, they would rather let it be so. Their calls to promote a *jatiya samaj*, that is, a national society, almost necessarily drew the required emotional appeal from historical and religious imageries. The precolonial history of India soon developed as a site for idealized promises and fabricated narratives. Fabrications, or at least selective erasures of collective memory, indeed were absolutely necessary to suit the nationalist purpose for projecting a sense of unity.[82] When around the time of the first pronouncement of Bengal parti- tion, a prominent lady of the illustrious Tagore family and a niece of Rabindranath Tagore named Sarala Devi rediscovered Pratapaditya, a lost historical hero of Bengal, and introduced the Pratapaditya Utsav in April 1903, her mission was to instill a sense of one-ness among the 'Bengalis' through the popularization of the glories of Pratapaditya. One of the famous *baro bhuyian*s of the Bengal *subah* (province), that is, the twelve local chieftains-cum-landlords known to have put up a brave fight against the Mughals, Pratapaditya was supposed to have saved Hindu rulers in an era of political turmoil. In her overenthusiastic 'national' mission, Sarala Devi completely neglected the fact that Pratapaditya had actually turned into an extortionist ruler, later deposed by his own rebellious subjects aided by the Mughal general Man Singh.[83] With this selective forgetfulness in propounding a story of a Bengali 'hero', Sarala Devi also allowed herself to be oblivious of the fact that her cherished hero could appear as a great anathema to Bengal's Muslims.[84] In fact, the problem went beyond the Muslim question. Pratapaditya, the landed elite ruler of Jessore in southern Bengal, was by no means a popular leader but a dominant power-figure with whom few other than the urban, upper-caste, well-educated Bengali Hindu champions of nationalism could identify. The same was true for Shivaji, the iconic Maratha warrior-ruler. Throughout the first few years of the twentieth century, the cult of Shivaji continued to spread in various parts of Bengal. It was celebrated in June 1906 by the extremists of the movement in a clearly Hindu manner. For the so-called Extremists, the task of mobilizing even a small part of the society in the name of nation became so urgent and desperate that these limitations of controversial historical symbols were comfortably glossed over. Taking a cue from Sarala Devi, Nikhilnath Ray (1905) and Satyacharan Shastri (1906) both wrote tracts titled *Pratapaditya*.[85] The Bengali theatre world also did not miss the chance: Kshirodprasad Vidyavinod launched the play *Pratapaditya* in the Star Theatre, while the Minerva Theatre in a competing bid began to stage a play by the same name, scripted by a different playwright, Amar Dutta. Religious symbols and customs were brazenly brought to the forefront. Significantly, in her search for a 'proper national festival' (*jatiya utsav*), Sarala Devi first came up with the idea of celebrating Virashtami (the eighth day in the auspicious fortnight of Devipaksha, that is, the fortnight during which the festival of Goddess Durga takes place). It was indeed celebrated for a couple of years before her next venture during Shivaji Utsav and then Pratapaditya Utsav. The last festival was to be deliberately celebrated on the auspicious first day of Bangabda (the Bengali calendar starting in mid-April). The cult of the Bengali nation began to be intricately connected with Hindu mythology on the one hand and historical myths on the other.[86]

The emergence of Extremists (the proponents of either passive resistance or more extreme methods of counter-aggression, that is, terrorism) played a major role in strengthening and popularizing this trend of self-consciously and deliberately Hindu notions of nation. In 1906, at a time when there was perceptible enthusiasm around the launching of the AIML, Rashbehari Ghosh in his speech at the twenty-second session of Indian National Congress held in Calcutta talked about 'nation' and the importance of having an active 'national platform', without a single reference to the possibility or the reality of alternative association(s). Aurobindo Ghose declared in 1907 that 'the political strife has assumed a religious character ... [by] men who have realized that the true secret of power is Faith'.[87] Other speeches and articles of Aurobindo Ghose in 1907–8 would similarly reveal his firm convictions in the *sanatan dharma* (classical faith), which, he believed, would salvage the nation from the imminent moral and political crisis embedded in the present state of subordination. This sanatan dharma would have to be 'applied as it has never been applied before to the problem of politics and the work of national revival'.[88]

Bepinchandra Pal, the 'high priest' of swadeshi activities, invoked the imageries of a Hindu nation in a similar fashion, but at the same time, never found it incongruous to base his ideas of a 'composite nationalism' on the fundamentals of Hinduism. He believed that while the compositeness of the future Indian nation was an absolute imperative, considering the interests of a multi-lingual and multi-racial country, the Hindu overtures of the nation could be blended with it in a comfortable way. Multiculturalism, for Pal, could provide the 'form' to the nation, whereas the 'substance' would be culturally more specific. In an editorial in *Bande Mataram*, one of the most important contemporary journals of the period, Pal explained why the 'bedrock' or 'groundwork' of his composite nationalism should be essentially Hindu:[89]

> The groundwork of what may well be called the composite culture of India is undoubtedly Hindu.... The different world religions representing different world culture that have already found a habitation in India will remain here always, *form elements of common national life*, and contribute to the evolution of the composite culture of modern India. The Hindu culture however, on account of its *age and superior numerical strength*, will always form the *groundwork* of this composite Indian culture and civilization [emphasis added].

Time and again, Pal pleaded for greater cultural contacts between two major communities of the country, and hoped that the spread of politics, of course the boycott and the related agenda of the Extremist variant of politics, would bring the communities closer.[90] That other communities would be given a fair-place 'common national life' was his proposition; however, during the swadeshi years, he did not address the obvious implication of his claim that the 'age and superior numerical strength' of Hindu culture might in the end indicate an 'inferior' place to these others. We should see in the next chapter how this view partially changed over a few years, when Pal, leaving out 'composite nationalism', would eventually develop the idea of a 'federalist nationalism'.

The divisive ideological position of swadeshi, more commonly known to us, was a continuous and self-sustaining trend. Ramlal Sarkar, the writer of a less-known tract represented this viewpoint with great persuasion when he recommended a division of two communities for all political and cultural realms.[91] It seemed important to safeguard the *swadesh*, the homeland, from the British and also from the memory of the 'past injustices of the Muslim rule'. He voiced the sentiments of many in claiming that 'people were impoverished and constantly threatened by the endless cruelties of the rulers as well as the subordinate Muslim state-officials'.[92] In a chronological account of 'Muslim atrocities' perpetrated to *Bangali* bhadraloks over the ages, Sarkar went on prescribing the duties of the neo-Bengali (*nabya Bangali*): it was no longer prudent to look up to the administration helplessly, rather it was time to take up power in one's own hands. It was now time for some 'manliness' (*purushochito karya*). The 'manly' duties would, however, be to strengthen the Bengali Hindu community on the basis of its own strength, not discarding or essentially antagonizing the Muslims, but bearing in mind that 'self-help is the best help'.

By now, the allegedly fast growth rate among the Muslims began to be seen as a serious threat by this section of Bengali Hindus. In the Bengal Provincial Conference held at Pabna (1908), the Chairman of the Reception Committee analysed in his address how the Hindus in Bengal had been transformed into a decadent race, evident in the census figures from 1871 to 1901. This surely meant an impending danger to the 'national society', he pointed out. Same alarm was raised by the publication of a book named *A Dying Race* by U.N. Mukherjee. First published in *Bengalee*, the book soon triggered off a heated controversy. Sakharam Ganesh Deushkar challenged his thesis in his well-documented work *Bangiya Hindu Jati Ki Dhwansonmukha?* (Is Bengali Hindu a dying race?).[93] Deushkar showed that the census figures were based on Bengal as an administrative unit, which changed in composition a couple of times in the preceding four decades, counting off either Malda or Kachhar or Manbhum at times. 'Bengal should be considered, not as an administrative, or linguistic or religious entity, but as a social–cultural entity.' Stepping outside the categories of colonial administration, this was an attempt to conceive Bengal in terms of the characteristic socio-cultural life of the region itself.

In this way, while the compositeness of 'nation' was suggested and explored by some nationalists, the principle of forging unity by erasure of difference seemed an absolute priority for some others. However, there emerged yet another, a third, view of 'nation', distinctive from the above trends. A handful of nationalist protagonists emphasized that the route to political unity must be conceived through a robust agenda of social regeneration. The neglect of socially constructive work by the so-called swadeshi agenda, they pointed out, would amount to a strategic lapse with dangerous consequences.[94] Champions of each trend of swadeshi had problematized the nation in their own distinctive ways. Their social views and political agenda followed directly from those basic premises of nationalist visions. Rarely were these contending trends watertight compartments with little mutual overlap; yet the defining features of the disparate premises of nation are hard to miss.

When Dwijendralal Roy, the eminent nationalist playwright of the time, mentioned in a number of letters written to his friend and biographer, Debkumar Ray, that he could be optimistic about the high-sounding swadeshi objectives of national unity and mutual tolerance only if the movement focused on 'people',[95] it can be seen as a nascent form of the third trend of swadeshi nationalism. Indeed, the immense political cost of the oversight in the swadeshi agenda could not remain unnoticed even by the contemporaries. Dhiren Chaudhuri, a swadeshi thinker, pointed out in *Nabya Bharat* that all reference to the Muslims as foreign invaders must be stopped, just as swadeshi practices of holding Shivaji and Pratapaditya festivals must be discontinued in the interest of national unity.[96] The reactions were often not strictly limited to the intellectual segments of the society. An anonymous pamphlet, published in Calcutta shortly after the city started erupting in political demonstrations in 1905, discussed the need for care and caution in invoking political unity:[97]

> Religion is the basis of our culture.... The religious practice of one community can hurt the same of another. Conflict is therefore unavoidable if we let religion enter into our political movement.... *So long [as] we have differences, it is not at all advisable to hold religion as the basis of our national polity.* However, that is not to say 'eliminate religion from your life if you want to participate in swadeshi movement'. We all can perform

our private rites at home, and come out to pursue our collective mission together [emphasis added].

The author of this circumspectly positioned tract explained why religious symbols, myths, and associations seemed important in the course of such collective imagining of the nation. However, he thought, these easy shortcuts should be resisted in the best interests of the society. Significantly, while an anonymous tract discussed this 'terrible illness' of the society, the very same argument was offered by the leading intellectual of the time, Rabindranath Tagore.

Once an enthusiastic proponent of the old Hindu institutions and ideals, Tagore gradually developed an awareness of the shortcomings of the essentially Hinduized nationalist vision. Even in the pre-swadeshi times, he had been strongly proposing the need to devote energy and enterprise in the creation of a 'swadeshi samaj' through the ground-level constructive programme of self-regeneration, termed by him as *atmashakti* (self-help). The deeply introspective speeches delivered in Minerva and Curzon Theatres (1904), and the resultant article 'Swadeshi Samaj' (1904) delivered a call for turning away from conventional politics in order to build up one's own strength through constructive and educational work, that is, swadeshi and national education.[98] This call found momentum during the swadeshi movement, was reiterated during the movement in his essays published in *Bhandar*, the swadeshi journal launched by him, and also in his presidential address in the Pabna Provincial Conference (1907) after the initial excitement of the swadeshi movement was over. Again, the term 'illness' came up, this time in one of Tagore's famously polemical essays titled 'Byadhi o Pratikar' (The illness and its remedies). What, according to him, was the cause of this 'illness'? The answer was simple: the inability to see plain facts. 'It is no use spreading lies. We must now accept that there is a huge discord between the Hindu and the Muslim societies. It is not only true that we are different. We are opposed to each other.' The root of such contradiction or opposition lay, he would insist, in the continuation of a 'crime', the crime of not acknowledging 'others' as people of similar dignity and similar abilities. Against what he considered as the facile calls for unity, he sounded a solemn note of warning:

All of us are wailing today that the British are secretly inciting the Muslims against the Hindus. If the charge is correct, why be angry with the British? Why should we be so foolish as to imagine that the British will not utilize our own weak points? Let us pause and ponder as to how the Muslims are being turned against the Hindus and not worry over who is doing it. The devil can enter our citadel, only if there is a chink in our armour. Hence our main task is to make our own defence impregnable, and not fume against the devil.[99]

Tagore had already been averse to the mendicant mode of prayer-and-petition politics of the Moderates. Now he started abhorring the Extremist techniques of political mobilization, an unthinking political hyper-ness ('asphalan', as he himself described such brand of politics in 'Byadhi o Pratikar'). All forms of the menacingly shortsighted political activities pursued for immediate gains would be done away with; instead, he would now advocate a complete focus on social work.[100]

His position already began to attract criticism, even from close quarters. In a reply to Tagore's 'Byadhi o Pratikar', first published in *Prabasi* (Sravan 1314 BS [Bangla Shon, the Bengali calendar], that is, July 1907), Ramendra Sundar Trivedi wrote an article by the same name in the following issue of the same journal (September 1907). There he would criticize Tagore for being 'over-anxious' and politely accused him of an exaggeration of inter-communal discord. He emphatically pointed out that the signs of discord arising in some parts of the province were just natural aberrations of a nascent national movement which were bound to subside with the maturity and success of the movement. 'We should not feel so scared at this temporary over-enthusiasm ("*asphalan*") of the Hindus or the temporary derailment of the Muslims.'[101] He, therefore, would rather stick to his espousal of swadeshi brand of activities, a fresh departure from the earlier 'non-action' and 'passive optimism', which would eventually sort the social crisis on their own.

Tagore, however, was unconvinced. By 1907, his disillusionment with swadeshi was so profound that he would dissociate himself from formal political activities. Although he would still carry on a 'political' life in the coming decades, as I will discuss in the next chapter, the termination of the swadeshi phase of his direct political engagement indeed contained a serious critique of the swadeshi nationalism. In the very same year, 1907, when he penned his critique in 'Byadhi o Pratikar', he also delivered his famously defiant speech in Pabna Provincial Conference. That same year, he also started writing *Gora*, one of his finest novels, in which an uncertain and evasive 'nation' would imperil the 'national' awareness.[102] The creed of 'nation through social regeneration' as opposed to that of 'nation through political unity', was most effectively voiced by Tagore in all these expositions, which pointed towards the emergence of a very differently conceived and passionately articulated alternative nationalism.

Tagore was not alone in struggling with the crisis of nationalism. There was at least one leader of swadeshi Bengal, who was as earnest but more successful than Tagore in promoting a directly political agenda based on this creed. Aswinikumar Dutta, a rather unexplored figure of this time, had preceded Tagore in many ways in the realms of socially constructive work and in the corresponding criticism of the 'Congress brand of politics'. As far back as in 1897, during the Amarabati session of the Congress, Dutta denounced the nature of Congress politics as 'three days' *tamasha*'. Later in the same year, he had the opportunity of meeting Vivekananda in Almorah to discuss the principle of national self-regeneration at great length. He outlined in an article the fundamentals of any robust national politics: 'national education, national arbitration, construction of local libraries and galleries'.[103] He established the Barisal Janasadharan Sabha in the early 1880s, even before the birth of the Congress, and spread health and educational amenities in the rural areas of this district through this association thereby anticipating the more widely known *Swadesh Bandhab Samiti* during the swadeshi movement. No wonder, this southeastern district of Bengal became the most successful site of swadeshi endeavours from 1904–5 onwards. Dutta was indeed supported by a huge mass following unequalled by any other leader of Bengal had at that time. Tagore called him 'deshbandhu', the first one to receive the epithet (1898) in the course of nationalist movement.[104] So consistent were his efforts at social reconstruction throughout the first decade of the century that Tagore's pre-swadeshi congratulatory title was repeated by Bepinchandra Pal in the late-swadeshi era, who considered Dutta 'the only person who has a large and devoted following among the masses', the true *loka-nayak* (leader of the people).[105] The leading school in the district of Barisal, Brajamohan Vidyalaya, was established by him, the model of which was followed in more than 200 relatively smaller primary schools in the same district during 1905–6. The Swadesh Bandhab Samiti succeeded in creating 41 branches within a year of its establishment in August 1905, and at least 159 branches by 1908, all of which performed in an exemplary way to extend education, offer arbitration to local disputes, and provide emergency relief during natural calamities.[106] His primary focus was on the rural Muslims, a majority community in Barisal and other districts of eastern Bengal. Colonial rulers found in him a more potent threat than leaders like Bepinchandra Pal due to the former's remarkable 'ability to reach and mobilize Mahomedans'.[107]

Dutta was considered to be an Extremist protagonist and a threatening figure by the district administration, although he was never close to the prominent political groups, either the Moderates or the Extremists.[108] But, an 'Aashwin' (a derivative of 'Aswini') brand of politics, as he himself used to depict his own politics, was indeed launched in his locality on a limited scale. This politics represented the third variant of Hindu political ideology of swadeshi times, approaching the problematic of 'nation' not from above or from the higher planes of large political organizations, but from below, through a careful everyday politics of rural regeneration. That this politics was received with admiration by his contemporaries can be inferred from the fact that his name was suggested for the position of president of Pabna Provincial Conference (1908), before Tagore's name appeared to replace it. Dutta continued to be seen by colonial rulers and nationalist leaders alike as an eccentric but dedicated social worker, with the potential of turning into a demagogue in the future.

The swadeshi movement started losing its initial optimism and vibrance after 1907. As it waned, bitter conflicts between the Moderates and the Extremists revealed, more than ever, their fundamental disagreements over the two trends of swadeshi, which, among their other disagreements, also displayed a deep ideological split: one favouring a composite nation, and the other, somewhat covertly, a Hindu nation. For the later radical leadership of the swadeshi era, and also for the emerging groups of militant nationalists, concerns about 'unity' seemed only a restrictive 'Moderate' ploy of stalling and shelving any agitational movement. They considered any constructive social programme only as an unnecessary hurdle in the way of the immediate goal of freedom. 'Unity versus Freedom' now became the crux of the controversy, as reflected in a protracted debate on 'national' priority between two leading newspapers, *Bengalee* and *Bande Mataram*, the former representing Surendranath Banerjea's views, and the latter the creed of Aurobindo Ghose. In his characteristically polemical style, Aurobindo Ghose asked his followers to refrain from the 'banya' (trader) mentality of 'buying' freedom from the rulers:

> We tried to prove from History that nations had been made free not by a scrupulous pursuit of unanimity or of unity in action but by faith, energy and courage.... Politics is for the Kshatriya and in the Kshatriya spirit alone can freedom and greatness be attained, not by the spirit of the

Banya trying to buy freedom in the cheapest market and beat down the demands of Fate to a miser's niggard price.[109]

The Moderate–Extremist debate remained a significant inheritance of the swadeshi years, finally, of course, marking the victory of the latter, that is, the more radical leaders. Under their auspices, the late swadeshi political agenda began to revolve around social networks grown mostly on the basis of Hindu religious–cultural affinities in various localities. The local associations in Calcutta and the districts were overwhelmingly Hindu in terms of membership, interests, and political programme. One of their naturally developed objectives was to protect Hindus from any real or perceived aggression. These local bodies often bordered on being Hindu in the narrowest sense of the term and, consequently, came perilously close to an aggressive exclusionist ideology. It is not a surprise that as early as in 1907, the Hindu volunteers of local associations played a critical role in the riots in Comilla and Jamalpur.

But who were these 'Hindus'? Of course, the gradual emergence of a different battlefront within the Hindu community can also be traced back to the late swadeshi years. The growing assertions of low-caste groups within the Hindu community were increasingly making themselves felt in the localities. Although still somewhat inarticulately pronounced and dissipated in nature, the ideas that began to govern the behaviour of these groups included a will to dissociate themselves from swadeshi. Neither the creed of unity nor the creed of faith promulgated during swadeshi offered them a comfortable ground for belonging to, or any prospect of equal membership in the imaginary of swadeshi 'nation'. It is worth remembering that the Barisal District Conference of August 1908 was not attended by the Namasudras of the region, and none of the upper-caste Hindu delegates there raised a single caste-related question, like the already politicized issue of accepting food and water from the hands of the 'lowly' people.[110] Instead, it was suggested by many at this conference as well as by some high-caste 'well-wishers' in a Namasudra Conference that followed in the same year that the Namasudras would not benefit themselves by engaging in 'quarrels' with the higher classes. Occasional efforts were made to build bridges, but rather sporadically and half-heartedly. In October 1909, Ambika Mazumdar took a tour across the Faridpur–Bakarganj area to enlist some Namasudra support for the boycott movement, but only with very humble success.[111]

The response of the marginal social groups towards the swadeshi leadership was often disapproving as well as sarcastic. When, under the leadership of Guruchand Thakur, the Namasudras in Gopalgunj in eastern Bengal welcomed the partition, a major Namasudra propagandist of the area began to preach low-caste self-help in order to oppose swadeshi. The level of bitterness was reflected in his anti-swadeshi songs: 'To become a nationalist, all round these ravings/ Do any of you know what a nationalist means?'[112]

In hindsight, such articulations would raise a doubt, though. Did the tone of condemnation here not entail a latent wish for gaining respectability instead of equality? In other words, were the low-caste protagonists like Thakur demanding an equal status with the high caste, or just eyeing for any status or any place, however indefinite and subordinate, within the nation? The incipient language and politics of 'identity' had yet to develop into a discourse of 'rights'. This would take place only when the politics of 'rights' would reveal itself more directly in the following decades. The low-caste discourse during swadeshi was essentially of a limited character, no doubt.

The same limited vision of low-caste politics also characterized the upper-caste construction of the 'national'. Tagore developed a strong critique of untouchability, but he also failed to circumvent this conceptual constraint.[113] Even the well-meaning swadeshi leaders like him could hardly venture to eradicate the entire caste system or to step beyond the primary task of condemning the oppressive practices of untouchability. The swadeshi agenda was not yet ready to embrace the notions of social or economic equality. This inherent limitation points towards a very critical characteristic of their 'nation', of course. It shows that the 'nation' of even the most liberal protagonists had to hold on to an essentially stratified existence, strangely enough, for the sake of its own authenticity. In the words of Tagore, the caste system or *varnashrama*, the 'classic feature of the Indian civilization', had to be maintained as a social inheritance, while the evil practices of untouchability had to be done away with.[114] The eminent nationalist writer Dwijendralal Roy also thought similarly and took the pain of arguing at length why caste system was to be preserved and upheld to maintain the uniqueness and the time-tested resilience of the 'Eastern-style' civilization of India. The 'national characteristics' of the English and the Hindus were so widely different that any hope to create a 'nation' on the Western model would be self-defeating, Dwijendralal thought.[115] The need was to effect a 'reform' of the present system only to make it work better, but not a 'revolution' to change the social structure altogether.[116] Since the complex history of the caste movement and caste politics in Bengal is outside the scope of this study, I would only point out that the swadeshi period was essentially marked by an opposition or, at best, an indifference towards the deeper questions of equal rights or equal representation within the 'national' society. For the most liberal swadeshi social reformer, the problem of untouchability was neatly separated from its concomitant notions of social stratification, and a pragmatic rather than an ideologically rebellious position was sought for the otherwise glorious construct of the 'nation'.

The inability to problematize difference in terms of caste inequality and the question of equal social rights would continue to haunt the structure and character of the Bengali nation, often surreptitiously. Remarkable is how on this question the demarcating lines used to collapse between the various competing trends within nationalism, between the Extremists and Moderates, and between the believers of the 'nation through political unity' and those of the 'nation through social regeneration'. The caste question did and would remain the most ubiquitous deterrent in the narrative of the nation, as is indicated in its early versions.

Still, a ray of hope began to emerge, not in the realm of the upper-caste construct of the nation, but outside it. The protests against the hegemonic claims of the 'nation' could no longer be avoided or stalled. Any national or regional imaginary immediately charged the marginal groups and communities with a sense of rebelliousness against the surreptitious project of 'other'-ing of the nation and a concomitant wish to harbour alternative territorial claims. 'When the country be true for us, will be our base, / We will bet our life to relieve her distress' (*Jedin bujhibo satyo amader desh, / Pran diye ghuchaibo jananir klesh*): the words of Guruchand Thakur of Gopalgunj contained the kernel of the challenge borne into the new awakening of the non-hegemonic societies. The hegemonic 'nation' would soon discover its own predicament in the proposed 'national' journey, and would variously attempt to address, by either assimilating or negotiating with, this challenge of 'otherness'.

The Emergence of the 'Local'

All these political and cultural contestations of the swadeshi 'nation' were nevertheless marked by a common quest, that is, the quest for roots, for a spatial or territorial attachment.[117] One of the most significant messages of the swadeshi movement was that 'nation', *swa-desh*, etymologically implying a place of one's own, had to be the search for an identity territorially bound and geographically defined. The immediate context of living and belonging became exceedingly important, leading to an altogether new and potent locus of identity, which is the region or locality. The question of locality became so central and vital both in Hindu and Muslim 'national' constructions during the swadeshi era that it eventually could not but provide an alternative dimension of unity and belongingness, or an alternative meeting ground within the meta-narrative of 'nation'.[118]

The wave of swadeshi activities spread from the metropolis to the mofussils. Popular organizations, both Hindu and Muslim, sprang up in different neighbourhoods (*paras*) in Calcutta and other cities, led by prominent professionals. These professionals had most often come to the city from their ancestral homes in mofussils or villages of Bengal, where, no less significantly, the spell of swadeshi had begun to be felt. The swadeshi period thus marked a tying up of the mofussils with the metropolis, and brought a distinct awareness as well as concern in the city about the districts and villages far removed from the urban settings. If terming it as a rural–urban integration would seem to be an undue glorification, the critical change in 'national' awareness could at least be called a moment of a new connection, hard to be missed. Most commonly, this introduction of a 'local' flavour to the nation was carried out by the innumerable grass-root level political associations or *samitis* (associations) that surfaced during the swadeshi movement. These samitis became the principal blood vessels of Bengali political life hence. If seen in contrast with a few developed earlier, the explicit emphasis of these local samitis established since 1905 was on political objectives and, very often, on revolutionary activities. From the Anushilan Samitis of Dacca and Calcutta to the Athletic Club (Balaram Majumdar Street, Calcutta), the Swadesh Sevak Samiti (Ahiritola, Calcutta), or the district-level associations like Brati Samiti of Faridpur, Suhrid Samiti of Mymensingh, and Swadesh Bandhab Samiti of Barisal: all were established between 1905 and 1907, and were enjoying parallel ties with the city and the countryside. Despite their projected image as recreational samitis, these associations used to possess full-time political cadres and organized special training programmes.

The swadeshi era witnessed new Muslim associations as well. In addition to the older ones like Anjuman-e-Islamia (1855) or Mohammedan Literary Society (1863), the Bengal Mohammedan Association (1906), the Indian Mussalman Association (1907), and the Bengal Provincial Muslim League (BPML, 1909) emerged during this time. More ceremonious was the foundation of the Provincial Mohammedan Association in eastern Bengal and Assam (16 October 1905) in Dacca. Established on the very day the partition was effected, this organization in fact provided critical leadership in the subsequent politics of 'difference' in the newborn province. With the foundation of the AIML in 1906 under the overarching leadership of Nawab Salimullah, presiding over both the premier organizations in the new province, the regional Muslims gained a new voice and a new standing in the politics of the province.

How the new identity of locality played a critical role in politics must be apparent in the events of inter-communal cooperation during swadeshi. Clearly, after the partition, the Muslims in the eastern Bengal mofussils were not alone in their support of the partition: they were joined by the low-caste Namasudra leaders. Even the upper-caste groups often crossed the line of religious divide to create a united 'local' front. A later writer called Girishchandra Sen recalled how in an eastern Bengal village he saw a new hope of material and cultural improvement after partition. The administrative decision, in his view, served as a unique opportunity of developing the hitherto backward localities into self-sustaining units. He wrote:

> I am not against but in favour of the partition of Bengal. It is my firm belief that it would surely contribute to the development of this hitherto neglected region.... The prosperity of the Bengalis might be an eyesore to many. In Calcutta and its neighbourhood, qualified persons from East Bengal can never have an easy entry to the offices, and are thwarted by the people of Calcutta. The clerical jobs in Calcutta are always the monopoly of the local people.[119]

In reality, even for the few who initially resisted partition, the making of a new province began to make sense after a couple of years. Nawab Atikulla, the defiant brother of Nawab Salimullah, one of the chief priests of pro-partition movement, was opposed to the whole idea of dissecting the province. In the 1906 session of the All India Congress Committee (AICC) in Calcutta, he attempted to correct the prevalent misperceptions about the support for partition:

> I may tell you at once that it is not correct that the Mohammadans of Eastern Bengal as a body are in favour of partition. The real fact is that it is only a few leading Mohammadans who for their own purposes supported the measure.... As a matter of fact, with the exception of Nawab

Salimullah, the view of the Khwaja family is that partition is a great wrong
done both to Hindus and Mussalmans, and it should be revoked.[120]

But within a couple of years, the younger brother changed his mind,
joined his elder brother Salimullah, and appeared in the Muslim
Conference in Dacca convened by the latter in protest of the revocation
of partition in 1911. As the neo-convert would explain his position, the
local interests of Dacca and its neighbourhood forced him to change
his earlier views. However, it can safely be surmised that power politics
played a critical role here, especially considering the larger prospects that
the partition brought to one of the most powerful families of Dacca—
the second metropolis of Bengal and the capital of the new province of
eastern Bengal. But in the same context we may review the examples of
Maniruzzaman Islamabadi and Ismail Hossain Siraji, as discussed earlier
in this chapter, for shifting from an earlier pro-swadeshi position to the
support for partition. As we have noted earlier, they were eventually
reconciled with the significant gains that the new province would generate for the local (Muslim) communities.

If the interests of eastern Bengal appeared paramount to some Hindus
like Sen who supported partition, the same interests of the districts led
most of the Hindus of East Bengal to oppose partition. They suffered
from the fear that partition might destroy the social and economic base
of their homeland by dissecting them from the more populated, more
prosperous, of course, more 'Hindu' parts of western Bengal. It would
be a sheer over-simplification to say that these eastern Bengali Hindus
resisted partition only because of their narrow 'communal' association
with the western district of Bengal. The resistance was more layered
and more nuanced than what a Hindu 'communal' outlook would
usually denote. The district of Barisal might be a case in point. Under
the stewardship of Aswinikumar Dutta, Satishchandra Mukhopadhyay,
Mukunda Das, and Brahmabhandhab Upadhyay, swadeshi agitation
took fierce shape in this district. All these leaders were charged with
a passion for their own district and their own local dialect of Barisal.
Sandhya, a popular newspaper edited by Upadhyay, adopted a linguistic
style suitable for the common village masses, and thereby departed from
the standardized swadeshi cultural trends. Apparently, a large number of
the village officials and zamindari staff like *gomasta*s and *naib*s, as well
as the local cart-drivers, street vendors, hawkers, and general villagers in
Barisal used to constitute a loyal readership of this newspaper. Spreading
national education was one of its chief objectives after 1906.

We say that we shall create a new independent system, which will regulate our education, the protection of our lives and properties, our trade and commerce, our agriculture, our laws and our courts, our rents and all our dealings. We do not wish to remain forever under the restraints of foreign domination…. We know that complete independence is impossible for the present. But nonetheless that it is the goal which should always be before our eyes.[121]

Even if the 'we' of Upadhyay did not provide the Muslims or the low castes an equal footing in the 'national' society (his edited journal *Swaraj* contained a full-blown picture of Shivaji in 1907),[122] his liberalism was much too complex to be branded as 'Hindu swadeshi'. The predominantly Hindu composition of the politically aware society left a distinct mark upon the nation, where 'others' would not rightfully claim but must be 'given' their commensurate space in this society as a mark of generosity.

Was Upadhyay in a better position to admit candidly this Hindu nationalist position because the swadeshi movement was better organized in his own district than in the others? Arguably so, and here lies one of the most important features of the swadeshi discourse of nation. The direct acknowledgement of difference was never in the swadeshi interest. Rather, a particular construction of 'nation' and thereby a particular resistance towards the problem of difference was a fundamental attribute and inheritance of swadeshi ideology. In a number of districts in eastern Bengal, where the swadeshi movement did not strike deep roots, Muslims actually joined hands with their Hindu neighbours in local development activities. Hasmatali Chaudhuri and his followers in Nawabgunj,[123] and Munshi Fakirullah and Munshi Suleiman, the locally prominent legal practitioners in Dinajpur,[124] stood out in their ardent opposition to partition in the interest of their locality. Muzaffar Ahmed describes in his autobiography how the small islands around Chittagong like Sandwip, mostly Muslim-inhabited, underwent immense upheavals during swadeshi and how movements took place both for and against partition. According to him, for a schoolboy (as he had been at the time), it would have been just normal to join either of the groups, as no pressure was felt on the count of religious affinities.[125] The Muslims in Chittagong warmly welcomed the new province, but the swadeshi agenda of boycott also found an equally favourable response. The Bengal Steam Navigation Company, one of the major swadeshi ventures, an inter-communal enterprise, was jointly run in Chittagong by Jatramohan Sen (father of Deshapriya Jatindramohan) and Abdul

Bari Chaudhuri.[126] Establishment of meagrely funded political associations, small-scale schools, makeshift student hostels in the interior, the temporary yet inspiring spurt of national education and national business enterprise all contributed towards an organically buoyant view of 'nation' where differences could possibly be obliterated. The Muslims often took the direct initiative in such local enterprises in eastern Bengal, be it in favour of or in opposition to partition. It was not uncommon for them to collaborate with their Hindu counterparts when it was a matter of local interest. The evocation of an affective bonding in the name of the locality or region opened up possibilities of greater rapprochement:

> If all sucks milk from the single mother's breast
> Same blood and same strength in each one would rest.
> We'll call them all brother, by brother we abide—
> If we drink this same milk, in our love we'll be tied.[127]

In short, the less organized the swadeshi activists were, the more was their chance to combine with the Muslims. Greater organizational consolidation alienated the voices of difference and hindered the swadeshi 'nation' to broaden itself. The instance of Barisal would support this proposition.

The affective bonding of a region or locality also helps us appreciate the strong emotive appeal of the 'Bengali' identity, a key territorial and cultural sentiment of swadeshi. Territorial loyalties, just as in other cases, were hopelessly overlapping in Bengal. Scholars have often found the terms 'Bengali' and 'Indian' so interchangeable in swadeshi discourse that they have accepted that most often the purpose was not to denote any particular location, but to underline the contrasting civilization of the East as opposed to that of the colonizer.[128] This study suggests that, while the terms 'Bengali' and 'Indian' were interchangeable in some cases, in some other, their respective use and context, in fact, signifies an additional dimension of affinity. It is not to be missed that the idea of a 'Bengali' nation had to be accompanied by strong cultural evocations or deep sentimental expositions, whereas the 'Indian nation' seemed relatively distant. Starting from Bankimchandra Chattopadhyay's *Bande Mataram, sujalang sufalang malayajashitalam shashyashyamalang Mataram* (I bow to thee, O Mother, the richly-watered, richly-fruited, cool with the winds of the south, dark with the crops of the harvests, Mother!) of the nineteenth century, to Rabindranath Tagore's *Banglar mati, Banglar jal, Banglar bayu, Banglar fal, punya hayuk he Bhagaban*

(Let the earth and the water, the air and the fruits of Bengal be sweet, my God!) of the feverish days of 1905, and the passionate calls of a not-so-famous Muslim poet, Mohammed Mozammel Huq, 'Nirjib Bangali tora ke dekhibi aye'[129] (Come and see the lifeless lot of Bengalis), the reader is sure to note the impassioned imageries and earnestly enlivening urges. A charged sense of intimacy characterizes the imagining of the 'nation' when the term refers to the Bengali homeland. On the other hand, in case of the 'Indian nation', one is bound to notice a striking absence of intimate evocations. It is hard to overlook how often a direct address to *desh*, referring to either Banga-janani or more specific localities within Bengal, was evoked with *tui*, the more intimate term of addressing someone in Bengali, while addressing Bharat-mata would usually call for a more respectful and also a relatively distant term, *tumi*. A closer look at the swadeshi songs evidently exposes this varying affective identification with desh.[130]

A similar modulation of the affective tone is discernible in the Muslim discourse also. The sense of distance and discomfort continued to be vexing for those Muslims who sought to extend their 'national' loyalties beyond the region–nation, either in the name of India or that of world Islam. The distance hindered them from imagining the ties with the larger 'nation' in an affective tone, hence required a leap of 'faith', that is, taking recourse to carefully crafted claims of religion on the larger national entity. Both the Hindus and the Muslims, curiously, found themselves employing religious imageries and mythical memories for imagining their bonding with a trans-regional nation. Just as Bharat-mata was idealized by the Bengali Hindus for her integral symbols of Hindu glory, that is, the sites of piety like Kashi, Prayag, Prabhas, Pushkar, Braja, Mathura, the sacred streams of Ganga and Jamuna, 'avatars' like Rama, Krishna, Buddha, and historical heroes like Prithwiraja or Shivaji, similarly the bravery and piety of the long-lost Islamic civilization in the Arab lands served as the only emotional platform where Muslims from various parts of India could hope to meet. Religion proved to be the most important vehicle of imagination whenever the urge was felt for the envisioning of a larger 'country–nation'. The challenge of transcending the compelling emotive appeal of the region and the linguistically or culturally defined regional community was met ingeniously by both communities through the help of religious metaphors and symbols.

It is natural, therefore, that 'desh' in Bengali also had a more intimate usage than its usual reference to 'country-nation' that is, Bharatvarsha. This alternative usage was very closely associated with the feeling of a community. In such contexts, 'desh' would refer to the village-home, infused with a very deep sense of emotional attachment. This was the era when, following the British administrative initiatives of retracing the 'locality', the indigenous attempts began to take place at the reconstruction of the local regions by collecting micro-history of various districts and villages as well as taking greater care to incorporate folk or native elements more vigorously into the national culture and nationalist rhetorics. The pioneering attempts by Nagendranath Basu (who wrote the history of northern Rarh), Achyutranjan Chaudhury (*Srihatter Itibritto*, 1910), Kedarnath Majumdar (*Mymensingher Vivaran*, 1904) only to be followed by their intellectual heirs like Jogeshchandra Basu or Rakhaldas Bandyopadhyay, as well as the institutional initiatives of the Bangiya Sahitya Parishat to collect local tracts and compile local histories, were significant achievements of swadeshi patriotism. 'Desh' simultaneously denoted countryside or locality in a more immediate context, as well as an overarching political community or nation with a set of more distant attributes. The sense of parallel belongingness to different communities was pervasive, though rarely formalized in a clear, unambiguous manner. At the same time, the locality or the region also proved to be a handy conceptual platform on which various different identities could combine together. The space for negotiation was far from eliminated in the process. Whereas the creed of individuality, a necessary derivative of Enlightenment modernity, was the cardinal principle of nationalism, links between the immediate and the distant, between individuality and collectivity, between the 'self' and the 'other', and between the 'local' and the 'national' revealed considerable freedom of manoeuvre in imagining the nation in Bengal.

Representation: The Political Domain of the 'Self' and the 'Other'

In the corpus of modern political thought, the compromise between the collective and the individual is often sought to be resolved by the principle of representation. In the colonial context, however, this inevitably led to certain ideological predicaments.[131] There emerged a dilemma for the colonial subject when he, infused by modern concepts of equality within a 'nation', was constantly pushed towards an erasure of 'difference'. On the one hand 'difference' from the colonial rulers as an ideological construct had to be evoked constantly in order to raise claims of self-assertion and self-rule, and on the other an erasure of 'difference' seemed a necessary condition within the 'nation'. Yet cultural assertions of difference, by their very nature, were ever-particularistic, and one set of claims or identities would inevitably give way to the next set of differentiation. It was necessarily accompanied by the question of representation on the basis of 'difference'. The colonial subject would now have to struggle for its right as a unified collective against the colonial ruler, and at the same time, deal with the haunting realities of more fragmented groups and communities within his own society and culture.

Perceptions of the 'self' and the 'other' began to reveal remarkable divergences in the face of such a conundrum. The 'self' would take different forms at different times, often without any implicit conflicts between its potential forms. Sometimes it was the communitarian self, sometimes it was the regional self, at other times it might even comfortably denote a supra-regional national self.[132] Identities and the layers of self could coexist side by side, combine with each other, manifest themselves in varying contexts, and negotiate between themselves about the pressing needs of anti-colonial nationalism. Clearly, one's own identity or belongingness would also necessarily follow from these varying constructions of the self, and would continue to be variable themselves. The early years of twentieth-century Bengal witnessed a visible change in the visualization and formulation of this self as the proliferation of swadeshi discourse would suggest. Not only did the number of tracts or journals or articles suddenly soar, the level of articulation around political and cultural identities also betrayed an unprecedented height. The claims of belonging to a collectivity of any sort as well as the claims of an assertive individuality were brought forth for the first time with so much clarity and force.

A lesser-known author of this period, Ramlal Sarkar, already mentioned in a previous section,[133] can be recalled in this context. Sarkar outlined the tasks of the 'New Bengali' (Nabya Bangali) of his times, called for 'manly' assertions and, in doing so, went on to a thoughtful exposition of his own position vis-à-vis his own society. He pondered on in a remarkable self-reflection how a common individual like him was now more potent as a social being and therefore more liable to the social and political developments around him. Individual agency was felt with a definite, hitherto un-experienced, urgency. It was no longer the duty or responsibility of the leader, or the ruler, to think about or speak for the common man. The ultimate responsibility resided with the common individual like him. Before detailing out the duties and liabilities of the Bengalis (the Bengali Hindus, for him), he would explain, therefore, why he troubled himself so much as to write all this, or why he wasted his time and strained his mind over such complex issues, and, more importantly, who he was in the end. After all, he was none but an insignificant Bangali. Yet he felt that he had the right to speak his mind, on behalf of his own 'nation': 'Here I am…. Am I not one of this larger "whole", this society, this country? Am I not one who has some rights and responsibilities towards this "whole", which is my "nation"? Yes, I do have the right to think, express, pursue and thus determine the welfare of the "whole" to which I belong!'[134]

The fast spread of the spirit of individuality and individual right or responsibility indeed marked out swadeshi Bengal from the previous era. Proliferation of vernacular tracts on political and social reality constituted this changing spirit: people were no longer followers, but the makers of their own destiny. With such a new sense of political urgency and individual responsibility, the contestations between 'unity' and 'difference' gained an altogether different momentum.

The growing urge to recover and represent the individual voice was not limited to writing and expressing oneself verbally. With the birth of innumerable associations, expressions of the self could expand beyond the realm of thoughts and change the character of the social and political life of Bengal. The local samitis were named after any district, town, or even a para where this sense of belonging was immediate. At the same time, large political bodies also emerged in the name of a community and along the principles of self-representation. Significantly, the expressions of self through a community or a collective always proved to be more desirable. Ramlal Sarkar's words can also be read in a different light if we see how his proclaimed self was not of an individual but 'a part of a larger whole'. The initial boldness of the expression, 'Here I am,' would soon give way to his belonging to a community, a community of his own choice. In an age of fast-spreading national consciousness, the self would still find its ultimate purpose and justification in its exercise of 'choice' of the community, but rarely transcend the community identity. One should not overlook that even the most articulate voices of this time were raised in the name of representing the community, instead of the particular individuals.

But which community was to be held as the most immediate one, or the most urgent to represent? The urge of community representation is laden with its own inevitable contradictions. For the largest community of Bengal, the question of representation already proved itself to be troubling enough during the swadeshi era. The founding of the AIML stood as an epoch-making event in the history of Bengali Muslims. It is through this organization that the utterances of religious–cultural difference were translated for the first time into a political ground of representation. One of the main grievances against the All India Congress Committee was that its claims to represent all communities and all interests within India were appallingly unfounded, regardless of any social–economic or political differences. The launching of an alternative organization therefore seemed urgent on the basis of such difference. The Muslim League was founded to redress this long-felt grievance of a different community. Yet in no time it revealed itself to be almost equally over-ambitious in its claim to represent the Muslims of all parts of the country.

Quite logically, therefore, yet another set of particular claims arose to counter this ambitious claim of the Muslim League. Much along the same line as in the case of anti-Congress agenda, the new organization soon triggered off certain oppositional sentiments within itself. While the projections of 'all India Muslim interests' started attracting great numbers of followers, so far relatively unperturbed about the 'Muslim' events beyond the boundaries of the province, the new association at the same time antagonized a large section of Bengali Muslims by neglecting their concerns.[135] By the latter half of the 1910s, all-India Muslim interests began to be perceived in aggregative terms, was given a clear priority, and a group of regional proponents came up to champion 'national' Muslim interests as against the Bengali Muslim interests. The question of representation was clearly a political question, or an issue of competitive strength. As early as in 1905, an article in *Nabanur* had urged to give rise to an 'Indian Mussalman' community, the true counterpart of Hindu national identity.[136] Whether the Bengali Muslim 'self' should be extended into a national–religious existence or a regional–religious one remained a deeply divisive question.[137] Significantly, by itself this search for a different ground, or a different identity, did not inherently force the 'Indian Muslims' to move away from the collective 'national' (namely Indian, in this context) interest. It only provided them with the standing of confident self-assertion. This helps us grasp the spirit of the conclusive plea of the author quoted earlier: 'Hindu Brothers! Let us first have the chance to be Muslims, to stand on our own feet, and then call us to join hands with yours in the matter of politics!'[138] The right to represent the Indian 'nation' could only be attained through a strengthening of their distinctive 'self'-image or, more correctly, the 'community' image.

It goes without saying that such an urge could only be felt by those who had remained on the margin or under the veil of 'otherness'. The hegemonic community always found it difficult to deal with the quest of the non-hegemonic community for a confident identity with sympathy or generosity. So, when the Reform Act of 1909 allowed the Muslims with separate electorate the right to vote in the general constituencies and made the income qualification for Muslim voters lower than that for Hindu voters, it was deeply resented by Hindus all over the country, including in Bengal.[139] The new Act, in practice, gave a non-official majority to the Muslims only in the Bengal Legislative Council, and hence was gravely criticized for injecting the 'communal poison of separate electorate' and a system of patronage. 'If this becomes the rule of the day to uphold our own tiny fragments instead of a larger whole, if we stop thinking of others in the pursuit of self-interest, never again would humanity be restored even if one acquires all sorts of freedom and rights, let alone the Morley Reforms.'[140] The frustration of swadeshi politics was neatly summed up in the strongly worded statement by Bepinchandra Pal: 'India will not sell her soul for Morley's mess of pottage.'[141] For most of the educated Bengali Hindus, with their fervent beliefs in the indivisibility of nation, the concept of separate representation for the communities appeared anachronistic:

> The system of class representation is unknown in all civilized countries and it is unworkable in India. If class representation is to be introduced in India, the division of the Indian people into Hindu and Muslim will not do. There are sub-divisions even among each one of the two communities. Can Government arrange to take in representatives from each one of the sub-divisions?[142]

The politics of 'self' had, by definition, entailed a game of mirror-images. The Muslim newspapers and journals therefore immediately put forward a few contrary examples from the 'civilized countries'.

> Considering that in Municipal elections a Mahommedan candidate is often defeated for want of Hindu votes, how can it be reasonably expected that justice will be done to a Mahommedan candidate for a seat on the Legislative Council? ... The principle of good government consists in this that a weaker race should be saved from the jaws of a stronger one. [143]

Just as the logic of numbers dragged a section of Bengali Muslims towards an 'all-India' representative body, the inevitability of their minority position in the context of India attracted them to the model of separate representation. In defense of separate representation, the famously polemical journal *Mihir o Sudhakar* posed the following question: 'Would the Mahommedan candidate have a chance for a seat on the Legislative Council if there be no separate representation for them?'[144] Just before the Act was announced, the suspicion that the Muslim interest might not finally be taken heed of led them to place the 'minority viewpoint' with forceful assertion:

> A nation had far better become wholly extinct than pass entirely under the control of another.... Perhaps partition of Bengal may come to be modified next year. The Hindus held meetings in every village and every town and that is why Mr. Morley has acceded to their prayers....We also must tell the Government that we cannot be content unless half of Indian members in all the councils consists of Muslims.... If the fear of being oppressed as a minority is removed from the minds of Muslims, they will not mind the new change and co-operate in a friendly spirit with Hindus, not otherwise.[145]

To sum up, the problem of political and social justice in the realm of 'difference' had already been troubling to the Bengali Muslims. With the introduction of representative politics through the new Act of 1909, they were now thrown into an all-India minority status, and the need of the day seemed to be safeguarding and enhancing their own domain of representation. For the first time in history, a section of Bengali Muslim leadership found their regional political realities about to be overshadowed by the challenge of all-India identity. If the multiplicity of identities appeared troubling in the social and cultural lives of the Bengali Muslims, the question of identity proved to be a bitterly contentious one in the context of the new ideas of political representation. A cursory glance at the end of the partition decade helps us to appreciate how this contested domain of representation would slowly develop into the most important site of struggle around the claims of 'nation'.

Towards a New Politics

The heated debates of the swadeshi years over the issues of 'difference' and 'unity' continued even after the colonial rulers announced that Bengal would again be re-united as a single province from 1 April 1912. The annulment of partition was an unexpected boon to the Hindus, and a heartbreaking betrayal for most of the Bengali Muslims. The unprecedented social and political prominence that the partition of 1905 had brought for the Bengali Muslim elite was now lost. For the Muslim social reformers or the emerging class of professionals in the mofussils, the end of partition meant an immediate loss of social and economic opportunities. The deputation of Nawab Salimullah, Nawab Syed Ali Chowdhury, and Fazlul Huq sent to the viceroy in January (1912) put forward a compensatory demand for a new and separate university of Dacca for protecting the disadvantaged Muslim interest in eastern Bengal.

On the one hand, there were deep resentments coupled with new demands for compensation.[146] On the other, there was the danger of providing the Hindu swadeshi nationalists a political victory and strengthening their position altogether. Confronted by these twin pressures, the colonial rulers came up with an ingenious strategic adjustment: the decision to revoke the partition was coupled with transferring the capital from Calcutta to Delhi. It was also considered that the transfer of the capital to Delhi would serve to appease the disgruntled Muslims, who still cherished the memories and traditions of an old Islamic capital city. The borders of the newly constituted province were adjusted in a way so as to make Muslims the majority community (the Musilm–Hindu ratio becoming roughly 21:19 million). The anxiety over the backwardness of the Muslim-dominated eastern Bengal was also sought to be redressed by appointing the Calcutta University Commission to prepare a scheme for the new university in Dacca. In this way, the losses for the Bengali Muslims were sought to be compensated in a well-calculated balancing game.[147] One thing had become clear by now. 'Difference' in interests, sentiments, and aspirations of religious communities was being seen as an integral part of the discourse and politics of the 'nation' by the end of the swadeshi era. Any political change of a 'national' dimension must henceforth be seen to cater to the interests of any constituent group which had developed a distinct subjectivity for its own claims of difference.

Interestingly, 'difference' was also being re-evaluated and redefined in the light of the newly emerging discourse of representation. Many Muslims were now able to envisage a future position of strength in a reunited province on the basis of the principle of representation. How the 'losses' could possibly be compensated was being contemplated in this new light:

The partition of Bengal was advantageous to the Mussalmans of Bengal in all ways. This is why we rejoiced at the partition and prayed to the

Government to uphold it. However that may be, the present arrangement in placing the two Bengals under one Governor has satisfied the
Mussalmans of Bengal. But their prayer to the Government is this that
the advantages which the Partition gained for the Mussalmans of Eastern
Bengal in District Boards, Local Boards and Municipalities, in the public
service, in education may be maintained. In short, it is the earnest desire
of all Mussalmans in Bengal that a system of separate representation like
that for election of members to the Legislative Councils may be introduced ...[148]

The possibility of a Hindu–Muslim coexistence in the consolidated
province was discussed even before the annulment actually took place.
I have already mentioned that in 1909, *Mihir o Sudhakar*, a conservative journal from Bengal, had reflected on such a distant possibility,
and stated that 'if the fear of being oppressed as a minority is removed
from the minds of Muslims, they will not mind the new change and
co-operate in a friendly spirit with Hindus'.[149] Hidden in this comment
was a remarkable, and mostly unnoticed, sense of optimism about the
long-term prospects of the Bengali Muslims who, after suffering from
a huge minority complex despite their majority position in the province, could now hope for a reversal of fortune on the basis of the new
principles of representation. The demands of representation were to be
articulated more clearly in the following years, and the mechanisms of
representative politics were yet to unfold their nature. But it was more or
less accepted that the representative structure of administration would
be more amenable to safeguard community interests than a separate
administrative unit.

However, at the same time, the politics of representation forced
the Bengali Muslims to face a hugely divisive question. It immediately
meant strengthening the numerical base and the political presence of
the community, which, in turn, would increase the importance of the
'Indian Muslim' identity. For the Bengali Muslims, this meant a challenge, perilous in proportion, although not novel in nature. Eventually,
a more decisive and self-aware Bengali Muslim leadership would emerge
in the second decade of the twentieth century and address this challenge
from a position of regional strength.

The swadeshi era was thus coming to an end, in more than one
sense. 'Region', a vital conceptual construct embedded in all varieties
of nationalist thought, began to be precariously vexed with the claims
and counter-claims of 'nation'. Throughout the earlier decade, shifting
and contending identities of jati underwent considerable conceptual

experimentations, a process through which regional and/or local senti-ments proved to be overriding. But the swadeshi discourse, in course of its experiments with the political implications of the religious divide running through the region, had so far only dealt with the social and cultural bearings of the identity based on region. That the regional iden-tity also had huge political potential in the context of new politics of nation was yet to reveal itself. In the next decade, this potential would begin to be exposed, and more assertive regional nationalisms would emerge with the rise of a more self-conscious regional leadership among both the Bengali Hindus and Bengali Muslims. The following chapter will explore the new politics of constitutional representation and the new nationalisms emerging around this new political ground.

Notes

1. The famous line from Secretary of State H.H. Risley's note can once again be remembered: 'Bengal united is a power; Bengal divided will pull in several different ways. That is perfectly true and is one of the merits of the scheme.' See his Note of 7 February 1904, Home Public Proceedings A, February 1905, no. 155, accessed at the National Archives of India (henceforth NAI). The British 'design' of 'divide and rule', transparent and widespread in high-level deliberations of 1903–5, much explored in scholarly works, indicates that the new idea of national unity, however facile and implausible to some of its native audience, were intimidating to the colonial rulers.

   The Bengalis who like to think themselves a nation, and who dream of a future when the English will have been turned out, and a Bengali Babu will be installed in Government House, Calcutta, of course bitterly resent any disruption that will be likely to interfere with the realization of this dream. If we are weak enough to yield to their clamour now, we shall not be able to dismember or reduce Bengal again.

   See Lord Nathaniel Curzon, 17 February 1905, Lord Curzon Collection, MSS. Eur. F. 111/163, India Office Collections, British Library.

2. Nur Ahmed, *Bangiya Mussalman* (Calcutta, 1905 [1312 BS]), pp. 9–18, Vernacular Tracts, India Office Library (henceforth VT, IOL). All transla-tions in this work, unless otherwise stated, are mine, and I am indebted to my father, Sankha Ghosh, for helping me translate many of the Bengali poems to be found in this book.

   The first set of italicized words in this quote constitutes a few of the derogatory terms used in Bengali Hindu parlance to denote the Bengali Muslims, considered to have been hailed from the lowly social strata. The second set of words, generally meaning 'accursed' or 'those deprived of

God's mercy', is used by the conservative Muslims to refer to the non-Muslims at large.

3. See Swarupa Gupta, *Notions of Nationhood in Bengal, Perspectives on Samaj, 1867–1905* (Leiden: Brill, 2009), pp. 97–103.

4. Even before the Indian National Congress was founded in 1885, it became the order of the day to name political and cultural associations as 'national'. Increasingly the need was felt to erect a 'national' political community, which would justify and support the cause of anti-British struggle. With the emergence of a class of English-educated, middle-class, professional Indians gradually exhibiting a spirit of self-assertion, 'national' ideas began to gain considerable momentum. However, before the late nineteenth century, 'a concrete expression to the feeling of oneness in the form of written words was absent'. See Swarupa Gupta, *Notions of Nationhood in Bengal*, p. 137. This began to change as imagining the nation acquired emphatic overtones and finally gathered a distinct momentum during swadeshi.

5. Surendranath Banerjea, *A Nation in the Making: The Reminiscences of Fifty Years of Public Life* (1925; reprint, Bombay: Oxford University Press: 1963), p. 184.

6. The agitation seemed 'serious' to the administration at the political level. It showed the potential for and the desire 'to rouse anti-European feeling, to excite racial hatred', as mentioned in a letter by Sir Andrew Fraser, Lt Governor of Bengal, to Lord Curzon, Lord Curzon Collection, MSS. Eur. F111/198, no. 55, 1905, India Office Records (henceforth IOR), British Library.

7. One important purpose of this chapter is to argue that it is historiographically incorrect to portray the whole body of swadeshi thought as Hindu in its spirit and tenor. Although the movement created an image of a nation and a national homeland on the symbols of Hindu mythology, it was just one aspect of the nationalist thought of swadeshi. As Partha Chatterjee has already emphasized, the swadeshi movement had an explicit theme of Hindu–Muslim unity. See Partha Chatterjee, 'On Religious and Linguistic Nationalisms: The Second Partition of Bengal', in *Reflections on Partition in the East*, edited by Ranabir Samaddar (Delhi: Vikas, 1997), pp. 35–58. Swarupa Gupta also suggests the same when she argues that 'inclusive strands in the literati's "Hindu" discourse co-existed alongside conceptions of communal otherness'. S. Gupta, *Notions of Nationhood in Bengal*, p. 349.

8. Sumit Sarkar, in the preface to the new edition of his book on the swadeshi movement considers 'self-criticism, debate, [and] internal dissent' to be the most important legacies of the movement in response to the question: 'What would I regard now as the most valuable legacy of those times?' He adds, 'Had I been able to revise this book before the present new edition,

I would certainly have taken [the cultural achievements] up as central features of the Swadeshi era', in *Swadeshi Movement in Bengal, 1903–8* (Delhi: Permanent Black, 2010), p. xxiii.

9. Not only the Muslim support for partition of 1905, but the entire history of Indian Muslim politics in the first half of the twentieth century has generally been read and analysed in terms of an inexorable fact of Muslim separatism. It is often presupposed that the Muslims of the Indian sub-continent *were* separatist, instead of the fact that a part of them *became* separatist during the course of history. The Partition of 1947 is attributed to a consistent and inevitable conflict between intrinsically irreconcilable forces. See Mushirul Hasan, *A Nationalist Conscience: M.A. Ansari, the Congress and the Raj* (New Delhi: Manohar, 1987). Recently published studies have questioned this assumption; see Neilesh Bose, *Recasting the Region: Language, Culture and Islam in Colonial Bengal* (Delhi: Oxford University Press, 2014). 'In current historiography there is an over-whelming emphasis on communal conflict, communal ideology and propaganda leading to such conflict,' says Sabyasachi Bhattacharya in *The Defining Moments in Bengal, 1920–1947* (Delhi: Oxford University Press, 2014), p. 108.

My PhD thesis on which this book is based emphasized on the urgency of this historiographical corrective 'Nationalism and the Problem of 'Difference', Bengal, 1905–47' (Tufts University, 1999). The same argument was presented in my book (Bengali), *Swajati Swadesher Khonje* (Calcutta: Dey's Publications, 2012).

10. Historians of early twentieth-century Bengal have often considered the Bengali Muslims who opposed swadeshi and supported partition as 'separatists', and those who resisted partition as 'nationalists'. Two important works in this context are: Rafiuddin Ahmed, *The Bengali Muslims, 1871–1906* (second edition, New York: Oxford University Press, 1988); and S. Sarkar, *Swadeshi Movement in Bengal*. When Sarkar mentions that 'even nationalist-minded Muslims' felt strongly against the swadeshi cult of Bankimchandra, it becomes clear that, according to him, 'nationalist-minded' were those Bengali Muslims who came forward to oppose the partition and join swadeshi. See his *Swadeshi Movement in Bengal*, p. 358.

11. As Sumit Sarkar points out, '[That the Muslim participation] attained quite respectable dimensions is a largely forgotten fact which deserves emphasis.' See S. Sarkar, *Swadeshi Movement in Bengal*, p. 360.

12. Abdul Gaffar Siddiki, 'Sangbadik Maniruzzaman Islamabadi' [origi-nally written in 1953], *Maulana Maniruzzaman Islamabadi Rachanabali* (Dhaka: Bangla Academy, 1986), p. 64.

13. Muhammad Abdul Hye, 'Maniruzzaman Islamabadi', *Maulana Maniruzzaman Islamabadi Rachanabali*, p. 67.

14. *Bengalee*, 21 October 1906.

15. Ekinuddin Ahmed, 'Banger Angachchhed', *Nabanur*, year 3, no. 6, Aswin 1312 BS (September 1905).

16. E. Ahmed, 'Banger Angachchhed'.

17. *Bengalee*, 21 July 1905.

18. Jogendranath Bandypadhyay, *Lanchhiter Samman*, 1905, p. 8, VT, IOL.

19. Abdul Rasul was a loyal supporter of Congress during the anti-partition movement. A successful law practitioner at Calcutta High Court and also a professor of law at Calcutta University, he devoted himself to spreading the movement in various parts of Bengal. Later he joined the Muslim League and contributed in drafting of the famous Lucknow Pact of 1916.

20. 'Atma-Pratishtha', *Aswinikumar Rachanasambhar* (Adhyayan: Calcutta, 1969), p. 5. One of Bayati's more famous compositions on the laxity of colonial administration and non-deliverance of public promises: 'E debo ta debo bole / Abaseshe bhujanginir pa dekhay' (After promises and pledges of this and that, / The outcome is nothing but a zero!).

21. *Bengalee*, 25 July 1905.

22. Description of common hardship in Muslim villages may be widely found in the contemporary vernacular tracts of that time. Mohammad Golam Hossain, the author of such a tract, narrated how swadeshi activists forced Muslim villagers to boycott cheap clothes and food commodities like sugar, salt, and grains, procured and marketed by foreign traders. Anonymous, *Bangadeshiya Hindu Musalman* (Calcutta, 1911), pp. 5–7, VT, IOL.

23. 'The Farcical Project of Hindu–Muslim Union', *Moslem Chronicle*, 26 December 1908.

24. See *Moslem Pratibha*, 1, no. 1(1907 [Agrahayan 1314 BS]), p. 23.

25. Anisuzzaman, 'The World of the Bengali Muslim Writer in the Nineteenth Century', in *Creativity, Reality and Identity* (Dhaka: International Center for Bangladesh Studies, 1993), p. 83.

26. *Maulana Maniruzzaman Islamabadi Rachanabali*, p. 70.

27. *Maulana Maniruzzaman Islamabadi Rachanabali*, p. 70.

28. Mohammad Golam Hossain, *Bangadeshiya Hindu Musalman* (Calcutta, 1911), p. 9, VT, IOL.

29. Hossain, *Bangadeshiya Hindu Musalman*, p. 9.

30. *Mihir o Sudhakar*, 11 August 1905, p. 21, and 18 August 1905, p. 12.

31. Mehraullah, and his follower, Jamiruddin, were staunch believers in the need for turning to the fundamentals of Islam. A part of the 'Sudhakar group' of Calcutta during the swadeshi period disseminated their firm resistance against swadeshi and wholehearted support for partition through their mouthpiece journal, *Mihir o Sudhakar*. It is also important to note that like Mehraullah and Jamiruddin, most of the sympathizers of this 'Sudhakar group' were landed gentry and, in many cases, zamindars

themselves. Their economic interests and political ambitions had a role to play in their opposition of the 'Hindu pre-eminence' in Bengal.

32. Muhammad Shadat Ali Ansari, *Munshi Mohammad Mehraullah* (Barandipara, Jessore, 1983), pp. 10–15. Also see *Maulana Maniruzzaman Islamabadi Rachanabali*, pp. 61–3.

33. Ansari, *Munshi Mohammad Mehraullah*, p. 11.

34. Maulavi Mohammad Hedayetullah, 'Swadeshi Andolana', *Nabanur* (1905 [Kartik 1312]).

35. There is a common structural pattern in the formulation of 'myth': a high point of past glory, followed by a sharp fall, then envisaging a new high point to be achieved in future. This three-point curve focuses on the difference between the first high point and the low point, greater the difference, more effective is the myth. Interestingly, in many of the expositions of this time on the past Islamic glory, this pattern is clearly traceable.

36. The Bengali Muslim discourse consists of innumerable such poems steeped in nostalgia about a glorious past, and complaints about the degrading Indian Islam. They contained a striking resonance of what Altaf Hussain Hali (1837–1914) had written earlier, or during the same period explored here. Ayesha Jalal shows how it would be grossly simplistic to hold Hali's *Shikwa-e-Hind* as merely a bigoted laments of a 'communal' mind. Jalal, 'Exploding Communalism: The Politics of Muslim Identity in South Asia', in *Nationalism, Democracy and Development: State and Politics in India*, edited by Ayesha Jalal and Sugata Bose (Delhi: Oxford University Press, 1997), pp. 76–103.

37. Naosher Ali Khan Yusufji, 'Chhilam Bijati Amra Bharate', *Nabanur* (1903 [1310 BS]). The original poem is as follows:

> *Bijati chhilam, achar-bichar sakal-i moder prithak chhilo*
> *Praner bandhan, samaj milan, tomar sahit kichhu na chhilo.*
> *Aj fate pran hoile smaran, jaha kichhu balo apon chhilo,*
> *Bharate ashiye khoyalem taha, adham kangal sajite holo.*
> *Manuswatwa, aha, aparthiba dhan, Moslemer jaha bhushan chhilo,*
> *Haralem taha Bharat-prantare, ei abasheshe lalate chhilo.*

38. Kaikobad, 'Abahan', *Nabanur* (1905 [1311 BS]). The original poem is given below:

> *Oisharya baibhab bijnan darshan*
> *Ki chhilo na hai Muslim ghare?*
> *Ki chhilo Muslim, ki hoyechhe ebe,*
> *Aro ki ba habe dudin pare!*

39. Kazi Imdadul Huq, *Nabanur* (1903), p. 21.

40. Anisuzzaman, *Muslim Banglar Samayik Patra, 1831–1930* (Dhaka: Bangla Academy, 1969), p. 27.

41. R. Ahmed, *The Bengal Muslims*, p. 116.

42. R. Ahmed, *The Bengal Muslims*, p. 116.

43. Naosher Ali Khan Yusufji, *Bangiya Mussalman* (Calcutta, 1907 [1315 BS]), VT, IOL.

44. Mohammed Mozammel Huq, 'Nirjib Bangali', *Jatiya Mangal* (Calcutta, 1910 [Aswin 1316 BS]), VT, IOL. The original poem follows: *Keho shishusiksha pare,/Moktab talash kare,/ Parite Parshi bhasha/ 'Bonsta''golostaye'./ Nirjib Bangali tora ke dekhibi aye!/ Moktaber shiksha hole/ Keho Hooghly jai chole,/ Sajibe Maulavi guru/ Pori Madrassah-e./ Nirjib Bangali tora ke dekhibi aye!/ 'Anjuman-e-Islamia'/ 'Anjuman-e-khairatiya'/ Title-e bhishito sabha/ Jathai tathai./ Nirjib Bangali tora ke dekhibi aye!*

45. Syed Abul Mohammad Ismail Hossain, *Bangiya Mussalman* (Calcutta, July 1906).

46. The new province of East Bengal and Assam supplied the largest number of delegates, that is, 38 out of 68, whereas it was allotted only 4 seats on the 60-member provisional committee. On the other hand, the total number of the delegates from the United Provinces (UP) was 16 while it secured 23 seats including the two joint secretaries. See S. Pirzada (ed.), *Foundations of Pakistan*, vol.1 (Karachi: National Publishing House Ltd., 1970), pp. 11–12.

47. See Viqar-ul-Mulk's address in Pirzada, *Foundations of Pakistan*, pp. 2–6.

48. N.K. Jain, *Muslims in India: A Biographical Dictionary*, vol. 1 (New Delhi: Manohar Publications, 1979), p. 15.

49. Abdul Karim, 'Bangabhashai Mussalmani Sahitya', *Nabanur* (1905 [Ashar 1312 BS]). A passionate call like his for the use of Bengali language foreshadows the struggle of East Pakistan against their rulers of West Pakistan after 1947. Right after the emergence of the 'Muslim nation-state' of Pakistan, Bengali Mussalmans engaged themselves in a bitter struggle demanding the right to use their mother tongue, leading finally to the great Language Movement of 1952.

50. Karim, 'Bangabhashay Mussalmani Sahitya'.

51. R. Ahmed, *The Bengal Muslims*, pp. 120–35.

52. Karim, 'Bangabhashay Mussalmani Sahitya'.

53. Karim, 'Bangabhashay Mussalmani Sahitya'.

54. R. Ahmed, *The Bengal Muslims*, p. 128.

55. Khademol Ensan, 'Bangalir Matribhasha', *Al Eslam* 1, no. 8 (1911): 23–30.

56. *The Mussalman*, 14 December 1906.

57. *The Mussalman*, 26 April 1907.

58. As the next section of this chapter will explore, the festival centring the seventeenth-century Maratha icon Shivaji, famous for his anti-Mughal expeditions, was sought to be introduced by swadeshi Hindus. A whole new body of Bengali literary tracts on Shivaji and his combats against the Yavanas emerged during this era. For a strongly negative take on this new Hindu trend of Shivaji Utsav, see *Soltan*, 8 June 1906.

59. 'Bhasha Bishaye Nur Al Iman-er Koifiat', *Nur Al Iman* 1, no. 2 (1905), pp. 12–17.

60. Hamed Ali, 'Uttarbanger Mussalman Sahitya', *Basana* 2, no. 1 (1909), p. 23.

61. Ekinuddin Ahmad, 'Bhasha-bichchhed', *Nabanur* 3, no. 4, (1906), p. 34.

62. Mir Mosharraf Hossain, *Mussalmaner Bangala Shiksha*, edited by Abul Ahsan Chauduri (Dhaka: Suchipatra, 2006), p. 13.

63. Mir Mosharraf Hossain, *Mussalmaner Bangala Shiksha*, p. 15.

64. Mohammad Shahidullah, Presidential Speech at the Second Bengali Muslim Literary Conference, *Bangiya Mussalman Sahitya Patrika* 1, no. 1 (1918) pp. 20–26.

65. R. Ahmed, *The Bengal Muslims*, p. 128.

66. R. Ahmed, *The Bengal Muslims*, p. 132.

67. For an overview of the impact of madrassa education on the Bengali Muslims, see Tazeen Murshid, *The Sacred and the Secular, Bengal Muslim Discourses, 1871–1977* (Delhi: Oxford University Press, 1995).

68. The assertion of a Bengali Muslim identity in the Language Movement of East Pakistan of 1952 and Mukti-juddha or War of Liberation (1971) has often been explained as an essentially postcolonial development, as 'a new linguistic nationalism' or 'the rise of Bengali nationalism' after 1947. See Joya Chatterji, *Bengal Divided: Hindu Communalism and Partition, 1932–1947* (Cambridge: Cambridge University Press, 1994); Joya Chatterji, *Spoils of Partition: Bengal and India, 1947–1967* (Cambridge: Cambridge University Press, 2007); Partha Chatterjee, 'The Second Partition of Bengal'. I would, on the contray, prefer to see it as the logical extension of the pre-1947 trends of Bengal Muslim nationalism conceived and realized through cultural contestations and political negotiations, which might be traced back to the swadeshi era.

69. Rabindranath Tagore, 'Introduction', in Kedarnath Dasgupta (ed.), *Shikshar Andolana* (Calcutta, 1905), pp. 2–9, VT, IOL.

70. Haridas Mukherji and Uma Mukherji, *The Origins of National Education Movement* (Calcutta: National Council of Education, 1957), p. 37.

71. Tagore, 'Introduction', *Shikshar Andolana*, p. 4.

72. Ekinuddin Ahmad, 'Bhasha-Bichchhed', *Nabanur* 3, no. 4, July 1905, p. 155.

73. Ekinuddin Ahmad, 'Bhasha-Bichchhed', p. 155.

74. See Partha Chatterjee, *The Nation and Its Fragments: Colonial and Post-colonial Histories* (Princeton: Princeton University Press, 1993), pp. 95–115; Sumit Sarkar, *Swadeshi Movement in Bengal*, pp. 450–60.

75. Surendranath Banerjea, *A Nation in Making: The Reminiscences of Fifty Years of Public Life* (1925; reprint, Bombay: Oxford University Press: 1963), p. 190.

76. Nagendranath Chattopadhyay, 'Biruddha-mater Samanjashya', *Nabya Bharat* 18, no. 10 (1903), pp. 547–9.

77. N. Chattopadhyay, '*Biruddha-mater Samanjashya*', pp. 547–9.
78. Sashibhushan Basu, 'Bangala Nationality', speech read in Rajshahi Sahitya Sammilan and published in *Prabasi* 10, part 2, no. 2 (January 1911 [Agrahayan 1317 BS]), pp. 119–27; no. 3 (February 1911 [Poush 1317 BS]), pp. 326–36; no. 4 (March 1911 [Magh 1317 BS]), pp. 415–20.
79. Alexis De Tocqueville, *Democracy in America*, vol. 1, translated by Henry Reeve (New York: Vintage Books, 1945), p. 251.
80. Sashibhushan Basu, 'Bangala Nationality', pp. 119–23.
81. See Sugata Bose, 'Nation as Mother: Representations and Contestations of India in Bengali Literature and Culture', in *Nationalism, Democracy and Development: State and Politics in India*, edited by Sugata Bose and Ayesha Jalal (New Delhi: Oxford University Press, 1997), pp. 50–75.
82. 'All profound changes in consciousness, by their very nature, bring with them characteristic amnesia,' Benedict Anderson pointed out in *Imagined Communities* (London: Verso, 1983), p. 200. The need for narratives is also critical: 'As with modern persons, so it is with nations. Awareness of being imbedded in secular, serial time, with all its implications of continuity … engenders the need for a narrative of "identity"' (p. 205).
83. *Bangadhip Parajay*, a two-volume novel by Pratapchandra Ghosh in the late nineteenth century (the first volume published in 1869, and the second in 1884), played a major role in popularizing the image of Pratapaditya. Inspired by this work, Rabindranath Tagore wrote his first novel, *Bou-Thakuranir Hat* (1883). Sarala Devi was also influenced by this novel. But the two volumes of *Bangadhip Parajay*, separated by more than a decade, differed on a cardinal question, whether to project Pratapaditya as a villain or a hero. It was only in the second volume of the novel, probably under the influence of growing nationalist pronouncements in Bengal, that the author of *Bangadhip Parajay* made him the saviour of 'Bengal': 'Nobody is in a position to understand my predicaments. All through my life I had one and only aim before me, to establish an independent Bengal.' Pratapchandra Ghosh, *Bangadhip Parajay*, vol. 2 (Calcutta: published by Gopalchandra Ghoshal, 1884), p. 530.
84. Rabindranath Tagore reacted strongly against this cult of Pratapaditya Utsav. In the preface to a much later edition of his novel *Bou Thakuranir Hat*, where Pratapaditya appeared as one of the characters, he clarified his stand: 'In the excessive passion of swadeshi Pratapaditya was attempted to be seen as the exemplary hero of the Bengali. The information I had collected at the time of writing this novel however point towards the fact that he was nothing but a cruel, unscrupulous and exploitative ruler.' See *Rabindra Rachanabali*, Sulabh Sangskaran (Calcutta: Visva-Bharati, 1986 [1393 BS]), vol. 1, p. 603. All future references to *Rabindra Rachanabali* will indicate this particular publication.

85. The tradition of upholding Pratapaditya as a 'national' hero of Bengal con-
tinued in later decades also, in *Jasohar-Khulnar Itihash* by Satishchandra
Mitra (1914), *Bangiya Bhowmik-gan-er Swadhinata Samar* by Nalinikanta
Bhattashalee (1927), or *Brihat Banga* by Dineshchandra Sen (1935).

86. Sarala Devi, *Jibaner Jharapata* (Calcutta: Saraswati Press, 1957), pp.
140–2.

87. Aurobindo Ghose, 'The New Faith', editorial in *Bande Mataram* (weekly
edition), 1 December 1907. Aurobindo saw in 'Faith' the essential ingre-
dients of national unity, and wanted to convert religion into a base of
political movement. Sugata Bose, 'The Spirit and the Form of an Ethical
Polity: A Meditation on Aurobindo's Thought,' *Modern Intellectual
History* 4, no. 1 (2007): 129–44.

88. Aurobindo Ghose, 'The New Ideal', *Bande Mataram*, 12 April 1908.

89. Bepinchandra Pal, 'The Bedrock of Indian Nationalism', *Bande Mataram*,
14 June 1908.

90. Ramendra Sundar Trivedi, a stalwart intellectual of the time writing
extensively on nationalism and historical consciousness of the Bengali,
would, however, agree with Pal. Trivedi, in his sharp criticism against
Tagore, held that the Hindu–Muslim situation was not as hopeless as
people like Tagore would think, but it could only be addressed by a strong
programme of swadeshi and boycott, with all their essential 'cultural'
attributes. The debate between Trivedi and Tagore is discussed in a subsequent section of this present chapter.

91. Ramlal Sarkar, *Nabya Bangalir Kartyavya* (Calcutta: Nabya Bharat Press,
1313 BS), VT, IOL.

92. R. Sarkar, *Nabya Bangalir Kartyavya*.

93. Sakharam Ganesh Deushkar, *Bangiya Hindu Jati Ki Dhwanshonmukha?*
(Calcutta, 1910), VT, IOL.

94. It is important to note here that when the different paths of swadeshi
movement were first outlined and explained by Sumit Sarkar, it was not
brought into attention how intricately these trends were related to the
divergent and contesting views of nation. See his *Swadeshi Movement in
Bengal*, pp. 30–70.

95. P. Guhathakurta, *Bengali Drama: Its Origin and Development* (London:
Kegan Paul & Co. Ltd, 1930), p. 160.

96. S. Sarkar, *Swadeshi Movement in Bengal*, pp. 420–1.

97. Anonymous, *Swadeshi Andolana* (Calcutta, 1313 BS [1906]), VT, IOL.

98. Rabindranath Tagore, 'Swadeshi Samaj', *Atma-Shakti* [1904], in *Rabindra
Rachanabali*, vol. 2, p. 632.

99. Rabindranath Tagore, 'Byadhi o Pratikar' (1907), *Rabindra Rachanabali*,
vol. 5, p. 782.

100. A detailed analysis of his change of heart during the swadeshi movement
both in terms of social principles and political views is found in Sumit
Sarkar's *Swadeshi Movement in Bengal*, pp. 43–8.

101. Ramendra Sundar Trivedi, 'Byadhi o Pratikar' *Prabasi* [1907], in *Ramendra Rachana Sangraha* (Calcutta: Bangiya Sahitya Parishat, 1964), pp. 632–4.

102. Written during 1907–10, and first published as a book in 1910 by Indian Publishing House, Tagore's novel *Gora* describes the self-discovery of an Indian patriot of half-Irish descent, who was finally able to 'find' his homeland not through the high ideals of nationalism but amidst the problems and promises of rural India. Even some of the Marxist critics of Tagore, usually antipathetic to his overt idealism, consider that this novel in its brilliant projection of the 'lower depths' of the society and its relevance to the upper-class political agenda far surpassed any other literary works in Bengali. Boudhayan Chattopadhyay, 'Gora: Bangla Upanyas o Jatiya Jiban', *Sahitya-patra* (Kartik 1358 BS [October 1952]), p. 147.

103. Aswinikumar Dutta, 'Congress-er Kartabya Ki?' (What Should the Congress Do?) *Bhandar*, Chaitra 1312 BS (April, 1905), pp. 409–12.

104. Tagore, *Rabindra Rachanabali*, vol. 5, p. 746. Chittaranjan Das would be hailed by the same term after 1921, following his decision to dedicate himself fully to nationalist activities after quitting legal practice.

105. Bepinchandra Pal, *Character-Sketches* (Calcutta, 1909), p. 60; Barisal Seba Samiti, *Swargiya Aswinikumar Dutta* (Calcutta, 1980), p. 46.

106. Mention must be made of the remarkable achievements of these branches of the samiti in the relief work during the famine of 1906. Sister Nivedita, the Scots-Irish social worker who spent most part of her life in India, also a leading disciple of Swami Vivekananda, was known to have commented that the role played by the Swadesh Bandhab Samiti was 'the greatest thing ever done in Bengal'. See Introduction to Badiur Rahman (ed.), *Aswinikumar Rachana-Sangraha* (Calcutta: Jibananda Academy, 1992).

107. Home Political A Proceedings, October 1908, nos 61–103, NAI.

108. In his own words, he would never preach any Aashwin (etymologically, belonging to 'Aswini') brand of politics, nor make it distinct from the Soura (the followers of Surendranath) or the Baipin (the followers of Bepinchandra) variants of national politics. A self-styled apolitical leader, he expressed an unwillingness to be a part of any of these reigning trends. The above comment is to be found in an article on Dutta by Sankha Ghosh, *Bhinno Ruchir Adhikar* (Calcutta: Talpata Publishers, 2010), p. 128.

109. Aurobindo Ghose, 'More about Unity', *Bande Mataram*, 8 December 1907.

110. Sekhar Bandyopadhyay, *Caste, Protest and Identity in Colonial India: The Namasudras of Bengal, 1872–1947* (second edition, Oxford: Oxford University Press, 2011), pp. 75–6.

111. S. Bandyopadhyay, *Caste, Protest and Identity in Colonial India*, p. 81. The reports of the local governments made clear that very few Namasudras actually attended the meetings organized and even smaller number of people were really interested in taking a 'swadeshi vow'.

112. The original Bengali lines are: *Swadeshi sajite sabe hoyechhe unmatto/Keho ki jano ki shei swadeshi-r tattwo?* This poem by Guruchand Thakur is quoted in Mahananda Haldar, *Guruchand Charit* (Calcutta, 1943), pp. 173–4. The rest of the poem was no less sharp than its opening lines:

> Let them who know their land, who know her content/ Be the nationalists with united strength./We are all poor, we've nothing to eat,/ Bound in debts we all are in retreat./ Our land may be one or divided in two/ Let the King do whatever he likes to do./ United or divided, how does that matter?/ Neither way shall we get food on some platter./ They cry for their country, most honored they are,/ Don't they even count that we exist ever?/ 'Never you touch them,' these people will tell./ Has ever one opened his heart enough?.... Well..../ When the country be true for us, will be our base,/ We will bet our life to relieve her distress.

The original Bengali poem follows after the first two lines:

> *Desh jara chene, jane desher khabor,/ Swadeshi sajuk tara hoye ekottar./ Amra daridra sabe ghare nahi anno,/ Dena-daye bandha sabe chiro-abasanno./ Bibhag houk desh, athoba juruk,/Ja achhe rajar mone shebhabe koruk./ Bhag hoyi, jure royi tate moder ki?/Konobhabe moder kapale nahi ghee ... /Desh desh kare jara shabe desh-manyo/ amadige desh-madhye kare naki ganyo?/ Chuyon na chuyon na bale Brahman Kayastha,/ Keho ki korechhe tader hriday proshoshto?/ Jedin bujhibo satyo amader desh,/Pran diye ghuchaibo jananir klesh.*

113. At least two of Tagore's poems, 'Apamanito' (The insulted) and 'Hey Mor Durbhaga Desh' (Oh my unfortunate motherland) deserve mention here. Tagore's premonition that the downtrodden classes of India, the victim of *varnashrama* (the four-fold division of Hindu society), if still left in oblivion, would soon emerge in rebellion and deliver a deadly blow to the existing social structure is expressed here more bitterly than ever. Some of his personal letters also dealt with the caste-related oppressions in society. See his letter to Saradacharan Dutta, Bhadra 1317 BS (September 1911), in Satyendranath Ray (ed.), *Rabindranath Tagore: Samajchinta* (Kolkata: Granthalay Private Limited, 1985), p. 151.

114. This point has been made by Sekhar Bandyopadhyay in an article: '[Tagore] too believed with Gandhi that *varnashrama* was a harmonious system of social division of labour—uncolonized—and therefore, a unique marker of Indian difference and her civilizational superiority over the West.' Sekhar Bandyopadhyay, 'Rabindranath Tagore, the Indian Nation and Its Outcasts', *Harvard Asia Quarterly* 15, no. 1 (2013): 34–9, see 30.

115. Dwijendralal Roy, 'Jati-bhed', *Sahitya*, Sraban 1314 BS (August 1908).

116. 'Reformation, not Revolution. We Hindus are proud as Hindus for all these 4000 years because of this structure, which had produced eminent sages like Vyas, Balmiki or Kapil. To destroy this structure is not to effect a revolution, but to invite vandalism of the worst kind.' D. Roy, 'Jati-bhed'.

117. The criticality of the notion of territoriality in the incipient nationalist thought in Bengal has attracted scholarly attention. See Reece Jones, 'Whose Homeland? Territoriality and Religious Nationalism in Pre-Partition Bengal', *South Asia Research* 26, no. 2 (2005): 115–31. Swarupa Gupta argues that these notions of fluid and incorporative boundaries of a greater Bengal contributed to the variations in nationalist discourse. See her *Notions of Nationhood in Bengal*, p. 349.

118. 'The community of sentiment', the term used by Max Weber, has been employed in the context of nationalism in India by Rajat K. Ray in his argument of the felt community which preceded the nationalistic notions. Rajat K. Ray, *The Felt Community: Commonality and Mentality before the Emergence of Indian Nationalism* (Delhi: Oxford University Press, 2003), pp. 4–5. As these notions began to spread fast during the swadeshi era, the territorial or local belongingness had a vital role to play in the historical process behind the formation of a 'felt community'.

119. Girishchandra Sen, *Atma-jiban* (Calcutta, n.d.), pp. 119–20.

120. Cited in Dr Muhammad Abdullah, *Nawab Salimullah: Jiban o Karma* (Dhaka: Islamic Foundation, 1986), p. 202.

121. Brahmabhandhab Upadhyay, *Sandhya*, Confidential RNP, no. 40 of 1906.

122. Mentioned in Haridas Mukhopadhyay and Uma Mukhopadhyay, *Upadhyay Brahmabandhab o Bharatiya Jatiyatabad* (Calcutta: Firma K.L. Mukhopadhyay, 1961), p. 126.

123. Sureshchandra De, *Swadhinata Sangrame Nawabgunj* (Calcutta: Jijnasa, 1971), p.2.

124. *Dinajpur Patrika*, Ashar 1315 BS, p. 45.

125. Muzaffar Ahmed, *Amar Jiban o Bharater Communist Party* (Calcutta: National Book Agency, 1977), pp. 7–8.

126. Purnendu Dastidar, *Swadhinata Sangrame Chattagram* (Chittagong: Boi-Ghar, 1970), p. 17.

127. Rajanikanta Sen, 'Samkirtan', in *Swadeshi Sangeet*, edited by Narendra-kumar Seal (Calcutta, 1907). The original poem was: '*Jodi ek mayer dudh sakal chhele khai,/ Sabar gaye ek-i sakti, rakta boye jai,/Amra bhai bole bhai chinbo sab mile/Preme porbo bandha ei mayer dudh khele.*'

128. Partha Chatterjee, *Nationalist Thought and Colonial World* (London: Zed Books, 1986), p. 58.

129. Mohammed Mozammel Huq, the poem titled 'Nirjib Bangali', mentioned earlier in this chapter, *Jatiya Mangal*.

130. Gita Chattopadhyay, *Bangla Swadeshi Gan* (Delhi: Delhi University Press, 1987), pp. 45–50.

131. Partha Chatterjee has offered the theory of the inherent ideological predicaments hidden within the position of a colonial nationalist. See his, *The Nation and Its Fragments*. However, while Chatterjee's focus is on the colonial nationalist's dilemma based on the connects and disconnects between

the colonial tenets and the nationalist's own project of nation, I want to focus here on the split within the nationalist's own self-image as a result of his preoccupations with the problem of 'difference'. A part of his self needed to be reaching out and connecting with others in order to mount an opposition against the colonizer by employing the rule of 'difference', whereas another part of this self had to engage in a larger projection of a national collectivity by negating the rule of 'difference'. The rule of difference, a phrase borrowed from Chatterjee, therefore became a conceptual trap for the colonial nationalist, torn between two conflicting purposes at one and the same time.

132. The new focus on the collective self in an age of emerging notions of nationalism has been brought into attention by Swarupa Gupta in *Notions of Nationhood in Bengal*. However, what I would like to argue here is that this collective 'self' was a necessary extension of a renewed understanding of the individual 'self', its location, and role in the larger society. A major part of the complexities and anxieties around the question of identity were, in fact, generated by the very uncertain relationship between these two dimensions of 'self' and the varying parameters of the imagined link between the individual and the collective.

133. R. Sarkar, *Nabya Bangalir Kartyavya*.

134. R. Sarkar, *Nabya Bangalir Kartyavya*.

135. For example, when Nawab Salimullah and Syed Nawab Ali Chowdhury earnestly insisted before the Simla Deputation (October 1906) that the League deputationists seek an assurance from the viceroy for the permanence of partition, the demand was finally not incorporated into the League memorial due to the disinterest of the members from other regions. See N.K. Jain, *Muslims in India: A Biographical Dictionary* (Delhi: Manohar, 1983), vol. 1, p. 15.

136. Lehajuddin Ahmad, 'Rajnitikshetre Hindu Mussalman', *Nabanur* 3, no. 3 (1905), pp. 117–19.

137. The above article also mentioned that Sir Syed Ahmed, the 'political genius', had apprehended this deep conflict in the previous century: 'He [Sir Syed] understood that in the event of a union between the big and the small, the small is who is bound to be the loser…. It is enormously easy for the big to get away with its own terms, to manipulate the small in its own interest, to associate and dissociate with the small at its own convenience, and to overrun the small's interest if that in the least bit infringes its own…. No doubt, many gestures of generosity are made by the Hindus nowadays. But one suspects that this has something to do with the pursuit of their own political interests.' L. Ahmad, 'Rajnitikshetre Hindu Mussalman'.

138. L. Ahmad, 'Rajnitikshetre Hindu Mussalman', p. 127.

139. From the official point of view, the reform was a fair deal: 'The weightage given to Muslims was seen as 'merely a further application of the principle of representation by classes and interest.' *Report of the Indian Statutory Commission*, vol. 1 (London: His Majesty's Stationery Office [HMSO], 1930), pp. 186–7.

140. Surendranath Bhattacharya, 'Hindu o Mussalmaner Rajnoitik Swartha', *Bharati*, Falgun, 1315 BS.

141. Bepinchandra Pal, *Swadeshi and Swaraj* (Calcutta, 1958), p. 128.

142. *Hitavadi*, RNP, no. 5, 22 January 1909.

143. *Mihir o Sudhakar*, RNP, no. 8, 23 April 1909.

144. *Mihir o Sudhakar*, 23 April 1909.

145. *Mihir o Sudhakar*, RNP, no. 5, 22 January 1909.

146. As published in an editorial in *The Mussalman*:

    It has become necessary for the Mussalmans to turn out agitators, to try to stand on their own legs and demand the satisfaction of their claims as a matter of right.... The claims of Muhammedans have been systematically neglected in the matter of making appointments, even in the new province of Eastern Bengal, which was ostensibly created for the benefit of the Mussalmans.

    Editorial, *The Mussalman*, 12 January 1912.

147. This point has been argued in my Bangla essay, 'Banga-bhanga Rad o Jati Rajniti', published in a collection of essays, *Swajati Swadesher Khonjey*, pp. 32–46.

148. *Muslim Hitaishi*, RNP, no. 1, 29 December, 1911.

149. *Mihir o Sudhakar*, 22 January 1909.

2 *Promises and Politics of a New Nation*
1912–25

The annulment of partition in December 1911 was hailed by the swadeshi Hindus in a curiously short-sighted way. They considered it a major moral and political victory in their anti-colonial struggle and organized celebrations to mark the moment of glory. In truth, however, the annulment was hardly a surrender of the British Raj to the Bengali Hindu lobby. On the contrary, it could only be explained as yet another well-calculated measure to maintain a balance of power within the province of Bengal between the 'Hindu interest' and the 'Muslim interest', more clearly shaped than in the previous decade. The experience of partition, the foundation of the Muslim League, and the granting of the principle of separate representation had by this time decisively changed the political climate of Bengal, and posed a stupendous challenge before the aspirations of a unitary 'nation'. As pointed out in the previous chapter, swadeshi nationalism was already negotiating with 'difference' in various ways. But, in one respect, its fight had been relentless and uncompromising: the swadeshi nation was against any political or administrative separation of its constituent elements, however 'different' they might claim to be. Yet the idioms of separate representation did emerge victorious by the end of this period. The end of 1911, therefore, could not be held as a moment of victory for the swadeshi nationalists, if judged by their own priorities. By heralding an era of new idioms of competitive representation, it indeed was a veiled defeat for them. From now on, the question of 'share' in constitutional representation would dominate the politics and the discourse of the 'nation', and seek a new political legitimacy for the old claims of cultural difference.

In the context of new idioms of 'difference' and 'share', new grounds were sought to assert 'national' heritage and interests, and check the possibility of political accommodation of various disparate interests. The idea of swadeshi nation was now extended in its political scope and spirit, and this new dimension of politics in turn gave rise to new ideological formulations.[1] With a central focus on these ideological experimentations, this chapter examines the 'new nationalism' against the changing contours of the Bengal politics, where the self-propelling logic of 'difference' steadily drove the earlier assertion of cultural identity to the demands of its political representation. I argue that these demands did not necessarily preclude the space for inter-community negotiation. Strong anti-colonial overtures as well as robust regional sentiments—the two characteristic bedrocks of Bengali nationalism—continued to serve as the potential meeting ground for its diverse interests and identities during this period.

Politics of Muslim Representation and Khilafat Universalism

During the short career of the new province of East Bengal and Assam (1905–11), benefits of reduced competition and greater material resources for the Bengali Muslim community confirmed the merits of playing the political card of difference. In the meantime, the Morley–Minto Reforms (1909) had institutionalized 'difference' in the political realms by introducing the system of separate electorate. Moreover, there was a major change in the Muslim politics of a reunited Bengal. As partition was overturned, many loyal members of the Muslim League began to be discredited, and an emerging agitationist leadership gave the 'Muslim interest' a new spin. Considering the revocation of partition a blessing in disguise, the new leaders sought to combine the theme of sociocultural 'difference' with the larger political objective of anti-colonialism. The task of launching a more effective struggle against colonial rule now required a more popularly based Bengali Muslim nation, as the changed rhetoric would prove.

The old swadeshi argument was given a curious twist here. It was accepted that 'national' existence should be safeguarded first in order to represent and establish its own rights. But then, this 'national' community became freshly defined as the 'Bengali Muslims', with a strong assertion of 'difference' as its cornerstone. The first step towards the making of this Bengali Muslim nation was to create an association of its own. On 2 March 1912, there took place in Calcutta the Amalgamation Conference of the Bengal League, which was preceded by the debate to establish a provincial branch of the League as an 'independent association', separate from the All India Muslim League (or the AIML).[2] Bengali Muslim leaders like Abdur Rasul and Abdullah Khan Suhrawardy considered the prospects of an independent association for the province of Bengal, as they thought that 'the League was confined within narrow limits', and that, therefore, an active affiliation to the AIML 'was bound to be detrimental to [the Bengali Muslim] interests'.[3] The all-India 'parent body' was also duly perturbed at this suggestion.[4] The 'crisis' for the AIML was initially averted by the masterly intervention of Nawab Salimullah in the Amalgamation Conference in Calcutta. The League retained its 'single body' status and the provincial voices of dissent were temporarily sidelined.[5]

Hidden in this historic conflict was the irreconcilability of interests and viewpoints of different sections of Muslim leadership. The Bengali Muslim leaders were already demanding for themselves a community primarily defined by their regional–cultural identity. While the foundation of the League in 1906 is hailed in history as the defining moment of the development of 'Muslim separatism', it often glosses over the critical juncture of 1912, a moment of possible split in the overarching category of 'All-India Muslims'. Far from its steady journey towards 'separatism', the League after 1906 underwent serious internal conflicts and shifts of balance.

Another shift within the League was its new policy of closer proximity to the Congress against the common adversary of colonial Raj. A sizeable section of Bengali Muslim leaders supported this policy. They thought that the survival of their 'new' nation could be guaranteed only in conjunction with other neighbouring communities. Maulavi Abul Kasem Fazlul Huq, an upcoming leader from a humble social background,[6] who would eventually develop into 'one of the ablest spokesmen' for the following decades, declared in 1913 the new 'policy of co-operation with all other advancing communities':

> The one definite policy to which the Moslem League is now committed is the policy of co-operation with all other advancing communities in working out the common weal of our mother country. If there are men who think that the salvation of Moslems lies in maintaining an attitude of perpetual warfare with the other communities, they must step out of the League or one day they will be forced to go.[7]

The confrontational stance on the British and the collaborationist approach towards 'the other communities' were reflected in the AIML activities also. *Al-Hilal*, the periodical edited by Maulana Abul Kalam Azad, a theologian and an anti-colonial spokesman of this time, had been voicing the need for embarking on an anti-British struggle along with the Congress. At the end of 1913, the AIML declared colonial self-government as its chief political aim. The same year, as many as 107 Muslim delegates attended the Congress session in Karachi.

Nevertheless, this was not the only trend of Bengali Muslim politics. There were staunch 'loyalists' who even preferred to leave the League in case of a pro-Congress overture. Huq's earlier comment was made in a press interview, soon after veterans like Ameer Ali had left the League. This divergence in Muslim voices was also reflected in the representation of the community in the legislative council.[8] Yet these representations bring out the centrality of accommodation, a favourite ideological theme among the Bengali Muslims during this time. It points to a distinct continuity between the swadeshi and the post-swadeshi times. Just as a large number of Bengali Muslims, either for or against the partition, had earlier taken up the project of Muslim self-assertion, in the post-swadeshi decade too, Muslims who emphasized electoral or political benefits in collaboration with Congress and those who resisted it were equally intent on furthering the interests of their own community. Earlier they had to juggle with the parallel or overlapping notions of Bengali jati and Bengali Muslim jati. Now, through a new stretch of political imagination, they began negotiating between the Bengali Muslim 'nation' and the larger Indian 'nation'.

This trend can be explained by the political ambitions of a rising middle class among the Bengali Muslims. The example of Huq showed that at the helm of this newly orientated agenda were the Muslim professionals of the urban and mofussil areas.[9] His rise in itself was a sign of a larger social, economic, and cultural change in Bengal, of a growing Bengali Muslim middle class and their much-awaited entry into politics.[10] Their emergence was greeted with an expected resistance from the traditional elites, who still nurtured an aversion towards any professed political goal of anti-colonialism as well as any common cause with the Congress.[11] The resultant conflict centred around the principle of representation, whether to be based on joint electorates of the Hindus and the Muslims or on separate electorates of Muslims. The younger professionals believed in accommodation based on their awareness of their sheer numerical majority in the province. They acknowledged this demographic feature as a key to their future political predominance and thus became open to the ideas of joint electorates. However, the Muslims whose regional commitment was less and vacillating, insisted upon separate electorates. There developed a clear conflict of interest between the new class of Muslim professional politicians who were more inclined towards a regional identity and the old loyalist elite vanguards, the 'Urdu Muslims' so to speak, with the former slowly replacing the latter.

The political conflict soon made its way into the discursive arena in Bengal. Two leading Muslim journals of Calcutta, *Mohammadi* and *Muslim Hitaishi*, represented opposite viewpoints of this exceedingly bitter conflict. The latter ridiculed the former's enthusiastic support for the new objective of 'self-government' as sheer 'subservience' to the 'Congressite' Hindus. An article published in *Muslim Hitaishi* glorified the traditional anti-Congress stance to be the 'one and the only' focal aim of the League. If the League deviated from this line and pursued self-government, the Bengal Muslims should 'cut off all connections with it'.

> The League has now forgotten its original objects of existence and is now blindly following the Congress. When it asked for self-government, we urged Bengal Muslims to cut off all connections with it.... Indeed under present conditions there seems to be no necessity for separate existence of the League.[12]

The *Mohammadi* retorted with equal alacrity. It declared that in this mood of confrontation lay the seeds of future national existence, 'Bengali Muslim national life now gains a fillip it badly wanted. Let them not forget that "Nations by themselves are made!"'[13] Whatever needed to be done for the 'nation' to 'arise' must be accomplished by the community itself. Even if a separate body was required exclusively to represent

Bengali Muslim interests, the leaders must take the lead. I have already noted how the need for a separate provincial organization was thus being felt and how the idea brought out adverse reaction from the all-India parent body. Although the split was finally averted, the spirit of dissent amongst the Bengali Muslims within the League left a permanent mark in the minds of the politically aware Muslim public in Calcutta.

With the outbreak of the First World War, an even larger number of Muslims developed anti-British feelings. At the Lucknow session of Congress in 1916, both the Muslim League and the Congress designed a united demand for a representative government and dominion status after the war. The agreed basis of a representative government, as laid down by the Lucknow Pact, was that the seven Hindu majority provinces would have over-representation for the Muslims while the Hindus would be over-represented in the Muslim majority provinces of Bengal and the Punjab. As a result, Bengal with a Muslim population of 52.6 per cent would secure 40 per cent legislative seats for its Muslim population. The terms of the agreement, initially welcomed by the Provincial Muslim League led by Fazlul Huq, soon became an enormously divisive issue for Bengal Muslims, left with an unsatisfactory terms of representation. The conservative loyalists emerged with a twisted sense of victory: the Indian Moslem Association was set up to oppose the Pact, and the *Muslim Hitaishi* launched its offensive against the League.

> As long as the League worked on the lines approved by its founder, the Late Nawab Salimullah, it enjoyed the support of the Bengali Muslims. The League is now only toeing the Congress line.[14]

The internal disagreements put the provincial League leaders in an uneasy position on the issue of representation, but they nevertheless continued to play an effective role in the Legislative Council in furthering what in their view appeared to be the 'Bengal Muslim' cause. 'Our share we claim as our indefeasible right, and the excess we claim by way of compensation for the wrong done to us by the annulment of Partition,' declared Fazlul Huq in the council.[15]

In the post-annulment days, the reduced importance of Dacca, the capital of the new province created in 1905, was apprehended to mark the beginning of yet another phase of official neglect of the whole of the eastern Bengal region. It is important to note that a whole array of Muslim council members, including Fazlul Huq himself who came from eastern Bengal, still retained close ties with the middling Muslim sections of that region.[16] With the intensifying bid for greater representation, the 'Muslim interest', therefore, started to project the lack of educational and employment opportunities for the expanding middle classes of this part of the province. Demands for special privileges became increasingly inseparable from the issue of community representation at various levels of administration for addressing the special needs of the community. For example, Huq and others demanded 'a wider recognition of the claims of our community on the resources of the state in educational matters'. They also complemented this by duly pressing for the appointment of Muslim officials in the educational department, because, they thought, it would 'greatly benefit the cause'.[17] Both Fazlul Huq and Abul Kasem maintained that '… officers should be appointed for inspection purposes who know local conditions, and it would not be difficult to find such men from the Muhammedan community'.[18]

In spite of a growing acknowledgement and enthusiasm for English education, Muslim leaders still laid stress on the traditional mode of education through madrassas and *maktab*s (centres of Islamic education). In the budget discussions for 1914–15, Muslim legislators criticized the Government for not allotting more funds either for the reorganization of Calcutta madrassas or development of madrassa education in general. The real intention was to strike a compromise by maintaining the madrassas in a reorganized form, because they thought that it would ensure the support of the masses. As late as in the early 1920s, Muslim public opinion continued to be deeply divided on the issue of madrassa education, and their legislators were forced to stick on to a middle path.[19] The majority of Muslim leaders viewed the spread of primary education as the cornerstone of the agenda for the 'national' community. Numerous questions were raised regarding the necessity of introducing a Government Bill for 'free and compulsory' primary education for the whole province. Tamizuddin Ahmed declared that 'Tax or no tax, we must have free and compulsory primary education.'[20] Although it was never denied that primary education was a universal concern, Aminur Rahman and Fazlul Huq still consistently underlined the 'special problems of Muhammedan education in Bengal'.[21] The demand for establishing an exclusively Muslim college at Dacca was first raised in the council in 1913. Huq held that '[fo]r more than half a century Government has maintained a purely Hindu college (Sanskrit College) at Calcutta … and the Muhammedan college at Dacca would only be a very tardy recognition of the long neglected claims of Muhammedan community'.[22] Similar demands also emerged for a Muslim institution in Calcutta, followed by the establishment of Calcutta Islamia College in 1925. Claims for adequate support for Muslim higher education in colleges and universities were also laid. These included special facilities for Muslim students like greater number of stipends and scholarships, reservation of seats in educational institutions, adequate hostel accommodation, and opportunities of professional and vocational training.[23]

As expected, the greatest concern was to ensure adequate Muslim representation in the government services. Especially after the annulment of partition, Muslim legislators consistently attempted to draw the attention of the government to the 'unfair' Muslim representation in various government services, and demanded reservation of positions at various levels. To ensure fair representation of the Muslims in public services, a direct resolution was moved by Huq, proposing to form a Staff Selection Board with official and non-official members with due 'proportion of Muhammedans'.[24] The motion was lost. But it served the purpose of adequately reflecting the intensity of 'community sentiment' on this matter. In the 1920s, the question of job reservation for the Muslims took a more concrete form and demands were put forward more forcefully as clear-cut suggestions: ' ... 80 per cent (of appointments) be given to the Muhammedans of Bengal till the number of Muhammedan officials in each class in the employment of the Government of Bengal becomes 55 per cent of the whole.'[25] However, the Muslim legislators had to wait for a more effective debate on this till Chittaranjan Das, the great nationalist visionary, came up with his own arrangement within Calcutta Municipality in 1923.

Such debates show a deep anxiety of being outnumbered, or marginalized. The post-annulment era also saw a sharp rise in Muslim anxiety about the discrepancy between the demographic composition of the province on the one hand, and the poor representation of their community in local administrations on the other. A fairer representation through the means of election was thought to be an objective almost impossible to achieve because of the overall backwardness of Bengali Muslims. The system of governmental nomination seemed more suitable in increasing their representation in the civic bodies. Nomination rather than election was the key demand of the Muslim legislators. The question of application of governmental power of nomination became even more critical in the intensive discussions on the formation of the Calcutta Corporation.[26]

The enthusiasm informing the demands for representation, electorates, or employment and educational opportunities was hardly matched in the realm of the more radical issues like tenancy reforms and reforming the terms of rural money-lending. The new Muslim leadership voiced a few agrarian grievances, but in general this period experienced only very limited representation of the rural Muslim interests. While leaders like Huq and Kasem strongly urged for 'free and compulsory' primary education, mostly for the benefit of the poorer multitudes in the countryside, a note of caution was forwarded by *Mohammadi*, the most vocal journal of the new professional leadership. The journal upheld the cause of the Indian self-government to be pursued by the League and the Congress alike, and expressed delight in the inadvertent popularization of the issue in the countryside where Maulana Muhammad Abu Bakr of Noakhali spitefully bashed the new political objective of 'self-government' in a public meeting. But at the same time, it hinted at the potential danger of such popular appropriation of political projects.

> Out of evil cometh good. Maulana's speech will enlighten the rustic masses on the topic of self-government which was hitherto familiar only to the educated classes. Of course, the participation of illiterate Muslims in politics is rather dangerous, because of their tendency to provoke breaches of peace.... Government ought to see that ideas of liberty and race-hatred are not rashly instilled into the brains of the ignorant masses.[27]

The same political groups which lost trust in the capacity and intention of the government to ensure protective measures for the middle classes were now hoping for timely administrative interventions if and when popular upsurges took place. 'Of course the participation of illiterate Muslims in politics is rather dangerous, because of their tendency to provoke breaches of peace.'[28] Clearly, the politics of representation was being cautiously fashioned by and for the Muslim middle classes, whose advancement and interests reflected in the new politics of a new provincial Muslim leadership.[29] 'Government ought to see that ideas of liberty and race-hatred are not rashly instilled into the brains of the ignorant masses.'[30] Hand in hand went the fear of 'liberty', that is, 'unrest', which might destabilize middle-class interests, and the fear of 'race-hatred', equally potent in unleashing forces of social turbulence.

With 'interest' thus defined and styled, the guiding spirit of the era was to 'leave the choice to the interest itself'. This was not a far cry from the ideological core of the larger nationalist demand for 'self-government'. In fact it was just given a twist to suit the interests of a 'community', or a differently defined 'nation', in this case the Bengali

Muslim 'nation' (Bangiya Mussalman jati). The growing pressure for self-government finally yielded the Government of India Act of 1919 (the Montagu–Chelmsford Act), which after much deliberation produced only a less-than-satisfactory arrangement through a system of dyarchy.[31] The criticism against the Act, nevertheless, came from both Hindu and Muslim communities of Bengal against the nominal transference of power to the province; the 'different' interests found themselves on a joint platform to voice deep resentments against 'colonial autocracy'.

While such anti-colonial resentments and questions of a joint Hindu–Muslim platform for the anti-British struggle kept the urban Muslim leadership (especially in Calcutta) utterly preoccupied during this time, and the rural people were mostly unaligned with these higher levels of policy-talk, there emerged a distinctly different group of Urdu-speaking immigrant Muslims in Calcutta and its suburbs, consisting of up-country traders, artisans, and labourers. Mostly belonging to the provinces of Bihar, Uttar Pradesh, and Punjab, these up-country Muslims had little vested interest in their temporary domicile and thereby began to play the role of a very different kind in Bengal politics. Against the bold regional expressions of the urban leaders of Bengal, this latter group clearly cherished their all-India Islamic ties, actively promoted preaching and teaching in Urdu, and often contributed generously in local communal tensions in their strongholds, resulting in the landmark Calcutta riot of 1918. In Calcutta, localities such as Burrabazar and Kalutola were fast becoming potential 'danger-zones' with their overlapping Marwari business community and the new Muslim groups—both imported from north India.[32] Note that the 1918 riots, first among its kind, were devoid of any deep-seated communal anxiety. Scholars showed it as a case of breach of law and order, given a distinct communal colour,[33] and thus setting a new trajectory for negotiating zones of competition through violence. Even if such a competition or collaboration argument does not seem convincing, one is tempted to see the riots of 1918 as an event not integrally linked to local Hindu–Muslim tensions, but as turbulence primarily caused by 'rumours and stories of designing outsiders'. The Bengal Muslim League declared with a palpable tone of alarm: 'The Working Committee strongly appealed to all, both in cities and rural areas, and to the Muslims in particular, to be calm and peaceful, to do everything possible to restore normal conditions of life and not to be carried away by rumours and stories of designing outsiders.'[34]

The Urdu Muslim lobby of Calcutta became a key player in the complex narrative of Bengali 'nation' in another significant way. This group was extensively politicized during the post-1916 Khilafat agitation. It is important to remember that when the agitation was spreading fast in India and stirring raw emotions among Muslim leaders outside Bengal, the new League leadership of Bengal could remain aloof. The initial inspirations evidently came from the Urdu protagonists of Muslim community, the promising leader Maulana Abul Kalam Azad being one of them. Azad, belonging to an old elite family based in Calcutta, enjoyed the political–cultural influence emanating from a large number of similar-minded Muslims in and around Calcutta, and also had an 'inter-provincial appeal'. The Jamiat-i-Hazbullah, founded by Azad, and promoted by the Urdu business lobby, contributed to promote pan-Indian feelings among Calcutta Muslims in the mid-1910s. Clearly anti-British in intent, Azad and his close group of followers, through their mouthpiece journal *Al-Hilal*, actively preached agitationist methods to register their protest against Khilafat arrangements, and stressed on the need to boycott European goods.[35] Although the movement slowly and steadily spread to various parts of the province, it was Azad, arguably the first major leader of the movement in Bengal, who delivered inflammable speeches on the 'Muslim insult' in the Balkan War.[36] In other words, Azad played a significant role in inviting a pan-Islamic movement into the province of Bengal, albeit with limited success.

At the local level, Bengal was a little late in catching up with the spirit of Khilafat. In spite of Azad's speeches in Calcutta and the efforts of eastern Bengali leaders like Maniruzzaman Islamabadi and Ismail Hossain Siraji to spread the message of Khilafat to the countryside, the reaction was lukewarm. A part of such lack of interest can be attributed to the ambivalence towards the British Raj.[37] A locally strong leader, Munshi Jamiruddin, even organized a movement of opposition in Rajshahi and resisted the Khilafatists rather successfully.[38] But another part of this initial disinterest was due to the inability to connect with the cause of the Caliphate. An article in *Mohammadi* took a bitter tone in criticizing such a trend: '*The Mussalman* reports that Mr. Abdulla Tonki of Calcutta Madrassa and Dr A. Suhrawardy have told the government that their opinion is that the Sultan of Turkey cannot be the universal Caliph of all Moslems and that the Caliphate agitation is spurious.'[39] It also mentioned that support for the Caliph was still weak in Bengal. This journal, the voice of professional Muslims of Calcutta, condemned the non-sympathizers in a scathing way. Urging upon the leaders to take lessons from the Sinn Fein (self-help) movement of Ireland, it remarked that the path of agitation should be the only self-respecting path to take:

'None pays heed to the beggars.' [40] Boycott of foreign goods began in Calcutta in August 1920; declaration forms were distributed among the people in the districts. One of the Khilafat posters urged for immediate '*Swadeshi Grahan o Sahayogita Barjan*' (adoption of swadeshi and non-cooperation) in the name of Allah to 'determine the nation's life and death question!'[41] Swadeshi Khilafat stores were set up in Calcutta, with purely indigenous goods of daily use, observed *The Mussalman*:

> As an auxiliary to the non-cooperation movement it has been resolved by the various Khilafat Committees and other public bodies like the Bengal Provincial Congress Committee that the people of India should boycott foreign, specially British goods ... we hope for the revival of the swadeshi spirit. Personally, we have been swadeshi sympathizers for the last 19 or 20 years. But what we are ashamed to say in this connection is that our co-religionists as a whole did not take to swadeshism even when the movement was in full swing. It is the duty of every Indian, be he a Muslim or a Hindu, a Parsi or a Christian, a Jain or a Sikh, to take to swadeshi and thus help in the bringing about not only the economic salvation but in righting the wrongs done to Turkey and the sacred cause of Khilafat.[42]

'Personally we have been *swadeshi* sympathizers for the last 19 or 20 years': the term swadeshi in this context denoted the agitationist mode of political movement, a trend apparent even among the pro-partition Muslims in the earlier era. This trend was now being revived again in the context of Khilafat, this time infused with the interest of the 'community' firmly in focus. However, assertion of community or community interests did not preclude upholding other interests. Internal differences gradually gave way to a broader, over-arching commonality of political agenda. Muslim associations were desperately looking for a combined path of Islamism on the one hand and a broadly defined nationalism on the other, a combination which would ensure their rights of 'self-assertion' against the British within and outside India. The 'self' being defined by various and overlapping characters, the search began for 'national' ways which would prove substantially 'Islamic' as well.

> The great leaders of our nation have, as a matter of fact, realized the basic need of the 'ummat-i-Islamiyah'. If the students of the Muslim institutions where modern sciences are taught, are kept ignorant of their religion, thereby forgetting their Islamic and national duties, then such institutions become instrumental in weakening the prestige of the Muslims. Therefore it has been announced that there will be laid the foundation of an independent university which has nothing to do with government

subsidy and interference and whose organization is based on *Islamic principles and national aspirations* [emphasis mine].[43]

The critical missing link between the 'national' and the 'Islamic' was the Hindu cooperation. In order to elicit Hindu support, four prominent Maulanas of the United Provinces and the Punjab issued a fatwa against cow slaughter as a gesture of community friendship. Appearing in the Congress pandals, Maulana Saukat Ali and Fazlul Huq strongly denounced cow slaughter. The Hindu journal *Bangali* commented, 'Differences and discord between Hindus and Muslims only arise during the korbani [the Islamic practice of slaughter/sacrifice of an animal, usually a cow]. If cow slaughter be abolished, there will be no cause for disunion.'[44] To match with the Muslim calls for unity, optimistic messages were also circulated in the Bengali Hindu journals:

> Now that the Khilafat Committee has decided to adopt non-cooperation, we appeal to all Hindus to help their Moslem brethren and fully sympathize with them. Those who do not like to take a practical part in it should at least help the Moslem brethren with money.[45]

The extent of the promises pronounced and gestures made by both communities during this time were undoubtedly compelling. For the first time in the history of colonial Bengal, the long-cherished ideas of unity seemed to have real prospects. The Congress under the leadership of Mahatma Gandhi had full sympathy with the Khilafat cause. After the Jallianwala Bagh tragedy, a mass movement was hoped for and a common line of action was to be decided upon with Khilafat providing a unique political opportunity for both. After observing the movement for over a year, an author commented that it puzzled him how the swadeshi movement, in spite of its widely nationalistic potential, had failed to generate enough Muslim involvement and ended up being a more or less 'Hindu affair', while the Khilafat movement, an absolutely religious one in terms of content and purpose, could arouse tremendous enthusiasm from other communities too.[46] Even when the *shuddhi* (the Hindu ritual for purification and often also for conversion) ceremonies for the revival of a more conservative and codified Hindu social order took place in different parts of Bengal, voices of resentment were heard against both this purification drive in general and its bad timing in particular: 'The distrust being spread among the Muslims never justifies any move of this sort. Hindu–Muslim unity, one of our greatest priorities of all times, has only been a reality recently, and now such activities can be extremely damaging. There can be damages beyond reparation.'[47]

Of course, the popularization of swadeshi as part of Khilafat agitation had its own pitfalls. The call for widespread Muslim participation in the boycott activities was sure to arouse self-doubt among many Muslims, so far aloof from the agitational politics. Local vernacular tracts often revealed the curiosity and bewilderment generated by the novelty of the political agenda. A pamphlet published from Barisal discussed the most troublesome questions for the Muslim villagers and sought to clarify those with an earnest optimism. The following part of the pamphlet, styled in the form of a dialogue between a leader and his followers, emerges as a brilliant example of how political principles, fashioned at the higher levels of society by the top-ranking leaders, had to be translated into common parlance painstakingly and mediated through popular cultural symbols:

Q. *Huzur*! Some of the Muslims are joining hands with Hindus and uttering *Bande Mataram*…. Do you think this is *jaiz* [acceptable] or not?

A. My child! *Bande Mataram* literally means 'We hail our Mother-country'. Hence this is *kaferi* [against the Religion] to say this for a Mussalman, because according to *Hadish* and *Feka* [religious texts], it is not permissible to hail anyone but Allah for the Mussalmans. So we would not say *Bande Mataram*. However, we would still join our hands with them in our common cause, with strong faith in mind and the cries of *Allah-o-Akbar* in our mouth.

Q. *Huzur*! Should *charkha* be a part of Khilafat then?

A. Yes, my child! *Charkha* will help us materially to cope with the strains of the time, hence it will please Allah if we take care of the community by doing so [italics original].[48]

Differences in social custom and religious practice remained an integral part of popular life, and at the level of day-to-day agitation politics, their implications could not be anything but complex. *Allah-o-Akbar* served the purpose of religious incitement, where threats of cultural distancing between the two major communities were latent. At the same time, needs for political collaboration also proved urgent, giving way to ingenious channels to overcome this 'distance'. The locally composed Khilafat songs evoked Hindu–Muslim union both in the rural areas as well as in Calcutta. The following song illustrates how 'unity' served as an important theme in popular support for Khilafat:

> Brothers, come and save Khilafat...
> The British have taken all,
> Save only some self-regard...
> We are not alone in this
> Hindu brothers will also come,
> Let us forget all hate and pain
> Protect our society and religion![49]

As the movement began to spread to the mofussils, the provincial Khilafat leadership developed district-level organizations, and adopted new techniques of mass approach. Leading Muslim personalities took up the responsibility for mobilizing their respective localities for *hartals* (boycotts or strikes) announced in Calcutta.[50] Local branches of the *Anjuman-i-Ulama-i-Bangla* were instructed to explain to the people the significance of the all-India decisions regarding Khilafat. *Ahsan Manzil* in Dacca became the centre of the Khilafat activities of that division. In Tangail under Maulavi Mohammad Wazad Ali Khan of Karatia, in the earlier Wahabi-inspired localities of Rajshahi, Dinajpur, Rangpur, Murshidabad, and Mymensingh, the movement gained great momentum through organized hartals and public demonstrations. The surge of mofussil activities also significantly contributed to a new spirit that encouraged local development projects. One would notice the launching of small-scale vocational schools, primary-level day and night schools, and numerous *rayat* (peasant) organizations in the mofussils of Bengal. Thus, what the swadeshi movement achieved in the case of Hindu communities of Bengal, the Khilafat movement did for the Bengali Muslims. A mighty trend of local development was their most lasting legacy.

Times had changed, nevertheless. The new politics of 'interests' and 'representation' had to go beyond the swadeshi mode of agitation and entail a stand on swaraj, that is, self-rule. Reassurances had to be provided that after Khilafat, swaraj could not but be a natural political priority for the Muslims. It was also declared, rather ambitiously, that the nature of swaraj would have to be both political and religious at the same time:

> Some Hindus are asking questions, suggestive of suspicion, regarding the attitude, present and future, of the Moslems towards the Swaraj agitation. Some even say that once the Khilafat problem is solved, the Moslems will sever themselves from the Non-cooperation agitation. We have repeatedly stated that if Swaraj is a political goal for the Hindus, it is

both a political and religious one for us, the Moslems. The hands of the British government have been detected almost everywhere underlying the attempts being made in Europe to destroy Islam and the Khilafat; so it will not be just to think that any peace with it will be possible on the part of the Moslems.... Is India's state of subjection intolerable only to the Hindus?[51]

'Political' and 'religious' swaraj, not mutually exclusive but essentially interconnected, was the message. Often latent or unspoken, this message was curiously delivered at a promising moment for the nation. For some, the intermingling of politics and religion appeared to be a matter of political pragmatism, a technique for mass mobilization. It might be argued that the Congress leaders never read the Khilafat movement as anything but a politically opportune moment to be seized. Significantly, for some others, like Gandhi himself, the question of combining politics and religion on a single ground of nation was a far deeper one.

The proximity between Gandhi's ideas of dharma (moral principles) and dharma-rajya (an ideal state governed by moral or ethical principles) and the fundamental premises of Khilafat ideology cannot escape attention. The unique combination of the temporal and the religious in Gandhi's thoughts, his signature rhetoric of Ram-rajya politics, unequivocally marked with religious–cultural symbolism, had often opened the floodgates of alternative nationalist viewpoints from various unsuspected quarters. A pamphlet published from the interiors of Barisal deserves mention here. Styled as a short play with two principal characters—Birendra, a young non-cooperation activist, and Sudha, his wife—both reflecting on the Gandhian creed of nationalism. They do not follow Gandhi's preachings merely as unquestioning followers, but instead attempt to come up with their own interpretation of Gandhi's dharma-based nation:

Sudha: ... You know, I feel what Lord Srikrishna has said will happen now: *Dharmasangsthapanaya Sambhabami Yug-e Yug-e*—[I will be here through ages in order to establish dharma]. Now Gandhi, the God-sent messiah of our times has come to remove all the immoralities we have so far nurtured in our life and society. Now is the time for the nation to wake up.

Birendra: Mahatma seems to me to be a political reformer; do you think he is a religious or social reformer too?

Sudha: Forgive me. It seems that you really consider these things—*dharma* and politics—as essentially separate, unconnected to each other. I do not think so. We, the Bengali, never understand politics without *dharma*. Politics, religion, society, education—every one of them are inter-connected, inseparable from each other.... The West might see religion and politics as different and separate things, but in our perception, they are not. That is why we have always had in the past a Kshatriya King, but a Brahmin minister. The Brahmin, being the keeper of religion, it could not be otherwise. It is he who guides the King, the watch-person of the political sphere [italics mine].[52]

A very different creed of 'nation' in Bengal thus emerged during this era, with intertwined trends of the religiously exposed Gandhian politics and a politics infused with great regional spirit. In a similar vein, the universalist overtures of the Khilafat ideology also provided a platform where religious sensibilities surpassed their apparent purpose, and the religious and regional identities were combined. From this perspective, the tying of the non-cooperation and Khilafat movements was not spurious in the province of Bengal, but provided an important key to the imagining of a cross-communitarian political ground. Whatever its merits or weaknesses were, this unique conjunction represented a moment of realization for the long-cherished dream of political collaboration between different religious–cultural communities. A historic irony may be found here: while 'difference' and 'rights' were asserted in the name of the indivisible temporal and religious sovereignties of the Khilafat and 'Muslim interests', this was also the historical juncture to effect a uniting ground between the two major religious communities within the region. The Bengali Muslims were drawn towards the political struggle in the name of the nation during this moment of religiously defined politics. Its eventual failure did not erase the fact that Bengal in 1920–1 witnessed an alternative concept of nation where religious differences would not recede, but cohere and converge in a politics thriving on regional identities.

The Conflict and Compromise of 'Bengali' Culture(s)

Any important moment of political transition like the Khilafat–non-cooperation moment in Bengali nationalism had to be embedded in its larger sociocultural context. Just as Fazlul Huq's new anti-colonial politics with a fervent call for representation in legislative bodies could not be divorced from his deep-rooted regional ties, which were never shared by leaders like Ameer Ali or Nawab Salimullah of Dacca, the resplendent moment of unity in political imagination during the early 1920s was also necessarily rooted in the social and cultural developments of the time. Bengal witnessed an unprecedented level of cultural exchange between its two major communities during this period. Nowhere was it more prominent than in the spheres of culture, or, more specifically, in literature, language, and music. Historians have often pointed out how Bengal's Muslims gradually shifted away from the Hindu bhadralok *samaj* (society).[53] But that would appear only as a part of the truth, perhaps even a misleading part, if one turns attention from the narrowly defined political discourse to cultural expressions and social realities of this time. These two communities had maintained their distinctive life-styles even in the earlier times, but there had also existed certain avenues of social and cultural exchange and cooperation. In the second and third decades of the twentieth century, these avenues continued to linger, flourish, and were even strengthened by a number of factors. The growing trend of cultural sharing, primarily urban in nature, and the social cooperation widely prevalent in rural areas, hardly received the historical attention they deserved. If, going beyond the political or state-oriented nationalism, cultural nationhood is to be deciphered through the shared memories, cultural artefacts, and social experiences—that is, through a shared cultural space of reckoning and a dynamic process of nation-formation—then the Bengali society in the early decades of last century undoubtedly held significant promises.

During swadeshi, any reference to the possibility of Bengal's 'national' life through Hindu–Muslim unity invariably relied on the instances drawn from the rural or small-town experiences of the region.[54] The idyllic village had to be the natural site where two communities shared quotidian pleasures and pains of life, often participating in each other's rituals and festivals. The sharing was achieved in the domains far removed from the din and bustle of urban life, naturally more differentiated and less accommodative by its nature. Around the 1920s, however, this frame of reference began to change. It was this period which saw the first emergence of a meaningful sharing between two communities in the cities and towns. A new distinctive interest was seen in the urban, middle-class, Bengali-speaking Muslim society towards the larger cultural milieu of the region, clearly defined and powerfully dominated by Hindu sensibilities.

The slow but steady development of an urban middle class of Bengali Muslims, aspiring to match the thriving Hindu bhadralok society, had much to do with this new cultural bridging. In both Calcutta and Dacca, two prime urban nuclei of western and eastern Bengal respectively, several Muslim literary groups flourished during this time. In a bid to strengthen their regional–cultural identity, these groups concentrated on upholding Hindu and Muslim literary traditions together and partaking in the life of both.[55] Following the model of Bangiya Sahitya Parishat of Calcutta, founded in 1897 with the aim of advancing the studies of Bengali language and literature, a group of Muslim intellectuals based in Calcutta started a new institution called Bangiya Mussalman Sahitya Samiti. One is bound to note the apologetic mood of some of the founding members of this samiti inasmuch as Muzaffar Ahmed, a leading figure of the group who would later develop into a well-known communist politician, offered a clarification on the use of the term 'Mussalman' in the title: 'At first glance, one might find Bangiya Mussalman Sahitya Samiti too much Islamic in its nomenclature. But in reality it was not so. It was never meant to be an exclusively Muslim, i.e., communal organization. In fact, neither did it aim to become a competitor to the Bangiya Sahitya Parishat.'[56] He emphasized that the primary purpose of the samiti was to represent these 'Muslim' accomplishments 'before the Bengali readers, especially the Bengali Hindu readers'. His articles appeared in the journal published by the samiti and showed how a tone of resignation mixed with resentment drove the Bengali Muslim intellectuals to look for a literary platform to which they could begin to belong with self-confidence.

Another new feature of the Bengali Muslim cultural enterprises of this time was the change in the nature of participation. During the early swadeshi period, major cultural figures like Sayyid Emdad Ali (editor of the journal called *Nabanur*) or Mohammad Akram Khan (editor of the journal *Mashik Mohammadi*) had mostly functioned on an individual basis in a mutually disjointed manner. But in the late 1910s, similar cultural enterprises were taken up by the Muslim literati working in a collective mode, giving their pursuit the shape of a movement. These groups acted as a social force towards their commonly perceived goal of attaining larger social and political fairness. Muhammad Shahidullah and Mohammad Mozammel Huq together published the quarterly journal *Bangiya Mussalman Sahitya Patrika* from 1918, and, in the same year, the journal *Saogat*, which was destined to become famous for its critical contribution in developing a regional Muslim movement and was published by Mohammad Nasiruddin. *Moslem Bharat* came up in 1920 with Mohammad Mozammel Huq as the editor. Their endeavours were significant not only because in them the Bengali Muslim community found certain isolated intellectuals pursuing similar aims, but also because their overlapping participation in literary and journalistic activities and the mode of collective functioning indicated a broader change of spirit for this community. One notices an upsurge of the educated, well-informed, and culturally aware social leaders, able to spearhead a new regional–cultural community. These were the people whose cultural inheritors would eventually come forward as powerful agents of Bengali Muslim identity in the late 1920s and 1930s in the 'Emancipation of the Intellect' movement (Buddhir Mukti Andolan), and thereafter in the Language movement (Bhasha Andolan) of East Pakistan in the late 1940s. Thus, here lies a significant cultural continuum in the Bengali Muslim society, which is often missed by scholars. Notably, this continuation made the late 1910s and early 1920s pregnant with immense possibilities for a 'different' socio-cultural negotiation in Bengali society.

Thus the regional–cultural nation for Bengali Muslims was never merely an abstract idea, but the lived reality of inter-communal cultural exchange in a very promising moment of national imagination. With the meteoric rise of the gifted poet Kazi Nazrul Islam, in whom the Bengali literary world immediately began to discover a talented star, this trend of inter-community cultural exchange grew even stronger. Later on, a prominent Bengali Hindu writer commented on Nazrul's emergence in the early 1920s: 'His appearance synchronized with that great upheaval in Indian life known as the first non-cooperation movement.... He wrote with equal ardour on Hindu and Muslim subjects, on the dark goddess Kali and on Kemal Pasha. His mind nourished on the myths and legends of both, was at home as much in the Gangetic plains as in the Arabic Desert.'[57] Syncretism was no longer a much-desired cult to this new literary legend, but a magically fertile ground for creative explorations. Nazrul's mastery over the language stood apart from almost every contemporary writer as he had an excellent gift of appropriating various strands of linguistic traditions—Sanskrit, Persian, and Urdu, along with various local dialects—in a remarkably natural way. 'Shat-it-Arab', 'Korbani' (The holy sacrifice), 'Kheyapar-er Tarani' (The boat to cross the river), 'Bidrohi' (The rebel), 'Kandari Hnusiyar' (Boatman, beware), and 'Kemal Pasha'—his masterpieces published one after another in the journal *Moslem Bharat* in the early 1920s—stirred the Bengali literary world precisely due to this unprecedentedly rich and eclectic language. It is possible to conjecture in this context that, apart from his literary contributions, Nazrul also made a larger impact on this shared space of Bengali culture through his songs, gaining immense popularity among the Bengali Hindus, both urban and semi-urban. Nazrul-giti, that is, the songs by Nazrul, soon occupied a position second in importance only to Rabindra-sangeet (the songs by Tagore) for the culturally hyperactive middle classes of Bengal. However different in genre and spirit Nazrul-giti and Rabindra-sangeet might have been, there is no denying the fact that together these musical traditions opened up a new horizon of cultural sharing. The unprecedented scale of such musical sharing may be inferred from various autobiographies or literary works reflecting on this time.[58] A new experience to the Bengali middle class comprising both Hindus and Muslims, Nazrul thus personified the linguistic–cultural unity of identities of Bengal. Muzaffar Ahmad, a close friend of Nazrul, reminisced: 'Nazrul had a magical spell during this time. Whatever he wrote attracted people of various different backgrounds, of different classes and communities.'[59] Mohitlal Mazumdar, a contemporary poet, also sought to place Nazrul's brilliance against the perspective of changing socio-cultural attitudes of Bengali Muslims, and observed: 'I have long been complaining that a large section of Bengali Muslims are to an extent unmindful to the potentials of their mother tongue, and due to this lack of participation, Bengali literature falls short of attaining its maturity', a trend which, Mazumdar thought, Nazrul could finally reverse with a great measure of success.[60] Rabindranath Tagore also noticed this rise of a new literary star of distinctly different genre with appreciation, as can be surmised from the favourable remarks of one of his close aides in Santiniketan.[61] However, it remains a matter of debate how much Tagore of the 1920s really approved of the novel experimentations with Bengali language that Nazrul, or some of his other Muslim contemporaries, were trying to do.[62]

The question of freely using Urdu/Arabic/Persian words in Bengali had been controversial even during the swadeshi era, as we have already seen in the previous chapter. Acknowledgement of 'difference' deemed to be an area of deep discomfort in the realms of culture and language. In the swadeshi days, the idea of an accommodative nation was torn from inside by its own cultural project of standardization. The same crisis was brought forward in the following decade and indeed deepened in a certain way.

The crisis was felt even outside the high political and cultural circles. A long tract written in 1925 on the Hindu–Muslim relationship considered it an absolute imperative for the Bengali nation and its smaller constituents to shed off unnecessary complexes and acknowledge the prominence of the more dominant cultural form, which had both genealogical authenticity and the advantages of widespread usage.[63] Bengali language might contain a rich repertoire of Arabic or Persian words, but it was still based on Sanskrit, hence, the author pointed out, essentially Aryan. 'When a Bengali Muslim writes Bengali, he must accept that what he actually writes is more than 90 per cent Aryan in terms of expressions and style.'[64] Such an overly assertive outlook was shared by a large chunk of the Bengali literary society including the cultural torchbearers who took up the task of promoting the language in the interest of a regional–national identity. The viewpoints and everyday functioning of the Bangiya Sahitya Parishat, the premier institution in Calcutta for the advancement of Bengali language and literature, was marked by a cultural complacence and high-handedness. The Parishat often defined the boundaries of 'national' culture in a 'classical' (Hindu) way,[65] yet, most unsuspectingly, resented the non-participation of Bengali Muslims in its activities. A scholar affiliated with the Parishat voiced this expectation:

> Both Hindus and Muslims have equal rights and claims over Bengali language. But we do not understand why the educated Muslims do not allow the Parishat to oblige them. We sincerely request them to come and join us here on this platform where we meet to celebrate the cause of our Mother Nation [*matribhasha-mandir*].[66]

For the majority of the Hindu authors and cultural activists of this time, raising a counter-offensive like the one above and shift the onus on to the marginal social groups was only too handy. Often they did not have to care for appreciating why the Parishat could never attract any substantial Muslim participation with the glaring examples of Munshi Abdul Karim Sahityabisharad (one of the ablest disciples of Dineshchandra Sen) and Gaffur Siddiqi. As a matter of principle, it maintained a specially designated position for a maulavi in the Parishat Committee. But the proceedings themselves show that this position was hardly filled.[67]

However, it is difficult to paint a monochromatic picture in this respect. Certain attempts were still made to bridge this ever-confounding gap between the two major regional–cultural communities, and one must not overlook how every such attempt at addressing the Muslim identity by the Parishat was received with great enthusiasm by the Bengali Muslim intellectuals eager to lay their own claims of the regional language. Dineshchandra Sen, one of the major historians of medieval and early modern Bengal, came to be highly regarded in the Muslim quarters for his stupendous effort to recover the literary and cultural accomplishments under the Muslim nawabs of Bengal. They took pride in the fact, as confirmed by Sen, that Bengali as a language prospered under the aegis of the late medieval nawabs who promoted poets like Alaol in the seventeenth century. In a way, Sen was a perfect fit in the Bengali Muslim project on nationalism, as he underscored the 'Muslim' contributions towards the Bengali 'nation'.[68]

Sen might have been one of the most distinctive scholars who gave due attention to the multiple components and complex heritages of the history of Bengal. But during this period some sections of Hindu literary circles showed a significant alacrity to new 'Muslim' cultural practices. The enormously positive responses to Nazrul and his various accomplishments are significant. Poems like 'Dhumketu' (The comet [1921]) proved that his appreciation ranged from the highest literary quarters to the barely literate sections of the society. Nazrul was, however, not alone among the newly discovered Bengali Muslim literary talents. A study of the literary discourse points out that a number of Muslim authors earned frequent favourable mentions, some of the most famous being *Abdullah* (1919) by Kazi Imdadul Huq, *Mir Paribar* (1919) by Abdul Wadud, and *Natun Ma* (1920) by Maulavi Ikramuddin.[69] This would surely strike us as a new development if the explicit condescension towards the Bengali Muslim writers of the earlier era, even to the finest ones as Mir Mosharraf Hossain, is borne in mind. The Bengali literary world perhaps attained a greater maturity in the post-swadeshi decade. A more direct engagement with 'Muslim difference' in this rather restricted world now became possible, or at least imaginable. Examples of such engagement deserve mention.

In a literary conference in northern part of Bengal (Uttarbanga Sahitya Sammilan) in 1911, the inaugural session started with a striking poem that focused on the Hindu–Muslim 'difference' and carefully juxtaposed the voices of two girls, the first one, a Hindu, and the other, a Muslim:

[Hindu girl:]

At this auspicious moment of an Indian homage
Our leaders are all here assembled
What have you brought for them, sister?

[Muslim girl:]

Here is the garland with the fragrance of rose...
Be it alien, don't ignore it dear
Many-splendoured surely is this garland of mine
Many a grace, many odours, from nay a sphere
In a band of love all of them smoothly combine.

[Hindu girl:]

Is our own garden, sister, bare and thin?
Is it not the plenty of God?
To adorn our speech-Mother would we be so keen
To borrow some flowers from abroad?

[Muslim girl:]

The flower that you label as of an alien brand
And neglect it, keeping it at rest—
Hasn't it drunk from the water of this land?
Hasn't motherland brought it up holding in breast?

[Hindu girl:]
Today you freed me from my deluded notions
The darkness of doubts now disappears.[70]

Jadunath Sarkar, the eminent scholar and historian, was the chief guest at this conference. Sarkar chose to address the problem of Muslim difference in his presidential address, with a clear emphasis on the 'other' claims on Bengali.[71] He asserted that the Muslims, forming more than half of the 'nation's population', must be taken along in the journey towards the creation of a strong national cultural heritage. He also appreciated that the Muslims themselves were not reluctant receivers in this project but enthusiastic partners in shaping this united cultural–linguistic platform. Neither an agenda of conscious Sanskritization nor that of Islamization of Bengali language was passed by him as an imperative. Rather he wished Bengali to have a standard of its own upheld and preserved by all communities within the region.[72] Dineshchandra Sen in one of his lectures reiterated the same idea and condemned the irrational tendencies to recover the lesser-known Sanskrit words to replace its more popularly used Arabic or Persian synonyms.[73] Any such self-conscious and wrongly motivated tinkering of the language was bound to be a self-defeating exercise in the end because, Sen thought, it would be nearly impossible to disown and destroy the characteristically rich and diverse linguistic traditions hidden underneath the commonly accepted form of the language.

The Muslim response to the question of language also reflected a change from the earlier era. The pro-Urdu lobby became less vocal than before. Their main focus had by now decisively shifted to Bengali or, at least, to a version of the Bengali language where Arabic and Persian words would be given their due place. What was meant by a 'due' place appeared to be the centre of controversy. Journals like *Al-Helal*, *Soltan*, *Moslem Bharat*, and *Bangiya Mussalman Sahitya Patrika* engaged in the debate over the 'desirable form of the language' for a regional nation. Mohammad Shahidullah spoke of a strong claim on Bengali, and turned his focus from literary to linguistic questions.[74] He also hoped that a 'comprehensive' history would necessarily include the marginal, or at least, the less vocal or visible segments of the society, and the Bengali Muslims would then be able to locate themselves on the cultural map of Bengal. The swadeshi project of culling and styling history from localities in the interest of the regional nation was given a new momentum by scholars like Hirendranath Dutta, Rameshchandra Majumdar, and Ramendrasundar Trivedi and pursued by meticulous researchers like Nagendranath Basu. In the second decade of the century, their project continued with greater vigour.[75]

The trajectories of the nation were strange, no doubt. The nation needed its own history, the accounts of its own 'people', but a nation's history and the search for its claimants would again point towards its endless inherent contradictions and limitations. Therefore, the nationalist's project ultimately had to be self-defeating, and the nationalist, in turn, had to be acutely aware of his predicaments. In this case also, the enthusiasts of national history and national language constantly stumbled upon the unbridgeable diversities of the region that defied the project of generalization and then looked for means to escape this conceptual labyrinth. Sometimes the task was to glorify the folk elements in different subcultures only to prove that those elements had necessarily been similar despite the diversification in their more cultivated forms: 'The folk literature is, by definition, collective. Every village or every locality becomes a part of that collective.'[76] Sometimes it would be considered necessary to locate the origins of inhabitants of Bengal outside Bengal and thereby efface and then equalize all their claims: '... not a single of the best-known races of Bengal were originally from this particular region.'[77] The Bengali language seemed to be the only connecting thread—the linguistic commonality being the strongest bond among a people otherwise diverse in racial constitution and historical background.[78] Who would not accept, the aspiring nationalist would ask, that ' ... the south-eastern part of Bengal populated by the descendants of Mongolian tribe, the south-western Bengalis largely belonging to Dravidian lineage, and the traditional Brahmins directly descending from the north Indian Aryan tribes'[79] had nothing much in common other than the language itself?

Lying at the centre of this common claim about the overarching national importance of the language was the assumption of its standardized form against which Muslim reactions were strongly pronounced. It is curious to see that while arguing vigorously in favour of the 'folk' or the 'locality', most of the stalwarts of the Bangiya Sahitya Parishat, as well as Tagore himself, proved themselves unwavering classicists regarding the form of language. Tagore's stand was unequivocal and, strangely or perhaps not so strangely, extremely political. The language of Calcutta, he argued, must be the standard form of the language because

> it is the capital of Bengal. The capital city is always like the stomach or the central organ of the body.... If it were Dhaka that had been the capital of Bengal, no doubt, the people of Dhaka would have had the advantage of ruling us with their own form of language, and provided the platform on which Bengali language would have based itself. If then the south and the west of Bengal wanted to move their faces away from it, they would have come to terms automatically in time, without much prayer and pleading.[80]

He would even extend this argument of the 'power–centre' in order to discredit the 'other' variants of the language: 'There is no reason why people of Birbhum would go on writing in their own language as a mark of protest against Calcutta. And even if some crazy people do so, the rank and file of the population would never really want that.'[81] The contradiction between Tagore's much-cherished creed of 'nation through social regeneration' and the consequent emphasis on decentralization of power on the one hand and the insurmountably hierarchical notions of his own cultural aesthetics on the other is easily discernible here. His ambiguity must have been an inheritance of the psycho-social conditions of Bengali bhadralok society in general. But the important point here is to note the deeply embedded hegemonic control over culture, language, and the related cultural aesthetics, which could effectively resist even the ablest intellectuals to step beyond the classical forms. If Tagore's consistent opposition to the uni-centric nation in the first decade of the century and his critique of the controlling, hierarchical nation-state in the following decade are read against his views of cultural and linguistic plurality, the disconnect is indeed glaring, a point I will return to in the next chapter.

However, one must also notice some early signs of an important post-Tagorean tendency in the Bengali literary world from this period. By the term 'post-Tagorean', I literally imply the generation of writers after

Tagore, and the new overtures in Bengal's cultural scene.[82] It was due to their new ideas that the language debate took a more vigorous turn. Their resentment against the old literary elite was now visible. The Sabuj Patra group, founded in 1914, led by Pramatha Chaudhuri, consciously invested in a form of Bengali that was more sub-literary and colloquial in nature, with a distinct flavour of its own. This debate inevitably raised the question of allowing the language to incorporate local dialects and local usages to a higher level. Nareshchandra Sengupta, a well-known novelist of this time, aggressively lampooned those who shrank at the prospect of the emergence of 'a number of Bengali languages, rather than one standard Bengali'.[83] Sengupta argued that there could not be a sensible argument in favour of debarring certain forms or usages due to their novelty or unfamiliarity. Any language would have a life of its own, and sift through the less worthy elements. It so happened in the case of many other languages of the world, evolving through a long, time-tested process or experimental practices. The major eighteenth-century English poet Robert Burns would be cited in this context, as his use of provincial English had discredited his unique position in the English literary tradition. Nor could Walter Scott be refused his due for the massive volume of Scottish influence in his writings. The Bengali classicists, who believed that their language belonged to the highest class of citizens, were reminded that, if any Englishman did not have an adequate knowledge of Scottish English and still wanted to treasure Scott's writing, he would 'courteously' invest in learning that particular dialect, and therefore,

> ... just in the same way, there should be no bar in acknowledging local dialects and local usages in Bengali literary tradition. If the work passes the test of time, if it has some artistic value, it will win automatically, and some of us will be obliged to acquire knowledge about the respective local forms and words. If it does not, no conscious interference is needed to push the work to the margins.... If Rabindrababu and others who follow his path can introduce the language of Calcutta, why can writers from Dhaka or those from Rajshahi not do the same thing without any hesitation? [84]

The above argument was followed by Sengupta's sarcasm about the puritanical attempt to rush to form an 'Arya Samaj of the language and marginalize the *antyaja* [outcaste] dialects once and for all [italics added]'. As expected, this elicited severe reactions from the conservative quarters. He was condemned for confusing 'literary style' with 'language', and irresponsibly inviting a dangerous trend of 'decentralization'. That the Bengali language attained a stable form (the standard language of Calcutta literary circles) after ages of experimentation, and that anarchy would only destroy its basis irreparably, was pointed out by one of his critics:

> Nareshbabu would not see that there is a discrepancy in the weightage of the writers. If Rabindranath suddenly starts writing in Noakhali dialect, we all will still read his writings taking as much trouble as it would need. But does the same apply for the lesser writers? If the ordinary writers of Bengal start writing in their own localized dialects, who would take that much trouble to read them? Would it not mean a loss for the whole Bengali literary tradition, if so much diversification ends up dividing the common literary world?... Does he really think that if one wants to use *polapan* [children] according to the Dhaka dialect instead of *chhelemeye* as we would say it in Calcutta, the Bengali language would prosper in any way [italics added]?[85]

Echoing Rabindranath's reactions about the 'Birbhum dialect', the classicists continued to foreground a universal, standard language, the lingua franca of the literary circles of Calcutta, and, by extension, the linguistic and literary form aspired by the entire region.

There may arise a question of how far these highly sophisticated articulations of literary–linguistic traditions were reflective of the broader society of the region. From a certain point of view, this doubt is natural and somewhat unsurpassable. People who engaged themselves with finer as well as deeper questions of culture came by definition from an elevated background, or at least with high credentials of literacy and awareness. However, this being said, I must argue that they were neither unconnected to the wider society to which they belonged, nor did they represent a discourse which was isolated from other contemporary discourses on identity and nation. The cultural and political ideas and movements in those times were so integrally interlinked, and interdependent, that any meaningful analysis of nationalism must retain a central space for these high-sounding cultural articulations. Significantly enough, this book finds these articulations full of the same contradictions and confusions that pervaded the nation's highly problematic connection with difference. The same hegemonic pulls proved indomitable; the same reluctance to give up one's smaller identity for gaining a place in the larger one. A more complex story of intense centre–margin contradictions, hidden in any narrative of nationalism, used to characterize the Bengali nationalist discourse as well. The second and early third decades of the nineteenth century, the era of an unprecedented degree of sharing and dialogue, and finally the failures in the realm of Bengali culture were still plagued by the internal crisis of nationalisms of Bengal. This shows that even at a moment of promise, all doubts raised and debates fought against the uniformity and indivisibility of national culture were adequately counterbalanced by a few powerful narratives of the 'national centre' refusing space to the marginal components of the 'nation'. While it was heard more strongly than ever that 'it is the language by which we aspire to build up the nation despite all differences of race, religion, and locality',[86] and a number of alternative nationalist visions made their presence felt in the linguistic–cultural domains, the objective of forging a nation owned by all its different elements continued to elude the nationalists. They seemed more eager to take the language to the people than to bring the people's languages together.

The Sceptics and the Advocates of Nationalism

The objective of forging a nation encompassing differences kept on eluding the nationalists. Yet it was constantly troubling for them that their ideas and activities had so little to do with the 'people', the larger society they all claimed to represent. From this ever-growing dissatisfaction, there appeared a number of strong critiques of nationalism by the nationalists themselves. It is hard to miss that the first experiences of a country-wide nationalist upsurge in the non-cooperation-Khilafat era actually coincided with the first major moment of critique of nationalism. Bengali nationalist discourse entered its most contentious and, by implication, most promising phase during this period. The towering voice amidst all contestations was that of Rabindranath Tagore, who during the years 1916–21 wrote and spoke vociferously on nationalism in a sharply critical tone. Even before the political movement began to spread under the aegis of Gandhi, Gandhian nationalism with its own set of rhetoric and the agenda of *satyagraha* (passive political resistance) found its first potent critic in Tagore. It is generally well known and explored in scholarly works that through protracted debates between these two major intellectual figures of colonial India, they finally agreed to disagree on the purpose of nationalism in general, and the specific ways of practising nationalism through satyagraha and non-cooperation in particular.[87] Scholars have often found underneath their disagreements a strong note of similarity, an ultimate proximity between Tagore's idea of swadesh and Gandhi's idea of swaraj, and their respective bids of building a swadeshi samaj or Hind Swaraj.[88] Yet some other scholars noted their differences as fundamental: 'Tagore and Gandhi were not equally, and in the same way, opposed to the modern state'.[89] However, while the Gandhi–Tagore debate had its own supreme value in the context of nationalist thought and its 'illegitimacies', from the viewpoint of this book it seems important to step back a little from this debate and to trace the line of Tagorean critique of the nation from the earlier swadeshi phase to the later phase. Instead of going into the intricacies of Tagore's vision of modernity, modern state or capital, all fundamentally connected with his understanding of nation, I find that his long-felt uneasiness about the politics of nationalism and his later full-scale critique of the 'ideology' of nationalism help us problematize the scepticism inherent in the nationalist ideology itself. Tagore in the present context is not Tagore the solitary rebel-artist struggling on the terrains of modernity (and nationalism as its product), but Tagore the most able spokesman of a time suffering from the agonies of self-experimenting nations.

It is usually said that Tagore had 'removed' himself from politics and lost his appeal to the contemporary politicians as an ideologue of the nation.[90] However, it is important to note that such claims of Tagore's 'dissociation' from politics are misleading.[91] Any appreciation of Tagore's nation, or, to quote Partha Chatterjee, his 'non-nation', must begin from this point, because what Tagore identified as the malaise of nationalism made him change his own outlook on nationalism in the post-swadeshi days. In the previous chapter, we have observed how Tagore had always been critical of the practices of nationalist politics. But he never developed an apathetic disposition towards either the 'political' or the 'national'. Tagore's alleged 'aversion to politics' can only be meaningful if we consider 'politics' in a narrowly defined sense. During these years, he became preoccupied in his search for an alternative form of politics, removed from its overtly institutional, hence inherently 'statist' version. The domain of formal politics had lost its charm for him, but his dream politics of empowerment, self-help, and constructive village regeneration refused to die. To him this alternative nationalism would lead to a 'realization' of the homeland or swa-desh.[92]

The context of 'people' which he found missing in the earlier nationalist imagination had begun to become 'politically' meaningful to him after his social experimentations with a few villages of eastern and western Bengal.[93] The agenda of village reconstruction was no less 'political' than 'social', he emphasized:

Time and again I had the opportunity to meet our politicians and insist them to consider an agenda of bringing the people to the political front for a proper national self-expression. They did not bother about any of my suggestions. And then I decided that this task must be taken up by no other than myself, without waiting for or depending on anyone else, because nowhere else it has its space.[94]

Thus, village became the 'other nation' for Tagore, and also, the proposed site for an alternative nationalism. In all these writings, we find him constantly employing the state–society ('rashtra'–'samaj') binary, and resting his critique of 'nationalism' on this particular binary.[95] Only a diversion from the powers of the state could unleash the internal forces generating within the village (*palli*). A true regeneration of the villages would necessitate social and economic developmental enterprises, essentially of a 'modern' nature. While too much reliance on the state was detrimental for the healthy development of a nation, the modern administration of the nation at large was not discarded by him. He would suggest alternative principles where the village population would be the direct agents of social reforms, which would then disseminate from the villages to the outside societies.[96] Tagore's 'national society' (swadeshi samaj) thus differed from Gandhi's Hind swaraj in major and fundamental ways.[97] To the latter, going back to the villages was primarily and essentially a crusade against modernity and its representations in urbanity or industrialization, and therefore a clearly moralist position. For Tagore, on the contrary, village was the most significant entity from where modern civilization should spread its wings, and with which the modern towns and cities should be integrally linked.[98] It was not a state versus society debate for him, but a model of regenerating the state through small-scale social organizations.[99] The power of the 'localities' denoted a geographical location and the abstractions of an imagined nation could only be handled from the political grounding of such locations. Thus a focus on the villages never precluded the criticality of the urban locations: 'Cities are essential as the central ground of all activities and creative energy. Just like in our body, energy is in some organs characteristically diffused while in some others, concentrated as well as intensive.'[100] How should the villages be linked to the cities? 'We need to collect information on the western efforts of village reconstruction through economic and social enterprises.... It is not possible, or advisable, to rush towards and impose on the villages all of a sudden. Perhaps for the doctors and teachers it might be easier for building ties with village societies, not for everyone ...'[101] Tagore would lay an explicit reliance on the machinery or other necessary apparatus of 'modern' life; more specifically, industrial machinery was seen to be a necessity by Tagore even in the swadeshi days. [102] Tagore's critique of modern capital and its growth did not leave much mark beyond the articles written at different times from 1908 and 1930.[103] Yet these writings had some significance. They served well as to indicate how an alternative national politics advocated by Tagore was essentially linked to his sociopolitical views of village reconstruction, and how the whole critique of the overtly politicized nation craved for a concomitant 'national' self-development (*atma-shakti*). I will argue that this 'local' project of nation, first emphasized by Tagore, would subsequently resonate through the thoughts of some of his contemporaries.[104]

It is important to note that, despite such stress on the society at large, Tagore was critical of the Gandhian movement even in its early days.[105] The non-cooperation and satyagraha movement fell short of Tagore's expectations.[106] A visionary looking for positive social energies to be unleashed, the calls for non-cooperation left him deeply unsettled.[107] In 1917, he already launched a lethal critique against the nation for its internal violence, its propensity to create 'huge organizations of slavery in the guise of freedom'.[108] Interestingly, the inverted violence of Gandhian satyagraha through the creeds of negation and obsessive protestation appeared equally unacceptable to him by 1921. He would term these traits in Gandhian doctrine as another form of violence and admit that he did not find it agreeable. He would rather look for a different collective enterprise of building a freewheeling political system which would be able to offer enough space to the diversities of mind and life.[109] In this adamant belief in India's potential to move beyond the self-limiting spirit of any violent or short-sighted breed of nationalism, Tagore put high premium on the deep diversity of culture and its enormous capacity to accommodate cultural differences.

A relatively 'long view' of early twentieth-century Bengal suggests that Tagore, despite being the most prominent critic of nation, was not a lonely voice in this respect. His scepticism cast its shadow on others too, some of whom were more vocal and active as the leaders of the nation. Chittaranjan Das, a highly successful barrister drawn into the ranks of Home Rule leaders, engaged himself directly in debates with Tagore on the questions of nationalism. The Tagore–Das disagreement demands a special mention here for two reasons. First, it has never received its due attention in scholarly studies. Second, if examined within the broader context of the variant of nationalism emerging within the Congress during this time, of which C.R. Das was a leading protagonist, one can identify its critical links with Tagore's views. Das, the master politician of this time, took vital cues from Tagore's deeply sceptic critique of nation. Through such links and cues, the apparently distant ideologues were actually connected in bringing subtle but critical insights into the mainstream discourse of nation. A review of Das's views and their connection with Tagore enables us to address the limits of nation, which was not only being explored in ideology and culture, but also left its direct mark in the realms of nationalist politics.

How the Tagorean challenge elicited reactions from Das on one level and cast influence on him on another is reflected in his historic speeches before and during the non-cooperation movement. Das's presidential speech at the Bengal Provincial Conference in Calcutta (April 1917) was a direct and rather personal attack on 'Sir Rabindranath Tagore', who was 'very unfortunately out to laugh away our newly gained national life':

> It is said nowadays that invoking nationhood would inevitably lead to national conflicts and national antagonisms, only to endanger the whole of mankind in due time. It is a rather old wisdom, but repeated with a vehemence in the present days. Even in India, we have some wise men who are very unfortunately out to laugh away our newly gained national life…. The Rabindranath of the swadeshi days who made the passionate pleas to God to bless the soil and water of Bengal has been turned into Sir Rabindranath now, who presumably has voiced this opinion during his trip to the Americas…. I have read the sections of those speeches which were published in *Modern Review*, hence I do feel the need for voicing a protest against that … [110]

Das was perhaps agitated by Tagore's speeches during his trip to the United States and Japan, published in *Modern Review* in 1917, where he doubted the legitimacy of 'nationalism'. To counter this, Das relied on two arguments: one, to seek the legitimacy of nationalism by giving it a clear regional twist, which I will focus on in the next section; and two, to defend and glorify nationalism like a true politician and reformulate the grounds of nationalism in substantial ways. The poet did not react publicly against this scathing critique, but some of his close followers did. Satyendranath Datta, Ajitkumar Chakrabarty, and others took on Das in *Prabasi* and *Bharati* rather aggressively. A few years later, Tagore resurfaced in Das's speech in 1921. This speech was written in the prison and read out by Sarojini Naidu during the Ahmedabad session of Congress. This speech by Das revealed, interestingly, a modified view on nationalism, different from his earlier stance, and was full of resonances of Tagore's own alternative model of nation, and its great capacity to assimilate and modify other cultural experiences:

> We stand then for freedom, because we claim the right to develop our own individuality and evolve our own destiny along our lines, unembarrassed by what western civilization had to teach us and unhampered by the institutions which the West has imposed on us. But here a voice interrupts me, the voice of Rabindranath, the poet of India. He says 'The western culture is standing at our door; must we be so inhospitable as to turn it away, or ought we not to acknowledge that in the union of the cultures of the East and the West is the salvation of the world?'
>
> I admit that if Indian nationalism is to live, it cannot afford to isolate itself from other nations. But I have two observations to make to the criticisms of Rabindranath: first we must have a house of our own before it can be ready to assimilate Western culture. And in my opinion, there can be no assimilation before freedom comes. The cultural conquest of India is all but complete; it was the inevitable result of her political conquest. India must resist it. She must vibrate with national life; and then we may think of union of two civilizations.[111]

Embracing the 'modern', or the 'Western modern' could not be unconditional but essentially a question of political priorities. The anti-West preoccupation of colonial nationalism was an inevitability which could only be reversed if it finally won and gained for itself equality of dignity. He conceded that colonial nationalism should not merely reflect the aggression, violence or inflated ego of the colonized, but aim to develop itself as a self-generating doctrine of cultural and political assertion. A year later, in the presidential address at the Gaya Congress (1922), he emphasized that, contrary to Tagore's fears, no fundamental conflict between nationalism and universal humanism should exist, provided freedom had been won. This was an 'ideal' that the 'other', that is, the anti-colonial nationalism, could deliver:

> What is the ideal which we must set before us? The first and foremost is the ideal of nationalism. Now what is nationalism? It is, I conceive, a process through which a nation obtains freedom, and then expresses and finds itself not in isolation from other nations, not in opposition to other nations, but as part of a great scheme by which, in seeking its own expression and therefore its own identity, it materially assists the self-expression and self-realization of other nations as well. Diversity is as real as unity. And in order that unity of the world may be established it is essential that

each nationality should proceed on its own line and find fulfillment in self-expression and self-realization.[112]

'The unity of the world' needed the 'self-expression and self-realization' of each individual nation as its constitutive parts:

> I desire to emphasize that there is no hostility between the ideal of nationality and that of world peace. A full and unfettered growth of nationalism is necessary for world peace just as full and unfettered growth of individuals is necessary for nationality.[113]

In Das's view, the essential truth of nationality lay herein: '[F]ull and unfettered growth of individuals is necessary for nationality', and, as for nationality, '… each nation must develop itself, express itself and realize itself, so that humanity itself might develop itself.'[114]

What must not escape our notice is that Das's later speeches revealed a change in both its tone and content. Whereas in 1917, he was more generously disposed towards the prevalent modes of nationalism, in 1922 he condemned its aggressive potential. By this time the need to distinguish the emancipatory nationalism of the colonial world from the self-aggrandizing models of Western nationalism was felt acutely, a need that must have been made urgent by the Tagorean critique.

From here followed the characteristic dilemma of the anti-colonial nationalist: what might constitute the nation's own distinctiveness or own 'self' in order to assert and uphold a separate identity? Here Das was faced with an impasse, exceedingly difficult to exercise in the cultural realm and almost impossible to handle on the platform of realpolitik. This confusion was amply reflected when he upheld the self-oriented nature of anti-colonial nationalism: 'Some measure of selfishness or self-defence will show us the path to solve this problem. Not the narrow-minded selfishness, we should aim for a self-centric creed which is intellectually open, advanced as well as universalized enough by its different outward manifestations.'[115] So nationalism would be inward enough to resist any generalized claim of the colonizer; again it had to be open in nature to engender a give-and-take equation with the same colonizer.[116] Due to its unabashed approval of the some fundamental tenets of Western modernity,[117] Das's take on modernity was different from the Gandhian critique of modernity and, at the same time, closer to the openness of the Tagorean approach.[118] The contradiction inherent in the spirit of nationalism, between its 'inward'-ness and 'open'-ness could be averted by the anti-colonial nationalist rather painstakingly.

The ideological challenge launched by Tagore against nationalism was thus received by the highest level of political leadership in Bengal, and influenced the formulations of a more liberal version of nationalism which developed from 1917 onwards. Das can be seen as the most promising architect of this 'new nationalism', a creed which through a period of introspective deliberations would finally combine its inwardness and openness, its opposition to the Western nations, and its aspired internationalism. No less significantly, some other political stalwarts of the swadeshi period, Bepinchandra Pal and Aurobindo Ghose, had also shifted towards this new nationalism of the late-1910s. For example, the opposition of Bepinchandra Pal, a rebel nationalist after 1920–1, against the Gandhian non-cooperation movement, also bore indisputable marks of Tagore's critique of nation. Pal firmly denounced nationalists for their aversion to the universalist messages of the West and the complete lack of constructive social work in the battle for swaraj. The remarkable affinity of his views to those of Tagore's cannot escape our attention, although they were never on the best of terms.[119]

Aurobindo Ghose, on the other hand, before choosing for himself a spiritual exile in Pondicherry, arrived at a differently conceived universalist platform through an entirely different psychological journey. His quest for spiritual unity with the world and its forces led him to espouse a theory of organic coexistence as a means to reduce the state of conflict. This theory, when translated into political terms, indicated that a national existence in India was possible through an *organic* assembling of the many different, even conflicting elements, and therein lay its claim to originality.[120] In this roundabout way, the new nation of this period attempted to address its own complex reality and distinct positioning.

Aurobindo was not the only one trying to grasp the essence of the national task of bringing many into one through the prism of religion. Both Pal and Das were also driven towards the pronounced spiritual imageries while interpreting the political implications of nationalism in colonial India. Pal spoke of the Hindu principles of cosmic harmony to be used in the project of nationalism. In essays such as 'Federalism: The New Need', 'Nationalism and Federalism', and 'From Conflict to Compromise', he argued that such a loosely joined existence of political nation could only be made comprehensible by the organic tenets of Hinduism, where the relationship between the part and the whole was imagined in a loose but critically connected way. Just as Hinduism, as Pal would argue, is essentially 'federal' in nature with a number of castes and sects, each more or less autonomous within itself but also dependent on each other, the ideal political structure of India should also be essentially federalized.[121] The political cult of the old Chakravarty Raja (a political head of an essentially decentralized state, bound only by the acknowledgement of the tutelage of that ruler) should be upheld in order to define the national 'self' in an authentically Indian way, rejecting its Western models: '... a federation of many cults and cultures, uniting under one common idea and ideal, but each cult and culture seeking to realize this common ideal in its own way.'

> This is how we find Hinduism, not a religion, but really a federation of many cults and cultures, uniting under one common idea and ideal, but each cult and culture seeking to realize this common ideal in its own way.... Similarly, when we had a national state of our own, that too was not a unitary state, but really a group of independent states, combined together under some central head or *Chakravarty Raja*. This federal idea has been a principal note or mark of the differentiation of our national *swa* or self from the other national *swas* or selves of the world. So this must find us the first element of our definition of Swaraj [italics mine].[122]

Pal, a highly articulate protagonist of nationalism in Bengal, would then define an internally 'differentiated' self or 'swa' in the interest of the nation and assert that the national 'self' in India must be made up of the different constituent cultures. But their peculiarities should be tied at the centre in the form of a 'state', the 'national state', to realize their fullest potential.[123] The 'Hindu Philosophy of Nationalism', written during the swadeshi movement, served as the bulwark of his new vision, which was articulated in the article written in 1917 called 'Federalism: The New Need'.[124]

> *Narayana*, or humanity is the whole, the different nations of the world are parts of that whole. *Narayana* or humanity is the body, the different tribalities, racialities and nationalities are limbs of that body. The whole is implied in the parts: the organism in the organs. *Narayana* or Universal Humanity is, therefore, logically implicit in every tribe, race and nation. *This is the philosophy of nationalism, as it is understood by the highest Hindu thought* [emphasis mine].[125]

The overtly Hindu metaphors notwithstanding, Pal's formulations had a curious proximity to Das's thoughts of new federated nationalism. Even an astute reader of nationalist discourse would, therefore, find it enormously difficult to guess who between these two leading ideologues could possibly have composed the following lines: 'The trends of modern social evolution seem unmistakably to be pointing to such a higher category. From nationalism to internationalism [*sic*]. No nation, in our time, can with impunity refuse to accept the lead of modern historic evolution in this matter and oppose the advance of this internationalism.'[126] Interestingly, along the same logic of induction, the particularities of religious–cultural entities, so far seen as stumbling blocks in the path of nation-building, were now seen as integrally constitutive parts of the nation by the leading visionaries of the 'new nation'.

Yet the two of them gradually developed major disagreements. Bepinchandra Pal and Chittaranjan Das, in spite of all apparent proximities of their own brands of nationalism, could not differ more on the required mode of 'national' activities when Gandhi called out for countrywide non-cooperation with the British. On 25 March 1921, in the opening ceremony of Bengal Provincial Conference of Barisal, Pal voiced his disapproval of the Gandhian programme and consequently of Das's leadership in Bengal, primarily on three counts: one, the unnecessary emphasis on exhibitionist acts like surrender of honorary titles; two, more emphasis on negative agenda than on the positive acts of self-construction; and three, the lack of any scope for harnessing the true socio-economic grievances of the people by the proposed movement. Pal's criticism was reminiscent of the critique of Gandhi by Tagore, made some years earlier. However, it had little political implication in the context of the ensuing movement. By dismissing the idea of non-cooperation for not implying a 'democratic swaraj', he declared a war against the all-India dictates of Gandhi and alienated himself in an irrevocable way.[127]

Das, on the other hand, was emerging as the most dedicated leader of the non-cooperation movement in 1921. An astute pragmatist, he never pondered for a moment before throwing his entire political weight behind the Gandhian agenda, however much his ideas had once been akin to Pal's. In a large meeting held outside the pandal of the conference the next day, Das, along with several other delegates, severely condemned Pal. In his most eloquent style, Das declared that the goal of swaraj was non-negotiable: 'Let (the others) not now add qualifying phrases such as "democratic" or "autocratic" to their ideal of Swaraj. It [is] no good to indulge in logical quibbling now about the form of *Swaraj* [emphasis original].'[128]

The Barisal Conference proved itself to be a landmark in the history of Bengali nationalist political ideology for two reasons. First, the Das–

Pal controversy left such a bitter mark that Pal withdrew from all public political engagements henceforth, and, by accepting his own defeat, also ensured that the agenda of social constructive works be defeated in the realms of nationalist politics.[129] Second, Pal's emphasis on the need for a distinctively different political movement in Bengal within the larger framework of non-cooperation underlined the strength of his beliefs in federalist national agenda. He boldly proclaimed that '[f]ederation is the way to democratic Swaraj,' and that 'the administrative machinery cannot be of the unitary type. Real democracy does not grow under unitary system of government. It is also against our spirit and traditions which have been essentially federal in character.'[130] Espousing the old Indian federalist traditions, and underscoring the need for a 'real democracy', Pal would thus claim a different path for Bengal's politics. In his views, various linguistic–cultural provinces of India must be very differently placed in terms of psychological and material preparation for any anti-colonial movement:

... conditions are different in different provinces, and though it may be conceded that the non-cooperation propaganda in the provinces should generally follow the non-cooperation resolution of the Nagpur Congress, complete freedom must be given to them to take up particular items of this programme and emphasize these more than the others with a view to suit the provincial temperaments or conditions...[131]

Rarely was a more cogent argument heard in favour of the 'region–nation', its position, and rights vis-à-vis the 'country–nation'.

A common commitment towards regional nationalism did not mean uniform conceptualization of the region–nation in question. Pal differed from Das on certain critical grounds. The latter's political priorities dictated a tying up of the region with the larger nation through a common political movement under the aegis of the Congress. The political alliances Das was privileging at this time made him sail in a different boat. Pal by this time had evidently rejected the Congress movement and thought that no anti-colonial movement should need to follow the principles of uniformity throughout the country: 'The practical shape of non-cooperation will have to be determined by practical considerations. It may take one shape in the Punjab, another shape in Bengal.'[132] So the most evocative calls for regional autonomy of Bengal by Pal failed to elicit any sympathy from Das, who would, somewhat ironically, soon emerge as the most vocal proponent of the region–nation. Das and Pal, two priests of regional nationalism, visualized the political needs of the region at this critical historical moment through different strategic prisms, and by doing so, belied the possibility of forming a solid regional alliance. Thus a moment of immense possibilities for the region–nation could not become a moment for its more meaningful realization.

The inability of two eminent leaders to join hands at a critical historical moment remained a significant failure of Bengali nationalism, which was about to be pitted against the 'national' political platform for the first time. The Bengal Provincial Congress at the Calcutta and Nagpur Congress sessions under Das's leadership in 1920–1 declared that some of the primary guidelines of Gandhian non-cooperation would be opposed in the province, and the continuation of government service and participation in government institutions would be advocated along with an economic boycott. That Das could take such a bold step against Gandhi and cut down the latter's urge for total non-cooperation with the colonial government to a significant degree indicates the strength of this regional leader and his political convictions. In terms of analysis, therefore, one can keep aside the personal and strategic differences between Das and Pal during this time, and focus on their ideological proximity instead. Both were in favour of a self-reliant 'Bengali' nationalism as opposed to any blind imitation of an 'all-India' nationalism.

Das's formulations of regional nationalism went back to his first presidential speech of 1917 at the Bengal Provincial Conference in Calcutta, which was also published as an article named 'Banglar Katha'. It began with an apology about the title of the speech: why Bengal, not India, had to be his ultimate focus. 'How does one define politics then, if that is not an integral aspect of the life of the "nation"? Is not the region of Bengal, or the Bengali nation, the starting point of all our political concerns?'[133] In all fairness to Pal, Das was the first to offer Bengali nationalism its first unabashedly 'regional' stance. The novelty of the approach was quite clear to the contemporary observers, many of whom might not look at his stance very favourably. Referring to this speech by Das, an article in *Calcutta Samachar* charged him of narrow provincialism, or to quote the author, 'a provincial spirit':

> The address evinces what we may term a provincial spirit. It is good to help oneself, but such a spirit has always the tendency to swallow up the *national* spirit. It also leads to the division of society into various groups. Recognizing fully that provincial conferences should deal with local questions only, we are constrained to remark that a time has come

when Indians should think of India first and of their respective provinces afterwards. Where there is broad-mindedness there is this feeling present. Charged with this spirit, the Muslims joined hands with the Congress platform, and a Gandhi comes from Guzerat to study the conditions of Bihari peasants.

[Das] has remarked, 'We are a *nation* which has its own individuality and its particular mission.' If every sentence of Mr. Das had not breathed out, 'we are all Bengalis,' his words would have deserved to be written in letters of gold [emphasis added].[134]

There is a clear divergence between the 'nation' Das had spoken about, and the 'nation' that this passage refers to: the former evoking the region–nation of Bengal and forging its links to the state above, and the latter indicating the country–nation and looking at regions as mere provinces of that overarching entity called 'nation'. This confusion was not striking at all; throughout this era 'nation' continued to be variously employed to refer to any of the following categories of country, region, religious community, or even caste groups, all signified by the same confounded Bengali word 'jati'. However, it is important to note that the late 1910s and the 1920s marked a high point in construction of the regionally defined nation of Bengal. By declaring that '[the region] has got a cast of its own; it has got a spirit of its own; it has got a distinct individuality,' Das maintained a strong position that all the demands for 'self-government' would actually stem from the assertions of the 'nationalities', which in this context would necessarily imply 'provincial autonomy':

If you consider what is the kind of self-government which is exactly necessary for us, what is the first point which suggests itself to you?... *Provincial autonomy.* I desire you to approach this question not at all from the European point of view, but from our own national standpoint. What is the exact meaning of provincial autonomy?... That people who have for hundreds and hundreds of years been living in Bengal, have come under the sway of a particular culture, have been animated by a particular genius, and the provincial government which will be established in Bengal must give the fullest expression to that ideal. That they have, for several centuries, been living in Bengal, and amongst them there have grown up a very great culture which has made itself felt in the domains of science, philosophy, religion, literature and art. It has got a cast of its own; it has got a spirit of its own; it has got a distinct individuality [emphasis mine].[135]

But how would Das conceive the contours of the distinct provincial space, which possessed such a 'distinct individuality'? How would he address the claims of the major communities figuring in this space? 'The kind of self-government' necessary for Bengal should not leave this question unanswered, because only a satisfactory solution to this problem would dictate the nature of political participation and cultural projects on the regional level. So Das immediately asserted:

> When I speak of the Hindus, I am at once reminded of the Mahommedans of Bengal. They have also lived in Bengal. When I am speaking of provincial autonomy, I am not forgetting any community or members of any particular religion. I want to include all of them, and I say, taking the whole of them, there is a distinct individuality of Bengal. It is on that individual nature that we must take our stand. Now, gentlemen, provincial government must be so formed that it will not lose the particular interest which that individuality requires.[136]

For the preservation of the individuality of the (region)–nation, the province should have a substantial measure of autonomy from the (country)–state. How exactly did he visualize the hierarchical relationship between various levels of administrative structures? There should be a 'central government', representing the 'wider interest', and the provincial governments would be consenting to form that central government, something like the 'United States of India' or a 'Greater Indian Nationality', with certain in-between ties loose enough to allow space for the regional individualities to grow and prosper:

> I believe, it was John Bright who said that the future of India was the United States of India. So far as that ideal is concerned, it is a grand idea. Provincial autonomy is only a part of that ideal. But John Bright went further; he said that the several provincial governments should be connected with British Parliament. To that view I do not assent because the result of that would be that wider interest of Indian Nationality would be overlooked. So we want a central government. It must be made fully representative of all the provincial governments and of the Greater Indian nationality.[137]

Das would thus envisage a 'federated government', where all the 'greater nationalities' should belong through the mediation of a 'federated parliament'. The swadeshi era had experienced the immediacy of a regional identity, and now, in Das's imagination, the region–nation of Bengal was consciously taking a 'political' shape to complement the idea of a greater Indian whole. For the first time in the history of Indian nationalism, such a clear agenda of a free and federalized 'India' could be seen through the bridging of different layers of social and political loyalty in a cogent vision of national administration. We would find Pal only echo, perhaps unwittingly, Das's persuasive reasoning heard as early as in 1917 when the latter insisted that India in the precolonial times was not accustomed to any politically integrated existence that was essentially signified by the term 'nation'. Pal's next argument for federalism was also anticipated by Das, almost literally, that the 'provincial nationality' would ideally be connected with a 'federated Indian nationality'. The similarities were not fortuitous at all; the discourse of 'nation' was surely elevated to a different level of political–cultural imagining by its sincere imaginative engagement with its most troubling problematic: 'difference'.[138]

The idea of region–nation had some impact on the larger political society as well. At the Bengal Provincial Conference in 1920 held in Midnapore, Upendranath Maiti, a scholarly politician, delivered the presidential address and set the tone for the meeting by pleading for a joint front of Bengali Hindus and Bengali Muslims for the sake of a 'Bengali provincial nation'. The geographical boundaries of Bengal being endlessly disputed, he implored for a settlement first on the question of mapping of the region, and expressed deep resentment at the colonial attempt of excluding Sylhet, Manbhum, and Singbhum, 'parts of Bengal from time immemorial' from the present province. 'We should press the Raj for paying a little more attention to the desperate pleas of the inhabitants of these districts; we should pray to God for building a united province of Bengal.'[139] Another author from Calcutta made a comparative estimate of Gandhi and Das, and weighed their respective contributions in delivering the 'nation'. Clearly an admirer of the Bengali stalwart, the writer noticed that Das, in his capacity of leading a 'provincial nation', was in a position to provide an effective ground for 'national' belonging in the end. This 'critic' of Gandhi would even point out that this was only natural because Gandhi had been and still was an outsider to his own province, and never found an opportunity to develop close ties with any 'regional' culture:

If following Das's example, all the provinces like the Punjab, Gujarat, Maharashtra, Ayodhya or the Deccan—all take effort to uphold their own provincial spirit which reigns over and above the communitarian cleavages, if the groups and communities of India champion the provincial identity, then only it would be possible to ensure a sense of 'unity' amidst such vast range of 'differences'. That is the only way to save India....

The Non-cooperation movement under Gandhi's stewardship cannot fulfil such promises. But if Das takes the charge of guiding the movement, if he returns to politics actively, this great politician cum visionary would surely become the most successful champion of nationalism.[140]

The trust in Das's leadership as opposed to that of Gandhi's was not uncommon in these years. Followers of Das began to oppose Gandhi's Congress openly and stood firmly beside the Bengal Congress,[141] which was seen as the association of the region, and therefore, a more trustworthy platform:

> As we in Bengal Congress have already connected ourselves to the world civilization, if we have to return, we cannot return erasing everything that we have so far experienced outside. We cannot go home and non-cooperate like the old Brahmin *pundit*s who would give up every single small thing which did not belong 'originally' to India. We cannot do that. It is no more a mission of negativism [*nibritti*] but indeed one of our positive desires of life [*prabritti*]—not to mention the fact that Indian tradition has always been a complex intermingling of the *prabritti* and the *nibritti* [italics mine].[142]

There could no longer be a journey back to the origins, but a journey ahead to some kind of a 'modern' future; one might not be guided by negativism (*nibritti*), but by positive (*prabritti*) impulses. Succinctly framed, the above passage explicated the connections between the ideological imperatives and the resultant politics born out of the 'new nationalism' of Bengal during non-cooperation. Much of Tagore's opposition to Gandhi's satyagraha, voiced roughly at the same time, indeed rested on a similar premise: too much negative obsession might not be an effective and desirable ground of a self-reliant anti-colonial nationalism.

The regional nationalism during this time may be seen as thriving to a large extent on an anti-Gandhi prejudice. But, having said this, this prejudice should be carefully weighed against the powerful nationalist visions launched by Das and the kind of strong support that leaders like him were able to muster. Scholars have often argued that much of the Gandhi–Das conflict over non-cooperation movement arose from their irreconcilable priorities, and had its roots in the typically Bengali bhadralok apathy towards Gandhian moralism and asceticism.[143]

The ideological component of this conflict has not been adequately emphasized. In reality, the steadfastly 'regional' leadership of Das was perhaps bound to clash with Gandhi's supra-regional agenda of nation, particularly at this historical juncture when the region had its strongest leadership in its colonial history. Das aimed at taking the movement to a level where rural and urban societies could be mobilized and the colonial government could be pressurized for an immediate compromise on the questions of representation at the Legislative Council. To focus on the latter half of his strategies, that is, to 'capture' the Legislative Council and dismiss the former part of his vision to mobilize various levels of regional society (in his case, Bengal) would be inordinately one-sided.[144] It was mainly due to Das that the Bengal Congress could successfully establish a province-wide village-level contact and turn itself into a grassroots organization during these years. Also, he was not alone in visualizing Bengal's national awakening in a different trajectory. We must note that, not only Das, but many Bengali leaders of this time, ranging from the great orator-leader Bepinchandra Pal to the more locally rooted organizer-leaders such as Birendra Sasmal, found themselves in a quandary vis-à-vis the Gandhian leadership, and their rebellious acts and gestures began to endow Bengal with a distinct character of a 'dissenter' against the tide of Gandhian movements. Sasmal, the undisputed leader of the non-cooperation movement in the district of Midnapore, deliberately defied the Gandhian dictum and led a local tax-refusal movement against the Union Board. At the same time, Das found himself disaffected with Gandhi to such an extent as to draw from most of the erstwhile Bengali non-cooperators and also from a number of revolutionaries huge support for the new-born 'Swarajya Party' or 'Swaraj Party'.[145] One of Das's followers and close aides, Subhas Chandra Bose, later recalled that in 1922 the whole nation had been aroused to passionate activity, when the 'commander-in-chief' (Gandhi) suddenly hoisted the white flag.[146] Bengal was clearly on a different track than the rest of India during this critical juncture of the first large-scale Gandhian movement of non-cooperation.

In conclusion, this was the time when the leading Bengali ideologues and politicians identified and debated over two fundamental dilemmas of nation and nationalist politics: first, how to nurture the nationalist cause and yet retain a place for themselves in the growing internationalism of the day, and second, how to bridge the smaller regional communities or cultures within the larger whole of the nation. They had to address both the interests of their regional homeland as well as those of the larger country. In whatever way they might have accommodated their many different nations on an imaginative or ideological plane, they found the representation of those overlapping emotional and cultural ties or identities, in political terms, to be enormously challenging. Any sensible politics had to be conceived through an acknowledgement of this plain fact of multiple national identities. The idea of federalism in this context proved itself most attractive. By a rather timely ideological twist, Das, Pal, and others emphasized the 'federal' links with the country, lying beyond the peripheries of the Bengali nation, while firmly setting the contours of a regionally defined nation as their focal point.

However, the second problem often proved to be more troubling and less likely to be solved by any such clinical prioritization. Even if the needs of the region–nation could co-exist with the larger needs of the country–nation, the needs and interests of the nation and those of its smaller constituent elements were hard to be synchronized. There were intellectual attempts to approach this vexing problem in Tagore's idealized prescriptions or Pal's federalist formulations based on the abstracted 'Hindu' idioms. But there was also a gaping need for a suitable political agenda by which the accommodation of the smaller communities or localities within any broadly defined nationalism would be conceivable. During this rather uniquely creative period of Bengali nationalism, we can identify certain attempts to skirt around this particular crisis, through the crafting of a new national politics devised to handle the reality of differences. The next section will explore the political and ideological negotiations of nation within its various smaller components.

Fragments of the Nation: Localities and Communities

When and how would the multiple self-asserting entities want to form a larger 'national' whole on their own? This question had attracted a great deal of attention in Bengal by the 1920s. But most of this attention was paid on the ideological plane. C.R. Das might claim to be the first leader who searched for a possible solution from a political angle. For the first time in India's national struggle, a political leader formulated a coherent agenda on tying up the various localities and communities in a plausible national structure, which would nonetheless ensure the preservation and advancement of the particular interests within it.

In the earlier section I mentioned how Das attacked Tagore in his presidential speech at the Bengal Provincial Conference of Calcutta in 1917. In the same conference, where Das's name was proposed as the chairperson by the old Moderate leader S.N. Banerjea, Das declared that bridging the gap between the educated community and common people should be the first priority of the Congress henceforth. Although he was not the first ever politician to underline this principle,[147] Das was the first front-ranking Congress leader to outline a scheme of village rehabilitation on the basis of the district boards, local boards, and municipalities. However, his ideas once again resonated with Tagore's, in many ways his ideological predecessor. The other ideologue who cast his influence on Das in this respect was perhaps none other than Gandhi. We can identify in his village development programme of 1917 various aspects of the Gandhian 'village India'. But there was one important mark of distinction. For Das, unlike Gandhi, this was more of a political project than a moral task. In his Provincial Conference speech of 1917, Das argued that village reconstruction should be an integral part of the political project of the nation, because 'if we begin to think where our "nation"-ness begins, we will find that poverty in the Bengali country-side is the critical element in our history which has been unchanged, yet providing the basic spirit of our culture':

> We have to pay good attention to what Bengali nation actually means. To do so, we need to go back to history and find out the essential features of the Bengalis, and the ways by which such essential 'Bengali'-ness would be realized in the present conditions in a natural but universally redemptive manner. If we begin to think where our 'nation'-ness begins, we will find that poverty in the Bengali countryside is the critical element in our history which has been unchanged, yet providing the basic spirit of our culture.... Therefore, to have our nation realized we first need to reform our village-life.[148]

'To have our nation realized we first need to reform our village–life': this was considered critically important not beacuse of any moral responsibility of upholding the true India that resided in its villages, but because, according to Das, one of the key identities and loyalties of an individual had to be rooted in his/her primary habitat. In another speech (Dacca, October 1917), he repeated his firm conviction in upholding 'parochial politics':

> You must not lose sight of what is called parochial politics. From Time immemorial, the village has been the unit of our national life. You must consider the reconstruction of our village life. You must consider the education of our villagers. You must consider the question as to how they may be represented in the district associations, which will be formed with

representatives sent by them, and you must so frame your scheme that the interest of what is called parochial government may not in any way suffer from what may be called the interests of the provincial government. Let the village be so connected with the province that it may not be felt as an obstruction but as a real and integral part of the province.[149]

The principal objective was to 'connect' the multiple identities within the nation than to seek the nation's prospect in the idyll of the village. The onset of the non-cooperation–Khilafat movement seemed to have stalled Das's agenda of active village reorganization for some years. Although he spent much time and energy in pressurizing Gandhi and the Congress to include the demand for swaraj in the non-cooperation resolution, it was not before 1922–3 that he could produce an 'Outline Scheme of Swaraj' designed on his own set of political priorities. In his speech at the Special Session of the Congress held in Delhi in October 1923, he announced this 'outline', already anticipated in the presidential address at the Gaya Congress (December 1922):

To form a scheme of government, regard must be had

1) to the formation of local centres more or less on the lines of the ancient village system of India;
2) the growth of larger and larger groups out of the integration of these village centres;
3) the unifying state should be the result of similar growth;
4) the village centres and the larger groups must be practically autonomous;
5) the residuary power of control must remain in the Central Government, but the exercise of such power should be exceptional, and for that purpose, proper safeguards should be provided, so that the practical autonomy of the local centers may be maintained.

Briefly, a maximum of local autonomy, carried on mainly with advice and co-ordination from, and only a minimum of control by, higher centers, which will have some special functions besides.[150]

The excessive concentration of power at the upper levels should give way to a genuine decentralization of administration and substantial redistribution of power; hence the formulation of local autonomy was the fundamental principle.[151] However, most of Das's 'village–scheme' remained only a dream, as he died in 1925 leaving behind many of his dreams unrealized.

A close contender of Das in this respect might be Aswinikumar Dutta of Barisal, one of the chief local leaders of swadeshi Bengal who did not give up his project of rural reconstruction even after the frenzy of the swadeshi movement had cooled off.[152] The president of the Barisal District Congress Committee till his death (1923), he believed that '[g]iven the condition of our country, I firmly think it is much more important to be a good District Congress-person than to be a member in the Legislative Council. That gives me the scope to serve my country in a real sense'.[153] He devoted tremendous organizational energy and resources to the development of village-oriented schemes, including provision of drinking water, establishment of schools, and medical facilities. The local programmes had a profound effect on the Muslim and Namasudra population of the region, and Barisal at this time was one of the most developed districts of eastern Bengal. There were a few rather disconcerted efforts towards this task of tying up of rural Bengal with the political centre of the province. A series of publications named *Rayat-bandhu*, published in Calcutta since 1924 under the supervision of Said Erfan Ali, a famous barrister of Calcutta High Court and also a member of the Legislative Council, testifies to the establishment of a Central Rayat Committee of Bengal in Calcutta for a district-based developmental programme.[154] The association had also planned to establish district branches later, which in all probability remained an unfulfilled dream. Two of their booklets titled *Permanent Settlement and the Bengali Rayats* and *Zamindar's Abwab* were circulated in the interior villages.

Finally, there was none other than Tagore. When Das and others were fighting with the Gandhian Congress over the issue of council-entry, Tagore dedicated himself to his dream project of building the Visva-Bharati Ashrama and its adjacent village of Sriniketan, modelled on the basis of self-sufficiency. He echoed Aswini Dutta: 'We should not think of the whole country but start with one or two villages ... that is the way to discover the true nation.'[155]

> When we all have finished discussing that the nation would have to be constructed on the strength its village-base provides, I understand that those who have conceded would nevertheless take initiatives about more discussions and planning, but not about the true work in the villages. So it seemed that I myself should take up the responsibility despite all my limitations.[156]

The day had come, he thought, when agriculture should no longer be the exclusive concern of the cultivating classes, but also of the whole society as such.[157] Under the leadership of Leonard Knight Elmhirst,[158] Sriniketan was developed as an ideal locus of the localist experimentations.[159] A person with a deep distrust for the creed of 'political nationalism', Tagore wanted to explore the 'localities' as against the 'centre', thus channelize the political project of nation towards a socio-economic and cultural project of nation, and enable the forces of unity and freedom negotiate between themselves at the local societies.

Village development became a passionate agenda for sections of Bengali Muslims too. As we have noted earlier, the Khilafat movement by its populist content and organizational success created a potent trend of local development projects in the villages of Bengal. The provincial Khilafat Committee took particular care to start permanent branch offices at some key mofussil centres, which encouraged local or individual initiatives for establishing primary schools and vocational training centres. In *Ranga Prabhat* by Abul Fazl and *Jiban-Kshuda* by Abul Mansur Ahmed, memoirs of Bengali Muslims who had themselves been politically active around the 1920s, new experiments with public necessities in small villages were mentioned. The local Khilafat leaders organized the rayats of Rangpur, Faridpur, Bakharganj, and Tripura. In Mymensingh, numerous rayat committees were set up during this time to undertake projects like abolition of various cesses and *abwab*s (arbitrary exactions above the formal rent) to relieve the burden of local cultivators.[160] Maulana Maniruzzaman Islamabadi at Munshigunj laid great stress on a system of education that would enable the students to learn social, moral, and religious laws.[161]

The local endeavours were connected to the new politics of representation in an important way. At the Legislative Council, the Muslim leaders unfailingly upheld the cause of the rayats who constituted the majority in the Bengal Muslim community.[162] In 1919, Abul Kasem and Fazlul Huq stressed the need for an immediate action to redress the awful condition of cultivators mostly due to the commercial overuse of the arable lands.[163] Yakinuddin Ahmed forcefully voiced the need to stop the export of rice from India.[164] The Muslim legislators routinely upheld the tenants' interests. During the Bengal Tenancy (Utbandi Amendment) Bill, 1923, both Ahmed and Syed Emdadul Huq discussed the conditions of the rayats.[165] These legislators used to draw their moral rights from their respective local bases. As an aspiring political class stepped into the arena of institutional representation for the first time in Bengal, the 'local' began to be critically decisive in politics.

The 'local' also immediately brought in another very critical dimension of nation in the nationalist discourse. As the 'local' inevitably involved the resident community of a locality, the question of internal dissensions and differences had to be addressed. The legislative representatives, including the premier leader himself, were acutely aware of the eternally vexing Hindu–Muslim question within the localities. Das, once again, deserves a special mention in this context. Under his leadership, the Swaraj Party became an alternative political institution functioning parallely with the colonial government. Due to his deft leadership, the Bengal Provincial Congress Committee (BPCC) and Swaraj Party were bridged in such a way as to appear like a single institution, drawing support from all social bases. The professional Hindu bhadralok society was made to cooperate with popular leaders of villages, revolutionary leaders, labour leaders, and, most significantly, the Muslim business and professional sections.[166] Key to this outstanding political success of the Swaraj Party and its 'domination' of the Council and the Calcutta Corporation around 1924 was the tremendous Muslim support behind it. Das was almost single-handedly responsible for this unique social bridging: no other politician of Bengal before or after him was able to secure such overwhelming support of the Bengali Muslim community. It is often argued that Das was excessively generous towards the Muslims in an attempt to win as much support as possible for his party.[167] However, Hindu–Muslim unity was not merely a strategic invention for him in the early 1920s, but a constant theme in his writings and thoughts right from 1917. While it might be difficult to conclude whether politics determined ideology or vice versa, it can be argued that throughout his career Das betrayed a remarkable readiness to walk an extra mile for a united front of the major regional communities. This eventually led him to undertake a concrete administrative step towards an inter-communal alliance. In December 1923, the historic proposal for Hindu–Muslim partnership in bearing the municipal responsibilities suggested by Das was formally translated into the Bengal Pact. The Pact stated:

> It is resolved that in order to establish real foundation of self-government in this province, it is necessary to bring about a pact between Hindus and Muslims of Bengal, dealing with the rights of each community when the foundation of self-government is secured.[168]

According to this Pact, first, representation in the Bengal Legislative Council would be on the basis of population ratio with separate electorates. Second, in the local bodies the proportion would be 60:40 (60 for the majority community, and 40 for the minority community) in every district. Third, 55 per cent of the government posts were to be earmarked for the Muslims.

The Pact, rather expectedly, elicited most acrimonious criticisms from the educated Bengali Hindus and an enthusiastic support from the urban professional Muslims. Both Congressmen and Swarajists opposed it bitterly. Three main charges were hurled against the Pact by the Hindu bhadralok quarters: extravagant concessions had been showered on the Muslims; the Muslims were 'too inefficient to deserve them'; and the very idea of communal representation in government services would encourage 'petty inter-communal bickerings, inimical to the growth of broader nationalism'. Indignant comments raged around Calcutta: 'Such pacts and compromises are likely to excite the rowdy elements among the Moslems to cry for more and more.'[169] The *Amrita Bazar Patrika* affirmed that by accentuating communal differences and inciting Hindu–Muslim tensions afresh, the Pact did 'a great disservice to the nation'.[170] With a tone of sarcasm, it also noted that national leaders like Muhammad Ali did not have much faith in such 'so-called' Pact, and yet this was being experimented with in the context of Bengal: 'The separation of the State from the particularistic, denominational religions in India must form the corner-stone of the composite Indian nationality and Indian Swaraj.'[171] The *Dainik Basumati* apprehended,

> A section among the Muslims would not shrink from demanding those excessive privileges which it has proposed to give them and, on the other hand, there is no doubt that the Hindus would refuse to give them those undue privileges. As a result, the two communities will come to conflict. The present action of the Swarajya Party is nothing more than the same divide and rule policy which the bureaucracy has pursued so long, only in another shape.[172]

Surprisingly enough, the divide did not strictly run along the inter-communal lines. A number of opposing voices within the Hindu community, who failed to see any injustice in the provisions of the Pact, were also heard. In journals like *Bande Mataram*, *Hindustani*, *Bengalee*, and, of course, *Forward*, the journal edited by Das's Swarajist colleagues, all published from Calcutta, the Pact was welcomed and considered as a brave move forward. The *Bengalee* commented: 'It is not a one-sided pact. The proposals have been framed on the principle of give and

take, and with a view to strengthening the solidarity of the nation.'[173]
Forward presented a persuasive argument to counter another common
charge against the Pact:

> We venture to say that the Pact gives to the Muhammedans nothing more
> than what they are entitled to get in fairness and justice. It is surprising
> that the argument of efficiency should be introduced against the claims of
> the Muhammedans. Is not that argument constantly invoked against our
> national claims by the bureaucracy? Is it not a fact that the European Civil
> Service is sometimes more efficient, if efficiency is only considered?[174]

The most powerful defence of the Pact obviously came from Das himself. He kept on asking his adversaries what they thought about a fair
adjustment of job opportunities and electoral representation: 'You are
believers in democracy and adult franchise.... What's the harm in arriving at a reasonable position where an adjustment can be made with the
Muslims in terms of the seats in legislature and percentage of jobs, more
or less in keeping with the ratio of the population?'[175] But he would also
remind everyone that it was more than a question of fairness, that it had
become a question of correcting historical wrongs, to move forward with
a brave spirit of generosity for the interest of the province: 'If the Hindus
do not behave magnanimously, they can never earn the confidence of
the Muslims.... Without Hindu–Muslim unity, our demand of Swaraj
shall ever remain a slogan, and never be transformed into reality.'[176]

Sharp replies to the critique of the Pact came from the Bengali
Muslims. After the iniquitous terms of the Lucknow Pact denying the
Bengal Muslims their fair share on the basis of their numerical strength
in the province, the Bengal Pact could only be seen as a 'historic justice', 'undoing the wrongs'.[177] At the Provincial Conference in Sirajganj
(Pabna) in June 1924, the East Bengal Muslims, under the leadership of
Maulana Akram Khan, recorded a strong support for Das. It was evident
in only a couple of months after the Pact was declared that words from
Das were enough to trigger a magical effect on the Bengali Muslims, and
compensate for the bitter Hindu reactions directed against the Pact. The
primary ideological challenge before nationalism was the question of
Muslim difference. Das's Pact took a stance that since the fact of difference could not be removed by an immediate change of heart, any 'new'
beginning to this direction must be effected by certain compromises and
adjustments at the political level, with the twin principles of sharing
of resources and redistribution of offices. As against Bengal Congress,

Das and his Swaraj Party clearly scored some extra points from 'other' communities by setting the tone of this new beginning.

The Bengal Pact could be held as a successful administrative experiment in spite of its eventual failure. Success may also be measured in terms of the promises and hopes generated. This bold experiment of Das betrayed a promising vision of the nation, inclusive by its intention and ambition, but at the same time eager to embrace its own internal differences. Das's nationalism was, no doubt, of an essentially limited character by its sheer lack in any transcendental or revolutionary objective of erasing social or cultural differences altogether. However, it signified an atypically defined liberalism, open to acknowledge the multiplicity of identities, and accordingly, to accommodate, not to write off, these identities within an overarching political structure. In this sense, he was more of a realist than an idealist in the world of Bengali nationalism. How much his realism paid off in his own times is a different question. But the trust he could generate among the Bengali Muslims, hitherto considered a marginal and unimportant part of the nation, delivered a potential ground for any 'combinational' unity for the nation. A Bengali Muslim activist-cum-author, later a campaigner of the 'Pakistan' movement, remembered after four decades while writing his memoir in the late 1960s the tremendous impact Das created by this single administrative proposal. 'The country is partitioned today. Much water has flown down the Padma. Yet that passionate call by Deshabandhu [Das] to come forward and make compromises for the sake of Bengal's unity still rings in my heart, and surely in the hearts of many Bengali Muslims of my generation.'[178] A similar articulation of 'trust' in Das was to be found in the writings of S. Wajid Ali, a more self-consciously liberal writer of colonial Bengal. By illuminating the supremely urgent task of putting Bengal's political and cultural interests first, he regretted the great 'misfortune' the province suffered due to his untimely death.[179] After Das's death in June 1925, his signature Pact was discarded rather hastily and his province had to wait for almost two more decades for another administrative effort of bringing various communities of Bengal together on the political platform of nation. By that time, however, more water would have flown down the rivers of Bengal; the structure of 'trust' would be hugely damaged.

The Limits of Swaraj

It was no simple coincidence that when Das's ingenious attempts at a pluralistic political arrangement created a stir in Bengal, an author named Nalinikanta Gupta voiced his grave concerns about the endangered 'nation', that is, the Bengali Hindu community. Gupta's anxious observations were published in a pamphlet called *Bharate Hindu o Mussalman* in 1925.[180] According to him, Bengali Hindus in particular and Indian Hindus in general were on the verge of becoming extinct. He would obviously use the word jati, which could by this time mean anything from 'race' to 'community', or 'nation'. The Hindus were seen to approach their final decimation as 'evidently the Bengali Hindus are decreasing in numbers as days pass'.[181] Although such claims were attempted on a statistical level, the dearth of supporting statistics had only to be compensated by a denigration of the political leadership, considered to be miserably oblivious to the Hindu jati in times of need. While such concerns had started to surface in the swadeshi days, the third decade of the century saw a great spurt in Hindu anxiety.

What might have contributed to such a sudden increase of anxiety among the Hindus? The conservative sectarian discourse would suggest that the reasons were three-fold: one, the Muslims overtaking the Hindus in Bengal resulting in the latter's marginalization; two, massive numbers of low-caste people being converted to Islam; and three, the alluring external opportunities of widow remarriage and polygamy. All three pointed to the more fundamental fact of the new visibility of Bengal Muslims in social, political, and cultural realms. The conservative Hindus found these new competitors unacceptable, if not due to their sheer number, then due to their assertive presence. However, we should note that these concerns were not shared in the same way by staunch conservatives like Gupta and a wider group of social reformers who began to feel that any task of social regeneration must begin with community-based reforms.

This critical point of a shared concern among both conservatives and relatively open-minded social reformers must be emphasized while exploring this Hindu anxiety. A large number of reformists used to believe that the Hindu community must be reformed through greater social integration of the lower castes and only the removal of their oppressive binds could strengthen the larger community. Digindranarayan Bhattacharya, a social reformer, was far from a conservative spokesperson when he single-handedly spearheaded a crusade against untouchability in the 1920s. His highly acclaimed book *Jatibhed* (1912) called for the immediate annihilation of the *Manusamhita*, the most important Hindu text for social codification. However, at the same time, he cautioned the lower castes not to unite with the non-Hindus under any circumstances.[182] Prafulla Chandra Ray, the well-known scholar-cum-nationalist warned the nation of the impending danger for the high-caste Hindus in his numerous essays.[183] He expressed dismay at the fact of the Hindus losing out in terms of number vis-à-vis the Muslims of Bengal.[184] It is curious to note how almost every organization for caste reform launched by high-caste leaders consistently suffered from a latent 'Hindu' concern and 'Hindu' sensibilities in their social activism. Under the supervision of Shibnath Shastri, a Depressed Classes Mission was established in 1909, which in 1913 changed its name into Society for the Improvement of the Backward Classes, offering educational facilities to the low-caste groups. The Bengal Social Service League and Bengal Social Reform League founded in 1925 were essentially 'Hindu' organizations for social reforms.

The trajectory of Digindranarayan Bhattacharya tells us a significant story. Initially he was a Congress sympathizer, but eventually joined hands with the Hindu Mahasabha. This was not an isolated case, but many of these Hindu reformers underwent remarkable vacillation between liberal and conservative ideas. This, however, does not nullify the need for drawing a separating line between the conservative Hindu protagonists and their relatively liberal counterparts who nonetheless shared the former's anxieties and believed that any social reform should necessarily begin with the task of strengthening one's own community, that is, the community of immediate belonging.

Alongside these somewhat blurred but vital lines of distinction, the potential and aspirations of a pluralist 'nation' continued to waver. The liberal-minded social agenda often overlapped with the conservative propaganda and exposed itself to a narrow nationalist vision. This was an idiosyncratic feature of nationalist discourse which, nevertheless, cannot be summarily discredited as Hindu communalism. A study of such a dithering discourse makes us wonder if the highly equivocal term 'jati' had played any major role in blurring the lines between various communities, attributing legitimacy to the interchangeable marks of identity. It was perfectly acceptable to become a proud protagonist of one's own jati, be it Indian, Bengali, Bengali Hindu, or Bengali Hindu Brahmin, by keeping the term adequately undefined. One could combine all of these together, or foreground any of these depending on the urgency of the occasion or purpose. The lack of clarity and the element of interchangeability between the different meanings of jati surely came in handy for the nationalists, eternally troubled in their frantic search for a hierarchy of their own belongingness.

Not surprisingly, the Hindu Mahasabha, established in the mid-1910s and catering to the conservatives and reformers alike, saw a rapid growth during the next decade in Bengal. This organization, from the very beginning, displayed a dual purpose: one, to strengthen the community by mobilizing the lower castes; and two, to assert the existing social hierarchy by restricting its leadership to the Brahmins.[185] However, while the problem of 'difference' in the case of low castes was being addressed, the very similar problem of 'difference' vis-à-vis the Muslims never found any sympathetic response from this organization, or from the conservative Hindus in general. Due to the spirit of political and economic competition and a pervasive social apathy, the Mahasabha's attitude towards the Muslims was frankly oppositional.[186] The rise of the Muslim middle class during the early years of this period was directly related to the growing Hindu middle-class discontent. The Muslims were the 'other' factor of the society, in view of which they needed to reform and reassert themselves. The Mahasabha's reform agenda designated a space for the low castes, however lesser and subservient that might have been, but was frontally opposed to the Muslims. Rumours like 'the abduction of Hindu women by the Muslims leading to a sharp fall in Hindu population' and 'the need for redressal' found bold headlines in the same journals, which also routinely lamented about 'the unfortunate fact of caste difference within our own society'.[187] When Viceroy Montagu was reported to make the statement that the Mohammedans of India were largely the descendants of Hindus, the news was greeted by these journals with great alacrity, with a perverse pleasure of sabotaging the Islamic pride: 'They must remember that special franchise which has been granted to them cannot make them a separate nation.'[188] This collective anxiety would soon develop into a social movement, bringing to Bengal from northern India the socially conservative Hindu reform movements of shuddhi and *sangathan* (organization and/or mobilization within the Hindu community).

If the reformist impulses forced a considerable part of the conservative Hindu society to address the caste question as a self-strengthening measure, for the liberal Hindus also, making headway into this caste conundrum was exceedingly difficult. Any internal erasure of varnashrama proving to be too challenging a task, the social status quo was accepted first, and political strategies were chalked out only thereafter. The already politicized low-caste society raised voices against such brazen attempts at political appropriation. A bold statement was published in a pamphlet published from Calcutta: 'Just as the body becomes dead when the heart is taken out, the nation (*jati*) is also no more than a lifeless entity if the depressed castes (*jati*) are not taken care of [italics original].'[189]

> If somebody wants to improve and unite the country for 'national' inter-
> est, he must change this four-fold division of Hindu society which had
> made this society an inhuman association in the history of the mankind.
> All the depressed castes are the main force of the whole nation, the basis
> on which it is erected.[190]

How the low-caste expectation was belied by the liberal nationalists, shying away from any radical reforms, is apparent from the example of Chittaranjan Das. In a bid to involve the low-caste groups in the movement of the 1920s, he extended a hand to ask for their support and sent a personal note to Guruchand, the great Namasudra leader of Gopalgunj. Guruchand rejected Das's request[191] and never warmed up to the idea of mobilizing the low-caste groups only to provide support to an agenda set exclusively by the upper-caste Hindus. Thus Das, the great nationalist visionary, who could generate significant amount of trust among Bengali Muslims, could never alter the structure of trust for low-caste societies. Hence, while the caste question was never left unaddressed by the liberal as well as the conservative nationalists, they could never go beyond their own terms of appropriation.

As the caste question and the Muslim question remained as vexed as ever for the Hindu nationalists, the lower castes and the Muslims were increasingly alienated from the mainstream Congress nationalism. The new politics of representation and self-assertion could not but hasten this alienation. Just as the conservative, urban middle-class bhadralok whipped up an unfounded anxiety in the name of 'a dying race' in the middle of the 1920s and the Muslim professionals began to feel the crushing need for mobilizing the larger Muslim society in a political climate of competitive representation, a similar momentum was gained by the low castes also. Caste associations emerged in great numbers, who rightly observed, in the prevailing political climate, that there was a unique opportunity to extract a firm political ground if a 'social basis' of their 'political society' could be properly established. The new era gave them hope for raising their own voice and raising their own representa-tion—entirely new possibilities for the socially backward and downtrod-den people.[192] This explains why, unlike the agitationist politics of the Muslims, the lower-caste demands for political rights and social and economic improvement were still voiced in a mendicant style.[193] Caste politics of the 1920s was almost a replay of the Muslim politics of the 1910s—the same political parameters at work, only with an obvious time lag. Caste associations like the Mahishya Samiti, the Kshatriya Samiti, the Purbabanga Vaisya Samiti, and the Kolkata Subarnabanik Samaj urged its members to join the government and took up the responsibility of organizing 'national' self-strengthening movements. The efforts at building bridges between the lower castes and the Muslims can also be explained by the same logic of new politics. Their numerical strength proving to be the best bargaining ground, their proximity often grew, and the possibilities of any rapprochement seemed lucrative. At a huge Muslim gathering in a village in Jessore, a Namasudra youth recited a poem where the Muslims and the low-caste Hindus were declared as 'natural brothers' as against their 'natural opponents', the Aryas (the Aryans) or the high-caste Hindus.[194] In the urgent need for erecting a common front of the marginal groups, it was necessary to project the Muslims as 'Aryans', the term which by itself implied an elevated social prestige and a resultant political legitimacy. The new politics of representation thus engendered a new breed of nationalism among the Bengali Hindus, Bengali Muslims, and the low-caste societies alike. This nationalism was more inward, root-searching, mutually differentiating, and hence more 'illiberal' in its essence. In the next chapter, we will deal with the new competitive politics of representation and its impact on society.

Crossing the Most Promising Moment

In conclusion, what makes the myriad cultural and political formulations of this period most significant were the new idioms and promises of the 'different' claims ushered in by the new politics of representation. Although the resultant focus on 'share' and 'difference' never erased the space for a common imaginative ground of 'nation' altogether, it changed the outlook and orientation of the politics of nation, slowly but irreversibly. The eventual failure of the political and cultural promises of this period must be examined in this particular context where a colonial society was becoming charged with its recently acquired weapons of political self-representation. The period ranging from the mid-1910s to the mid-1920s thus showcased a dual force—the height of creative imagination around the nation and its difference on the one hand, and the inexorable political forces of colonial modernity on the other.

Towards the end of this period, there was an increased surfacing of communal and caste tensions. The liberal protagonists of the nation would now be facing an altogether new challenge of constitutionalized legitimacy of difference. In a sense, hopes for an 'inclusive' nation began to recede. Bengal just crossed a critical historical juncture. However, in another sense, this new reorientation of the socio-cultural identities did not foreclose the prospect of unity. As the later years would prove, this alternative unity would be of an essentially different kind, distinct from the model of unity once envisaged by swadeshi nationalists. By the mid-1930s, to espouse a project of national unity without a due acknowledgement of the religious or caste identities, therefore, turned out to be unworkable.

But if this different notion of unity was given its legitimate due in the narrative of nation, the familiar historiographical stereotype of nationalism as an essentially intolerant body of ideology comes to face a major challenge.[195] This chapter has shown that both in the cultural and political lives of the province, there were ingenious attempts of carving out a different nationalist belonging, more heterogeneous in nature, willing to unite the diverse self-asserting components of the nation, albeit with their own limits. The premier regional leader of this era was able to locate the role of the 'people' at the heart of his own version of swaraj, respect rather than denounce their parallel belongingness of different kinds, and declare that swaraj must have a 'settlement not only between the Government and the people as a whole, but also between different communities'.[196] The potentials of the swaraj of the early 1920s might not be revolutionary, but were surely generous and forward-looking. Despite its ultimate non-realization, the significance of this concept of swaraj should be appreciated in terms of the new, ambitious, and sincere pledges it had entailed. The 'nation' in Bengal had seen the era of its greatest promises and most imaginative politics.

Notes

1. There is a historiographical trend to view the gradual emergence of nationalism mainly as a response to the colonial administrative policies. As the 'Cambridge School' of historians believe, 'Government impulse had linked the local and the provincial arenas of politics and the general trend among Indian politicians ... was to react to this initiative by copying it. In so doing, they altered the working of Indian politics.' See John Gallagher, 'Congress in Decline: Bengal 1930–39', in *Locality,*

Province and Nation: Essays on Indian Politics, 1870–1940, edited by John Gallagher, Gordon Johnson, and Anil Seal (Cambridge: Cambridge University Press, 1973), p. 270. They argue that the claims for 'representation' and 'share' raised by the Muslims as a parallel to the claims of representation by the Congress leaders were mostly born out of a political opportunism, and were devoid of much ideological content. The Cambridge view has been later modified or challenged by subsequent historians. Rajat K. Ray, for instance, has pointed out, 'Expectation of advantage will explain the manoeuvres of a considerable number of politicians, but not the sacrifices of large bodies of ordinary men and women. In the complex politics of the subcontinent, pursuit of power by politicians and search for identity by people acted as interlocking forces and it is inadequate analysis which ignores either.' See his *Social Conflict and Political Unrest in Bengal, 1875–1927* (Oxford: Oxford University Press, 1984), p. 2. There is, however, enough scope to argue that the reality of Hindu nationalist claims and the parallel Muslim or low-caste claims was all integrally linked with an intense search for identity, an urgent and necessary prerequisite for any 'national' awareness. Even the 'pursuit of power by politicians' must be understood in the context of the larger society which had produced them, a society teeming with the fervour of nationalism. The 'politicians' and the 'people' must be seen together in the light of a continuing ideological journey of a colonized public, deeply torn by cultural and social differences among themselves. Claims of the 'nation', however, could not but be followed and endangered by the concomitant claims of 'share' within that nation. Swadeshi nationalism was not all about passion and frenzy in the name of a homeland. It also imparted a deeply troubling quest for identity, later reflected in the demands of a political expression of such identities.

2. Harun-or-Rashid, *The Foreshadowing of Bangladesh: Bengal Muslim League and Muslim Politics 1936–47* (Dhaka: Asiatic Society of Bangladesh, 1987), p. 12. It was held that any fixed affiliation with the AIML might be 'detrimental to their interests'. The same confusion was noticed by the *Bengalee*, 5 March 1912.

3. This letter from Aziz Mirza to Sheriff on 15 January 1912 was mentioned by Harun-or-Rashid in *The Foreshadowing of Bangladesh: Bengal Muslim League and Muslim Politics 1936–47* (Dhaka: Asiatic Society of Bangladesh, 1987), p. 11.

4. The reaction was evident from the letters of Aziz Mirza, the central League secretary, where he affirmed that the 'All-India Muslim League claims to represent the whole Muslim population, and if the important presidency of Bengal does not accommodate it, its (that is, the League's) position will be undermined and it will never be able to speak on behalf of the Muslims of India.' See Rashid, *The Foreshadowing of Bangladesh*, p. 11.

5. Salimullah gave the League a second life by this step. He helped the Muslim League become the sole representative organization of a fuzzy and uncertain community of 'Indian Mussalmans'. See Rashid, *The Foreshadowing of Bangladesh*, p. 11.

6. Fazlul Huq was born in a highly respected Qazi family of Bakhargunj in the district of Barisal in East Bengal. His father was a government pleader at the district court. Huq, a brilliant student throughout, started his career as a lecturer at Rajendra College, Faridpur. Later on, he became a pleader at the Calcutta High Court, and then a deputy magistrate and collector. In 1912 he resumed legal practice.

7. *Bengalee*, 6 November 1913. Huq's bold assertions were mentioned in the Minute of *Shams-ul-Huda*, September 1913, in Government of Bengal, Political Confidential File no. 66 of 1913, accessed at the West Bengal State Archives (henceforth WBSA).

8. Leonard A. Gordon, 'Divided Bengal: Problems of Nationalism and Identity in the 1947 Partition', *Journal of Commonwealth and Comparative Politics* 16, no. 2 (1978): 136–68, 140.

9. The process of a slow but continuing emergence of a middle class among Bengali Muslims is also mentioned by L.A. Gordon, 'Divided Bengal: Problems of Nationalism and Identity in the 1947 Partition', *Journal of Commonwealth and Comparative Politics*, p. 141; R.K. Ray, *Social Conflict and Political Unrest in Bengal*, p. 218.

10. Two of the prominent leaders of this era, Fazlul Huq and Abul Kasim, came from the provincial towns of Barisal and Burdwan respectively.

11. Ray explains that the younger Muslim leaders were different from their earlier generation in the sense that 'their political influence derived more from professional competence than from British patronage', and hence they could afford to be critical of the official policies. R.K. Ray, *Social Conflict and Political Unrest in Bengal*, p. 218. Huq declared, 'Our quarrel is not with the Hindus but with the officials', in *Bengalee*, 26 April 1913.

12. *Muslim Hitaishi*, 29 December 1916, RNP, no. 1 of 1917.

13. *Mohammadi*, 26 January 1912.

14. *Muslim Hitaishi*, 29 December 1916, RNP, no. 1 of 1917.

15. Bengal Legislative Council Proceedings (henceforth BLCP), vol. 14 (April 1913).

16. Huq was termed as a leader of 'a new kind' by John Broomfield, 'The Forgotten Majority: The Bengal Muslims and September 1918', in *Soundings in Modern South Asian History*, edited by D.A. Low (London: Weidenfield and Nicolson, 1968), p. 203. Rajat K. Ray also compares Huq and Kasim with the old oligarchic Muslim leaders of Calcutta and comments that '[the former] fully appreciated the value of mass agitation and mofussil support'. See R.K. Ray, *Social Conflict and Political Unrest*, p. 218.

17. BLCP, vol. 46, January 1914, p. 146.

18. BLCP, vol. 46, January 1914, p. 147.

19. An insightful article on madrassa education is Mamtajuddin Ahmed, 'Problem of Education', *Shikha* 1, no. 1 (1927). Reflections of Muslim public opinion on madrassa during this time may also be found in some other articles, for instance, 'Educational Problems of the Muslims', *Saogat* 6, no. 8 (1929) and 'Muslims in Education', *Saogat* 6, no. 12 (1929). See Mustafa Nurul Islam, *Samayik Patre Jiban o Janamat: 1901–1930* (Dhaka: Bangla Academy, 1977).

20. BLCP, vol. 30, no.1, p. 548.

21. BLCP, vol. 49, p. 755, September 1917.

22. BLCP, vol. 45, p. 580, April 1913.

23. BLCP, vol. 45, p. 349, March 1913.

24. BLCP, vol. 49, p. 876, November 1917.

25. BLCP, vol. 14, no. 4, p. 57, March 1924.

26. The introduction of the Calcutta Municipal Bill (1917) put an end to plural voting and introduced the election of Muslim representatives through separate electorates. It could not but attract bitter criticism from the Hindu-dominated organizations like the Indian Association, the Bengal National Chamber of Commerce, and the Bengal Provincial Congress Committee. As a result, the bill was withdrawn in 1919. The warm welcome to the bill already offered by associations like the Central National Muhammedan Association or the Bengal Provincial Muslim League was quickly transformed into strongly worded rancour. The subsequent Calcutta Municipal Bill (1921) was crafted by S.N. Banerjea, a nonbeliever in separate electorates, who recommended that thirteen seats out of fifty-five elected members be reserved for Muslims. This aroused strong reactions from the Muslim legislators. See Keshab Chaudhuri, *Calcutta: Story of Its Government* (Calcutta: Orient Longman, 1973), pp. 217–18.

27. *Mohammadi*, 1 June 1917, RNP, no. 23 of 1917.

28. *Mohammadi*, 1 June 1917.

29. *Mohammadi*, 1 June 1917.

30. *Mohammadi*, 1 June 1917.

31. According to this system, the provinces were entrusted with minor departments (education, health, and agriculture) and little funds, while the vital departments (law and order or finance) were designated to the centre. The electorate was considerably enlarged to 5.5 million for the provincial legislative councils and 1.5 million for the Imperial Legislature. The system of communal representation and reservation was maintained as before, even little expanded, which, surprisingly, was not the primary reason for the endless attacks it elicited. All the leading journals of the day vigorously attacked the Act because of its design to retain effective governing power for the imperial body. 'One can easily detect in this

scheme the same old Morleyan policy of reconciling the Moderates....
We want constitutional reforms, but of a character which would help
us to get full self-governing right.' *Dainik Bharat Mitra*, 12 July 1918.
Dainik Basumati asserted, on 7 July 1918: '... The British have taught
us there can be no real freedom without democracy. That is why we
want the full rights of Citizenship.' Other journals like *Bangali*, *Amrita
Bazar Patrika*, or the local ones like *Khulna*, *Jashohar*, or *Bangaratna*
(Krishnanagar), expressed equally indignant reactions to 'the denial of
any substantial rights conferred on the people.' RNP, no. 30, July 1918.
None of these reports dealt with the issue of communal representation in
this context. *The Mussalman*, *Moslem Hitaishi*, and *Islam Pracharak* made
similar observations.

32. R.K. Ray, *Social Conflict and Political Unrest in Bengal*, p. 222.
33. Broomfield, 'The Forgotten Majority'. Although the Cambridge histori-
    ans overemphasize the role of competing interests as the primary guiding
    force of the Indian national movement, this distinctive view point appears
    useful in one respect: in explaining the making of the climactic points of
    riots or violent clashes, either on inter-communal or on inter-caste lines.
    Petty politics of power and interest played an extremely important role in
    destabilizing the everyday social negotiations of 'difference'.
34. Press statement of the Working Committee of the Bengal Provincial
    Muslim League, IOR/L/PJ/8/655, IOR.
35. R.K. Ray, *Social Conflict and Political Unrest in Bengal*, p. 223.
36. Ayesha Jalal points out that there are some less known, and less celebra-
    tory, aspects in Maulana Abul Kalam Azad. A major theologian of Islamic
    law and ethic, Azad was the most prominent Muslim leader of the Indian
    National Congress in pre-independence India. He is best remembered in
    retrospectively constructed statist narratives as a 'secular nationalist'. Yet,
    during the decade of the First World War, he was one of the major theo-
    rists of a trans-national 'jihad'. See Ayesha Jalal, 'Striking a Just Balance:
    Maulana Azad as a Theorist of Trans-National Jihad', *Modern Intellectual
    History* 4, no. 1 (April 2007): 95–107.
37. Salimullah, the Nawab of Dacca and a staunch loyalist, exercised a great
    deal of control in order to keep the Muslims inert during this period.
    R.K. Ray, *Social Conflict and Political Unrest in Bengal*, p. 223. The
    Muslim Hitaishi opposed the 'extreme proposals', in the apprehension
    that such non-cooperation would, in fact, provoke the British to con-
    tinue the wrongs being done to Turkey and the Muslim world. *Muslim
    Hitaishi*, 30 April 1920, RNP, no. 17 of 1921.
38. Mustafa Nurul Islam, 'Munshi Jamiruddin', *Journal of Bangla Academy*
    14, no. 4 (December 1968–April 1969): 1–21.
39. *Mohammadi*, 2 January 1920, RNP, no. 1 of 1921.
40. *Mohammadi*, 11 June 1920, RNP, no. 20 of 1921.

41. *Mohammadi*, 11 June 1920.
42. *The Mussalman*, 20 August 1920, RNP, no. 34 of 1920.
43. Madani, *Naqsh-i-Hayat*, vol. 2 (Deoband, 1954), p. 257, cited in Ziya-ul-Hasan Faruqi, *Deoband School and the Demand for Pakistan* (London: Ring House, 1963), p. 66.
44. *Bangali*, Calcutta, September 16, RNP, no. 39 of 1920.
45. *Viswamitra*, Calcutta, July 6, RNP, no. 28 of 1920.
46. Satyendranath Majumdar, *Gandhi O Chittaranjan*, Ashahojog Granthabali, vol. 4 (Calcutta: Saraswati Library, 1921).
47. 'Hindu–Mussalman Samasya', *Prachi* 1, no. 2 (July 1924).
48. Abu Bakr Siddiqi, *Khilafat Andolana Padhati* (Barisal, 1921), p. 5, VT, IOL.
49. *Bhai re, chalo Khilafat uddhare/Ingraj eshe shab niyechhe/baki ar je roilo na re!/... Eka mora jabo na bhai/Hindu bhaira jaben sangete/Dwesh-hingsha bhule aye bhai sakale/Jati-dharma shab jete boshechhe!* 'Khilafat Sangeet,' by a village bard, compiled by Mainuddin Hossain, *Khilafat Prasanga* (Calcutta: Saraswati Library, 1921), p. 23.
50. Government of Bengal, Political Confidential D.O. no. 3043, Sl. no. 1, dated 9 March 1920, WBSA.
51. *Mohammadi*, 15 April 1921, RNP, no. 17 of 1921.
52. Upendranath Dutta, *Desher Ahwan ba Ashahayog Andolane Narir Sthan o Kartabya* (Barisal, 1921), p. 3, VT, IOL.
53. See Sufia Ahmed, *Muslim Community in Bengal, 1884–1912* (Dhaka: Oxford University Press, 1974), Anisuzzaman, 'Introduction', *Muslim Banglar Samayik Patra, 1831–1930* (Dhaka: Bangla Academy, 1969).
54. For example, Aswinikumar Dutta of Barisal, the renowned swadeshi leader, was respected by all Hindus, Muslims, and lower-castes alike in the peaceful villages of his own district in the early years of the twentieth century, as described by Saratkumar Ray, *Mahatma Aswinikumar* (Calcutta, 1926), p. 98.
55. Mustafa Nurul Islam, *Samayik Patre Jiban o Janamat*, pp. 226–8; Humaira Momen, *Muslim Politics in Bengal* (Dhaka: 1972), p. 120.
56. Muzaffar Ahmad, *Amar Jiban o Bharater Communist Party* (Calcutta: National Book Agency, 1977), p. 19.
57. Buddhadev Basu, *An Acre of Green Grass* (1948; new edition, Calcutta: Papyrus, 1982), pp. 36–7.
58. Muzaffar Ahmad observed,

So many people wanted to hear [Nazrul's] singing. If he had time, he would not refuse a single soul. He visited many Hindu and Muslim student hostels or clerical quarters and sang for them. Gradually he even started to get invitations from Hindu families who organized musical evenings for him.... They were extremely hospitable to him while he sang for them. That is why I say that not only his popularity increased during this time, he was also serving as an important agent to break down the walls of social separation.

See Ahmad, *Amar Jiban o Bharater Communist Party*, p. 27. It may also be mentioned that Nazrul was an ardent 'preacher' of Rabindra-sangeet, that is, the songs composed by Tagore. His friends reminisced in private conversations about how Nazrul used to consult notation books to learn Tagore songs. See Arun Kumar Basu, *Nazrul Jibani* (Calcutta: Pashchimbanga Bangla Academy, 2000), p. 39. Many of the characters depicted by Nazrul in his novels are found to sing Tagore songs. Muhammad Shahidullah once informed Tagore that, on his way to Santiniketan, he had been accompanied by Nazrul singing the songs of *Gitanjali* one after another throughout their journey (A.K. Basu, *Nazrul Jibani*, p. 40). It can be speculated that Tagore songs by this time were more or less familiar among literate Muslim middle classes. Gradually, Tagore and his songs would even become a site of 'national' contestation between the hardcore conservative Muslims of Bengal who rejected Tagore and the large sections of Bengali Muslims who drew their own regional–cultural identity from his writings and songs. This latter section of Bengali Muslim intelligentsia as well as the average, literate Muslim would later play a critical role in the Language movement (Bhasha Andolan) of East Pakistan in 1952, and subsequently in the Freedom Movement of Bangladesh (Mukti Juddha) in 1971. Today, many of the ablest and finest singers of this musical tradition are arguably from Bangladesh where they virtually dominate their national cultural world.

59. Ahmad, *Amar Jiban o Bharater Communist Party*, p. 23.
60. Mohitlal Mazumdar, in his 'Letter to the Editor', *Moslem Bharat*, September 1921 (Aswin 1327 BS), p. 21.
61. Sudhakanta Raychaudhuri spoke of Nazrul's appreciation in the cultural circles of Santiniketan. See A.K. Basu, *Nazrul Jibani*, p. 36.
62. Tagore made extensive comments on the use of Islamic words in Bengali in general and on Nazrul Islam in particular during the next decade, in the 1930s, which will be discussed in the next chapter. However, in the 1920s Nazrul or his literary style and use of language could not elicit any direct comment from Tagore, who is hailed as the Gurudeva (saint) of the Bengali literary world.
63. Nalinikanta Gupta, *Bharate Hindu o Mussalman* (Calcutta, 1925), p. 12.
64. N. Gupta, *Bharate Hindu o Mussalman*, p. 14.
65. From the very beginning, the Parishat maintained an indifference towards the Bengali Muslims. L. Leotard, one of the original founders of the Parishat, presented its main 'objectives' before the Parishat Committee in 1893, which included an assessment of 'Hindu literature as portraying society and ethics among the Bengalis, past and present'. However 'absent-minded' this comment had been, it was reflected in the Parishat's activities throughout the first half of the twentieth century. While able biographers were regularly commissioned by the Parishat to write the life stories of a host of Bengali littérateurs, only a single Muslim author, Mir

Mosharraf Hossain, figured as the subject of such biographical explorations. Later, in the post-Independence days, only two more names were added in this 'biography' series: Muhammad Shahidullah and Nazrul Islam. Dilipkumar Biswas, 'Bangiya Sahitya Parishat: Uttar Swadhinata Parbo' (Parishat in the Post-Independence Days), *Sahitya Parishat Patrika*, centenary volume, Kolkata: Bangiya Sahitya Parishat, 2007.

66. 'Maulavi Sadasyer Niyamabali', Ekabingsha Barshik Karya-bibaran (Minutes of the 21st session), in *Sahitya Parishat Panjika*, vol. 2 (Calcutta: Bangiya Sahitya Parishat, 1915–16 [1322 BS]), p. 6. Laments over the shortage of the Muslim members of the Parishat were followed by a desperate plea for a greater Muslim involvement in its activities.

67. Gautam Bhadra and Dipa Dey, 'Chintar Chalchitra: Bangiya Sahitya Parishat, 1300–1330 B.S.', in *Bangiya Sahitya Parishat Patrika*, edited by Satyajit Chaudhuri, centenary number (Calcutta: Bangiya Sahitya Parishat, 1997), p. 51.

68. Syed Emdad Ali, 'Matribhasha o Bangiya Mussalman', *Nabanur* 1, no. 9 (1903): 348.

69. Kazi Imdadul Huq, *Abdullah* (first published in periodicals in 1919, published as a book in 1933; reprint, Dhaka: Afsar Brothers, 2006); Abdul Wadud, *Mir Paribar* (a story first published in 1918, compiled in later in his collected orks, *Wadud Rachanabali* [Dhaka: Bangla Academy, 1993]); Ekramuddin Ahmad, *Natun Ma* (first published in *Saogat*, April 1927).

70. [Hindu girl] *Bharatiya Puja-jajne—mahendra lagane/ Samagata netribrindo-gane.../ Tahader tare Bhagni ki enechho saji?/* [Muslim girl] *Golap-modito bash ei pushpohar/ ...Hok na bideshi pushpo korio na hela/ Bichitra e phulohar mor,/ Nana jati nana gandha sushomar mela,/ Bendhechhe sabare jeno ek sneho-dor./* [Hindu girl] *Moder malancha bhagni etoi ki deen?/ Suprotul nahe she ki hai?/ Kori bidesher pushpo-abharan rin/ Sajaite habe bhasha-matrikar kai?/* [Muslim girl] *Tumi je kusum diye 'bideshi' akhyan/ Phele rakho upekshar bhare/ She ki janmobhumi payah kare nai pan?/ Pale ni e janmobhumi bokshe tare dhore?/...* [Hindu girl] *Ghuche gelo aji mor bhranto e dharona/ Tute gelo samsay-andhar*

'Karya birani', in Jadunath Sarkar, *Presidential Address, Uttarbanga Sahitya Sammilan*, session 4, Maldaha, 1911 (Calcutta: India Press, 1912), pp. 19–22.

71. J. Sarkar, *Presidential Address, Uttarbanga Sahitya Sammilan*, 1911, p. 14.

72. J. Sarkar, *Presidential Address*, p. 11.

73. Dineshchandra Sen, Ramtanu Lahiri Fellowship Speech (1915–17), published as the Introduction in *Mymensingh Gitika* (Calcutta: Calcutta University Publications, 1923), pp. 1–31.

74. He chalked out three priority research areas by this time. The first on his priority list was a differently modelled Bengali dictionary, following the *Oxford English Dictionary* model; second, a dialect dictionary (*bibhasha-grantha*), and, third, a comprehensive history of Bengal. See Mohammad

Shahidullah, 'Bangla Sahitya O Chhatra-Samaj,' *Bangiya Mussalman Sahitya Patrika* 3, no. 3 (1920): 168.

75. The projects of history-writing and collecting local traditions by Bangiya Sahitya Parishat were critical for a 'national' imagination to develop. See Bhadra and Dey, 'Chintar Chalchitra', pp. 39–64.

76. Rabindranath Tagore, 'Gramya Sahitya', *Loka-Sahitya*, in *Rabindra Rachanabali*, vol. 3 (Calcutta: Visva-Bharati, Sulabh Sangskaran, 1986), p. 794.

77. Nagendranath Basu, 'Bangla Itihasher Upadan', mentioned in Bhadra and Dey, 'Chintar Chalchitra', p. 62.

78. Sashibhushan Basu, 'Bangala Nationality', speech read in Rajshahi Sahitya Sammilan and published in *Prabasi* 10, part 2, no. 2 (January 1911 [Agrahayan 1317 BS]), pp. 119–27; no. 3 (February 1911 [Poush 1317 BS]), pp. 326–36; no. 4 (March 1911 [Magh 1317 BS]), pp. 415–20.

79. S. Basu, 'Bangala Nationality'.

80. Rabindranath Tagore, 'Bhashar Katha', *Bangla Sabda-tattwa* (Calcutta: Visva-Bharati, 1984), pp. 9–10.

81. Tagore, 'Bhashar Katha', p. 9.

82. The revolt of the new trendsetters against the old literary vanguards was not an unknown thing in Bengal. The 'diluted Sanskrit' of Vidyasagar was once vigorously condemned, or the more conversational prose of Tekchand Thakur was discredited in the previous century. In a similar fashion, Tagore's literary style also began to be strongly disowned by the next generation of authors in the 1920s.

83. Nareshchandra Sengupta, 'Bhashar Akar o Bikar', *Sammilan* 6, nos 5–6 (1916): 167.

84. N. Sengupta, 'Bhashar Akar o Bikar', 167–8.

85. Jatindramohan Singh, 'Abar Bhashar Katha', *Sammilan* 6, no. 7 (1916): 195.

86. Satishchandra Vidyabhushan, Presidential Speech, Bangiya Sahitya Sammilan, Session IX (Jessore, 1917), published in *Sammilan* 7, no. 9 (1917): 31.

87. The first collection of the correspondence and public statements exchanged between Tagore and Gandhi was published in R.K. Prabhu and Ravindra Kelekar (eds), *Truth Called Them Differently: Tagore–Gandhi Controversy* (Ahmedabad: Navajivan Publishing House, 1961). Tagore had several reservations against Gandhi's satyagraha, the most important of which was his discomfort with its easy instrumentalist application towards nationalism and the potential of using it as a political stratagem, only to enhance the existing impatience and inertia of the political society as a whole. The doubts raised by Tagore in *Modern Review* were responded to by Gandhi in *Young India*, the journal he himself edited. Tagore's criticisms did not

seem to trouble Gandhi too much as he thought that those must be considered in view of Tagore's 'poetic license'. The Tagore–Gandhi debates are also reviewed in Sabyasachi Bhattacharya, *Rabindranath Tagore: An Interpretation* (New Delhi: Penguin Books India, 2011), pp. 135–9. Also see Sabyasachi Bhattacharya (ed.), 'Introduction', in *The Mahatma and the Poet: Letters and Debates between Gandhi and Tagore, 1915–1941* (New Delhi: National Book Trust, 1997).

88. According to Rajat K. Ray, the Tagore–Gandhi closeness lay in the fact that both of them were eager to distance themselves from politics and to chalk out a programme of social regeneration against that politics. See Rajat K. Ray, Presidential Address, Indian History Congress, Calicut, 2007, later published as *Nationalism, Modernity and Civil Society: The Subalternist Critique and After* (School of Historical Studies, Visva-Bharati), pp. 23–4. This view, however, does not take into account that Tagore would eventually see Gandhi's vision of swaraj degenerating into the narrow binds of the 'political', by some direct or indirect imposition of tactical position and organizational discipline on the people at large. Ashis Nandy has on the other hand argued that Tagore, by employing the 'high' classical traditions of Indian civilizations, and Gandhi, through the notions of 'little' traditions of folk culture, had essentially arrived at a common position: the position to build a anti-statist critique of 'nationalism' and to replace 'nationalism' with an alternative form of 'patriotism'. Ashis Nandy, *The Illegitimacy of Nationalism: Rabindranath Tagore and the Politics of Self* (Delhi: Oxford University Press, 1994).

89. Partha Chatterjee, 'Tagore's Non-Nation', in *Lineages of Political Society* (Delhi: Permanent Black, 2011), p. 114.

90. Historians and Tagore scholars alike point out that Tagore disapproved of the use of violence perpetrated on the people opposing swadeshi, and link it directly to his decision of 'removing himself' from the movement. Some even assert a clear 'break' in Tagore's political phase and the post-swadeshi non-political phase. See Nepal Majumdar, *Bharate Jatiyata o Antarjatikatabad*, vol. 1 (Calcutta: Dey's Publishing House, 1983), p. 312. Similar suggestions are to be found in Sumit Sarkar, *Swadeshi Movement in Bengal, 1903–8* (New Delhi: Permanent Black, 2010), p. 52; P. Chatterjee, 'Tagore's Non-Nation', pp. 105–6. I would like to argue that Tagore maintained a low and different political profile during these intervening years and did not exactly 'resurface' after a decade of self-exile from the political arena. Although he had turned away from his earlier involvement with swadeshi-style preachings and activities, he was noticeably consistent and relentless in his critique against the creed of 'nation' as propounded by his contemporary leaders. It is eminently possible to trace the thread of his criticism from the very early essay 'Swadeshi Samaj' (1904), through his brilliantly polemical article 'Byadhi

o Pratikar' (1907), the novel *Gora* (1907–10), articles like 'Kalantar' and 'Palli-Prakriti' (1910–24), and the unabashedly political novel *Gharey–Bairey* (1916–17) as well as his self-professedly 'alternative' political projects of village reconstruction in the second and third decades of the century.

91. Tagore's name did not disappear altogether from the formal political circles after swadeshi, which showed that neither Tagore himself nor the Tagorean critique of nationalism was seen to be disconnected with the political society of Bengal. In the mid-1910s, the fighting clans of the Congress turned to him as a mutually respected figure, equally distant from the Moderates led by Surendranath Banerjea and the radicals like Bepinchandra Pal and Motilal Ghose. In 1917, Tagore's name was proposed as for chairman of the Reception Committee for the Calcutta Congress by the more radical leaders like Motilal Ghose and C.R. Das as opposed to the Banerjea group, who nominated Baikuntha Nath Sen. Tagore also was not averse to the proposition, which did not materialize for various reasons. Nepal Majumdar, *Bharate Jatiyata o Antarjatikatabad*, vol. 1, p. 312.

92. A deep disappointment in Tagore was palpable by 1908: 'We need to achieve the nation at first through our duties to the nation. Even in selecting our representatives, the people of the nation must be allowed to have their say,' (Presidential Speech at Pabna, *Samuha*, in *Rabindra Rachanabali*, vol. 5, p. 698). His tone became scathing in 1914 when he lampooned at the oversight of nationalist leaders: 'Very recently, we have had a lesson on this. During the swadeshi days, in our sudden burst of emotion, we started calling the Muslims as 'brothers', as our very near ones, with a rather loud voice. They somehow did not respond well to those ardent calls of love and we were indeed enraged at their obstinacy!... If we have not been able to accept [the Muslim folk] as our own in daily life, sudden gestures of intimacy in political life motivated by certain cautious calculations of our immediate interests are doomed to fail,' ('Loka-Hita', *Kalantar*, in *Rabindra Rachanabali*, vol. 12, p. 549). It was precisely during this phase that he insisted on a programme of village reconstruction which would serve twin purposes of bridging the gap between communities and raising the living standards of the poor.

93. Tagore's connections with the vicinities of his zamindari in Silaidaha in eastern Bengal, and then in Sriniketan near Visva-Bharati gave him the scope of experimenting with the principles put forward in the essays like Swadeshi Samaj (1904) and 'Bharatbarshiya Samaj' (1901) written before the onset of Swadeshi movement, or the later articles and speeches like 'Loka-Hita' (1914), 'Chhoto o Baro' (1917), 'Samaj' and 'Samadhan' (1923) in *Kalantar, Rabindra Rachanabali*, vol. 12, pp. 537–611, and then the speeches at Bengal Provincial Conference in Pabna (1908),

'Karma-Yajna' (1915) and 'Pallir Unnati' (1915) at the meetings of Hitasadhan-Mandali, 'Bhumi-Lakshmi' (1918), later compiled in *Palli-Prakriti* (Calcutta: Visva-Bharati, 1962), pp. 1–40. See also *Rabindra Rachanabali*, vol. 14.

94. Rabindranath Tagore, speech delivered at the inaugural ceremony of Sriniketan Manufacturers' Store (Shilpo Bhandar), *Palli-Prakriti*, p. 89.

95. Rabindranath Tagore, 'Samasya', *Kalantar*, in *Rabindra Rachanabali*, vol. 12, p. 601.

96. Rabindranath Tagore, 'Bhumi-Lakshmi', *Palli-Prakriti*, p. 38.

97. Swaraj in the Gandhian sense was vastly different from swaraj that the Extremists spoke of. According to Gandhi, Swaraj represented a moral principle: 'It is Swaraj when we rule ourselves.' See M.K. Gandhi, *Hind Swaraj and Other Writings*, edited by Anthony J. Parel (Cambridge: Cambridge University Press, 1997), p. 73. In this sense, swaraj is achieved by the abolition of state and power would naturally revert to the community from the clutches of the state.

98. Tagore's moral critique of the modern state could not be matched by a political process suitable for the requirements of creative freedom of the individual, Partha Chatterjee argues in his 'Tagore's Non-Nation', pp. 122–3. It is, however, possible to view Tagore's obsessive preoccupation with samaj (usually translated as society or community) as opposed to rashtra (state) in a different way, as a suggestion of reorientation of power through decentralization and localization, which would not be in contradiction with the essential purposes of the state, or of modernity. In all probability, Tagore's samaj was more of a small locality, where voluntary participation of the inhabitants, irrespective of any social divisions, would generate different kinds of power to counterbalance, or possibly replace, the homogenized power of an overarching state.

99. At the centre of Tagore's ideas about the village would be the principles of liberal democracy by which the communities would join with each other on the basis of fair and just procedures of representation. See Asok Sen, *Rajnitir Pathakrame Rabindranth* (Calcutta: Visva-Bharati, 2014), pp. 130–2.

100. Rabindranath Tagore, 'Palli-Prakriti', in *Palli-Prakriti*, p. 48. In stark contrast to Gandhi, Tagore was positively enthusiastic about the spread of modern education, science, medicine, and technology in the villages and urging the educated youth who otherwise were 'inherently dismissive and indifferent towards the uneducated downtrodden masses' to take up these tasks. A combination of modern education and ancient knowledge should provide the basis of any 'national enterprise', according to Tagore. He even advocated for the building of a modern-style science laboratory with the help of Tata, the nationalist-minded capitalist. See 'Prasanga Katha 5', *Samuha*, in *Rabindra Rachanabali*, vol. 5, p. 747.

101. Tagore, 'Pallir Unnati', *Palli Prakriti*, p. 30.

102. Tagore, 'Swadeshi Samaj', *Atmashakti*, in *Rabindra Rachanabali*, vol. 2, p. 634.

103. 'Much to do yet, much too formidable a task. I warned them many a times—they never listened to me because I am a poet—I asked them to consider the ways social energy could be generated from within the society itself through collective efforts. I have tried on my own, have established village associations [*palli-samiti*], but could not think of what more to do ...' The candour as well as the deep pain borne in this statement is remarkable. Rabindranath Tagore, 'Malaria', *Palli-Prakriti*, p. 137.

104. Tagore's ideas on local reconstruction as the real core of the nation-state certainly bore similarities with the rural developmental programme envisaged by C.R. Das, the premier nationalist leader of this time. It is in this context that I question Partha Chatterjee's conclusion that 'Tagore's idea of a modern community that could be an alternative to the nation-state found no political support either in his own lifetime or later'. See P. Chatterjee, 'Tagore's Non-Nation', p. 122. Das's image of a 'modern community' suggested fundamental changes in the structure and functioning of the nation-state and provided it with an alternative form.

105. Of course, initially Tagore was overwhelmed by Gandhi. His first reaction was: 'Mahatma Gandhi came and stood at the cottage door of the destitute millions, clad as one of themselves, and talking to them in their own language. Here was the Truth at last, not as a mere quotation out of a book.' Rabindranath Tagore, 'The Call of Truth', *Modern Review*, October 1921, p. 428.

106. Tagore's discomfort with Gandhian doctrine can be summarized in two main points. First, the instrumentalist approach of satyagraha and the cult of the charkha appeared too imposing, therefore repugnant to him. The poet's heart revolted not only against the closed-minded creed of 'spin and weave, spin and weave', but also to the mindless application of satyagraha, already reduced to a political mantra, devoid of much conviction or dedication. Second, Gandhi's call for non-cooperation with the entire colonial socio-political system, and by implication, with the corresponding knowledge and value system of Western modernity, appeared to him as an unnecessary closure of the self before the world, and therefore an inverted violence on the inner psychological level. In the Gandhian agenda, he could not locate the liberty of the mind he so valued in any civilizational form, and instead found an ideological straitjacket refusing any space for the freedom of expressions. Tagore detected an inherent dogmatic inflexibility, almost bordering on coercion, in Gandhi's strictly charted mass movements or in his rigidly idealized models of village. Tagore, 'The Call of Truth'.

107. Rabindranath Tagore, 'Nation ki?' *Atma-shakti*, in *Rabindra Rachanabali*, vol. 2, p. 619.

108. Rabindranath Tagore, *Nationalism* (London: Macmillan, 1950), p. 21. This book was first published in 1917 as a compilation of the above-mentioned essays.

109. 'India has never had a real sense of nationalism and it is my conviction that my countrymen will truly gain their India by fighting against the education which teaches them that a country is greater than the ideals of humanity.' Tagore, *Nationalism,* p. 125.

110. Chittaranjan Das, Presidential Speech at the Bengal Provincial Conference, published in *Narayana,* June 1917.

111. Chittaranjan Das, Congress Presidential Address, *Deshbandhu Rachanasamagra,* edited by Manindra Datta and Haradhan Datta (Calcutta: Tuli Kalam, 1977), vol. 2, p. 437.

112. C.R. Das, Congress Presidential Address, p. 568.

113. C.R. Das, Congress Presidential Address, p. 570.

114. C.R. Das, Congress Presidential Address, p. 569.

115. Chittaranjan Das, Speech delivered at Bengal Provincial Conference at Faridpur (1925), in *Deshbandhu Rachanasamagra,* p. 168.

116. This is where Das, an able leader of the colonial world, would draw upon the modernity of the colonized, and thus, could not but be 'deeply ambiguous' towards modernity itself. Thus, in Das we identify the same colonial 'ambiguity' that Partha Chatterjee has underlined as the characteristic feature of 'Our Modernity': '… the uncertainty is because we know that to fashion the forms of our own modernity, we need to have the courage at times to reject the modernities established by others. In the age of nationalism, there were many such efforts which reflected both courage and inventiveness.' Partha Chatterjee, 'Our Modernity', in *The Present History of West Bengal: Essays in Political Criticism* (Oxford: Oxford University Press, 1997), p. 210.

117. Rajat K. Ray has underlined the difference between Gandhi and Das in their respective advocacy of village reconstruction programmes as a vital part of nationalist movement. Das saw it more as a part of a broader agenda of cultural regeneration, quite dissimilar to Gandhi's rural moralism. R.K. Ray, *Social Conflict and Political Unrest in Bengal,* p. 247.

118. For the widely varying approaches of swadeshi nationalists towards Western civilization, see Kris Manjapra, 'Knowledgeable Internationalism and the Swadeshi Movement, 1903–21', *Economic and Political Review* XLVII, no. 42 (20 October 2012).

119. Bepinchandra Pal, Presidential Address, in *Bengal Provincial Conference Session, Barisal–1921: Presidential Address* (Calcutta: Suresh Chandra Deb, 1921), p. 44. How Pal almost habitually engaged himself in criticizing Tagore can be found in Baridbaran Ghosh (ed.), *Rabindranath o Bepinchandra Pal* (Calcutta: Puthi Patra, 2010).

120. 'In a country full of the most diverse religious opinions ... spirituality is much wider than any particular religion.... [By this] we shall understand man's seeking for the eternal, the divine, the greater self, the source of unity, and his attempt to arrive at some equation.... This alters necessarily our whole normal view of things; even in preserving the aims of human life, even in politics, it will give them a different sense and direction.' Aurobindo Ghose, *The Renaissance in India* (Chandenagore: Rameshwara and Co., 1927).

121. Bepinchandra Pal, Presidential Address, *Bengal Provincial Conference Session, Barisal–1921*.

122. Bepinchandra Pal, *Swaraj: What Is It?* (Calcutta: Vadhwani and Co., 1922), p. 9.

123. Pal's 'national state' would be distinctly different from the modern 'nation-state'. Although Pal would not engage himself with any elaborate clarification of what he actually meant by a 'national state', its character- ization as essentially 'federal' and 'decentralized' by Pal immediately sets it apart from the modern nation-states which self-consciously thrive on a cultural homogenization and political centralization.

124. Bepinchandra Pal, *Nationality and Empire: A Running Study of Some Current Indian Problems* (Calcutta: Thacker, Spink and Co., 1917), pp. 37–40.

125. An alternative ontological vision was thus proposed with great persua- sion by this nationalist stalwart: '*Narayana*, or humanity is the whole, the different nations of the world are parts of that whole. *Narayana* or humanity is the body, the different tribalities, racialities and nationalities are limbs of that body. The whole is implied in the parts: the organism in the organs.' See Pal, *Nationality and Empire*, p. 37.

126. Pal, *Nationality and Empire*, p. 40.

127. Bepinchandra Pal, Presidential Address, *Bengal Provincial Conference Session, Barisal–1921*, p. 44.

128. *Amrita Bazar Patrika*, 29 March 1921.

129. From Pal's writings during the following decade, before his death in 1932, it was clear that while Pal's critique of non-cooperation in 1921 and his subsequent pronunciations remained at best an insightful refuta- tion of the Gandhian movement of the 1920s, it contained within itself kernels of an alternative politics as well. But effectively speaking, his new thoughts were never translated into a political agenda because of his self- chosen remoteness.

130. Bepinchandra Pal, Presidential Address, *Bengal Provincial Conference Session, Barisal–1921*, p. 44.

131. Bepinchandra Pal, Presidential Address, *Bengal Provincial Conference Session, Barisal–1921*, p. 81.

132. Pal, 'The Non-cooperation', in *Nationality and Empire*, pp. 52–3.

133. C.R. Das, 'Banglar Katha', in *Deshbandhu Rachana-samagra*, pp. 74–7.

134. Anonymous, *Calcutta Samachar*, 25 April 1917, RNP, no. 18 of 1917, May.

135. Das, 'The Nationalist Ideal', speech at Dacca, 1917, in *Deshbandhu Rachanasamagra*, p.19.

136. Das, 'The Nationalist Ideal', p. 19. Tagore also saw the chance of bridging of the contentious communities through a regional/local identity.

> ... it is only through economic life of the society that we can hope for some union of different groups and communities [*goshthi* and *sampraday*], it is only here where our interests meet, and not only that, where we desperately need other's co-operation.... So, the only way to create a platform for Hindu–Muslim unity is to call them to participate in the economic projects [*arthanoitik anushthan*] in the villages, which would cater to both Hindu and Muslim interests beyond any doubt.

> Tagore's interview with Mrinal Kanti Basu, editor of *Bijali*, August 1923, pp. 5–7.

137. Das, 'The Nationalist Ideal', p. 23.

138. Das, 'Was India Ever One Whole?' Speech at a meeting held at Barisal, 14 October 1917, *Deshbandhu Rachanasamagra*, p. 37.

139. Upendranath Maiti, *Proceedings of Presidential Speech at Bengal Provincial Conference* (booklet published from Calcutta, 1920), p. 12.

140. Satyendranath Majumdar, *Gandhi o Chittaranjan, Asahayog Granthabali*, Pustika IV (Calcutta: Saraswati Library, 1921), pp. 23–5. The author seeks the historical reason why the swadeshi movement was a thoroughly 'Hindu' endeavour in the end, and the non-cooperation–Khilafat movement in Bengal was not. He would, however, credit Das greatly for providing a platform where Hindus and Muslims could freely unite, leaving their differences behind.

141. Majumdar, *Gandhi o Chittaranjan*, p. 26.

142. Kshitishchandra Bandyopadhyay, *Hak Katha* (Calcutta, 1921), p. 29, VT, IOL.

143. R.K. Ray, *Social Conflict and Political Unrest in Bengal*, pp. 300–3.

144. Historians have often portrayed Das as an ambitious and unscrupulous politician, mainly a manipulator–strategist of a high order, even 'the most brilliant opportunist in Indian politics'. See Gallagher, *Locality, Province and Nation*, p. 275; John H. Broomfield, *Elite Conflict in a Plural Society: Twentieth Century Bengal* (Berkeley: University of California Press, 1969), p. 259). In explaining the Gandhi–Das breach during the non-cooperation movement, Ray would refer to Das as a master strategist as against the less 'political' objectives of Gandhi. To do so, he would even juxtapose the 'intentions of Das' against the 'vision of Gandhi'. R.K. Ray, *Social Conflict and Political Unrest in Bengal*, p. 310. Das has been reduced in this analysis to a mere political opportunist whose only aim

was 'bringing the British to a constitutional compromise'. I challenge this view by suggesting that Das had a deeper nationalist view where the 'intention' of gaining control over the administration was to be adequately complemented by a 'vision' of applying the structures of constitutional politics to every level of society in order to create a 'national' existence. If we take into account Das's extensive deliberations on the intricacies of national/regional socio-political life, it becomes enormously difficult to denude Das's political position of its ideological component and dismiss his ideal of 'nation' beneath or beyond all his political strategization.

145. The revolutionaries were uncompromising fighters and as such had little love for the programme of being a part of the Council and creating a constitutional deadlock there. Das therefore, would arrive at a tacit agreement with them: the Swarajist leadership would give benevolent patronage and a legal platform to the revolutionaries, as also fight for the release of all revolutionary political prisoners. The revolutionaries, on the other hand, would enter the Congress, run the Congress machinery at the primary and district levels, and popularize the Swarajist programme, but they would be free at the same time to carry on their illegal, revolutionary activities. Home Political Files, no. 103/3, 18 December 1922, NAI.

146. Subhas Chandra Bose, *Fundamental Questions of Indian Nationalism* (Calcutta: Netaji Research Bureau, 1970), p. 54. The influence of Das on Bose in the matters of nationalism and representation will be addressed in Chapter 3.

147. Motilal Ghose, one of the front-ranking politicians among the 'Extremists' in Bengal, had been addressing this problem even before Das. In fact, in the Provincial Conference of 1917, Ghose also put special emphasis on the need for a village rehabilitation programme for advancing the cause of the 'nation'. The speeches of Ghose and Das were mentioned together in this context in *Bengalee*, 22 April 1917. Rajat K. Ray therefore points out that Das's address could not be considered as 'unique'. However, if not 'unique', Das's speech was definitely exceptional, marking a new beginning, as he would not leave the issue only at that and keep on hammering it henceforth in almost all his major speeches and writings. See R.K. Ray, *Social Conflict and Political Unrest in Bengal*, p. 211.

148. Das, *Bangalar Katha* pp. 16–20.

149. Das, 'The National Ideal', pp. 20–1.

150. Das, 'Outline Scheme of Swaraj', *Deshbandhu Rachanasamagra*, p. 170.

151. The scheme advocated administrative divisions like local centres (*grams*) or town centres (*nagars*), district centres (*zillas*), provinces (*soobas*) and all-India (Bharatavarsha or Hindustan) organizations. The three-tier administrative system would require all villages in a district to be grouped into a number of unions, and all adult males of a village to form an assembly and elect a panchayat body and then report to a district

assembly for overall supervision. The panchayats would deal with the day-to-day local affairs like sanitation, water supply, night schools, petty disputes, local schools, vocational and technical education, appointment of a troop of watchmen and local militia, arbitration courts for civil and criminal cases, establishment of hospital and medical facilities, supervision of pasture lands, village commons, playgrounds, groves, orchards, and also the establishment of co-operative organizations like banks and stores, and cooperative running of tanks, wells, canals, and so on. See Appendix in Das, 'Outline Scheme of Swaraj' p. 180.

152. Nibaranchandra Dasgupta, a successful advocate of Barisal during the 1910s, observed in his memoir:

> While our politicians wanted to be worshipers of 'India' [*Bharat-sevak*] first, Aswini Kumar wanted to belong to his own locality [*palli*] first. He became known for his steadfast representation of his homeland of Barisal. At a Congress session he reminded others that if the nationalist leaders did not go out to the villages and localities far removed from the centres of institutional politics, Congress would soon really cease to be anything more than a three-day tamasha.

See Saratkumar Ray, *Mahatma Aswinikumar*, p. 112.

153. Aswinikumar's letter to Haji Chaudhuri Ismail Khan, Dutta's ardent follower and also, the first elected non-official secretary of the Barisal District Board, in Sureshchandra Gupta, *Mahatma Aswinikumar* (Barisal, 1928; reprint, Calcutta: Barisal Seba Samiti, 1984), p. 325.

154. *Rayat-Bandhu* (Brahmanbaria, Dacca), September 1924 (Aswin 1331 BS), pp. 1–5.

155. Tagore, *Palli-Prakriti* (1915), in *Rabindra Rachanabali*, vol. 14, p. 380.

156. Tagore, *Palli-Prakriti*, p. 356.

157. Tagore, 'Bhumi-Lakshmi' (1918), in *Palli-Prakriti*, p. 360.

158. Leonard Knight Elmhirst (1893–1974) was a British specialist on agriculture who stayed in Santiniketan during 1921–4 and was hand-picked by Tagore to serve as Director of the School of Agriculture at Sriniketan.

159. Tagore, *Samabay 1* (1918), and *Samabay 2* (1922), in *Rabindra Rachanabali*, pp. 313–32.

160. Abdur Razzak, *Mymensingher Rajnoitik Andolon o Aitihya* (Mymensingh, 1987), p. 56.

161. *Mohammadi*, July 1926, p. 76.

162. A remarkably high number of Bengali Muslims was peasants. In fact, according to Bose, religion was an important factor which 'bound the peasantry together.' Sugata Bose, *Agrarian Bengal* (Cambridge: Cambridge University Press, 1986), p. 184. According to the Census Report of 1911, out of the total Muslim population of 24 million in Bengal, 83.3 per cent depended on cultivation. On the other hand, among the landlords, only a handful were Muslims. The reason behind such skewed social distribution was that in the post-Permanent Settlement years, Muslim *ashrafs*

(upper-class, 'noble-born', and, in most cases, the immigrant sections of the community), unlike the wealthy Hindus, had depended on political and military employment rather than trade, and consequently experienced a reduction in their access to jobs, liquid cash, and hence in the landed estates in the times of growing commercialization of land during the Company era. Among the urban sections, in 1911, only 0.4 per cent Muslims were educated, and of them, 0.25 per cent knew English. In the professional jobs, the Hindu–Muslim ratio was the following: civil servants 3.5:1, teachers 7:2, lawyers 9:1, doctors 5:1 (*Census of India,* 1911, vol. 5, part 1, pp. 58–60, 315, 350).

163. BLCP, vol. 9, p. 21, September 1919.

164. 'We must take into consideration the interests of the peasantry of Bengal and not of a few paddy dealers.' BLCP, vol. 10, p. 43, November 1921.

165. BLCP, vol. 12, pp. 72–3, September 1923.

166. R.K. Ray, *Social Conflict and Political Unrest in Bengal,* p. 323.

167. R.K. Ray, *Social Conflict and Political Unrest in Bengal,* p. 321.

168. Das, Speech at the All-India Swarajya Party Conference held in Calcutta, August 1924, *Deshabandhu-Rachanasamagra,* p. 287.

169. *Viswamitra,* 23 December 1923, RNP, no.1 of 1924, January.

170. *Amrita Bazar Patrika,* 23 December 1923, RNP, no.1 of 1924, January.

171. *Amrita Bazar Patrika,* 30 December 1923, RNP, no. 2 of 1924, January.

172. *Dainik Basumati,* 24 December 1923, RNP, no. 1 of 1924, January.

173. *Bengalee,* 25 December 1923, RNP, no. 1 of 1924, January.

174. *Forward,* 23 December 1923, RNP, no. 1 of 1924, January.

175. This particular comment of Das was remembered by Gopal Halder, in the latter's interview with Gautam Chattopadhyay; see Chattopadhyay, *Bengal Legislature in India's Struggle for Freedom 1876–1947* (Delhi: People's Publishing House, 1984), p. 75.

176. Das, Speech at Sirajganj, 1924, *Deshbandhu Rachanasamgra,* p. 296.

177. Letter by Abdul Matin Chaudhuri, *The Mussalman,* 11 January 1924, p. 6.

178. Abul Mansur Ahmed, *Amar Dekha Rajnitir Panchash Bachhor* (Dhaka: Maola Brothers, 1970), p. 55. Das's acceptance among the Bengali Muslim public was noted with grave concern by the government. On receiving news of his death, the secretary of state for India wrote to the governor of Bengal: 'I shall be interested to hear from you whether you expect any individual to succeed in seizing the unique pposition which C.R. Das held...'. See Letter from Lord Birkenhead to Lord Lytton, 18 June 1925, Mss. Eur. D 703/2, IOR.

179. In 1945, reflecting on the need for a regional nationalism through Hindu–Muslim unity in Bengal, he wrote: 'The late Mr. C. R. Das realized this obvious truth and tried to solve the problems of the country in this light. But after his death the people of this province have moved a long way away from his ideas and ideals.' S. Wajid Ali, 'Bengal's Misfortune', in *Bengalees of Tomorrow* (Calcutta: Das Gupta and Co., 1945), p. 83.

180. Nalinikanta Gupta, *Bharate Hindu o Mussalman* (Calcutta, 1925), p. 18.

181. As Nalinikanta Gupta observed,

> Some would say that it does not matter if the number of Hindus goes down. They are still leading in every sphere of life—in education, in wealth, or in terms of sheer intellect. *Ekashchandratamohanti na cha taraganairapi* [Sanskrit, meaning the moon alone removes all darkness, while so many of stars together cannot do so]. But we should remember that time for such self-confidence is gone: Muslims are making rapid advances in all fields—economically, socially, politically. Moreover, survival does not always depend on intellectual abilities. (See Gupta, *Bharate Hindu O Mussalman*, p. 30.)

182. Bhattacharya offered this warning in 1926 at a meeting in Mymensingh, which was attended by at least 200 Namasudras. See Sekhar Bandyopadhyay, *Caste, Protest and Identity in Colonial India: The Namasudras of Bengal, 1872–1947* (second edition, Oxford: Oxford University Press, 2011), p. 137.

183. Prafulla Chandra Ray, 'Jatibhed Samasya,' *Prabasi*, June 1920.

185. Matilal Ray, *Hindu Jagaran* (Calcutta: Calcutta Burrabazar Hindu Sabha, 1935), p. 6

186. M. Ray, *Hindu Jagaran*, p. 7.

187. *Prabasi*, December 1923, p. 429.

188. *Prabasi*, March 1923, p. 729.

189. By a clever juxtaposition of the same term with two different connotations, it was asserted how these two identities were deeply connected, the one relying on the other in a crucial way. 'National' advancement of a larger society would never succeed without a radical agenda to elevate the downtrodden 'nations' (that is, the smaller communities), so went the threat. See Madanmohan Bhowmik, *Jat-er Nam-e Bajjati* (Calcutta, 1924), p. 12. A curious interchangeability of the terms 'jat' and 'jati' has been a very common feature in the low-caste discourse of this time. But although often described as jati (nation), the assertions in the name of jat (caste or the ancestral group) do not leave much doubt about its contextual signification. In this context of juxtaposition of the two related but different terms jat and jati, one may be reminded of a famous line of one of Nazrul's poems ('Kandari Hnusiyar', 1926): '*Aji poriksha, jatir athaba jat-er koribe tran…*' (Now is your test—will you save your own caste or your own nation?) Bhowmik's above tract was also named after another famous phrase of Nazrul, *jat-er nam-e bajjati* (the perilous incitement to social dissension in the name of caste politics).

190. Bhowmik, *Jat-er Nam-e Bajjati*, p. 12.

191. Mahananda Haldar, *Guruchand Charit* (Calcutta, 1943), pp. 414–15. The refusal letter was also a piece of advice to the most important leader of Bengal. '*Amantran-patra dile manyo dite hoi/Kintu bartaman-khetre ami ati nirupai./… Satya katha Deshbandhu! Kori nibedan/ Ei pathe swadhinata ashe na kakhono./Samajer ange achhe jato durbolota/ Age taha dur kara*

abashyak katha./ ... Dalito-pirito jato pichhe pore achhe,/ Shuddho budhhi niye jan tahader kachhe.' (One should honour an invitation, yes, /But in this case, I'm utterly hopeless!/ Deshbandhu, allow me to state a plain fact -/It's not the way that our Swaraj would act./ The foremost thing you need to do/Eradicate the ills which the society grew./ ... Have a proper sense to reach those in haste/Who're the most backward and the most oppressed.)

192. Bandyopadhyay explains that these groups, with a new reading of historical events, created a different ontological vision essentially opposed to that of high-caste Hindu nationalists. Instead of the typical national myth of a golden past and dark present, they cherished the image of a golden present. See S. Bandyopadhyay, *Caste, Protest and Identity*, p. 111.
193. S. Bandyopadhyay, *Caste, Protest and Identity*, p. 139.
194. Raicharan Biswas, Introduction to *Jatiya Jagaran* (Calcutta: Kuntaleen Press, 1921), p. 17. The poem, as originally written by Raicharan Biswas, goes as follows:

Jatibhed kshudra swartho jar mone nayi/sparsho-dosh jar kachhe nahi pai thnai/'Paka' jati, 'paka' dharma, 'paka' karma jar,/Ekatai sarbo-shreshto sahoshe apar, Aryajati gananai/ Shreshto sankhya tulonai/Itihashe bhugole ujjwal proman/ Jagate Badshahi jati dhanyo Mussalman./ ... Banger bhandari mor bhai Mussalman,/ Namasudra bhai tar daler kishan./ Dui bhai tulyo bale/ Dui bhai ek dale/ Namasudra bale tai buk kori tan,/Jagate Badshahi jati dhanyo Mussalman./ ... Loye bhai namasudra hoye aguyan/ Elahi bharosha kori jago Mussalman!

(From casteism, from narrowness—those who are free,/Those who don't care for untouchability,/Whose religion, whose race, whose actions are from/Are best in their broad-minded union./ If Aryans you count/They are best in amount/History or geography will prove that no less,/ Blessed are the Muslims—the world's royal race!/ ... The treasurer of Bengal is my Brother Muslim,/Sudras are peasants, they make a nice team./In strength they are same,/Two brothers—both of them -/So Sudras can proclaim with a straightforwardness,/Blessed are the Muslims—the world's royal race./ ... Come forward and take the Sudras with you/Rise up all Muslims with your faith in Allahu.)

195. Nationalism in India has almost always been equated with its particular brand espoused by the Indian National Congress, and very often this equation is immediately followed by the charge of its championing of Hindu majoritarianism. Starting from the Cambridge School of historians, neo-Cambridge historians, to the subaltern historians, all share this view on nationalism. See Gordon Johnson, C.A. Bayly, and John F. Richards (general eds), *New Cambridge History of India* (Cambridge: Cambridge University Press, 1987); John A. Gallagher, *The Decline, Revival and Fall of the British Empire* (Cambridge: Cambridge University Press, 1982). The most noteworthy contribution in this respect has been Joya Chatterji, *Bengal Divided: Hindu Communalism and Partition, 1932–1947* (Cambridge: Cambridge University Press, 1994). Also Bidyut Chakrabarty, *The Partition of Bengal and Assam, 1932–1947* (London:

Routledge, 2004). The historians of Bengal Muslim politics also have corroborated this from the other end. See Neilesh Bose, *Recasting the Region: Language, Culture and Islam in Colonial Bengal* (New Delhi: Oxford University Press, 2014). My study finds this assumption problematic and questions its characterization as wholly and overtly Hindu. One must distinguish between the nationalist thought at large and its Congress version in particular, and focus on the various ways of dealing with the ideological and political implications of difference. Especially in case of Bengal, the imaginations of the nation and political experiments with the nation were only too variegated to be lumped together as a 'Hindu' discourse. I would like to rescue nationalism from this simplistic and monolithic characterization and argue that the discourse of nationalism in Bengal indeed displayed a remarkable insight and alacrity to handle 'difference', and even a process of 'otherization' did not immediately imply that combining with the 'others' was impossible. I would also assert that these variegated experiences of the nation must be remembered, as they contained within themselves remarkable possibilities of pluralist existence against the backdrop of identity politics. Recently 'the implicit assumption made too often about the monolithic 'Muslim mind' has been questioned. See Sabyasachi Bhattacharya, *Defining Moments in Bengal, 1920–1947* (Delhi: Oxford University Press, 2014), p. 111. I want to extend this argument even further, and question the monolithic depiction of the 'Hindu mind' as well.

196. These are C.R. Das's lines from his presidential speech (also his last public speech) at the session of the Bengal Provincial Conference, Faridpur, 2 May 1925:

> Till *Swaraj* comes, a sure and sufficient foundation of that should be laid at once. What is a sufficient foundations, and must necessarily be a matter of negotiation and settlement—*settlement not only between the Government and the people as a whole, but also between the different communities*.... Nationalism is merely a process in self-realization, self-development and self-fulfilment. It is not an end in itself.... And I beseech you, when you discuss the terms of settlement do not forget the larger claim of humanity in your pride of nationalism [emphasis added].

In this context, it is also worth noting that Subhas Chandra Bose, one of Das's closest disciples, later remembered him as the pioneer in interpreting swaraj as 'the uplift of the masses, and not necessarily of the upper classes'. This view, evoked at great length by the late nineteenth-century thinkers like Swami Vivekananda or the early twentieth-century ideologues like Rabindranath Tagore, however, had to wait till its first meaningful 'political' exposition in Bengal by Das. See Sisir Kumar Bose and Sugata Bose (eds), 'Deshbandhu Chittaranjan Das', in *The Essential Writings of Netaji Subhas Chandra Bose* (Delhi: Oxford University Press, 1997), p. 68. In the following chapter, we will see how Subhas Bose himself was deeply influenced by the views of his political mentor.

3 Politics of Enumeration and the Changing Nation
1926–36

The last chapter traced how Bengal experienced the height of creative imagination for the nation and its difference against the backdrop of the newly gained political tools of self-representation. We also explored the role of Chittaranjan Das as the architect of a 'new nationalism' of Bengal in the early 1920s. Das seemed to have grasped the essence of the unique moment of the nation, when the claims of 'difference' emerged from within its folds, and demanded a broadly defined and loosely interconnected 'national' framework. His 'new nation' was based on a principle of representation of various communities. In this sense, Das's nationalism was more cross-communitarian than supra-communitarian; its inclusiveness meant accommodation, not assimilation, of socio-religious differences. With his death on 16 June 1925, immediately followed by the abrogation of the proposed Hindu–Muslim Pact and the disintegration of the Swaraj Party, the enormous potential hidden in this 'new nationalism' began to fizzle out. The idea of allowing the communities their own representation on a national forum based on cooperation and mutual trust came to an abrupt end. Birendra Sasmal, one of Das's loyal followers and a defender of the Pact, was defeated in the election of the Bengal Provincial Congress in 1926, where the main political slogan happened to be 'Hinduism in danger'. Muslim representatives left the ranks of the Bengal Congress as well as the Swaraj Party. The strong ill feeling and murky factionalism generated by the Pact and its sudden collapse vitiated the political climate.

In spite of the efforts of Subhas Chandra Bose, another close follower of Das, to uphold and expand the 'Das politics', the late 1920s saw an upsurge of conservative politics of nation both against the Muslim claims of a different nationalism as well as against the demands of the low-caste communities. Condemnations of the idea of community representation during the Communal Award debate of the mid-1930s also contributed to this rapid change in political climate. Difference was no longer limited to cultural contestations or to the question of institutional representation. It now emerged as an effective weapon for extracting share in social or political power and resources, only to generate strongly adverse reactions in its course. 'Politics of representation', slowly but inescapably, was translated into a 'politics of enumeration', and began to unleash forces of political segregation in the name of community identity in a colonial society, only partly literate and unevenly modernized.[1]

However, due to the same forces of competitive and enumerative representation in provincial politics, the latter half of this period witnessed the slow emergence of a new politics oriented towards the common masses. The more difficult the solution of the conflict between nation and its hopelessly heterogeneous society appeared to be, the more pressing became the need for the 'politics of people'. This 'people'-oriented politics suffered from an intrinsic tendency to degenerate into a 'politics of numbers' and gradually proved itself incapable of rising above its basic urge of ensuring a committed number of followers. Projecting and employing an ideology became important only in view of this narrow political end. As a result, the old trends of ideology were readjusted into new forms, according to the new political needs of the time. Amidst many contending agendas of 'mass contact', there was one principal, vexing question: What kind of 'national' identity could be the most suitable ideological vehicle for this supremely urgent 'politics of people'—

region, religion, caste, or class? Or, could it still be a broader identity surpassing all these?

In this new context, the prospects of region–nation were not insignificant at all. Although 'Das nationalism' had been on the wane, and the religious–communitarian nationalism was evidently on the rise, regional sentiments were amply manifest in new trends of national imagining. The self-consciously 'Bengali' literary–cultural programme of the *Shikha–Saogat* group of the urban middle-class Muslims of Calcutta and Dacca, and the Buddhir Mukti (Emancipation of the Intellect) activists among the Muslims of eastern Bengal represented this new trend of 'national' culture, which implied a new strand of cultural politics as well. Although essentially urban, these cultural movements generated potent regional rhetoric and tied themselves with the emerging socio-economic radicalism of the *praja* (cultivators) politics of agrarian Bengal.

The gradual rise of praja politics must be seen as an important landmark of this period. Lack of any substantial commitment and involvement in Bengal's countryside on the part of the Congress during the Great Depression (1929) created a serious social and political vacuum, eventually filled up by radical socialist organizations like the Workers' and Peasants' Party of Bengal (1925–6) or Nikhil Banga Praja Samiti (1929), and, finally, by the Krishak Praja Party (1936). The last organization would soon fashion itself in a way to cater towards a diverse range of communitarian, class, and regional identities, which will be focused on in the next chapter. The present chapter traces the conflict-laden journey from the Das variant of 'new nationalism' of the early 1920s to a fresh project of praja politics of Bengal in the mid-1930s.

The Uncertain Legacy of Das's New Nationalism

It is commonly held that the ideological and political legacy of Chittaranjan Das was short-lived. However, one needs to be careful in claiming so. Although in some respects the Das trend of combinational nationalism was no more in practice after 1926, in some other sense, the ideal of the multi-layered, internally differentiated nation, based on cooperation and mutual trust, stayed alive and continued to face challenges during the next decade.

Such continuity was inevitable. Just as Das's ideological dilemma around unity and difference within the nation was not unique but a natural inheritance from the liberal nationalist thought of the Swadeshi period, the same notions of a federated nation would persist to haunt the liberally exposed nationalists even after his death. Bepinchandra Pal was one such link between the pre-Das and post-Das nationalist ideology, although we must bear in mind that in terms of practical political agenda, Pal had already become one of Das's principal adversaries.

As noted in the last chapter, during and after the non-cooperation movement, Pal formulated the idea of a Federation of India. In the latter half of the 1920s, he argued that despite the typically Western categorization of oriental societies as inherently monarchic or autocratic, hence far too resistant to any form of democracy, a substantially decentralized polity with huge internal diversities had been one of the prominent ancient Indian traditions.[2] It was only by the 'Modern Empire', Pal pointed out, that the idea of a centralized political entity following the political logic of *samrajya* (empire) was made popular in India. This new, modern, essentially colonial notion of a centralized polity began replacing the old visions of a 'Federation of many monarchies' and, by implication, the multiple power centres coexisting side by side.[3] Unlike the less heterogeneous European nationalities, the questions of democracy and federalism must be understood by Indian nationalists in this context.[4] Pal's notions of 'Federation' bore strong resonance with Das's ideas of 'provincial autonomy', and with the idea of parallel political structures suggested by Das only a few years earlier.

Pal, however, was already on the margins of the Bengali political community because of his decision of distancing himself from the Bengal Congress. Neither did he sympathize with the legislative activism of the Swaraj Party enthusiasts and their pro-agitation stance.[5] Yet his resistance to legislative activism was not akin to the Gandhian critique of the Swaraj Party. Pal by this time had developed into a deep disbeliever of the 'politics-only' approach of nationalism, and craved for a 'social' agenda in politics. However, on the margins, he was not without a loyal band of followers.[6] His critique of the prevalent modes of politics and his alternative ideas of a liberal but anti-Congress politics of nationalism often resonated through some contemporary journals like *Dhaka Prakash*, *Bangashree*, and *Bangabani*.[7] There we find the celebration of regional identity set in the broader context of Indian polity and culture, and arguments on a regionally diffused political structure. In a way, these articles explicated the intricate connection between the ideas of Das and Pal, two chief Bengali ideologues of the non-cooperation era. In the context of a future Indian federation, *pradeshikata* or provincialism was defended in the hope that every region should be given a chance to emerge with its own distinctive characteristics before combining with each other to form a larger Indian whole. The overtly defensive tone of such utterances, nevertheless, indicated the pressure exerted by the opposite view, that is, the dominant creed of a singular and unified nation.

One thing must be noted here. On the larger all-India plane, nationalists of younger generations during this time were increasingly leaning towards the left, getting embroiled in power conflicts within the Congress dominated by the Gandhian High Command, and also in a bitter fight for the goal of complete independence instead of pursuing the limited objective of dominion status. In the course of this struggle, no larger debate on the nature of the present or future nation seemed attractive. It seemed that as if for the time being any idea on the form and the nature of the nation was shelved for the sake of a more immediate political objective. Consequently, the deliberations on the 'federal nation of India' in the vernacular journals of Bengal were destined to remain only dispersed or isolated. Unfortunately, this bit of 'federalist' discourse did not find attention even in the later historical research.

The historiographical neglect is regrettable because the regional nationalism presenting itself hand in hand with an advocacy of federalism distinctly marked the early writings and speeches of another new leader of Bengal: Subhas Chandra Bose. A close follower of Das in the early 1920s, Bose repeatedly acknowledged his profound indebtedness to Das in the realms of political ideology. This intellectual and ideological debt is discussed in Bose's letters and diaries written from the Manadalay prison in 1926–8, shortly after Das's death. Bose considered it to be his own duty to give shape to his mentor's 'unfulfilled dreams'.[8] Das, he believed, was the first political leader of India who attributed to the much-cherished aim of swaraj a specific 'popular' character. By defining the basic objective of swaraj as 'the upliftment of the masses, and not necessarily the protection of the interest of the upper classes', Das, he thought, was the first leader to create 'many possibilities' within the politics of nationalism.[9] The emphasis on the 'masses' inevitably brought Das to questions of popular culture, diversities of cultural groups, and multiplicities of communities. The new nationalism had thus been, for the first time, bound to set off a new political and cultural agenda for Indian nationalism with a realistic goal of bridging the gap between different peoples or communities of the nation, the starting point of which was a frank and fair acceptance of difference.

Bose also suggested a strange connection between Das's religious orientation and his political vision. Das's religious beliefs in general or, specifically, his belief in idolatry, devoid of any dogmatism, made it easier for him to grapple with the reality of difference— Bose would think. It was neither strange nor random that 'Islam found the greatest friend' in this devoutly Hindu Vaishnavite leader.[10] In Bose's view, the acknowledgement of the value of religious difference barred Das from giving 'countenance [to] any struggle or conflict between classes and communities', and to sympathize with any doctrine of social dialectics.[11] On the contrary, 'differences could be resolved by concluding pacts between different religious communities, so that all Indians, irrespective of race, caste, and creed, would come forward to join the fight for swaraj.'[12] The pragmatist in Das argued that if the human society itself could be based on pacts and contracts as well as compromises, why would such a negotiated pact not succeed as the ground for political existence? Bose would, therefore, read Das in the following way:

> Whether it be in family life, in friendly circles, in community life, or in the political field, men could not possibly live as social beings unless they came together in a spirit of compromise though possessing different tastes and views. All over the world, trade and commerce are carried on through pacts and contracts. The question of love and affection does not come in there.[13]

However, not wholly comfortable with the excessively pragmatic or functionalist principle of Das's politics, Bose wished to read the latter in a more nuanced way. To the younger leader, deeply idealist and optimistic in nature, 'pacts' seemed useful but only as a mere 'patch-up work'.[14] The starry-eyed radical found it hard to digest that the negotiations among difference would have to depend primarily on contractual agreements instead of 'deeper remedy' of 'love and affection'.[15] He therefore hastily looked for complementary means for enhancing social amity between various communities in Das's legacy. This brought him to foreground Das's 'love for Islam'. Irrespective of Das's political philosophy, Bose would argue, the former had succeeded in bringing the communities closer by his significantly exuberant love for others and a high measure of tolerance. Clearly, both love and tolerance inhabited outside the sheer functional ground of pacts and contracts, or the dry political calculations. 'We might settle our disputes through pacts but [Das] did not believe that that was the *only* means of securing cordial relations between Hindus and Muslims [emphasis added].'[16] So Bose would prefer to see Das as the visionary of a lasting Hindu–Muslim unity through 'a kind of cultural synthesis'. Such cultural synthesis was not perceivable without the prior recognition of 'difference'.

Taking this cue, Bose would strongly propose the need for cross-cultural exchanges, some kind of a 'synthesis', to be pursued in greater intensity than the need of fostering 'pacts'.[17] 'I venture to think that the fundamental basis of political unity between different communities lies in cultural rapprochement.'[18] In the political directives sent out to the Congress workers of various localities, Bose would resolutely stick to this belief.[19] In reality, however, this had only a limited impact on the political society of Bengal, as inter-communal tensions were visibly on the rise during this time. But these limits of politics were more indicative of the nature of the control of the larger political organization on its local bodies than of a lack of awareness in the leadership of the need for inter-community 'synthesis'.

Did social disharmony alter the scope of such liberal visions of 'community'? This appears to be a complex question. Reading Bose, one can notice a significant departure from Das in the former's use of the term 'communalism' in a negative way. This rather loosely and frequently used term became a synonym for 'fanaticism' in his writings.[20] He was also, perhaps, one of the pioneers in using the word 'secular' as an oppositional term to religious fanaticism. In many speeches, he underlined that fanaticism or communalism was 'the greatest thorn in the path of cultural intimacy and there is no better remedy than secular and scientific education.'[21] The question naturally emerges here: How would Bose then distinguish 'communalism' from the utterances of difference, keeping in mind that a true national unity must be achievable only by recognizing the pronounced cultural or religious differences? Where would he draw the line between community sensibilities and community obsession?

Although this question was never directly addressed by Bose, the answer must have been hidden in his repeated assertions that 'cultural' differences should not be allowed to become a hindrance to the path of 'political' unity. Bose's impatient criticism vis-à-vis the organizations like the Hindu Mahasabha might be taken as an important pointer in this context. The Hindu Mahasabha, he thought, should limit its work to social and cultural realms and not aspire to 'dabble in problems which come primarily within the purview of the Indian National Congress'.[22] The strictly and narrowly defined 'community' as prevalent in the Hindu Mahasabha agenda thoroughly disgusted Bose, who threw a frontal challenge to the Mahasabha leaders like Moorji asserting that '80% of the workers and members of the Bengal Hindu Sabhas are nationalist to the core'. The underlying message was plain enough to read: while the community and its associations should maintain their sociocultural agenda, they should not be allowed to occupy the terrain of the 'political' nation. The ground of nation's politics should be left to the overtly political organizations like the Congress, which would begin with an effective struggle against communalism in the sense of fanaticism. About how to devise an agenda of cultural self-awakening of the communities without any political implications, the young radical only maintained a strategic silence.[23]

Thus the communalism/fanaticism versus nationalism dichotomy transpired in Bose's thoughts, as did the 'political' versus 'cultural' binary of modern life. The Das variant of nationalism once attempted to redefine such binaries by giving some parts of the 'communal' a place in the 'national'. But for Bose, a reformulation of 'communal' seemed necessary in the late 1920s. By 1928, 'nation' and 'national' found a well-defined space in Bose's writings, and that space was primarily 'political', guided by a singular aim of attaining freedom, and a singular purpose of building 'the will to be free'.[24]

In redefining the 'national', Bose differed from his ideological predecessor in another respect—the idea of the region–nation. In his formative years, Bose was greatly inspired by the images and plights of 'Mother Bengal', and also discussed with Basanti Devi, Das's wife, about the inheritance Das left in the form of 'Bengal's Spiritual Quest'. He used to express a lot of pride that no other province in India showed such adaptability towards the politics and ideologies of nationalism:

> Bengal may be lagging behind in other spheres of life but I am firmly convinced that in the fight for Swaraj she goes far ahead of others.... Although Mahatma Gandhi, who is the sponsor of the national movement, happens to be a non-Bengalee, still no other province can claim national activities on such a tremendous scale as Bengal.[25]

However, over time, Bose became increasingly more engaged with the mission of India rather than with the problems and perspectives of Bengal as a region. His expressions of regional sentiment became more of a vehicle of mobilizing the supra-regional national sentiments, and less of the reserve of a provincial spirit. One may identify a significant reversal here— because the ideological journey of Das, Bose's mentor, was just in the reverse direction, from an all-India vision towards the realities and plights of his own region. On the other hand, Bose became more of a promising 'national' leader, especially after the All Parties Conference in Calcutta and Calcutta Congress in December 1928, and during the course of the agitation inside the Congress against the clause of Dominion Status in the Nehru Report.[26] To ensure a stronger and surer footing within the Congress became increasingly important to him; the spread of the organization throughout the country seemed to be the foremost priority.[27]

This new role of Bose was, no doubt, a response to the new political challenges of his own times. Those who focused exclusively on the provincial (*pradeshik*) awareness and socially constructive works to build a nation from below, like Bepinchandra Pal in his later phase, had been effectively marginalized by this time as a result of the increasing internal turmoil within Congress.[28] Anti-colonial politics started to steer its course in a different direction: the goal of freedom emerged as the first and foremost objective. The Bengal Congress as well, fraught with tremendous factional squabbles, was engaged in a fierce debate on the question of complete independence instead of dominion status as the political goal of India. Alongside, there was a visible growth in the socialist ideology within and outside Congress. This also gradually shifted the focus on to the rift between the Gandhian High Command and the younger radicals like Bose. Against the backdrop of such intense infighting, the rival political factions of the region could not but keenly await the support of their respective blocs of colleagues from the all-India platform.

There was another pivotal factor behind the new focus being pushed away from provincial concerns. The dilemma of joint versus separate electorates soon revealed its complex implications within the province of Bengal, which possessed a very special demographic spread. So far elections for legislative council had routinely been held in the province since 1909, which made the Bengali Muslims realize the strength of their position in Bengal in a joint-electorate system. In eastern Bengal they were by far the clear majority, while in western Bengal they were in a losing position. The case was just the reverse for the Bengali Hindus, eastern Bengal being not only a lost game to the Muslims in case of a joint electorate, but also a hotbed of conflict within the Hindu community due to its substantial and antagonistic low-caste, especially Namasudra, population. However, the Hindu-dominated Congress was still overwhelmingly in favour of a joint electorate, because that ensured for them the key to maintain a more secure position in western Bengal, the part of the province where the metropolis of Calcutta, the bird's eye for every political party, was located. The importance of eastern Bengal began to diminish in the Congress view; the need for a provincial politics became less urgent. The Bengal Congress now began to lean explicitly on its all-India platform to strengthen its own position in the joint-electorate system.[29]

No doubt, the ideological preferences for unity and unified existence bolstered its support for a joint electorate. But it would be hard not to appreciate the electoral calculations amidst the new, unfolding system of electoral politics. It is of critical importance to note how the Bengal Congress at this phase decided to follow the all-India commands and virtually cut itself off from the districts of eastern Bengal. During the civil disobedience movement, the Congress seldom bothered to spread the movement to the distant localities in the east.[30] Instead of the tremendous spurts of revolutionary activities in various parts of Bengal, the larger national movement would refuse to mobilize local grievances to a satisfactory extent, and even alienate the masses in the eastern provinces. The Muslim and low-caste groups of Dacca, Faridpur, Bakarganj, Mymensingh, and many other districts even rose in opposition to the civil disobedience movement.[31]

If this was the shifting position of the political establishment in the late 1920s, the reverberations of this shift from 'region' to 'country' were also felt in the world of ideas and opinions. The principle of consolidating regional communities in the name of national unity, a principle once foregrounded by Das, now began to exasperate many, both conservatives and liberals. Some thought that such a process of anticipating a Hindu–Muslim unity in the region had practically been futile, often disintegrating the society, and weakening its politics in the end.[32] Some even went further and considered that an over-emphasis on provincial politics had a direct communal bearing because it meant sacrificing prospects of the Bengali Hindus for the sake of Bengali Muslims. They thought that instead one must ensure the spirit of Hindu unity within and outside Bengal.[33] If this could be called a conservative challenge against the regional nationalism, a larger and more liberal ideological challenge also surfaced during this time. Nirad C. Chaudhuri[34] was amongst those who consistently mocked the self-styled provincialism of the group of Bengali politicians inspired by Das. To champion provincial cultures and identities, Chaudhuri argued, was nothing but an exercise in parochialism, bringing 'the particular expressions of the same general Indian mould of existence' instead of its whole. A generality behind 'the particular forms' was systematically missed out in such a political discourse. Chaudhuri did not find the idea of a 'Bengali nation' anything but a cultural or political chauvinism of a repugnant sort, a product of the typically 'Bengali intolerance and high-handedness' vis-à-vis the 'other' cultures. He would rather fall back on the theme of 'unity' among various provincial cultures and societies of India. 'There is indeed something like a "derivative" (*tadbhaba*) form of "Hindu civilization", which we can describe as "folk civilizations". But, surely that cannot and would not provide the basis of a respectable "nationalism" as that of India!'[35]

Most certainly, this view sounded akin to the 'reformulated' national politics of Bose in its compulsion to look beyond the region. At the same time, dissimilarities between these two approaches must also be underscored. First, despite the outward thrust of Bose's view, Bengal still continued to play in it a pivotal role, just like 'a starting point of a long journey'.[36] Indeed, this continued preoccupation with the region reflected in Bose's thoughts was what in Chaudhuri's grudging analysis seemed to be 'the all-round climate of federalism and democracy.'[37] Second, there was a clear dissociation from the masses, and an attempt to returning to the classical or elite folds of the society in the views of Chaudhuri (and of many others of this time, as we will see in this chapter). Bose, on the contrary, never endorsed this self-consciously classicist, anti-folk, and therefore, sanitized version of nation. For him, the national journey might have become less regional and more out-bound than before, but the need to find, reach, and locate 'people' into its centre was acknowledged more strongly than ever. It was important for the nation to be tied to 'the people and their communities', but at the same time the nation must not be limiting itself by the particularism of these identities.

In all these debates between regional versus supra-regional or between communitarian versus supra-communitarian visions of the nation, we can then identify a new ideological straitjacket. The logic of the politics of representation inevitably pushed its frontiers further towards the common masses, but, at the same time, approaching or addressing the 'popular' inevitably implied negotiations with the deeply embedded smaller identities, either belonging to community or caste.

Culture and Language: Rebels against the Classical

Nowhere was this contradiction more pronounced than in the domains of language and culture. The more the need was felt for broadening the base of the imagined national community, the more resistant the internally limiting lines in culture and language proved to be. These limits had already made themselves apparent in the earlier years, as we have noted in the last chapter. But the resistance and acrimony only grew over time, and the newer implications of community stimulated by new modes of politics began to reflect themselves heavily in the cultural discourse.

Understandably, the most urgent call was to distinguish between the different types of claims or characteristics of a community, thereby posing a hierarchy among its various demands of self-assertion. Cultural claims had to be weighed against the other accompanying, mainly political, claims. The task was not easy. For example, when Subhas Bose condemned 'communalism' in the sense of 'fanaticism', and at the same time looked forward to a cultural self-strengthening of communities, he essentially implied a separation between the 'political' and the 'cultural'. An endlessly plural and multicultural society, India, in his views, had its best hope in a cultural federation of various self-confident communities and a political federation of various self-reliant national communities.[38] This view immediately raised the question of the slippery passage between the 'cultural' and the 'political'. How much 'cultural' was still 'cultural' and not 'political'? How far could one bend for the sake of the 'cultural'? Or, in the end, on what grounds must the 'cultural' never be 'political'? These riddles were not simply theoretical but practically relevant day-to-day worries for the nationalist leadership during these years.

Yet, very often, the cultural and political overlapped so hopelessly in the nationalist mind, often of the most liberal sort, that it proved stupendously challenging to step beyond the position of power. This was evident in the debates around the form and content of the Bengali language, as the task of developing a widely acceptable common lingua franca of the region–nation turned out to be an enormously complex one. The fundamental problematic was: should it be endowed with a standardized, classical character, with its multiple local variations being done away with? Significantly, within the fold of this one question, all the existing identity anxieties, relating to community, locality, or even class, were patently manifest. Bengal Muslims, of course, had the deepest stake in pushing for a wider acceptance of local dialects in literary culture and vernacular sociopolitical discourse. On the other hand, the more tolerant, accommodative and influential Hindu Bengali literary figures often found the idea of departure from the classical form unnecessarily complicated.

The clearest evidence of this conflicted national–cultural outlook can perhaps be found in Rabindranath Tagore. His discomfort regarding the self-conscious expressions of different or 'other' forms of language is already noted in the previous chapters. He adopted a firmer position on local or communitarian dialects and refused to accept the idea that these dialects could ever develop themselves as a match for the language of Calcutta. Having started his argument in the voice of an aesthetic conservative, he unwittingly subjected himself to the logic of social positioning or the forces of cultural hegemony. It has been mentioned in the last chapter that it seemed to him that the mere fact of geographical distance of these other dialects from Calcutta, the supreme locus of Bengal's national–cultural identity, had assigned to them their own inferior position:

> [Calcutta] is the capital of Bengal. The capital city is always like the stomach or the central organ of the body.... If it were Dhaka that had been the capital of Bengal, no doubt, the people of Dhaka would have had the advantage of ruling us with their own form of language, and provided the platform on which Bengali language would have based itself.[39]

While this reservation on the forms of Bengali language was expressed a few years earlier, the communitarian variants of language began to trouble him distinctly during this period. Faced by the continuous, deliberate attempts by the new Bengali Muslim writers, he was now persuaded to engage with the legitimacy of these 'other' languages. His position was, nevertheless, more cautious than before and, in some of his articles written between 1932 and 1934, an assimilation of 'alien' words and expressions was even considered acceptable, but only conditionally. He would have approved it only if the language was 'enriched' by those.[40] This qualified support for 'alien' or non-standard words and expressions indicated his fundamental discomfort with any deliberate or self-conscious attempts of modifying the language. His firm displeasure at the efforts of 'Urdu-ization' of Bengali by many of his Muslim contemporaries was even expressed in case of Kazi Nazrul Islam, by this time one of the most prolific Bengali poets, whose writings were bursting with Urdu, Arabic, and Persian words. Indeed, Nazrul invited pervasive attacks from the bhadralok, which also included strong retorts from Tagore. Of course, the lines between the purpose of enrichment and the purpose of deliberate tinkering of the language, either in a vengeful or in a reformatory spirit, were clearly thin, arbitrary, and subjective. Tagore's writings themselves bore the kernel of the dilemma:

> Every language has a life of its own. It actually loses its spirit if stretched too far. It would be self-defeating if we attempt to go against the basic nature of the language, because then it would only be made crippled

forever. The language would imbibe into itself the usages it is able to assimilate, but it would decide on its own to what extent this absorption can be done.[41]

The subjectivity inherent in his apparently non-subjective position made itself obvious in these lines. When was such 'assimilation' desirable, and when did it appear artificial, over-stretched, self-defeating? Part of Tagore's resentment was due to the unfamiliarity, and partly due to the non-literariness, of these alien words. One such word used by Nazrul, *khun*, Persian in origin, etymologically meaning 'blood', but also denoting 'murder' in an extended sense, attracted Tagore's brazen disapproval:

> The word *khun* in the sense of murder is very much in vogue, but if you now want to make use of the same word in its other original sense, that is, blood, then the language would turn its face away from us [italics mine].[42]

Note the use of 'us' in the statement, which could not but render the subjectivity hidden in any such position evident. The liberal ideologue was thus inadvertently pushed to his 'own' position, a communitarian position, on the question of language. The position was also one of sociocultural elitism, which could hardly be made to fit into a neat Hindu–Muslim binary. Judged from this position, the 'others' in the language map of the nation might include all marginal positions in terms of community, class, location, or any combination of these factors.[43] The established 'classical' standard of language was thus given an excessive sanctity by liberal nationalists like Tagore. When Abul Fazl, a sensitive young intellectual, prodded him on the subtle connections between the cultural practices of a community and its language of daily use, his response was that he would rather set a 'condition' to that alleged 'connection'.[44] 'The flexibility of a language must remain within a certain limit. Greater interference in a language jeopardizes its natural modes of expressions,' Tagore commented. His displeasure was even mixed with a tone of aggression. 'I feel ashamed to see how it is in the province of Bengal, nowhere else, that such a cruel and mindless endeavour of [crippling its own native language] is taking place [through the incorporation of 'alien' words and expressions].'[45]

The position of Tagore on Bengali language illustrates how, in an era of the emerging challenge of difference against the imagined 'national', the liberal protagonists of nation used to feel threatened by the 'other' faces of nation despite their intention to broaden the national society as much as possible. It is precisely here that the 'cultural' quickly merged with the 'political', and the hidden spirit of majoritarianism in the form of classicism crept in to deny the 'other' a legitimacy it deserved. Tagore, who had already dismissed the local dialects on the basis of their distance from the political or cultural power centre, would now by a curious twist of the argument warn the Muslims of extending communal differences beyond the matters of politics into the realm of language. The language, the glorious possession of the 'Bengali nation', an exceptional site 'where the two communities doubtlessly meet' should not be made a site of contestation. Reckless experimentations with this common property seemed nothing but 'burning up the old ancestral house out of petty family quarrels'.[46] The logic was one of urban over-sensitivity, as well as one of an inherent high-culture elitism, sometimes veiled in the arguments of convenience, sometimes in those of aesthetic value, and, in most cases, patently dismissive towards the rights of marginal societies.

Consequently, a note of caution is in order here. To view this dismissiveness as simply a Hindu cultural nationalism does not seem adequate or even a fair historiographical exercise. Going beyond the overused and hackneyed analytical prism of the Hindu–Muslim binary, debates on Bengali as a national language must illuminate the multiple anxieties at play within the project of nation, based on the multiple loci of the nationalist as an individual, as well as a part of an undefined collective.

Against the resistance put up by the elitist defense of the classical, the Bengali Muslim reaction was naturally defensive. Difference was not merely an ideological vehicle of political ascendancy to them, but also a fairer ground of social coexistence. To assert the cultural and linguistic individuality of Bengal's Muslims seemed a crucial imperative, a necessary step to lay their own claims to 'national' or Bengali life: 'Posterity will decide which forms of language would perish and which would survive. Is it worth our time and energy to split hairs over judging the legitimacy or acceptance of expressions or usages?... [The diversification] is necessary precisely because we think that it is here that the interests and the identity of Bengali Hindus and Bengali Muslims meet.'[47] The self-justifying tone in pursuing Mussalmani Bangla is clearly audible. There would also be a quick cautionary advice towards fellow Muslims for restraining the impulse of overdoing the 'Islamization'.[48] An article by Nurunnesa Khatun read in the session of the Bangiya Sahitya Sammilan (1926), expressed deep resentment that after investing so many years in Bengal, some Muslims suddenly felt the urge to disown its language and traditions.[49]

Nazrul, however, took the pain to explain his position on the use of 'alien' words like 'khun' in particular, and the theme of Islamization of Bengali in general. The 'goddess of world literature' could not be as averse to the Islamic (Mussalmani) style as not to allow many 'flowers to bloom', he argued with a mild sarcasm. His choice of the word 'khun', unpalatable to the 'literary masters', was not intended to 'give any particular colour, either *Mussalmani* or Bolshevik, to the language', but merely represented his very own style. He hastily added that Tagore would perhaps not warmly react towards either of these 'colours', Mussalmani or Bolshevik, but that in the end the literary style must only be a matter of the author's personal choice.[50] The name of this particular article by Nazrul was also subtly poignant: 'Baror piriti balir bandh', that is, 'the love of the big for the small cannot but be short-lived'.

A profound insecurity and self-defense on one side and a distinctly elitist, classicist preference on the other—the twin trend in the everyday cultural life of Bengal—and the resultant sense of cultural dismemberment for the Bengali Muslims was silently assuming a political character, something which very few noticed during the time. In the Bengali Hindu nationalist perception, it was not only unacceptable but hugely insulting that the Bengali Muslim writers would harbour such animosity towards the classical forms of language and tradition. The Muslims, they would insist, 'must' internalize the basics of classical literature like the Vedas, the Upanishads, and the two epics Ramayana and Mahabharata, surely by definition Hindu, only in order to share the foundational spirit of the nation. Curiously, such majoritarian ideas were sometimes echoed by the liberal Bengali Muslim ideologues as well, who saw the intellectual merit in assimilating the classical Bengali language and literature and broadening their own cultural vista for the sake of their own good. In 1928, at a meeting of the Bangiya Mussalman Sahitya Samiti, an association headed by Mohammad Shahidullah and Mohammad Mozammel Huq, two leading Muslim intellectual leaders of the time, a Muslim speaker elaborated this argument. He indignantly mentioned that although it was hard to find a single Bengali Muslim unfamiliar with Ram's respect for his father, Lakshman's love for his brother, or Sita's loyalty towards her husband, there suddenly emerged a disquieting tendency of cultural dissociation with these regular and commonly practiced cultural references. The Sahitya Samiti played an important role in disseminating a spirit of cultural confluence in this era of divisive contestations. It is no exaggeration to argue that, in fact, the Bengali Muslim protagonists often moved far ahead of their Hindu counterparts in developing cross-communitarian cultural bridges. By virtue of their sustained and secure claims on the language and culture of the region, the Hindu Bengalis seldom exposed themselves to the Islamic cultural traditions. For the Muslim writers, on the contrary, there was indeed an unavoidable imperative to extend the definition and meaning of 'national' outside their own cultural heritage. It was precisely here that the latter had to stretch the problematic up to the question of 'assimilation' beyond 'tolerance', and felt the pressing need of generating a shared space of cultural memory rather acutely.

The Bengali Muslim anxiety over language was also reflected in their views on education. The staunchly Islamic protagonists were in favour of establishing as many madrassas as possible. They were routinely countered by their Moderate co-religionists, possibly infused with a stronger awareness of regional–cultural identity. Arguments were heard that for the professional and vocational training of the Muslims, the principle of uniformity in education should not be compromised. This would mean an eventual decline of the madrassas, and, in a deeper sense, a separation between 'social practices' and 'religious faith'. The argument was cogently put: 'It is not only about which languages are to be taught in the madrassas, and which are not. It is about the whole madrassa system as such. Do we really think that learning four or five languages at one and the same time in the junior madrassas prepares our children for any good?... This is what we call the New Madrassa Scheme, the revised and developed version of what has been the "old" system.'[51] How would this 'new' system bring a change in educational outlook?

> Only a dose of English coupled with Urdu, Arabic, Persian and Bengali would not solve the problem. There must be a focus of some sort in the education system. That is the only way to recoup our long-lost touches with the civilized world…. Therefore, in my humble opinion, *the problem of education of the Bengali Muslims is the most important national problem. It immediately needs a remedy* [emphasis mine].[52]

Abul Hussain, the writer of the above argument, belonged to the Dacca region, outside the liberal literary or educational circles of Calcutta. But his relative locational marginality did not hinder him from balancing the assertion of 'difference' with robust pragmatism and self-confidence. Different interests had to be adjusted and oriented in a way to curb the impulses of insecure indigenism and promote a modern national profile, he thought. In doing so, a reformulated, forward-looking education system seemed necessary. Such were the moderate Muslim voices in

Bengal, heard even beyond the enlightened society of Calcutta, allegedly the cultural–political 'centre' of the region. An open advocacy of the old madrassa system was diminished by the latter half of the 1920s. To combine the fundamentals of the Islamic culture with the needs of an increasingly self-conscious regional community was becoming more urgent than before.

The liberal Muslim circles of Calcutta were perhaps at the height of their imaginative national–cultural endeavours during this time. The Bangiya Mussalman Sahitya Samiti mobilized greater number of people than ever before in Calcutta. Following its example, the Muslim Sahitya Samaj was established in Dacca in 1926. Both contributed significantly to the dissemination of the liberal ideal of a region–nation with multi-faceted cultural identities. The Sahitya Samaj would even launch a broader cultural movement of Buddhir Mukti, headed by literary stars of the region such as Kazi Imdadul Huq, Kazi Abdul Wadud, Abdul Kadir, Abul Hussain, and Abul Fazl, most of whom maintained close connections with another prominent liberal-minded group around the journal *Saogat*. The interconnected intellectual nexus of the late 1920s reminds us of a similar cultural cosmos in the earlier decade comprising the groups gathering around *Bangiya Mussalman Sahitya Patrika*, *Saogat*, and *Moslem Bharat*. There is enough ground to conclude that the vibrant cultural milieu of Bengali Muslims in the late 1920s and early 1930s was an inheritance from those cultural trends of the previous decade. The Bengali Muslim literary liberalism perpetuated itself in this way over a considerably long period. The Sahitya Samaj crowd of 1926–7 gradually came to be referred to as the *Shikha* group after the name of the mouthpiece journal it used to publish. Essays were read out by Muslim writers and students of *Shikha–Saogat* group in each session of the Sahitya Samaj, where the forms of Bengali language were debated with the cultural predicaments of Bengali Muslims in focus. Two articles must be mentioned in this respect: —'Bangali Mussalmaner Bhabishyat' (The future of Bengali Muslims, 1927) and 'Bangali Mussalmaner Shiksha Samasya' (Problems of education for Bengali Muslims, 1928), both written by Abul Hussain, who espoused the purpose of a national language on the basis of a shared heritage of Bengali culture.

As the Calcutta University Committee proposed Bengali as the universal medium of instruction within the province, Mr M.A. Rahman, Chairman of the Reception Committee of the first annual conference of the Sahitya Samaj, pointed out, 'The language of the country where we live is our language,' and thereby dismissed the claims of the contending anti-Bengali groups in this committee.[53] This position was reinforced by Golam Mostafa, Dr Lutfar Rahman, and Said Abdul Latif, leading to a unanimous acceptance of the proposal. Both Abdul Wadud and Abul Hussain fought hard against the more obscurantist version of Islam, which, they thought, only aimed to deny the complex enmeshing of various influences and the resultant richness of the Bengali Muslim culture.

Abul Hussain also upheld a strong case for a modernist and federalist political system suited for different communities living harmoniously together.[54] He made a sharp distinction between the religious cultures to be observed in a 'society' and the political culture of the 'state', and thus reached an ideological position significantly close to the ideal of a separation between the 'cultural' and the 'political', advocated by Subhas Bose roughly around the same time. Cultural self-expressions were considered essential for the community, but the foundation of a liberal and workable polity must be made 'democratic', a system best suited to nurture diversity. The only imaginable way of self-advancement for the Bengali Muslims was to have 'trust' in and 'share' with the Hindus, going beyond the traps of the words like 'fear', 'slavery' or 'begging'. By insisting on doing away with a particular set of words and relying on another, he definitely suggested a psycho-linguistic solution for extending the spirit of community cooperation within a national space. He was not alone in this respect. For another anonymous author of the same period, the Bengali Muslim identity would have to rest on the capacity and readiness for participating in the freedom movement of the 'country':

> Bengali Muslims should join the Hindus on equal terms in the struggle for the freedom of the country. We believe that it is an important duty of every Moslem to strive for the freedom of their own country. But if after joining the struggle for freedom the Mussalmans have to give up their individuality and allow themselves to be merged in the Hindus, then we say a hundred times that such national movement will bring them freedom with nothing but slavery.[55]

There was one serious problem though. The outlook of the Muslim Sahitya Samaj of Dacca and the *Shikha–Saogat* group of Calcutta would often amount to claim an effective inseparability of Hindu and Muslim cultural worlds in Bengal. This eventually antagonized not only the Islamic purists but also the groups of Bengal Muslims craving for a 'different' identity altogether. The long-protracted debates between two major journals of this time might be taken into consideration in this context. In the world of Bengali Muslim journalistic literature, there emerged a bitter split between the radical *Saogat* group and the self-professedly Islamic group of *Mohammadi*, led by Mohammad Akram Khan. The former consistently resisted the attempts of the latter 'to tie up religion with all literary endeavours.'[56] *Mohammadi* would in turn retort to such allegations with a typical sarcasm:

> It is a pity that some of us think that in order to claim a respected position in 'world literature', it is mandatory to dissociate oneself from one's own culture, which happens to be necessarily infused with religious sentiments and religious ideals. To belong to one's own cultural ground is becoming 'parochial' and 'communal'. What can be more lamentable than this![57]

The Bengali Muslim proponents of national–cultural synthesis of the 1920s had to face resistance and even acrimony, but they left a distinct effect even after the disbandment of the *Shikha–Saogat* group. In later years it served as a model for the Moderate *mentalité* in the Bengal Muslim world, where the evocation of a regional–national identity would be considered a vital task. It must be noted that despite contestation over the form and the extent, or the conflicts and controversies between the liberals and the conservatives of this world, the essentially regional character of the Bengali Muslims was no longer doubted. Even the staunchly conservative protagonists of *Mohammadi* did not fail to recognize, or even foreground, their Bengali identity. The region–nation by this time proved its vitality among various sections of Bengali Muslims. The following poem is just one of the innumerable similar evocations of the regional Muslim sentiment, published in *Mohammadi*, and more significantly, written by the same author who proudly declared that 'being a Muslim' could not imply 'parochial' or 'communal', but a primary claim to be 'national':

> Sing for Bengal, oh you Moslem, sing of Bengal, open your heart—
> This is our own native land, offer her homage, your devotional word.
> That this land we do not own
> Is a wrong notion, false in tone,
> Bangla is ours, India is ours, ours is the whole of world.
>
> Like alien here we do not stand, this is our own, very own land
> We are the true Bengalis, and ours is the right demand.
> In India or in Bangladesh
> We are the new-age Aryan race
> Here is flying the victory-flag of Bakhtiar the great valiant.[58]

'Muslim interests' mingled with 'Bengali interests' provided the base of the bold assertions of Muslimness, and thus the assured ground of regional nation was pronounced. Being Muslim was no longer contradictory to, or even conflicting with, being Bengali. To view the contestations within the Bengali nation solely through the prism of Hindu–Muslim binary would have left this narrative of owning up to a linguistic regional culture woefully uncharted. The growing world of a self-confident, self-assertive Bengali Muslim intelligentsia, socially influential and political vocal, would have been left unaddressed. To note that the Bengali versus Muslim dilemma receded by the 1930s to a significant extent, paving the way for the wide range of Bengali Muslim assertions is enormously important in the history of Bengali nationalist thought. Those assertions are best explained in a resistance–accommodation–assimilation model vis-à-vis the elitist or classicist position on Bengali language and culture, where the constant intermingling of regional and community identities could, in the end, produce multiple possibilities of the nation.

Not surprisingly perhaps, amidst the assertions of a Bengali regional self, the Bengali Muslims consistently betrayed a strong discomfort regarding the all-India 'nation', being constantly defined and shaped in terms of non-Bengali and non-Islamic terms. Even the non-Bengali but Islamic construction of identity often appeared distant to them. In an age of constitutional experiments of new kinds in the early 1930s, the Bengali Muslims were thus going through the same dual conflict of interests as was experienced in the late 1910s and early 1920s.[59] The all-India Muslim leadership was bitterly criticized in Bengal for 'selling out Bengal's interest' for the 'larger Muslim interest' even by the conservative Muslim groups: 'We are constantly kept hypnotized in the name of Muslim community at large,… but what about our own fortune in Bengal?'[60] The project of guarding their 'own fortune in Bengal' was fast becoming their abiding political imperative by this era.

The Predicament of the Moderates

Contradictions between the regional and Indian realities for the Bengali Muslims were apparent by the 1920s. The new constitutional politics of colonial India made these contradictions glaring. At the same time, the constant enmeshing of regional, communitarian, or cultural–linguistic identities continued to intensify those conflicts.[61] There had already emerged an ideology which championed the 'Muslim' identity in Bengal, but this Muslimness was sought to be upheld in a distinct way, that is, with a characteristically regional or Bengali twist. There was a large section of vocal 'Moderates' in Bengal making their presence felt in the political and cultural discourse of the time and reassuring that community identity needed to be protected for its further advancement, but that identity should not be an end in itself. The 'communitarian', or to use the more regular term, 'communal' politics and culture became increasingly more visible, but it was also becoming apparent that the battle between the 'good communalists' and 'bad communalists' was more relevant and more fierce than ever before.[62] Significantly, this battle was embittered by the question of privileging an extra-regional Islamic identity, or an all-India identity for the Bengali Muslim community in the late 1920s. To appreciate this point better, it is important to review the constitutional deals taking place at an all-India level during this time.

Looking back, the Lucknow Pact of 1916 had actually left a permanent mark on Bengal Muslim politics, as the nature of negotiations at the time of the Pact had revealed the necessity of regional sacrifices for the sake of the 'Muslim interest' at an all-India level. The logic behind the interplay of Muslim-minority and Muslim-majority provinces brought the Bengali Muslims a less-than-proportionate representation. Those negotiations had left the Bengali Muslims clearly displeased, or, at best, confused. So when in 1927 Jinnah made the dramatic offer of joint electorates with reservation of seats fixed in proportion to the population in Muslim-majority provinces, it was also not meant to please the Bengali Muslims. It was simply designed to guard the interests of the Muslim-minority provinces. The breach between the all-India Muslim leadership and the Bengali Muslims would only be widened in the following years.

Moreover, the question of separate electorates left the Bengali Muslims perturbed. Prospects of the joint-electorate system were surely brighter in Bengal than those in any Muslim-minority provinces. Fazlul Huq and his followers still favoured separate electorates as a means to safeguard the Muslim interests in an aggregative way. But many regional leaders like Abdul Karim, Mujibur Rahman, and Akram Khan chose to disagree with them and supported joint electorates with their eyes fixed on Bengal. They even held that the communal electorates would prove 'detrimental to the interests of the community' as they put them in the position of an under-represented community on a fixed basis, whereas adult suffrage or 'lowering of franchise qualifications could have earned for Bengali Muslims a representation commensurate with their numerical strength'.[63] It must be kept in mind that this latter group of leaders was in control of the Bengal Provincial Muslim League when the Nehru Report was put forward in 1928.[64] The general mood in Bengal after the Report was one of approval, as it seemed to have brought for them an opportunity to correct the injustice done to the Bengali Muslims in Lucknow. At least two of Bengal's leading Muslim journals, Mujibur Rahman's *The Mussalman* and Akram Khan's *Mohammadi*, campaigned in favour of the report. They pointed out that while Muslim interests of eastern Bengal were safe with joint electorates, in western Bengal, where they were generally in a small minority, Muslims still had 'a fair chance of winning' through an alliance with the Congress and various regional parties.[65] Most importantly, they thought that 'one of the most striking features of both the Nehru Committee and of the All Parties Conference was that no attempt was ever made in any stage of their proceedings to shelve the legitimate demands and rights of the minority communities'.[66] However, the arrangement suggested by the report naturally frustrated the minority-province Muslims, as it effectively discarded the advantages they enjoyed for years in the form of 'weightage'. The positive impact the report had on Bengali Muslims was lost in the course of a direct clash of the potentially irreconcilable interests of the Muslim-majority and Muslim-minority provinces in matters of representation. Eventually, the constitutional compromise suggested by the Nehru Report went in vain. What was left behind was the realistic possibility of a future 'sacrifice' expected to be imposed on the Bengal Muslims by the all-India leadership at the centre.[67]

The Nehru Report was clearly the first major attempt to draft a constitutional framework for the country, complete with lists of central and provincial subjects and fundamental rights. The issue of adult suffrage was raised for the first time, something never conceded in any constitution made by the British so far, and, while the issue of adult franchise brought out a lot of possibilities amidst the regional diversities of India, the possibilities were also effectively truncated by crippling the powers of the provincial legislatures. This last point did not escape the notice of the Bengali Muslim leaders, no less because they saw their community interests irredeemably bound with the prospects of the province. In fact, the neglect of the 'federal' principle seemed to be the fundamental flaw of the report, otherwise acceptable by proposing a joint electorate without reservation of seats with an extended adult suffrage. Its recommendations for a relatively stronger centre were strongly resented:

One of the principal defects of the Nehru Report is that it has unnecessarily crippled the powers of the Provincial Legislatures and given much wider powers and privileges to the Central Legislature. This will be highly unjust to the Muslims who will always remain a minority in the Central body. [68]

If it was for the first time that Bengali Muslim leaders proved amenable to the constitutional adjustments of various kinds, and even willing to accept less than what the more radical section of Muslims would like to have, the critical importance of the Nehru Report lay elsewhere. Its failure, coupled with the experience of the Communal Award of 1932, made sure that the Moderate Bengali Muslim voices would continue to reign in cultural realms but become gradually marginalized in the political realms by a combination of historical forces. These forces included: first, the growing visibility of a leadership outside Bengal hinging themselves upon an 'all-India Muslim interest', and second, the steady political opposition of the conservative groups of their own region, both from Muslim and Hindu quarters. Rather inevitably, from now on, the Muslim conservatives would begin to appear stronger than their actual strength in the region due to their ready acquiescence with the deals and dictates presented in the name of an extra-regional Islamic identity or, to put it simply, an 'all-India Muslim interest'.

It is in this context that we should assess the significance of certain desperate efforts made by a handful of Bengali Muslim leaders to come to an understanding with the Bengal Congress leaders. They did so before the All Parties National Convention (December 1928) following the Nehru Report. Abdur Rahim, Fazlul Huq, Abdul Karim, Mujibur Rahman, Akram Khan, and Maniruzzaman Islamabadi held an informal meeting with Dr B.C. Roy, J.C. Gupta, J.M. Sengupta, Sarat Chandra Bose, and Nalini Sarkar in the office of the journal *The Mussalman* to explore the possibility of reviving the Bengal Pact in some modified way. The meeting ended as a failure, as a unanimous decision could not be reached on the Muslim share in public service.[69] Many were in favour of reconsidering the issues of reservation and representation. According to a news report in a contemporary Hindu journal, a meeting was arranged by the Muslim Sahitya Samaj in Calcutta in March 1927, where Maulavi Abul Hussain allegedly condemned the Muslim demands for special privileges: 'It would be far beneficial for the community not to look up to the special privileges like concessions or reservations but strive for greater self-expression and self-strengthening.'[70] Even with a discount for an interest-driven bias, the absence of any rebuttal of the story in the contemporary Muslim journals demands attention. Similar views are found elsewhere. 'Why such obsession with reservations and concessions?' wrote another Muslim author, 'Is not there enough reason for us to succeed if we just try to be what we are? Just stand up and claim what is yours and none else's. After all, God helps those who help themselves.'[71] At the Barisal Muslim Conference (May 1927), the proposal for separate electorates was strongly opposed. The unanimous opinion of the conference was that the representation in the legislature by communities only on the basis of their population could generate confidence of the Bengali Muslims at the national level. It was expressed in resolute terms in that conference that with the growth of national solidarity, the two major communities (that is, Hindus and Muslims) would solve by themselves the riddle of replacement of the separate communal electorates by mixed or general electorates.[72] Just on the eve of this conference, it was argued in *The Mussalman* that community consciousness was not incompatible with nationalism:

A man's duties to his own community are not necessarily incompatible with his duties towards the nation and if he can perform both to the best of his ability, why can he not be a good communalist, as well as nationalist?[73]

How this notion of good communalist-cum-nationalist was defined by these Moderates of the late 1920s might be explained by this following opinion piece published in *The Mussalman*:

The nationalism we contemplate for India ... will not be uniform in nature but multiform. It will be a weft of many different strands and in order that we may make a stable and durable fabric of it, we must ensure that each one of its component parts may attain its maximum strength, durability and resilience.[74]

Thus the prospect of being a good communalist-cum-nationalist appeared eminently practical in the late 1920s, both culturally and politically. The first identity did not foreclose the pronunciation of the second at a different time, in a different context. Hence community and nation could both be served at one and the same time. This prospect seemed to be meaningful even to the student organizations and youth meetings of this time. At the initiative of Maulavi Mujibur Rahman and Fazlul Huq, the All Bengal Muslim Youngmen Association and the All Bengal Muslim Student Union started functioning from 1927.[75] The question that was raised in the early meetings betrayed remarkable clarity: '[I]f we believe in democracy, and if we form a majority [in Bengal], why all this noise about "communal representation"?'[76] *Mohammadi* published the proceedings of the BPML conference held at Faridpur in 1931 under the presidentship of Dr Mukhtar Ahmed Ansari, by this time a major all-India leader. The proceedings show that the importance of adult suffrage was underlined even there. It was argued that the Muslim-majority provinces should logically have joint electorates, with seats allocated to each community on the basis of their numerical strength.[77] In this conference also, the greatest discomfort was expressed against the tendency to overrule the principle of federalism when the questions of the structure of the state and centre–province relationship were raised. It was deliberated at this meeting that in the next framework for the future constitution, the principle of federalism should be strictly adhered to, relegating the 'residuary powers' to the 'federated units', that is, the provinces.[78] However, the 'next framework' arrived only about a decade later, and the intervening years saw a substantial change in the Bengali Muslim views of nationalism.[79]

The Communal Award of 1932 strengthened the feeling that the 'rightful claims' of the Bengal Muslims were undervalued. The Award offered them 48.4 per cent representation in the provincial legislature as against their population strength in the province of nearly 55 per cent. Although at the AIML session Huq moved a resolution confirming support for the Award, the mood in Bengal was not very positive. Much of the Muslim displeasure during this time was in response to the conservative Hindu reactions against the new proposals. Against raising the Muslim seats from what had been the arrangement since the Lucknow Pact, the Hindu Mahasabha erupted in anger during several meetings. N.N. Sircar, Pandit Malaviya, and B.S. Moonje spearheaded the agitation. The Congress press also voiced similar reactions, and once again began to press for the urgency of the agenda of social self-strengthening like shuddhi and sangathan.[80] The Muslim press was defensive and, at times, aggressive. The BPML statement was scathing in debunking the Hindu nationalists on account of their 'double-standards': 'The most significant fact that strikes us is that the so-called nationalists are not much concerned with the allocation of seats to the Europeans who have got their quota abnormally out of proportion, but in season and out of season they would cry that some seats must be taken from Muslims.'[81]

Is this nationalism? Muslims can understand to some extent the actions of the Hindu Mahasabha ... but the attitude and actions of the sponsors

of liberty, freedom and self-determination is an enigma to them. The attitude taken up by Hindu men at large will surely widen the gulf between
the two communities in Bengal and in India.[82]

Reactions against the 'unfairly' inflated claims of the Muslims did
not come from the Mahasabha alone. When Ramananda Chatterjee,
editor of the *Modern Review,* participated in the Unity Conference at
Allahabad, organized to propose correction in the Award in favour of the
caste Hindus, the line between the conservative and the liberal circles got
blurred in an unfortunate way.[83] Tagore also expressed his deep concern
at the new proposals, but finally he was the only signatory who accepted
that 'Muslim interests' should be addressed at some level, though not at
the risk of segregating 'national interest':

> It is not that we wish to deny our Muslim countrymen the benefit of their
> numbers, neither that we suspect them of dangerous designs. It is only
> that we refuse to accept the fate of all future prospects of mutual coop-
> eration blighted by a scheme which puts a premium upon communal
> allegiance at the expense of *national interest*.... I beg to remind our rulers
> of the fact that, this political poisoning of our *national blood* is even worse
> than the commercial exploitation of our economic life, or punishing the
> subjects without trial [emphasis added].[84]

The administrative attempts at 'dividing and poisoning the national
existence' seemed to be the worst outcome of colonial rule, 'worse than
the commercial exploitation of our economic life ... worse than pun-
ishing subjects on suspicion, without trial', because it was designed to
cripple the 'nation' even in its future existence. The 'nation' and 'national
interest', by implication, could not but appear singular, at least in its
idealized form, not extending any endorsement to 'communal allegiance
at the expense of national interest'. Whereas on the cultural levels, leaving space for different identities might still be a matter of negotiation,
for many liberal nationalists, it was hard to consider the 'political' as a
divided or multi-form space.

It was through the practice of dismissing and discarding of even
the fair claims of certain less powerful 'communities', and bolstering
the more powerful ones in the process, perhaps unwittingly, that the
Moderate Muslim voices began to lose their strength. As already evident from the discourse on 'national' language and culture in the earlier
section, in the late 1920s, a substantial section of the Bengal Muslims
was approaching the issue of representation in an accommodative way,

and therefore could legitimately be labelled as Moderate. At the Barisal session of the BPML (May 1927), the basic premise of the political debate on representation was put forward in clear terms: 'We expect other communities to have the same opportunities and rights, which exactly we would like to claim for ourselves. Conversely, we would never go for anything what we cannot allow others to have.'[85] Reasons behind such explicit caution were two-fold: first, to assure the Hindus of the real intentions of the Muslim deliberations, and second, to present an earnest appeal to the more extreme groups of Muslims to practice restraint and not impart an intolerant image. Driven by the same concern, some even envisaged a battle between 'the Islam for liberty and freedom' with 'Islam of the mullahs'.

> The common people in our country are very backward in terms of education and other respects. Taking advantage of their ignorance and simplicity, and also of their religiosity, the mullahs are creating havoc all over the place. They are after their own interests, and therefore are completely opportunistic and unconcerned of the consequences of their own acts.... But this is not what true Islam is all about. Islam does not want us to hate and attack others. It has been a long overdue project for the reasonable Muslim minds of Bengal to fight the Islam of the mullahs for the sake of the Islam of liberty and freedom.[86]

The Moderate Muslims disposed towards a regional–cultural identity thus found themselves in an unenviable position. Concerns about misrepresenting the substance of 'Muslim identity' were grave; the Extremist Muslim protagonists were as fiercely opposed to their moderate reasoning as the more prominent Hindu voices of distrust and intolerance.

Most unfortunately, the trend of Muslim bigotry on the one hand and the trend of Hindu intransigency on the other began to reinforce each other so well that the process of social polarization was significantly hastened in the 1930s. Urgent pleas on the need for treating the 'extreme' and 'moderate' Muslims with more caution and discernment appeared in some Muslim periodicals and journals. An article in *Saogat* made a request to the 'more level-headed men of the country' to reconsider the song 'Bande Mataram' as national song, because '... there are enough reasons for even peace-loving Mussalmans to get upset with the history of the song and some of its phrases'.[87] The persistent use of catchphrases like 'destruction of Bengali Hindu community' or 'Muslim aggression on Hindu music' in nationalist agitations were strongly resented on the assumption that these facile and baseless charges would polarize the society even more.[88] Concerns were also expressed at the spread of the shuddhi movement in Bengal, often in a rather nuanced and veiled language.[89] The reactions of *Saogat* after the murder of Swami Sraddhananda, resulting in frantic demands for shuddhi may be mentioned in this context: 'How is this going to influence the common Hindu minds? Is it at all fair to make such generalizations after a clearly unfortunate incidence of homicide? Do the Hindu people really want to accuse the whole body of Indian Muslims for this heinous crime and thus alienate them forever?'[90] Such lack of discernment proved to be detrimental to 'Muslim confidence', who had already been suffering from a 'deep anxiety', the above article would point out.[91] By the early 1930s, a strong feeling of insecurity, later termed as 'minority anxiety', started being voiced extensively by the Bengali Muslims, who were, in reality, the majority community of Bengal. Far from a historical puzzle, this was a direct outcome of the twin trends of this time: one, their indiscriminate 'otherization' by the Bengali Hindus, who happened to be numerically not as strong but socially and politically hegemonic in the region; second, the constant reinforcing of this anxiety by the strategic tying up of an all-India Muslim perspective with that of the Bengali Muslims.[92]

Intrinsically connected to such gradual marginalization of the Moderate Muslim voices was the rise of an oppositional binary— 'national' versus 'communal'—which would rule the Indian political and social reality henceforward. Just as we have already noticed in the context of Subhas Bose's ideological evolution the steady penetration of a secular or communal binary, on a larger scale too, the inter-related terms of nationalism or communalism would begin to figure in the mainstream discourse from the late 1920s with their very rigid and specified connotations. During this phase of the Nehru Report and Communal Award, the nation and national interest as defined by the Congress would serve as the only model. Nation, henceforth, would be zealously projected as an indivisible whole than a multi-tiered, differentiated concept. It would now decisively reject its 'other' contesting notions, like that of a loose-knit political conglomeration with voluntary and self-asserting constituent communities, or that of any regional particularity. This being so, any individual or organization outside the self-professedly nationalist peripheries of the Congress would immediately run the risk of being labelled as 'anti-national', even 'communalist', and any deviation from the resounding singularity of this very specifically defined 'national' would be viewed as 'anti-national' or 'communal'.[93] For the non-hegemonic groups like Muslims and low-caste Hindus, therefore, 'community interest' would now be a matter of utter intransigency or rebellion. It would mean a regressive mentality, which must be addressed, cured, and reformed before being brought back to the mainstream. 'Difference' had already turned antithetical to the 'national', and any alternative or Moderate vision of nation began to lose its legitimacy by the mid-1930s.

Nation and Its Caste Twist

As the third decade of the twentieth century was coming to a close, nationalists in Bengal faced a curious predicament. On the one hand, in the context of the new discourse of adult suffrage, the need to reorganize the nation's base through greater popular mobilization was felt more accurately, and addressing the particular religious/caste/class identities became more critical. On the other hand, the nation was assuming a more 'unitary' character even within the relatively liberal circles with a renewed emphasis on the indivisibility and uniformity of the national purpose. Confronted with this challenge, the nationalists had to approach the fact of social differences with a new vigour and attempt to resolve the issue from within the fold of the 'Congress' variety of 'unitary nationalism'. This task was not easy. Any serious acknowledgment of difference would have belied the principal 'nationalist' objective of uniting people regardless of any caste, class, or community difference. Again, in the midst of vigorous self-assertion of the non-hegemonic groups and communities like the Muslims or the low-caste groups, not to address the question of 'difference' altogether was an impossibility, even self-defeating in the end. The nationalists therefore had to take into account the fact of difference, and somehow find a way out of this ideological conundrum. Difference was fast becoming a 'problem' to be 'solved', and to be solved within the given parameters of the nation, which included its singularity and indivisibility.

The problem of caste before the nationalists in Bengal in the 1930s thus needs to be examined against this background of the larger predicament. It is for this reason that the caste question is briefly brought into focus in this chapter, although I will almost entirely rely on the existing scholarly works in this respect, with some corroborative references. Even in the absence of new findings, the issue of caste demands a summary review in the present context in order to offer a proposition. I argue here that the deep and complex connections between the caste problem and the troubling nationalist project of unity made the larger problem of difference suddenly more acute. The long-waged debates and conflicts over difference assumed a sharper character in the wake of the Communal Award (1932). The questions of disparate distribution of resources and lack of social respectability were intensified in a way that changed the tenor of nationalist discourse and turned a part of it more openly chauvinistic than ever before.

The decade preceding the declaration of the Communal Award saw an increased awareness about the caste question and social evils like untouchability from both directions—among the high-caste Hindu associations as well as in low-caste groups. As for the high-caste bhadralok initiatives, we can identify various social regeneration agendas, largely inspired by an aim of strengthening the 'Bengali Hindu nation' through greater incorporation and heartier cooperation of the lower castes. On a closer look, two separate trends are discernible here. If the first trend included mass purification movements of shuddhi and sangathan in the conservative Hindu circles, the second trend implied the Gandhian mode of long-term social reconstruction by the relatively liberal sections. The main difference between the two lay in their underlying ethical principles, although there was often very little divergence in terms of their agenda. The conservative Hindu purpose was to emphasize and empower the Hindus as one single community to counter the 'other' challenges raised against it, whereas the Gandhian purpose of strengthening the community was mostly defined in terms of the humanitarian principle of social fairness. But, significantly, their disparate orientations did not often imply dissimilarities in actual practice. For example, in 1924, the Bengal Provincial Hindu Mahasabha held a mammoth meeting at Calcutta, presided over by Swami Avedananda, to preach the urgency of eliminating untouchability and establishing solidarity among the Hindus through shuddhi. Two years later, the Burrabazar Hindu Sabha declared that all Hindus should have equal access to Hindu temples,[94] and in 1929 Swami Satyananda of the Hindu Mission led a temple-entry satyagraha in Munshiganj, Dacca, where a large number of Namasudras were reported to have participated enthusiastically.[95] During the same time, the Gandhian agenda of countering untouchability was gathering momentum in the Bengal countryside. A series of meetings were held in rural areas to discuss 'the programme of Gandhi Maharaj', a number of voluntary associations were formed to this end, and also, a few eminent Congress politicians like J.M. Sengupta were being drawn to this vision of social reconstruction. Gandhi himself placed the right of the low castes to enter Hindu temples at the forefront of his agenda, and even observed a fast on that demand.

The visible overlap of two trends of reform was often somewhat accentuated by some other factors. First, the Gandhians seldom intended to extend the principle of social fairness up to a demand for abolishing the caste system. They only envisaged a less discriminating and more tolerant society with well-defined ties between the higher- and lower-caste strata, but not a thorough overhauling of the social structure. To the Hindu nationalists too, an essential idealization of the indigenous society deemed urgent, with a residual 'nationalist' task of cleansing it of its excesses and abuses, and rendering it more harmonious than before.

Second, as Bandyopadhyay showed, all such attempts from both ends were clearly marked with a high-caste Hindu chauvinism.[96] Both the Gandhian reformers and conservative community-builders used to believe that it was only under the aegis of the high-caste activists that lower sects could ever hope to gain more rights and privileges. The reorganization of the Hindu community would be a Brahmin/nationalist-dictated programme. Not surprisingly, the whole structure of chauvinism or goodwill began to crumble on both ends as soon as the low castes began to spearhead their own movements around their own interests and rights. The underlying tone of upper-caste high-handedness never drew any spontaneous trust from the low-caste groups, which was only affirmed by the political incidents of the 1930s.

Third, possibly as a consequence of these internal proximities, there was a peculiar tendency of the two trends to come together on the same platform. More often than not this platform proved to be that of the Congress Party. As we have already mentioned in the last chapter, during the civil disobedience movement, the renowned social reformer Digindranarayan Bhattacharya, who would later be associated with Hindu Mahasabha, delivered an open call to the 'Depressed Classes' to join the Congress, in return for which he promised that the Congress volunteers would work for the elevation of their social status by accepting water from their hands.[97] The call, however, only evoked a partial and mixed response. Similarly, when the Bengal Provincial Hindu Sabha, in the meeting held at Faridpur in 1925, was blessed by Gandhi's personal presence, and a warm welcome was forwarded by Prafulla Chandra Ray who presided over the meeting, these separate reform movements lost much of their distinctiveness. They coalesced in a way that one might not be able to distinguish between the majoritarian overtures of Hindu Sabhas and the crusade for social tolerance on Gandhian lines. The latter's inability to carve out a space and ideology for itself won it the ill reputation that the Mahasabha had gained, and the prospect of creating a middle ground of social reform movements, where liberal and radical endeavours could successfully meet, was eventually frustrated. In low-caste perceptions, both Gandhian social reform and Congress politics with their own respective brands of nationalism were becoming increasingly associated with the condescending Hindu conservative groups and their target-oriented agenda.[98]

Considering the background, it is understandable how divisive the question of separate electorates or reservation of seats could be for the low-caste Hindus in Bengal in the early 1930s. The low-caste initiatives of empowering their own community had indeed been taking place from the earlier decade. In 1926, various associations for separate caste groups were brought to a common platform with the establishment of the Bengal Depressed Classes Association at a conference held in Kanchrapara. The Namasudra leader Mukunda Behari Mullick served there as the first president. Through this Bengal Depressed Classes Association, caste politics in Bengal was tied up with larger all-India caste movements. In 1930, Bengal representatives were present when the national association condemned the civil disobedience movement in no uncertain terms.[99] At the same meeting, the Report of the Indian Statutory Commission was discussed at length and its recommendation for reservation of seats through a joint electorate was unequivocally criticized. It was argued that to safeguard the Depressed Classes' interest, separate electorates were an absolute necessity.[100] In August 1930, the Depressed Classes representatives in the Bengal Legislative Council voted against a resolution that recommended dominion status for India and demanded 'their right as a minority to separate electorate' and condemned the Congress for its efforts to repudiate it.[101] The declaration of the Communal Award in August 1932 made the Bengal low-caste leaders content with the realization of their long-cherished dream, but the number of seats allocated to them was still not satisfactory. With a renewed enthusiasm, and, more specifically, an indomitable urge to counter the sharp and bitter reactions of the Bengali bhadralok in the aftermath of the Award, the All Bengal Depressed Classes Federation was formed in 1932. The situation, however, changed after Gandhi's decision to fast unto death as a protest against the system of separate electorates, and by the signing of the Poona Pact (September 1932). In a following modification, the Hindu joint electorate was retained with reserved seats for untouchables, now given greater representation than by MacDonald's Award. Understandably enough, the revocation of separate electorates left the Bengali low-caste groups infuriated and deeply frustrated about their much-cherished aims of self-representation.[102]

The high-caste Hindu reactions were, expectedly, sharp and bitter. The divisive provisions put forward by the Award were fiercely attacked. The idea of social segregation as the basis of representation in the administrative bodies used to trouble the bhadralok since the swadeshi days. But evidently, their reactions against the principle of separate electorate or reservation of seats were now sharper than ever, definitely more bitter and pronounced than their stance on the same principle relating to Bengali Muslims. The reason was perhaps not difficult to grasp. 'Difference' was now viewed as an aggressor within one's very own territories, as the proposal for low-caste reservation was about to divide the Hindu community itself and thereby weaken its position before 'other' communities. It is striking that the ideological resistance against the Award became so fierce and sensitive when its implications for the low castes (as opposed to the implications for the Muslims) were in question. The philosophical principles were not the only problematic aspect of the Award; the arithmetical calculations appeared more unsettling. Taking away a good number of seats meant a substantial reduction in the traditional Hindu political base. Democratic principles were defended and upheld not in view of their intrinsic liberal intent but on the merit of their efficacy in giving the society an undifferentiated and united character. The anti-Award discourse could be reviewed here briefly in this light.

Several anti-Award meetings were organized in Calcutta in 1932. The first one, held on 20 August, was presided over by Narendra Kumar Basu. In the meeting at the Town Hall in Calcutta on 4 September 1932, the Award was characterized as one 'of a highly retrograde character, as it has deepened the foundation of communalism and has also extended the principle in new directions contrary to all enlightened and democratic ideas of the age.'[103] Obviously here the 'enlightened and democratic ideas' referred to the spirit of a transcendental social existence where minor sociocultural or economic differences were of no relevance. According to such 'ideas', the question of representation or, more specifically, of self-representation, would apply only to the colonized society at large, but never to its myriad constituent segments. The smaller segments might be provided with wider acceptance and even some extended rights, but not with any political rights which could in turn acknowledge a virtual separation from the imagined 'national' society. As Gandhi started fasting to register his protest against the Award, the Bengali political society was greatly perturbed. Meetings were held in a rush in Calcutta, where prominent leaders and intellectuals such as Prafulla Chandra Ray, Nirmal Chandra Chunder, Ramananda Chatterjee, Shyamaprasad Mookherjee, Basanti Devi, and Nellie Sengupta figured along with the one organized in Santiniketan by Tagore. The demand for a change in the government's decision to save Gandhi's life was consciously supplemented by a forceful condemnation of the social practice of untouchability. It was important for the nationalists to denounce the highly derogatory custom of untouchability in order to convince themselves that they were only opposing the low-caste claims of political separation, not their demand of a fairer social order.[104] It was in this way that the democratic foundations of the national society were being interpreted in a very specific and limited way. The process of nation-building required the extension of liberal democratic principles only to assimilate and appropriate the marginal groups and communities, not to allow them their much-craved space for self-representation. The nation, naturally, had to be founded on the basis of the idealized and abstracted existence of its 'people', not on the basis of its felt and expressed sociocultural interests.

Conceived and defined in such a limited way, the nationalists continued to lament over the undemocratic nature of the Award. A meeting in Calcutta organized around the same issue even as late as July 1936, presided over by Rabindranath Tagore, brought together an impressive array of eminent leaders and ideologues from very different political backgrounds and orientations. Prafulla Chandra Ray, Radha Kumud Mukherjee, Brajendranath Seal, Nilratan Sircar, Saratchandra Chattopadhyay, Shyamaprasad Mookherjee, and Hemchandra Raychowdhury registered their protest in that meeting.[105] In his speech delivered at this meeting, Saratchandra Chattopadhyay, the stalwart author and novelist of Bengal, also marked by an innate social conservatism and a Hindu bhadralok (that is, the middle-class professional most often belonging to high-caste) brand of the unitary nationalist view,[106] denounced the idea of social or religious segregation in political arena in strong and clear terms. He asked, 'Is one's religious faith from now on to become a dominating factor in matters political?'[107] That the caste question, not only divisive but undoubtedly exclusionary in social and political realms, might have deserved greater and deeper consideration was never acknowledged by this conservative strand of Hindu nationalism.[108]

Tagore, on the other hand, stuck to the basic principles of liberalism in a more pronounced way. The foundational principle of Indian civilization had been considerably illiberal, he thought, due to its reliance on a viciously divisive system of caste. From the early days of his literary career, his writings reflected a deep pain and resentment at the way the lower castes were banished outside the peripheries of the bhadralok lands.[109] Even in 1932, when he was deeply agitated about the Communal Award in general, he could not but condemn the Indian society for its 'unforgivable' practices.[110] However, his disapproval of untouchability was never duly matched by his attitude towards the varnashrama, that is, the caste system, which, he thought, although not ideal, was a naturally evolving system in the context of India's endless social diversity. He often expressed an element of indifference towards complete eradication of the system, which was coupled with a hope of getting the residual inequalities removed through the spread of national awareness.[111] In other words, for him, caste was a tolerable evil while untouchability was not.[112] The solution must lie in creating and spreading a spiritual unity across the society and cleansing it of the age-old impurities. He thought the primary onus lay on the high-caste Hindus to take the initiative of reform and do away with the excesses of the system and only then could the lower castes, emboldened by a spiritual sense of uplift, unite with them. As synchronous with his other ideas, he would never favour any socially disruptive method of reform by envisaging or supporting any agitational or political movement by the low castes themselves. So he would not hesitate to take a negative stand on the Award: 'If the low-caste initiatives were seen as disruptive, no wonder their demand for their own representation was equally so. The Communal Award, carrying the malediction of a separated political life, has been pronounced even upon groups and communities of our country that did not want it.'[113]

However, Tagore's opposition to separate electorate or reservation of seats for the low-caste Hindus arose out of a liberal intent to establish a spirit of harmony among all social groups and communities, not out of a conservative impulse of maintaining the high-caste dominance.[114] But here lay the ideological trap. Since Tagore's critique never entailed a commensurate urge of eradicating the caste system, 'harmony' and 'spiritual unity' often failed to make much practical sense in the face of corrosive and persistent demands for self-representation by the low castes. As a result, Tagore's reaction against the Communal Award, just as that of Gandhi, stood deeply ambivalent and opaque, and unduly dismissive of demands of social fairness. By harbouring a neglect of even the basic emotional and practical content of such demands, both Tagore and Gandhi appeared uncharacteristically cold and unsympathetic to the question of caste 'difference' in a very critical juncture of anti-colonial nationalism.

Democracy, as Tagore understood it, was meaningful only in its ability to represent individual or national interests; any middle ground between the individual and the nation was reactionary in spirit and retrograde in nature. If we remember his position on the Communal Award, 'the separated political life' was a 'non-idea' for Tagore, because the 'groups and communities of our country did not want it'. The level of wishful thinking involved in this and many other similar observations appears rather bewildering, especially considering the contemporary political climate. Internal dissensions on the question of community or caste representation proved to be intensely searing at the time. The typical bhadralok indifference, or more charitably, unawareness, could not be incidental but very fundamental in shaping the polemical ground for their critique of the Award. It was also a pointer to the way the claims of difference were totally overlooked or dismissed in the context of caste while envisaging a national and/or democratic society. Of course, beyond the ideological aspirations for a unitary society, there were equally troublesome apprehensions about the future 'prospects' of Hindu bhadraloks, now reduced to a statutory minority position. One must pay attention to the resigned desperation in Tagore at the colonial attempt of crippling the 'Hindu community', and his unquestioned acceptance of the Hindus as being *'one* [unified] community' even after his thoroughly steadfast and pointedly pungent denunciations of the system of caste discrimination:

> For reasons which need not be explained, the Hindus are handicapped most in the coming constitution. Though a tacit compliment, it is an open assault employing a novel political arithmetic invidious enough to turn the methods of responsible government into most irresponsible means by which one community is made permanently independent of the co-operation of the other.[115]

The alternative system imagined or idealized was not one of a different arrangement of social redistribution, but one where 'differences' were not to be tolerated for the sake of 'national unity'. How to implement such a state of ideal accomplishment was, nevertheless, a question consistently ignored. As a result, while there was certain legitimate ground for a larger bhadralok anxiety during this era of divisive administrative experiments, the unaddressed question of social fairness in the end sabotaged even the legitimate parts of the critique of the Communal Award.

It was exactly here that the demarcating line between the conservative majoritarian position and the liberal critique began to get blurred. Even the argument against the notion of separate electorates lost a large part of its reasonableness when it repeated the acrimonies routinely expressed against the Award. Commenting on the 'underprivileged status' of the upper-caste Hindus, the same report commented:

> ... the Hindus have never stood either for separate electorate or fixed quotas and weightages of representation setting up statutory majorities and statutory minorities in the legislature against all conceivable canons of democracy. The Award has grievously denied the claims of Bengal Hindus to such weightages. And yet in the Bengal legislature, the scheme of weightages has given full scope for other communities.[116]

The report pointed out that many of the so-called backward classes made impressive advancements in recent years, and that the Namasudras and Rajbanshis, therefore, hardly needed any special constitutional protective arrangements.[117] In all deliberations and debates on the Communal Award, never had the fact been addressed that the constitutional arrangement was not entirely a brainchild of the British alone, or with their remarkably insidious calculations to cripple the 'Bengali nation', but was, to a very large extent, a response to the vigorous demands and grievances posed by the communities and low-caste groups. The voicing of difference from the indigenous communities and low-caste groups had thus remained an unrecognized fact in the mainstream Hindu nationalist thought, even in its most liberal versions and during its most liberal moments.

The reactions against the Poona Pact, which provided for joint electorates of caste Hindus and untouchables with a reservation of seats for the latter, eventually led to some organizational endeavours. The Congress Nationalist party was born (1932) to defend the rights and interests of upper-caste Hindus in Bengal. True, this new party never gained much political prominence, but together with the Hindu Mahasabha, they constituted an extreme pole of social conservatism, thereby tearing the Bengali political society further apart. Roughly at the same time, there also followed a lull in the caste-centric agenda of the Congress, finally leading to its disappearance from 1935 onwards.[118] While the reasons behind such withdrawal of bhadralok interests were manifold (like Gandhi's repeated cancellation of visiting harijan villages of eastern Bengal or the organizational or financial difficulties faced by the local leaders), in the eyes of the low-caste Namasudra peasants of Bengal, it seemed nothing less than a resounding negligence to their claims of rights and representation. One must note that the 'shift'—both real and perceived—of the Congress politics, and the body of nationalist ideology associated with it, towards conservatism became decisive only in the mid-1930s. Only a few years earlier, Subhas Chandra Bose was seen to voice a moving call in favour of a joint electorate with the provision of 'reservation' from the platform of the Congress itself. In his opinion, the proposition of separate electorates being a negation of the idea of nation, joint electorates must be guarded, even at the cost of conceding reservation to some sections of the society.[119] Evidently, Congress nationalism in the early 1930s, in spite of its endless internal dissensions and factionalism, began to be viewed as the principal contender for all the alternative claims of difference. It seemed to the upholders of such claims that the conservatives and the liberals of all shades were only acting in unison to oppose these differences. The 'others' of the nation, as a result, shifted more towards the resigned belief that the chances of obtaining fair representation in any future constitutional arrangement under the aegis of the self-professed 'nationalists' of the Congress sort were, at best, scanty.

The New Radicalism: 'Nation' from Below

When Subhas Bose considered that concessions such as reservation of seats within a system of joint electorates might be necessary for an inclusive nationalism, he was, in fact, appreciating the enormous importance of the principle of self-representation for the Muslims and low-castes. The pragmatist in him came to the fore; the idealist in him stepped back. Despite being ideologically and temperamentally in favour of a unitary nation with all its internal differences, and a steadfast enthusiast for preserving the 'umbrella' character of Congress where all interests and identities were to be accommodated side by side, he ultimately found himself in a position to concede to the demands for self-representation of the marginal communities. His understanding of the multi-dimensional popular interests had something to do with his own political journey. Bose recognized the emergence of the national spirit to be the most spectacular achievement of Gandhian movements, which had the potential for arousing the youths and workers all over the country by its sheer 'spontaneity'.[120] But the pragmatist also did not fail to figure out that Congress politics continued to suffer from an important lacking—the failure to transcend the social class barriers in its political and economic agenda. During 1930–3, Bose, placed at the helm of municipal politics in Calcutta, devoted a lot of time to the youth groups and trade unions of Bengal, for which he even subjected himself to bitter criticism from various quarters.[121] The focus on the youth was bolstered by his connections with the revolutionaries of Bengal, primarily the Jugantar and Anusilan samitis, and with the 'Bengal Volunteers' serving as an effective organizational meeting ground for all these forces. Bose's statement at the Maharashtra Provincial Congress in Poona (1928) that 'democracy is by no means a Western institution; it is a human institution', may be understood in his growing awareness of the mass base of the Congress as a national organization.[122] He also became involved in three major labour strikes during this period: one by the railway workshop workers at Liluah; the second by the jute workers of Bengal; and the third, by the workers of Tata Iron and Steel Corporation in Jamshedpur.

Bose's example is telling, because, during the late 1920s, one can identify a decisive break in the terrain of the nation in Bengal—never before were the 'people' placed as a central focus of the entire framework of nationalist thoughts and politics.[123] After Das's death, the Swarajists were being squarely charged for neglecting 'the constructive programme'.[124] One of the leading journals pointed out that 'people' were gradually losing all faith and hope in the Congress because both the Swarajists and the Congress leaders had long been neglecting their cause and interests.[125] The ideological discomfort around the inherent limitations of the 'nation' was also suitably bolstered by its political logic. It was becoming increasingly clear that without a strong support base amongst the working classes and peasant societies, the nationalist claims could not be strengthened further. However, one needs to be cautious while appreciating this political logic. It cannot minimize either the long-standing ideological tussle between the nation's urge to transcend differences and its inability to do so, or the impact of global ideologies like socialism or Bolshevism. The emerging leftist-socialists, like those in the Communist Party of India (CPI), the Congress Socialist Party, or the 'Royists' who followed the great theorist–politician M.N. Roy, had various levels of connections with this international Left movement, while their support base in the region often overlapped with those of Subhas Bose, the Bengal Labour Party, and, last but not the least, the Nikhil Banga Praja Samiti (1929), later renamed as Krishak Praja Party (1936).[126]

The importance of the KPP needs to be examined carefully. While this is done in the next chapter, it is important to mention here that around 1936, this party represented the question of 'difference' from within the folds of a larger nation more successfully than all other previous and contemporary political associations of Bengal. Once again it was the momentum of the competitive and representative politics that paved the way for mobilization of lower classes within the Muslim community, and an effective, though temporary, tying up of the demands of rural societies with those of the urban middle classes.[127] By the same logic, it was even hoped that only through the promotion of local welfare that communal disharmony or occasional clashes could be minimized. [128]

Ideas were not the only plane on which Bengal was bearing the impact of the global trends. The rural societies of Bengal underwent severe strains due to fluctuations in the agricultural market during the Depression years. The excessive dependence on cash crops like jute led to a virtual disintegration of the small-holding peasant economy, as jute lost its viability as a global cash crop in the late 1920s. At the same time, fiscal policies hit the regional agrarian economy very hard. The crunch in the credit inflow into the rural societies caused abject helplessness for the eastern Bengal peasantry, long inhabiting a highly monetized agrarian system, critically bound by credit relations. In fact, as a result of these two major changes, eastern Bengal villages were more hard-hit compared to the relatively less monetized peasant societies of western Bengal, where small-holding peasantry and large-demesne labour co-existed.[129] However, the latter did not escape the dire consequences of the crisis that took place in the grain-redistribution system throughout the province. The usual practices of grain-lending were disrupted by the general trends of credit squeeze in the colonial markets.[130] On the whole, this period experienced a gradually disintegrating credit market, which resulted in threatened agrarian relations of production.

The changing rural society slowly gave rise to a larger political discontent, co-mingled with the general anti-zamindar grievances of the Muslim or low-caste peasantry. The complex social–economic dissensions eventually saw the emergence of a small but determined urban youth network upholding the interests and demands of the peasants in the countryside and the factory workers in the towns and cities. These groups exerted considerable pressure on the political leadership, a part of which was already infused with a socialist or communist spirit. This rather potent trend of socialist politics opened up a new platform for the claims of difference, and gradually emerged as an alternative site of nation-building. Muslims and Hindus jointly organized some of these associations and formulated socio-economic and political agenda together.

Some remarkable instances of such cross-communitarian socialist projects demand mention. Towards the close of 1925, the Labour Swaraj Party was founded within the Indian National Congress in Calcutta by Maulavi Qutubuddin Ahmad (a former associate of Maulana Abul Kalam Azad), Muzaffar Ahmed, the poet Kazi Nazrul Islam, Maulavi Shamsuddin Hussain, and Hemanta Sarkar (a dissident Swarajist). A promise of a new kind was surely brought forward by this venture. Nevertheless, it was mainly with the formation of Bangiya Krishak o Sramik Dal or Bengal Peasants' and Workers' Party, born out of the annual Nikhil Bangiya Praja Sammilan held in Krishnanagar in 1926, that the inter-community divides were blurred with an ambitious stroke. The conference was opened with an 'Ode to Labour' (*Sramiker Gaan*), composed and sung by Nazrul himself, and conducted deliberations on the Tenancy (Amendment) Bill of 1928. Nazrul enthusiastically took charge of *Langal*, a weekly news magazine published by the party. In its very first issue, the objectives of the new party were elaborated, along with a set of stern criticisms of Congress nationalism. Projecting itself as a party for the peasants and workers, and for attaining Swaraj for the country, it attempted to strike a common ground for all marginal societies:

> The cultivators have got no proprietary right over the land they cultivate, nor have they got full share of the crops produced by their labour.... It is said that all these grievances will disappear after we have attained swaraj. But if swaraj dawns, who will benefit? Those who eventually will, have never done anything to other members of society. The system of one class of men getting nourished at the expense of others must be ended now. The society should no longer decide the fate of the sudras who live in the villages. Rather, these sudras would henceforth direct the course of the society.[131]

A movement for swaraj or self-rule with the sudras of the village at its forefront—a curious mingling of the class objectives, caste movement, and a nationalist purpose. What else was needed to set the 'nationalist agenda with a difference'? Muzaffar Ahmed in several articles sharply criticized the educated urban middle class for keeping themselves confined to the Congress-brand nationalist movement and for 'championing the cause of the rich'. The labouring classes were called upon to 'come forward holding aloft the standard of liberation'.[132] In 1926, *Ganavani*, which replaced *Langal* as the mouthpiece of the new party, launched scathing criticisms of both the Muslim leaders for their excessive preoccupation with religious symbolism and the national leadership for its failure to provide a clear definition of swaraj.[133] No wonder, while these writers and their mouthpiece journals celebrated the cause of a broad-based, supra-communitarian nation, they were also careful to underline the 'class angle' of their own national aspirations. Muzaffar Ahmed wrote in *Ganavani*, 'All of us want to achieve swaraj. But what indeed swaraj is has not yet been defined, even though the movement has been going on for ages.'[134] When the famously conservative Bengali Muslim journal *Mohammadi* bitterly criticized *Ganavani* for undermining religious identity for the sake of championing class-interest,[135] it was squarely accused by Ahmed for misguiding 'class-struggles of the Muslim rayats into a communal channel'.[136] The *Ganavani* group organized a special youth conference of Dhaka district in 1927. While presiding over this session, Ahmed condemned the nationalist leaders and the revolutionary activists for never taking into account the interests of the oppressed and exploited classes of society:

> Destruction of the old system and its replacement by a new one is what is called revolution. Destruction of the capitalist mode of exploitation and establishment of the rule of peasants and workers alone can be termed as revolution…. Judged from this angle, it is doubtful whether we can call these secret terrorist movements truly revolutionary.[137]

With the dismissal of the 'Congress nationalism' and terrorist movements alike, the Bengal Peasants' and Workers' Party painstakingly dissociated itself from the local organizations which had so far been operating in the countryside. There had already been a trend of tenant movements in rural Bengal among the Muslim prajas or rayats against the oppressive zamindari system. However, the radical revolutionaries refused to acknowledge the prevalent modes of the praja movement as a progressive interest group as it was primarily led by the people of intermediary *talukdar* (landlord or tenure-holder, usually the rent-collector) and *jotedar* (holder of cultivable land) classes.[138] The lack of cooperative ties even at the initial stage with such intermediary groups did not lead the new party into a strategic position to mobilize substantial sections of peasantry. Many of them were already tied up into the mesh of local-level organizations, led by the praja leaders. As a result, although the Bengal Workers' and Peasants' Party played a leading role during the Calcutta Corporation Scavengers' strike in Calcutta and jute-mill strikes in Chengail and Bauria near Calcutta in 1928, it hardly achieved any success in developing a mass-base in the countryside. Perhaps the climax of its career was reached in December 1928, when thousands of industrial workers under its aegis stormed the Congress session in Calcutta and successfully moved a resolution demanding complete independence. With Ahmed's arrest, as well as the onset of the famous Meerut conspiracy case for the trial of Ahmed and his associated trade union activists, the party began to decline, finally being disbanded at the beginning of the next decade. In spite of great promises and organized activities on a limited scale, the task of the Workers' and Peasants' Party remained only half-accomplished. The failure in mobilizing the peasantry figured in stark contrast to the party's short but vibrant career in Calcutta. Apparently, an exclusive focus on the economic issues kept leaders like Ahmed unaware of the potential of the leadership of a communitarian elite working with a similar agenda in the localities. Since the basis of the localized praja movement was often the communitarian ties of the villages, socialist leaders like Ahmed denounced these endeavours. Their aversion to religious practice also extended to an aversion towards the religiously informed social networks of the Bengali countryside.[139] To what extent this social radicalism was acceptable to the rural people still remains unclear. What is clear though is its relative failure in the peasant issues compared to the workers' movements. Unfortunately, this radical leadership mostly kept itself busy with political deliberations, planning and executing demonstrations, and meetings in the urban areas within and outside Bengal. To establish branches of the Workers' and Peasants' Party in other provinces as well, especially in Bombay, and also to publish a weekly journal named *Kranti* were some of the immediate objectives around 1927–8.[140]

These praja leaders played the critically important role of intermediaries between the politics and the ideology of nation. They were keen on ensuring greater representation of agrarian issues in the literary–cultural space, as well as in the politics of the Legislative Council. The tenets of socialism cast a significant influence on a number of prominent Muslims. Shahidullah, the Bhashacharya (Great Linguist); Kazi Nazul Islam, the poet; Kazi Motahar Hussain Chaudhuri and Said Abul Hussain, the two leading stalwarts of the Muslim Sahitya Samaj all served as principal ideologues behind the praja movement. Shahidullah sought to connect the tenets of brotherhood and egalitarianism of Islam with the

basic principles of socialism, though in a somewhat amateurish way.[141]
Motahar Hussain Chaudhuri and Abul Hussain made it clear that they
believed in the 'Emancipation of the Intellect' (Buddhir Mukti), and
therefore remained respectful towards socialist principles without directly
belonging to any radical party organizations of contemporary Bengal.[142]

Inside the Legislative Council too, the local praja leaders were represented by a host of Muslim legislators. The Bengal Tenancy (Amendment)
Bill was introduced in the council in 1928 with the aim of granting the
occupant rayats the right to transfer their occupancy rights. While the
Congress spokesmen were divided on the issue, the Muslim legislators
mostly spoke in favour of the rayats and vehemently opposed the bill.
Abdur Rahim argued that the proposed 'Right of pre-emption' given
to the zamindars would result in '… really transferring of all the land
gradually into the hands of the zamindars', and the rayats 'will be turning
into mere serfs'.[143] The Muslim legislators, in their attempts to remove
the controversial clauses from the bill moved amendment after amendment to protect the right of the tenants. The actual tenant was defined
by Tamizuddin Khan, who championed their cause as most urgent: 'The
*bargadar*s are in fact the most helpless class of peasants in this country …
and we should try not to rob them of their present rights [italics origi-
nal].'[144] Fazlul Huq unequivocally claimed that even the 'under-rayat
shall acquire a right of occupancy in his holding in the same manner and
in the same extent as a rayat.'[145] The amendments received support from
most Muslim legislators. The bill was nevertheless passed in the council
in the teeth of opposition, marking inside and outside the council a
clear line between the pro-zamindar and pro-rayat groups. The swarajists eventually sided with the pro-zamindar interest groups of Congress
inside the council, while the majority of the Muslim legislators opted
for the path of resistance. Outside the council, *The Statesman, Amrita
Bazar Patrika, Forward* (representing the swarajists) strongly supported
the bill, and most Muslim papers, including *The Mohammadi* and the
The Mussalman, adopted a severely critical stance. The *Soltan* wrote,

> Nothing can be more regrettable than that the Swarajists … join[ing]
> with the Government against the rayats….The serious injury done to the
> rayats this time by the treachery of the Swarajists, is indeed more fatal
> than even what has been brought by the Permanent Settlement.[146]

The Act 'reduced the 80 per cent of the population engaged in agricultural pursuits to mere serfs', thought *The Mussalman*.[147] *Anandabazar*

Patrika, a prominent 'Hindu nationalist' paper, significantly enough, did not follow the usual pattern of reaction to the proposed amendment. It supported the cause of the rayats and opposed the pro-landlord lobbies at the assembly. Almost along the lines of argument the Bengal Muslim leaders upheld at this time, this newspaper accused the swarajists of double-standards. It alleged that while the latter had posed themselves as the 'worshippers of democracy', 'representatives of the rayats', and the well-wishers of the nation, they belied the trust placed on them by the 'people' at a critical juncture.[148]

The objective conditions for forming a peoples' organization as an alternative to the provincial Congress seemed to be present at this juncture. At a big protest rally (on 13 September 1928) in Calcutta, urges were made to form a party to represent the tenants both inside and outside the council. A few days later, even *Mohammadi* came out with the same proposal, pointing out that the interests of the non-Muslim peasants and non-Muslim zamindars had forever been at odds with each other, leaving almost nothing in common between the rich Muslims and their co-religionist cultivators working in the fields. The shift in tone of the *Mohammadi*, known to be a mouthpiece of the more conservative Bengali Muslim community, is significant. This shift was temporary in nature, no doubt, clear from its many other usual stances like the insistence on the Urduization of Bengali language, or the frantic calls for the right of cow slaughter. It is indicative of a shifting definition of the 'Muslim interest', cautiously attempted by *Mohammadi* in the late 1920s, in the face of the need to popularize their claims of Muslim Bengali identity. This same journal also pleaded for the formation of at least one rayat committee in every village and every sub-division,[149] and convene an All Bengal Rayats' Conference in order to give the 'Bengali Muslim interests' their long-deserved recognition. The simultaneous stances of sympathizing with the non-Muslim rayats and taking on the non-Muslim rural landed gentry and urban professionals thus illustrated the complex nature of the *Mohammadi* brand of 'Bengali Muslim' politics in Bengal. Its main target being the high-caste, urban (mostly Calcutta-based) Hindu cultural and political domination in the province, it did not have qualms in appealing to the underclasses and low castes for a joint regional front. In doing so, the most meaningful political task in the late 1920s and early 1930s seemed to be aligning with radical rhetoric of the time, and not complying with the mode of Congress politics.[150]

Radical politics in Bengal towards the end of the 1920s, therefore, had several strands. The mainstream Congress leaders who tried hard to draw in the communists and socialists, the local level praja organizers operating in the villages, and then the urban middle-class Muslim or Hindu professionals gathered in small groups to voice the peasants' and workers' grievances—all these represented simultaneous trends, with limited overlap and varying degrees of success. The radical politics of the Congress was bound to fail because of its internal ideological contradictions. The civil disobedience movement (1930–1) brought only limited success as far as the workers' movement was concerned.[151] The post-Depression era was marked by a long-drawn industrial depression. Yet the Congress–communist platform began to disintegrate fast, marking the decline of a potentially promising trend of events in nationalist politics.[152] Changes in the communist strategy also contributed to the decline of the united front. The earlier communist strategy of unity-cum-struggle, of lending support to the Congress on issues of anti-imperialism while resisting its bourgeois tendencies,[153] had to be replaced following the injunctions of the Sixth Comintern Congress (December 1928) by a more 'revolutionary' strategy of all-out resistance to the bourgeois forces, and by implication, to the Congress itself.

The workers' movement, gaining momentum steadily during this era, thus failed to draw in stable and unswerving leadership in the realm of formal politics. In a similar way, the peasant unrest in the Bengal countryside in the early 1930s did not find much political guidance from the nationalist arena. We have seen that the swarajists opposed tenancy status to bargadars (sharecroppers) or enhancement of zamindari power over the rayats. The Congress representatives also steadfastly blocked the amendments to give bargadars tenancy rights and thus reduce jotedar domination.

In this situation, the only sympathetic champions of the rayat cause appeared to be the Muslim legislators, who often maintained connections with the local praja leaders. It's important to note that the Namasudra and Muslim bargadar movements in the mid-1920s in districts such as Mymensingh, Dhaka, Pabna, Khulna, and Nadia failed to draw any significant nationalist effort to integrate such dispersed agitation into a broader movement.[154] More alarmingly, when the specific demographic composition of the eastern Bengal countryside increasingly turned the bargadar movement into a religiously fanned agitation against the Hindu upper-caste rural elites, and the latter still stuck to their habitual demonstration of socioeconomic superiority,[155] little attention was paid by the Congress leadership. No doubt, this failure had much to do with the fateful lack of coordination between the local community-based praja leaders. Slowly but inevitably, many sections of the Muslim rayats began to perceive these 'class' conflicts in 'community' terms, while the Namasudras linked up the 'class' issues with broader movements for 'caste' upliftment.[156] As a result, while the need for broadening the base of the 'nation' was felt more acutely than ever by the political societies, and the need for choosing representatives to voice their grievances became unmistakably urgent for the disadvantageous and downtrodden 'people', a dual trend became remarkable in the Bengal countryside. The 'community' leaders strengthened themselves by representing and verbalizing the concerns of 'difference', and proved to be the only political champions of the cause of the peasantry, predominantly Muslim in composition. On the contrary, the political groups or activists who were averse to interpreting and mobilizing the nation around the marks and demands of community and/or other identities gradually began to recede. As a result, the distance between the leading champions of the nation and the vocal defenders of difference was widened by the course of rayat politics in Bengal.

New Constitution and New Political Alliances

The links between the Muslim praja leaders and the agrarian societies of Bengal were established by the middle of the 1930s. Though dithering and tenuous in nature, these links began to be reflected in political reorganizations taking place after the constitutional declaration of 1935. The existing political parties and groups started reinventing themselves, and along with it emerged new compromises and alliances among various competing regional parties, based on their shared concern for the politics of the masses. It is interesting to examine how this politics of the masses contained from the very beginning the strong internal pulls of identity differences on the one hand, as well as a non-negligible potential of surpassing those very differences on the other.

The Muslim League of Bengal enjoyed a near autonomous existence by this time, loosening their ties from the all-India body.[157] The relative independence in its functioning generated an impetus for the Provincial League to further its stronghold in the region. It developed closer ties with the praja samitis, while many leaders associated themselves directly with the villages.[158] But in its new agrarian overtures, the BPML was often outmanoeuvred by the Praja Party, known as Krishak Praja Party from April 1936. When, on the eve of the provincial elections, the Government of India Act laid down the new constitutional parameters in 1935, the KPP succeeded in entrenching itself in rural

Bengal in an unprecedented way. No doubt, the party was troubled by factional clashes between the leaders with a strong rural following in eastern Bengal such as Fazlul Huq and the 'urban bosses' such as Akram Khan and Abdul Momin of western Bengal. Momin was nominated for the post of the president of the Praja Party against Huq (1935) and was defeated decisively. This was because the young radicals inside the party threw their support behind Huq, as did the English-educated professionals like Abul Mansur Ahmed of Mymensingh, Shamsuddin Ahmed of Nadia, and Syed Nausher Ali of Jessore. Soon Huq emerged as the first Bengali leader who served as the most effective bridge between the rayat lobby and the urban professional middle classes of the Bengali Muslim society. In this way, the rise of Fazlul Huq as the primary leader with an undisputed command on the Bengal Muslim society ensured a radical and progressive alternative to the old-style leadership, namely, the old guard of the BPML and the Provincial Congress.

The Krishak Praja Party was surely not the only political body to represent agrarian grievances during this period. A new party called the United Muslim Party was also launched in 1936 by the relatively conservative sections with Suhrawardy as their spokesperson, and Ispahani, Abdur Rahman, and the aggrieved deserters of the KPP like Akram Khan and Abdul Momin as its prime members. This new party soon raised the charge of being oblivious to the 'real' Muslim interests against the KPP, while the latter debunked the former as a 'ministerial' or a 'zamindar' party. While several regional parties competed with each other on the legitimacy of their representation of agrarian issues, their ties with the all-India League still remained loose and insignificant. Not a single representative from Bengal was present at the Bombay Session of the All India Muslim League in 1936.[159] Evidently, even three decades after the birth of the Muslim League, 'Muslim politics' in general, or its 'Bengal chapter' in particular, never had one single united or uniform trend of activities or ideology. With deep internal contestations and contradictions, Bengali Muslims were still in search of a political movement which would direct them to combine a mass politics with their own identity markers.

Events, nevertheless, took a drastic turn after 1936. The AIML was sought to be revived by Muhammad Ali Jinnah as an effective bargaining counter against the Congress before and during the regrouping of power under the provisions of the new Government of India Act of 1935.[160] He even began a skilful dealing with the regional leaders of Bengal and ensured a better control of its regional organization. Most of the United Muslim Party was quickly won over by the AIML with a sharp eye on the upcoming elections.[161] Jinnah presented the image of 'Muslim solidarity' in Bengal. The alleged 'solidarity' was, of course, a figment of his imagination, put forward rather deliberately. The challenges before this claim of Muslim solidarity were patently discernible. First, the KPP remained determined to maintain its independence from the League, and second, tough resistance was also put up by the BPML, making a rather bold, though temporary, move to align itself with the KPP.[162] Before the elections, nevertheless, Jinnah's relentless persuasions made the BPML concede to not contesting the elections despite its extended support to the KPP. As a result, finally, during the elections, the KPP was the only remaining force to oppose the League Parliamentary Board, the League's provincial counterpart in Bengal. Thus, on the eve of the elections in 1937, the conflict between the two Bengali Muslims organizations came to a head with the KPP and the League Board directly opposing each other in the elections. More interestingly, this conflict necessitated a settlement of regional claims between these two parties. The KPP, the more 'Bengali' organization, pressed Jinnah to present his case in a deliberately regional context, and also in an inter-communal context. As a result, during his visit to Calcutta in August 1936, Jinnah delivered two rather exceptional speeches, one at the Town Hall, and the other, at the Ashutosh Hall in Calcutta University. On both occasions, he had to mention in clear terms that any meaningful advance of national politics would essentially rely on a Hindu–Muslim alliance, and a successful negotiation of the contentious matters between the two communities in Bengal.[163]

With such an acute internal conflict within the Bengali Muslim community, the elections of 1937 were now about to take place—the first major election with the new perspective of provincial assembly.[164] By this time, Bengal had a significant increase in the electorate, from six million to about thirty million, and already carved out a distinct position in all-India constitutional calculations due to its characteristic population ratio. The critical importance of Bengal, one of the two prominent Muslim-majority provinces of British India, was becoming clear to both Hindu and Muslim all-India leaderships. The AIML was desperate in its bid to control the Bengali Muslim politics. However, its desperation was still counter-balanced by the regional Muslim forces already out to test their strength against the League through the robust platform of the KPP. The tasks before the KPP were unenviable. At one level, it had to raise a fight for its legitimacy to represent the Bengali

Muslim interest on electoral grounds. At another level, it needed to go beyond the trap of any singular identity in order to further its influence in the mixed and diverse rural societies to establish and assert its own legitimacy. In the next chapter, we shall see how this particular strand of Bengali Muslim politics would rise to meet this dual agenda of taking its proposed Bengali Muslim 'nation' to the localities and to mobilize support around the local agrarian grievances.

Alienating a Torn Identity

To sum up, although the variously imagined ideas of region–nation faced critical challenges with the Nehru Report and Communal Award during this period, their potential was still thriving. The immense internal dissensions among Bengali Muslims on the cultural or political self-representation during the late 1920s and the first half of 1930s were the key factors behind keeping this idea of regional identity afloat. Just as in earlier periods, their deep, idiosyncratic bonding with the region–nation still continued to be reflected even in their communitarian ways of imagining the nation. For many Bengali Muslims, usually dismissed as 'communalists', identities were indeed multiple, layered, and co-existing, and nation was, somewhat indefinably, multiform rather than uniform. Even faced with the needs of mass politics, the urge for uniting the Muslim rayats did not inevitably preclude the possibility of upholding a joint front with the non-Muslim peasant societies.

At the same time, the reception of this deeply torn but steadfastly upheld Bengali Muslim identity was often not recognized or appreciated by the dominant Hindu Bengali nationalism.[165] This rather deplorable failure was pronounced in all cultural, linguistic, or even political questions raised during this period, as this chapter has argued. Yet it would be historiographically misleading to depict this failure as a chauvinist communalism on the part of the Bengali Hindus in general. The crisis was much deeper, more fundamentally structural, and therefore, in a way, more inescapable. While the majoritarian orthodoxy of the conservative Hindu nationalists, an indubitably apparent trend, is easier to understand, we should not fail to appreciate that many of the liberal Hindu nationalists of this era found themselves in a quandary on the question of striking a compromise between their respect for differences on the one hand and the occasional need to transcend the same differences on the other.

In fact, the compromise, if any, seemed viable only within the region–nation of Bengal than in the context of larger Indian nation, where contradictions and conflicts were larger and more complex in nature. At the juncture of 1936–7, the provincial politics thus reflected a still buoyant prospect of region–nation, with its sharp contradictions lurking underneath. Whether it would be possible to address or resolve these contradictions in the interest of the region–nation was yet to be seen.

Notes

1. For the idea of 'enumerated communities', see Sudipto Kaviraj, 'The Imaginary Institution of India', in *Subaltern Studies*, vol. 7: *Writings on South Asian History and Society*, edited by Partha Chatterjee and Gyanendra Pandey (Delhi: Oxford University Press, 1993).

2. Bepinchandra Pal, 'Rashtra-niti', *Basumati*, March 1926, p. 679.

3. Pal, 'Rashtra-niti'.

4. Pal, 'Rashtra-niti'.

5. Right from the non-cooperation days, Pal developed an inherent dislike towards the agitationist nationalism of Gandhi. This political stalwart, once so celebrated for his fiery Extremist brand of politics, had turned into a 'pacifist' by the 1920s. In Pal's own words, 'I am so determinedly opposed to the Gandhi cult and campaign, because it seeks to replace the present Govt. by no Govt., or possibly by the priestly autocracy of Mahatma.' *Hindu*, 5 March 1932, quoted in 'Parishishta 1' (postscript 1) in Pal's unfinished autobiography, *Sattar Batsar* [Seventy Years] (Calcutta: Patralekha, 2013), p. 192.

6. Unlike Surendranath Banerjea, Bepinchandra Pal did not dissociate himself formally from the Congress. When Banerjea left the Congress, he formed a Liberal Party along with Dinshaw Wacha, Chimanlal Setalvad, and Tej Bahadur Sapru, and availed the new political opportunities of the Montagu–Chelmsford Reforms. Pal, on the other hand, left mainstream politics in silence, never attempted to form any new organization, and kept himself more or less aloof from the political scene till his death in 1932.

7. To mention only a few: 'Bangalar Pradeshikata' (editorial), *Dhaka Prakash*, August 1936; 'Bangali Jati', *Bangabani*, September 1927; 'Bangalar Katha', *Bangashree*, July 1933.

8. Subhash Chandra Bose, 'Bengal's Spiritual Quest', *The Essential Writings of Netaji Subhas Chandra Bose*, edited by Sisir K. Bose and Sugata Bose (Delhi: Oxford University Press, 1997), p. 79. The legacy of Das is explained in one of Bose's letters written to Hemendranath Dasgupta, 'Deshbandhu Chittaranjan Das', in *Essential Writings of Netaji Subhas Chandra Bose*, pp. 61–70.

9. Bose writes: 'Swaraj for the masses is not a new thing in the world. Europe preached this doctrine long ago; but it is comparatively new in the field of Indian politics. Of course, thirty years ago, Swami Vivekananda spoke in that vein in his book entitled *Bartaman Bharat*, but that message of the Swamiji was never echoed from our political platforms' ('Deshbandhu Chittaranjan Das', p. 68).

10. Bose threw a question to other leaders: 'Let me ask, how many of our Hindu leaders can declare on oath that they do not hate the Muslims? On the other hand, how many of the Muslim leaders can likewise say that they do not hate the Hindus? In religious belief, the Deshbandhu was a Vaishnavite, but people of all faiths had a place in his large heart' ('Deshbandhu Chittaranjan Das', p. 68).

11. S.C. Bose, 'Deshbandhu Chittaranjan Das', p. 67.

12. S.C. Bose, 'Deshbandhu Chittaranjan Das', p. 67. Das's faith in the efficacy of 'pacts' between different but negotiating communities reminds us of the other contemporary ideologue of India, approaching the problem of religious and class differences with a similar sense of urgency and imagination. Mahatma Gandhi, much during the same time, was elaborating his concepts of 'contracts' between various communities and classes in the society to achieve a common platform for social and political actions. However, Gandhian 'contracts' had also retained a space for 'trusteeship', while Das would emphasize on the mechanism of common interests. The links and distance between Das's idea of 'pact and the Gandhian idea of 'contracts' have not yet been explored.

13. S.C. Bose, 'Deshbandhu Chittaranjan Das', p. 67.

14. Subhash Chandra Bose's presidential address at the Maharashtra Provincial Conference, Pune, 1928, cited in Sisir Kumar Bose (ed.), *Netaji: Collected Works*, vol. 5 (Calcutta: Netaji Research Bureau, 1985), p. 248.

15. Subhash Chandra Bose's presidential address at the Maharashtra Provincial Conference, Pune, 1928, p. 248.

16. *Essential Writings of Netaji Subhas Chandra Bose*, p. 68.

17. In explaining how important it was to know the 'others', Bose pointed out that, while in jail, Das used to have frequent discussions on the affinity between the two cultures with Maulana Akram Khan, an emerging radical leader of the Bengali Muslims. See *Essential Writings of Netaji Subhas Chandra Bose*, p. 86.

18. *Essential Writings of Netaji Subhas Chandra Bose*, p. 86.

19. *Netaji: Samagra Rachanabali*, vol. 4 (Calcutta: Ananda Publishers, 1992), p. 148.

20. For example, Bose reminded the youth and the students of Bengal that 'if we are to rid India once and for all of the canker of *communalism* and fanaticism, we have to begin work among our youth [emphasis added]'. See *Essential Writings of Netaji Subhas Chandra Bose*, p. 87. The evolution

of the term 'communal' in colonial India demands scholarly attention. It underwent a remarkable journey from a simple term denoting identities or interests or cultural particularities of a 'community' to its very specific and derogatory use, deliberately 'othered' first by nationalism, and later by secularism, in the context of twentieth-century India. To pinpoint when and how this transition took place might be difficult. However, it is important to remember that 'communalism' in its usual pejorative sense was becoming quite familiar in Indian nationalist discourse by the 1920s. The journey of a word from a positive, constructive sense to a negative and dismissive expression left its various silent marks on the entire nationalist discourse. Sometimes the reincarnation of this word even evoked reactions from the defenders of community identity. In a prominent journal of this time, we come across an article, later mentioned in this chapter, which problematized this term and raised the question about why it would be inherently wrong to be 'a good communalist', keen on upholding the community identity for the sake of its overall advancement. See *The Mussalman*, 12 May 1927, p. 6.

In this context, mention may be made of Tagore's writings on Hindu–Muslim disunity in the late-1920s, which revolved round the word *sampraday* (community) in its negative and restrictive meaning. The term *sampradayikata* (that is, 'communalism'), considered to be the chief hindrance in the path of the attainment of 'national unity', was routinely denounced by him only in the late 1920s and early 1930s. See the essays 'Dhaka Muslim Hall-e Abhibhashan', *Prabasi*, February 1927 (Falgun 1333 BS); 'Hindu–Mussalman', *Prabasi*, July 1931 (Sraban 1338 BS); 'Bhasha-Shikshai Sampradayikata', a set of three letters written in 1934 (Chaitra 1340 BS), to be later compiled in 'Bangla Sabda-tattwa' later in 1935. This latter book is incorporated in *Rabindra Rachanabali*, vol. 16 (Calcutta: Visva-Bharati, 2001 [Magh 1407 BS]), pp. 359–524. All these essays are available together in Nityapriya Ghosh (ed.), *Hindu–Mussalman Samparka: Rabindra-rachana Sangraha* (Calcutta: Mrittika, 2003), pp. 138–70.

21. S.K. Bose, *Netaji: Collected Works*, vol. 4, p. 248.
22. Statement on Dr Moorji, 1 January 1928, in S.K. Bose, *Netaji: Collected Works*, vol. 4, p. 236.
23. 'Democracy in India', *Essential Writings of Netaji Subhas Chandra Bose*, p. 87.
24. Appeal for Workers, 22 February 1928, in S.K. Bose, *Netaji: Collected Works*, vol. 4, p. 237.
25. Subhas Chandra Bose, *The Mission of Life* (Calcutta: Thacker, Spink, and Co., 1953), p. 5.
26. The Motilal Nehru Report (August 1928), the first major attempt to draft a constitutional framework for the country, outlined a proposed

Dominion Status for India. There were two strands of opposition against this report. First, although the Congress accepted it, the younger sections within the Congress led by Jawaharlal Nehru and Subhas Chandra Bose pressed for the deletion of the Dominion Status clause and the insertion of the demand of Purna (complete) Swaraj in its place. Second, the Muslim League and a section of the Khilafat Committee opposed the report. M.A. Jinnah led this opposition and refused to accept the kind of communal settlement proposed in it. Three amendments were proposed: greater representation for the Muslims, full adult suffrage to enable Muslim-majority provinces to have Muslim-led governments, and for residuary powers to be vested not in the centre but in the provinces.

27. 'How to rouse the national will within the shortest possible period is, then, the problem before us: our policies and programmes have to be drawn up with a view to this end…. The Congress offices are, therefore the forts where we have to entrench ourselves and whence we have to stir out every day in order to raid the bureaucratic citadels. Congress committees are our army…' (S.K. Bose, *Netaji: Collected Works*, vol. 4, p. 250).

28. Difference in visions led to different nationalistic goals. While Pal in the 1920s believed that leaders should pay more attention towards the tasks of social regeneration instead of political freedom, Bose strongly reversed the underlying logic of priorities. 'You may ask what we shall gain by this resolution of Independence. I say, we develop a new mentality. After all, what is the fundamental cause of our political degradation? It is a question of mentality, and if you want to overcome the slave mentality you do so by encouraging our countrymen to stand for full and complete independence.' See his speech at Calcutta session of Congress, December 1928, in S.K. Bose, *Netaji: Collected Works*, vol. 4, p. 276.

29. John Gallagher, 'Congress in Decline, 1930 to 1939', *Locality, Province and Nation: Essays on Indian Politics 1870–1940*, edited by John Gallagher, Gordon Johnson, and Anil Seal (Cambridge: Cambridge University Press, 1973), pp. 286–8. Putting a disproportionate emphasis on the arithmetic of politics would tantamount to a narrow and limited analysis of nationalist politics and its discourse. However, one must note that the change of political priorities at different moments cannot be explained without a fair appreciation of political calculations of gains and losses or advantages and disadvantages.

30. For the weak performance of the Bengal Congress during the civil disobedience movement, see Gallagher, 'Congress in Decline', pp. 286–90; Leonard A. Gordon, *Bengal: The Nationalist Movement, 1876–1940* (New York and London: Columbia University Press, 1974), pp. 244–50.

31. The Namasudras organized two anti–civil disobedience meetings in Faridpur, and some more in Bakarganj. In Pirojpur, Jessore, and Khulna, the Congress picketers were actively resisted by both the local Muslim

and Namasudra population. See Sekhar Bandyopadhyay, *Caste, Protest and Identity in Colonial India: The Namasudras of Bengal, 1872–1947* (second edition, Oxford: Oxford University Press, 2011), pp. 152–3.

32. 'Milaner Joratali', *Bangabani*, June 1927.

33. Jogeshchandra Pal, 'Dhawangsher Mukhe Bangalar Hindu', *Bangabani*, March 1928.

34. Nirad C. Chaudhuri later turned into a major author and essayist, as well as possibly the sharpest critic of urban Bengali literati. One of his most well-known literary assaults on the Bengali was *Atmaghati Bangali* (The suicidal Bengali) (Calcutta: Mitra and Ghosh Publications, 1991). In the 1920s, he was an editor based in Calcutta, working for several liberal journals like the *Modern Review*, *Prabasi*, and *Shanibarer Chithhi*.

35. Nirad Chandra Chaudhuri, 'Bagalitwer Swarup', *Bangashree*, February 1932.

36. Even amidst the busy negotiations over the Nehru Report and the demand for complete independence from the Congress platform, Bose reiterated on the importance of the Bengal province in Indian 'national' life. His address in March 1929 as the president of the Bengal Provincial Conference at Rangpur put an emphasis on 'the message of Bengal': 'A message of her own to deliver to the world. That message is the sum total of life and history of Bengal as a whole.' Leonard A. Gordon, *Bengal: The Nationalist Movement*, p. 244.

37. In the course of his joint political endeavour with Jawaharlal Nehru to establish and promote the independence of the India League, which did not succeed much despite their efforts, Bose's persistent engagement with the youth of Bengal in running the provincial branch of the League invited condemnation from Nehru. Nehru feared that Bose was rapidly being sucked into a 'provincial separatism'. See Rudrangshu Mukherjee, 'Immersion in the Congress', *Nehru and Bose: Parallel Lives* (New Delhi: Penguin, 2014), p. 49.

38. Subhas Chandra Bose, Opera House Speech in Bombay, 22 May 1928, in S.K. Bose, *Netaji: Collected Works*, vol. 5, pp. 256–7.

39. Rabindranath Tagore, 'Bhashar Katha', in *Bangla Sabda-tattwa* (1935; reprint, Calcutta: Visva-Bharati, 1984), pp. 9–10.

40. Rabindranath Tagore, 'Maktab-Madrassa-r Bangla Bhasha' [1935], *Bangla Sabda-tattwa*, p. 302.

41. Tagore, 'Maktab-Madrassa-r Bangla Bhasha', p. 302.

42. Rabindranath Tagore's letter to Abul Fazal in 1934, cited in 'Bhasha-shikshai Sampradayikata', *Bangla Sabda-tattwa*, p. 308.

43. Tagore's disapproval of the local dialects was mentioned in Chapter 2: 'There is no reason why people of Birbhum would go on writing in their own language as a mark of protest against Calcutta.' See 'Bhashar Katha', *Bangla Sabda-tattwa*, p. 9.

44. Tagore's letter to Abul Fazl, p. 307.
45. Rabindranath Tagore's letter to Altaf Chaudhuri, cited in 'Bhasha-shikshai Sampradayikata', *Bangla Sabda-tattwa*, p. 306. The claim is evidently incorrect. The domain of the English language had already been fraught with challenges posed by the Irish or Scottish cultural self-assertion, and this information might not have been wholly inaccessible to the colonial literati in India.
46. Tagore's letter to Altaf Chaudhuri, p. 306.
47. Sayyad Emdad Ali, 'Bangla Bhasha o Mussalman', *Mohammadi*, April 1928, p. 329. A very similar argument was put forward by S. Wazed Ali, 'Bangali Mussalmaner Sahitya Samasya', *Mohammadi*, May 1929, p. 443.
48. S.E. Ali, 'Bangla Bhasha o Mussalman', p. 329.
49. Nurunnesa Khatun, 'Banga Sahitya o Mussalman', *Manashi o Marmabani*, Calcutta, June 1926.
50. Kazi Nazrul Islam, 'Baror Piriti Balir Bandh', *Atmashakti*, Calcutta, 30 December 1927.
51. Maulana Abul Hussain, *Bangali Mussalmaner Siksha Samasya* (Dhaka, 1928), pp. 22–4.
52. M.A. Hussain, *Bangali Mussalmaner Siksha Samasya*, p. 24.
53. *Shikha*, Dhaka, 1927, p. 4.
54. Abul Hussain, *Abul Hussain-er Rachanabali*, edited by Abdul Kadir (Dhaka, 1968), pp. 146–88.
55. *Hanafi*, 12 March 1928, RNP, no. 2 of 1928.
56. 'Kabya Sahitye Bangali Mussalman', *Saogat*, December 1926.
57. Golam Mostafa, 'Muslim Sahityer Gati o Lakhya', *Mohammadi*, January 1928.
58. Golam Mostafa, 'Bangladesher Gan', *Mohammadi*, November 1930. The mention of 'Bangladesh' obviously points towards the undivided Bengal of the pre-partition days. The original song was:

Pran khule aj gao re Moslem, Bangladesher gao re gan,
Ei amader janmabhumi, Bhakti-arghya dao re dan.
Edesh moder noi aponar
Bhul katha e- aleek, ashar,
Bangla moder, Bharat moder, apon moder shab jahan.

Hethai mora noyi bideshi, e je moder apon desh-i,
Morai khanti khash Bangali, desher dabi moder beshi.
Bangladeshe, Bharate bhai
Nutan juger Arya Morai,
Bir-Keshari Bakhtiyar-er urchhe hethai jai-nishan.

This evocation of the Aryan status, however, was not typical. Long histories of claiming Muslims as merely a part of a larger indigenous Hindu society had antagonized the culturally assertive Muslims enough to dissociate themselves from the sanctifying traditions of Aryanism. But the poet Golam

Mostafa did not find it hard to claim a neo-Aryanism, as far as it denoted the heightened cultural confidence needed for the Bengali Muslims.

59. It is already mentioned in the previous section of this chapter how the system of joint electorates placed the Muslims of eastern Bengal in a favourable position, thus demarcating them from the Muslims of the rest of the country. What was rather new in the 1930s was the sincere attempt to keep the Bengali interests separate as much as possible. This point will be elaborated further in the following section.

60. 'Itobhrashtastatobhrashta', *Mohammadi*, May 1931.

61. The regional politics of Bengali Muslims has recently been explored in Harun-or-Rashid, *The Foreshadowing of Bangladesh: Bengal Muslim League and Muslim Politics, 1936–47* (Dhaka: Asiatic Society of Bangladesh, 1987); Neilesh Bose, *Recasting the Region: Language, Culture, and Islam in Colonial Bengal* (New Delhi: Oxford University Press, 2014). However, what these works do not adequately consider is the need to explore the critical interdependence between these two domains of politics and culture. The true bearing of the conflicting Bengali Muslim interests and the all-India Muslim interests would never be adequately grasped if the connections between the Bengal Muslim politics and their cultural concerns are not examined together, side by side.

62. The idea of being a 'good communalist' imparted a lot of sense to the Bengali Muslims during this period. It was considered to be an important task of nationalism of any genre to espouse smaller cultural identities, and also, political self-enhancement of those communities. 'Why can [a Muslim] not be a good communalist, as well as nationalist?' See *The Mussalman*, 12 May 1927, p. 6. The Muslims were not alone in this belief. The pivotal importance of the community, either to be equated with or to be viewed as a part of the 'nation', was highlighted by the Bengali Hindus as well. Community loyalty was asserted as an integral part of national politics since the Swadeshi days.

63. Abdul Karim's presidential address at the annual session of the BPML in 1933, *The Statesman*, 30 November 1933.

64. The Nehru Report recommended: (*a*) reservation of seats for Muslims only in provinces where they were in a minority and at the centre in strict proportion to the size of the community; (*b*) abolition of separate electorates; and (*c*) discarding reservation of seats for the Muslim majorities in the Punjab and Bengal. Understandably, the reaction of the BPML was favourable towards the report while that of the Muslim-minority provinces were not so. In Bengal, the support for joint electorates was openly expressed in a resolution passed by the BPML in September 1928, which demanded that, first, adult suffrage would be introduced in the province, and second, the Muslim community was accorded the option of reopening the issue after a period of ten years. Abdul Karim, the

Vice-President of the BPML, even described the report in his address at the Calcutta Session of the AIML (December 1928) as a 'good basis for final deliberation and an effective presentation of [Hindu–Muslim] joint demand'. See Harun-or-Rashid, *The Foreshadowing of Bangladesh*, p. 36.

65. *Mohammadi*, 23 August 1928, RNP, no. 38 of 1928.

66. *Mohammadi*, 14 September 1928.

67. Abdul Karim categorically explained in the general meeting of the BPML in 1933 that the all-India priorities necessitated one of the costliest sacrifices for the Bengali Muslims during the Nehru Report controversy: 'It was a strange irony of fate that Lucknow Pact, in the drawing up of which the Bengal Muslims were very weakly represented, and the Muslims of Bihar and the U.P. who were over-anxious for their weightage had upper hand, relegating the Muslim majority in the [Bengal] Presidency to the intolerable position of a permanent minority.' See Harun-or-Rashid, *The Foreshadowing of Bangladesh*, p. 36.

68. *Mohammadi*, 14 September 1928.

69. Abul Mansur Ahmed, *Amar Dekha Rajnitir Panchash Bachhor* (Dhaka: Maola Brothers, 1970), pp. 60–1.

70. 'Ashare', *Bangabani*, June 1927.

71. *Swaraj Pratishthar Bichitra Namunai Hatabhagya Mussalmaner Durgati*, anonymous pamphlet (Calcutta, 1923), p. 12, VT, IOL.

72. *The Mussalman*, 12 May 1927, p. 6.

73. *The Mussalman*, 23 April 1927, p. 4.

74. *The Mussalman*, 23 April 1927, p. 4.

75. The first meeting was held at Town Hall, Burdwan, September 1927. *The Mussalman*, 26 February 1927, p. 7.

76. Abul Mansur Ahmed explained how people of his generation, primarily middle-class professionals in nature and less exposed politically, looked at the problems of representation and 'communal' politics in an open-minded way. He held that it was possible for Bengal to carve out a comfortable solution for itself in spite of its political divergences. For people like him, the 'Indian Muslim' problem was fundamentally different from that of the 'Bengali Muslims'. He, therefore, considered himself no more than a side-watcher for the turns and twists of Indian politics. 'When non-Bengali events sought to influence Bengali political mood, we thought it an outside interference into our home politics.' A.M. Ahmed, *Amar Dekha Rajnitir Panchash Bachhor*, pp. 170–1.

77. 'Faridpur Sammilaner Prastab', *Mohammadi*, July 1931, p. 789.

78. 'Faridpur Sammilaner Prastab', *Mohammadi*, July 1931, p. 794.

79. At the All Parties Conference in Calcutta in 1928, Jinnah made a plea for giving out residual powers to the provinces, one-third of central assembly seats to the Muslims, and reserve seats in Bengal and Punjab till adult suffrage was established. The Hindu Mahasabha leaders succeeded in

brushing aside these demands decisively. Jinnah was then ready to launch his famous 'Fourteen Points', which virtually repeated all these demands. Jinnah later described the acceptance of the conference of Jayakar's standpoint as the 'parting of the ways'. It might be simplistic to attach excessive weight to the breakdown of 1928, but, surely, the hardened Mahasabha stance substantially contributed to the growing aloofness of the Muslim leaders in the civil disobedience movement and to the marginalization of the Moderate voices within the Muslim community.

80. Upendra Nath Mukhopadhyay, 'Atmaghati Moho', *Bangabani*, July 1933.

81. 'A New Version of the Situation', statement by the BPML, *Star of India*, 22 November 1933.

82. 'A New Version of the Situation'.

83. This conference proposed that 51 per cent of seats would be reserved for the Muslims in Bengal only for ten years. The Muslim League representatives, among whom, strikingly enough, no Bengal leaders were present, discarded the suggestion and stuck to their demand of separate electorates. See *Dainik Azad*, 19 November 1932.

84. Mentioned in *Bengal Anti-Communal Award Movement—A Report* (Calcutta: Secretaries Bengal Anti-Communal Award Committee, 1936), p. 15.

85. 'Ebarer Bangiya Pradeshik Mussalman Sammilan', *Dhaka Prakash*, May 1927.

86. Mohammad Wazed Ali, 'Dharma-jibane Ajnanata o Kusanskar', *Saogat*, March 1929.

87. Editorial, 'Jatiya Sangeet', *Saogat*, March 1928.

88. Editorial, *Saogat*, June 1926. The reference to 'the Dying Hindus' also directs our attention towards the continuing discussions over Hindu decline. To mention just one, see Jogeshchandra Pal, 'Dhwangsher Mukhe Bangalar Hindu', *Bangabani*, March 1928.

89. Editorial, 'Shuddhi Andolan', *Saogat*, September 1927.

90. Editorial, 'Delhir Hatyakando', *Saogat*, February 1928.

91. Editorial, 'Delhir Hatyakando'.

92. Partha Chatterjee argued that the 'minority' perception of the Bengali Muslims was due to the all-India position of the Muslims in general. 'There is no way of explaining this [non-hegemonic ambition in relation to the Hindu society] except by connecting Muslim politics in Bengal with that in India as a whole where, of course, it had the character of the politics of a minority.' See his 'The Second Partition of Bengal', in *The Present History of West Bengal: Essays in Political Criticism* (Delhi: Oxford University Press, 1997), p. 36. I would disagree with him and suggest that this conclusion is followed from the assumption that Bengali Muslim politics was just an integral part of all-India Muslim politics. My

proposition on the contrary is that it was mainly due to the social, cultural, and economic realities of Bengal that the Bengali Muslims developed a distinct 'downtrodden' syndrome. Despite forming a numerical majority, they had been reduced to a non-hegemonic position and marginalized rather decisively. This syndrome was palpable even during the swadeshi times when the 'all-India Islamic connections' used to be drawn primarily with a purpose of glorification of the community. In other words, it was an essentially Bengali phenomenon, not a necessary imprint of the all-India Muslim realities. I would extend my argument to explain the contradictions and conflicts between the Bengali Muslim interests and all-India Muslim interests in the light of such dominance of regional realities. The entire Bengali Muslim discourse on 'nation' would illustrate the importance of the construct of the Bangiya Mussalman, who had so far been 'denied' their rightful claims in the region. The mainly agrarian character of the Bengali Muslim society and the late coming of the Muslim middle-class in the professional ranks all contributed to this sustained and entrenched sense of 'deprivation'.

93. Bose and Jalal pointed out how a departure took place in the acknowledgement of religious differences by the 1930s. For example, when Mohammed Ali made a passionate plea for Indian independence but at the same time advocated the 'Muslim case' for separate electorates, he was immediately branded as 'communal'. 'A perfectly legitimate "nationalist" position in 1920, such an expression of the multiple identities of India's Muslims in 1930 by a former Congress President now entailed his being nailed a "communalist".' Sugata Bose and Ayesha Jalal, *Modern South Asia: History, Culture and Political Economy* (Delhi: Oxford University Press, 1998), p. 143.

94. Matilal Ray, *Hindu Jagaran* (Calcutta: Calcutta Burrabazar Hindu Sabha, 1935), p. 6.

95. S. Bandyopadhyay, *Caste, Protest and Identity*, p. 145. He mentions that the high-caste nationalists began to undertake such patronizing acts of social upliftment of the Namasudras, or of lending support towards the endeavours of low-caste self-assertion (pp. 144–6).

96. Bandyopadhyay showed that the feeling of upper-caste superiority was pervasive during this era and naturally resulted in deep social suspicion and rancour. A high-caste Bengali nationalist noted that the 'depressed classes', 'the younger brothers', deserved from 'us', 'the elder brothers', love, affection, and sympathy (1924). See *Caste, Protest and Identity*, pp. 145–8.

97. Digindranarayan Bhattacharya, *Hindur Nabajagaran* (Calcutta, 1931), p. 27.

98. During the political crisis of Communal Award of 1932, the low-caste groups would, therefore, easily discard both the Congress and the Hindu Mahasabha by a single stroke as 'sister organizations' for having

'conflicting political interests with the depressed classes'. See Sekhar Bandyopadhyay, *Caste, Politics and the Raj: Bengal, 1872–1937* (Calcutta: K.P. Bagchi, 1990), p. 175. They consequently requested the government not to accept any proposal coming either from the Mahasabha or the Congress regarding the inclusion or exclusion of any caste in the listing of the 'depressed castes' as a category of social representation.

99. S. Bandyopadhyay, *Caste, Protest and Identity*, p. 153.

100. S. Bandyopadhyay, *Caste, Protest and Identity*, p. 153.

101. S. Bandyopadhyay, *Caste, Protest and Identity*, p. 154.

102. It must be remembered that the constitutional arrangements in independent India in 1950 were largely in keeping with the terms of Poona Pact, signed by Gandhi in 1932. However, in the early 1930s, both the Pact and the great signatory of the Pact had been severely criticized by the nationalists in Bengal. To them it seemed nothing but an unfortunate capitulation before the separatist demands of the 'non-national' forces. Even Tagore bitterly disapproved of Gandhi's stand, and fervently hoped for the former's change of mind. See Rabindranath Tagore's statement on 21 August 1933 read in the protest meeting in Calcutta, in C.R. Bandyopadhyay (ed.), *Rabindra-Prasanga: Anandabazar Patrika*, vol. 2 (Calcutta: Ananda Publishers, 1995), p. 169.

103. Tagore's statement on 21 August 1933, *Rabindra-Prasanga*, p. 167.

104. During this period the untouchables, for the first time, entered the Kalighat Temple in Calcutta in the presence of Congress workers led by Basanti Devi. C.R. Das's widow implored the Bengali Hindus to take a vow on the auspicious Mahashtami day to put an end to untouchability and unite the Hindu community. See C.R. Bandyopadhyay, *Rabindra-Prasanga: Anandabazar Patrika*, p. 169. Apparently, she alleged that this was a continuation of the unfulfilled mission of her late husband.

   For the historian, however, this declaration by Basanti Devi is of great significance. While this was an attempt to appropriate the historical legacy of a past visionary leader of Bengal, one may infer, with the risk of being a bit speculative, that Das's brand of inclusive nationalism would perhaps not have limited itself to such a rhetorical 'removal' of untouchability but could have negotiated with the principle of proportional representation more seriously. The logic of the Bengal Pact of 1924, if maintained in its essence and character throughout the last decade, would have pointed towards that possibility. The politically defensive and conservative nationalists of the 1930s would, of course, not want to bear that possibility in mind. History does not always have to be distant in its temporality in order to be appropriated with a twist of convenience.

105. See *Bengal Anti-Communal Award Movement—A Report*, p. 9.

106. In spite of some of his literary expositions being sympathetic towards the Muslim or Brahmo communities, Saratchandra Chattopadhyay is generally seen as a conservative Hindu. His Hindu sensibilities domi-

nated the greater part of his writings. An assessment of Chattopadhyay's outlook and viewpoints is to be found in Joya Chatterji, *Bengal Divided: Hindu Communalism and Partition, 1932–1947* (Cambridge: Cambridge University Press, 1994), pp. 173–7.

In this context, one should also remember that the Brahmo movement, a social–religious reform movement grown out of the Hindu society in the late nineteenth century, essentially a Bengali phenomenon, was losing its edge by this time, due to its rapidly diminishing influence, and also due to the strengthening of the Hindu community amidst new sociopolitical changes.

107. See *Bengal Anti-Communal Award Movement—A Report*, p. 12.

108. Saratchandra Chattopadhyay's dismissive outlook on the question of caste in the context of nationalism may be traced through a range of essays or speeches written in the 1920s and 1930s. For example, in a speech delivered at Bikrampur on 15 February 1929, he sarcastically referred to the 'nationalist' advice of eradicating the caste system. He emphasized that he would never align himself to such a moralistic position. He would rather believe that there could be no such absolute moral position on caste, the time-tested social structure of Hindu society. It being so, one could only hope for a consistency in the beliefs and actions on an individual level. Interestingly, as an individual, while Chattopadhyay himself did not want to take a reformist position on caste, or change the exclusionary practices of Hinduism, he was averse to allowing the lower castes a separate political standing on the basis of their 'excluded' status. Saratchandra Chattopadhyay, 'Satyasrayee', *Sarat Rachanabali*, centenary edition, vol. 3 (Calcutta: Sarat Samiti, 1976), pp. 480–1.

109. From the paradigm poem '*Bharat-tirtha*', written in 1910, to his play *Chandalika*, written in 1933, Tagore's disgust towards the custom of untouchability was unambiguous. However, about the eradication of the caste system, he was less certain, and his position was, at best, shifting.

110. Tagore wrote in a letter to the Bengali revolutionary leader and organizer Motilal Ghose in 1932: 'God Almighty will not forgive us if we ignore and dishonour a class of people merely because of their name. He has not forgiven India also.' Satyendranath Ray (ed.), *Samajchinta* (Calcutta: Granthalay Private Limited, 1985), p. 256.

111. Tagore's 'optimism' reflected in the social, individualistic solution to the problem of untouchability rather than going for a political solution is discussed by Sekhar Bandyopadhyay, 'Rabindranath Tagore, the Indian Nation and its Outcasts', *Harvard Asia Quarterly* 15, no. 1 (2013): 28–33, at 32–3.

112. Possibly one can suggest a gradual evolution in Tagore's thoughts. The early Tagore rested his belief on the efficacy of the varnashrama due to its critical role in shaping the classical Hindu society. See 'Swadeshi Samaj' (1904), *Rabindra Rachanabali*, vol. 2, p. 639, where he glorified the

Brahmins as the only worthy people for the perpetuation of knowledge, religiosity, or meditative qualities, all of which together characterized the essence of the Indian society. As the focus on traditionalism, Hindu society and culture later shifted in his ideals of 'nation', so did his views on caste. The later Tagore would denounce the psychological and institutional resistance on the question of caste divisions rather strongly ('Sudra-Dharma' [1914], *Rabindra Rachanabali*, vol. 12: *Kalantar*, pp. 611–17). However, at least in this context, the shift was perhaps not complete, and the vacillation, still persistent. In my views, this inner contradiction and hesitation in Tagore led him to make a deviation from his earlier nuanced ideological position in the 1930s, and joining the conservative high caste lobby in the wake of the debate on low caste reservation.

113. See *Bengal Anti-Communal Award Movement—A Report*, pp. 14–15.

114. Sekhar Bandyopadhyay refutes the idea that Tagore was 'opposing' the untouchables' demand for self-determination. He cites in favour of his argument Tagore's 'message' sent to Gandhi at fast at Yeravda Jail: 'No civilized society can thrive upon victims whose humanity has been permanently humiliated.' See his 'Rabindranath Tagore's Nation and Its Outcasts' *Harvard Asia Quarterly* 15, no. 1 (2013): 28–33. I would, however, argue that his position was perhaps not one of 'opposition', but even with all due benefits of doubt, it was neither one of support for the low-caste demands. I would maintain that while Tagore was abstractly defending the untouchables' demand for self-determination and envisaging for them a spiritual emancipation from the ties of bondage, the path leading to social and political freedom for the lower castes in general still eluded him. The idea of reservation was clearly repugnant to him, given his universalistic belief system. But that he could never prescribe any alternative way for the lower castes to claim their rightful demands paves the way for concluding that he was against their self-determination. It is perhaps more accurate to say that for the liberal nationalists like Tagore, caste empowerment in the end had to be a social struggle, not a political one.

115. See *Bengal Anti-Communal Award Movement—A Report*, p. 15.

116. See *Bengal Anti-Communal Award Movement—A Report*, p. 7.

117. N.N. Sircar, *Bengal under Communal Award and Poona Pact* (Calcutta, 1936), p. 40.

118. S. Bandyopadhyay, 'Rabindranath Tagore's Nation and Its Outcasts', p. 169.

119. 'Nationalism and separate electorates are self-contradictory. Separate electorates are wrong in principle and it is futile to attempt to build up a nation on a bad principle.' Subhas Chandra Bose, Speech at Maharashtra Provincial Conference, Poona, 3 May 1928, in S.K. Bose, *Netaji: Collected Works*, vol. 5, p. 253.

120. Bose, Speech at Maharashtra Provincial Conference, Poona, 3 May 1928, p. 248.

121. Both B.C. Roy and Nalini Ranjan Sarkar opposed Bose for his encouragement of 'disruptive activity' by students and workers. Gordon, *Bengal: The Nationalist Movement*, p. 250.

122. Bose, Speech at Maharashtra Provincial Conference, Poona, 3 May 1928, p. 243.

123. The 'populist' or 'localist' ideas had, no doubt, been of a much older lineage, though. The emphasis on the 'people' had been haunting nationalist discourse right from the Swadeshi days, from the first instance of a political movement in the name of the 'nation'. Both Tagore and Das had forcefully outlined the localist potential of the 'nation'. But never before the late 1920s had the politics of people found any real ground in Bengal.

124. *Atmasakti*, 15 January 1926.

125. *Anandabazar Patrika*, 16 January 1926.

126. For a detailed account of the foundation and development of Nikhil Banga Praja Samiti, see Rashid, *Foreshadowing of Bangladesh*, pp. 30–5.

127. Various essays of this time published in journals like *Swaraj*, *Sonar Bangla*, and *Manashi o Marmabani* dealt with the value of local self-development projects.

128. To give just one example, see Shashadhar Ray, 'Hindu–Mussalman, Banglar Samaj', *Manashi o Marmabani*, April 1927.

129. By questioning the old classification of the peasantry into rich, middle, and poor, Sugata Bose makes a useful typology of the Bengal peasantry on the basis of its various local characteristics. According to his study, East Bengal was a predominantly peasant, small-holding society overlaid by various rent-collector and creditor groups; West Bengal possessed a combination of peasant, small-holding, and landlord-dominated demesne labour; and north Bengal was typically marked by rich farmer–sharecropper system. See his *Agrarian Bengal: Economy, Social Structure and Politics, 1919–1947* (Cambridge: Cambridge University Press, 1986), pp. 20–30. The earlier 'middle peasant' theory is to be found in the works of Eric Wolf, *Peasant Wars of the Twentieth Century* (New York: Harper and Row, 1969); Hamza Alavi, 'Peasants and Revolution', in *Imperialism and Revolution in South Asia*, edited by Kathleen Gough and Hari P. Sharma (New York: Monthly Review Press, 1973). Bose's typology also fundamentally challenged the assumptions of the 'jotedar' thesis of Rajat K. Ray and Ratnalekha Ray, 'Zamindars and Jotedars: A Study in Rural Politics in Bengal', *Modern Asian Studies* 9, no. 1 (1975): 81–102, whereby the political turmoils of the twentieth century were sought to be explained by the growing tensions between the revenue-collecting landlord and the village-controlling dominant jotedars.

130. Bose shows that the critical centrality of the rural credit networks rather than zamindar–jotedar sociopolitical contest was the primarily important factor in debilitating the village societies of East Bengal in the post-Depression era. By implication, the peasant politics acquired newer trajectories against the rapidly radicalizing social background. Sugata Bose, *Agrarian Bengal*, chapters 6 and 7.

131. *Langal*, Special issue, 25 December 1925, RNP, no. 1 of 1925.

132. *Langal*, 18 March, 1926, in Muzaffar Ahmed, *Prabandha Sankalana* (Calcutta, 1970), pp. 204.

133. An insightful article in *Ganavani* focused on the nationalist's 'characteristic lack of concern for people's interests':

> It is because of this attitude of our national leaders to popular interests that the Congress has not yet evoked a real response from the people. Moreover, the present politics of our country is lacking in the economic basis which is conducive to the real peace of the people in the practical world. On the other hand, many of the principles of our so-called leaders are reactionary from the standpoint of the interests of the people. It is nevertheless true that the people are uniting and slowly awakening, a fact which is evidenced by the recent strikes. Hence a little consideration shows that our foremost duty is to awaken the masses, to tell them the reason of their destitution ... What is now wanted is the union of the peasants, the worker, and the people of the lower classes. Popular government will never come without that.

See Ranajit Kumar Barman, 'Which Way to Go?' *Ganavani*, 28 June 1926 RNP, no. 2 of 1926.

134. *Ganavani*, 19 August 1926, in Ahmed, *Prabandha Sankalan*, p. 29.

135. *Mohammadi*, 21 May 1926, RNP, no. 2 of 1926.

136. *Ganavani*, 12 May 1927, RNP, no. 2 of 1927, p. 106.

137. *Ganavani*, 12 May 1927, p. 163.

138. *Ganavani*, 12 May 1927, pp. 196, 202–7.

139. One of Ahmed's articles reveals the standard Left attitude towards religiously informed culture: 'In every country and in every age, religious spirit is something infused into the people's mind in the interests of the rulers and the ruling classes. Religion is only being used as an instrument of exploitation, hence is becoming totally "irreligious".' Muzaffar Ahmed, 'What Is the Basic Point?' *Ganavani*, 12 May 1927.

140. Muzaffar Ahmed wrote about the workings of the party and its members rarely operating beyond the urban, educated society up till this point in *Amar Jiban o Bharater Communist Party*, pp. 350–85.

141. Shahidullah, *Al Islam* 13, no. 2 (1921), p. 23.

142. Kazi Motahar Hussain Chaudhuri, *Sanskriti Katha* (Dhaka, 1958), p. 3. Abul Hussain's preoccupation with economic issues of Bengali society was reflected in his essays published in *Bangiya Mussalman Sahitya Patrika*. Some of them were 'Banglar Balshi', 'Krishaker Artonad', 'Krishaker Durdasha', and 'Krishi Biplaber Suchana'.

143. *Bengal Legislative Assembly Proceedings*, 1928, vol. 1, pp. 399–401. While 1928 amendment to the Tenancy Act legalized the right of transfer of occupancy rayat holdings, it provided for a 20 per cent transfer fees payable to the landlord who was also given a pre-emptive right to purchase the holding. It was therefore seen by many as a legal intervention not wholly in favour of rayat interests.

144. The Bengal Tenancy Amendment Act, 1928, *Calcutta Gazette*, part 3, 1929, p. 50.

145. The Bengal Tenancy Amendment Act, 1928, p. 400.

146. *Soltan*, 26 August 1928. The assembly voting on this amendment revealed three clear groups: the Muslim group, the Swarajya Party group, and the official/European group. The first bloc voted in favour of the rayat and the under-rayat, the second bloc voted against the rayat interests, and the third bloc generally opposed the idea of amendment to the original bill. For details, see Partha Chatterjee, *Bengal 1920–47: The Land Question* (Calcutta: K.P. Bagchi, 2010), pp. 77–84.

147. Editorial, *The Mussalman*, 6 September 1928.

148. *Anandabazar Patrika*, 9 September 1928.

149. *Mohammadi*, 28 September 1928, RNP, no. 1 of 1928.

150. The Congress plea of forming a peasants' party was already heard in 1928. One cannot but observe that *Mohammadi* repeated the same plea on its pages after a few days without even mentioning the Congress' proposal. The conspicuous absence of any mention of the Congress position is difficult to interpreted in terms of anti-Hindu bias, as the journal was at the same time conducting a campaign on Hindu–Muslim unity. It was urging the Muslim peasants to unite with the non-Muslim rayats. An opposition to Congress politics, rather than an anti-Hindu bias, might be a more plausible explanation behind this. *Mohammadi*, 28 September 1928.

151. After its initial sparks, the civil disobedience movement was not followed by any proletarian agitation in the following years. See Sumit Sarkar, *Modern India, 1885–1947* (Madras: Macmillan, 1983), pp. 290–5; Tanika Sarkar, *Bengal 1928–1934: The Politics of Protest* (Delhi: Oxford University Press, 1987).

152. This is not to deny that some important attempts at labour organization took place during this time. When deflationary policies of the government led to a considerable contraction of market, prices as well as wage rates were slashed, working hours reduced, and agricultural prices remained high. The resultant industrial strikes (1928–9) took place among the Calcutta Corporation Scavengers, railway workers in Howrah and Burdwan, the oil depot at Budge Budge, and some jute mills around Calcutta, where the task of labour organization was taken up by L. Hussain, K.C. Roychowdhury, Kiran Mitra, and Prabhabati Dasgupta.

Subhas Chandra Bose built up several labour organizations, and was given the charge of the Budge Budge strike. A handful of Congressmen like Bankim Mukherjee and Radharaman Maitra worked in close conjunction with the union leaders and also, with the more self-conscious labour organizers like those in the Workers' and Peasants' Party.

153. In the early 1920s, the communist faction growing under the leadership of M.N. Roy wanted to cooperate with the nationalist bourgeoisie in the struggle against imperialism. Leadership, it was thought, should not be surrendered to the bourgeois democratic leaders. It was regarding this particular issue that Roy and Lenin parted their ways. Lenin was acutely apprehensive of the possibility of an understanding between the bourgeois of the exploiting countries and those of the colonial countries in a joint struggle against all revolutionary movements. However, Roy was slowly changing his mind on the issue. In 'The Aftermath of Non-cooperation' (1926), he expressed concern over the course of the movement, 'too afraid, too hesitating to follow a revolutionary channel'. It was thought necessary to shake off the compromising elements once and for all, and move forward with the proletariat alone. With this end in view, Roy suggested the creation of a broad-based 'People's Party', with a programme of revolutionary nationalism, which would bind together all the oppressed classes, namely, the petty bourgeoisie, the peasantry, and the proletariat.

154. *Mohammadi*, 22 August 1928, RNP, no. 38 of 1928.

155. A.M. Ahmed, *Amar Dekha Rajnitir Panchash Bachhor*, pp. 34–6. Based on his childhood memories of the native village of Mymensingh, he mentions a number of everyday instances of this Hindu Brahmin 'superiority'.

156. The role of religion in reshaping class conflict was noteworthy. A rayat movement took place in Narayanganj sub-division in Dacca over the issue of rent adjustments on the entry of a new zamindar, who was a rich Hindu merchant and bought the property of an old Muslim zamindar. The rayats in this case were directed by a Mymensingh pir who advised non-payment of rent. In this case, no explicit use was made of the obvious communal divide. In many other instances, religion turned out to be a handy weapon to evoke communitarian ties in the process of organizing a class conflict. Tanika Sarkar, *Bengal 1928–1934*, pp. 40–6.

157. Scholars have noted that during the first half of the 1930s, the dwindling condition of the AIML was matched by the flourishing state of the BPML. Rashid, *Foreshadowing of Bangladesh*, pp. 30–48. The impoverished condition of the All India Muslim League was caused due to a number of factors. Some of the hitherto prominent League leaders died by this time, while securing enough finances to keep the organization afloat proved increasingly difficult.

158. A.M. Ahmed, *Amar Dekha Rajnitir Panchash Bachhor*, pp. 86–92.

159. A.M. Ahmed, *Amar Dekha Rajnitir Panchash Bachhor*, p. 48.

160. For a detailed analysis of the re-emergence of the League under Jinnah, see Ayesha Jalal, *The Sole Spokesman: Jinnah, The Muslim League and the Demand for Pakistan* (Cambridge: Cambridge University Press, 1994), pp. 7–14.

161. Jinnah gave an address to a gathering at the Town Hall in Calcutta in August 1936. He delivered a passionate plea for accommodating the Bengali Muslim interest with those of the Muslims in the minority provinces. His anxiety about the support of the Muslim-majority provinces like Bengal and Punjab was clearly reflected in this address. *Anandabazar Patrika*, 21 August 1936, p. 11.

162. Rashid, *Foreshadowing of Bangladesh*, pp. 50–4.

163. *Anandabazar Patrika*, 21 August 1936, p. 11

164. The end of dyarchy and the beginning of the era of so-called provincial autonomy began with the Act of 1935 which provided for the setting up of responsible government in the eleven provinces of British India, qualified by a string of safeguards. It also provided for a Federation of India, consisting of both provinces and the states, with excessive weightage in favour of the latter. The Congress in its Lucknow Session (1936) had rejected the Act in its entirety, but eventually agreed to participate in the elections to be held in 1937.

165. It is left to the historian's imagination if the long absence of the two most liberal leaders, Subhas Bose and Sarat Bose, from the region's political scene became a critical factor behind this failure. Sarat Bose was in jail from 1932 to 1935, while Subhas Bose was either in jail or in exile from 1932 to 1937. The latter's absence also had an impact on the course of left-wing politics emerging within and at the edges of Congress in the context of Bengal. When Subhas Bose reappeared in the political scene with his radical social and economic programme based on a form of socialism adapted to Indian conditions and also a creed of militant nationalism, and thus virtually threw a challenge to the Gandhian leadership, he was almost without a strong organizational footing for himself. For more details, see Sugata Bose, *His Majesty's Opponent: Subhas Chandra Bose and India's Struggle against Empire* (Cambridge, MA: Harvard University Press, 2011).

4   Two Coalitions and Three Moments of Failure

1937–45

Towards the end of 1936, local and popular mobilization for the ensuing provincial election altered Bengal politics in a distinctive way. Never before was politics brought to people so decisively, with mass meetings, processions, pamphlets, and manifestos all directed at bringing out popular support. What must not be overlooked in this new incipient political culture is its specific orientation and targeted nature, born out of the electoral necessities. Political parties competing with each other knew only too well that they were to address specific communities and groups in Bengali society, which by this time was seen as a conglomeration of different and demarcated quarters like Muslim, Hindu high castes, Hindu low castes, and so forth. The preceding decade of politics of enumeration had changed irrevocably the structures of imagination for the Bengali nation.

Yet this change was more a matter of perception than reality. Social compartmentalization was never as neat and complete as it was claimed to be. There still existed ample opportunities of a common political platform for these disparate quarters. Of course, 'nation' could no more be 'united' in the sense the swadeshi nationalists had once envisaged. But a different kind of unity was still conceivable through social and political negotiations among these differentiated quarters. One such alternative negotiating platform was regional interest. The previous chapter has outlined how, around 1936, almost all regional parties began to broaden their base and uphold their own claims of representation based on regional identity, which bore within itself potential for a possible meeting ground. On the eve of the first provincial election of 1937, one of these political organizations emerged as the most capable champion of regional identity—the Krishak Praja Party.

One of the focal points of the present chapter, therefore, is the KPP, its success and failure and its struggles through the challenges thrown by two all-India organizations—Congress and the Muslim League. Primarily a Muslim organization, its political and electoral success sprang from its close ties to the localities and villages, to the region. It is commonly held that the failure of the Congress to strike an alliance with the KPP after the elections of 1937 was one of its huge strategic mistakes, because such an alliance could have meant the building of a 'secular' national platform. This chapter, however, supports this assumption only partially. It argues that this failed alliance, indeed a turning point for Bengal, was not so for its aborted promise of developing a secular or radical movement, but for its frustrated potential for providing a broad-based provincial or regional agenda. The assumption that follows from this argument is: had the KPP survived and flourished for a longer time, a KPP–Congress partnership might perhaps have generated the capacity to address the problem of 'difference' in this Muslim-majority, Hindu-dominated province of Bengal.

From the regional perspective, two other moments of 'failure' can also be identified during this period. Fazlul Huq, the premier of the KPP–League coalition government, joined the Muslim League towards the end of 1937, thereby allowing the potential of the KPP politics to be hijacked and appropriated by the League. A good number of KPP politicians eventually joined the BPML, which, instead of toeing the all-India Muslim line, embarked on a struggle with the latter. The all-India League's overarching narrative of 'Muslim' identity contained a threat to any regional diversity. In this struggle between the two levels of the

League, the latent contradiction between the larger Muslim interests and the regional Muslim interests was starkly obvious. After the launching of the Pakistan proposal at Lahore in 1940, this conflict was more direct and visible. However, fighting with a larger Muslim organization for the sake of upholding regional interests was not the same as jeopardizing what was seen as the Muslim identity. The third moment of crisis, therefore, came subsequently when Huq joined hands with the Hindu Mahasabha in 1943, distinctly known for its anti-Muslim stance. As a result of this association, Huq lost much of the grip over his erstwhile huge following in the Muslim society of this region, and the Bengali Muslim world lost a very promising leader keen on building regional and inter-communal alliances. Chances of creating a region–nation were deplorably cut short by these three critical political conjunctures.

The gradual rise of the League from the 1930s in Bengal is usually explained in terms of growing Muslim separatism or communalism. But this chapter argues that the real significance of the League ascendancy in Bengal lies in its double-edged fight on the question of difference. On the one hand, it deftly politicized the claims of Muslim difference in the larger Indian context and toyed with the potentials of a 'two–nation theory'. On the other, for the consolidation of its own rights on behalf of an alternative 'nation' based on difference, the All India Muslim League had to bulldoze all voices of difference within it, emerging from the diverse segments of the Indian Muslim world. In such a situation, the Muslim-majority province of Bengal inevitably found itself in a tight corner, while the all-India League was kept under the firm control of the Muslim-minority provinces. Regional heavyweights like Huq had to bear the worst brunt of this homogenizing drive of the League. Seen in this light, the growth in the League's hold in Bengal served as a blow more to the hope of building a resilient provincial platform on a possible compromise between various communities of the region than to the chances of a secular anti-colonial struggle. I emphasize this point because it is important to note that the primary danger in the rise of the AIML was its excessive stress on larger Muslim interests by sidelining the provincial or regional concerns. These concerns could have otherwise provided a basis for regional negotiation so far as the KPP and, later, the BPML leadership stuck to their unrelenting preoccupation with the 'Bengali' identity. The alternative identity the Bengali Muslims were carving out for themselves might not be wholly 'secular' in the conventional sense of the term, but had the potential to serve as a bridge between various identities in the interest of the broad-based provincial politics.

Somewhat counter-intuitively, when the unlikely alliance between Fazlul Huq and the Mahasabha leader Shyamaprasad Mookherjee (1941–3) irrevocably discredited Huq's leadership, the most creative regional alternative of an inter-community administration was perhaps to be found in the project of 'Pakistan'. The Pakistan proposal, still devoid of any clear practical implications, was undergoing complex conceptual manoeuvrings in Bengal where it was given a curious regional twist. A section of Hindu nationalists also showed interest in negotiating between different communities within the region. I will argue in the next chapter that even after the Great Calcutta Killings of 1946, the potential of framing a new inter-communal administration was not eliminated. From these arguments follows my observation that the partition of Bengal in 1947 should not be seen as a 'logical' result of the 'communal' politics of either the Muslims or the Hindus in Bengal.[1] On the contrary, even in the early 1940s, the provincial leadership of Bengal—both Muslim and Hindu—still considered alternative options with a great degree of flexibility. The story would nevertheless only become one of failure and defeat. In the very last years of the Raj, the Congress and the League at the all-India level, the two reigning variants of 'unitary' nationalism, would successfully steal the show by silencing their regional counterparts.

Provincial Elections: People's Politics?

When the three major political parties—the Congress, the League, and the KPP began preparing for the provincial elections in 1937, the excitement surrounding this watershed event was unprecedented. Elections brought new promises and fresh hopes. Waliullah, an eminent Muslim journalist of late colonial Bengal, described the moment later in his memoir:

> Starting from the Vedic Age down to our *Kali-Yuga* [the last of the four Puranic periods in the history of the world], never before have the 'people' of this country seen the prospect of being represented by a government directly elected by them. As a student of history, I considered this as no less momentous an event than Balmiki's composing of *Ramayana*, Asoka's conquest of Kalinga, Alauddin Khilji's market-price regulations, Sher Shah's building of the Grand Trunk Road, Akbar's propagation of Din-i-Elahi, or the creation of Shah Jahan's Taj Mahal! People of Bengal were acutely aware of the enormous significance of 1937 ... [italics original][2]

The tone of enthusiasm was striking, especially in view of the fact that the franchise was still very limited. Only about 10 per cent of the total population qualified as the electorate. In reality, the explanation of such enthusiasm lay elsewhere, in the mass mobilization techniques adopted as a vital part of the election preparation. It seemed important to bring the agenda to the people, to enlist as much popular support as possible, and demonstrate the strength of the following in political rallies and meetings prior to the elections. The elections constituted a moment of demonstrating public acceptability, if not to the people at large, to the electorate as well as the bureaucracy. The formal and informal arenas of politics were bridged for the very first time in Bengal. Despite the fact of limited franchise, the elections therefore meant a democratization of politics in a significant way. No wonder, under the circumstances, the political agenda also had to undergo a massive change. Both the Congress and the KPP came up with election manifestos filled with promises to the 'people'.[3]

However, the tone and intent of the 'popular' agenda showed some intriguing variations. The Bengal Congress, dominated by landed interests in a province where (unlike the United Provinces which had large numbers of Muslim talukdars) the zamindars, mostly Hindu in composition, proved themselves largely unsympathetic to peasant interests as well as averse to the growing demands for agrarian reforms. 'People' in Congress rhetoric was carefully kept mostly undefined, relating to an unspecified mass, while the economic (that is, agrarian) concerns of these people remained mostly outside the purview of its agenda. Rayat associations or *krishak samitis*, set up in mofussil towns and villages across the province, did not receive much backing from the Congress: '[N]ot one senior Congress leader appears to have addressed or attended the rallies they organized.'[4]

On the contrary, 'people' found a specific definition as 'rural masses' in the KPP schema of politics. Unlike the Congress, the KPP even denominationally claimed to represent the peasant interests, embodied the inheritance of the praja politics of the earlier period, and, in terms of its expressed agenda, consistently upheld radical proposals like the abolition of zamindari without compensation and immediate rent reduction in addition to the more general demands of compulsory primary education. The 'socialist' leanings of the KPP, nevertheless, had its limits: neither its composition nor its objectives were devoid of class contradictions. That its class character was never as radical as alleged is particularly important to remember in appreciating the KPP itself and Bengal politics of the late 1930s in general.[5]

Before the elections, the KPP leader Fazlul Huq styled himself to be a politician of the 'people' in his speeches and declarations. The following message of *dal* and *bhat* politics (that is, lentil and rice, the basic food for the rural population of Bengal) was delivered in August 1936:

> ... it is not a civil war in the Muslim community but it is a fight in which people of Bengal are divided on a purely economic issue. This issue must be decided first before we take up any matter for consideration ... the problem of *dal* and *bhat* and some kind of coarse cloth is the problem of problems which stares us in the face and which must be solved immediately.... An obvious and immediate solution to the problem will be reducing the cost of administration, reducing taxes on the poor and a thorough overhauling of the Bengal Tenancy Act ... [italics added][6]

As Huq's 'people' agenda and his vision of an 'economic' conflict between the 'people' and the elite within the Muslim community suggest, his political stance was different from the existing modes of politics, practiced both by the League and the Congress. The question is: How radical was his agenda in the end? Huq and the KPP leaders regularly took pride in their stake for peasants' issues, but their essentially jotedar background, or their reliance on the jotedar elements within the party, also hindered them from pushing these beyond a certain point.[7] The class profile of electoral candidates was never conducive to the tall claims of a comprehensive 'peasant representation'; yet it was never overwhelmingly elitist in nature. Of the 24-member election board of the KPP, 11 were professionals, 2 landlords, 5 jotedars, and 2 former government servants.[8] With the influential talukdars and jotedars as leaders, it enjoyed the support of the occupancy rayats on the one hand and succeeded in drawing support even from a number of Muslim zamindars as its props on the other. The class composition was mixed, although that did not hinder the party from maintaining a consistent focus on the abolition of zamindari.

One must remember in this context that to abolish zamindari was never merely a 'peasant demand'. More often it was a demand raised by the jotedar or middling power-brokers of the rural society as well. These newly enfranchised groups of jotedars became more important in the political arena of Bengal and provided strength to the KPP.[9] This partial jotedar domination of the KPP immediately explains why the demand for abolition of zamindari was not automatically supplemented by an agenda of giving occupancy rights to lower strata of the peasantry like *bargadar*s. When Abul Mansur Ahmed, a prominent KPP leader, later recalled that many KPP members had flinched at the suggestion of any extension of occupancy rights to the bargadars or under-rayats, he indeed pointed towards this inherent limitation of the praja agenda of the KPP.[10] A closer look at their election manifesto also reveals how, alongside the populist appeals of Huq and other leaders and a war cry on the abolition of the Permanent Settlement, there were somewhat veiled but persistent concerns about the capping of the land rent, the annulment of the zamindari right of pre-emption, abolition of cesses like abwabs and *nazar-salami*, and the establishment of debt-settlement boards, measures designed to benefit the richer peasants, tenant-proprietors, and jotedars as such.[11]

However, to characterize and understand KPP only in terms of its 'jotedar' character would, again, be an over-simplification.[12] The combination of interests KPP had as an organizational platform was complex. A large chunk of the middle-class professional people found this party an important vehicle for their identity-based but liberal politics. Once again Abul Mansur Ahmed's autobiographical account provides us a critical key to realize the nature of this party. He mentioned that KPP could best be characterized as a forum of the Muslim middle class against the 'feudal' elements in Hindu as well as Muslim societies, represented respectively by the Congress and the League. Clearly, as an inheritance from the widely spreading urban radical groups in the earlier era, the latter half of the 1930s saw a swelling of middle-class and student support for the popular slogans put forward by KPP. When the League leaders poured out their wrath on Huq in the most organized fashion through the Muslim press, almost entirely under the League's control (for instance, the *Azad*, the *Mohammadi*, or the *Star of India*), KPP relied on the weekly journal, *Chashi*, to support its cause. The writings in *Chashi* unmistakably betrayed a middle-class language and sensibility. The aim of addressing the peasantry directly meant that there emerged new ways of political mobilization. One method was taking the party agenda to the rural masses by bands of its dedicated volunteers, covering miles after miles on foot, talking to the peasants in their own language taking a door-to-door approach. The second was the publication, popularization, and a creative translation of KPP agenda and spreading it among the village and small-town people inhabiting the middling zones between the rural peasantry and urban elites. These publications served more than just a literary purpose and became a vital part of the KPP populist politics. A poem by Nazrul rephrased a widely known folk rhyme, transforming the old peasant-style fatalism into a theme of subaltern resistance:

In our slumber we shudder, for the robbers descend.
The land is filled with swarms of locusts, how to pay the rent?
Children will sleep, all be quiet, hold a rod in hand
Oh you ploughmen, never leave your own land.[13]

The focus on economic hardship of the peasantry and the conflict of
their interests with those of the higher classes automatically brought
KPP activists and ideologues in a position to counter the homogenized
construction of a 'Muslim' community. In the above poem, the conflicted
economic programme of the liberal–radical Muslims was given a clear
'praja' twist: '... ploughmen, never leave your own land'. In a less direct
way, literary expressions of other leader–writers betrayed a connection
between the urban and rural classes. The following poem by Humayun
Kabir revealed an urban Muslim apologia, rather typical of the professional middle classes, for the detachment from their rural co-religionists.

A whole year passed, now there is the first moon of Eid
Everyone is in glee, but I rest aggrieved ...
When there will be no rent for landlord, no interest for lender
All will get new attires irrespective of gender.
On their lands tillers will have their rightful claims
No rich no poor, no difference, all be the same.
In that Id's congregation when all get unified
No conflict among brothers, no one can divide.
No more want, no suffering, everyone in tune
I wait for that Eid, the rising of that moon.[14]

The waiting for the Eid when people would be equal in rights and
entitlements: surely a call for solidarity, but solidarity not in terms of
simplistic Islamic ties. This call was for the consolidation of an economically divided society of Muslims and in order to effect greater social fairness. At one level, these politically motivated literary works showed an
intermingling of 'Muslim' and 'peasant' interests. At another, with the
radical objective of ending economic exploitation on various ends, it was
sought that the rural society be connected with the urban professional
classes. The peasantry, heavily Muslim in composition, and the urban
professional Muslims, acutely aware of their relative economic and cultural backwardness, could thus unite on an ideological platform which
was not overtly Islamic neither staunchly socialist, but instead a regionally defined, multi-class front, informed with a deep religious–cultural
sensibility.

Such a combined front was envisaged to wage a battle against both Hindu and Muslim vested interests in the towns and the countryside, against the landed elites as well as the professional bhadralok classes. Religious symbols (like the crescent of Eid in Kabir's poem) proved handy in evoking the sense of cultural solidarity. No doubt it was very different from the religious war cries raised by the League during the same time. We will examine the use of religion in KPP rhetoric in the following section, but it is urgent to mention here that the ideal of social fairness began to serve well for several social groups within the Bengali Muslim community: middle classes, rural jotedars, and the upper echelons of rayats. Even a cursory view of the KPP cannot support the label 'radical'. But it would also be enormously difficult to describe it by the inherently limiting term 'jotedar'. Like all broad-based radical organizations, it must have suffered from deep inherent constraints, arising out of internal conflicts of interests, but there were also visible efforts at initiating a mass movement of a limited sort. In its electoral battle against the League in 1937, the KPP rarely lost the populist directions. A common question that came up during the election campaign was: Why were the KPP and the League, two 'Muslim' parties, fighting each other, and wherein lay their true differences? This was precisely why the KPP had to repeatedly emphasize its difference with the League in terms of their professed social objectives.[15] By this time, the KPP had more or less developed a character of its own—a cross-class organization, self-consciously Bengali in nature, mainly Muslim in composition, representing peasant issues more resolutely than any other party. Rural issues were central to the party's politics and the province-wide agrarian interests were sought to be addressed. The KPP fought mostly on the basis of their local organizational strength. Following Huq's rhetoric, other KPP leaders underscored during their campaign in different localities that the term 'Muslim interest' being illusory, the vested interests in the rural and urban societies had to be the primary target.[16] The urban people were not counted out in the process, rather sought to be mobilized on broader principles of social fairness. With a distinctly middle-class party structure, the KPP election programme suggested that at least on the level of political rhetoric and social aspirations, the objective was first to inherit and then to surpass the strength of the hitherto localized and limited praja movement.[17]

Such a cross-class character of the KPP was deliberate and not accidental or random. However, it has rarely been emphasized in the studies of the Bengali Muslim politics of the late 1930s. But the multi-class character of the KPP seems significant for two reasons. One, it was in a position to provide a bridge in a highly stratified society, a novel and effective handle on the question of 'difference', and a fresh hope for a broad-based politics of the region. Two, it is only natural that, due to its precarious middle path and a vacillating leadership, it had to suffer from certain inevitable and dangerous shortcomings in the post-1937 politics.

The KPP did not choose a middle path only in terms of class interests. On the question of religion too, it positioned itself on a middling ground. We will see in the following section how its rhetoric employed religion in a curiously imaginative way, mainly as a vehicle of a culturally embedded politics rather than an instrument of enhancing the notion of 'difference' with other regional communities. The uniqueness of the KPP's middle path, of course, had its pitfalls from which it could not finally recover. Although the fall of the KPP had much to do with the personal choices Fazlul Huq would eventually make, the structural idiosyncrasies of this party were no less consequential in the end.

Promises and Pitfalls of the 'Middle Path'

The KPP was not 'secular' in the way the word 'secularism' is usually understood. At the same time, it was never Islamic in the way the conservative Muslim politics would have liked it to be. To appreciate the complex nuances with which Huq approached and employed religion is extremely important for exploring the possibilities of the 'nation' from the fold of the KPP. Huq appropriated religious idioms to arouse Muslim masses even in his early phase, that is, before his joining hands with the League. This move possibly seemed handy in his attempts to bridge the gaps between disparate social groups within the Muslim community. However, at the same time, throughout the period he remained at the helm of Bengal politics, he was particularly receptive to the Hindus and repeatedly spoke about a common Bengali homeland. One may identify in such a dual strategy of Huq's politics a conscious adoption of a middle path.[18] However, such a precarious balance between religious idioms and cross-communal regional sentiments was not easy to maintain and depended heavily upon the circumspect approach and strength of the leadership. Although Huq displayed those in the initial years, he began to lose control over his own party very quickly. Only in a couple of years, KPP politicians were drawn close to the Muslim League. The catchy religious idioms began to be used in a more random and reckless manner by the League. The rural reform programme like the abolition of zamindari was sidelined, and the cross-class, multifaceted, pluralistic agenda of 'Huq nationalism' had to recede to the background. In all, the transformation of cultural Islamism into a political Islamism was hastened by the weaknesses of the KPP. Nevertheless, one needs to be cautious in bringing out the caveats of Huq's nationalism. Instead of blaming it squarely as doomed, or an inevitable failure, we must appreciate that the promises inherent in his politics were misappropriated by the unrelenting pulls and pressures of all-India Muslim politics. The 'middle-path' nationalism of Huq brought about its own demise only in the sense that, due to its own internal weaknesses, it could not resist such pulls and pressures from the AIML with adequate strength.

The use of religious symbols in KPP politics, culturally motivated in the beginning, increased significantly due to the electoral compulsions. Huq had been serving as a prominent politician from the middle of the 1910s when the Bengali Muslim middle class made their first entry into the arena of formal politics. Indeed his occasional portrayal of the 'Muslim cause' in legislative deliberations was pivotal in his political rise. But he seldom relied so critically on religious rhetoric before the late 1930s. Similarly, the Praja Party, the KPP's predecessor, had also so far preoccupied itself with the economic interests of rayats, despite the fact that the majority of the cultivator population of Bengal shared one religion. Till the latter half of the 1930s, the Praja rhetoric did not include religious overtones as it began to do in the wake of the elections. One identifies this change in the KPP manifesto published in September 1936. It first talked about the 'economic grievances of the masses in Bengal', and then had to supplement it with the demand of 'full responsible government for India with adequate and effective safeguards for Mussalmans'.[19]

Outwardly too, the KPP was more of a Muslim organization than a secular one, despite its non-religious nomenclature and the professed class character. With 21 out of 25 members in its Election Board being Muslim, the party structure was visibly erected on the dedicated service of leading Muslim professionals like Shamsuddin Ahmed, Syed Nausher Ali, Abul Mansur Ahmed, Humayun Kabir, and Rafiuddin Ahmed as well as groups of madrassa-educated maulanas like Pir Badshah Khan of Faridpur, Maulana Maniruzzaman Islamabadi of Chittagong, and Maulana Abdullahil Baqui of Dinajpur. 'On account of predominant membership of the community and the confinement of leadership almost exclusively among them,' the KPP, therefore, was a Muslim party.[20] By Huq's own admission, the KPP 'can no more be called a Hindu–Muslim party than the Congress be said to represent the Muslims'. He explained: 'We have kept the door open for Hindus to come in, because the problems with which we deal are all of provincial concern where united action by all sections seems to be essentially necessary. But as facts stand, the Hindus are practically non-existent in the Council of the Praja Party.'[21]

Thus the peculiar demographic composition of the province helped the earlier praja movement in Bengal grow into a Muslim movement rather surreptitiously. The Hindu high-caste groups with a clear stake in the zamindari system deliberately kept themselves away from this movement and hence from the KPP. As for the low castes, whose material and constitutional interests were very similar to those of the Muslims,[22] the KPP's failure to incorporate them into its fold in significant numbers was due more to the lack of systematic organizational plans than to any pronounced policy of the party.[23] In fact, it enjoyed some support amongst the low-caste groups in the countryside but, in the system of separate electorates, that support had little relevance for the Muslim constituencies. After the elections, the party claimed that two of the successful candidates in depressed-caste constituencies had been put forward by the party, even though they contested as independent candidates.[24] However, this cannot escape attention that the 'natural' transformation of praja politics into a religiously coloured Muslim party clearly coincided with the flurries of pre-election mobilization activities.

The pre-election days also showed how the KPP strenuously kept itself away from the overt and aggressive Islamic propaganda. It was mandatory to do so to dissociate itself from the League. The seemingly facile 'talks of Muslim unity' were shunned as 'worse than useless'.[25] But why was it at all important to maintain distance from the League before the elections? Both Abul Mansur Ahmed and Mohammad Waliullah spoke of the heightened animosity between the KPP and the BPML during this time.[26] Their negotiations broke down on the question of the professed aims and objectives of the two parties, primarily on the KPP's insistence on the abolition of zamindari.[27] But this lack of unity between the two 'Muslim' parties was not merely about their conflicting 'class interests' in a conventional socialistic sense. There was an additional dimension in this conflict, which in Huq's own words represented a different sort of 'class contradiction'. This was the conflict between the non-Bengali business community of Calcutta and the Bengali Muslim community. As far as the League Board was concerned, it was a party dominated by the Muslim landed and urban elites. Closely tied to the all-India parent body, the main steering of the League Board in fact lay in the hands of big industrial interests like the jute-mill owners of north India. The non-Bengali Muslim magnates of Calcutta such as the Ispahanis and Adamjee Haji Daud realized that they must count on the political support of a Muslim organization in their competition with the Hindu industrial interests, the Marwaris and Bhatias.[28] The League under Jinnah appeared the most likely launching platform for this purpose.[29] It was these groups in Calcutta that provided the strongest support for Jinnah, who, until then an unfamiliar name in Bengal, readily found favour among the non-Bengali Muslim groups. Two rising Muslim leaders of Calcutta, both businessmen and non-Bengalis, A.H. Ispahani and Abdur Rahman Siddiqui, became Jinnah's close aides. Thus, in the mid-1930s, doubts arose about whether the AIML and its provincial representatives truly cared for the Bengali Muslim interests.[30] In contrast, the KPP from the very beginning projected itself as authentically 'local', both in terms of composition and agenda. Most of the chairmen and minor officials of the zilla boards, local boards and union boards with their large followings joined the Praja Party, imparting a local colour to the organization. The KPP base was actually rather weak in the urban areas, its popularity being mostly concentrated to the mofussils. Its stronghold was in the districts of Khulna, Jessore, Barisal, Mymensingh, and Faridpur. Due to its 'local' character, the KPP's claims to represent the true 'Bengali Muslim' interests appeared well-founded.

The disparity in terms of composition and organizational techniques leaves no doubt that the AIML rose in support of the League Board in Bengal, while the KPP steadily began to lose favour with the AIML. Huq and his KPP consistently explicated the distance between the Bengali Muslim community and the non-Bengali business and capitalist Muslims on two grounds: first, economic interests; second, culture and language. He would dismiss the League simply on account of these 'Ispahanis' who, in his views, would unfailingly symbolize the oppositional realities of the Bengali Muslim and the non-Bengali Muslim worlds. 'In the [League] Board, out of 28 members, as many as 11 are non-Bengalis who hail from Ispahan, Tehran, Badakshan and Samarkhand, and other places outside Bengal, and 89 per cent are landlords and capitalists. These landlords and capitalists cannot certainly join us in this fight, because they are the very people with whom we will have to carry on a life and death struggle.'[31] During the election campaigns in Patuakhali constituency, known for its Nazimuddin-versus-Fazlul Huq ('Khwaja versus Praja') contest, Nazimuddin's followers asked Huq why he refused to represent the League. Huq allegedly replied that since the League had become 'a power-machine for rich people like Ispahanis and Suhrawardys', he did not find it mindful of the 'Bengali Mussalman interests'.[32] The raison d'être for the KPP lay in its dissociation from the League, and to this end, the unbridled cries of Islamic unity needed to be carefully avoided throughout the elections. The League also did not lag behind in hurling at Huq its counter-offensive of betraying the 'Muslim cause'.[33] Even in the late 1930s, the myth of a single Muslim identity did not hold true even in this most vocal and politically active moment for Bengal's Muslims.

It can be concluded that despite the KPP's overwhelmingly Islamic composition and regular use of Islamic symbols, it could resist the lures of self-projection as an overtly Islamic party. However tough this tight-rope walk of dual strategy might seem, it served an important purpose in resisting a head-on collision between Muslim politics and Hindu politics in the province, or a clear electoral division between the Congress and the League. By maintaining this precarious middle ground, the KPP no doubt represented the possibility of offering a platform on which an inter-community provincial nation could be acted upon.[34]

When Huq joined the League in 1938, it meant an organizational decline for the KPP, but the possibility of a regional front mentioned above, as well as the traces of the KPP dual strategy lingered on for a considerable time. The reasons were simple. The League leadership in the province meanwhile underwent a compositional change due to its merger with the KPP, and some of the objectives and outlook of the latter were transferred to the newly reformed version of the former. The conservative spirit of pan-Islamism, which the all-India League used to uphold, could not curb the vitality of Bengali Muslim identity, although by this time the Bengal Muslims perceived themselves as separate from the social and political realities of the Bengali Hindu. The continued strength of this Bengali Muslim identity turned out to be an effective dampener in the so-called and all-too-magnified story of the spread of Muslim separatism. Despite its ultimate failure, the middle-path politics of the KPP served as a critical component in this story unfolding in Bengal.

Region–Nation and Its Three Moments of Failure

The Moment of an Unborn Alliance

A.K. Fazlul Huq, leading two coalition governments (1937–41, 1941–3) of the province, may be considered a paradigm figure of this era. In the middle of an ideological crossfire, he embodied both the agony and the hope of the Bengali Muslim world.[35] We have already mentioned that he represented the regional spirit of Bengali Muslims, and became the face of their identity confronting the homogenizing tendencies of League politics. Moreover, his politics was more authentically populist than many of his contemporaries in the sense that he could cast an enormously positive image in the minds of large sections of people, rural as well as urban, or professional middle classes as well as the uneducated mass of cultivators.[36] With such a strong popular endorsement behind him, Huq was described by a foreigner as the 'magician' of Bengali politics.[37] Jinnah, the self-proclaimed 'cold-blooded logician' of India could not but be wary of this 'magician' or the living legend of Bengal, more because the election climate of the mid-1930s made it patently clear that without the critical support of two Muslim-majority provinces of Bengal and Punjab, the all-India League would be a negligible political institution.[38] The contradiction between Huq's KPP and Jinnah's League, therefore, needs to be understood in the parallel contexts of their disparate ideological and political interests.[39] Although Huq himself underwent a political decline by the mid-1940s, the regional spirit he had embodied for so long continued to reign through the new League politics as his legacy, and drew the battle lines deep within the Bengali Muslim society.

At the critical moment of ministry formation, the Congress refused to come in to join the coalition with the KPP, and the latter had to ask for the League's support.[40] The Congress's decision of keeping itself out of any coalition in Bengal was unquestionably a mandate from the High Command.[41] Praja leaders like Syed Nausher Ali, Maulavi Shamsuddin Ahmed, Maulavi Ashrafuddin Choudhury, and Humayun Kabir who took active initiative in securing Congress support were greatly disappointed.[42] For most of the contemporary observers, the breakdown of the Congress–KPP understanding and the formation of the KPP–League ministry as a result were of enormous significance: 'It was a cursed day for Bengal.'[43] Interestingly, when historians later judged the significance of this event, it was interpreted as a lamentable failure of the 'secularist, radical politics' of the region.[44] I disagree with this interpretation and argue that the real importance of the moment of loss lay instead in the non-realization of a region-based and locally grounded popular political movement, which could only have been possible through a merger of the Hindu-dominated Congress and the Muslim-dominated KPP. The conflicted class character of the KPP has already been described above which negates the idea that an alliance with it was a sure way to a radical–leftist movement. I also pointed towards the key role the Muslim identity played, albeit in a subdued style, in KPP rhetoric. The complex use of religious symbols and religious ties by the KPP was in many ways remarkably similar to the 'Hindu' undertones of political culture of the Congress.[45] Yet both these organizations valued Bengali identity to such an extent as to surpass or at least overlap with the religion-based identity. The reliance on Bengali language was equally vital for both the organizations while the League was still struggling with its Urdu-speaking leaders campaigning in the interiors of the province.[46] In spite of its electoral successes, it still lacked in mass-contact techniques and lagged behind in many of the districts like Nadia, Murshidabad, Bogra, Pabna, Noakhali, Chittagong, and Tippera (present Tripura).[47] However, when the AIML played its brilliant strategic move by offering Fazlul Huq the cooperation of the League and also the premiership of the province, this weakness was removed to a significant extent.

The critical mass links of the KPP and the long-standing praja politics of its predecessor were thus won over by the League instead of the Congress. Had the Congress–KPP alliance taken place, the failure of Congress to design and implement its much-advertised 'Muslim mass contact campaign' could have been reversed by the KPP network.[48] It was already clear to many contemporaries that any Congress mass-contact campaign had an intrinsic limitation of not making much inroad into rural Bengal. This was partially due to its total lack of appreciation of the role of religion in the popular psyche.[49] No popular campaign in Bengal could possibly ignore the strong emotive appeals of the crescent of Eid, just like the blessings of Goddess Durga. But it was never admitted either by the hyper-secularist nationalists of the late colonial period, later to be termed as 'Nehruvians' in postcolonial India, or by the conservative nationalists marked by a deeply entrenched majoritarian syndrome. Both were equally distraught by the severity of the challenges that 'difference' threw on the face of the aspiring 'nation'. It is in this context that the failure of this moment is significant. If the combined strength of the Congress and the KPP could have opened up the possibility of a joint front for various identity-based regional parties, it would have marked a distant inheritance of the Das nationalism of the 1920s. With the removal of this possibility, the Muslim identity politics was hijacked by the League, by all means a more aggressive upholder of 'difference'.

The Moment of Surrender

If July1937 was the first lost opportunity of this period for the politics of region–nation, it was soon to be followed by the second one in October

1937, when Huq joined the League. It is usually suggested that Huq's KPP could not avoid the pressures of the more authentically Muslim organization, that is, the League.[50] However, this proposition needs to be modified. This is because the intensification of slogans like 'Islam in Danger' did not have much role in the power play between the two parties. The nature of negotiations was primarily interest-driven, and strategically determined.

From the very beginning of the ministry, the League strategy was to sideline the KPP agenda as far as possible. The fourteen-point parliamentary programme that the League and the KPP chalked out together was brought under enormous pressure from the League and finally took place only at the expense of the toning down of the KPP pre-election manifesto. Instead of an outright abolition of the zamindari system that the KPP had earlier pledged, the ministry finally decided only to appoint a committee of inquiry on the matter. The overwhelmingly non-agrarian background of its members played an important role here.[51] The clash of economic interests between the representatives of different sections of Bengali Muslim society ensured the defeat of the KPP's legislative agenda.

The formation of the ministry had to take place amidst bitterly contentious negotiations. A number of influential zamindars mobilized support behind their claims of seats in the cabinet, and made the situation so vicious that it needed three weeks to form the ministry. The preponderance of zamindari elements troubled Huq from the very beginning, and he was forced to shelve his populist and rayat-oriented politics for some time and make strategic overtures to the League members to keep the ministry going. The rural agrarian interests could not be adequately represented on the floor.[52] This capitulation to the League's pressures led to infighting within the KPP, resulting in a split as seventeen disloyal members, including two leading figures, Shamsuddin Ahmed and Maniruzzaman Islamabadi, were purged. Placed in an awkward situation, Huq took the decision of joining the League in October 1937. He was forced to make some other political compromises on the floor after joining the League. In November 1938, the ministry set up a Land Revenue Commission (known as Floud Commission), consisting mostly of the representatives of big zamindars.[53] The tremendous pressure on Huq and the tenant lobby right from the time when the Tenant Bill had first been proposed in 1937 finally led to a virtual eclipse of the KPP on the assembly floor.[54] The multi-class, multi-identity popular politics of the KPP was the prime reason behind its failure. It would thus be wrong to look for the reasons in its limited use of religion compared to that by the League.

However, even if religion did not explain the League's initial ascendancy within the assembly, it did so afterwards. Failure in matters of tenancy legislation made Huq somewhat desperate in looking for an alternative ground for legitimacy. The rayat-friendly image having suffered tremendously, his only hope now seemed to rely on the 'Muslim' popular appeal and specific 'Muslim' grievances were now taken up for redressal. He lent himself to become a signatory to the Report of the Inquiry Committee appointed by the council of the AIML to enquire into Muslim grievances in the Congress provinces, published as *Pirpur Report* in 1938. In December 1939, he published a pamphlet titled *Muslim Sufferings under Congress Rule*, where he accused the Congress of displaying 'the blatant arrogance of the militant Hindu'.[55] At the general meeting of the BPML, on 8 April 1939, Huq gave a speech particularly marked by a new tone of intolerance:

> The Muslims ruled India for seven hundred years. If you will so, you can again be the rulers of this country. We can establish an independent kingdom in Bengal, if we want to, therefore I ask you—once will it be so brethren, awake once and resolve…. If in Bengal the Congress gets the power of Government in its hands, here also it will begin similar oppression of non-Congressmen. The Congressmen are always ready to oppress, but they are silent only because to do so is beyond their power.[56]

Outside the assembly, the Muslim crowds were stirred up by the oratorical and organizational skills of H.S. Suhrawardy. The left-wing KPP leaders such as Humayun Kabir and Abul Mansur Ahmed, who had criticized Huq for his 'short-sighted' surrender to the League, were assaulted. After Huq's controversial 'surrender', his legitimacy needed to be tested by a no-confidence motion within the assembly in August 1938 by the militant wing of the KPP. Congress gave its strong support to the KPP motion. Tamizuddin, a radical KPP leader, launched a brutal offensive against Huq:

> A false and insidious cry of religion in danger has been raised and this has poisoned the very atmosphere of the country … and the Ministry is fostering the cry and has all but dragged the country into a mouth of volcano. How long should Bengal be allowed to groan under the dead weight of a ministry like this? When is Bengal get rid of this nightmare [*sic*]? [57]

Jogendranath Mandal, the depressed-caste leader, known for his long-standing rapport with Huq, also gave a speech on this motion which revealed his disillusionment with his former colleague:

It is with a very mixed feeling that I am constrained to take part in the motion.... [Huq] has aroused great hopes and great expectations when he acclaimed himself as the champion of the depressed classes and down-trodden peasants of Bengal. But today I stand disillusioned.... To our eternal shame and disgrace he has found his most congenial allies in the cream of Bengal aristocracy, whose heads, he had only a few months back, demanded on the charger. Today we find him in strange surroundings, amidst strange bed-fellows ...[58]

The motion against Huq who betrayed such 'great hopes and great expectations' was, however, defeated with a small margin, a pointer to the tough opposition he had to face because of the sudden conservative twist in his political stand.[59] The conservative League supporters found a strong boost at this victory: 'On the particular day, thousands of Muslims from Calcutta and even the suburban areas started approaching to the Governor's House, with the Muharram flag in their hands, and fiery slogans in their mouth ... a number of pro-motion members of the Assembly in fact spent the night in the Council in the fear of mob-violence ...'[60]

The authenticity of Huq's new leaning towards a pronounced Islamism was soon put to test by the League. At the Lahore Conference in 1940, he was asked, as the premier of the province which had the largest Muslim population, to move the momentous resolution known as 'Pakistan Resolution'. He appeared to have taken great interest in representing the Muslimness, and declared, 'I am a Muslim first and Bengali afterwards. I will take revenge on the Hindus of Bengal if Muslims are hurt in Congress-ruled provinces.'[61] Understandably, there was a huge reaction outside the formal political quarters against Huq's message. In fact, the change in Huq's public image and his government was doubly unfortunate because it confirmed the suspicions harboured against the new ministry for being 'communal'. Neither was it possible for Huq to convince the people about the initial compulsions of the KPP to form the coalition ministry with the Muslim League, or about his subsequent capitulation to the League pressure in the late 1937. In the Congress view, this ministry became no less than a reminder of 'the dark age'.[62] The conservative Hindu propaganda against the 'Khwaja–Praja' ministry gained momentum; the 'fear' of 'Muslim rule' rapidly spread.[63] In the Hindu-dominated districts, the Huq–League era saw a strengthening of the Mahasabha hold. An erstwhile Congress supporter of Noakhali confessed that the new 'Raj' convinced him of the importance of the Mahasabha, and the need to redress 'the wrongs perpetrated against the Hindus':

So far I was inspired by the Gandhian political ideals of village reconstruction and social service. However, the Muslim acquisition of political
power around 1940 gradually turned me into a rebel.... In my district, a
sizeable number of Hindus took refuge to the Hindu Mahasabha during
this period. Because of my professional life as a teacher, I became quite
close to Dr. Shyamaprasad: teaching and Mahasabha, this was my life
henceforward.[64]

No doubt the identification of the Huq–League ministry as the keeper
of the 'Muslim' interest both by the Hindu and the Muslim press was the
most critical development of this era. The political narrative of Huq and
his tryst with the League shows how the new context of electoral politics
had pushed a leader from Moderate politics to a conservative and an
intolerant political creed.

There still remained a few unresolved riddles. Why would a Moderate-
turned-hardliner still care to woo the Hindus in his own province, as he
would be seen doing afterwards?[65] Much attention has been directed to
his calamitous declaration of being 'Muslim first and a Bengali afterwards.' But this utterance needed to be weighed against the innumerable
occasions when he prioritized his Bengali identity rather unwaveringly,
even after this above declaration. It has recently been argued by a historian that 'Huq was placed in a precarious position'.[66] Put in a wider
perspective, his declaration itself raises doubts about Huq's own convictions. The rhetorical emphasis was perhaps strategically employed,
and stands in stark contrast to his not-so-'communal' expressions of
the preceding and following years.[67] Whereas his 'Save the Muslims'
type of slogans have been emphasized time and again by historians, his
reservations against the non-Bengali Muslim interest were not traced
carefully. Most ironically, we must note that when Jinnah pressurized
him to resign from the Defence Council, the 'Muslim first' leader wrote
a letter to Liaquat Ali Khan, secretary of the AIML, as late as in 1941,
where he said:

> I wish to record a most emphatic protest against the manner in which the
> interests of the Moslems of Bengal and the Punjab are being imperiled by
> Moslem leaders of the provinces where the Moslems are in a minority....
> I will never allow the interest of 33 millions of Moslems of Bengal to be
> put under the domination of any outside authority.[68]

Instead of reading Huq's statements and declarations with a facile
haste, and bringing charges of rabid communalism against him, it still

remains an important imperative for the historians to decode the complex nature of his 'Muslim' rhetoric. It is possible to locate numerous occasions where he championed his Bengali identity with equal passion, and with a focus on inter-community cooperation.[69] In a conference organized by the nawab of Murshidabad in 1940, Huq gave a speech on Hindu–Muslim unity in the province: 'Hindus and Muslims must realize that they have got to live together and, if need be, lay down their lives together for the good of their motherland.'[70] This conference even proposed to establish a permanent non-party organization to carry on the work of creating an atmosphere of communal harmony and co-operation.[71] We must also remember that in February 1940, the same month when the Lahore Resolution was being placed, Huq convened a joint Hindu–Muslim conference (by inviting both Congress and the Mahasabha) in Calcutta. He was also desperate to make a fresh bid for Congress cooperation, envisaging a new inter-communal party. We will return to this point later. For now, it is important to note that however tenuous this combination of Muslimness and Bengaliness might appear to us, in all probability, just like many other Bengali Muslims of those times, Huq was keen on upholding both, and dreaming of a regional politics to foreground his Muslimness, and yet accommodate others.

Whatever his ideas and intentions had been, his political steps jeopardized Bengal's interests. It meant a subordination of Bengal's regional interest to the evasively homogenized 'Muslim' interest of the AIML. We must note that by merging with the League, Huq not only compromised the regional Muslim identity but also gave a new life to the League in one of its very difficult moments. If Huq and Sikander Hayat Khan, who was heading the Unionist Ministry in Punjab, had not joined the League formally in 1937–8, and thus not strengthened the latter by the significant weight of 'numbers' of the two Muslim-majority provinces, the political trajectory of the League would have been locked in the quagmires of minority-province politics. Chaudhury Khaliquzzaman, a prominent leader of the League, later described the importance of the event:

> What would have happened if the Punjab and Bengal Premiers had not agreed to come to the rescue of the Muslim League organization in the U.P.… Briefly it would have remained merely the Muslim League of the Minority provinces and in time to come would have had to surrender to the Congress. Sir Sikander and Fazlul Huq saved Muslim India by throwing their weight at the crucial hour behind the Muslim League.[72]

The moment of surrender was even more unfortunate than the first moment of failure, because, in all probability, Huq's decision to merge with the League was only strategic and not born out of his personal convictions. His continuous vacillation, his still desperate bids to strike a balance between various interests indicated that, for him, joining the League was just a question of political survival. A deadly blow to the region–nation of Bengal was unwittingly delivered by a Muslim leader, in whom some Hindus had once discovered a 'perfect Bengali'.[73]

The Moment of a Damaging Entente

The second coalition ministry formed in December 1941 by Fazlul Huq and Shyamaprasad Mookherjee of Hindu Mahasabha, was by all standards an odd political entente. It was odd as well as damaging, primarily on two counts. First, once more the Congress had failed to provide a political lifeline to Huq, which meant that the moderate trends of Hindu and Muslim politics were stripped of another chance. Second, there was the further loss of Huq's personal political stature due to his new Pact. Had the Congress been successful in making use of this critical moment and extending a hand to Huq, it could have been a different political trajectory for Bengal.

A brief look at the preceding developments is perhaps called for to indicate the plausibility of a Huq–Congress ministry at this historical juncture. During the war, Huq withstood great pressures from the AIML[74] in order to provide the government wartime cooperation.[75] Skirting his way through pressures from different quarters, Huq wanted to come out of the League fold and to strive for a different power configuration within the province. On the eve of the viceregal talks with Jinnah and Gandhi in February 1940, this fiercely independent provincial leader of the League did not hesitate to issue a statement suggesting an alternative course of action on the part of the ministries in the provinces:[76] 'Whatever may be the result of these talks in high quarters, I stick to my resolve to try and bring about a peaceful solution of the problem that concerns Bengal ... and object which must be dearer to the heart of every Bengali.'[77] Disregarding the already standing resolution of the AIML Working Committee forbidding any negotiation by individual province for any communal settlement on an independent basis, he convened a conference of Muslim and Hindu leaders (Congress and Mahasabha) in Calcutta. This conference, held on 24 February 1940,[78] found him making a passionate appeal 'to find out a lasting solution of all differences'.[79] It took place at a time when Huq was fast heading to a conflict with the League authorities. The final disciplinary action (26 December 1941) was taken against him as he tactfully dismissed the ministry and was about to form the Progressive Coalition Ministry with the support of the Congress and the Hindu Mahasabha.[80] The experiences of the past coalition made Huq especially aware of the fact that he needed to look for the support of 'other' quarters because of the urgency of mobilizing numbers within the assembly. The purpose of provincial interest also pointed towards a satisfactory accommodation of other community interests. To put it simply, Huq now became desperate for a large measure of Congress cooperation. He even envisaged the formation of a new inter-communal party:

> The formation of this party, bringing together the diverse elements,... is an event unprecedented in the history of India, and should, I hope, be an augury not only for the cessation of communal strife, but also for the good of all sections of the people in this country ...[81]

The Congress, too, was not wholly averse to the idea. Its stance of blocking the League, not Huq, was evident from a telegram sent by the governor of Bengal to the viceroy: 'The attitude of official Congress is that they will oppose any Ministry formed by Nazimuddin but will remain neutral in the case of any Ministry formed by Huq.'[82] The broader political climate also was not uncongenial to such a possibility. As Huq began to distance himself from the AIML, it was reported from the Chittagong division that the 'dissensions in the Muslim League have for the time being promoted more amicable relations between the two major communities'.[83] However, Huq's all-time favourite dream of forging an alliance with the Congress did not come true. Sarat Bose, the most important leader of the Congress at that time, was arrested under the Defense of India rules on the very day of forming the new cabinet, and therefore was barred from any possible cooperation with Huq.[84] In an extremely well-calculated move, the governor frustrated the enormous possibilities of this historical moment. This was a real tragedy for Bengal and an hour of silent victory for the Raj. The promising combination of Huq and Bose, full of potential, was never allowed to materialize, although the public mood was not averse to give this project of inter-community ministry another chance.[85]

Rather ironically, this public support began to wane quickly after the formation of a very different type of inter-community coalition in 1941.

The belief in an inter-community rule suffered a great deal due to the increased social and political polarization during this time, and due to the tremendously damaged reputation of the leaders at the helm of the administration. The ignominy Huq already suffered in the Hindu society due to his excessive Islamic rhetoric earlier was now ironically combined with an alienation from his Muslim followers due to his breakup with the League and his joining hands with the Mahasabha. Huq was personally attacked for his 'betrayal' of the Muslim cause.

Thus, notwithstanding the fact that the Huq–Mahasabha ministry in fact fared reasonably well in terms of administrative competence, its political acceptance quickly diminished. The Bengal Muslim community at large showed signs of rapidly growing intolerance during this Huq–Mahasabha ministry. At a time when 'Pakistan' had already been proposed as an ideal by the League, and the Mahasabha had already engaged itself in fierce opposition to the political claims of Muslim difference, the alliance could not but be deeply suspected. The hope for a future inter-communal regional nation gradually receded to the background with this unlikely entente, seen primarily as untrustworthy, untenable, and one devoid of any ideological basis.[86]

Indeed, it was during this time that Huq finally lost the political ground he had so painstakingly earned in the province, leaving the AIML an unchallenged authority in provincial matters of Bengal. Suhrawardy, the primary League spokesman and the most aggressive opponent of Huq, rose to prominence during these years. He began to appropriate the widespread popular base Huq and his KPP had so far built. That base was still not insignificant. Despite being a mercurial politician, even up till 1941 Huq had enjoyed a tremendous amount of popular support. A journalist like Waliullah, never particularly sympathetic to Huq, observes that in 1941,

> [h]ad it not been Shyamaprasad, Muslims of Bengal would have continued to provide their support to Huq that day, however much the League fought against him. Because, for large sections of Bengali Muslims still used to think that all differences between Huq and the League ministers were nothing but quarrels for power, and *Huq did not yet lose his image of savior of the masses—it had no connections with their dreams of Pakistan* [emphasis mine].[87]

The huge significance of this moment in Bengal's history can perhaps be best assessed with the projection of a counterfactual. Had it been

Huq and Bose together, with their respective organizations and popular followings behind them, Bengal politics might have gained a new lease of life. Just as Bose was the only Hindu leader in good terms with the regional Muslim community, Huq was the only Muslim leader whom large sections of Bengali Hindus still considered fair-minded. The failure to strike a coalition with Sarat Bose and his Congress, therefore, quickly provided a potent argument to the League leaders that Fazlul Huq was courting a self-professed anti-Muslim organization only for personal gains.[88] He still had his followers in the province. An administrative report in August 1941 mentioned that 'Huq's followers have started a campaign of criticism of the Muslim paper *Azad*, the editor of which is Akram Khan, the Vice-President of Bengal Provincial Muslim League.'[89] In anticipation of his breach with the League, he even started to publish a newspaper called *Navayug*.[90] But, no doubt, the lack of popular trust in his leadership was plainly visible and irreversible after this odd experiment of 'Shyama–Huq' coalition. Even the relatively sensitive, politically aware Muslims were thrown off-balance by this sudden change in the course of events.[91] The Mahasabha, rather expectedly, did little to ward off the common Muslim's apprehensions. In order to counter the League propaganda, it observed an 'anti-Pakistan day' by holding meetings and rallies in the province.

The League, somewhat discredited by Huq's bold move of this second alliance, also enthusiastically drummed up this anti-Huq sentiment.[92] Suhrawardy and his followers warned the masses on their visits to towns and the countryside that the chances of Pakistan would evaporate if support was extended to Huq. The significance of the League was being put in the simplest and strongest terms: 'The goal of Pakistan, which now is part of its creed, will benefit Bengal Muslims far more than Muslims in any other part of India, hence it is here more than in any other province that the Muslim League must be strongest.'[93] It can be argued that the distrust and ignominy incurred by Huq's second ministry contributed substantially to further strengthening of the League in Bengal countryside.

Huq, however, had to remain cautious on the issue of 'Pakistan', and assert that his differences with Jinnah's League did not have anything to do with the idea of 'Pakistan'. By this time, Pakistan began to be seen as the most important element in the League programme. Consequently, Huq's fight with the League made his own stand on the question of Pakistan dubious in the public eyes. In the absence of a dependable party-base, he now found a 'growing threat' to his position even in eastern Bengal, his erstwhile citadel of power. He toured with some of his colleagues in certain districts to mobilize support for his new stand. But the Muslim students and youth, whom he had consistently championed, were rallying around Suhrawardy instead of him.[94] In Dacca and Noakhali, many of the students organized black-flag demonstrations with slogans of 'ghaddar murdabad' (down with the traitor).[95] The most violent incident took place at Feni College in Noakhali where, during Huq's visit, students appeared naked all over the college as a form of protest.[96] Huq's efforts to mobilize support through district tours were more than adequately matched by similar organized efforts of the BPML leadership. Local League heavyweights like Tamizuddin Khan, Khwaja Nasrullah; student leaders like Abdul Waseq and Fazlul Quadir Choudhury; Waliullah, the journalist; and Suhrawardy himself together undertook extensive tours in districts like Comilla, Brahmanbaria, Mymensingh and, of course, in Dacca. They were offered enthusiastic support and promises for cooperation in these districts, including Muslim small-peasant areas of Mymensingh, the traditional bastion for the Praja Party. They succeeded in convincing the less-informed people of the villages and mofussils that Huq, having proved himself unworthy of taking their responsibility in the political rough and tumble, they should look up to the League for an able leadership. The role of Maulana Akram Khan, the editor of the journal *Mohammadi*, was significant in this propaganda mission: villagers placed great trust in Maulana, a person without much political ambitions for himself.[97]

Amidst all this, one thing was clear. The Shyama–Huq ministry led to the political decimation of Huq, and no other Bengali Muslim leader had yet emerged to replace him. The eclipse of Huq did not imply that the Bengal Muslim world was readily subjected to the creed of Islamic exclusionism, as some historians would suggest.[98] But the hugely discredited leadership of Huq implied that the chances of building a regional political platform were diminished. Just as the dismissal of the Bengal Pact after Das's death in 1925 had once damaged this dream irrevocably, the three historic moments in Bengal's politics in early 1937, late 1937, and in 1941 delivered severe blows to the regional capacity of Bengal for addressing the problem of 'difference' on its own terms.

Twin Trends of Concern and Confrontation

The inter-communitarian political project of the region seemed to be a lost dream in 1943 when the Muslim League ministry with Khwaja

Nazimuddin, the premier, followed the Huq–Mahasabha government. However, an overall assessment of the period 1937–43 points towards the fact that at the social level, questions on community were being discussed and debated with great depths of concern. The conflicted nature of Bengali society can only be properly appreciated if we assess these trends of collaboration and confrontation together. Unfortunately, it has been a long tradition in the historiography of pre-Partition Bengal to overlook the forces of concern and coalition between the two major communities, and focus exclusively on the forces of disruption instead. A different perspective is urgently needed, therefore, by highlighting the complex social and political forces at work, which were sometimes complementary, and sometimes contradictory to each other. Only such a perspective enables us to grasp the true nature of Bengal's experiments with the problem of 'difference', and the multiple possibilities of 'national' solution in the 1940s.[99]

New Leadership and Bengali Identity

In the search for such a perspective, the bearings of the symbol of Pakistan in Bengali Muslim society assume a critical importance. Till the end of this period, the Bengali Muslim leaders resisted the pressures and priorities of the AIML. The latter indeed achieved a good measure of organizational success in Bengal, owing to the favourable disposition of the provincial ministries. Its branches came up at various sub-divisional towns like Pabna, Noakhali, Chittagong, Dacca, and Faridpur. Yet the support for the AIML from Bengal fell much short of what it would have expected, which caused a great deal of anxiety for its all-India leadership.

The instance of Shahidgunj Conference may be telling in this context. In 1938, this conference was convened in Calcutta as a part of a country-wide League movement against the Sikh intransigence over a disputed gurdwara at Shahidgunj. The conference in Calcutta, however, was a great failure.[100] Even the government failed to pull support for the advertised cause.[101] Similarly, at the Lahore session of the League (March 1940), no more than 400 delegates could be mobilized from Bengal.[102] The aware journalists of that time observed the striking lack of interest among Bengali Muslims about this conference and its proposal which would soon be famous.[103]

On the assembly floors too, the League's show of strength did not go unchallenged. Between 1938 and 1940, the Huq ministry withstood a lot of internal resistance and achieved notable success in pushing its recommendations.[104] During this first ministry, Huq's efforts at addressing various peasant issues were highly praised. The no-confidence motion against the ministry in 1938 could be defeated because of the support he still used to muster within the assembly.[105] However much Huq was accused for his capitulation to the League forces, it was his unmitigated 'Bengali' image that still served well in resisting the pressures of the League, a conglomeration of diverse, heterogeneous elements, with a strong non-Bengali character.

During this time, the craving for a pronounced Bengali identity against the desperate attempts of constructing a singular Muslim identity advocated by the League was reflected in various contemporary accounts. From one such account, we come to know of a local incident, revealing in this context. When Jinnah presided over a meeting at Berhampur Muslim Council, attended by thousands of illiterate poor Muslims, he was not treated well by the crowd. The Bengali way of organizing popular meetings demanded an inaugural song before the speeches. The popular folk-singer Abbasuddin Ahmed was about to take the stage when, suddenly, Jinnah, the chief guest, announced, 'No music!' The whole gathering fell silent for a while before almost several hundred people shouted: 'No music, no sabha! We want Bengali songs by Abbasuddin!' As the entire crowd stood up in protest, Jinnah had to concede. 'This is what the Bengali identity was like those days,' Biswas, a contemporary journalist, commented.[106] The memoirs and journalistic accounts of the time also suggest that the ascendancy of the League during this era should not blind us to overlooking the emotive appeals of the region–nation still at work. The political rhetoric of Huq on a 'united Bengali society' was not devoid of its social content. His opponents, too, conceded that even when Huq had difficult times within the assembly, he had the unwavering support base of the Muslims in the rural areas where the 'Bengali' identity was the most natural inheritance.[107] For this community, maintaining and upholding of a 'Bengali' heritage often was not a matter of negotiation but simply an everyday sociocultural practice.

The urban Muslim youth was still looking for a potent leader to rally around. When Subhas Bose, one of the most prominent 'national' faces of the region by this time, sent a call to the Muslim students and middle-class professional Muslims of Calcutta, the impact was immediately visible. Bose intended to popularize the image of Siraj-ud-Daula as the last independent ruler of pre-British Bengal, and by virtue of that historical fact, a 'national' hero. He received an enthusiastic response in Calcutta for a student movement launched by him for the removal of the Holwell Monument. Siraj Day was observed on 3 July 1940. The Muslim students joined these movements en masse along with the Hindus. Former League workers recall how, with the declaration of Holwell Day and Siraj Day, Bose was able to create a stir among the Muslim students and youth, most of whom were involved only with the League.[108]

In the contemporary Bengali Muslim discourse, the abundance of regional sensibility was striking, to say the least. A host of writers, authors, poets, and composers like Kazi Motahar Hossain, Humayun Kabir, Abul Mansur Ahmed, and Abdul Sadaq actively engaged in preserving and spreading this heritage. In one of his articles, 'Swadhinata-Jatiyata-Sampradayikata', Kazi Motahar Hossain urged the Muslim intellectuals to come forward with their own views of Bengaliness and thus help the community (sampraday), as well as the nation (jati).[109] Abul Mansur Ahmed wondered why the Bengali Muslims failed to counter the hegemonic culture in Bengal in an effective way. He proposed that they should take part in and contribute to the cultural life of the Bengali community through the development of Muslim cultural events into general regional festivities like Durga Puja or Christmas.[110] On the principles of representation and practical politics, Abdul Sadaq put forward the following insights in his article 'Nikhil Bharat Federation Gathan ki Sambhab?' (Is it possible to develop an all-India federation?): 'Hindu–Muslim unity is indeed possible in Bengal for two reasons. One, Bengal has its special characteristics, and two, the people of other provinces cherish a distinct anti-Bengali sentiment.'[111] The sessions of Bangiya Mussalman Sahitya Sammilan were held with great enthusiasm, where scholars like S. Wajid Ali, Abdul Karim Sahitya Bisharad, Muhammad Hedayetullah, Kazi Motahar Hussain reiterated their faith in the prospects of Muslim Bengali literary accomplishments. Kazi Nazrul Islam's electrifying presence was by this time missed in the Sammilan due to his illness, but Golam Mostafa, another poet of reputation, came forward to lead the meetings. The extent of popular involvement in these meetings used to surprise even the organizers.[112]

During the second Huq ministry, the increased popularity of Akram Khan as the editor of the *Mohammadi*, the regional mouthpiece journal of the AIML, did not, however, reduce the distance between his own political views and those of the leaders like Tamizuddin, Suhrawardy, and Abul Hashim. The latter group was still heavily discontented with the AIML involvement in the regional issues, and their discontent was intensified on the issue of Pakistan.[113] Huq himself continued to be the key figure in spreading the spirit of the region–nation, already frustrated and jeopardized to a great extent by his own political choices. During 1941–2, in order to project his government as inter-communal, a scheme for promotion and maintenance of communal harmony was drawn up in consultation with local officers and a handsome amount was earmarked in the budget of 1942–3 for this purpose.[114] Huq also participated in a February 1942 meeting of the Muslim Majlis in Calcutta with the same view and formed a Provisional Standing Committee with a group of young activists and leaders like Humayun Kabir. In June 1942 a conference at Calcutta under the auspices of the Hindu–Muslim Unity Association was attended by leading Hindu and Muslim leaders of Bengal under the presidentship of the nawab of Dacca.[115]

The AIML faced resistance from the BPML, reorganizing itself in terms of agenda and composition. Suhrawardy proposed that the former KPP members should join the League and thus strengthen the peasant wing of the BPML. Following this idea, Abul Mansur Ahmed and Maulana Abdullahil Baqui, two KPP stalwarts became formally associated with the League,[116] with some others like Nawabzada Hasan Ali Khan and Shamsuddin Ahmed of Kushtia. In order to organize the party at the mass level, greater attention was given to local grievances. An enquiry committee was formed in the Bengal League 'to investigate the cases of oppression of League workers and the Muslim public in general'.[117] A standing Disputes Settlement Committee was set up for the settlement of intra-party disputes. The district and sub-divisional League committees were organized on a regular basis. The working committee held as many as twenty two meetings in 1944.[118] To popularize the BPML in the countryside, abolition of zamindari was adopted as one of its leading goals. Disregarding the all-India League's opposition to the issue of tenancy rights, the proposal was passed by ceaseless persuasion of the former Praja Party leaders Abul Mansur Ahmed, Ghiasuddin Pathan, and Nurul Amin, all representing the Praja stronghold of Mymensingh. As a consequence of these attempts at reorienting the agenda and the organizational basis of the League, a host of new leaders emerged in Bengal, among whom Abul Hashim was the most promising face.

It was mostly due to Hashim's relentless endeavours that the BPML would now strengthen its already pronounced regional image. When in some other context, Hashim commented that during 1942–4 the BPML attained 'manhood',[119] he tried to indicate this process of transformation within the BPML. A leader with overtly socialist leanings, he had the vision of freeing the peasantry from the 'rusty shackles of the Permanent

Settlement'.[120] The younger generations of Bengali Muslims found in him a sincere and open-minded leader, marked by idealism and steadfastness. His approach was to bring the League 'out of the folds of the few into the broad world of the many'.[121] The League workers engaged themselves in enrolling new primary members in the localities. In 1943–4, in Dacca and Barisal alone, they enrolled as many as 160,000 and 105,500 respectively.[122] Although the AIML central command found Hashim too democratic and too 'communist' for its own good, Hashim retained his hold in the BPML as the most effective leader, with an added legitimacy for being hailed from the ranks of the young Leaguers.[123]

The 'Fifty's Famine', or the devastating famine of 1943, one of the major landmarks in the social history of colonial Bengal, had a role to play in strengthening the hold of this new League leadership of Bengal.[124] The huge toll taken by the famine undermined the League administration led by Nazimuddin, which took charge in the same year.[125] However, the administrative failure on the top was compensated to some extent by the admirable relief work of younger brigade of the League, led by Suhrawardy himself.[126] In mofussils and rural areas, Muslim students were mobilized on a large scale.[127] Kamruddin Ahmed, a League worker in the outskirts of Dacca, remembers later how medical teams were organized for mass-vaccination projects, while Hashim himself took personal interest in spreading medical facilities in distant localities.[128] Ahmed also mentions that these projects of the League were supported by the local Krishak Sabhas in districts like Dacca, Faridpur, and Mymensingh.[129] From the early 1940s, the local sabhas functioned with relative independence, as the Provincial Krishak Sabha and the National Krishak Sabha lost their interest in the larger prospects of any *adhiar* (sharecropper) movement after 1939–40.[130] By the mid-1940s, they had already carved out an existence of their own by various agitations organized locally, and threw their weight behind the Communist Party in certain districts and behind the Muslim League in others. Connections with the local sabhas strengthened the Bengali League leaders, and Abul Hashim and Suhrawardy emerged as two prominent leaders of the invigorated League politics at the provincial level. The regional Muslim movement found in Hashim an able successor to Fazlul Huq.

Social Reforms and Polarization

During the coalition governments of the late 1930s and early 1940s, a constant tension between the Bengali identity and a vigorous fabrication of 'Muslim interests' plagued the social and political discourse. The role of the overzealous Hindu protagonists of nationalism must also be taken into consideration here. A continuous indifference and impatience towards difference often jeopardized the expressions of the Bengali Muslim identity and polarized the society even more. The case of the Mohammedan Sporting Club may be a good case in point. The decision of the League government to develop this club as a 'Muslim' cultural symbol attracted vicious criticism from the Hindu Press.[131] No less as a result of this acrimonious reaction, the question of this club soon turned into a 'political' concern.[132] The club contributed to the enhanced popularity of the League in Bengal.[133] A number of branches of this club were established in the districts and sub-divisional towns, which soon became a target of political discontent.[134] Actions and reactions from the conservatives of both communities bolstered each other, leaving the Moderates helpless and endangered.

Consider the more reasonable reform of job reservations. This reform was aimed at attending to a longstanding grievance of the Bengali Muslims, who were visibly underrepresented in government jobs. On 25 August 1938, a resolution was brought by the Huq government recommending a 60 per cent reservation of all government jobs for the Muslims. In 1939, it was decided that the percentage of reservation for the Muslims in direct recruitment would be 50. Even this climb-down left many Bengali Hindu representatives in the assembly extremely agitated, in whose views the 'jump' from the 'minimum one-third' to 'minimum fifty per cent' for the Muslims to bring parity in government services seemed a 'reign of bias' under Muslim rule.[135] The government was squarely blamed for sacrificing the principle of 'efficiency' and 'quality' to the 'Muslim cause'.[136] Even Sarat Chandra Bose, the eminent Bengali Hindu nationalist known for his liberal inclinations, criticized Huq for this 'anti-nationalist' measure: 'What you advocate is the denial of nationalism and the apotheosis of the communal spirit at its worst.'[137]

The same argument was employed in case of the Secondary Education Bill. The purpose of the bill was to demand 'fair treatment': to transfer the charge of the Matriculation Examinations from Calcutta University to a government-elected council, which would call for necessary reforms in the educational field. Abul Mansur Ahmed commented in his autobiography:

> The objective seemed sensible. In most countries, even in the present West Bengal, this is the system that prevails now. Madhyamik [matriculate]

education is no more a concern of the University as such, rather a government concern. But, at that time, all Hindus irrespective of class and creed, burst into protest against the Bill. In fact, even before the Bill was brought on the floor, the Hindu papers started fierce propaganda against it.[138]

A heated debate took place in the university senate, where, among others, Shyamaprasad Mookherjee and Fazlul Huq presented two opposing viewpoints with great persuasion. The Hindu bhadralok opinion was near unanimous: the Bill was considered to inflict the 'taint of communalism' on the 'sacred shrines of learning'.[139] Ahmed recalls that his arguments in favour of this so-called 'communal' bill in some of his articles published in the 'secular' journal Krishak put him in severe conflict with Hemendra Nath Dutta, the managing director of the journal. As a result of this conflict, Ahmed was forced to give up his editorship of Krishak. 'Not the Bill, but [it was] the Hindu stand on the Bill that was "communal"', went his assessment.[140]

The attempts to remove the traditional symbols like the word 'shree' and the emblem of padma (lotus) from the logo of Calcutta University were fiercely debated as well. The Muslim leaders thought it was too 'Hindu', a direct invocation of the image cult. Maulana Akram Khan, the editor of Mohammadi, delivered a speech on this at the Town Hall, Rangpur, immediately after which the cue was taken up by some other Muslim ideologues. Leading intellectuals of Calcutta like Ramananda Chattopadhyay came forward to explain in Prabasi that neither shree nor padma had any such direct connection with any Hindu deity.[141] Anandabazar Patrika expressed concern at the 'recent traits of obsessive disorder [suchi-bayu-grastota] of the Muslims. They have started to shrink even at the remotest hints of something non-Islamic, and recognize anti-Islamic signals all over the place'.[142] On the other hand, the Muslim resentment spread among the student communities in far-off villages, as reflected on the pages of the Saptahik (weekly) Mohammadi and the Mashik (monthly) Mohammadi.[143] After long deliberations, the university conceded to the demand.

While the obsessive disorder (suchi-bayu-grastota) as indicated by Anandabazar Patrika was indeed manifest in the Bengali Muslim psyche, one cannot but notice that these contested symbols were vividly displaying Hindu undertones. The reactions were excessive, but not ungrounded. They demanded serious attention from the ideologues of both the communities. However, an informed and level-headed debate never took place at that time, excepting only one case: the case of the disputed song 'Bande Mataram'.

After its long, intimate association with Hindu nationalism, the song by this time was attributed the status of the 'national anthem' by the Congress. The Muslim outrage assumed grave proportions in many parts of the country. In a mass meeting at Calcutta in August 1937, thousands of copies of the book *Anandamath* were burnt. Challenging the common Muslim allegation against the song as being 'anti-Muslim and anti-nationalist', *Anandabazar Patrika* published a protracted and heated exchange of thoughts. Condemning the act of burning, Rezaul Karim, a leading nationalist Muslim, wrote an article in this newspaper, saying: 'In an age of growing faith in individual liberty, freedom of expression and greater tolerance of difference, where are we going in our country? With our heart heavy with deepest pain and shame, we should record our protest.'[144] Ramananda Chattopadhyay, the editor of *Prabasi*, sent a request to Gandhi asking about the 'national' status of the song, and published numerous persuasive articles in his own journal. Gandhi as well as Nehru and Subhas Bose were unsettled by the extent of the unrest. Tagore, nevertheless, championed the song, at least initially, and argued in favour of conferring a 'national' status on it.[145] He wrote in a letter to Nehru that although he did not hold the entire song to be a great one, but the patriotic disposition of its first stanza stood out on its own.[146] But the course of events made him reconsider the case and acknowledge that the song might be offensive to many, hence not fit for the epithet 'national'. He openly conceded that the phrase 'Bande Mataram' indeed retained a sectarian flavour. In his letter to Subhas Bose, Tagore's transition was clarified. In this letter he stated that addressing the Muslim grievance over the song was indeed necessary, as the song evoked the image of Goddess Durga:

> True, the idea is to imagine Mother Bengal as an embodiment of Durga herself. But should we expect that the Muslims will accept such a ten-armed Mother Goddess as their Mother Bengal?... *Anandamath* is literary creation; the song has been a good fit there. But in the national association of Congress it should not be the national anthem.[147]

Tagore's sensitive and circumspect argument was mixed with a grave note of caution, which demands special mention here. 'Let me remind you that even in this year's Puja magazines we have seen many cases where this song has been religiously used. What is so easily acceptable to us for being religious expressions might also easily be unacceptable to another religious creed.'[148]

Significant is his use of the term 'we' while admonishing the Bengali Hindus for their impatient ways: 'We resent strongly when a certain section of Muslims becomes unfairly rigid and unaccommodative. Is not our own rigidity merely a replication of such attitude?... In our national pursuit, we need patience, tolerance, good sense. We do not want endless tussles spurred by our rigid attitude towards each other.'[149] After handling the problem of difference for several decades, Tagore's own expressions thus began to reveal a clear and confident community identity, which was, however, impossible to brand as 'communal'. This was an enlightened sense of identity, eager to negotiate between itself and a larger one, in this case, presumably, the 'national', through the principle of patient and generous accommodation. According to Tagore, there was a crucial difference between condemning the Muslims for their intolerance towards Bankimchandra's disputed novel on the one hand and insisting that this song be attributed with a 'national' status on the other. The national leadership, he thought, should be more discerning and judicious about this overtly 'negative' feeling of the conservative quarters.

It was finally decided that only the first stanza of the song was to be sung in the national meetings. Tagore was directly instrumental behind this decision, and became the target of strong reactions.[150] *Anandabazar Patrika* criticized Tagore as well as Bose and other Congress leaders involved in the verdict and described it as nothing but 'a blatant act of appeasement':

> Why so much anxiety and deliberation? Even after collecting the mandate from the old poet, why refrain from honoring the song in its totality as 'national'? Why saying that other songs would be equally welcome when knowing fully well that in all the provinces *Bande Mataram* has already been taken up as 'the' national anthem? Do we not know what is there behind such an attitude?[151]

Alongside the 'Bande Mataram' debate, another controversy erupted around the staging of a play, *Gairik Pataka*, based on the life and times of Shivaji, the famous Maratha warrior of the late Mughal period. Abul Kalam Shamsuddin recollects in his memoir that the liberal Bengali Muslims felt deeply 'pained' at the exalted Maratha glory in curbing the medieval Islamic culture and politics conveyed in the play:

I was surprised having read the explanatory article Buddhadev Basu wrote about this [*Gairik Pataka*] event; it seemed he could not even realize what was causing us pain. In fact, why singling him out? No Hindu of that time could possibly realize what we used to think and say. Otherwise, what could have led our country to its present shape and state? [152]

No doubt, this 'pain' caused by the staging of a historical play was indeed indicative of a collective social anxiety (or 'suchi-bayu-grastota', the obsessive disorder, as suggested by *Anandabazar Patrika* in a different occasion, mentioned earlier). This is where one comes perilously close to a divisive agenda of a community, which can legitimately be described by the derogatory term 'communalism'. One finds it difficult to infer from this narrative whether a more flexible stand on 'Bande Mataram', that is, to strip the song of its 'national' status, could have comforted the Bengali Muslims at large. The insight Tagore provided about the latent religious underpinnings of the song implied that it was best to glorify it as a literary gem but not as a 'national' symbol. At the same time, there is no denying the fact that, for a substantial section of Bengali Muslims, addressing the problem of difference began to mean campaigning for a reverse sectarianism, upheld for some political advantage. The situation got worse because of the lamentable lack of a competent leadership at the helm of political affairs after Huq's decline. Slowly but steadily, the gap between 'community sensibility' and 'communalism' was getting blurred in both Hindu and Muslim discourse.[153] The positive, liberal orientations and the inter-communal cultural efforts of the Bengali Muslims were being expropriated by the mid-1940s by the conservatives of their own society—a process which could perhaps have been averted if there were an able and insightful cultural and political leadership at the top.

Significantly, the Hindu Bengali over-reactive communal onslaughts were more a characteristic feature of Calcutta than of the mofussils or small towns of Bengal. This perhaps suggests that the problem of difference was more vitally relevant to the educated Muslim middle class rather than the rural Muslim masses to whom the leaders used to look for their own social and political legitimacy. One must see in this narrative of mutual distrust a competition around material gains and opportunities; but at the same time, a sense of deprivation felt in the cultural and social spaces also played a critical role. It is hugely sensible to read this story of Bengal's political society as one of conflict between the centre and the margins, religious identity (or caste identity) being only a vehicle for such heightened resentment. The reaction, or over-reaction, of the

Hindu bhadralok society, mostly with its urban locations and assertive cultural expressions, was also distinctly marked by centre–periphery tensions, and their community sensibility was only partially defined by religion. This sensibility, on the contrary, was loaded with various engraved identity markers like caste, class, community, urbanity, cultural elitism, or a combination of all/some of these. The deceptive tag of 'communalism', therefore, should not blur the inherently overlapping identities, or restrain us from delving deeper into the questions of cultural space and social fairness, unfolding themselves in a society frantically rummaging around a collective self called 'national'.

The Question of Community Representation

'There is today dark uncertainty before us ... but all this will vanish in no time if we can achieve two things—unity among Congressmen and a Hindu–Muslim settlement', hoped Subhas Bose in the 1920s.[154] By the 1940s, politics of difference became tremendously challenging in Bengal. On the one hand, it bore the onslaughts of divisive communalism, and on the other, it needed to deal with the legitimate questions of community difference. An inter-community government could have been the best way to counter the challenge by addressing the fair demands of representation, and at the same time, by harnessing the excesses of such demands as well.[155] The demands of representation need to be examined more closely in this context for a better understanding of the challenges of the time. The most intriguing questions were: if state machinery had to accommodate various communities and groups, what would be the fair basis of the government representation at a formal level? Also, what should be the ratio of representation of the civil institutions at a more general level? In other words, was it at all sensible to consider communal representation or group representation in the assembly, or the administrative departments, or in the non-elected fields of job recruitment and educational opportunities?

Even within the limited span of the first Huq ministry, the Bengal Legislative Assembly underwent debates on separate electorates, community representation, and community rights and privileges. The well-formulated and emotionally charged expositions proved the urgency of 'representation' in the context of late colonial Bengal. Huq argued that the communities should get representation on the basis of population ratio: 'We feel that, under present conditions, the Moslems do not get that opportunity to which they think they are entitled on the basis of their numerical strength. All that I plead for is that we should be given opportunities to take our proper share in the administration of the affairs of our country and to be partners with the other sections of the community in the civic and administrative life of the Province.'[156] Although the goal of having a 'proper share' in the 'civic and administrative life of the province' would apparently sound most innocuous, the matter was not simple if liberal principles of modern governance were to be attended. A modern state in the Western model, it was already known in the late 1930s, demanded equal power over all its citizens, although it could not guarantee an equal participation by all of them. The space for hegemonic control in the garb of 'representation' was allowed in the modern statecraft, as well as in the modern civil society. This naturally brought back the question of the pre-existing social–economic conditions and cultural power balance to the minds of relatively marginalized members of the society. After decades of assertions of social and political rights and the stubborn resistance put against those assertions, leaders like Huq were only too familiar with the caveats of nationalism. He considered it vital that in Bengal 'the participation of all classes and communities in the work of administration should be so arranged that all the communities may have equal opportunities'. In Huq's view, it was not mandatory to 'depend merely on theories in order to decide whether a particular course should be taken or not':

> If Swaraj really attends this message for all, I submit that the progressive realization of responsible government in India demands that the participation of all classes and communities in the work of administration should be so arranged that all the communities may have equal opportunities to show how much they are prepared to contribute to the common good. If the situation needs adjustment in certain matters, then adjustments should be made. You need not depend merely on theories in order to decide whether a particular course should be taken or not.[157]

To ensure that 'all classes and communities' would participate in administration, it might be necessary to formulate new principles of governance more imaginatively.[158] Huq's pleas might have sounded desperate and fraught with anxiety, but they were also highly cogent, and well-defended in the face of strongly negative reactions.

'Theories' could not be avoided though, in the way Huq would have liked it. It could not but put leaders like Sarat Bose into trouble that the principles of communal representation or communal job quotas should necessarily be introduced in order to enable all classes and communities participate in the task of national administration. Bose's reaction at this suggestion that 'each community might be led to believe and be encouraged in the belief that its interest would not be furthered and protected by public servants belonging to communities different from its own' was one of sheer bewilderment:

> Do you really hold that the principle of nationalization of the public services in India should be carried down from the national to the communal plains so that each community might be led to believe and be encouraged in the belief that its interest would not be furthered and protected by public servants belonging to communities different from its own? If so, when and where do you think there would and should be an end to this process of splitting up?[159]

He would ask: what, then, would be the ingredient of commonality, if 'the process of splitting up' was to be given such a free hand? 'Your argument regarding the employment of Muslims and Scheduled Caste Officers for looking after the Muslims and Scheduled Castes is really the "reductio ad absurdum" of the principle of Indianization. I wonder how you are going to put this principle (really negation of principle) into operation.'[160] Bose raised the most relevant logical riddle that the 'theories' of modern state suffer from, when faced with the claims of its constituent particularities. What would 'nationalization' of the public services at all mean? Also, where would such splits end, if started once? 'Supposing you begin by differentiating between the so-called Caste-Hindus (a stupid and misleading classification) and the Hindus belonging to the Scheduled Castes (an entity so artificial and unreal that no better label could be attached to it), could you logically refuse me, if I, a Kayastha, demanded that my case shall be governed by Kayasthas alone ... ?'[161]

Undoubtedly, in 1939, Bose was caught right in the middle of the conceptual impasse created by the nation and its differences. He did not dismiss the importance of the question of representation. He also added that special arrangements might be made in case of particular communities. But he did not endorse reservation on 'communal' lines in all matters of 'national' representation and participation.

> I can understand the eagerness of the members of a particular community to take part in the administration of the province and also their desire to have a fair share of the economic advantages of public services. It is necessary to remove such grievances, and it is from this point of view that I

have supported communal reservation as a traditional arrangement. But what you advocate is the denial of nationalism and the apotheosis of the communal spirit at its worst.[162]

He would not place himself fully against the principle of 'communal reservation' as long as it did not amount to the 'denial of nationalism'. This debate did not reach its logical end, but at least revealed promises of coming to a compromising ground.

Bose perhaps missed a point here, that more than a question of communal interests being satisfied, it was a question of voices being heard. The concern was not what was being said, but who was saying it. Self-representation, although enormously troubling as an administrative principle, indeed bore great significance in the context of an incipient democracy in a supremely heterogeneous society. Claims of representing oneself developed into a demand for group representation in the realms of practical politics in its course, and it was the formation and identity of the groups in a politically fluid society that led to all these debates of self-signification. Far from a communal volcano waiting to erupt, Bengal politics in the late 1930s and early 1940s was experimenting with a very familiar logical riddle of modern democracy, where the 'politics of presence', seeking to replace the 'politics of ideas', began to accentuate the narrower identities.[163]

Pakistan: A 'Province-Based Solution'?

With the spread of the League's power in Bengal in the early 1940s, the word 'Pakistan' was transformed into a symbol signifying almost everything for everybody. The widespread construction of a notional 'Muslim' identity and its political articulation led to a whole new imagined world of rights and freedom borne within a single word, 'Pakistan'. Such overloaded subjectivity of the word inevitably led to many internal contestations among the Bengali Muslims, as is evident from the contemporary writings, memoirs, or other narratives. Many Bengali Muslims continued to find solace in the thought that Huq, however much he might oppose Jinnah and his AIML, was in fact a believer in 'Pakistan'. When, subsequently, many of their most informed leaders came to conclude from Huq's alliance with the doggedly anti-Pakistan Mahasabha that he possibly was not as serious about 'Pakistan' as he himself had claimed to be, some would still believe there must be some other 'Pakistan' in Huq's mind which would only slowly reveal itself.[164]

This pointed out the tremendous potential of the idea of Pakistan, at least of the version circulated in Bengali society in the 1940s, with a circle of endless confusion and evasiveness around the word. The confusion was even visible in some of the contemporary literary flourishes on Pakistan, consciously endowing it with a magical character, as the 'Aladin' incarnate in Bengal politics. Golam Mostafa, the prominent Muslim poet of the time, tellingly used the old imageries of 'Aladin' and 'Sinbad' in his ode to Pakistan.[165] How these multiple possibilities gradually became eradicated to produce a single vision of Pakistan appears to be an immensely interesting story, yet to be traced historically.

What did 'Pakistan' mean to the Bengali Muslims in the early 1940s? How far could it be related to the 'Pakistan' that Jinnah and the AIML proposed during all these years? Interestingly, the Lahore Conference initially failed to arouse much enthusiasm among Bengal's Muslims, possibly because the three League meetings before this particular session had in fact set off a sense of disinterest and disappointment in Bengali Muslims.[166] Around 400 delegates from Bengal finally participated in the conference, where Fazlul Huq, the chosen presenter of the famous Lahore Resolution (later to be referred to as the Pakistan Resolution), was greeted with rapturous slogans like 'Long Live the Bengal Tiger'. Amidst tremendous excitement and loud cheers, it was declared that the Pakistan scheme was, 'planting a vision of unlimited hope and enthusiasm'.[167] The 'hope and enthusiasm' possibly touched delegates from Bengal; one of them, Abul Hashim, then only an upcoming young leader of the Burdwan wing of the BPML, later recalled how he was moved by the Conference.[168] From his own admission, the Lahore Resolution was viewed by the leaders of Bengal as a scheme aimed to establish a number of independent and sovereign Muslim-majority zones in India, among which Bengal would be one. Neither the boundaries of such a zone, nor its definite political status was clear in their minds, not to speak of its connections with the non-'Pakistan' India. But by the phrase 'sovereign and independent states', the Lahore Resolution itself created the space for multiple interpretations. The peculiar imperatives of the AIML politics dictated the necessity of maintaining such confusion in the interest of an all-India Muslim politics. Clearly, the demands generated by the majority provinces and minority provinces had to be disparate, often contradictory. Jalal pointed out how Jinnah and his AIML could not afford to be precise about the Pakistan demand, 'since what suited one local faction might upset another'.[169] In her later work, Jalal verified her earlier claim by exploring the Pakistan politics in the regional context of Punjab.[170] The present work also shows that the Pakistan politics of Bengal also developed in an independent, often oppositional way to what Jinnah and his AIML had expected. By not toeing the all-India Pakistan dictates, the Muslim-majority provinces were clearly experimenting with their own versions of Pakistan according to own particular needs.

The temporary autonomy of interpretation and politics of Pakistan was bound to land the Bengal Muslims later in tremendous anxiety and disappointment. However, in the early years of the 1940s, Bengal Muslim ideologues exercised a great deal of liberty in translating the ideal of Pakistan both in political and cultural realms. The idea of an independent state was an obvious assumption in this context. A few months after the passing of the Lahore Resolution, Akram Khan, the vice-president of the BPML, thought that if Bengal and Assam formed an 'independent state in eastern India', there would be no lack of resources or military might for its defense.[171] 'How an independent state in eastern India' would be related to India itself was obviously left vague and fluid. If this meant a separate state of Bengal, its great appeal to a large section of Bengali Muslims was easily understandable, as they fervently believed in the distinctiveness of their regional community. Hashim once put it succinctly: '[The Resolution] did not contemplate creation of a single Pakistan State but two independent sovereign States as homeland for the Muslims of India. One in North-West India consisting of the Punjab, Sind, Baluchistan, North-West Frontier Province and Kashmir, and the other in North-East India consisting of Bengal and Assam.'[172] He unhesitatingly added that, it being so, 'in Lahore Resolution I saw my complete independence as a Muslim and as a Bengali'.

The confusion over such a 'sovereign state' reflected itself in the Pakistan discourse of Bengal. That the Bengali vision differed in a substantial way from that of the AIML was first signified by Huq's own statement after the conference. When most of the League leaders severely criticized Maulana Azad's idea that the Muslim fate was irrevocably linked with India,[173] Huq refrained from doing so and lent support to the idea of a 'confederacy'.[174] While Huq admitted the need for negotiations, it remained unclear how he anticipated the compromise between being a part of a 'confederation' on the one hand and retaining 'sovereignty' on the other. This built-in confusion in the Lahore Resolution about the political implementability of the 'federation', in which the diverse entities would have the fullest measure of 'sovereignty' was first pointed out by a particularly insightful politician, B.R. Ambedkar, in 1940.[175] However, for Huq, this confusion either escaped his attention, or was allowed to be kept so, only to allow him the freedom to work around a future political arrangement. It is only in Hashim's later biographical account that one finds an explanation of this envisaged connection between any future 'Muslim' state in eastern India and India at large. With a characteristic clarity on the terms of nation, country or continent, Hashim declared, 'India is a Sub-continent, not a country', and, 'I never believed in Mr. Jinnah's two-nation theory and I never preached this in Bengal. I preached the multi-nation theory.'[176] A 'multi-nation theory', as he would specify, is the theory which conveys the sense that Europe does. 'When a citizen of Bengal says that he is a Bengali he is correct and he is also correct if he says that he is an Indian too.'[177] It is not clear if Hashim only thought of this argument of 'parallel identities' only later in his life. If he did not, he never made any attempt to communicate this in public previously. The Bengali Muslim discourse in the early 1940s remained hopelessly torn over the vision of Pakistan, as well as its relations with India.

The torn-ness was also evident in the deliberate silence of some prominent leaders. Huq rarely made any explanatory comment on Pakistan. One of such rare comments was: 'The ideal of the Progressive Muslim League will be Islam first and Islam throughout, but without ignoring the legitimate rights of other communities.... Unity between Muslims and other communities has got to be regarded as a fundamental necessity for the political advancement of India.'[178] Later on, in response to Akram Khan, his principal intellectual adversary in the province, Huq bared his anxieties: 'On many occasions I felt that the Muslims of Bengal were being misled by false ideas as to the scheme itself, but I have intentionally kept silent, because I thought my comments may be misunderstood.' As the Pakistan scheme stated that geographically contiguous units would be demarcated in a manner where the Muslim-majority areas would be grouped to constitute 'independent states', Huq concluded that Bengal did not stand a chance to qualify and therefore had to rely on the rest of India anyway:

> We have to remember that the three provinces geographically adjacent to Bengal are Assam, Bihar and Orissa. In Assam, the Muslims are only 35%, in Bihar, 10%, and in Orissa, barely 4%. It is not therefore evident that Bengal as constituted cannot form autonomous state with adjacent provinces. If however, Bengal has got to be divided into two, the result will be that the Eastern zone which will be a predominantly Muslim area will be surrounded by 4 provinces in which Hindus will be in a majority. It is therefore no use hoodwinking the Muslims of Bengal that the

formula which may hold good in the Punjab will also hold good in Bengal. At the same time Bengal Muslims realize that they have got to fall into line with the rest of India.[179]

The above letter of Huq can be considered as the first document pointing towards the implausibility of the Pakistan idea in Bengal. However, the general mood of the Bengali Muslim world was not such as to pay much attention to these logical incongruities of the resolution. What snatched their imagination was the vision of a new administration, new economy, and new polity, devoid of any Hindu hegemonic control. So when Huq launched his brief and ingenious alternative campaign of 'Chashistan' in early 1943 and tried to tie it with the scheme of Pakistan, his audience was not particularly impressed.[180] Chashistan, formulated out of the term *chashi*, that is, cultivator, seemed to be a natural political extension of the much-wanted economic liberties, where the rights of the peasants would be protected from the zamindari system. Huq and a handful of his supporters began to popularize this idea of Chashistan in the countryside, possibly hoping to make a last effort to bridge the new 'Muslim' politics of Pakistan with the remnants of the earlier praja movement.

By the middle of the 1940s, therefore, the Pakistan movement was no more conducted by the 'party', that is, the League, alone; it was rather a joint movement of the League, Muslim literati, youth, and the masses. Not only did the Muslim intelligentsia accord their fullest support to the movement but they also gave multiple shapes to the Pakistan ideal. In course of such attempts, there emerged a more self-conscious campaign for 'Purba Pakistan' than Pakistan, following the hints provided in the Lahore Resolution, indicated by Huq and Hashim earlier. The previous disparate comments of the leaders were now replaced by a series of comments and contemplations by the Bengali Muslim intelligentsia in general on the specifically 'Bengaliness' of Pakistan. 'That the Mussalman chashi of Bengal can make friendship with Kabuli Mahajan [moneylender] can only be imagined by those who do not have any connection with the soil of the country,' commented Zahur Hossain, one of the writers of a popular pamphlet.[181] He also strongly predicted a clash of languages within an undifferentiated entity of Pakistan: 'Sometimes it is said that Urdu is the mother-tongue of Indian Mussalmans. But the leaders of Pakistan movement in Bengal have clearly said that the state-language of "Purba Pakistan" will be Bengali and not Urdu. Peshawar and Chittagong cannot be brought under one state. Pakistan idea accepts this truth only.'[182]

'The leaders of Pakistan movement in Bengal' were then dreaming of a 'nation' of their own, where Bengali identity would reign supreme and at the same time Pakistan would ensure their much-awaited protection of Muslim interests. Young leaders like Abul Mansur Ahmed and Sheikh Mujibur Rahman described that with Mujibur Rahman Khan's above-mentioned Bengali pamphlet on Pakistan, a couple of other contemporary publications like Ambedkar's *Pakistan* and Habibullah Bahar's *Pakistan* cast a deep influence on 'people like them', still reeling in confusion and doubt about the efficacy of the new idea. Ahmed felt that any conceivable 'Pakistan' must be realized in practical terms by a clear demarcation of territories and clarification of objectives, but at the same time could not be effected solely on the basis of religion, which might transform it into a mullah nation. The latter trajectory could only be avoided if the cultural basis of 'Purba Pakistan' (East Pakistan, that is, East Bengal) was hammered upon. Not quite arbitrarily, in 1942 a group of Muslim literati and journalists of Calcutta founded the 'Purba Pakistan Renaissance Society', with Mujibur Rahman Khan as the convener, and Abul Mansur Ahmed and Abul Kalam Shamsuddin among others as members. During the same time, the Dacca Muslims launched the 'Purba Pakistan Sahitya Samsad' with roughly similar objectives. The idea was to pronounce their difference not only from the Hindus but also from Muslims of other provinces. In his presidential address at the Dacca session of the Renaissance Society, Abul Kalam Shamsuddin explained that the ideal of Pakistan meant a self-awakening in the field of politics as well as in literature and culture of the Bengali Muslims.[183] *Bangali*, a formerly KPP-influenced journal from Rajshahi, expressed grief as the Gandhi–Jinnah meeting in 1944 failed to reach an agreement. It seemed that while the nation was ready for a peaceful settlement among its communities, the leaders proved unable to fulfil the promise of the time:

> What a wretched lot of people we are! We are born in a country where no matter how much you want to have an agreement between yourselves, you cannot achieve so because of the incompetence and intolerance of your leaders. Let us now pray to God—may you bring good sense to these leaders—the deciders of our fate and future, may you bring peace and unity to our cottage-doors.[184]

The National War Front, organized on a provincial scale. arranged for an 'Eid–Puja-Sammilan' (Eid–Puja Festival) in October 1944, for which both Hindus and Muslims were supposed to take initiatives. M. Rahman, Justice N. Khondakar, and Khash Bahadur Wali-ul-Islam along with with J.C. Gupta and Satyen Majumdar were the speakers at this conference, all of whom emphasized the urgency of a united Bengali organization of some sort to enrich and uphold Bengali literature and culture (Bangali Muslim Sahitya Sanskriti).[185] When S. Wajid Ali, a staunchly liberal writer of this era wrote that '... if the people of every province in India, try earnestly to solve their provincial problems keeping in view the peculiarities of their provincial life ... the Indian problem would move towards solution at a faster pace, and with a fewer hitches than at present', he was definitely pointing at this province-based solution.[186]

Significantly, the quest for a 'provincial solution' also meant a renewed interest and passion for the locality. Just as ever, and very much like the swadeshi times, anxieties over a regional identity pushed the Bengali Muslim intelligentsia towards a rediscovery of the 'true Bengal', essentialized in the village life of the region. In the meetings of Calcutta and Dacca, repeated urges 'to go back to roots' were heard in speeches and papers read at the meetings (sammilans) organized by both Purba Pakistan Renaissance Society and Purba Pakistan Sahitya Samsad. Ahmed analysed at the Renaissance Society that any 'national' culture (*jatiya sanskriti* or *tamaddun*) was essentially retained and upheld by the villages of the region, desh (locality, in this context), and *paragana* (countryside).[187] As the term nation (jati) in its abstract sense primarily relates to the people of a territory, and in the context of Bengal, village–folk in particular, what could be more accurate as a standard of determining people's that is, a nation's, culture? 'Purba Pakistan', according to Abul Mansur Ahmed, therefore, was destined to uphold people's culture, and 'Pakistan' would denote several implications for them, among which the most important would be the cultural autonomy (*tamadduni azadi*) or 'swaraj':

> Whatever the politicians may understand by 'Pakistan', to us, the literate Muslims of Bengal, 'Pakistan' means tamadduni azadi or swaraj. If you want to know whether a nation could survive without political autonomy, you can go and ask the political leaders. We only know that without cultural identity of our own, without the tamadduni azadi of Bengal, we will not survive.[188]

The idea of swaraj or self-representation thus re-emerged with an opposite spin, with a confirmation of a regional Muslim 'nation' pitting itself against the totalitarian claims of the more general 'nation' as such. It was no more about any political control, but about a philosophical ideal of social and cultural freedom. The notion of 'rights' was emphasized and re-explored. The self-assertion of culture or tamaddun being the need of the day, it was also important to redefine the nature and location of the tamaddun more carefully, and to acknowledge its essentially regional nature: 'Religion can go beyond geographical boundaries. But tamaddun cannot. It is limited and defined by the very boundaries of a region'.

> ...'Pakistan' is not about political doctrine. It is a cultural, philosophical doctrine. 'Pakistan' is also not about Muslim-ness only, it is about the rights of a culture, be it Hindu, or Muslim, or any other cultural tradition of the world. Now let us turn our face to Purba Pakistan. Hindus and Muslims do not share one culture, so they do not belong to one nation. This is very clear by now. But, do the Indian Hindus and Indian Muslims by themselves constitute distinct 'nations'? The answer is: no.... Religion may be the foundation of tamaddun or cultural nationality. But religion cannot be an adequate marker of a tamaddun. Where does the difference lie? Religion can go beyond geographical boundaries. But tamaddun cannot. It is limited and defined by the very boundaries of a region.
>
> This is where Purba Pakistan is distinctly different from other nations. This is where Purba Pakistan has its own claims to nation-hood. We are therefore different from the Hindus, as well as from the Muslims of other regions.[189]

'This is where Purba Pakistan is distinctly different from other nations. This is where Purba Pakistan has its own claims to nationhood. We are therefore different from the Hindus, as well as from the Muslims of other regions': by far the clearest and most confident articulation of Bengali Muslim 'nation', and at the same time the boldest refutation of Jinnah's 'two-nation' theory, upon which the idea of Pakistan was based. The vagueness and flexibility maintained in the idea of Pakistan, therefore, not only produced in Bengal a 'different' vision of Pakistan, but also helped the Bengal leaders into waging a deliberate ideological challenge against the foundational principles of Pakistan.

That the much-publicized 'two-nation' cult was so vigorously and self-consciously challenged by a 'multi-nation' theory by the Bengali Muslim leaders is a little-appreciated fact of history. This is unfortunate, because the intermixing of region and religion indeed produced a strong and fairly persistent cult of nation or 'tamaddun' in Bengal. Significantly enough, this insightful speech by Ahmed was later also published in *Azad* and

Mohammadi, two journals so far steadfastly popularizing the singular identity of Islam. During the next few years, the following lines by Ahmed would be quoted in numerous articles and speeches of various Bengali Muslims, and would be the favourite propaganda for 'Purba Pakistan':

> Religion and culture are not the same thing. Religion transgresses the geographical boundary but '*tamaddun*' [culture] cannot go beyond the geographical boundary, but flourishes within the '*seema*' [geographical limits] of the area. Here only lies the difference between Purba Pakistan and Pakistan [italics mine].[190]

The geographical boundary of the culture was also being envisaged in various other imaginative ways. Mujibur Rahman Khan's *Pakistan* also contemplated a boundary for this Purba Pakistan whereby it would consist of the eastern parts of Bihar, Bengal except Burdwan division, and the whole of Assam province. A map was also enclosed to show that 'Muslim Bengal' wanted a demographic as well as a cultural solution to the problem of tamaddun or the cultural nationality.

All these attempts to reorient Pakistan in the specific regional interest of Bengali Muslims did not go unchallenged in Bengal. The national vision upheld by *Dainik Azad* was fiercely opposed by these sections of Bengali Muslims, not only in Calcutta and Dacca, but also in the mofussils. The views on Bengali Muslim tamaddun were lamented at on the pages of the *Dainik Azad*:

> There is this growing unfortunate tendencies among the Bengali Muslims to believe in a united Bengali nationality. What can be more deplorable than this? This only strengthens our rival's position. True it is not entirely unimaginable to have Bengali nation and Pakistan both realized at one and the same time. But to claim a Bengal on the basis of united Hindu–Muslim existence? We call it a *sonar patharbati*, that is, an impossibility. Come brothers, show these people that we will not tolerate such nonsense any more![191]

In its bid to win political ground in the region against the adversaries, the *Dainik Azad* group strongly aligned itself with the AIML.[192] However, this mainstream AIML view had to recede finally due to the institutional changes taking place within its regional wing, the BPML, where Abul Hashim played a pivotal role.

The ideas of 'Eastern Pakistan' and the 'multiple nation' were also propagated by Abul Hashim, one of the most prominent young leaders, and a visionary with leftist leanings. Utterly dissatisfied with the League propaganda or random drawing of boundaries of the cherished land, he lamented that few had any real idea what this land of Pakistan stood for. He expressed the need for a 'well thought-out and clear-cut manifesto', not as a 'handy vote-catching contraption', which through an effective medium of education 'will concretize our cherished ideal of Pakistan'.[193] His manifesto demanded that 'the time has come for defining the clear outline of what the contents of Pakistan are':

> The BPML feels that the time has come for defining the clear outline of what the contents of Pakistan are—political, social, economic and moral—as related to the life and conditions of the people of this Eastern Zone. Such an outline will be effective not only in inspiring the entire Muslim community of Eastern Pakistan but will be equally helpful in instilling confidence and understanding among the millions of non-Muslims, steeped in prejudices and misgivings against the Muslim national movement.[194]

The manifesto published in 1945 embodied the fundamental rights of people of 'Purba Pakistan', highlighting: (a) the sovereignty vested in the people, (b) universal adult franchise, (c) equality before law, (d) guarantee of civil liberties, (e) guarantee of employment, (f) free and compulsory primary education, (g) free hospitals for the poor, (h) nationalization of the key industries, (i) minimum living wages for the labourers, and (j) equality of opportunities and rights for women. It also spoke of a regional solidarity with all other marginal interests of the province. The low-caste groups with similar interests should, it said, find in Pakistan a remedy for their age–old political and cultural obscurity. According to the manifesto, 'The Muslim League leadership in Eastern Pakistan enjoins upon it the solemn responsibility of acting as the custodian of the interests of the non-Muslims including the depressed classes and backward peoples to whom it guarantees not only common rights but also provision for their betterment in accordance with their own respective traditions and culture.'[195]

The manifesto was not just an intellectual exercise but contributed significantly to the process of moulding common Muslim minds and enabling them to imagine an ideal state of Pakistan. The experience of 1942–3 brought about one important change in the League's organization.[196] There already emerged a Bengali middle-class upsurge against the aristocratic leadership. Although Suhrawardy undertook sincere personal efforts to ameliorate the conditions of Bengali Muslims, the long-term grievances against the oligarchic structure of the party and its non-democratic organizational stances stirred up a formidable reaction within the party.[197] From these rebelling groups, Abul Hashim by now emerged as the most potent leader, who criticized Suhrawardy in the severest manner for the latter's alleged irresponsibility exposed in the aftermath of the Great Famine. In November 1944, Hashim replaced Suhrawardy as the secretary of BPML. The agenda he now put forward was to wage a crusade against 'the mortgages League had been using so far: leadership to the Ahsan Manzil, publicity to the *Azad* management, and finances to the Ispahanis.' It also called for an organization of the Bengali middle classes.[198] Although initially it all seemed high talk, Hashim soon proved to be the fittest leader to reform the base and orientation of the BPML, and transform the BPML to grow phenomenally in size and popularity. He undertook regular district tours and made his ideas accessible to the masses.[199] From 1943 to 1945, a large number of Pakistan meetings and League conferences were held by him in various mofussil towns. In the cities, Muslim boys developed a ritual of addressing Jinnah about the urgent need for Pakistan: 'Often we used to write those letters on the back of the money-order forms sent out to the Jinnah front.'[200] The ideal of 'Purba Pakistan' was transformed into a common vision in these years. With the League in Bengal undergoing a massive change in its character, the Pakistan movement was turned into a combined movement of the Muslim middle classes and the Muslim masses henceforth.

That the slogan of Pakistan spread in the countryside was evident in various personal accounts, either in the published memoirs or in the oral anecdotes. Even the little boys in villages recited poems exalting Jinnah and Pakistan, and discussed with their Hindu friends whether Pakistan would mean for the Muslim schoolboys an end to the studying of 'Hindu' history altogether.[201] It is important to remember in this context the political vacuum created in the Bengal countryside due to the elimination of the KPP brand of 'praja politics', [202] and the failure of the Congress to defend peasant interests.[203]

The Communist Party also failed miserably on this account. There is reason to suspect that the latter's failure also resulted from its inability to come to terms with the growing community consciousness, which was often dismissed as 'communalism', a factor arising out of 'narrow social base', expected to be 'rapidly liquidated' by the 'progressive forces'.[204] After more than a few decades of nationalist politics of cultural self-assertion, common people in the interior villages grew adequately aware of their collective backwardness on the one hand, and their sociocultural identities on the other. It was enormously difficult for any political ideology to make any inroad by denouncing the community ties, or the religious–cultural identities.[205] With the spread of the League in the Bengal countryside, a fervent adherence to the regionally informed cultural identity began to grow, along with the awareness of the regional socioeconomic interests of the marginal communities. The direction of the movement was clearly from the urban areas to the rural areas, from the more socially exposed and politically advanced Muslim societies to the backward and peasant societies. The rise of 'Pakistan' in Bengal needs to be understood in this context.

Therefore, contrary to what some historians argue, the multiple meanings of 'Pakistan' cannot only be understood as 'peasant utopia', or a quasi-political ideal harboured by the illiterate, less-informed, economically backward peasantry of rural Bengal. It needs to be appreciated primarily as a self-conscious ideological construct of the Muslim middle classes in Calcutta and mofussil towns, politically aware and articulate, literate and culturally informed.[206] For this aspiring professional and educated class of Muslims, the jargons and evocations of Pakistan, however uncertain and undefined these might have remained, only proved to be excessively handy tools for political mobilization of the larger society—a goal they had long been chasing. Only a solid base of numbers could guarantee shorter routes to social and political success in their project to handle marginalization and exalt difference. So the primarily urban middle-class movement of Pakistan was rapidly spread as a peasant movement. In this Janus-faced phenomenon of the Pakistan movement, it is possible to locate the multi-level aspirations of Bengali Muslims. These aspirations arose out of a two-fold narrative of 'difference': first, their difference from the Bengali Hindus, and second, their difference from the non-Bengali Muslims. Hidden in this two-fold narrative was the call for a new politics of region–nation: a politics where differences, instead of being obliterated, could finally be addressed and accommodated.

The 'Other' Reaction to Pakistan

The Pakistan Movement in Bengal has so far been depicted as a steady and gradual conquest of the 'two-nation theory'. This interpretation, by definition, limits the political and ideological dialectics within a Hindu–Muslim binary. A closer look into the conceptual dissentions and digressions, nevertheless, suggests a different reality. It tempts us to argue that 'Pakistan' in its very distinct Bengal version seemed to be 'a province-based solution' for a larger and long-drawn battle between the nation and its differences.[207] One may argue that the notion of 'Purba Pakistan' was more than a mere verbal twist and contained real political bearings of a region–nation, and, viewed in this way, was in fact an inheritor of the long-drawn trends of regional nationalism. Breaking the overused binary of Hindu nationalism and Muslim communalism, it is even possible to see this very different 'other' political ideology as a third strand, or a 'regional' strand of nationalism, unfolding in a Muslim-majority but erstwhile Hindu-dominated province. It was, of course, unclear how this provincial solution was to be associated with the larger Indian reality and 'extra-territorial' power equations. However, the terms of association, though unclear, were never unthinkable, as we have already noted in this chapter and, therefore, the vitality or merit of this third strand of politics should not be dismissed. Even if one does not empathize with the terms like Pakistan or Purba Pakistan, it still remains tempting to consider the essential spirit beneath its Bengali interpretation with more seriousness, and contemplate a historical counter-intuitive. Had the concerns and pressures of the larger Indian reality not exerted themselves on Bengal with such force, the idea of a province-based solution might perhaps have proven its worth and work-ability. The refusal to see this in fact denies an acknowledgement of the plausibility of a different kind of nation, which might not necessarily manifest itself in the form of Pakistan as it finally evolved.

It is, nevertheless, not a simple task to disentangle the complex Hindu receptions of the idea of a provincial solution in general and that of Pakistan in particular. It is important to note that the launching of the Pakistan proposal was not immediately followed by a severe con-demnation of the proposal in the Hindu quarters. The Hindu Bengali public opinion was not distinctly formed outside the Hindu Mahasabha circle. It took a few years for the idea of Pakistan to take centre-stage in political discourse, while only a few segments of the political society engaged themselves directly with the implications of the new proposi-tion. To these understated Hindu reactions to Pakistan during the early 1940s was added the complex tenor of their responses to the ministries at work within the province. During the coalition ministries, the com-mon antipathy towards a Muslim Raj was often mixed with occasional praise being showered upon Huq's government, as we have seen earlier. In short, while Pakistan, the uncertain dream of the Bengali Muslims, generated deep discomfort in Hindu society, the realities of the League administration did not appear wholly unacceptable.

Against this perspective, it is sensible to trace certain Hindu intellectual reactions to the idea of Pakistan. In the midst of 'Hindu communal' overtones, there also emerged some notes of dissonance among the urban, literate intelligentsia. As the Second World War broke out, hasty political negotiations began to take place in the context of which 'rights of self-assertion' became more important than before.[208] While for the majority of Congress politicians Pakistan was abhorred for its highly divisive content, for a small section it also meant the 'self-assertion' of a regional community with a demand for fair representation. The Cripps Mission offer included a phrase that in the post-war Indian dominion, any unwilling province would be given the choice of not acceding to the Indian Union. The Congress response was naturally one of rejection, while the non-Congress political forces, including the Bengal ministry, gave a positive reaction to the suggested form of union. By the Congress standards of unitary nationalism, the principle of non-accession for a province was considered a straight negation of the nation. The Muslim League, on the other hand, endorsed the principle with a note of caution at the 'rigidity of the attitude of His Majesty's Government with regard to the fundamentals not being open to any modification'.[209] The overemphasis of the Congress on the theme of unity in case of a proposed independent national structure, clear in the refusal of Cripps Mission, already irked many others even outside the League circles. B.R. Ambedkar, the great protagonist of low-caste rights, thought that the attitude of the Congress towards the idea of Pakistan was too hasty, almost unwarranted: 'It was not even considered with seriousness but discarded outright.'[210] The Congress High Command was also put into trouble by C. Rajagopalachari's formula presented in 1942, which outlined the need for an understanding with the Muslim League through recognition of the right of Muslim-majority provinces to secede through plebiscite after independence.[211] Finally there were the Communists who from an entirely different ideological position questioned the Congress stance at the Bombay All India Congress Committee and pleaded for a joint front with the League on the basis of the right of secession.

The Communist endorsement to the basic principle of Pakistan needs to be taken into serious consideration, as it seemed to have stemmed from a commitment to the principle of the 'right of self-determination'. In 1940, the banned and underground Communist Party declared that it stood for a free India that would be a voluntary federation of peoples and nationalities, a federation of 'provinces where Muslims form over-whelming majority of the population could form autonomous units and even have the right to secede'.[212] Following this guideline, Gangadhar Adhikari, the major ideologue of the party, observed in his report to the Central Committee that although there was no difficulty in demarcating Baluchistan and NWFP in Pakistan, Bengal would pose a more complex situation. The character of the Bengali community being 'a distinct nationality', they should be given 'the right of self-determination'.[213] He argued that there was much more in common between the Bengali Hindu and the Bengali Muslim than between the Bengali Muslim and the Pathan Muslim. Within the framework of a common nationality, nevertheless, the Muslim peasantry of eastern Bengal had a distinct cultural complex of its own which had made its impression on eastern Bengal as a separate entity: 'In the case of nationalities, there are such things as transitional forms, and we have to recognize in eastern Bengal precisely such a transitional stage of development.... The crux of the matter is how best can we unite the oppressed peasantry of eastern Bengal for the common struggle, recognizing their special position.' Adhikari came up with a solution based on an emphasis on the regional–linguistic culture that the Bengali Muslim rural population shared with their Bengali Hindu counterparts, and asserted that 'the solution' enables the leaders to convince them 'that they would be better off if they remained within the Bengali state':

> The solution put forward in our party resolution, on the one hand, enables the peasantry of east Bengal to share and enrich the common national heritage of Bengal; on the other hand, it enables us to unite them and to convince them that they would be better off if they remained within the Bengali state. Such a solution alone will enable us to isolate the separatists and pave the way for a political unity of the Bengali people.[214]

Adhikari's statements are of enormous significance in our context: one of the clearest expositions of the 'Bengali state' where distinct and constituent 'nationalities' could belong during their 'transitional' stage. Second, his statements signified the priorities set by his own party, at least during the early stage of Pakistan movement, which included as a first choice the political realization of a 'Bengali state', with full right of self-determination.

Although the 'Adhikari Thesis' would soon be sidelined within the Communist Party itself, the impact of his theory of self-determination for each nationality lingered as one of the guiding principles for the left-liberal nationalist ideologues in Bengal. This lineage may be clear from the way the questions of 'unity' and 'difference' were subsequently taken up by Sushobhan Sarkar, a leading Bengali communist intellectual of the era. In one of his speeches at a meeting of the Purba Pakistan Renaissance Society, Sarkar commented: 'Any fixed or inflexible stand on the structure of a partitioned India is as vain as the principle of unity behind the concept of *Akhand Bharat*.'[215] In a nuanced defense for the ideal of federalism, he pointed out that while the fight for freedom from colonial rule based itself on the pronunciation of 'difference', ironically enough, it also inherently set limits on the similar rights for self-determination claimed by the smaller 'nations'.

> If India wants to rebuild herself on the basis of 'national difference', she must remember that all the smaller nations inhabiting the territories of India do possess the same right. It is not possible to erase others' rights while asserting one's own. Secondly, why this fear of losing the Indianness? All these nationalities can form a confederation on the basis of their own free will. [216]

The 'smaller nations' might find sooner or later the federation a more stable form of structure, Sarkar thought, because 'if it does not mean forfeiting one's uniqueness and particularities, diversity may agree to accept unity'.[217] But, such a unity had to be based upon free agreement, not on force or persuasion.

> Let these nationalities feel the threads of unity which still exist amidst nationalistic particularities. If and when they do feel so, it is only then we can think of any effective 'unity'.... 'Self-determination' is the key word here; let each constituent part decide if it feels it beneficial to willingly form a confederal existence. Only one nation can hope to have a unitary state; where it is a question of more than one, then it is only suicidal.[218]

A rather strong statement: 'Only one nation can hope to have a unitary state; where it is a question of more than one, then it is only suicidal.' Did India then not constitute one single nationality? Sarkar's answer would be: it did not. 'I will argue that in India we do not have "one" nation, neither do we have "two" nations, but a number of nations!'[219] With the claims of geographical unity untenable ('Then why not [expect] the whole Mediterranean region comprising North Africa or, for that matter, the whole of Europe, [to be] one single nation?'), India in its own historical past seldom underwent any such moment of grand unity in the precolonial past, nor did the existing polity in colonial India point to its feasibility. In matters of cultural lifestyle, 'religion undoubtedly being the life-line of culture, Hindus and Muslims could at best be connected, but never be one'. However, as different as Hindus and Muslims might be from each other, none of them constituted an integrated whole to support the 'two-nation theory':

> [To believe in two nations] could have been possible if religion could be held as the singular determinant of nationality. It is not so…. That is why you are using the prefix 'Purba' before Pakistan; using this qualifier, you are actually asserting a sense of 'difference' (swatantra) from some of your co-religionists … so I will argue that in India we do not have 'one' nation, neither do we have 'two' nations, but a number of nations! Today, we are being overwhelmed by the enormity of Hindu–Muslim question, tomorrow we will be pressed with other similar contestations. *The only solution therefore is to acknowledge with a liberated mind the existence of numerous nationalities, and their equal and full rights of 'self-determination'* [emphasis added].[220]

The same notions of 'multiple' (or, 'numerous') nationalities thus kept on haunting both Hindu and Muslim discourses on nation in Bengal. Sarkar's expositions remain especially significant since many Bengali Muslims present at the same meeting of Purba Pakistan Renaissance Society had independently, if less articulately, reiterated the same conclusions in their observations on the questions of 'rights', 'nation', or 'Pakistan'. Despite certain temporary and subtle shifts, championing of the rights of self-determination for smaller communities (or 'nations') seemed to be an ideological imperative in the context of ensuing decolonization.

As a matter of fact, the attempt to address the problems of Bengal in isolation from those of India was a consistently visible trend until 1942. Sarat Chandra Bose was another noteworthy champion of this provincial identity. The efficacy of a united front, especially in the context of Bengal, a Muslim-majority province charged with a very rich regional–cultural sprit, was highlighted by him. A fuller cultural identity through peaceful negotiations seemed attainable between its constituent communities. The possibility of such negotiations was seen in the prospect of strengthening the 'economic and social foundations' by him, just like Das whom he considered his political mentor (*guru*):

> The poverty of the masses should be removed; livelihood must be secured for the middle-classes; the Hindus, the Muslims and all classes of Bengalis

must be brought together.... We must carry on the fight for political and economic swaraj simultaneously.[221]

Not accidentally perhaps Das's hopes for a federated India were now reiterated by Bose in order to allow the regional distinctiveness to grow and flourish:

[E]ach part of the Federated State of India should not only be allowed to preserve its own distinctiveness but also to develop that distinctiveness to its full capacity with a view to give a new tone to the civilization of the whole of India. It is inevitable that India should find unity in diversity. So there is no substance in the argument that in order to think in terms of India one has to forget Bengal.[222]

Significantly, what had changed from the times of Das was that for even a liberal protagonist of difference like Bose, the emphasis on 'unity in diversity' had clearly gained supremacy. Perhaps the primary reason behind this renewed and inexorable emphasis on unity was the reaction to the idea of Pakistan itself, which had entailed in it a sharp attack on the Congress creed of unitary nationalism. Consequently, when Sarat Bose outlined the needs for maintaining and strengthening 'cultural' diversities of the country, he, unlike Das, had to underplay the 'political' expressions of such diversities. Just as we have noticed in the case of Subhas Bose in the previous chapter, Sarat Bose also remained insistent on the singularly supreme political association (that is, the Congress) representing all sects and communities of India, bound by the threads of unity among all cultural diversities. He had been delivering this argument in the most sophisticated manner during the entire period we have discussed here. His task was unenviable, even during the first provincial ministry of Huq. On the one hand, he had to acknowledge that Congress had often deplorably failed to meet people's expectations, rendering its own claims for representing them dubious.[223] On the other, he would still strongly believe that 'in the Congress provinces the Ministers themselves are the real representatives of the people and are supported by the united body of the real representatives of the people. How many Bengal [KPP–League] Ministers can make that claim on behalf of themselves?'[224] He would have to address tirelessly the fact of cultural difference and the need for a diversified political agenda directed to the dissimilar interests of various communities. But at the same time he would also have to appeal to 'make the [Congress] organization more coherent, more unified, more disciplined'. In an urge to combine a broad-based popular agenda with a unified national purpose, he looked for inspiration from the contemporary European and Asian experiences, especially Soviet Union and China, both showing 'the strength of a political organization depended on its faith in itself, on the discipline that it enforced on its members, on the readiness that it showed to serve national interests'.[225] 'National' thus emphatically brought into the fore-stage, Bose would approach the problem of difference only in terms of representation from within the folds of Congress. In one of Bose's letters to Shyamaprasad Mookherjee, the former had to clarify that his position on 'Pakistan, self-determination and all the rest of it' was not inconsistent with 'the views of the Congress', but at the same time, was sympathetic towards the Muslim cause. He would emphasize that the only way to counter Jinnah's politics was to incorporate and uphold Muslim voices from within the Congress in greater numbers. In the end, he believed that it was not by an oppositional Hindu Mahasabha but a more accommodative Congress that the excesses of League politics would have to be tackled: ' ... it is the Congress and the Congress alone that will be able to defeat Mr. M. A. Jinnah's claim for Pakistan.'[226]

The nature of popular reception of such sophisticated expositions of nation was not unexpected. In an era of sharp and bitter attacks on Pakistan, many of Bose's contemporaries as well as the society at large found such positions either one of capitulation or one marked by impracticality.[227] Yet, it is important to assess them with utmost care as only then can the pitfalls of treating nationalism as synonymous with the Congress vision of unitary nation become clear. Leaders like Bose valued the role and the potential of Congress immensely, yet did not fail to see its serious shortcomings. Ideologues like Sarkar would even want to go a step ahead to reject the Congress brand of unitary nationalism altogether on the same argument. Not surprisingly, in a political climate where taking an all-or-none position on Pakistan was called for, the Boses and Sarkars were indeed marginalized and so were their nuanced positions vis-à-vis the principle of representation and 'difference', the hardest problematic before the 'nation-to-be'.[228]

The importance of Bose lay elsewhere too. His relentless stress on the needs of community representation earned him a tremendous respect in the Bengali Muslim society. After Das, he was the next, and possibly the last, Bengali Hindu leader, able to extract so much confidence from both the communities, especially from the Muslim youth. Political workers like Abul Mansur Ahmed and journalists like Waliullah represented different strands of Muslim ideology, yet they both recollected with same passion in their autobiographical accounts that, among the rank and file of Congress leaders of the 1940s, Bose alone kept ablaze the hope of a fair negotiation with the Bengali Muslim interests.[229] The League workers often reminisced later that Sarat Bose was 'unusually sensitive' towards the 'Muslim problem', 'the only bridge between Congress and the Bengal Muslims'.[230] The continued Muslim trust in him in the mid-1940s, despite his unfazed loyalty to Congress nationalism, conveys an important message. It signifies the enormity of the potential of an inter-communal provincial politics even in the mid-1940s. Bose, for the Bengali Muslims, was not only an individual mustering a huge amount of political trust, but indeed an exemplary icon of the waning spirit of inter-communal region–nation.

Retreat of 'Other' Nationalisms

To sum up, although no inter-community government could prove itself successful in the usual sense of the term, the nature of political and cultural experiences during the new provincial administration demonstrated its plausibility and promises. The instances of Bengal ministries in the late 1930s and the early 1940s suggested that, if freed from the pressures of all-India politics, it might have perhaps been possible for Bengali Hindu and Bengali Muslim leaders to erect a functional political structure in the province, based on a workable amount of trust and mutual cooperation. In spite of the forces of conservatism and estrangement, there were parallel, adequately potent, forces of liberal nationalism working out their ways in an enormously complex context.

Of course, a part of this liberal view was nothing more than an enlightened, broader version of communitarian nationalism, which placed community interests more centrally within the framework of nation than its secular variant would ever consider to do. The nation envisaged by Fazlul Huq might not be secular and radical in conventional ways. But, unmistakably, it had a different, or an alternative, vision where various regional interests might well be accommodated. The 'Huq nationalism' would be carried forward by Abul Hashim of the BPML on the one hand, and 'Bose nationalism', on the other, would still kindle a ray of hope for inter-community negotiation within the Congress. No wonder, the seemingly singular domains of both national politics and Muslim politics turned into sites of great contestations in the mid-1940s.

Rather counter-intuitively, in Bengal, 'Pakistan' did not nullify all possibilities of inter-community exchanges, although it had indeed reduced the space for political dialogue. While this dialogue was still taking place on various levels, the sociocultural promises of the region–nation were finally denied a chance due to the frenetic search for political shortcuts by the all-India Congress as well as the all-India League. The next chapter will explore how these contradictions between regional and extra-regional politics led to an acute political impasse in the final two years of colonial Bengal.

Notes

1. It is commonly accepted in the historiography of colonial Bengal that the steady growth of Muslim communalism culminated in the Partition of 1947. Joya Chatterji has offered a counter-theory that Hindu communalism was the most important contributing factor behind Partition. See Joya Chatterji, *Bengal Divided: Hindu Communalism and Partition, 1932–1947* (Cambridge: Cambridge University Press, 1997).

2. Mohammad Waliullah, *Yuga-Bichitra* (Dhaka: Maola Brothers, 1967), p. 343.

3. The spokesmen of the Muslim League in Bengal complained that there was even an unwritten understanding between the Congress and the KPP. In November 1936, Maulana Abu Bakr Siddiqui, the president of the Jamat and a member of the League, pleaded to the Muslim voters to reject the KPP because 'you should not bring about the destruction of your community by casting votes in favour of the nominees of the Praja Samiti or any groups subservient to the Hindu Congress'. See Harun-or- Rashid, *The Foreshadowing of Bangladesh: Bengal Muslim League and Muslim Politics, 1936–4* (Dhaka: Asiatic Society of Bangladesh, 1987), p. 76. The basis of such a charge was the fact that the Congress in Bengal did not set up candidates in the 119 Muslim seats, extending their support informally to KPP-backed candidates. The KPP, on the other hand, did not contest from a single general seat. In the general seats, Congress had a relatively easy fight, having as their opponents either independents, the Mahasabha candidates, or the loyalists (candidates set up by the British government). However, historians point out that even if there was some tacit understanding, there was no evidence of any formal agreement between the two parties. See Rashid, *Foreshadowing of Bangladesh*, p. 70; Humaira Momen, *Muslim Politics in Bengal: A Study of Krishak Praja Party and the Elections of 1937* (Dhaka: Sunny House, 1972), p. 66. It may be mentioned that Huq himself debunked such charges and even issued a statement after the elections, declaring: 'It is a most malicious

lie to say that the Praja Samiti is only an off-shoot of the Congress ... it is absolutely false that I have been helped by the Hindus as such.' See *Amrita Bazar Patrika*, 30 January 1937. Nevertheless, one must note that whether there was an 'agreement' or not with the Congress, the fact remained that in the Muslim constituencies the contest was bitter, with either the League and the KPP locked in straight fights, or independents backed by the League and the KPP facing each other. Huq as the KPP leader challenged the Bengal Muslim League leader Khwaja Nazimuddin in two constituencies, and soon this royal battle between 'Khwaja' and 'Praja' became a spectacle for the Bengali press.

4. Chatterji, *Bengal Divided*, p. 100. Chatterji points out that even in the places where these samitis were nominally connected with Congress, the latter did not exercise any real control over them. The local samiti leaders resented any such control because of their more radical leanings. It being so, when the Congress rose up to assert itself in the matters of the krishak samitis just before the elections in 1936 and began to send speakers here and there to spread its message, the strong resistance against the Congressmen led to a widespread anticipation of its defeat in the elections soon to be followed. After one such speech, a local stood up to comment: '... the Congress only came when they wanted votes but when there was distress Congress was not to be found.' Chatterji, *Bengal Divided*, p. 100.

5. For a detailed analysis of the political programme and the election manifesto of the KPP, see Rashid, *Foreshadowing of Bangladesh*, pp. 75–80; Momen, *Muslim Politics in Bengal*; Shila Sen, *Muslim Politics in Bengal, 1937–47* (Delhi: Impex India, 1976), chapter 3; Shyamali Ghosh, 'Fazlul Haq and Muslim Politics', *International Studies* 13, no. 3 (July–September, 1974): 441–64, see 442; Shapan Adnan, 'Fazlul Haq and the Bengali Muslim Leadership, 1937–43', *Bangladesh Historical Studies* 1, no. 1 (1976): 1–18, see 4; and Chatterji, *Bengal Divided*, pp. 76–83.

6. *Amrita Bazar Patrika*, 16 December 1936. Also quoted in Kalipada Biswas, *Yukta Banglar Shesh Adhyay* (Calcutta: Orient Company, 1966), p. 27.

7. Abul Mansur Ahmed, *Amar Dekha Rajnitir Panchash Bachhor* (Dhaka: Maola Brothers, 1970), p. 63.

8. Rashid, *Foreshadowing of Bangladesh*, p. 65.

9. Chatterji, *Bengal Divided*, p. 77. The local boards of Bengal were largely dominated by the Muslim jotedars during this time. By 1936, thirteen districts were firmly under control of these groups; in two others, they constituted exactly half of the seats. Chatterji also shows that by this time, the Muslims fared well even in those districts where they used to be in a minority position.

10. A.M. Ahmed, *Amar Dekha Rajnitir Panchash Bachhor*, p. 180.

11. S. Sen, *Muslim Politics in Bengal*, p. 80.

12. Joya Chatterji is the most recent historian to emphasize this 'jotedar' profile of the KPP. 'The Krishak Praja Party was thus the agency by which the jotedars ... came out of the wings onto the centre stage of Bengal politics.' See *Bengal Divided*, p. 77.

13. 'Krishaker Gaan', Kazi Nazrul Islam, *Chashi*, Eid issue, 1938. The original poem follows:

    Ghumer majhe chomke uthi, bargi elo deshe,
    Pangapale desh chheyechhe, khajna debo kishe?
    Chhele ghumabe para jurabe, dhar phire tui lathi,
    chasha chharish ne tor ghanti.

14. Humayun Kabir, 'Krishaker Eid', Eid issue, 1938. The original poem follows:

    Bachhor-pare dekha dilo Id-er banka chand
    Sabar mone khushir dhara—amar bisambad ...
    Mahajoner roibe na sud, khajna jamidari,
    Jutbe sabar notun kapor, jutbe notun saree.
    Nijer khete habe chashir nijer adhikar,
    Gorib dhonir roibe na bhed sabai ekakar.
    Shedin habe Id-er jaamaat sakale ek thnai,
    Bhai-e bhai-e kono bibhag kono bibhed nai.
    Ghuchbe duhkho ghuchbe doinyo ghuchbe bisambad,
    Achhi boshe uthbe kabe shei Id-eri chand.

15. In 1936, Huq's press statement declared: 'All talks of Muslim unity and solidarity for merely political ends are worse than useless when it is remembered that the Mussalman cultivating classes constitute more than 90 per cent of the total Muslim population in Bengal, and it is, therefore, their interest which must be fundamental in any scheme we may lay down for ourselves...' (*Amrita Bazar Patrika*, 11 September 1936).

16. Huq was trying to tie in various aggrieved classes under the same political umbrella of the KPP, as reflected in his call to wage a war against rural as well as urban wealthy classes. 'My fight is with the landlords, capitalists and the holders of vested interests.' *Amrita Bazar Patrika*, 11 September 1936.

17. Huq's declaration that he was not fighting against Sir Nazimmuddin, but against Sir John Anderson, the Governor of Bengal in this 'all out battle between the zamindars and the peasants' may well be discounted as a mere election stance. It is hard to overlook the amount of popular appeal and rural contacts Huq used to muster during the late 1930s. Thousands of landless labourers in the East Bengal countryside were addressed by Huq in an age when the rural poor classes were clearly of no real significance as far as voting games were concerned. Harun-or-Rashid mentions

that Huq's ties with landless peasants 'became insignificant' in view of their non-enfranchisement. See *Foreshadowing of Bangladesh*, p. 65. However, one may argue that such ties assumed much greater significance in ascertaining the nature of Huq's political propaganda, if this fact of non-enfranchisement is borne in mind. Huq perhaps wanted to carve out a distinct political positioning for himself.

18. The 'dual strategy' in Huq's politics referred to here is close to what Sana Aiyar describes as 'dual politics' in 'Fazlul Huq, Region and Religion in Bengal: The Forgotten Alternative, 1940–43', *Modern Asian Studies* 42, no. 6 (2008): 1213–49, see 1217–19. In Aiyar's analysis, Huq's dual politics point towards his double responsibilities of invoking the all-India Muslim identity as a Muslim League politician as well as representing Bengal's interests in particular and, as the Bengal premier, 'playing the provincial card very carefully'. I intend to show that Huq's original dilemma went much deeper, to an uncertainty as to the use of the cultural potentials of the 'Muslim identity' on the one hand, and the need to step beyond this Muslim identity in the interest of carving out a combined Hindu–Muslim regional interest. In other words, Aiyar sees Huq's 'dualism' primarily through the prism of political compulsions, while I prefer to characterize this dilemma as intrinsically ideological. That the cultural promises of the religious symbols and traditions proved only too overwhelming in the path of constructing a cross-communitarian regional politics is beyond doubt. Huq was a leading figure as well as a major victim of the dilemma-ridden journey of the region–nation.

19. *Amrita Bazar Patrika*, 10 September 1936.

20. Humayun Kabir, 'Among the Bengal Peasants', *Hindustan Times*, 20 May 1945, p. 4.

21. Huq's statement on 7 July 1936, quoted in Rashid, *Foreshadowing of Bangladesh*, p. 66.

22. For the relationship between the KPP and the Namasudras, see Sekhar Bandyopadhyay, *Caste, Protest and Identity in Colonial India: The Namasudras of Bengal, 1872–1947* (second edition, Oxford: Oxford University Press, 2011), pp. 168–72.

23. Sekhar Bandyopadhyay comments that on the eve of the elections of 1937, the KPP had to project itself as an exclusively Muslim party, and thereby alienated the Namasudras. This observation needs to be qualified by pointing out, first, that the so-called 'KPP *volte face*' was not as decisive as it is made out to be and, second, the instances of later negotiations between the KPP and low-caste leaders explained how their support bases often overlapped. Mention may be made of Tamizuddin Khan, an opposition KPP leader in 1938, who amidst the furious reactions of Congress representatives rose up in the assembly to underline the united grievances of the Bengal Muslims and the low-caste

population. See Bengal Legislative Assembly Proceedings (henceforth BLAP), 10 March 1938, pp. 129–30, WBSA. Huq also assured that he would serve both the Muslims and the depressed castes 'in order to bring them on a line at par with other advanced communities'. BLAP, 18 March 1938, pp. 37–8. At the level of leadership, the twin demands of extending representation and education brought the caste politics closer to Muslim politics of the province. This point is illustrated in Dwaipayan Sen, 'Representation, Education, and Agrarian Reforms: Jogendranath Mandal and the Nature of Scheduled Caste Politics, 1937–1943', *Modern Asian Studies* 48, no. 1 (2014): 77–119. A recent literary work that has dealt with Mandal's complex relationship with Bengal Muslim politics is Debes Ray, *Barisal-er Jogen Mandal* (Calcutta: Dey's Publication, 2010), pp. 560–630.

24. Shamsuddin Ahmed's statement in *Amrita Bazar Patrika*, 4 February 1937, p. 13. The two members were Birat Chandra Mandal and Upendranath Edbar. The former was originally a member of the KPP Election Board. Immediately after the elections they recorded their names as Praja Party members.

25. The League propaganda was thus dismissed in Huq's speech of 11 September 1936, printed in the *Amrita Bazar Patrika*.

26. A.M. Ahmed, *Amar Dekha Rajnitir Panchas Bachhor*, p. 71; Waliullah, *Yuga-Bichitra*, p. 376.

27. Kamruddin Ahmad, *A Social History of Bengal* (Progoti Publishers, 1970), p. 33, Shyamali Ghosh, 'Fazlul Haq and Muslim Politics in Pre-Partition Bengal', *International Studies* 13, no. 3 (1974): 441–64, see 445.

28. Coming from an elite business family of Calcutta, M.A. Ispahani and his brother Hasan Ispahani were critical political figures in Muslim politics in Calcutta during the 1930s. The latter was made treasurer of the United Muslim Party launched in 1936, right before the provincial elections. Adamjee Haji Dawood was the founder of a jute mill in Calcutta and the head of the first Muslim public company. In the 1930s, he along with the Ispahanis started to contribute lavishly to the Muslim League of M.A. Jinnah, and became vocal proponents of the Pakistan movement in the 1940s. Both the families shifted their business to Pakistan after 1947.

29. K.alipada Biswas, *Yukta Banglar Shesh Adhyay*, p. 9.

30. 'League o Bangalar Mussalman', *Krishak*, September 1938.

31. Huq's speech of 11 September 1936.

32. Rashid, *Foreshadowing of Bangladesh*, p. 75.

33. Shyamali Ghosh, 'Fazlul Haq and Muslim Politics', p. 445. The pro-League newspapers screamed: 'Muslim voters, beware! Do you want Hindu Congressmen to rule Bengal? If not—send Fazlul Huq to the Wall: smash up the Praja Party!' See *Star of India*, 13 January 1937, p. 5.

34. In view of this 'middling ground' in Bengal Muslim politics, Shila Sen's conclusion does not appear tenable that 'although no single Muslim party emerged in a dominant position, the election results proved beyond doubt that compartmentalization of politics into Hindu politics and Muslim politics was complete in Bengal'. S. Sen, *Muslim Politics in Bengal*, p. 89. I would argue that there was no such 'compartmentalization' in the late 1930s because the continued internal dissensions among the Bengali Muslim community precluded any clear 'Muslim' pole to emerge. Even after the League's fast growth during the coalition ministries, the battle lines were drawn between the contending blocs of Muslims alongside the separating threads between Bengali Muslims and Bengali Hindus. The extent of mutual bitterness and conflict was great among these opposing factions within the League leadership. The ferocity of anti-Huq sentiments during 1941–3 showed how these intra-communitarian conflicts potentially created the space for inter-community negotiations.

35. In the capacity of the premier of two coalition governments during these periods, Huq made quite a few clumsy attempts to preserve the cultural identity of Bengali Muslims amidst pressures coming from other regional political groups on the one hand, and from the AIML leadership on the other.

36. The extent of the popular craze around Huq is described by a number of contemporaries. Mention may be made of the autobiographical writings of Abul Mansur Ahmad and Sheikh Mujibur Rahman. See A.M. Ahmad, *Amar Dekha Rajnitir Panchash Bachhor*, pp. 131–9; Mujibur Rahman, *Asamapta Atmajibani* (Dhaka: The University Press, 2012), pp. 22–5.

37. Having seen the thousands of the barefoot, ill-clad village-folk following Huq for mile after mile during his periodical trips to the Bengal country-side, a Canadian journalist once commented in an informal gathering in Calcutta, 'If Mahatma Gandhi is a saint, Nehru a patriot, Rajagopalachari an astute politician, Jinnah a strategist, Maulana Azad a wise man, Fazlul Huq is then the magician of Indian politics!' Waliullah, *Yuga-Bichitra*, p. 357.

38. As for Jinnah's epithet as the 'logician', his followers in Bengal must have felt awed of him. In 1936, the Bengali Muslim League journal *Dainik Azad* proudly translated Jinnah's self-description as the 'cold-blooded logician' (*him-rakta noiyayik*). No doubt, the distinctly challenging, almost threatening overtone was quite deliberately employed. Abu Zafar Shamsuddin, *Atma-smriti* (Dhaka: Jatiya Sahitya Prakashani, 1989), p. 186.

39. Commenting on the huge significance of Jinnah–Huq conflict, Sana Aiyar comments: 'Huq thus emerged as the regional Other for Jinnah. He could not be accommodated within the singular mould of the communalism, which had manifested itself in the political ideology of the

Muslim League.' See Aiyar, 'Fazlul Huq, Region and Religion in Bengal', p. 1222. However, as I have already mentioned, Aiyar thus downplays Huq's deep-running regional loyalties and prefers to explain his conflict with Jinnah as primarily political. I argue that, on the contrary, his dilemma was no less ideological than political.

40. The results of the elections to the Bengal legislature opened up a number of possibilities. In a house of 250, Congress had won 60 seats, the League 40, the KPP 35, independent Muslims 41, independent Scheduled Caste group 23, non-party caste-Hindus 14, and the Europeans 25. The course of events in Bengal took an interesting twist here. In spite of sweeping the polls in all six provinces except Bengal and Punjab, the Congress High Command under the influence of its leftist elements, including Nehru, was against the idea of accepting office under the 'unacceptable' Government of India Act of 1935. The same reluctance was shown by Sarat Chandra Bose, who in conjunction with Subhas Bose and the revolutionaries, opposed the Gandhiites like Kiran Shankar Roy and the recalcitrant leaders like Nalini Ranjan Sarkar.

41. See Chatterji, *Bengal Divided*, p. 223. She mentions that a contemporary whom she interviewed asserted that Sarat Bose on behalf of the Bengal Provincial Congress Committee (BPCC) could have been successful in forming an alliance with the KPP had the Working Committee not tied his hands by their mandate. The Congress Working Committee was absolutely insistent upon the immediate release of the prisoners to be the foremost priority in the ministry's programme, as opposed to the KPP's keenness on pushing its electoral promises of tenancy reforms.

42. Abul Mansur Ahmed describes the KPP position during this negotiation with a deep sense of betrayal:

> [T]he new Ministry should have first passed in the new Assembly the Bill ensuring tenants' rights as well as the Moneylender's Bill, thus consolidating its hold of the vast masses of peasantry, especially the Muslim peasantry. Only after that we should have possibly pressed for the release of political prisoners. If the Governor opposed this, then we should have resigned from the Ministry and the legislature and sought fresh mandate from the people. In that case, the Congress and the KPP would have swept all general and Muslim seats respectively.... But if we stuck on the contrary to the present serial order [that is political prisoners' issue on the top] and insisted on release of political prisoners first and resigned, then the KPP would lose to the ML. The League would then successfully paint us as the B team of the Congress and debunk our pro-peasant program.... Almost all the KPP leaders supported me but the Congress leaders refused to see the point. They passionately insisted that in the far-off Andaman Islands, hundreds of sons of Bengal were suffering, their lives were at stake and hence the issue must get priority over the economic demands of the impoverished peasants.

A.M. Ahmed, *Amar Dekha Rajnitir Panchash Bachhor*, pp. 135–8.

43. A.M. Ahmed, *Amar Dekha Rajnitir Panchash Bachhor*, p. 138. Biswas, the Hindu journalist expressed similar disappointment at the fallout of two 'like-minded parties'. Kalipada Biswas, *Yukta Banglar Shesh Adhyay*, p. 32. For Hindu Congressites like Biswas, however, this 'like-mindedness' between the Congress and the KPP did not mean much beyond a common line of opposition to the Muslim League.

44. '... [W]hat proved disastrous was not the rejection of a coalition, but the failure to develop and implement... a genuinely socially radical measure ... secularist and radical rhetoric in the end merely alarmed Muslim vested interests without winning over Muslim masses.' Sumit Sarkar, *Modern India, 1885–1947* (Delhi: Macmillan, 1983), p. 355.

45. Joya Chatterji has captured the continuous inner flow of Hindu sensibilities in Congress politics in *Bengal Divided*. However, the similar role of religion in the KPP politics has so far not invited much historical attention.

46. M.A. Ahmed, *Amar Dekha Rajnitir Panchash Bachhor*, p. 136.

47. Momen, *Muslim Politics in Bengal*, pp. 62–4. The League's success in Bengal was mostly due to the charm of Jinnah's political moves in the mid-1930s. Before then, the League was nothing but a political lightweight. But Jinnah single-handedly paving the way for the acceptance of the Communal Award and the Provincial Autonomy Scheme in the Central Assembly as well as for the rejection of the Federal Part of the Act of 1935, had a lasting impact in Bengal.

48. The Congress anxiety regarding its own failure on this matter rose to an alarming extent in only two years from this event. Sajjad Jahir, a Congress socialist and a close aide to Jawaharlal Nehru, later commented: 'I remember very well the worries and anxieties of Nehru and my friend Dr K. M. Ashraf in regard to the Muslim Mass Contact Movement from 1937 to 1939. On the one hand, they had to face the virulent and vicious communal propaganda launched by the Muslim League against the then forces of national unity, and on the other hand the discouragement and sabotage inside the Congress ...' Sajjad Jahir, 'Recent Muslim Politics in India and the Problems of National Unity', *India and Contemporary Islam*, vol. 6 (Simla: Indian Institute of Advanced Studies, 1971), p. 207.

49. Maulana Abul Kalam Azad, *India Wins Freedom* (Delhi: Orient Blackswan, 2014), p. 160. Later politicians like Sajjad Jahir also admitted this failure; see Jahir, 'Recent Muslim Politics in India and the Problems of National Unity', p. 210.

50. See Rashid, *Foreshadowing of Bangladesh*, p. 110.

51. The divided nature of the League and the interplay of opposing forces within the ministry during this period was mentioned by Bose. The pressure created by their more extreme supporters and by the opposition prevented the ministry from reneging on the Tenancy Act

Amendment when it was presented in April 1938. Sugata Bose, *Agrarian Bengal: Economy, Social Structure and Politics, 1919–1947* (Cambridge: Cambridge University Press, 1986), p. 213.

52. Out of eleven members of the Huq–League ministry, six were zamindars, three were lawyers, and one was a capitalist apart from Huq himself.

53. This Commission included the maharaja of Burdwan; B.K. Roychowdhury, the zamindar of Gouripur; and apologists of the Permanent Settlement like Radha Kumud Mukherjee. Huq clearly allowed himself to be influenced more by powerful zamindars like Bijoy Prasad Sinha Roy and Nawab Khwaja Habibullah of Dhaka (respectively the Minister of Revenue and the Minister of Agriculture and Industry in his ministry) than by the Praja leaders like Maulavi Shamsuddin or Abul Mansur Ahmed. The tenancy legislation of 1938 bore the impressions of this latent class tensions, amply reflected in the speech of Sarat Bose, the leader of the Congress, on the assembly floor. The Congress, suffering from the same anxiety as the League, declared, 'Congress was definitely not in favour of perpetuation of landlordism … but at the same time it discouraged any attempt on the part of any section of the people to describe another section as exploiters.' BLAP, 30 September 1937, p. 2093.

54. Sugata Bose discusses at length the essentially limited nature of the bill, and the heated exchange between the pro-rayat lobby and its opponents. See *Agrarian Bengal*, p. 210.

55. R. Coupland, *Indian Politics, 1936-1942* (London: Oxford University Press, 1943), p. 185.

56. Quoted in Sarat Bose's letter to Huq, 12 May 1939, in *Sarat Chandra Bose: Commemoration Volume* (Calcutta: Sarat Bose Academy, 1982), p. 262.

57. BLAP, 9 August 1938, p. 66.

58. BLAP, 10 August 1938, p. 121.

59. Prafulla Chandra Ray, an eminent nationalist and a scientist by profession, generously described Huq as 'the perfect Muslim and the perfect Bengali'. Ray was also deeply disappointed by the early 1940s. Huq's helplessness was coming through, nevertheless, when he made a direct appeal to Sarat Bose in the assembly:

> I would appeal to my friend Mr. Bose to come and tell me what is it that he wants me to do. He says he is not going to accept office. I should be very glad to sit with him and see what kind of programme he wants us to follow. If I fail in my duty after that, then will be the time for them to condemn us. But please give us respite at least for another year. (BLAP, 10 August 1938, p. 118)

60. Waliullah, *Yuga-Bichitra*, p. 351.

61. H.N. Mitra (ed.), *Indian Annual Register, 1940*, vol. 1 (1940; reprint, Delhi: Gyan Publishing House, 1990), p. 312.

62. Kalipada Biswas, *Yukta Banglar Shesh Adhyay*, pp. 35–9.

63. '"Muslim Raj" in Bengal is Complete! Division of Portfolios: All Nation-building Departments Go to Muslims, Hindu Ministers Offered Inferior Positions in the Bengali Cabinet'. *Amrita Bazar Patrika*, 1 April 1937, p. 1.

64. Dineshchandra Singha, *Noakhalir Mati o Manush* (Calcutta: Gyan Prakashan, 1992), p. 103.

65. 'I notice in the newspapers that there are apprehensions of a "Moslem raj" or "Hindu raj" here and there, but I take this opportunity of emphasizing the fact, that there can no more be a Moslem raj in Bengal than there can be Hindu raj in Bihar or the United Provinces.... The ideals throughout will be the British ideals of administration.' Huq's statement at a Press Conference, *Amrita Bazar Patrika*, 1 April 1940, p. 5.

66. Aiyar, 'Fazlul Huq, Region and Religion in Bengal', p. 1219.

67. While in Lahore, during that same conference, he indeed described himself as first and foremost, 'the leader of Bengal'. The omission of the word 'Muslim' might not be accidental. Huq's speech in Lahore session, K. Ahmad, *A Social History of Bengal*, p. 48.

68. Shyamali Ghosh, 'Fazlul Haq and Muslim Politics in Pre-Partition Bengal', p. 453.

69. Even when he spoke of 'being a Muslim first', Huq did not want to address the meeting in Urdu even though the crowds urged him to do so. It was also quickly supplemented by the talks of his Bengali lineage and the demand for a provincial autonomy. See Shyamali Ghosh, 'Fazlul Haq and Muslim Politics in Pre-Partition Bengal', p. 1220. In Aiyar's views, 'Huq's talk of "independent states" [in Lahore Resolution] that were autonomous and sovereign amounted to more provincial autonomy than the Act had so far provided, for it gave independence not only from the central government but also from the central policy of the Muslim League.' Aiyar, 'Fazlul Huq, Region and Religion in Bengal'.

70. Shyamali Ghosh, 'Fazlul Haq and Muslim Politics in Pre-Partition Bengal', p. 453.

71. Shyamali Ghosh, 'Fazlul Haq and Muslim Politics in Pre-Partition Bengal', p. 453.

72. Chaudhury Khaliquzzaman, *Star of India*, 18 October 1938, p. 4.

73. Sarat Bose underlined the contradictions he noticed in Huq. In his correspondence with Huq, he wanted to discuss the problem in a frank tone. Had he not been aware of the worries that kept Huq tormented during this time, he would not have written so. In one of his letters, he wrote: 'I have noted with keenest disappointment the progressive heightening of the communal complexion of your Government and Party, in which process I have watched with even greater disappointment and dismay the part played by you personally.' Sarat Chandra Bose's letter to Huq, 12

May 1939, *Sarat Chandra Bose: Commemoration Volume*, p. 261. Again, 'May I appeal from Philip the Drunk to Philip Sober, may I appeal from Mr. Fazlul Huq, the Chief Minister, to Mr. Fazlul Huq, the man, may I challenge him to say whether in his opinion ours is not the best workable program that can possibly be devised in this province?' BLAP, 10 August 1938, p. 102.

74. When the Second World War broke out in 1939, India experienced a new wave of political turmoil. In national politics, Bengal Congress leaders clashed with the all-India leadership. The Bose–Gandhi conflict over the presidentship of the Congress led to a split in the BPCC—the bulk supporting Subhas Bose and the rest going with the AICC. The Government of India tried to mobilize all the provincial ministries behind the war effort. While Congress High Command was in a severe confusion looking for a middle ground between India's anti-imperialist struggle and a broader anti-imperialist stand regarding the war, and the BPCC, despite its split, was more or less sharing the confusion of the High Command. The Huq Ministry was placed in a difficult situation. Although Huq was not over-enthusiastic in rallying support for the government, finally, in December 1939, he had to give in and offer 'full co-operation in the successful prosecution of the War'.

75. The AIML through two of its most trusted Bengal leaders, Siddiqui and Ispahani, opposed his decision. They held that any unconditional support before the reaching of an agreement between Jinnah and the viceroy, which was supposed to take place soon, would prejudice Jinnah's negotiation and lower his prestige. So Huq, in moving the official war resolution, had to declare in the assembly that he would look up to the AIML and follow it if asked not to cooperate with the government's war effort.

76. *Star of India*, 5 February 1940, p. 5.

77. Huq's statement, *Star of India*, 6 February 1940, p. 5.

78. Yet in the very next month the same person moved the famous Lahore Resolution (March 1940). The curious juxtaposition of events suggests that the Lahore proposal might not have appeared to Huq as necessarily divisive in content.

79. Huq's statement, *Star of India*, 27 February 1940, p. 4.

80. The final purging of Huq from the League followed from two incidents. The first incident of discord took place around the time of the 1941 census. During the census, communal tensions suddenly grew in Bengal as both Hindus and Muslims were equally keen to ensure 'proper' enumeration. The Hindu Mahasabha was accused of having inflated the Hindu position. Huq immediately expressed his apprehensions to Jinnah that Muslims in Bengal might be reduced to a minority, and that the AIML might lose one of the so-called majority provinces in India. Jinnah, when asked 'to be ready for an appeal from Bengal to launch an all-India

agitation', seemed to be lukewarm about this and his response disheartened Huq. The other incident was the observance of Pakistan Day on 23 March 1941. The census tensions already led to two cases of riot in Khulna and Dacca, and in fear of further violence, Huq instructed the district and sub-divisional Leagues to postpone the Pakistan Day celebrations in Bengal. Jinnah and AIML took exception at such a move, and Huq was put into a more difficult corner in the central body.

81. Huq's letter to Bose, Home Political Files, no. 232/41, p. 147, December 1941, NAI.

82. Governor's telegram to Viceroy, 8 December 1941, Home Political A (Confidential), file no. 37 (II), NAI.

83. Sugata Bose, *Agrarian Bengal*, p. 217. The quote is from the Fortnightly Report from the Commissioner, Chittagong Division, to the chief secretary, Government of Bengal, Political Confidential File no. 13/41, November 1941, West Bengal Home Department.

84. Sarat Bose demanded the Home portfolio in case of a possible ministry, which the government was not ready to acquiesce to. Viceroy Linlithgow wrote to J.A. Herbert, the governor of Bengal:

> This definite request by Sarat Bose and his followers for Home portfolio aggravates situation. While I await your future comments I am clear myself that given what we know of Bose's association with Japanese we cannot contemplate him as a member of a Ministry still less as Home member or the like. The counter-proposal was to arrest Bose, 'however risky it might be for local repercussions'.

Governor Herbert of course consented to this proposal. See telegram dated 9 December 1941, Home Political A (Confidential), file no. 37 (II).

85. The extent of Huq's acceptability can be assumed from the observations of the government before the new ministry was formed: 'Leaders of Progressive Party, Independent Scheduled Castes, Hindu Nationalists and Krishak Praja Party all affirmed their support to Huq.' Governor Herbert's telegram to Viceroy Linlithgow, 8 December 1941, Home Political A (Confidential), file no. 37 (II).

86. Aiyar contradicts the 'historians [who] tended to emphasize the incompatibility of cross-communal alliances in Bengal and accept [the] assertions that Huq–Mookerjee alliance was a failure,' and argues that during 1941–3, 'Huq and Mookerjee were able to reconcile their religious differences within an identity politics that privileged provincial identity but did not fall back on secular claims.' See Aiyar, 'Fazlul Huq, Region and Religion in Bengal', p. 1235. I agree with her to a large extent. In terms of administration, this coalition indeed proved workable, even peaceful at times. However, the consequences of this alliance were alarming. In an extremely volatile sociopolitical situation, the external perception of the ministry was growing more and more unfavourable in both Hindu and Muslim quarters, and neither Huq nor Mookherjee any longer enjoyed

any substantial support in their own communities. Both began to be seen as 'outsiders', either as opportunists, or Extremists. If the inter-community 'alliance' was kept limited only in upper-most levels of provincial administration, it might not ensure stability of such an alliance, as history proved soon. In this sense, the Huq–Mahasabha alliance could never fulfil the promises hidden in the prospect of a Huq–Congress alliance, and made only a futile attempt to bring together unbridgeable ideological adversaries.

87. Waliullah, *Yuga-Bichitra*, p. 387.
88. Rahman, *Asamapta Atmajibani*, p. 22.
89. Fortnightly Report of the Commissioner, Presidency Division, for the second half of 1941, Home Political File, 17 April 1941—Poll. (I), 1941, NAI.
90. A.M. Ahmed, *Amar Dekha Rajnitir Panchash Bachhor*, p. 219.
91. Huq had already earned the reputation for being a mercurial politician. But this move, as Abul Mansur Ahmed recalls, 'was clearly unimaginable. The sky fell on me, I was baffled as well as upset, and stood still for quite some time.' At Huq's attempts of justifying his own move, Ahmed's reaction could only be 'incredulous'. Although not entirely convinced himself, Ahmed, then the editor of *Navayug*, finally took up the challenge to popularize this Progressive Coalition ministry to the masses, which indeed proved to be an ideologically strenuous job. See A.M. Ahmed, *Amar Dekha Rajnitir Panchash Bachhor*, p. 222.
92. The bitter Huq–League rivalry caused Huq's political marginalization, though he was the supreme leader of the province at that time. It was alleged that Shyamaprasad Mookherjee made the situation worse for Huq by wooing the League rather unnecessarily. Waliullah alleges that Mookherjee did not hesitate to provide financial support to the Orient Press of the Muslim League, while it was none other than Huq who had been resisting this administrative effort. In the end, 'it only benefitted the League', says Waliullah, *Yuga-Bichitra*, p. 408.
93. Suhrawardy's report of the Sirajganj Conference to the BPML, *Star of India*, 14 February 1942.
94. Rahman, *Asamapta Atmajibani*, p. 11.
95. Rahman, *Asamapta Atmajibani*, p. 11.
96. Waliullah, *Yuga-Bichitra*, p. 414; Shila Sen, *Muslim Politics in Bengal*, p. 152.
97. Abul Kalam Shamsuddin, *Atit Diner Smriti* (Dhaka: Naoroj Kitabistan, 1968), p. 194.
98. Shila Sen, 'Some Aspects of Muslim Politics in Bengal, 1937–46 and Fazlul Huq', *Bangladesh Historical Studies* I (1976): 19–76, 53.
99. Aiyar, 'Fazlul Huq, Region and Religion in Bengal'.
100. Waliullah, *Yuga-Bichitra*, p. 362.

101. Even those Muslims sympathetic to the League noted the 'failure' with some frustration. *Mohammadi*, December 1938, p. 78.

102. *Mohammadi*, December 1938, pp. 372–3, 378.

103. *Mohammadi*, December 1938, pp. 372–3, 378.

104. Although not an all-out supporter of Huq, Ahmed, one of the leading KPP leaders, said that 'these 2–3 years of the Huq ministry, for the peasants of Bengal were indeed a golden age'. A.M. Ahmed, *Amar Dekha Rajnitir Panchash Bachhor*, p. 177.

105. A.M. Ahmed, *Amar Dekha Rajnitir Panchash Bachhor*, p. 176.

106. Kalipada Biswas, *Yukta Banglar Shesh Adhyay*, p. 42.

107. Mujibur Rahman, a young companion of Suhrawardy, was growing into a major figure of League in Bengal, and a sworn opponent of Huq. He later recollected that his father had sullenly warned him not to 'do anything that might discredit Huq-saheb', 'the last ray of hope for the Bengali'. See Rahman, *Asamapta Atmajibani*, p. 22.

108. 'Times were strange. We already started believing in "Pakistan", its urgency in realizing "Muslim" rights. But Pakistan, Holwell, Siraj never seemed to be at odds with each other. Subhas's calls were as ardent and irresistible as those of the League leaders.' Interview conducted on 28 July 1997 with Mustafa Nurul Islam, a former League activist of Calcutta, and later a retired professor of Bengali Language and Literature, Dhaka University.

109. Kazi Motahar Hossain Chaudhury, 'Swadhinata-Jatiyata-Sampradayikata', *Mohammadi*, June 1939.

110. Abul Mansur Ahmed, 'Muslim Jibane Ananda,' *Krishak*, Eid number, 1939.

111. Abdus Sadaq, 'Nikhil Bharat Federation Gathan ki Sambhab?'

112. A.K. Shamsuddin, *Atit Diner Smriti*, p. 210.

113. Debates on Pakistan, introduced in this chapter, will be explored further in Chapter 5.

114. H.N. Mitra, *Indian Annual Register, 1943*, vol. 1 (Calcutts: Annual Register Office, 1943), p. 93. While historians generally tend to characterize the 1940s as a decisive journey towards religious solidarity leading to the Partition of 1947, Aiyar has concluded that Huq's second ministry was an overall success in 'keeping the communal feeling low', and thus thrown a different light on the years 1941–3. See Sana Aiyar, 'Fazlul Huq, Region and Religion in Bengal'.

115. *Dainik Azad*, 21 June 1942.

116. A.M. Ahmed, *Amar Dekha Rajnitir Panchash Bachhor*, pp. 242–4.

117. A.M. Ahmed, *Amar Dekha Rajnitir Panchash Bachhor*, pp. 242–4.

118. *Dainik Azad*, 15 December 1944, p. 3.

119. Shamsul Huq (ed.), *Bengal Provincial Muslim League: Annual Report* (henceforth *Annual Report of BPML, 1944*) (Dacca: Bengal Provincial Muslim League Office, 1944), p. 11.

120. *Annual Report of BPML, 1944*, p. 8.

121. *Annual Report of BPML, 1944*, p. 9.

122. *Annual Report of BPML, 1944*, p. 8.

123. Confronted with a stiff opposition from the all-India League and its trusted lieutenants like Khwaja Nazimuddin and Akram Khan, Hashim had at least one heavyweight patron within the League, H.S. Suhrawardy. By this time, Jinnah's explicit preference for Nazimuddin as opposed to Suhrawardy gradually pushed the latter to a position where he, like Hashim, concentrated on the building up of a loyal following within the territories of Bengal. Suhrawardy and Hashim thus were on their way to become the two most prominent and popular leaders of Bengali Muslims. Their combination also offset Nazimuddin's influence in parliamentary politics. Again, the association of Suhrawardy, who was much more entrenched to League politics by the 1940s, enabled Hashim, the new radical leader of the youth, to continue with his own agenda from within the League.

124. This terrible famine is known in Bengal as 'Panchasher Manwantar' (the Great Famine of 1350 BS, that is, 1943), named after the year of its occurrence according to the Bengali calendar.

125. Humayun Kabir, 'Muslim Politics, 1942–47', in *Muslim Politics 1906–47 and Other Essays* (Calcutta: Firma K.L. Mukhopadhyay, 1969), p. 58.

126. The local League efforts at providing one-time meals through gruel kitchens (langarkhana) were commendable, according to many contemporary observers. Abul Mansur Ahmed was one of those who, during the famine, were actively involved in condemning the League ministry for its lack of adequate remedial measures. His widely publicized booklet on this issue referred to Suhrawardy as kutta-e-Bangal (the dog of Bengal). However, it is he who very generously remembers how important Suhrawardy's personal and organization contributions were in ameliorating conditions, at least in Calcutta. Abul Mansur Ahmed, *Amar Dekha Rajnitir Panchash Bachhar*, p. 237. Also, on Suhrawardy's role during the famine, see Kamruddin Ahmed, *Bangali Madhyabitter Atmabikash* (Dhaka: Naoroj Kitabistan, 1975), pp. 20–1.

127. The League workers collected large amount of subscription from locally resourceful people and organizations. K. Ahmed, *Bangali Madhyabitter Atmabikash*, p. 23.

128. K. Ahmed, *Bangali Madhyabitter Atmabikash*, pp. 23–4.

129. K. Ahmed, *Bangali Madhyabitter Atmabikash*, p. 29.

130. Sugata Bose, *Agrarian Bengal*, pp. 260–1.

131. The claims and counter-claims of 'nation' were reflected in Indian football to explain why the victory of the first Indian team called Mohun Bagan in the Indian Football Association (IFA) Shield Tournament in 1911 was always perceived as a greater nationalistic triumph than Mohammedan Sporting Club's five straight Calcutta Football League titles between

1934 and 1938. Kaushik Bandyopadhyay, 'In Search of an Identity: Muslims and Football in Colonial India', *Soccer and Society* 10, no. 6 (2009): 843–65.

132. A.K. Shamsuddin, *Atit Diner Smriti*, p. 168.

133. The victories of the club were seen to enhance the prestige of the League. The Muslims idolized this club more passionately than they had initially intended to do. It was also seen by the Hindu press as an alarming instance of Muslim self-assertion. An inspirational poem by Golam Mostafa was published in Saptahik Mohammadi, 'League Bijoy na Dig Bijoy?' (Merely a victory of the League, or a conquest of the world?). It was so hugely popular that 'hundreds of additional copies of that newspaper were sold that day'. A.K. Shamsuddin, *Atit Diner Smriti*, p. 168.

134. Nazimuddin allotted a single plot to the club, while the general rule of the day was sharing plots among a number of football clubs, including the big ones like the Mohun Bagan Club or the East Bengal Club. Government of Bengal, Home Political File, no. 7M of 1–3, 1937.

135. *Anandabazar Patrika*, 12 July 1940.

136. *The Statesman*, 25 July 1940.

137. Sarat Bose's letter to Huq, 12 June 1937, Sarat Chandra Bose: Commemoration Volume, p. 271. We will discuss Bose's stand on this issue in greater details in the section on 'representation' in this chapter.

138. A.M. Ahmed, Amar Dekha Rajnitir Panchash Bachhar, p. 211.

139. N.N. Mitra (ed.), *Indian Annual Register, 1941*, vol. 2 (Calcutta: Annual Register Office, 1941), p. 143.

140. A.M. Ahmed, *Amar Dekha Rajnitir Panchash Bachhar*, p. 212.

141. Ramananda Chattopadhyay, 'Bibidha Prasanga', *Prabasi*, June 1937 (Ashar 1343 BS). Akram Khan had interpreted the 'lotus' as the symbol of Saraswati, the Hindu goddess of learning.

142. Editorial, *Anandabazar Patrika*, 22 August 1937.

143. A.K. Shamsuddin, Atit Diner Smriti, p. 174.

144. Rezaul Karim, 'The Burning of Anandamath', *Anandabazar Patrika*, 19 September 1937.

145. *Anandabazar Patrika*, 27 October 1937.

146. Letter to Nehru, published in *Anandabazar Patrika*, 30 October 1937.

147. Rabindranath Tagore's letter to Subhas Bose, 19 October 1937, quoted in Nepal Majumdar, *Bharate Jatiyata, Antarjatikata ebong Rabindranath*, vol. 4 (Calcutta: Chatushkon Private Limited, 1971), p. 255.

148. Rabindranath Tagore's letter to Subhas Bose, 19 October 1937. Krishna Kripalani, a confidante of Tagore, confirmed the latter's revised stand and explained his own in that light:

    My sympathy, at any rate, is with the Mahommedans in this controversy, for I believe that if I were a Mahommedan I should have resented the particular garb this song gives to my love of my country. One can have no sympathy with the fanaticism of the Bengali Mahommedans, out to smell idolatry in all literary use of Hindu mythology. Still I should say that the spirit of the imagery and invocation employed in this song is merely literary and is such that it is unfair to force the monotheistic followers of the Prophet of Arabia to swallow it in the name of Indian Nationalism.

See Krishna Kripalani, 'Bande Mataram and Indian Nationalism', *Visva-Bharati News*, October 1937, pp. 45–56.

149. Krishna Kripalani, 'Bande Mataram and Indian Nationalism', pp. 45–56.

150. Tagore's stand underwent a slight change in the meantime, as was evident from his formal note to Nehru, where he gave a green signal to the first stanza of 'Bande Mataram'. He thought that it should be acceptable to the Muslims unlike the song in its entirety. Rabindranath Tagore, *Anandabazar Patrika*, 30 October 1937.

151. *Anandabazar Patrika*, 31 October 1937.

152. A.K. Shamsuddin, *Atit Diner Smriti*, p. 175.

153. The Congress intransigence in upholding the claims of its own tri-colour flag and its own chosen 'national song' 'Bande Mataram' began to be widely resented. Even the governor expressed concern at the recurrent complaints 'regarding the Muslim charges against the Congress Ministries,... Congress tactlessness in the singing of Bande Mataram in the schools and the unfurling of the Congress flag upon public meetings'. Governor Herbert to the Secretary of State for India, 21 February 1940, Zetland Collections, Mss. Eur. D 609/9, IOR.

154. Subhas Chandra Bose, *The Alternative Leadership: Netaji Subhas Chandra Bose, Collected Works*, vol. 10, edited by Sisir K. Bose and Sugata Bose (Calcutta: Netaji Research Bureau, 2004), pp. 103–4. As if to demonstrate the efficacy of the principles he put his trust in, he managed to execute a pact with the Muslim League in the Calcutta Corporation. This was effected on behalf of the Congress after a lot of persuasion by his own group within the Congress, and could not but estrange 'a certain number of communally minded Hindus'. Abdur Rahman Siddiqui of the Muslim League was offered the seat of the Mayor of Calcutta, 'after futile attempts to foster an understanding between the Congress and Muslim League'. Sugata Bose, *His Majesty's Opponent: Subhas Chandra Bose and India's Struggle against Empire* (Cambridge: Harvard University Press, 2011), p. 175.

155. How the idea of an inter-community government on the provincial level was constantly haunting Huq can be apparent from official records also. The governor wrote in a letter: 'I agree that much credit is due to Sikander [the Premier of Punjab Ministry] and Fazlul Huq for their willingness to contemplate the inclusion of Congress representatives in their Minsteries in the event of coalition governments being agreed to as part of a general

settlement.' Governor Herbert to the Secretary of State for India, 28 February 1940, Mss Eur, D 609/9, IOR.

156. Huq's speech in the assembly in 1939, in A.K. Zainul Abedin (ed.), *Memorable Speeches of Sher-e-Bangla* (Dhaka, 1978), p. 125.

157. Huq's speech in the assembly in 1939, p. 125.

158. Much attention was drawn to Huq's statement published in the Hindustan Times where he stated that ... 'no community had the right to hold up the progress of the country: the deadlock must be resolved by immediate agreement between the warring parties'. Governor Herbert to the Secretary of State, 28 February 1940, Mss Eur D 609/9, IOR.

159. Sarat Bose's correspondence with Huq, the Chief Minister, 12 June 1939, *Sarat Chandra Bose: Commemoration Volume*, p. 271.

160. Sarat Bose's correspondence with Huq, the Chief Minister, 12 June 1939, p. 271.

161. Sarat Bose's correspondence with Huq, the Chief Minister, 12 June 1939, p. 271.

162. Sarat Bose's correspondence with Huq, the Chief Minister, 12 June 1939, p. 271.

163. In this context, we can remember Ambedkar's observations about the connection between democratic rights and the demand for Pakistan. We have already quoted how he repeated a slogan used in Ireland's movement for secession from the British to explicate the basic principle of this demand of self-rule as a primary democratic right: 'Damn your safeguards. We do not want to be ruled by you.' Kalipada Biswas, *Yukta Banglar Shesh Adhyay*, p. 237.

164. In his unfinished autobiography, Sheikh Mujibur Rahman mentions such an instance of popular trust in Huq. See Rahman, *Asamapta Atmajibani*, p. 22.

165. Golam Mostafa, Pakistani Gaan (Dhaka, 1962), p. 12. The original song and its translation are given below:

Naya zamanar Aladin tumi mayabi murtiman
Nurer cherage Hindustane anile Pakistan
Sonar kathir parashe tomar jagilo Mussalman
Sat sagarer nabik tumi - tumi je Sindabad.

(You're the Aladin of the new age, the magic incarnate,
In Hindustan you brought Pakistan– by the bright light effect.
Muslims are roused today by the touch of golden reed
Oh you sailor of seven seas, the Sinbad indeed!)

166. Waliullah, *Yuga-Bichitra*, p. 373.

167. *Dainik Azad*, 24 March 1940, p. 3.

168. Abul Hashim, *In Retrospection* (Dhaka: Maola Brothers, 1998) p. 22.

169. Ayesha Jalal, *The Sole Spokesman: Jinnah, The Muslim League and the Demand for Pakistan* (Cambridge: Cambridge University Press, 1994), p. 119.

170. Ayesha Jalal, *Self and Sovereignty: Individual and Community in South Asian Islam since 1850* (Delhi: Oxford University Press, 2000). For the provincial Muslim politics in Punjab, also see D. Gilmartin, *Empire and Islam, Punjab and the Making of Pakistan* (Berkeley: University of California Press, 1988). Recently, Venkat Dhulipala has argued on the contrary that 'Pakistan' was never a vague idea that serendipitously emerged as a nation-state but was popularly imagined as a sovereign Islamic state, a 'new Medina'. His findings on the role played by Deobandi Ulema in UP have led him to this position. Venkat Dhulipala, *Creating a New Medina: State Power, Islam, and the Quest for Pakistan in Late Colonial North India* (Cambridge: Cambridge University Press, 2015). This observation is however exceedingly difficult to hold if the Bengal Muslim discourse on Pakistan is closely examined. The present study insists that the case of Bengal is not at all comprehensible through the prism of the Deobandi experience of northern India. Instead, in this eastern Muslim-majority province, the 'vagueness' of the Pakistan idea, sometimes wishfully preserved, sometimes strategically upheld, was a major contributing factor behind the rapid spread of this idea in Bengal. I refuse to relegate the Pakistan versions of Huq and Hashim to the realms of marginal significance, because, in terms of popular mobilization and popular perception, both were the most influential figures in the Bengal Muslim world in the 1940s. Neither does the general popular discourse on Pakistan in late colonial Bengal prove to be wholly synchronous with the new Deobandi political vocabulary fusing ideas of Islamic nationhood and its unquestioned supremacy.

171. Editorial, *Dainik Azad*, 14 September 1940, p. 4.

172. Abul Hashim, *In Retrospection*, p. 22.

173. At the Ramgarh Congress (March 1940), immediately preceding the Lahore Conference, Azad gave this speech where he asked Muslims to come out of the minority anxiety. By the merit of their numerical strength, they would be in a secure position in the five provinces where they constituted the majority and also form a very substantial minority in others. He emphatically pointed out the 'diverse' nature of India's culture and society, which demanded a flexible federal structure. See H.N. Mitra, *Indian Annual Register, 1940*, vol. 1, p. 300. On the other hand, the official League line presented in Lahore denounced any such 'constitution which must necessarily result in a Hindu majority Government. Hindus and Muslims brought together under a democratic system forced upon the minorities can only mean Hindu Raj.' Jinnah's Presidential Address, Lahore, March 1940, in H.N. Mitra, *Indian Annual Register, 1940*, vol. 1, p. 300.

174. However, Azad's opposition to the struggle for Muslim rights was not acceptable to Huq. He thought that 'even in Punjab and Bengal our position is not very safe. In the Legislature we are not in such large majority; we have to seek the help of other interests and minorities to form coalition governments which are the weakest form of government known to constitutionalists'. Mushirul Hasan, *India's Partition: Process, Strategy and Mobilization* (Delhi: Oxford University Press, 1993), pp. 44.

175. B.R. Ambedkar, *Pakistan or the Partition of India* (Bombay: Thacker & Co., 1946), p. 5.

176. Hashim, *In Retrospection*, p. 23.

177. Hashim, *In Retrospection*, p. 23.

178. *Hindustan Standard*, 21 June 1942. Also cited in Amalendu De, *Pakistan Prastab o Fazlul Huq* (Calcutta: Paschimbanga Rajyo Pustak Parishad, 1989), p. 119.

179. *The Statesman*, 3 February 1943.

180. *The Statesman*, 15 February 1943.

181. Zahur Hossain, 'Pakistan and Soviet Union', in *Mujibur Rahman Khan, Pakistan* (Calcutta: Mohammadi Press, 1942), p. 66.

182. Hossain, 'Pakistan and Soviet Union', p. 67.

183. *Mohammadi*, March 1943, p. 21.

184. 'Milaner Age Malinya', *Saptahik Bangali*, vol. 2, no. 33, October 1944.

185. 'Eid–Puja Sammilan', *Saptahik Bangali*, vol. 2, no. 33, October 1944.

186. S. Wajid Ali, 'A Talk on Tea', in *Bengalees of Tomorrow*, (Calcutta: Das Gupta and Co. Publishers, 1945), p. 57. This writer repeatedly emphasized the need to 'place nationalism on a firm basis in Bengal', or 'to carry on a propaganda on the basis of Bengali nationalism'. According to him, a Bengali nationalism would be 'far more acceptable to the people of this province than the vague ideal of Indian nationalism, the foundations of which are more or less mythical and geographical, and in the factual world, largely a creation of the administrative genius and Military efficiency of the British race.'

187. Abul Mansur Ahmed, Speech at Renaissance Society meeting in Calcutta, 1944, in *Pak Banglar Culture* (Dhaka: Ahmad Publishing House, 1966), pp. 1–14.

188. Abul Mansur Ahmed, Speech at Renaissance Society meeting in Calcutta, 1944, p. 156.

189. Abul Mansur Ahmed, Speech at Renaissance Society meeting in Calcutta, 1944, p. 161.

190. Cited in Shila Sen, *Muslim Politics in Bengal*, p.179.

191. 'Pakistan o Banglar Mussalman', *Dainik Azad*, 12 May 1944.

192. Jalal has already pointed out that 'Provincial Muslim politicians tended to align themselves to the League out of calculation not commitment ...' Jalal, *The Sole Spokesman*, p. 119.

193. *Annual Report of BPML*, 1944, p. 13.

194. *Annual Report of BPML*, 1944, p. 13.

195. Abul Hashim's Draft Manifesto of the Bengal Muslim League, *Star of India*, 23 March 1945, p. 3.

196. Bengal famine (1943) and Tebhaga movement (1946–7): The nature and course of Muslim politics seemed to have been critically affected by these historical events in the mid-1940s.

197. K. Ahmed, *Bangali Madhyabitter Atma-bikash*, pp. 20–3.

198. K. Ahmed, *Bangali Madhyabitter Atma-bikash*, p. 23.

199. K. Ahmed, *Bangali Madhyabitter Atma-bikash*, , p. 23..

200. Interview on 26 July 1997 with Dr Anisuzzaman, former Professor of Bengali Literature, Dhaka University.

201. Interview on 18 July 1997 with Jatin Sarakar, Professor, Mymensingh College. Also, interview conducted on 15 February 1997 with Kamaluddin Ahmed Khan, a former Muslim League worker of Chittagong, and a former advocate, Bangladesh Supreme Court, Chittagong.

202. In its ability to draw rural masses, overwhelmingly Muslim in composition, the KPP in the mid- and late 1930s played a more critical role than that of the Communist Party of India.

203. During the first Huq ministry when most of the tenancy regulations were passed, the role of Congress was equivocal. Sugata Bose argues that Congress stand in pressing the ministry to pass the tenancy regulation was as 'radical' as 'indefinitely whetting the appetite of the cultivator' while the ministry had retaliated by whetting communal passions. Sarat Bose criticized the Tenancy Amendment Bill for not going far enough in protecting the actual cultivators. See Sugata Bose, *Agrarian Bengal*, p. 210. The quote is from Governor Linlithgow to Governor-General Herbert, 7 September 1937, L/P & J/5/141, IOR. It can be fairly argued that although the Congress members did not vote against the bill en masse, no more than a few such as Sarat Bose really offered their strong support to it.

204. Gene Overstreet and Marshall Windmiller, *Communism in India* (Berkeley: University of California Press, 1959), p. 263.

205. As compared to the Congress, the KPP employed the community identity more pragmatically in its agenda. 'Muslim unity and solidarity' was blended well with the economic grievances of the peasant societies, with 'the problem of dal and bhat, and some kind of coarse cloth to cover our nudity … the problem of problems which stares us in the face which must be solved immediately.' Huq's election speech, *Star of India*, 12 September 1936, p. 12.

206. Taj ul-Islam Hashmi, *Pakistan as a Peasant Utopia: The Communalization of a Class Politics in East Bengal, 1920–47* (Boulder: Westview Press, 1992), p. 125.

207. Hashim, *In Retrospection*, p. 28.
208. The one-man mission in March 1942, called the Cripps Mission, triggered fresh hopes in Bengal despite the call for 'Pakistan' and the tensions of provincial politics in Bengal under the Shyama–Huq ministry. K. Ahmed, *Bangali Madhyabitter Atma-bikash*, p. 15. A graphic description of middle-class excitement and the heightened expectations at the news of Cripps Mission is presented in the autobiographical novel of a Bengali author, Jajabor [Binoy Mukhopadhyay], *Drishtipat* (Calcutta: New Age, 1946), p. 35, 40–5.
209. C.H. Philips (ed.) *Evolution of India and Pakistan* (London: Oxford University Press, 1962), p. 375.
210. Ambedkar's interview, in Kalipada Biswas, Yukta Banglar Shesh Adhyay, p. 236. 'Efforts at understanding began only when the "idea" transformed itself into a "demand". The Arabian monster has by then been given the full shape!' Biswas asked: 'Would it have been reasonable to grant League's demand for equal number of seats in the Central Legislature?' Ambedkar replied, 'Why not? Did the League not come up as the single Muslim party in 1946 elections? Even if League did not have the right, Congress did not either have the right to represent the Muslims any more—specially after its failure in 1937 to have even its only Muslim candidate back in the Legislature!' He concluded with the following anecdote, which he had often mentioned in his public speeches of mid-1940s, 'The Irish leader told the Ulster representative, "Consent to the united Ireland. Ask for any safeguards and they will be granted to you." The reply was, "Damn your safeguards. We do not want to be ruled by you."'
211. There was a small group of Bengali Hindus who became influenced by this C.R. Formula and favoured Pakistan as early as in 1944, shows Joya Chatterji in *Bengal Divided*, p. 231. She mentions how the Mahasabha campaign against the C.R. Formula was questioned by some Hindus who urged Shyamaprasad Mookherjee to see the wisdom of the plan. However, what is surprising here is her easy tying up of such positions with the Bengali 'bhadralok communalism' in general, thus providing evidence to his thesis that the Bengali communal-minded Hindus were those who actually wanted the Partition. To say the least, the C.R. Formula was not driven by any communal undertones and, consequently, it would be deeply flawed to associate any follower or defender of this formula with a 'communal' mentality. Given the fact that there was a number of ideological positions from where some Bengali Hindus began to consider the idea of 'multiple nations', like that of the Communists, that of the followers of Adhikari, or that of the defenders of Rajagopalachari, a historical assessment needs to be much more discerning before branding any dissenter of the 'one-nation' theory as 'communal' in general, or a supporter of Partition in particular.

212. Organ of the Underground CPI, *Communist* 2, no. 9 (July 1940), p. 9.
213. Gangadhar Adhikari's Report to Central Committee of the CPI, *Communist* 2, no. 9 (July 1940), pp. 20–4.
214. Gangadhar Adhikari's Report to Central Committee of the CPI, pp. 20–4.
215. Sushobhan Sarkar, 'Rashtrabijnan Shakhar Sabhapatir Abhibhashon', speech given at Purba Pakistan Renaissance Society, *Mohammadi* 17, nos. 10–11 (1944), p. 451.
216. Sushobhan Sarkar, 'Rashtrabijnan Shakhar Sabhapatir Abhibhashon', pp. 451–2.
217. Sushobhan Sarkar, 'Rashtrabijnan Shakhar Sabhapatir Abhibhashon'.
218. Sushobhan Sarkar, 'Rashtrabijnan Shakhar Sabhapatir Abhibhashon'.
219. Sushobhan Sarkar, 'Rashtrabijnan Shakhar Sabhapatir Abhibhashon'.
220. Sushobhan Sarkar, 'Rashtrabijnan Shakhar Sabhapatir Abhibhashon', p. 453.
221. Sarat Bose, 'Bengal and Her Problems', Presidential Address at Rajshahi District Political Conference on 2 July 1938, in *The Voice of Sarat Chandra Bose: Selected Speeches, 1927–41*, edited by Sisir Kumar Bose (Calcutta: Netaji Research Bureau, 1979), p. 25.
222. Sarat Bose, The Jalpaiguri Address at the 36th session of Bengal Provincial Political Conference, 4 February 1939, in *The Voice of Sarat Chandra Bose*, p. 77.
223. 'Achievements of Congress had fallen short of our own program as outlined in the Congress election manifesto and the resolutions of the Congress.' Bose, 'Bengal and Her Problems', p. 27.
224. Bose, 'Bengal and Her Problems', p. 27.
225. Bose, 'Bengal and Her Problems', p. 30. This speech was delivered in April 1939.
226. Bose would add here that the Congress was the only party to compete with the Muslim League in setting up Muslim representatives. He would ask in a tone of sarcasm, 'Which are the organizations that are today fighting Mr. Jinnah's Muslim League candidates over the Muslim seats?' Letter dated 12 November 1945, in *I Warned My Countrymen: Being the Collected Works (1945–1950) of Sarat Chandra Bose* (Calcutta: Netaji Research Bureau, 1968), p. 62.
227. Sarat Bose was arrested in December 1941, by when Subhas Bose had already made an exit from the political scene in January 1941. The conservative Hindu Press of Bengal continued to suffer nightmares with the hypothesis that the Boses might again take over, leading to a 'Hindu demise': 'We sincerely hope Mr. Subhas Bose would not do any harm to the Hindu community. The Hindu interest in Bengal has been jeopardized in many ways by our politicians. We would not tolerate any more of that. The Boses should be aware of the fact that the Bengali Hindus would not take that from them.' *Basumati*, July 1941, p. 32.

228. With the more liberally exposed leaders now removed from the scene, the conservative elements within the Congress gained in strength. Hopes for a 'Bengal-based solution' were jeopardized to a great extent. The divide-and-rule policy of the British government had a silent laugh here. By arresting Subhas and keeping him behind bars against the wishes of both Nazimuddin and the Huq ministry, they successfully destroyed the ground on which revolutionary Hindus and Muslims could join together. This is significant that Governor Herbert in his memo to Viceroy Linlithgow expressed his anxiety over the Holwell movement and asserted that the agitation must 'be stopped'. Chatterji, *Bengal Divided*, p. 183.

229. Ahmed, *Amar Dekha Rajnitir Panchash Bachhor*, p. 225; Waliullah, *Yuga-Bichitra*, p. 328. Waliullah was disposed towards the League even in the KPP days and developed a strong anti-Huq stand quite early in his career. Eventually he became the director of Orient Press, the leading mouth-piece for the League in Bengal. Abul Mansur Ahmed, on the other hand, although later joined the League, was a loyal and active Huq supporter right through 1942, when Huq's growing ineffectiveness and the appeals of 'Pakistan' won him over to the side of League.

230. 'We used to rush to hear Sarat babu speaking. He and Subhas babu seemed the most sensible among the Hindu leaders.' Interview with Kamaluddin Ahmed Khan, 15 February 1997.

5 Pakistan, Partition, and the Province 1946–7

I t has been an accepted practice in history to identify the last two years of colonial Bengal as the climax of the divisive politics of the preceding decades. The period covering 1946–7 has indeed been engraved in the Bengali psyche for the terrible acts of violence in different parts of the region. But to read these two years as a moment of climax or a point of no return appears to be a teleological exercise. This chapter questions this reading of history and argues that the eruption of Hindu–Muslim violence in these years and the subsequent partition of the province should not be seen as a 'logical' culmination of the earlier politics. Instead, it argues that, just as in the past decades, the divisive ideologies coexisted and overlapped with the continuous and compelling attempts at striking negotiation and mutual accommodation till the very last months of the British rule. The only difference was that while the trends of accommodation were perceptible on the social or cultural realms of the region, those were not commensurately reflected in the political developments taking place during this time. By emphasizing such a disjuncture between the social possibilities and political options available before the society, this chapter concludes that the last two years of colonial rule in Bengal should be seen as an unfortunate deviation from the preceding events, not their logical conclusion.

How should one then understand the historical context of the partition of Bengal in 1947? If the view of a sure and steady progress of the separatist Muslim politics in Bengal is not accepted,[1] how do we then hope to explain partition? The answer proposed here is: while inter-community tensions as well as pressures for the realization of Pakistan were growing fast, political alternatives before the Bengali Muslims and the Bengali Hindus began to disappear quickly. Due to the rapid changes in all-India political negotiations before and during the momentous Transfer of Power, they found partitioning the province to be virtually the only effective solution at their disposal. In other words, partition finally took place due to a structural impasse resulting out of the contradictions of the trends of competitive politics of a Hindu-majority country on the one hand and a Muslim-majority region on the other.[2] To look for its cause in the increasing communal or separatist tendencies in the region alone, therefore, would be immensely misleading. Surely Bengal reached a difficult point in trying to negotiate 'differences' within the vortex of competing nationalisms; partition was offered as a rather hasty solution to break that difficult notch. This is enormously significant, because during the previous decades, even in the early years of the 1940s, both communities of Bengal had sought to uphold the ideas of a 'regional nation' with a remarkable consistency. Through these viewpoints on the region–nation, and the political experiments based on such viewpoints, they had even sought to deal with the fact of 'difference' within their own province. The political and ideological experiences of swadeshi, Khilafat, Bengal Pact, praja movements, and provincial ministries had provided various levels of impetus to this regional solution of the communal difference. Even during 1946–7, the prospects of the same region–nation were kept afloat by the anti-Partition demands of the Bengali proponents of Pakistan, as well as by the champions of the United Sovereign Bengal. However, in the course of rapidly orchestrated processes of decolonization, it became exceedingly difficult to pursue any option other than the one suggested by the centre, that is, from the totally different perspective of a Hindu-majority country beset by the compelling demands of the Muslim-minority provinces: to dissect the country and, by implication, to dissect the Muslim-majority province of Bengal.

The new political realities could not have magically altered the social or cultural life of the region, nevertheless. Even in an atmosphere of penetrating mistrust and violence, trends of inter-community sharing and coexistence continued to make their way. To view the society only as the recipient of the highly divisive political events would lead us to portray a picture of total social neurosis, characterized by a deep and pervasive communalization of all spheres of life. But the contemporary non-political sources of 1946–7 do not validate such a view and urge us to look beyond violence and hatred. Bengal's life indeed continued to revolve around the quotidian inter-community exchanges, both in the countryside and in the cities, and showed sustained attempts to resist violence, open up new channels of communication, or fight the forces of segregation. While the extremist elements of the society gained in strength, especially because the political parties found the appropriation of this militant popular mood hugely handy in furthering their own agenda, that was not, and could not have been, the complete picture. There was another part of the picture which must not be lost sight of. The former part being well portrayed by now, this chapter will focus specifically on the latter set of social realities.[3] Perhaps that will enable us to juxtapose the moments of rupture against the moments of inter-community cooperation and collaboration, and realize why people of one community resisted members of the other community to vacate the villages, took pains to 'normalize' a conflict-laden situation through countering the *goonda*s (hooligans) or troublemakers, or offered minority safeguards in case of a territorial reconstitution. Relying mainly on the unofficial public documents like newspapers, journals, literary sources like autobiographies or memoirs, and some oral interviews conducted in Bangladesh, this chapter will highlight this 'other' history—the story of a remarkably resilient regional society at a most trying moment of colonial Bengal. To say the least, the overarching efforts to 'normalize' the society would appear to be striking during the most 'abnormal' or traumatic phase of decolonization.

Pakistan versus Purba Pakistan

In the earlier chapter, we have seen that the ideal of 'Pakistan' was given a distinct regional twist by some Bengali Muslim leaders. They sought to define Bengali Muslims as a regionally specified community (or, a 'nation', the most common term of reference being Bangiya Mussalman 'jati') and invoked the possibilities of a regionally diffused political structure to suit their own interests. The present chapter will trace how this regional version of Pakistan thrived during the 1946 elections and the last year of colonial rule, and how the hopes for a 'province-based solution' survived during the newly elected ministry in 1946.

'Pakistan', for most Bengali Muslims till the mid-1940s, was an 'ideological' instrument for differentiation, in the absence of any hard political context or content of the idea itself. For them, it was necessary to differentiate 'Muslim interests' from 'Hindu interests'. Moreover, during the course of the politics in the last few decades, it became clear that it was also equally urgent to dissociate 'Bengali Muslim interest' from 'other' Muslim interests. The 'Pakistan' idea as it developed in Bengal, therefore, had to fit into these complex demands of the Indian Muslim community. This is why the conceptual framework of 'Purba Pakistan' proved attractive to many of them. By this conceptual instrument, they could address the cultural and political particularities of their own familiar community, while the critical issues of rights and representation were being translated into the notion of Pakistan. The demand for provincial autonomy was also a possible implication of this regionalized version of Pakistan, a 'national' ideal opposed to the indivisible and unitary national creed of the Congress. Some Bengali Muslim leaders actively propagated the idea that the region should be given a free hand to attain its own version of 'Pakistan' in the Muslim-majority province. Such a 'version' would imply fair and simple principles of political and cultural representation on the basis of population ratio, and the regional majority community would negotiate within the region with the minority communities on the basis of their respective strengths.

In this context, the elections of 1946 seemed to be an important moment, in which the Muslim League won all six Muslim seats from Bengal to the central assembly, and captured all the urban seats in provincial legislature and 103 out of the 111 rural Muslim seats. The League finally turned out to be the supreme political party of the Bengali Muslims, and arguably, the most successful party in the region. The other victor was the Congress, whose success in general and special constituencies was just as spectacular. In Muslim constituencies, its performance was poor, despite its strategy of setting up independent Muslim candidates removing the Congress label which might have proved self-defeating. There were some other groups like the Hindu Mahasabha, the Communist Party, M.N. Roy's Radical Democratic Party, the Scheduled Caste Federation. But the battle line was rather sharply drawn between the provincial wings of the two leading parties, the League and the Congress, over a single issue—Pakistan. In fact in its capacity to bridge the formal and informal arenas of politics, the elections played a critical role in developing and spreading the Pakistan agenda by the regional leaders. If we want to explore how Pakistan was interpreted and popularized during this time, the election campaign might prove to be a meaningful entry point.

Jinnah declared that the general elections to the central and provincial assemblies would be 'a plebiscite of the Muslims of India on Pakistan',[4] for 'the Muslims of India to prove to the world that the All India Muslim League represents the Muslim nationals in this country'. In Bengal, the war cry waged by the League reached a serious proportion, and it definitely affected in an adverse way the smaller or more marginal voices which were still questioning or reformulating the League's agenda. One must bear in mind that there was a remnant of the KPP even in 1946. Moreover there was the Jamiat-ul-Ulema-i-Hind, the Muslim parliamentary board, and the nationalist Muslims—all of whom participated in the 1945–6 elections along with the League. No doubt, in terms of respective visibility, the targeted campaign, the cohesive nature of the organization, and above all, the strong emotional pull of their catch-term 'Pakistan', the League prevailed upon other Muslim voices in the mid-1940s. Nevertheless, the League in Bengal had a two-fold task before it during the campaign: first, to address and interpret Jinnah's 'Pakistan' in its own way, and, second, to eliminate any possible doubts on the eventuality of Pakistan, in some form or other, thus making it a question of honour and pride for the League.

As the Lahore scheme left open the space for such an interpretation by its confounding phrase 'sovereign and independent states', the leading League protagonists of Bengal considered establishing two independent and sovereign states in two Muslim-majority zones in India.[5] A few months after this resolution, Akram Khan, the vice-president of the BPML, stated that if Bengal and Assam formed 'an independent state in eastern India', there would be no lack of resources or military might for its defense.[6] To him, independence and self-sufficiency of Bengal seemed most natural and unquestionable as the Bengali Muslims were a different nationality. In the previous chapter, we referred to an article by Zahur Hossain, where he argued how Purba (East) Pakistan and Paschim (West) Pakistan would be very different in content. According to Hossain, the Bengali Muslim peasants could never imagine their material interests to be similar to those of the 'Kabuli Mahajans'.[7] The booklet where this article by Hossain was published became popular among the Bengali

Muslims, as has been acknowledged by Abul Hashim himself.[8] Yet it might not be easy to assess how this view was being received by the common Muslims. We can only deduce from this often-expressed hope about a state of 'Purba Pakistan' in 'eastern India' that possibilities of negotiation within the idea of Pakistan were not unthinkable to them.

However, when Abul Hashim wrote about the 'Free State of Eastern Pakistan', he surely takes his readers beyond all such shaky inferences. His draft manifesto of 1945 (March 1945) stood as a major example of the 'Bengali Muslim interpretation' of Pakistan. It is equally significant that even after the publication and spread of the manifesto, Jinnah never questioned or contradicted the claims made in it. The same equivocal stance from him was seen even in the case of C. Rajagopalachari's formula, proposing a joint Congress–League interim government, with the demarcation of contiguous districts in the north-east and east of India to be granted the right to secede in future. The situation began to change towards the middle of 1946, when, at the Delhi Convention, Suhrawardy was entrusted by Jinnah with the task of moving a resolution for a revision of the original Lahore Resolution, and subsequently the new resolution changed the critical word 'states' into 'state' in the central sentence of the resolution: '... the areas in which the Muslims are numerically in a majority, as in the North-Western and Eastern Zones of India, should be grouped to constitute Independent States in which the constituent units shall be autonomous and sovereign.' From then on, the demand for a single Pakistan state, not obligated to any constitution for a united India, became the official line of AIML. Ruling out any independent dealing with the Muslim-majority provinces or majority zones, the resolution specified that 'the zones comprising Bengal and Assam in the North-East and the Punjab, North-West Frontier Province, Sind and Baluchistan in the North-West of India, namely, Pakistan zones where the Muslims are in a dominant majority, be constituted into a sovereign independent State and that an unequivocal undertaking be given to implement the establishment of Pakistan without delay'.[9] The new conditions were designed to bar any independent individual or collective arrangement with any province or any Muslim zone by the British government.[10]

Whether and how Jinnah himself changed his position on the word 'states' and underwent a shift about the structure of Pakistan is outside the purview of this study. More significant in the present context is the Bengali Muslims' reactions to this change. Abul Hashim later claimed that although he had been acutely aware of the significance of this change during the convention, 'he was not allowed to talk'.[11] In any case, one must notice that the Bengali Muslim leaders maintained an apparent public silence on this very critical change made in the resolution and did not acknowledge its implications for them, at least in formal discussions. Considering this silence, the questions remain: how did the League elaborate this concept before the people, and what did it at all mean for a Bengali Muslim public in 1945–6 to take a stand regarding 'Pakistan' in the election agenda? The first question demands a close look at the booklet by Hashim, named *Let Us Go to War*, published towards the end of 1945. He later claims that '… this booklet became the guideline of election campaign of the Muslims of Bengal and Assam'.[12] Even if that seems a tall claim, we can safely assume that this booklet provided the basic framework within which the major leaders of the BPML operating under the leadership of Hashim and Suhrawardy used to function. The Pakistan formula for which the war cry was being waged by Hashim was explicated as 'a fairly simple one': one with 'real democracy, freedom, equity and justice, and opposed to imperial domination and economic exploitation, as well as to the favourite *Akhand Bharat* of the Congress [italics added].'[13] He explains what he means by 'imperial domination' of the Congress and how to bring an end to it:

> Free India was never one country. Free Indians were never one nation. In the past India was Akhand under the domination of the Mauryas and the Mughals, and is now Akhand under the domination of Great Britain. Liberated India must necessarily be, as God has made it, a sub-continent having complete independence for every nation inhabiting it. However much weakness the Congress may have for the capitalists of Bombay, however much they may help them open opportunities for exploiting the whole of India under the cover of Akhand Bharat, Muslim India to a man will resist all attempts of the Congress to establish dictatorship in India of any coterie, group, or organization. Pakistan means freedom for all, Muslims and Hindus alike…[14]

The 'unity' of India was thus something to be realized only under any state of political domination, illustrated by the examples of Maurya rule in the ancient era, of the so-called Hindu or pre-Islamic history of India, or of the Mughal rule of the so-called Muslim age of Indian history, or of the British Empire, which sought to provide an unwarranted legitimacy to this tenuous claim of Indian 'unity'. Hashim thus clearly directed his opposition to the carefully crafted cult of unity of India (*akhanda-ta*). This unity had always been 'political' rather than cultural or social.

Therefore, the future nation of India, which would aspire to be free from any political subjugation, either Hindu, Muslim, or colonial, needed to be conceived outside the glorified parameters of such superficial 'unity'. On a more practical level, upholding the glory of Indian 'unity' would necessarily signify a perpetuation of Congress domination, by all means an unacceptable premise for Hashim, and the other Bengali Muslim leaders, hailed from a Muslim-majority but Hindu-dominated province.

The lack of freedom that the Bengali Muslims identified with the Congress creed of unity and the notions of freedom idealized in the concept of 'Pakistan' provided the dual foundations of a new 'national' imagination in 1945–6. I call the 'Pakistan' movement of Bengali Muslims 'national' rather deliberately, because during this time the idea of 'Pakistan' in the Bengali Muslim world categorically entailed the essentials of a new territorial 'nation', endowed with certain political and cultural characteristics, and aspirations for a modern, postcolonial existence on its own merit. Hashim's ideas emphasized the necessity of upholding resistance against exploitation of a region against the over-arching extra-territorial domination that sought to bulldoze the rights of the regions inhabiting it. Amidst the rhetorics of a glorified 'nation' or a grand 'nationalism', this was a potent challenge thrown by the region. Hashim even tried to trace this notion of 'regional resistance' historically. He pointed out that the commonly held 'national idols' in India, like Rana Pratap, Shivaji, Haider Ali, Tipu Sultan, or Siraj-ud-Daula, were all regional rulers in reality, usually upright in their resistance to some kind of central or imperial expansionism. The centrist obsession in mainstream nationalism, he thought, was nothing but a modern colonial import, fabricated in accordance with the logic of imperial domination.[15] He conceded that regional autonomy also often meant a mechanism of domination, to be operated on local or regional basis. But he argued that it usually ensured cooperation among its component communities. 'Pakistan' of his own vision would likewise also mean the freedom 'for all, Muslims and Hindus alike' in the province of Bengal.

By the mid-1940s, the 'Hashim creed'[16] of Pakistan thus positioned itself as staunchly opposed to the idea of a 'united India'. This was a long way from the ideas of Huq, expressed only a couple of years earlier. Huq, the presenter of the famous Lahore Resolution, did not have any qualms to accept Maulana Azad's idea that the fate of the Indian Muslim was irre-vocably linked with India,[17] but he was never clear about its relationship with the proposed Pakistan. In order to realize and safeguard Pakistan in Bengal, Huq thought, 'We have to seek the help of other interests and

minorities to form coalition governments.'[18] But how should one strike
a compromise between being part of a 'confederation' on the one hand
and retaining 'sovereignty' on the other? He could identify the logical
puzzle as evident in one of his public statements:

> It is ... no use hoodwinking the Muslims of Bengal that the formula
> which may hold good in the Punjab will also hold good in Bengal. At
> the same time Bengal Muslims realize that they have got to fall into line
> with the rest of India.... We depend upon the Quaid-i-Azam to modify
> the Pakistan idea so as to enable the Muslims of Bengal also to assert their
> self-determination along with the Muslims of other provinces ...[19]

Hashim's later 'war cries' against a united India or the 'Akhand Bharat'
also stemmed from this fundamental dilemma. The lines of continuity
between the two Pakistan models presented by Huq and Hashim were
thus unmistakable: a strong emphasis on a provincial administration
and a new economy in a Muslim-dominated 'national state' in eastern
India. This can be considered as the first main characteristic of the
Pakistan model of Bengal Muslims. A pamphlet by Mujibur Rahman,
Pakistan, very popular among the educated and informed Muslims, used
to provide a map in which this new 'national state' was shown inside the
Indian borders, comprising the eastern parts of Bihar and Bengal (except
the Burdwan division) and the whole of Assam province.

The second important characteristic of this model lay in its staunch
resistance to the Congress. During the elections of 1946, the League
sought to channelize the 'Pakistan' movement in Bengal in a way that
might represent the grievances of the Muslim literati, urban educated
youth, and of the rural masses, and tie all these grievances together
by a single thread of anti-Congress politics. The Muslim intelligentsia
accorded their support to the movement assuming that Congress would
never guarantee them self-representation. The kernel of the Pakistan creed
was to be found in this emphatic rejection of the Congress claims of representing 'all' communities and classes in India. The electoral failure of
the Muslim candidates set up by the Congress in the Muslim constituencies might also be understood in this light. The spread and success of the
'Pakistan' creed cannot therefore, directly and exclusively be linked with
the growing trends of religious fanaticism, as has often been suggested.
Such an interpretation, however convenient, would never enable us to
appreciate why relatively open-minded, liberal Muslim politicians like
Abul Hashim, ideologues like Abul Mansur Ahmed, youth leaders like
Mujibur Rahman, never known for any religious bigotry or communal

outlook, were so deeply inspired by Pakistan. The missing link appears extremely critical here: the powerful waves of Pakistan politics can only be appraised by the logic of competitve politics and the rapidly growing opposition against the Congress, which by itself turned into a symbol of majoritarianism, veiled by the terms of 'unity'.

The Bengali Muslim leaders and ideologues who were in a position to be politically influential in the 1940s tried their best to explore the linguistic possibilities within the discourse of 'Pakistan', the most powerful signifier at their disposal, and align it with the demands of self-representation. As a politically charged catchword, 'Pakistan' was made powerful enough to trivialize the uncertainties and evasiveness within it. It was exactly here that the depiction of the Congress played a vital role. Amidst the overall confusions around the keyword 'Pakistan', the leaders' task was to assert that the demands of self-representation in the political realms could only be realizable through a staunch resistance to the Congress. Elections were only a starting point in this project. In Hashim's words:

> The General Election is just the beginning of our struggle. Immediately after recording our votes in favor of Pakistan at the polling centers, and liquidating the false claims of the Congress to represent the Muslims, we shall direct our attention towards British Imperialism and demand immediate transference of power to the peoples of India on the basis of Pakistan.[20]

In the pre-election propaganda, therefore, the BPML leaders chose to highlight the principles of self-representation and freedom instead of the more practical issues of ministry formation, or the ratio of community representation. The argument heard all over was that in a country with very diverse identities and interests, no 'all-India' organization could speak for all. *Dainik Azad*, the hardliner journal of the Bengali Muslims, even urged in its editorials that other backward castes and communities should join the Muslims to question the legitimacy of the Congress and its unwarrantedly heavy reliance on Hindu cultural and political rhetoric like 'Bande Mataram', Bharatmata Mandir (temple of Mother India), *akhand jyoti* (the flame of unity), *Hindi prachar* (spread of Hindi), or *go-raksha* (banning of cow slaughter).[21] India needed 'majority-led provincial representative governments' rather than 'unicentric Congress rule from Delhi': declared in its editorial articles.[22] In Bengal, the League deserved more prominence because it alone upheld the principle of representing 'difference', not 'unity'.[23] It aimed to enable the 'other' communities speak of their own interests and consolidate their own identity instead of obliterating them.[24] The proximity of economic interests was considered to be the main bridge between the 'other' communities like low castes and the Muslims.[25] Partition of the province was considered conducive to high-caste Hindu domination. Therefore, the League leaders were not only keen on developing an 'other minorities' angle to the Pakistan scheme, but also asked the low castes to join them in their opposition to Partition.[26] Even during the movement of the 'united, sovereign Bengal' in 1947, to which we will return later in this chapter, this reliance would be evident.[27] It is in the context that we must read Suhrawardy's pre-election declaration: 'Believe us, this is no longer a question of political games or individual success or failure. Neither does this involve the question of Ministry by League or by the Congress. The question is one of much greater fundamental importance, one of freedom, not only yours but others.'[28]

The key messages of the League leaders like Suhrawardy were spread by the leading journals of Calcutta as well as by the local vernacular dailies. *Satyabarta*, a local newspaper of Chittagong, published an article by a self-proclaimed League functionary who placed a direct question: Why Congress failed to see that India was not 'one, singular nation', but 'the home for many communities [sampraday] and many nations [jati]'. The ideal of 'Pakistan', as opposed to the India of Congress, it argued, was a more amicable solution for these multiple nations of India, 'who do not refuse to come out of their own narrow, confined definition of nation'.[29] The Congress 'nation' was thus curiously condemned for being 'narrow', in the sense of its one-dimensional nature, and its restrictive scope and orientation, and therefore, unsuitable for the country which had many nationalities. 'Why could the Hindus not see that the love for the country [desh] was not a monopoly of the Hindus? The Muslims and the other minority communities share the same patriotic feelings, but they differ from the Hindus regarding the nature and future shape of the country.'[30]

The clear anti-Congress stance of Pakistan brings us to the third feature of the League politics in 1946. Its focus before and during the elections was shifted towards the principle of representation and free-dom rather than religion. This does not imply a diminished intensity of the religious slogans, but that the slogans were constantly balanced by a more pragmatic political agenda, often downplaying religious fanaticism. For example, in case of the spontaneous youth movement in Calcutta in February 1946 against the INA trials, Suhrawardy had little option but to publicly espouse the cause and support the agitation, which was essentially nationalist in a larger sense.[31] As it was proved by the course of the movement, the extremist groups also found a chance to actively appropriate the mass militant mood, but they could not be equated with the agitators or their League leaders by the same stroke.[32] In other instances also, religious conservatism and fair minority demands went hand in hand during this time. Journals like *Azad* treaded a dangerous path when it called for the rule by the non-Muslims or 'heretics' (*bidharmi-shashan*), yet it never deviated from the questions of minority freedom and rights on its pages.[33] A close look at these routinely explored questions would make it enormously difficult to argue that the question of rights was needed to back up the question of religion, and not vice versa. Waliullah, a League journalist of the 1940s, recalled their wary avoidance of the more conservative and bigoted sections of the community and the constant need to keep them at bay.[34] Hashim's memoirs tell us that during his district tours before the elections, Suhrawardy or he himself had to counter these Extremist leaders and 'bring them to sense'.[35]

The fourth feature of the League campaign was its distance from the non-Bengali elements of the organization. The non-Bengali business community in Calcutta, the traditional power base of the AIML in the province, was severely challenged by the radical BPML wing in the 1940s. In 1937, this community held an influential position, while in 1946, League stalwarts like Ispahani and Adamjee Haji Dawood were clearly discredited by the Hashim–Suhrawardy group.[36] The close connections between Jinnah and these business interests of Calcutta explained the discomfort of the Bengal leaders. The misgivings started taking a toll after mid-1946, once the League High Command arranged for the meeting to lay down the boundaries of the proposed state of 'Pakistan'.

The emphasis put by the regional leaders on the 'agricultural interests' and 'socio-economic justice' served to widen the gap between the Bengali and non-Bengali lobbies. This represents the fifth characteristic feature of the Pakistan movement of this period. To ensure the maximum turnout in Muslim constituencies in favour of 'Pakistan', Hashim and Suhrawardy adopted a thoroughly localized election strategy. They visited the district League offices and chose popular candidates after carefully discerning all contesting claims. District-level, even village-level, student leagues were set up and vigorous student campaigns were launched.[37] In particular, Hashim's election tours had a great impact in rural Bengal. Right before the elections, a new journal called *Millat* was introduced to bolster and popularize the Hashim–Suhrawardy faction of the BPML against the *Azad* group operating under the influence of the Nazimuddin–Maulana Akram Khan axis, known as the 'Jinnah lobby'. Kazi Muhammad Idris, a former *Azad* loyalist, became the editor of *Millat*. Soon it became one of the most critical opinion-maker journals in Bengal. The high-pitched encounter between *Millat* and *Azad* in 1946–7 serves as an inheritance of the conflict between *Saogat* and *Mohammadi*, which were respectively the liberal and conservative Bengali Muslim journals of the late 1920s.

Under the supervision of Hashim and Suhrawardy, big and impressive 'Pakistan' meetings were organized in the traditional KPP strongholds.[38] In one of such meetings in Mymensingh, 'abolition of zamindari' was proposed as one of the major objectives of 'Pakistan', to be passed amidst huge clamour.[39] In another traditional Praja stronghold in Kishoregunj (Mymensingh), the League candidate Tamijuddin Khan had convinced the masses about the potential of Pakistan in ending the deprivation of the cultivators.[40] He skilfully interpreted 'Pakistan' as primarily a question of 'social fairness'. During the campaign, thousands of posters and placards were sent to the mofussils from the town offices of the BPML, with radical popular slogans such as: 'Langal jar mati tar' (Land belongs to those who hold the plough), 'Bina khoti purone zamindari uchchhed chai' (Abolish zamindari without compensation), 'Kayemi swarther dhwangsho chai' (Down with vested interests), 'Sramik je malik se' (Labourers are the owners), 'Janaganer Pakistan' (Pakistan for the people), 'Krishak-sramiker Pakistan' (Pakistan for peasants and labourers).[41] Abul Mansur Ahmed, a key member of the earlier KPP propaganda team, provided plenty of such slogans from Calcutta and played an effective role in disseminating them. BPML, in fact, finally adopted a programme of the abolition of the zamindari system.[42] *Millat* asserted in its editorial enthusiastically that this step was just the beginning of the true 'emancipation of the proletariat' through 'Pakistan'.[43] Suhrawardy also chose to focus on this programme in his election speeches:

> [Pakistan] will mean raising the standards of living for the poor, the oppressed and the neglected; more food, more resources, more work, better living conditions, more happiness for the common people; opportunities for all and the establishment of the reign of truth and justice, of toleration and fairplay.... Without political independence, it is impossible to achieve all these ...[44]

A local pamphlet circulated in the Dacca district of 1946, a rather typical one, unequivocally declared that the 'Muslim League wants to free the country and then to establish the order of Pakistan, the order for the poor'.[45] The League workers, closely connected to the respective localities they were entrusted to, proved more useful campaigners than the League stalwarts in popularizing these social–economic objectives of Pakistan. Their enthusiasm and effectiveness were exemplary.[46] They 'knew how to approach the people' and made tireless efforts to carry their message to the less exposed, illiterate villagers in the countryside, with their own narratives of why, how, and when Pakistan was to be realized.

Scholars often suggest that the speed and extent of the success achieved by the Muslim League and the rise of 'communalism' in Bengal were direct outcomes of the failure of the Communist Party in the Bengal countryside.[47] This may well have been true, but acknowledging the fact that the League succeeded in providing the rural peasants a political dream as well as a suitable political platform to chase that dream was more important than comparing these two organizations. The overall mood of peasant militancy substantially influenced the politics of Bengal in the 1940s.[48] When the north Bengal districts and the reclaimed areas of 24 Parganas in the south were affected by the Tebhaga uprising,[49] much of eastern, central, and western Bengal remained virtually unstirred by this communist movement.[50] In a substantial part of these areas, the peasant societies rapidly fell under the Muslim League's sway. The League provided them with an even bigger dream. As a contemporary observer puts it: 'Pakistan promised them of a greater freedom from socio-economic bondages: freedom from zamindars, jotedars, mahajans, even from the indirect exploitation of the urban lot of *daktar–ukil–moktar* [doctors–lawyers–attorneys]. It was no longer a truncated demand for *tebhaga* [two out of three shares], rather it now meant a *chaubhaga* (right to all shares)!'[51] Why some areas responded to the communists and some did not might possibly be explained by the varying social configurations of different localities.[52] The electoral logic of the separate electorate coupled with the sense of community solidarity, often described somewhat impatiently as 'deliberate attempts to communalize the situation', accounted for the failure of class politics in these areas.[53] It can also be assumed that the overwhelmingly non-Muslim population of northern and southern Bengal accounted for the failure of the Pakistan politics in these parts. The enmeshing of their respective agendas suggests that the same classes of people used to rally around either the communists or the Leaguers. The League meetings used to begin with songs and slogans of Tebhaga, thereby making similar promises to the lower peasants. In the course of the League meetings, it was emphasized that the number of Muslim zamindars being negligible, the purpose of socio-economic revolution was no less served by League politics.[54] In fact, one may identify behind the rise of the League a remarkable social resilience in the form of a cross-class patronage network, where seasonal support used to be provided by the upper- and middle-class Muslim households to the under-rayats, and often to the low-caste groups.[55] In view of this, it is possible to argue that while the Communist politics remained mainly an 'outside' force acting upon the inner fabric of a village, the League agenda was seen to be resting on internal or local power networks through dedicated social workers coming from the same locality. The effective strength of competing political ideologies, therefore, considerably depended on the respective strength of mobilization by the two parties.

By 1946–7, the Muslim League had already achieved an impressive extent of support across various social classes. Most of the former influential KPP leaders like Abul Mansur Ahmed, Abdullahil Baqui, Shamsuddin Ahmed, Hasan Ali, Nurul Islam Choudhury, and Ghiasuddin Ahmed were then in the League, and promptly appropriating peasant grievances to further the League interests. Many League members of the assembly, including the revenue minister, Fazlur Rahman, came round to the view that the Tebhaga demand ought to be conceded. A draft was presented to the governor, and due to the latter's indisposition, it was decided that a bill would be attempted in the assembly.[56] The news of the Tebhaga Bill, as it came to be popularly known, gave tremendous fillip to the agitation in the northern Bengal districts. The often explicit support for the peasant cause, commonly known to be the 'communist' cause, but in many ways also a 'League' cause in Bengal, often elicited sharp rebuke from the AIML High Command and its representatives in the provinces. During the agitation in the north Bengal districts, the more radical, populist groups of the BPML took an openly supportive stance while the conservative groups refrained from doing so. The journal *Millat* voiced the former group of provincial leaders while *Azad* criticized the Tebhaga agenda bitterly.[57] Abul Mansur Ahmed mentioned that the Mymensingh lobby was strengthened within the League during this agitation and, consequently, zamindari abolition was finally adopted as a League objective. However, to many former Praja leaders like Abul Hashim, the proposition of abolishing zamindari with compensation was not radical enough. The clause for compensation to the zamindars was also vehemently opposed.[58] In Dacca, the rising leadership of Fakir Shahabuddin or Taj-uddin Ahmed, later to become the leading political figures in East Pakistan, drew leftist bearings into the League fold, as well as large numbers of radically minded university students with them.[59] The radical and populist Maulana Bhasani, the so-called pir of Mymensingh, Rangpur, and Assam, or Sheikh Mujibur Rahman, the 'people's leader' of Gopalgunj (Faridpur), also rose to prominence riding on the back of their rural following.[60]

The overlaps between the League politics and the communist or Leftist politics should not be under-emphasized. Indeed it was the local contacts of the ranks of provincial League leaders, either endowed with or devoid of communist leanings that played a vital role in Bengali politics of the late 1940s. Their impressive identification with the masses of a particular region and skillful mobilization of popular support behind the League agenda of 'Muslim rights' was what ultimately dictated the course of events in Bengal both in the period leading to and following Partition. It is not an accidental fact of history that Bhasani and Mujibur Rahman gained popularity during this time by playing a critical role in the 1946 elections in their respective localities. 'They talked people's language, ate their food, dressed like them, knew them personally, and exercised an impelling influence in people's everyday life.'[61] They represented many social classes at one and the same time, just like the spirit of 'Pakistan' itself. They were agile on peasant issues, and as well as articulated the middle-class 'Muslim' grievances against all forms of social discrimination and economic exploitation by the Hindus. The Bengali Muslim world of the 1940s experienced a curious intermingling of various class issues behind the apparently confusing generic term 'Muslim interest', and, to a significant extent, these local popular leaders lived up to the potential of such historical conjuncture. After a few decades of relentless cultural movement of 'Muslim difference' and large-scale politicization of 'Muslim rights', it was difficult for CPI to erect a stronghold in Bengal with their typically dismissive outlook on religious–political identities. They regarded such identities as 'narrowly defined', 'socially regressive', or 'communal'; but the truth was that community identity was too vitally entrenched in the quotidian life of Bengal's peasants.

At the beginning of the narrative provided in this book, three distinctive trends have been identified among the Bengali Muslims during the Swadeshi movement:[62] one, those who believed so fervently in the sanctity of their homeland that they opposed partition of Bengal in 1905 and supported swadeshi; two, those who supported partition of the province at that time solely with the view to ameliorate the 'Bengali Muslim' conditions and idealized a separate Bengali homeland to flourish; and three, the self-professedly radical groups who saw a hope of Islamic revivalism in the partition of 1905. By 1947, the internal differences among these groups were not resolved by any means. Nevertheless, despite their deep divergences they could collectively keep faith in the power of 'Pakistan', a magic ideal for all practical purposes. The first two groups maintained their strong regional identity and did not see any incongruence between this identity and their imagined Pakistan. The third group was too radical and too entrenched in their pan-Islamic belief-system to care for such regional attachments. What ensured the phenomenal rise of the Bengal Provincial League during this late colonial era was neither the rise of a flagrant religious fanaticism of the last trend, nor a class struggle entrenched in the peasant societies. Its success instead depended on the remarkable capacity of the League leaders to accommodate all available trends of politics in a remarkable fashion, and their particular agility in coalescing various socio-economic classes behind their local and cultural agenda. Contrary to Jinnah's intentions, the firmly rooted *regional* aspirations of Bengal Muslims incorporated themselves within the ideal of 'Pakistan' in a remarkable way.

'Pakistan' and Changing Cultural Paradigms

When the Bengali Muslims found in 'Pakistan' or 'Purba Pakistan' a hundred creative potentials, they sought its appropriation in all possible fields of life: political, economic, social, and cultural. We have already commented on the ways Pakistan was being conceptualized in the political or economic worlds of Bengal's Muslims. Now, what exactly did they claim for themselves by this new-found notion in the realms of cultural expression? Exploring the cultural content of the politics of difference in mid-1940s Bengal, we are able to see that the new horizons in politics were duly matched by, and suitably bolstered with, a surefooted linguistic–cultural identity of Bengal Muslims. Their own legitimate rights to the regional culture emerged more clearly than ever, with an unprecedented degree of what used to be described by them as 'national self-assessment'.[63] A former CPI member commented in a personal interview on the burdens of his own Muslim lineage:

> With the idea of Purba Pakistan, through a tortuous process of mistakes and misappropriations, we, the Bengali Muslims, could finally decide

for ourselves where we belonged, where we came from, but still did not know where we were heading. The journey seemed tortuous because, as we often forget that unlike for the Bengali Hindus, for the Bengali Muslims, nation was something to be 'earned', not 'inherited'.[64]

The idea of an 'inherited' nation of the Hindus may sound simplistic. Even for the Bengali Hindus, the imaginative construction of a 'national culture' was never easy or straightforward. Yet there is some value to this contrast posed between the Muslim and the Hindu cultural projects of nation, as the attempts at historicization of their cultural difference amply suggest. With a haunting sense of extra-territoriality inherent in the idea of 'Islamic'-ness, and a constant Hindu hegemonic challenge to their political and cultural life within the territories, the Bengali Muslims indeed required an extra measure of cautious awareness as well as some irregular compromises. The religious–cultural and regional–territorial sensibilities of the Bengali Muslims had to be combined with a high degree of clarity and discretion. The intermingling of various inheritances was made to carve out the imprints of their own identification.

In the previous chapter we have seen how the Purba Pakistan Renaissance Society played held an important role in the early 1940s to pursue a project of cultural self-awakening and at the same time provided political leadership in the newly emerging course of League politics. What is to be noted here is that the connection between the domains of culture and politics became critical during the elections. Cultural and political leaderships were often seen together, hand in hand. Abul Kalam Shamsuddin, one of the founders of the Purba Pakistan Renaissance Society, was also a successful electoral candidate.[65] So was Shamsuddin Ahmed, a newcomer in the League and the former secretary of the Bengal Muslim Parliamentary Board.[66] Although not chosen as candidates, leaders like Abul Mansur Ahmed or Maulana Abdullahil Baqui, the former secretary and president of the KPP respectively, also joined the League before the elections, and contributed greatly to the election campaign by propagating their views. What they used to preach in the urban literary societies confined to elite activities thus used to trickle down to the lower sections of the population. The election speeches and pamphlets served as 'meeting points' in a literal way and bridged different classes and groups of the population. Note that the Renaissance Society intelligentsia constituted the bloc opposed to the Nazimuddin–Akram Khan group within the BPML, which was known for its support for

Jinnah. Thus the more self-consciously 'Bengali' bloc found a very effective means to propagate their own version of nation. Suhrawardy and Abul Hashim, the two leading regional political figures of the 1940s and the most respected leaders by the members of the Renaissance Society, indirectly found a massive preaching ground through such distinctive cultural–political connects. The 'Hashim creed' of Pakistan, already discussed in the previous section, could reach the people at large. The speeches popularized a vision of 'Pakistan' portrayed with the colour of Muslim 'difference' and explained that this essential 'difference' was not to be seen as an irreconcilable 'antagonism' with other cultures of the region.[67] Shamsuddin's speeches clarified that the 'territorial bearing' of the name of the 'Purba Pakistan Renaissance Society' was by no means incidental: 'It encapsulates the essence of our linguistic, literary, cultural and economic disparateness from others.'[68]

Neither was the choice of the word 'renaissance' random or meaningless. By directing the focus on the inheritance of the Buddhir Mukti (Emancipation of the Intellect, as they named their project) movement of the 1920s, the word 'renaissance' served to legitimize the claims of the Society to a much larger project of 'national' self-strengthening and self-construction.[69] 'We will not return to the past. That was the greatest mistake we have committed time and again. We will now move forward by the newly attained spirit of freedom or self-confidence and the new intent of self-realization.'[70] The Society was covertly political in its mission to attain freedom and to translate 'difference' through the 'mission of freedom'.

This indivisibility of the cultural and political leaderships of the Bengali Muslims was explained in great detail in Abul Mansur Ahmed's speeches and writings during this period. Renaissance, Ahmed explained, could only mean cultural, economic, and political 'reinstatement' of a Bengali Muslim nation, which was integrally tied in the past as well as in the present.[71] With the advent of the British in Bengal and the concomitant social changes in this region, 'a whole community was suddenly deprived of the value of their own cultural heritage: knowing our own language and following our own culture led to nothing but economic impoverishment'.[72] The changes were not only economic and political, but also social and cultural. 'Changes in the dress-code left the whole lot of Muslims unfit and embarrassed in the modern political society. Those who were respectable [*khandani*] before have now become the poor agriculturists.'[73] In Ahmed's views, the renaissance must be sought in disjunction with but not in opposition to the Hindu Bengali nationalist problematic already set in motion. Instead of 'disinheritance', he called for a 'revision'. The literature of Purba Pakistan would not only include Iswarchandra Vidyasagar and Bankimchandra Chattopadhyay to Rabindranath Tagore and Saratchandra Chattopadhyay, men occupying the highest level of sophistication in terms of literary merit, but also incorporate literary works for and by the Muslims.'[74] Why was disinheritance not a practical or a sensible option? Ahmed had a compelling argument: 'Even if we refuse to accept, the fact remains that religion cast a major influence in forming the essence of a literature: do you think Rabindranath could have been what he ultimately was if he chose to write only about Muslim life and culture, and in local dialects?'[75] One of the major objectives of the Society was to parallely uphold and develop the classical language, local dialects as well as the 'Mussalmani Bangala'. 'Mussalmani Bangala', according to the Society, would be widely used in Purba Pakistan, so that 'no longer would the literary and university authorities dismiss a whole body of language by effectively banning the Muslim daily usages such as Allah/khoda (the God), roja (fast during the Ramadan), namaz (the daily prayer), Haj (the holy trip to Mecca), jakat (the holy ritual of distributing world goods during the festival of Eid), oju (Bengali word for 'wudu' or washing various parts of the body), gossal (bathing), khana (food), and pani (water)'.[76] The entire gamut of puthi-sahitya, 'the real inheritance of Purba Pakistani Mussalmans', would not only be revived but also reinstated in setting the course of creative writing in Purba Pakistan. Struggling against a hegemonic political and social culture, the self-proclaimed 'Renaissance movement' aimed at azadi or freedom of the Bengali Muslims, in terms of a cultural regeneration, political reinstatement, and economic uplift together, all denoted by the magical term Purba Pakistan.

The fundamental role of a religious–cultural identity in determining the course, and even quality, of literary endeavours was reasserted in a more polemical way by Kazi Mohammad Idris, the editor of Millat.[77] An awareness of 'self' could often lead to a sense of parochialism, but nonetheless provide the essential foundations on which the structures of identity could be erected, he argued. If Muslims were 'communally motivated' in raising claims of their own literature or their own language, that might be considered regressive in all fairness. But was it not true that the 'communal' propensities of Hindu literary culture were far more unfortunate, because they already possessed the necessary foundational elements? The Hindu national culture had long attained a substantial measure of self-confidence; why then such a profound and self-limiting aversion towards 'other' trends? Any extension of the 'self' to the 'other' could only mean enriching the 'self' in the end. In this way Idris rather skilfully reversed the charge of 'self'-obsession from Bengali Muslims to Bengali Hindus.[78] What is needed, his argument continued, was to transcend the excesses of 'self', something which must start with individuals, not the society as a collective. This task of transcendence, a cognitive process of self-subversion (*swa-droha*), would then free an individual from the inherently limiting tendencies and practices.

Now, even if an individual eventually treaded such a course of self-subversion or swa-droha, could it be ever possible for the collective? Idris squarely faced this fundamental riddle lying at the basis of his arguments, and confessed that, in reality, the appropriation of 'self' in social and cultural expressions of the region had proven to be woefully short-sighted, and as a result, 'difference' had turned out to be unnecessarily antithetical or antagonistic. In the absence of a true spirit of self-extension or accommodation, the cultural as well as political options were becoming dangerously narrow: either integration or disownment.[79]

However, there still existed some middle ground, as the concept of Purba Pakistan had already proven in its claims. A closer study of the exclusionist Islamic trends of thought which essentially favoured disownment of all other cultural influences reveals their distance from the Purba Pakistan Renaissance Society and thereby illuminates the middle ground the latter occupied. The relatively emaciated trend of cultural absolutists dismissing regional–linguistic identities often resulted in internal dissensions. One such example was Golam Mostafa, a prominent poet of the Renaissance Society, who gradually developed a preference for an exhaustively 'Arabized' Bengali. When the Renaissance Society pronounced the need for originality instead of grudging simulation, Mostafa indulged in an exercise of caricaturing in the name of poetic liberty. One of his songs to hail Pakistan was nothing but an imitation of the much celebrated nationalist song by Dwijendralal Roy: *Sakal desher cheye piyara duniyate bhai she kon sthan, Pakistan, se Pakistan!* (Which is the dearest of all countries, oh which one? Pakistan, it is Pakistan!)[80] Such juvenile excesses notwithstanding, it is important to note that a regional–linguistic sensibility was palpable in the Purba Pakistan movement, which was sometimes even met with opposition.

The gradual change in the spirit of *Mohammadi* also serves as an appropriate example. This journal which had once famously disparaged Tagore for his 'inertness' in alleviating the Hindu cultural chauvinism, now revealed greater appreciation for the same poet.[81] One is rather struck by noting how *Mohammadi* during this time followed *Millat* in its newly conceived 'Bengali Muslim' inheritance, projected through a selective celebration of 'national' figures like M.A. Jinnah, Kazi Nazrul Islam, Rabindranath Tagore, and, not suprisingly, Siraj-ud-Daula. The last one, of course, was deliberately chosen as 'national' icon to embody the very specific intermingling of contemporaneous notions of region, religion, and also of freedom. The Bengali Muslim identity had already acquired a new self-confidence which helped them elevate their national claims to a higher level.

From the Bengali Muslim writings of this period, it is possible to identify signs of difference growing more pronounced in extent but less disinheriting in spirit. The earlier discomfort and antagonism around the question of 'Muslim difference' was by this time remarkably settled and resolved; newer models of cultural inheritance were now being put forward with a good measure of self-assurance. These models traversed but did not discard the dominant paradigms of the existing cultural world. No doubt this cultural confidence based on accommodation added an element of buoyancy to the unique project of Purba Pakistan. However, the same kind of resolution could not yet be attained in the political realm. The complex enmeshing of the regional interests with larger Indian concerns placed the provincial leadership in an inherently limited space in the field of politics, where manoeuvring and negotiating of multiple identities proved more strenuous, and finally, a failure.

Dictates for a 'Course Correction'

The multiple dimensions of 'Pakistan' in Bengal developed somewhat independently of the Pakistan politics as directed by Jinnah and the AIML. Right from the days of the Lahore Proposal up to early 1946, the real implications of Pakistan were never clarified by the AIML and neither was any response given by them to the various regional interpretations of the concept.[82] In the Muslim-majority provinces of Bengal and Punjab, the idea became prevalent that each of these provinces would form a unit by itself, if not independent, only loosely connected to the federation. The absence of any noise about such interpretation from the AIML supremo appeared conspicuous enough to even suggest a tacit approval. The situation could have changed after the Muslim Legislators' Convention at Delhi (April 1946) when the key word 'states' was changed into 'state' in the Pakistan Resolution, and instead of two 'Independent States', it was finally demanded for Pakistan a single 'sovereign Independent State' and two separate constituent assemblies for the Muslim and the Hindu provinces.[83] However, strangely enough, Bengal Muslim leaders did not pay any attention at that time to this critical development. Earlier in this chapter, I have mentioned Hashim's later claims of recording his displeasure at the change somewhat 'unofficially'. But there is little historical evidence to support his claims.[84] Neither is the true reason known behind the silence of Suhrawardy, whom incidentally, Jinnah had vested with the responsibility of moving the resolution at the Delhi Convention. Shila Sen's conjecture that Bengal leaders at that time did not take adequate notice of the change and were therefore not clear in their minds to protest against the move thus sounds plausible. There is also a merit in Harun-or-Rashid's argument that Suhrawardy could not afford to estrange Jinnah any further by registering any protest, or declining the task of moving the resolution personally.[85]

There are reasons to believe that even if Bengal leaders had opposed this move at the Convention, it could not have altered the course of events because Jinnah had already established the trend of turning a deaf ear to the Muslim-majority provinces. In fact, the League leaders of Bengal had perpetually been sidelined by AIML decision makers. Before the 1940s, the twenty-three–member Working Committee of AIML included only three members from Bengal, and after 1941, none other than Khwaja Nazimuddin, Ispahani, and Akram Khan were close to Jinnah. These three leaders, the first two considered 'outsiders' in Bengal politics due to their non-regional descent, constituted the hard-liner camp. They opposed any regional interpretation of Pakistan due to their deep dislike towards Hashim and Suhrawardy, the two most potent and popular leaders of the region. No wonder then that Hashim and Suhrawardy, despite their huge regional importance, never found a solid platform in the central bodies of the League. Even after the elections in 1946, when Suhrawardy emerged as the only League premier in India, he did not obtain a place in the Working Committee.[86] After having recorded one of the most spectacular electoral successes only recently, the Bengal League was struggling its way through political complexities within the province, with Jinnah and his hand-picked advisers being remarkably unsympathetic to its predicaments. *Dainik Azad*, the most influential daily with Akram Khan as the editor, became profoundly critical of Suhrawardy and his close association with Hashim. It did not find it difficult to overshadow *Millat*, a newspaper edited by Hashim himself. The financial means of the latter was never impressive enough to put up a fight against the 'Khwaja group'.

Considering the context, that the regional League under the steward-ship of Suhrawardy was able to maintain some measure of identity after the elections is a point worth taking note of. This was made possible mostly due to the political acumen of Suhrawardy, the premier himself. His potent intrigues in the elections of Calcutta Corporation in June 1946 snatched from his rival group an unexpected victory for his own group by defeating a weighty candidate, Hasan Ispahani.[87] Some of his political steps also revealed a measure of independence. In context of the insignificant role he played at the Delhi Convention in 1946, it is important to note that the same leader had asked for the post-election Congress participation in his government early in the same year. Negotiations with the Congress failed at that time: Suhrawardy and Kiran Shankar Roy, the leader of the Bengal Congress Parliamentary Party, accused each other of having drifted away from earlier rapproachment.[88] Suhrawardy would again join hands with Sarat Chandra Bose, Kiran Shankar Roy, and Abul Hashim in the move for a United and Independent Bengal in April 1947, to which we will come back later. Significantly, even the League premier who exercised such power of political maneuvring in a Muslim-majority province was never allowed any prominence in the AIML Delhi conference.

The Cabinet Mission plan of dividing India into three groups made the suggestion that the provincial assemblies could combine together and form a grouping, and all the groupings could then form a loose Indian federation. The power relegated to the provincial legislature was thought to address the demand of autonomy and self-determination Jinnah had so strongly voiced earlier. At the central level, both Congress and the League initially agreed to accept the plan. Congress registered its opposition to the grouping system, and the League found the rejection of Pakistan 'highly deplorable' but found it workable on the merits of the grouping scheme.[89] However, the situation changed fast. The AICC meeting in July 1946 condemned the 'imperial designs' of splitting India behind the scheme. Nehru repeated the Congress position that 'the Constituent Assembly would never accept any dictation or any other directive from the British Government in regard to its work ...', and also, more significantly, '... the probability is, from any approach to the question, that there will be no grouping'.[90] The AIML responded to this revised position of AICC with alacrity, in a bitter and angry tone. Their approach on the issue changed radically from one of moderation to that of radical pressures. Jinnah's famous announcement was heard all over the country: 'This day we bid good-bye to constitutional methods. Today we have also forged a pistol and are in a position to use it.'[91]

For the Bengal Muslims, this meant a sudden change of course. Such a major political reversal in the high quarters of politics implied a reversal in their fortune as well: a quick transition from political stability to new confusions and uncertainties. The memoirs and political commentaries of this time bear testimony of the post-election peace and order in the province. The Suhrawardy ministry was stable and functioning, and even included Shamsuddin Ahmed, the former KPP leader predisposed in intercommunal administration, and Jogendranath Mandal of the Scheduled Caste Federation who spoke in a different voice in the assembly. Waliullah remembers signs of 'hope and peace' in Calcutta, finally emerging out of the chaos and distrust during the elections. The signs of peace seemed even annoying to him and some of his exasperated fellow Leaguers:

> The relief was clearly in the hope for resolution of differences in the newly instituted structure. But if Muslims are so contented with a majority even inside the Akhand Bharat, why did we spend so much time and energy on the question of Pakistan? Popular mood was evidently pointing out that what is needed urgently is negotiation of some sort to restore political stability. We should have pitched our movement to this end, or so I thought during those days.[92]

To this young journalist of the 1940s, it was exasperating that it was only a majority rule in a democratic system was enough to maintain the 'peace', and that perhaps for them any prospect of negotiation was desirable than to launch a movement against the Congress creed of Akhand Bharat. He found that 'even in the Calcutta City Muslim League office, part of which had so far been a bastion of conservative Leaguers to our discomfort, the only concern seemed to restore peace in the province, and opt for the Grouping system as early as possible.'[93] Ahmed also noted the level of elation at the announcement of the Cabinet Mission proposals. He was very relieved himself, '...as if it had reconfirmed the solution I was toying with in my own mind'.[94] According to him, even the rank-and-file League workers saw the feasibility and desirability of the plan, and so did the staunchest supporters of Jinnah, who were the most vocal advocates on Pakistan: '... a huge of sigh of relief, all around'.[95]

Against this background, the Congress rejection of the Mission meant a total breakdown: '[T]he Congress refusal of the Grouping scheme only confirmed our worst fears.'[96] Nehru's declaration that the Constituent Assembly was 'not bound by a single thing', appeared as a repudiation of the whole basis of goodwill and cooperation, and the Bengal Muslims were shocked by its implications. Nehru's declaration seemed like 'sabotage' to these League leaders. Ahmed commented: 'I already geared my thoughts in the hope for the League's final participation in the Assembly and Central Government alike, which would have surely opened space for amicable negotiation between the major interest groups.'[97] The shock was soon surpassed by a deep sense of betrayal and distrust. 'What struck us most was what would have happened if after joining the Assembly, Nehru uttered these words of disownment regarding the basis of the Scheme. The League would have been left with no option other than resigning and coming out of the Assembly, only to trigger off a stronger distrust, more violent opposition, bloodshed and fury.'[98]

'Bloodshed and fury' could not be avoided though. The breakdown of the Cabinet Mission immediately led Jinnah to give a call for 'Direct Action Day' to be observed on 16 August 1946. A relatively peaceful climate came to be ruptured violently by the turns of political bargaining in the high quarters. On Direct Action Day, a massive communal riot broke out in Calcutta. The British police and army remained deliberately passive, and the governor's role was blatantly insignificant, allowing the holocaust to last for three whole days, with over five thousand people lying dead in the main streets and narrow lanes of the metropolis. In the eyes of one of Bengal's most talented poets of all times, it was as if Calcutta had suddenly inundated by a 'blood river swelling up'.[99] 'Men who knew from where fell assailed on the streets and in the alleys of the metropolis on that fateful day'; the poem by Jibanananda Das titled '1946–47' still serves as the poignant pointer to how the world changed as 'siblings' fought and killed each other with an unprecedented ferocity.

Scholars and observers have long been engaged in debates on whether the British authority, the Suhrawardy ministry, or the Hindu extremist groups led by the Mahasabha held the major part of responsibility for this mass carnage.[100] Both the Muslim extremists in the province and the 'communal' Bengali Hindus were jointly incriminated for their stupendous indifference to humanity in resorting to heinous violence against each other. However, what has often not been adequately highlighted here is the huge responsibility of the central commands of both the League and Congress at disregarding all attempts at moderation and negotiation on the eve of such disastrous riots. The regional politicians were mostly at the receiving end of such a high-handed strategic move by the central leadership. In a League-ruled province where the Muslims had no apparently compelling reasons to resort to such a bloody fight, the announcement of the Direct Action itself indicates the fateful disconnects between the central and regional levels of politics at this critical juncture.

In a different way, similar conflicts between the central command and the regional Congress also had their role to play behind the final rejection of Cabinet Mission Plan. When after the short-lived but 'glorious event' of agreement between the Congress and the League on the acceptance of the Mission[101] the Congress High Command suddenly hardened its initial stand on the 'grouping system', the argument was that it would contradict the principle of provincial autonomy and endanger the federation by allowing the provinces the right to opt out. The stand on provincial autonomy being never clear in the political calculations of Congress,[102] there was reason to suspect that its resistance primarily stemmed from the clause of the possibility of opting out, in which a challenge to a united India was apprehended. The apprehension was legitimate, no doubt. Through this particular clause, there indeed emerged a back-handed way of granting Jinnah's Pakistan, albeit within certain constitutional limits.

However, whether the fear was legitimate or not, it was essentially a priority set by the Congress High Command. When Nehru, the new president of the Congress, accepted only the provisions for an interim government from the Cabinet Mission Plan with a clear reluctance to include League members within the government, and as a result the League backed away from the entire agreement, one of the regional heavyweights of Bengal sounded cautious, if not defiant. Before the Cabinet Mission left India, Sarat Bose declared:

> I need hardly say that if any proposals are made in future for the dissection of the Punjab or of Bengal they will be strenuously resisted. There is absolutely no case for dissection.... Redistribution of Provincial boundaries on linguistic basis is another matter and it will have to be considered on its merits at the proper time.[103]

In his earlier visit to Abul Kalam Azad to record his protests against any Working Committee plan towards partitioning Bengal, Bose was accompanied by Kiran Shankar Roy, J.C. Gupta, and Sasanka Sanyal.[104] The much-maligned bhadralok politicians of Bengal did not then wholeheartedly toe 'the priorities of the Central High Command'.[105] To keep Bengal intact as a province with necessary readjustments of borders continued to be a serious priority for the regional Congress leaders, even when the province was being ruled by the League. Even after the Great Calcutta Killings of August 1946, Bose demanded the formation of an all-party ministry on the resignation of the League ministry. However, any idea of a coalition government in Bengal was not welcome to the higher quarters.[106] Bose was sought to be neutralized by Sardar Patel. He identified in Bose an 'undue' eagerness for inter-communal provincial administration, for which 'blocking' Bose was critical for him.[107] Later on, in April 1947, Bose once again tried to gather support for the same project of a 'United, Independent Bengal', only to find himself by then a solitary voice in the Bengal Congress.

In late August and September 1946, right after the Great Riots, the condemnation by the Hindu press of the premier in particular and the League ministry in general, was complemented by a vocal demand for the dismissal of the League ministry and the formation of an all-party ministry in its place.[108] Sarat Chandra Bose, the leader of Congress in Bengal, issued a statement in Calcutta demanding the recall of the Bengal governor and dismissal of the ministry: 'I entirely agree with what *The Statesman* writes in its editorials. If anything, the criticism of the Bengal Ministry is mild.'[109] A week later, he presented a proposal for an all-party ministry for Bengal.[110] He was not without public support. *Anandabazar Patrika* represented certain sections of Bengali Hindu society who felt in less than two weeks that 'what is needed urgently is the removal of Suhrawardy and the construction of a coalition ministry for Bengal'.[111] They expressed relief that the Muslim League politicians, primarily the League secretary, Abul Hashim, had showed keenness and optimism regarding this.[112] In the next few weeks, the newspaper maintained an optimistic stance about the possibility of a League–Congress partnership in the ministry, albeit with the demand of curtailing the extent of League's prevailing power.[113] Evidently, another 'province-based solution' was not unthinkable even at this violence-torn moment. This proposal for an all-party ministry in the immediate aftermath of the riots, nevertheless, found less than its due mention in historical research so far.[114]

The riots were followed by another trend of activities, which has also rarely been brought into historical attention. While violence and distrust spread like a bushfire, help and cooperation across community borders also continued in a desperate desire to return to normalcy. In many cases, violence was perpetrated by the 'outsiders', not integrally linked with the locality, and introduced in the locality only to unleash terror and communal vengeance. Scholars of riots tell us about official records testifying the presence of a large number of goondas, mostly from outside.[115] In many first-hand accounts too, we have heard or read a lament about how the peace in neighbourhoods was suddenly breached and blood-tainted by the 'outsiders', or the anti-social elements hustling in the localities from the margins.[116] However, at the same time, we also come to know how indescribable acts of violence perpetrated by the mobs and hooligans also determinedly countered by members of the same communities. As the news of Calcutta and Noakhali riots spread to the villages of eastern and western Bengal, local resistance was put up to preempt or stall communal skirmishes. A major part of these local initiatives to resist such onslaughts came from the volunteer groups, who organized community patrol or relief measures and urged terrified and timid people to watch out for outsiders. From Sarat Bose's account of his tours in the countryside in eastern Bengal, the towering importance of these volunteer corps can be inferred.[117] He mentioned that in Tippera district, 'Muslim men have already joined the volunteer organizations'.[118] The post-War growth of volunteer organizations in various parts of Bengal had an enormous significance in the local power-politics. However, contrary to the assertion of historians like Chatterji, these volunteer groups not only served as the 'private armies' of the political parties, but also had a positive role of community patrolling.[119] But, help and assistance was not provided by the organized volunteers alone. Independent members of the community and the locality or para also played a tremendously brave role in an effort to 'normalize' the abnormal levels of violence. The young people of the paras emerged as the saviours of women and men of different communities in Calcutta as well as in other parts of the province, as some reported incidents suggest.[120] An account of local disturbances, provided in a personal narrative of Anisuzzaman, the eminent historian of Bangladesh who had been a resident of Calcutta till 1947, gives an idea of how the local volunteer associations were working in unison with the larger body of residents of a community.[121] A boy in his early teens, he participated in relief activities of a volunteer association called 'Mukul', a children and youth wing of the conservative Muslim daily *Azad*, and was a part of enthusiastic community services.[122] In Pirojpur division in the district of Barisal, well-known for its long active engagement in anti-colonial movements, members of the local communities made sure to preserve peace when the news of riots reached the villages from outside during 1946–7.[123] If this was a story of a 'Hindu' area in the Muslim-majority eastern Bengal, similar stories can be heard from 'Muslim' villages of the Hindu-majority western Bengal too. Hasan Ajijul Huq, an eminent Bangladeshi author reminisces about his own experiences. In his ancestral village of western Bengal, tension and rumours did not escalate even after the news of riots reached the locality. This was not because of any unique character of the village community, but because of 'commonsense' prevailing among the village folks belonging to both the communities.[124] He raises the most relevant question regarding how far this rioting and violence was related to religion or 'difference' at all, and how far it was a politically orchestrated social unrest. Difference, in his views, is something that naturally existed in village life of Bengal, and accepted by a collectivity sharing the same spatial zone. When faced by unusual challenges, it often by itself opened up new spaces for compromise and cooperation. All these narratives throw light on an important feature of Bengali way of life, which had its own way of negotiating differences. These narratives, even if not accepted as representative, should indeed make us reconsider if revenge and retaliation were the only pervasive realities of this time, or if we must read the latter alongside the accounts of restoration and reconciliation. Notwithstanding the fact that these efforts often proved ineffective in halting the spates of brutality, these voices and narratives deserve a special mention in any historical account of the 1946 riots, usually packed with endless accounts of communal tension and violence.[125]

The tone of cooperation and sanity was found in the organized political bodies as well. The working committee of the BPML issued the following statement to the press in December 1946: '... the Working Committee appeal to all, both in cities and rural areas, and to the Muslims in particular, to be calm and peaceful, to do everything possible to restore normal conditions of life and not to be carried away by rumours and stories of designing persons.'[126] The colonial officials posted in Bengal did not seem utterly hopeless either. When Governor F.J. Burrows visited Dacca to adorn the annual convocation ceremony of Dacca University in November 1946, he made an extensive enquiry about the conditions of this major city of eastern Bengal and commented in his speech delivered at the convocation, 'Speaking as a comparative newcomer to this province, I confess that the lives and interests of the two major communities in Bengal seem to me to be closely intertwined.... It is for Bengal's political leaders to say whether this closely woven fabric is to be torn asunder or not.'[127] The riots of Noakhali indeed took place in April 1947 as an aftershock to the Great Calcutta Killings. The frequency and intensity of communal clashes quickly soared. Yet these were just one part of the history of Bengal in 1946–7. There were other histories too.

It is not my point to doubt the lethal nature of the communal violence during the riots, or reduce the importance of the fear and the pervasive helplessness generated due to riots. I would only take into account these 'other' histories in order to reassess the causal connection between the Great Calcutta Killings and the fateful Partition that would eventually follow. This connection has long been established in common wisdom as well as in scholarly studies.[128] But, while the riot resulted in a frenzied communal antipathy in many parts of the society, it did not bring about a complete rupture of social ties. The hugely damaged structure of trust could possibly be restored to a significant extent by a different type of administration with greater stress on law and order. A different type of provincial government might well have been possible if the central political interests would not have meddled themselves in the province so desperately. To locate the reason of a devastated regional society in the communal hyperactiveness of the region, therefore, although handy as an explanation, may be simplistic as well as misleading. The post-election realities in Bengal led to Partition primarily due to the extra-regional political dictates, which damaged the potentials of regional politics rather irredeemably.

Reconstituting the Region: United Bengal Plan

When Sarat Bose made an appeal against a dissection of the province of Bengal in 1946, his idea was to serve two purposes with one single move: to keep Bengal united, as well as to register support for the unity of India. A year later, he joined to uphold the 'United, Independent Bengal' scheme along with Suhrawardy and Abul Hashim. By then he was prepared to give up on 'united India', if it meant losing one part of the province (that is, the Muslim-majority eastern part) forever. He had always been vocal about the possibility and desirability of an inter-community government in Bengal, and garnered critical support from the Bengali Muslim politicians on this much-cherished dream. Now, as on the eve of decolonization, prospects of Partition appeared so frightfully grave that he had to change his course of action.[129]

How did the Bengali Hindus, most of whom had long defended unity and singularity of nation, cope with this new idea of dividing the nation on the basis of difference? What were the reactions of Bose and other liberal leaders who had so far fancied an accommodative inter-community provincial administration? Were there traces of any political solutions emerging from within the province?[130]

Before delving into these questions, one must appreciate that 1946–7 was a time when the power-games in Delhi pushed the province into a thorny situation. The Congress, dedicated in a formal way to India's 'national' struggle on behalf of its long-asserted claims of unity and indivisibility of the nation, was no longer in a position to set the terms for fresh negotiations within the nation itself. In this context, after four decades of uneasy tussle between the two, the problems of 'unity' and 'difference' finally came to face each other in a directly oppositional way: to defend one inevitably meant to give up on the other. A review of the centre–province structure in a really meaningful way seemed no longer feasible without an open capitulation to the challenges thrown against its own projected claims. Whenever the Congress wished to project its central principle forcefully, that is, to assert the cause of 'united India' or Akhand Bharat, it meant that it had to bulldoze any provincial or regional autonomy. On the other hand, if the Congress decided to acknowledge the rights of the provinces, it immediately had to open a pandora's box called 'Pakistan', that is, the right of self-assertion of the Muslim-majority provinces.

Caught in this desperate dilemma, Congress now betrayed its deep confusion about provincial autonomy. On a theoretical level, there was still an open window to acknowledge rights of the provinces. The twelve-point manifesto issued by the High Command in October 1945 outlined that the Congress's objectives were to establish a free democratic state, a 'federal' constitution with a great deal of 'autonomy' for its constituent units. It would ensure the freedom of each group and territorial area to develop its own life and culture within the larger framework, regrouping of provinces on a linguistic and cultural basis, removal of poverty, modernization of industry, and so forth.[131] However, at a practical level, such pledges remained hopelessly vacuous, because the Congress still wanted independence to come before settling the communal question. This condition meant ensuring an essentially unitary form of government in the soon-to-be independent India, with a strong centre and accompanying promises to the provinces and minorities about some future adjustments. The same obsession with a centralized unitary India was responsible for the final rejection the Cabinet Mission Plan. In reality, the Congress could never accept the rights of the states to opt out through 'grouping system' because of its commitment to a single, unitary nation.

This conviction only grew stronger during the short experience of a coalition with the League in the Interim Government which the Congress had in late 1946 and early 1947. After the formation of the Interim Government at Delhi, one of the main policymakers of Congress commented, 'Lord Wavell had allowed such power to go to the Provinces that they could defy the Central Government, and by the introduction of the Muslim League members, against the advice of the Congress, had so weakened the centre that India was rapidly disintegrating into a lawless state.'[132] In Bengal, despite the disagreement between the provincial and central Congress leaders on the question of regional autonomy, the former began to converge with the latter at a remarkable pace as the moment of decolonization approached. The idea of a strong Indian centre at any cost gained momentum after the riots. Any regional nation in Bengal based on inter-communal trust now receded to the margins, as that was arguably the lowest priority amidst such high-stake principles and prestige issues.

Even in popular psyche, it was clear that among the limited political options at disposal, the only possibility was to have a viable nation through Delhi. One of the most vocal nationalist papers of Bengal, *Anandabazar Patrika*, pleaded for bringing an end to all communal violence which could only be ensured by a membership of the Indian Union.[133] A contemporary political worker described later why Nehru's Congress became so important to them: 'We wanted a "nation". We wanted "India". "They" [Muslims] were only out to destroy all our dreams. The idea of Pakistan was based on an anarchic and anti-nationalist spirit. We placed our trust on Nehru, Gandhi and Congress lest it surrender what it itself had generated,' said a former Congress worker of Bengal.[134] Such an emphasis on nation or 'membership of the Indian Union' was a desperate attempt to cling to the Hindu domination; a stress on nationalism of unitary/centrist nature, therefore, became urgent like never before.[135] It is difficult to say which was more important in shaping the heightened dependence of the Bengali Hindu on 'India' at this moment: the recent experiences of unrest and violence or the imminence of transfer of power, which would clearly involve a grant of 'Pakistan' in some form or other, and thereby reduce them in a position of permanent minority. However critical the first had been in reducing the trust quotient between the communities, the second consideration appeared overwhelmingly paralysing. One can argue that even without the experiences of mid-1946, Calcutta would have raised the 'One nation, One India' slogans to an unprecedented pitch. In the course of events, 'One India' was becoming to them the safest repository of nationalist dreams, surpassing all previous regional sentiments. The all-India Congress to them was emerging as the most important keeper of 'Hindu interests'. While the swadeshi nationalists privileged territorial unity more than anything else, their inheritors in 1947 foregrounded the rights of separation or partition of the province. The vengeance of 'difference' had finally completed a full circle.

Against this perspective of growing pro-centre sentiments among Bengali Hindus, British prime minister Clement Attlee made the historic announcement on 20 February 1947 that the British were to leave India by June 1948, even if that necessitated transferring power in some cases to the existing provincial governments. Immediately, a panic descended on the province. The Hindu Mahasabha, an apostle of Akhand Bharat since its inception but recently converted to the most vocal pro-Partition lobby, read in the announcement a stark danger as Pakistan now seemed an inevitability. Under the leadership of Shyamaprasad Mookherjee, it launched a vigorous campaign for partitioning Bengal into Hindu-dominated West Bengal and Muslim-dominated East Bengal. The Congress High Command also revealed two major shifts in policy at this turn of events. Giving consent to some form of Pakistan in order to avoid 'frictions and conflict' with the League was the first shift. The second one was indicated in the Congress recommendation of division of Punjab and also of employing the same principle in Bengal. The BPCC made a declaration on 4 April in favour of the partition of Bengal, which gave the Mahasabha politics a huge fillip. At the three-day annual session held between 4 and 6 April at Tarakeswar (Hooghly), the Mahasabha laid down the 'line of action' and made a request to the existing Constituent Assembly. This request included several heads: to appoint a Boundary Commission for the demarcation of the area of the proposed West Bengal province; formation of a separate legislative body by the Hindu members themselves; enrolment of one lakh volunteers; and a demand for the immediate setting up of two regional ministries.[136] It also began mobilizing public opinion through numerous meetings and memoranda.

As the Hindu 'nation' began to flaunt its own claims of 'difference' through Congress and Mahasabha lines of action as against those who had long been used to see themselves as 'different', and the Muslim League was already celebrating its victory in the grant of a Pakistan, the passion for a united homeland of Bengal was still burning. The first overture came from the League itself, in fact, from the most prominent regional leader of the Bengal League. Already in April 1947, Suhrawardy, the premier of Bengal, had officially initiated a move for an 'independent, undivided and sovereign Bengal', and found at least two enthusiastic political heavyweights by his side: Abul Hashim and Sarat Bose. This was by no means a novel idea for the League premier. As early as in September 1946 (after the Great Calcutta Killings), Suhrawardy commented in an interview with *Millat* that a real solution could only be achieved if only Bengal was given more freedom to negotiate among its own communities.[137] He also argued that if Bengal is allowed to function autonomously, and not as an integral part of the Akhand Bharat, 'that would certainly assuage tensions and distrust between the two major communities residing in Bengal for ages'.[138] When asked about the feasibility of the idea of regional autonomy, Suhrawardy pointed out that the economic and cultural dependence of Bengal on the neighbouring regions should not be a major obstacle in realizing this objective. He presented the examples of many other such autonomous states functioning on the basis of mutual cooperation:

> When we asked the Prime Minister why he refrained from taking an initiative to this end, he replied: 'The truth is most of us still cannot think of Bengal in disjunction from India. At a practical level, Bengal Congress feels the necessity of such reorientation of attitudes. But it is reluctant to admit and pursue this in terms of principle.'[139]

After a long history of championing the cause of provincial autonomy in a Muslim-majority province, starting from the pro-partition enthusiasts of 1905 to the upholders of the regional ideal of Pakistan like Huq and Hashim, Suhrawardy now appeared as the great defender of provincial autonomy in the form of a 'united, sovereign' state. His proposition never found any solid political backing. Among the all-India leaders, Gandhi initially maintained a strategic silence on this effort, but later, when Bose directly asked for his support, he turned out to be more unyielding. Patel and Nehru actively persuaded Mountbatten that no such 'united Bengal' should be an alternative to be put before Bengal Assembly for voting.[140] Amidst an absence of any real political alternative, the Bengal Legislative Assembly met to take a decision on Partition on June 20.[141] The motion was designed in a way where voting against Partition meant joining the new constituent assembly of Pakistan which would in that case include all of Bengal.[142] A 'united, sovereign Bengal' separate from both India and Pakistan was not even a choice. It is therefore hard to predict what could have been the choice for someone who had a 'no' for Pakistan, but a 'yes' for a united Bengali homeland. Hindu–Muslim difference in this way was hopelessly made into a stand for or against the unity of Bengal.

Although the United Bengal plan in the end did not receive any serious political attention from the leaders and the assembly members, its plausibility and consistency need to be measured in terms of the legacy of the earlier trends of regional nationalism, and the foreshadowing of the future nation-state of Bangladesh, a relatively truncated form of 'sovereign Bengal'. In support of this plan, an article in *Millat*[143] evoked a united Bengal, which should neither erase nor essentialize Hindu–Muslim differences, but base itself on the spirit of regional cultural traditions. An image of the whole province of Bengal, stretched to include Assam in the east and parts of Bihar and Orissa in the west was also presented with the article. In January 1947, Hashim and Bose held a series of meetings on the same idea.[144] Although none of them made any public statement in those months, soon the news came out in *Swadhinata*, the communist newspaper.[145] For certain sections of Hindus in eastern Bengal, this plan brought new promises of a region–nation despite the possibility of a Muslim majority.[146] However, for the Hindu press of western Bengal, these opinions were only of marginal importance, and therefore Bose's seemed to be the only truant voice: '… his was the lone voice decrying the proposal for Partition.'[147]

During this time, Bose issued a statement where the cry of partition for Bengal was described as 'the result of defeatist mentality':

> By accepting religion as the sole basis of the distribution of the provinces, the Congress has sent itself away from its national moorings and has almost undone the work it has been doing for the last 60 years…. To my mind a division of provinces on the religious basis is no solution of the communal problem.[148]

He knew by this time that the plan and his suggestion of a 50–50 Hindu–Muslim representation in the new united Bengal had very little chance of realization. Therefore, making another shift in his stand was necessary for him. He would now give a 'reformed' but 'centrally united' India a last chance by demarcating 'the provinces on a linguistic basis and give them full measure of independence':

> Let them reform the provinces on a linguistic basis and give them full measure of independence. Let them introduce in the reformed provinces adult franchise and joint electorate. If they do that, they will be sowing

the seeds out of which will grow an independent and united India, an India not of Hindus against Muslims, or Muslims against Hindus, but an India of Hindus and Muslims ...[149]

The protest against Partition was becoming more severe at a time when Bose was making multiple suggestions on a possible solution. Large numbers of students of Dacca University issued a warning to Jinnah that in case he accepted partition of their province they would treat him as a 'traitor' and continue their struggle to realize 'real' Pakistan.[150] Articles in *Millat* stressed on Bengali regional identity surviving through the attempts of central domination in the ancient, medieval, and the early modern ages.[151] The irony, one article pointed out, was that in Bengal's history, those who had so far upheld the biggest claims to immortality like Suleiman Karrani, Daud-Shah, the twelve Bhuiyans including Pratapaditya and Isha Khan, Alivardi Khan, and lastly Siraj-ud-Daula, all used to represent the regional kingdom of Bengal rising in resistance against central aggression. The historical narrative was also often brought to its logical end, holding Congress, and sometimes even AIML, responsible for crushing the prospects of a regional state through inter-community negotiations within the province.[152] A former League worker who had been based in Calcutta during 1946–7 recollects that 'Hashim and Suhrawardy talked in terms of regional individuality against the bulldozing politics of the central League. We understood this clearly.'[153] Waliullah notes that in the political climate of 1946–7 Bengal, it took a high degree of authoritarianism on the part of AIML to completely ignore such a widely shared sentiment of Bengali Muslims against partition. 'We had instead been preparing ourselves for a victory of this Plan, where Assam also became eventually interested, when the news of breakdown reached us.'[154]

The anti-Partition sentiment of the Bengali Muslims is usually explained in terms of the desperation to win Calcutta, the one and the only coveted centre of Bengali culture and politics. This explanation is not wrong, though a little inadequate: to consider the Hindu advocate (that is, Sarat Bose) of the United Bengal plan a regional patriot, or a champion of Bengali nationalism, while branding the Muslim campaigners of the same plan to be politically motivated opportunists does not appear to be a fair historiographical exercise. It is immensely possible to find in this Bengali Muslim enthusiasm for the United Bengal plan a strong espousal of regional nationalism. The four-decade-long trends of such a different 'nationalism' do not lose its entire merit only due to the Muslim-majority profile of an imagined future of Bengal. At a time when realization of Pakistan in some form or other was beyond any doubt, excessive enthusiasm about such a plan was distinctly significant, especially because it could even have postponed or imposed a limit on the acquisition of Pakistan. The risks entailed in Muslim involvement with this plan were evident in the reactions of the opposite camp, which did not care about the 'region' any longer. Maulana Akram Khan, the staunchest protagonist of a separate Pakistan with a divided Bengal, lashed out to these region enthusiasts: 'Muslims of India constituted a single united nation and we aim at setting up a single united state, even at the cost of partitioning Bengal.'[155] The Hashim–Suhrawardy group was warned by him in no uncertain terms: 'Those who talk of a Bengali nation consisting of Muslims and Hindus and of a separate sovereign Bengal upon that basis are clearly playing into the hands of our enemies.'[156]

A major confusion arose regarding the relationship of the envisaged 'united Bengal' with the greater India. When Suhrawardy made an appeal to the Hindus, he did not categorically spell out the possible status of the 'united Bengal' vis-à-vis the rest of India. Consequently, in April 1947, speculations ran high and the situation seemed fluid. It became clear shortly that such a move for united Bengal could also mean an 'independent, sovereign' Bengal. As for the Muslim League leaders, with the clear dismissal of the idea of a united Bengal within an undivided India, the new prospect implied either a united Bengal with a sovereign status, or a united Bengal within the scheme of the AIML view of Pakistan containing both western and eastern parts. The first view therefore suggested a united, independent Bengal against the demand for one Pakistan, as well as against that of one India. Shila Sen holds that there were two groups within the supporters of 'sovereign' Bengal. One of these groups claimed 'an independent Bengal where Muslims by virtue of their numerical strength would be the dominant power', and the other, 'a microscopic section led by Abul Hashim', claimed 'an independent Bengal ... strictly according to the Lahore resolution, and therefore ... [embodying] the Pakistan demand of Bengal Muslims'.[157] The distinction between these two trends is difficult to understand from her analysis. However, it is worth noting that during the United Bengal debate, Hashim spoke more in terms of 'Pakistan' ideals and 'Muslim self-determination' within Bengal, and Suhrawardy talked more about 'Bengali culture' and 'Bengali identity' among the Muslims. Dissonance in Bengali Muslim views was still conceivable through a complex mesh of linguistic–cultural and religious identities, in which the regional loyalties continued to remain prominent in some way or the other.

For the Hindu protagonists of 'united Bengal' also, the idea conveyed a number of possibilities. Sarat Bose, Kiran Shankar Roy, and Satya Ranjan Bakshi outlined the proposal in a way where Bengal occupied a sovereign status. Among other things, it was decided that first, Bengal would be a free state and would decide its relationship with the rest of India. Second, the constitution would provide for a joint electorate and a representation of communities through reservation of seats proportionate to the population ratio. The new interim ministry to be instituted in case the proposal was accepted would constitute a Muslim chief minister and a Hindu home minister.[158] Sarat Bose pointed out that this was the first time after several decades that the Congress and Muslim League leaders of any province in India had agreed to the introduction of joint electorates and adult franchise.[159] However, about the future connections between India and the new sovereign state of Bengal, Bose stood to prefer some kind of a Union in future:

> I have always held that India must be a union of autonomous socialist republics, and I believe if the different provinces are redistributed on a linguistic basis and what are today called provinces are converted into autonomous socialist republics, those socialist republics will gladly co-operate with one another in forming an Indian Union. It is not the Indian Union of British conception and British making. I look forward to that Union and not to the Union of British conception and British making.[160]

Bose would further elucidate on ideas in the above terms during the meetings with the INA leaders, where he was accompanied by the League leaders like Hashim and Shamsuddin Ahmed.[161]

Congress protagonists not only made themselves distant from this plan, they also gave it a new twist to bolster their own uncompromising position on the question of India's unity. To put it simply, the united Bengal plan was declared workable only as a 'united Bengal in united India' format. Reconciliation between the Bengal communities was only conceivable within a clear framework of India: 'The supposed terms on the face of it are absurd and unacceptable to any sensible and patriotic Indian. Our nation is one and indivisible.'[162] Dwelling on the issue of undivided Bengal, Surendra Mohan Ghosh, the BPCC president, said in a statement: 'We too dream of a united and greater Bengal in a united India. We have lived for it, worked for it, and suffered for it. We shall continue to do so till the temporary partition is annulled and we have achieved an undivided and free Bengal in an undivided and free India.'[163] Ghosh clarified his idea again: 'Over and above the ghost of communalism he [Suhrawardy] has evoked the ghost of provincialism.... This is not the way to prevent partition. An undivided Bengal in a divided India is an impossibility. Let Mr. Suhrawady repudiate the two-nation theory and abandon communalism and he will be able to prevent the partition of Bengal.'[164] Other Congress leaders like Akhil Chandra Datta and Kamini Kumar Datta took the same position and commented that 'partition amounted to the acceptance of the basic principle of Pakistan, namely the territorial division or readjustment on the basis of community or religion'.[165] A letter published in a major daily persuasively presented the same ideological argument: 'By making our demand for a partition of the province on the basis of denominational religious communities we are likely to cloud the real issue. India cannot be communally divided, neither Bengal nor any other part of it. That will smother our progress; we will be going back to a perverted type of religious medievalism, absolutely unacceptable in the modern world.'[166] Thus we arrive at the regional reverberations of the Congress High Command's dictate: negotiations on matters of rights and differences could only follow the confirmation of India's unity and indivisibility as a nation. In other words, unity first, differences thereafter.

A large chunk of Hindu public opinion by this time was, of course, opposed to a united Bengal and championed a divided Bengal in divided India. It is important to recall some of the arguments already discussed above. P.C. Ghosh, a member of the Congress Working Committee, declared in a meeting: 'People who want to remain within the Indian union should be allowed to do so. Division of India under present circumstances seems inevitable. If the Hindus press for a united India, it will only increase bitterness between the two communities. Hence we should accept the inevitable.'[167] This statement revealed a plain 'acceptance' of the political realities, where no other option was even ponderable. By the industrial and commercial organizations of Bengali and non-Bengali Hindus in Calcutta, a resolution was passed supporting the demand for a separate West Bengal province. A committee was formed, including influential members like Birla, Goenka, Jalan, and politicians like Nalini Ranjan Sarkar, in order to mobilize support for partition. Most of the Hindu dailies such as *Amrita Bazar Patrika* or *Anandabazar Patrika* engaged in relentless arguments against the United Bengal Plan. *Amrita Bazar Patrika* decided on a poll in order to 'make a correct estimate of public opinion about the creation of a separate homeland for Bengali Hindus'. The result of this poll was 98.3 per cent in favour of partition and only 0.6 per cent against it.[168] As already mentioned, the essence of this position was to protect and safeguard the Hindu strongholds of power, both in politics and in society. The comparative estimates of numerical position in a united province in a divided/undivided country were what appeared particularly alarming.

Driven by the same logic, a part of the Hindu opinion, primarily in eastern Bengal, favoured a divided Bengal in a united India. Much like the provincial partition of 1905, these Hindus conceded the majority claims on eastern Bengal and the ground for demanding a separate state on the basis of such claims, but desperately wanted a link with the Hindu-dominated Indian centre to counterbalance a Muslim-majority province. *Dhaka Prakash*, a weekly newspaper published from Dacca, published a series of articles roughly on the same line. One such article reads: 'A strong state of Hindu western Bengal would allay the inevitable fears of discrimination and exploitation by the Muslims on the Hindu minorities.'[169] The use of the word 'state' (*rashtra*) instead of 'province' (*pradesh*) is startling, nevertheless. In many such pieces, curiously, the word rashtra apparently replaced pradesh when referring to West Bengal, possibly pointing towards the ambiguity latent in 'autonomy' and 'sovereignty' to be exercised by the future provinces constituting the larger nation-state of India. The point remains that the Hindus would seem to be a minority either in the united and sovereign Bengal, or in eastern Pakistan in case of Partition. Consequently, the prospect of a West Bengali domain of the Hindus seemed to many an adequately counterbalancing threat in order to exert pressures on Muslim majoritarianism in East Bengal. The above article advocated a return to the joint electorate system in the province of West Bengal, which would reduce minority interference in the shares of power and resources, and thus the 'powerful national state of west Bengal would necessitate peace and order for the Hindus in east Bengal'.[170] Such anticipations of safeguards were followed by the ultimate assurance: '... from within Pakistan, east Bengal [read the east Bengali Hindus] is determined to remain a member of an all-India union.'[171]

All this shows that, even amidst the overall climate of pro-centre, 'One India' Hindu Bengali sentiments, negotiations continued till the very last moments of colonial rule. These negotiations were not always based on abstract ideals. More often than not, these were results of practical estimates of potential gains and losses. But, significantly, an important variable in such estimates was the identity based on region, which had to be abstract in its nature. The burning question was: whether to forego this identity at this critical juncture, or still foreground it. Those who decided to uphold the assertions of the region against the centre could not successfully translate it into a political solution. In the Bengali public discourse of 1946–7, this distinct openness towards regional reconciliation remains a matter of great importance.[172] Of course, there was too much rush and impatience in the overall climate to consider the element of political fluidity in Bengal, one of the most critical provinces in the bargaining game with Jinnah's Pakistan. We have already noted previously how Patel took pains to frustrate the possibility of a coalition government in Bengal in 1946. Even in 1947, he in association with Nehru left no stones unturned to thwart all political options other than Partition before Bengal. Patel believed that the viceroy should make an announcement of the partition of Bengal as early as possible to force Jinnah to climb down from his bargaining rostrum.[173] Patel was so consistent in his opposition to anything except partition of Bengal that he even tried to manipulate public opinion by leaking transfer-of-power plans.[174]

In such a situation, Patel and others must have found the conservative Hindu pro-partition sentiments very handy. They chose to overlook all other regional efforts as a result. It is in this light that Gandhi's pronouncement in 1947 that the fear and suspicion in the aftermath of the riots 'was at the root of the partition fever' partly holds true.[175] However, even if the contemporaries missed it or chose to miss it, that there were multiple strands of deliberations at work should not escape the attention of historians. One particular strand of opinion must not be conflated inordinately to obliterate all others as well as other possibilities. It appears unfair on three counts. One, we tend to forget that the Bengali public discourse might have taken a different trajectory if any other political options could be offered before them, and if there would be a climate of a relatively free negotiation at the centre. Second, by holding riots and their resultant disorder the most crucial element in shaping the subsequent course of events, the historiography falls into the old trap of conflating 'communal bigotry of a few' with the 'communal sensibility of many'.[176] This book has explored the hidden layers of the discourse of 'difference' where the potentials for negotiation among communities reigned during four decades. I have showed that alongside the very rich discourse on difference, the Bengali society also consistently generated political and cultural compromises among differences. To view the entire Bengali psyche being flooded with communal bigotry would therefore not only be far from the truth, but also be terribly misleading as a historical viewpoint. Third, from the angle of purely political pressures and counter-pressures in the late colonial years, it is possible to argue that the centre–province dichotomy was no less fundamental as a site of contradiction and conflict than the Hindu–Muslim dichotomy. In the end, it was not the reality of the province that pushed the central leadership towards a deadlock where the only key seemed to be the axe of Partition. On the contrary, it was the centre whose political bankruptcy finally necessitated the partitioning of the province of Bengal.

Scholars who suggest that communalism and communal conflicts in Bengal were the sole cause of the Partition of 1947, therefore, may be challenged.[177] The timing of the opinion movements also should be taken note of. The official pro-Partition views of the Congress and the Mahasabha could be dated back to the early months of 1947, that is, exactly at a time when the central leaders were moving fast towards the agreement on partitioning two Muslim-majority provinces of India.[178] However, the overwhelming popular response to Partition only followed a political negotiation, forgone in nature and uncertain in its content.[179] My conclusion, therefore, is that it was the dialectics between the priorities of the players of the major political parties based outside the province and the calculations of the regional political entities on their potential gain and loss that brought about the deadlock Bengal witnessed in 1946–7. Bengal was partitioned due to the power bargains taking place far away from the rough-and-tumble of its own politics and society. Of course, the promises entailed in such high-level bargains proved to be especially alluring for the regional power-groups.

Partition: A Non-Permanent Settlement?

If the Great Calcutta Killings and Noakhali riots could not be directly linked to the massive exodus associated with Partition, in what other ways could we then possibly explain the connection between the riots and the Partition? Bengal Congress leaders converged with their all-India counterparts in the interest of maintaining a strong Hindu centre. But a strong centre would necessarily be attained with the cost of dividing their own province, which was still not palatable to large sections of Bengali society. There is no denying that the riots triggered off prolonged conflicts between the extremists of both communities in various parts of Bengal, and that the structure of trust was severely jeopardized at this historical juncture. Did the post-riot stress and anxiety gradually but inevitably lead to the partition of the province?

Localities or paras already marked as Hindu or Muslim started turning more polarized and exclusive after the riots. Both in Calcutta and in the countryside, people turned paranoid with fear; talks of riots were being heard among all who could think logically and who could not. Fear of mob fury sometimes resulted in spatial movements in Calcutta and also in the urban parts of eastern Bengal. What must be noted here is that this spatial movement was of limited nature, like the usual consequence of any instance of rioting, and rarely entailed any large-scale dislocation. Public writings and autobiographical accounts noted that rehabilitations followed a localized pattern, in the hope of a 'new normal' situation, with internal adjustments between the communities.[180] For example, when 'evacuation' took place in Chittagong, a classic locus of 'syncretist' society and culture, the traditionally divided Hindu, Muslim, and Buddhist areas of the city saw a spatial relocation of the population within themselves, but never meant a flight or desertion for any major section of the population out of the city.[181] 'Synthesis meant coexistence,' says a Muslim communist who used to be an inhabitant of Chittagong in the 1940s: 'We perfectly knew that it was not possible to mix the Muslims and Hindus within one and the same locality. But Hindu and Muslim paras coexisted side by side in peace, even in 1946 and afterwards.'[182] Another resident of colonial Chittagong remembered during an interview session that the co-existence went hand in hand with fear and distrust: 'We, the rank and file of League cadres of Chittagong came out to the streets to resist the disturbances, but what we could not address was the psychological wounds. The Muslims and Hindus were still living close by, but for the time being, hardly any Muslim dared to enter the Hindu zone and the Hindus remained as apprehensive and exclusive.'[183] If this was the case of Chittagong, accounts from Barisal district in eastern Bengal indicate that the huge numbers of professional Hindus of this district, occupying the ranks of teachers, headmasters, principals, police inspectors, and judges, all held in high esteem in their own localities, remained in their own places at least till the fatal moment of 1947, and often were provided protection from the League goondas (hooligans operating under the aegis of the Muslim League) by the local Muslim community itself.[184] The autobiographical account of a Hindu nationalist, who was Gandhian by creed, and a veteran politician of repute, mentioned a similar experience in the district of Mymensingh in eastern Bengal.[185] After the riots, a period of terrible fear and uncertainty ensued but 'not a single case of dislocation or violence' was recorded. Initially, almost all schools, colleges, and health centres got closed; normal life was denied for a couple of months. By December, however, life regained normalcy, mostly due to the attempts taken up by the local inhabitants, both Hindus and Muslims, to bring back trust and cooperation. The schools reopened and the doctors returned to the respective medical centres.

Significantly, no newspaper reports mentioned events of large-scale exodus from any localities either in Calcutta in the suburban or rural areas in late 1946 and early 1947. On the contrary, the reports on violence were often followed by the references of new readjustments within localities. *Anandabazar Patrika* published a report on a number of administrative steps especially taken to 'normalize the situation', such as increased police patrolling in the localities and the constitution of self-help groups in the city and its suburbs.[186] Steps were taken to counter spates of rumours, a normal occurrence after violent disturbances.[187]

The prospect of dislocation nonetheless emerged in a big way in the mid-1947 when it became clear that the Delhi Congress was anyway considering the partition of Bengal in its bid to secure its control over the rest of India. When Nehru told Wavell in March 1947 that 'the Cabinet Mission Plan was the best solution if it could be carried through: the only real alternative was the Partition of Bengal and Punjab',[188] he pointed towards a political impasse generated in the power-bargain at the centre, not a hopeless regional scenario. While there were pressures for partition exerted by the Congress and the Mahasabha, both eager to cash on the fear and trauma of the riots, what Sarat Bose reflected on the extent of such 'pressures' may be mentioned:

> ... it is not a fact that Bengali Hindus unanimously demand partition. As far as East Bengal is concerned, there is not the slightest doubt that the overwhelming majority of Hindus there are opposed to partition. As regards West Bengal, the agitation has gained ground because the Congress came to the aid of Hindu Mahasabha and also because of the communal passions that have been roused among the Hindus on account of the happenings since August last.[189]

Partition, nevertheless, happened, whether one wanted it or not and campaigned for it or not. If large sections of Hindu population in East Bengal were apprehensive of Partition and the prospect of being uprooted from the ancestral ground (*bhite-mati*), most of the Muslim families in West Bengal, particularly those based in Calcutta, found the displacement that Partition implied utterly deplorable. Suspicion of the 'other' community and the uncertain future of religious ties had to be the only determining force behind their decision of moving out to the 'appropriate' parts of divided Bengal. Many who even ideologically supported 'Pakistan' found themselves averse to pay such a high price of relocation. 'My family was not scared, neither convinced, but hoped that we might eventually be better off in the long run if we move out to east Bengal ...', says a scholar of Bangladesh whose family took the decision of leaving Calcutta in September 1947.[190] He remembers the same experiences later in an article. It was mostly his mother's decision, whereas his father 'used to smoke the pipe, listen to Mother, and ponder on and on'.[191] The dilemma of a Muslim professional of Calcutta was put succinctly by Anisuzzaman in this personal narrative: 'Most of [Father's] acquaintances, his journalist friends chose to stay back. None of the Muslim papers, either the monthly magazines or the dailies were transferred. The kind of riots were expected to take place after in August 1947, did never happen. There were lots of Muslim families staying on in Calcutta. My father did not care much about his place of origin ... but Calcutta? He had spent his entire childhood in this city, developed a bond of a lifetime. Where would he go now?'[192] Finally, his father reached the 'decision', rather unwillingly. Similar stories can be heard from other Muslim families as well, who left Calcutta with reluctance. Often enough, it was a matter of social obligation to leave West Bengal just because the entire peer group had shifted there.[193] Taking decisions of either staying back or leaving behind was thus predominantly a choice made on the basis of uncertainties in store rather than present hardships.

This reluctance to relocate was not difficult to imagine. In the backdrop of new electoral politics, the Muslim-majority province had their first few provincial ministries, all headed by the regional Muslim parties. Bengali Muslims found themselves in a very different situation in the middle of the 1940s, and gained a new social and political confidence. On the other hand, the Hindus were also accustomed to a certain extent to the new political realities. The willingness to form an all-party government even in the aftermath of the riots in Calcutta can be taken as an evidence of their new psychological adjustments. In this context, for the Bengali Muslims of western Bengal, severing local ties naturally meant the loss of a long-earned mesh of emotional and economic resources, or the security provided by a familiar cultural milieu with all its imperfections. To this were added the anxieties and uncertainties of a new territory. As for many Bengali Hindu families of the eastern part of the province, the anguish of the 'final decision' was a common experience. 'My father felt tormented all the time, and asked other Hindus who had already left the village if he could manage or protect the family by staying back. In spite of Mother's extreme discomfort about staying in East Pakistan, Father could not take the "decision" finally.'[194] For the Gandhian Congressite of Mymensingh we have mentioned before, 'staying back' in his own village was not only a choice, but also a 'moral obligation'. In his view, leaving one's one locality was a 'middle-class decision'. Despite the gradual intensification of communal distrust, the poorer sections often could not exercise that option, either due to their lack of means or due to their fear of an uncertain economic future. 'So many people were staying back. I also decided that I should not afford the luxury of leaving even if I could; I must stay back and serve the people of Purba Pakistan by Gandhian constructive work. I will transform my own village into a "model village", working in cooperation with the Gandhian camps [Gandhi ashramas].'[195] Another former Gandhian of Rajshahi also asserted that, 'Gandhiji asked us not to leave our own places': 'I found it only sensible. We did not support this partition, so it was our moral obligation not to remove ourselves from our own places out of fear and distrust of the Muslims.'[196]

Note that Suhrawardy, the eminent League leader and the premier of the League since 1946, did not himself leave Calcutta. Contemporaries debated on the real reason behind such a decision on his part. However, there might be some credibility to the apparent reason provided by him. He could not take the decision to relocate considering that there was an enormous number of Muslims who struggled for the realization of the dream of Pakistan, but had to stay behind in India in a permanent minority position. Even observers like Abul Mansur Ahmed, not particularly sympathetic to Suhrawardy, admitted that the latter indeed spent substantial time and energy in responding to the Muslims of Calcutta and the surrounding regions immediately after Partition.[197] The former head of the state now set up an all-India Muslim Federation in Calcutta (November 1947) to safeguard minority interests, and sought to formulate a uniform minority charter to be applicable to both the newborn nation-states. He convinced Prafulla Ghosh, the newly appointed chief minister of West Bengal, to visit East Pakistan, and address in popular meetings the issues to eradicate discomfort and fears of the minorities there. Prafulla Ghosh, who was from Dacca, was himself keen on this trip to alleviate tensions between the two neighbouring Bengals.

To sum up, despite severe disruptions in the social fabric, locational ties often triumphed over the concerns of community, nation, religion or even peer pressure. In some other cases, the uncertainties of dislocation seemed to have far outweighed the anxieties and fear associated with the option of staying back. In both cases, there was a distinct optimism for some eventual 'normalization' of the situation. West Bengali Muslims mostly chose to stay in India, as a result of which the state of West Bengal in an independent India became the home for almost twenty percent Muslim population, a very significant minority.[198] East Pakistan also continued to have a substantial Hindu population, a significant 'minority' in the newly constituted state.

Notwithstanding millions of such instances of staying back, the partitioning of the two provinces of Bengal and Punjab involved one of the largest mass exoduses in contemporary history, accompanied by massive human misery. This history of migration is well-explored by historians and sociologists alike.[199] However, a certain fact is often neglected in most of these historical studies. For many such hapless emigrants in Bengal, it appeared to be a temporary shifting rather than permanent uprooting. Many hoped that this would be an irregular adjustment due to some political crisis, and they could return to their own places in the near future when their leaders would be able to reach a political compromise more successfully. Even for the stalwarts of the Muslim League, the possibility seemed bleak that eastern Bengal, cut off from its more vibrant western part and surrounded by a different nation-state on practically all sides, would truly survive the tests of time. 'There was enough scope for doubting the whole question of workability, especially as Jinnah himself started treating East Pakistan in a step-fatherly way.'[200] Anisuzzaman's father, who after much hesitation and dilemma decided to leave Calcutta, headed for Khulna, a nearby western district in East Pakistan, because 'in case Pakistan did not survive, it would be easier to return to Calcutta'.[201] Many families adjusted themselves into a 'wait and see' approach in the months following Partition.

This was more because, in spite of the political boundaries drawn between two parts of Bengal, demarcation for all practical purposes remained fuzzy for quite a long time, at least till 1950, when official passports were introduced. Abul Mansur Ahmed mentions that those who could not make up their mind travelled back and forth. Due to the non-transference of journals like *Azad* and *Ittehad* from their original location, many League journalists like Ahmed himself could not leave Calcutta. Significantly, Abul Hashim, who preferred to stay back in Calcutta, was in two minds about the relocation of the journal *Millat*. His first impulse was to shift it to Dacca, but later on the decision was reconsidered and changed by the thought that the Muslims 'staying back' in Calcutta would perhaps need it more.[202] Even after Partition, these journals continued to discuss the same old 'Muslim interests', primarily because in their view, Partition did not really come as a solution to the problem of 'difference' so far problematized in terms of representation and rights. The needs of the 'thirty-five million Muslims of India' were thus considered to be taken up as a part of the project initiated long ago during the swadeshi days.[203] Occasional assaults were directed by the radical Hindu groups on the *Azad* office, but those were more than compensated by the generous protection offered towards these 'Muslim newspapers' by other important dailies of Calcutta like *Anandabazar Patrika*, *Amrita Bazar Patrika*, or *The Statesman*.[204] All these daily groups arranged for a sub-committee to look after the safe and secure publication and circulation of the so-called 'Muslim League' papers.[205] Suhrawardy asked the West Bengal Muslims to address the issue of their cultural and political interests in a multi-community society. In East Bengal, now constituted as East Pakistan, the firm belief of the Bengal Muslims in their national heritage of Bengali language and literature already began to be seen as endangered by the overarching domination of West Pakistan. Just before Partition, an article in *Millat* derided those who apprehended that Bengali might have been replaced by Urdu in the newborn state of East Pakistan. 'If any group of people somehow again seeks to impose a chain of slavery on East Pakistan, if East Pakistan is deprived of its national claims to Bengali, the Bengalis would storm to bring those conceited fools back to senses.'[206]

There is, therefore, enough ground to doubt that Partition was seen in 1947 to have marked a sense of irredeemable loss. Possibilities were still considered open and flexible; expectations did not die. Not surprisingly, to social observers like Waliullah and Abul Kalam Shamsuddin, this did not look like 'the last word' but 'just another' historical development in the life of the region, which might well be changed in case of 'a change in the circumstances':

> Partitioning a country, or a province, or even a smaller region for that mat-
> ter is nothing new in the history of the subcontinent. Bharat-varsha has
> been united into one and divided into many four times each at least, either
> through political deals or through warfare. So we could not be in a position
> to know if the partition of 1947 was the last word for us even for the time
> being. A set of circumstances led to the event of partition; who could tell
> that a change in the circumstances might not soon lead to its reversal?[207]

The hope for 'a change in circumstances' was kept alive for a considerable time, as Partition did not serve as a solution to any of the fundamental questions raised so far in the course of the 'national' journey around the problem of 'difference', either on the ideological issues of equality or fairness, or on the political negotiations of rights and interests.

A Remarkable 'Non-Solution'

In conclusion, the Partition became a climactic moment or a logical inevitability only in hindsight. For the partitioned people in the eastern side of India, it was neither as conclusive nor as permanent as it was later made out to be. This uncertain character of the event was only natural, because the controversies on freedom, representation, and sovereignty taking their cue at the moment of the first partitioning of the province in 1905 and traversing four decades remained unresolved even in the so-called final partition of Bengal. The spectacle of 'national' freedom from colonial rule was perhaps too overwhelming to realize the consequences of this massive failure and shortcoming. The question of freedom of the citizen within the new 'nation-state', especially the freedom of those who 'differed' from the quintessentially 'national' models, remained temporarily shelved. The postcolonial history of the subcontinent would only show that these questions re-emerged with their previous intensity and even in their previous form. 'Difference' continued to be an enormously vexing problem for the citizens of India, West Pakistan, and East Pakistan or, later, Bangladesh alike. The interconnected issues of freedom, representation, community identity, and regional autonomy, all returned after Partition only to unsettle the apparently settled claims of the nation-states born at midnight of 15 August 1947.

Notes

1. The above argument has been central in many historical works, some of which are Shila Sen, *Muslim Politics in Bengal, 1937–47* (Delhi: Impex India, 1976); Suranjan Das, *Communal Riots in Bengal, 1905–47* (Delhi: Oxford University Press, 1991); Joya Chatterji, *Bengal Divided: Hindu Communalism and Partition, 1932–1947* (Cambridge: Cambridge University Press, 1994); Bidyut Chakrabarty, *The Partition of Bengal and Assam, 1932–1947* (London: Routledge, 2004). According to Chatterji, the communalization of Bengali bhadralok public opinion decisively pushed the province towards a partition. See *Bengal Divided*, pp. 240–1. However, while the radicalization of politics was a clear and visible trend during the late colonial years in Bengal, one must wonder if the cause of partition of the province should also not be looked for outside the realms

of politics in the province. The complex political bargains and pressures at work at other levels seemed to have played a particularly critical role in this respect. The speculation develops itself into a historiographical problematic because, as this book suggests, it is difficult to hold the intolerant 'communalism', both of the Hindu and Muslim variants, as the *only* prominent trend in Bengal in 1946–7.

2. The contradictions of Pakistan politics arising in the late colonial years essentially rested upon the majority–minority question. This view was first explained by Ayesha Jalal, *The Sole Spokesman: Jinnah, the Muslim League and the Demand for Pakistan* (Cambridge: Cambridge University Press, 1985). Neeti Nair's work has also drawn attention to this argument in the context of Punjab in *Changing Homelands: Hindu Politics and the Partition of India* (Delhi: Permanent Black, 2011).

3. A recent article on the Indian National Army (INA) trials and a joint Hindu–Muslim movement in Calcutta against these trials in November 1945 and February 1946 has also pointed out that while this movement galvanized hundreds of people belonging to different religious communities against the colonial authorities, 'the political sentiment in the city was essentially anti-colonial and non-communal'. By studying this movement, this author has also questioned the common depiction of 1945–6 as 'the most decisive period of conflict among religious communities in the history of Bengal'. Sohini Majumdar, 'A Different Calcutta: INA Trials and Hindu–Muslim Solidarity in 1945–46', in *Calcutta: The Stormy Decades*, edited by Tanika Sarkar and Sekhar Bandyopadhyay (Delhi: Social Science Press, 2015), pp. 235–66. Previously, Leftist historians have even found the movement of February 1946 as constituting a 'revolutionary situation'. See Gautam Chattopadhyay, 'The Almost Revolution: A Case Study of India in February 1946', in *Essays in Honour of Prof. S.C. Sarkar*, edited by Barun De (Calcutta: People's Publishing House, 1976). Later historians have discarded this alleged 'revolutionary' potential of the moment on the ground that the movement clearly lacked direction regarding the most urgent political issue of the time: the unity or division of India. Nariaki Nakazato, 'The Role of Colonial Administration, "Riot Systems", and Local Networks during the Calcutta Disturbances of August 1946', in *Calcutta: The Stormy Decades*, p. 309. My point is: by keeping 'the most urgent political issue' out of its purview, this large-scale students' movement could at least indicate that there was enough scope for other political priorities to be put forward, or to make a Hindu–Muslim joint action on the streets possible. This 'possibility' itself should be brought into sharper historical focus regarding Bengal in 1946–7.

4. Jamil-ud-din Ahmed, *Speeches and Writings of Mr. Jinnah*, vol. 2 (Lahore: Shaikh Muhammad Ashraf, 1964), p. 202.

5. Before the formal clarification of 'Pakistan' by Jinnah in April 1946 at a convention of Muslim League legislators of the central and provincial assemblies in Delhi, there was enough evasiveness on the issue even in Jinnah's own mind. Scholars disagree on whether Jinnah used to mean one single state or two separate states by 'Pakistan'. Shila Sen and Harun-or-Rashid differ on this question. Referring to Jinnah–Gandhi correspondence where Jinnah talked about 'units of Pakistan', Sen concludes that he either meant that 'there would be two Pakistans' or that 'there would be a Federation of Pakistan'; see *Muslim Politics in Bengal*, p. 206. Harun-or-Rashid emphatically disagrees with her by pointing out that even this correspondence bears ample instances where Jinnah categorically argued for one Pakistan and, it being so, 'unlike the Bengal Muslim leaders and the East Pakistan Renaissance Society, Jinnah viewed the Lahore Resolution in terms of one Pakistan state, not two' see *The Foreshadowing of Bangladesh: Bengal Muslim League and Muslim Politics, 1936–47* (Dhaka: Asiatic Society of Bangladesh, 1987), p. 186.

6. Editorial, *Dainik Azad*, 14 September 1940, p. 4.

7. Zahur Hossain, 'Pakistan and Soviet Union', in Mujibur Rahman Khan, *Pakistan* (Calcutta: Mohammadi Press, 1942), pp. 66–7.

8. Abul Hashim, *In Retrospection* (Dhaka: Maola Brothers, 1998), p. 94.

9. *Dainik Azad*, 9 April 1946.

10. There is enough ground to infer that this move by Jinnah was clearly in view of the fact that the Cabinet delegation was coming to India and also that the election victories in provinces like Bengal might serve as the basis for individual or separate arrangements with the government. Shila Sen, *Muslim Politics in Bengal*, p. 205.

11. Hashim's interview by Shila Sen, *Muslim Politics in Bengal*, p. 207. In this memoir, Hashim comments that he could only challenge Quaid-e-Azam on the methods of the change: 'The convention of the Muslim League legislatures is not competent to alter or modify the contents of the Lahore resolution...which is now accepted as the creed of the Muslim League'. See *In Retrospection*, p. 134. Leonard Gordon confirmed the suggestions made by Sen that 'Hashim did object to this change in a closed session of that Convention and was put in his place by Jinnah'. Gordon, 'Divided Bengal: Problems of Nationalism and Identity in the 1947 Partition', *Journal of Commonwealth and Comparative Politics* 16, no. 2 (1978): 136–68, see 166.

12. Hashim, *In Retrospection*, p. 94.

13. Abul Hashim, *Let Us Go to War*, issued by Abul Hashim, 6 September 1945 (Dhaka: Society for Pakistan Studies, 1970), p. 5.

14. Hashim, *Let Us Go to War*, p. 6.

15. Hashim's speech in support for the United Bengal Plan, Calcutta, May 1947, discussed in Kamruddin Ahmed, *Banglar Madhyabitter Atmabikash* (Dhaka: Naoroj Kitabistan, 1975), p. 85.

16. While the Muslim League or the BPML are often analysed in their entirety by the scholars of Muslim nationalism in Bengal, L.A. Gordon appears to be an exception to suggest that Hashim personally stood out in this case, as his view of India differed from both the Congress and the League views. Gordon, 'Divided Bengal', p. 150. Although Gordon did not elaborate on the points of departure for Hashim, his insights regarding Hashim's multi-nation theory seem right on the mark. I would only like to add that through Huq and Hashim's forceful articulations, this 'other' creed of Bengali Muslim 'nation' made a distinct place in the Bengali Muslim mind.

17. At the Ramgarh Congress (March 1940), immediately preceding the Lahore Conference, Azad gave a speech where he asked the Muslims to come out of their minority anxiety. By the merit of their numerical strength they would be in a secure position in the provinces where they constituted the majority, and also form a very substantial minority in others. He emphatically pointed out the 'diverse' nature of India's culture and society, which demanded a flexible federal structure. H.N. Mitra (ed.), *Indian Annual Register, 1940*, vol. 1 (1940; reprint, Delhi: Gyan Publishing House, 1990), p. 300.

18. H.N. Mitra, *Indian Annual Register, 1940*, vol. 1, p. 301.

19. *The Statesman*, 3 February 1943.

20. Hashim, *Let Us Go to War*, p. 8.

21. Editorials in *Dainik Azad*, 'Paschatya Dharoner Government Bharate Achal', 23 March 1945; 'Akhanda Bharat O Ek Jatiyata', 14 June 1945; 'League O Anyanya Sankhyalaghu Jati', 10 April 1945; 'Pakistan O A-Mussalman', 21 November 1945.

22. 'Pakistan O A-Mussalman', *Dainik Azad*, 21 November 1945.

23. 'League O Anyanya Sankhyalaghu Jati', *Dainik Azad*, 10 April 1945.

24. 'League O Anyanya Sankhyalaghu Jati', *Dainik Azad*, 10 April 1945.

25. 'Asprisya Jati ki Hindu?' *Millat*, March 1947 (13 Falgun 1353 BS). Notwithstanding the Bengal Muslim displeasure at the AIML nomination of Jogendra Mandal as one of the League candidates from Bengal to the Interim Government in October 1946, Bengal leaders were open to negotiations with the low-caste groups, as these writings would suggest.

26. By this time, low-caste politics in Bengal was sharply divided into two rival camps. The first and the major camp with most of the Dalit leaders was in a pre-election alliance with Congress–Mahasabha, while the other, led by Jogendranath Mandal, was an ally of the Muslim League. Animosities ran high between the two groups before and after the elections. Meetings and campaigns arranged by Mandal's group, the Scheduled Caste Federation (SCF), were disrupted, even forcibly postponed by the Mahasabha and the Mahasabha-supported anti-SCF dalit leaders like Mukunda Behari Mullick. Surely, Mandal was a lone figure by then; nonetheless, his own following was not negligible at all. It is important to remember that even

when the election fight between the two Dalit political camps was made out to be a referendum on 'Pakistan' due to the constant campaigning of Mahasabha and Congress, Mandal still managed to snatch a victory with big margin in the reserved constituency of Pirojpur in the district of Bakharganj near Barisal. SCF, however, was virtually routed in the elections. For more details, see Sekhar Bandyopadhyay, *Caste, Culture and Hegemony: Social Dominance in Colonial Bengal* (New Delhi: SAGE, 2004), pp. 210–15; Anirban Bandyopadhyay, 'Orchestrating a Signal Victory: Ambedkar, Mandal and the 1946 Constituent Assembly Elections', in *Invoking Ambedkar: Contributions, Receptions, Legacies,* edited by Biswamoy Pati (Delhi: Primus Books, 2014), pp. 42–4.

27. 'Tafsilira Bangabhanga Chai Na', *Dainik Azad,* June 1947 (22 Jaishthya 1354 BS).

28. *Millat,* 2 November 1945.

29. Kamaluddin, 'Milan-sankat', *Satyabarta,* Eid issue, 1946.

30. Kamaluddin, 'Milan-sankat'.

31. The February Protests in Calcutta (1946) against the INA trials, which was joined by hundreds of Muslim students who engaged spontaneously into militant activities on the streets, had a clear political message that was neither linked with the demand of Pakistan, nor with any 'Muslim' interest as such. Yet Suhrawardy understood that 'with elections round the corner, [he] could not afford to lose popular support'. Sohini Majumdar, 'A Different Calcutta', p. 263. As the agitators assembled to protest vehemently against the conviction of the INA prisoner Captain Rashid Ali, '[Suhrawardy] knew that he had to agitate for the conviction of Abdul Rashid even if the agitation led to violence'.

32. Over the course of the movement, Suhrawardy and other League leaders became sympathetic to the agitator students. See Fortnightly Report for the first half of 1946, February, Government of Bengal, Home (Political) Confidential File, no. 18/2/46, IOL.

33. 'Bharatiya Muslim Jati', *Dainik Azad,* 3 February 1946.

34. Muhammad Waliullah, *Yuga-Bichitra* (Dhaka: Maola Brothers, 1967), p. 460.

35. Hashim described a situation in Faridpur where in a League meeting in 1946, groups of armed people led by some local power brokers got involved in a skirmish between themselves. Suhrawardy came off the stage, walked straight into the crowd, and urged for peace. The main impulse of the chief Muslim politicians of Bengal at that time was to popularize the basis of League politics in terms of representation rather than violent and antagonistic politics of any kind. Hashim, *In Retrospection,* pp. 87–8.

36. For a detailed account of the political strife between the non-Bengali and Bengali leaders of the League during these years, see Rashid, *Foreshadowing of Bangladesh,* p. 200.

37. Abul Mansur Ahmed, *Amar Dekha Rajnitir Panchash Bachhor* (Dhaka: Maola Brothers, 1970), p. 245.
38. Fornightly Report, March 1946, Home Political File, no. 18/2/46.
39. Sen, *Muslim Politics in Bengal*, p. 197.
40. Waliullah, *Yuga-Bichitra*, p. 469. He wrote the song before the Kishore-gunj elections. The song and its translation follow here:

Barisal-er Huq saheb, Dil-duar-er Gaznavi
Ratanpur-er Nawab saheb, korchhen vot-er dabi.
Jani mora ora shab Congressi-der dal-e
Shujog pelei chhuri deben Mussalman-er gale.
Hnakiye tader de re bhai Muslim League-er nam-e
Baron kore de ar kobhu ashen na e gram-e.
Khoda, tumi Tamij Khan-er purao mon-er shadh
Muslim League zindabad, Pakistan zindabad!

Huq Shahib of Barisal and Gaznavi of Dildwar
Ratanpur's Nawab Shahib—each claim to be a vote-catcher.
But we all know for sure, Congress is their real stance
They will butcher Muslims whenever there comes a chance.
Take the name of Muslim League, and drive them away with a rage,
Let them never come again to this our own village.
Fulfil the wish of Tamiz Khan, oh you almighty God,
Zindabad for Muslim League, Quaid-e-Azam Zindabad.

41. A.M. Ahmed, *Amar Dekha Rajnitir Panchash Bachhor*, p. 246.
42. *Millat*, 25 January 1946.
43. *Millat*, 22 February 1946.
44. Suhrawardy's Presidential Address at a public meeting in Calcutta, *Dainik Azad*, 28 December 1945, p. 3.
45. Anonymous, *League O Muslim Rajniti* (Dhaka, 1946 [preserved in Dhaka University Library], p. 10.
46. 'Although, we had been League workers even during the 1937 elections, at that time we did not exactly know how to approach the people. 1946 was totally different. We were so confident, so full of enthusiasm. For meetings after meetings, we the young Leaguers, toiled with relentless enterprise to make them a spectacular success!' says Kamaluddin Ahmed Khan, in an interview conducted on 15 February 1997.
47. The leaders and workers concentrated more on the urban industrial workers resulting in a weak grip on the peasants. 'Paradoxically, the party was more concerned about the impact of proposed abolition of the zamindari system on the non-peasant classes than putting an alternative program to that of the League to draw mass support after the War.' Taj-ul-Islam Hashmi, *Pakistan as a Peasant Utopia: The Communalization of a Class Politics in East Bengal, 1920–47* (Boulder: Westview Press, 1992), p. 250.

48. Jatin Sarkar, 'Communist Party o Krishak Sabha', *Pakistaner Janma Mrityu Darshan*, first published in *Kagaj*, a newspaper published from Mymensingh, in 1997 (reprint, Dhaka: Jatiya Sahitya Prakash, 2005).

49. The Tebhaga movement first started in September 1946 in parts of Dinajpur–Rangpur sub-region, supervised by the kisan sabhas and the CPI leadership behind them. Mainly directed by the local middle-peasant leadership, the peasant agitators of Dinajpur–Rangpur sub-region challenged the rights of petty landlords including jotedars, mahajans, middle peasants, and the bhadralok who had sublet their holdings to sharecroppers.

50. It is important to remember that even before the Tebhaga movement gathered momentum in the Bengal countryside, the CPI penetrated the local krishak sabhas of this area and was visibly active in mobilizing local movements in the northern districts of Dinajpur, Rangpur, and Jalpaiguri. It also had its strongholds in Mymensingh, Netrokona, Tippera, and Noakhali, and had organized the unprecedentedly grand All-India Peasant Conference in Netrokona in 1945. New names and new imageries were getting absorbed in the peasant myths or in the songs of village bards like Khabir Sheikh of Phulbari (Dinajpur), Majid Mian of Netrokona (Mymensingh), Akhil Thakur of Kishoregunj (Mymensingh), and Nibaran Pandit of Mymensingh. The old Baul tradition of Bengal was temporarily rejuvenated by the imaginative exercise undertaken by these revolutionary populist singers. At the same time, due to partial Communist penetration, the non-local bhadralok influence was also more visible in the villages, when the peasants enthusiastically participated in the communist conventions thriving on the songs of Binay Ray, Abbasuddin, Nirmalendu Chaudhuri, Hemanga Biswas, Jiten Sen, and Salil Choudhuri, that is, the entire Indian People's Theatre Association (IPTA) group. This small-peasant area of Mymensingh was predominantly Muslim, but the initial charm of the communists did not find such social composition an effective barrier to begin with. However, even with such a formidable support base in several pockets of Bengal, the communists could hardly make any significant electoral headway in 1946, primarily because of the system of separate electorates operating in a peculiar class–caste–community configuration.

51. Jatin Sarkar, a retired college teacher and a researcher based in Mymensingh, in an interview conducted on 18 July 1997.

52. A report from Bogra shows how the communal question was limiting peasant upsurges: 'The movement has failed to evoke sufficient response. The main reason appears to be the communal cleavage within the society. The Muslim *bargadars* have not so far joined the movement and the Communist leaders seem somewhat nervous in directing their operation against Muslim landlords who are numerous ... [italics original]'

See Sugata Bose, *Agrarian Bengal: Economy, Social Structure and Politics, 1919–1947* (Cambridge: Cambridge University Press, 1986), p. 271.

53. For example, it is claimed that in Netrokona, Jamalpur, and some other areas of Mymensingh, the Tebhaga movement could not strike any root because the Muslim jotedars actively neutralized Muslim adhiars 'by playing the religious card'. See Hashmi, *Pakistan as a Peasant Utopia*, p. 245. A general process of such neutralization is described in a major novel written by Akhtaruzzaman Ilias, the leading radical novelist of Bangladesh; Akhtaruzzaman Ilias, *Khoaab-nama* (Calcutta: Naya Udyog, 1996), pp. 121–30.

54. Anonymous, *League o Muslim Rajniti*, p. 18.

55. We have learnt from Sekhar Bandyopadhyay's study on Namasudra politics that 'their responses to the partition issue clearly shows that they had completely identified themselves with the Hindu sentiments and apprehensions on this matter' See his *Caste, Protest and Identity in Colonial India: The Namasudras of Bengal, 1872–1947* (second edition, Oxford: Oxford University Press, 2011), p. 224. However, even if the talks of partitioning the province eventually polarized the situation, there are enough instances of cooperation between the Namasudras and the Muslims in 1946–7. Even after the news of the Noakhali riots (where the Namasudra peasants were among the primary targets) reached the interiors of rural Bengal, especially its eastern terrains, the inter-community links between the low-caste day-labourers and Muslim cultivators continued to thrive well in the villages. For example, in northern parts of Bengal, Rajbansi and Muslim adhiars fought together against Rajbansi and Muslim jotedars. Sugata Bose refers to a village shooting by police against the rebelling adhiars in Chirribandar Thana in Dinajpur on 4 January 1947, where two peasants, a Santal and a Muslim, were killed. Sugata Bose, *Agrarian Bengal*, p. 265. In the brilliant literary reflection on the village politics by Akhtaruzzaman Ilias, one of the ablest novelists of Bangladesh, we can also come across images of Muslim–Namausudra cooperation during Tebhaga and Pakistan movements. Ilias, *Khoab-nama*, pp. 48–50.

56. Sugata Bose, *Agrarian Bengal*, p. 268.

57. Several articles supported the peasant cause, and even attacked the League ministry for neglecting the Tebhaga question. See for example, Kazi Mahmud Ali, 'Chashider Tebhaga Dabi Rodh Kara Jaibe Na,' *Millat*, January 1947 (10 Poush 1353 BS).

58. *Millat* had a strong stand on the problem of 'pointless resolution of zamindari abolition with compensation'. In several articles, it explored the following question, 'How, and more importantly, why should the Bengali people pay compensation?' Editorial, 'Zamindarir Khesharat,' *Millat*, May 1947 (18 Baisakh 1354 BS).

59. Abu Zafar Shamsuddin, *Atma-smriti* (Dhaka: Jatiya Sahitya Prakashani, 1989), pp. 220–2.

60. Abu Zafar Shamsuddin, *Atma-smriti*, p. 222; K. Ahmed, *Banglar Madhyabitter Atmabikash*, p. 46. These two men would emerge as the most prominent leaders of East Pakistan after 1947, and the foremost champions of Bengali identity politics against the state of Pakistan.

61. K. Ahmed, *Banglar Madhyabitter Atmabikash*, pp. 45–6; Abu Zafar Shamsuddin, *Atma-smriti*, pp. 220–2; Interview with Mustafa Nurul Islam, 28 July 1997. The latter comments: 'Who else could really claim to represent the real people—the Congressites? The Communists? The aristocrat Leaguers? When Bhasani or Mujibur Rahman thundered in their local dialects, it could trigger off a movement at once. Movements are made by such appeals, not by the sophisticated speeches of far-off leaders.'

62. See Chapter 1.

63. During 1944–6, this term (*jatiya atma-bishleshan*) was frequently used in the writings and speeches of the members of the Purba Pakistan Renaissance Society. See the speeches of Abul Kalam Shamsuddin and Abul Mansur Ahmed, *Mohammadi* 17, nos 10–11 (July–August 1945): 433–45.

64. Interview conducted on 28 February 1997 with Mahbub Alam Chaudhuri, a lawyer in Dhaka, previously a Communist Party worker in Chittagong before the Partition.

65. The former president of Purba Pakistan Renaissance Society, Abul Kalam Shamsuddin also served as the chairman of the Reception Committee of the Renaissance Society Summit at Kolkata in 1944. In 1946 he was elected to the Central Legislative Council. It is also to be noted that he would become a member of the Language Committee of the East Pakistan government in 1949, thus demonstrating a remarkable continuity in his political and cultural priorities before and after the Partition.

66. This organization was founded by Huq in October 1945 with the help of some former KPP compatriots. However, the board soon disintegrated before the elections with Ahmed joining the BPML in December 1945.

67. Abul Kalam Shamsuddin 'Speech of the President of the Reception Committee', *Mohammadi* 17, nos 10–11 (July–August 1945): p. 434. In the Renaissance Society expositions, 'freedom' and 'culture' were inevitably translated as '*tamaddun*' and '*azadi*' in place of '*sanskriti*', and '*swadhinata*', the regularly used Sanskrit words used in the Bengali. Contestations on language were thus extended to the political discourse.

68. Abul Kalam Shamsuddin 'Speech of the President of the Reception Committee', p. 434.

69. Abul Kalam Shamsuddin 'Speech of the President of the Reception Committee', p. 435.

70. Abul Kalam Shamsuddin 'Speech of the President of the Reception Committee', p. 435.

71. Abul Mansur Ahmed, 'President's Speech', *Mohammadi* 17, nos 10–11 (July–August 1945), p. 440.

72. Abul Mansur Ahmed, 'President's Speech', p. 441.

73. Abul Mansur Ahmed, 'President's Speech', p. 441.

74. Abul Mansur Ahmed, 'President's Speech', p. 441.

75. Abul Mansur Ahmed, 'President's Speech', p. 443.

76. Abul Mansur Ahmed, 'President's Speech', p. 444.

77. Editorial, *Millat*, October 1945 (30 Kartik 1352 BS), pp. 158–62. It was claimed to be the 'views-paper', not the 'newspaper' of the new regional face of the BPML.

78. According to Idris, such obsession with cultural self-promotion was only self-defeating when national regeneration was in question. 'One may have weaknesses and faults, limitations and inadequacies, but it is important to know and express oneself fully before absorbing the outside influence. Muslims might have not liked Bankimchandra for what he had written, but they must understand that Bankim attained excellence because he wanted to be himself, none other!' Editorial, *Millat*, October 1945, p. 160.

79. Idris referred to various common misperceptions about Muslim culture, such as, 'Despite the fact that it is written by a Muslim, the Bengali prose seems satisfactory'; or 'Who will realize that he is a Muslim? He behaves just like a bhadralok!' He also mentions the famous statement found in one of the most well-read novels by Saratchandra Chattopadhyay, called *Srikanta*, where one football match had been described by the author as being played between the 'Bangali' and the 'Mussalmans'. Chattopadhyay, whom Idris considered one of the greatest humanist writers of Bengal, could not but fall into this common habit of equating the Bengali with the Bengali Hindu only, and thereby treating Bengali Muslims as non-Bengali. Editorial, *Millat*, October 1945, pp. 159–60.

80. Golam Mostafa, *Pakistani Gaan*, song no. 1, p. 2. The original song by Dwijendralal Ray went as follows: '*Emon deshti kothao khunje pabe na ko tumi/ Sakal desher rani se je amar janmabhumi, se je amar janmabhumi!*' (Nowhere in the world you will find such a great country/ She is the queen of all the countries, she is my own motherland!)

81. 'Milan-prayasher Antarale', *Mohammadi*, May 1946, p. 592; 'Barshar Kabi', *Mohammadi*, July 1946, p. 634; 'Path O Pathik,' *Mohammadi*, May 1947, p. 511.

82. In spite of Jinnah's relentless stress on Pakistan for the whole of 'Muslim India', the 'powerful provincialism rather than commitment to 'Pakistan' continued to be the demand of most groups in the Muslim provinces. Ayesha Jalal, *The Sole Spokesman: Jinnah, The Muslim League and the*

Demand for Pakistan (Cambridge: Cambridge University Press, 1985), p. 179.

83. Jalal argues that, in his unstoppable journey towards developing himself into the 'Sole Spokesman' of the Muslims, Jinnah's plan was 'not to discuss the practicalities of Pakistan ... [but] to demonstrate that Muslim opinion was solidly behind its spokesman'. Jalal, *The Sole Spokesman*, p. 182.

84. See Gordon, 'Divided Bengal', p. 166. At this point, the only opposition to Jinnah's 'correction' of the Pakistan idea came from Khizar Hayat of Punjab, who under the old Unionist political tradition of that province looked out for a 'Punjab alternative' through Pakistan at this point. Jalal points out the difference between the viewpoints of Khizar Hayat and Jinnah: 'Jinnah needed control over the Pakistan provinces (themselves a constituent element of a weak central federation) whereas Khizar wanted no Pakistan centre or at most a weak centre over the Muslim provinces.' See Jalal, *The Sole Spokesman*, p. 181. Neeti Nayar has also traced how the premier of the Unionist Party had to distance himself from Jinnah's conception of Pakistan in order to maintain the priority of the Unionist-led cabinet to form a 'coalition government' with the non-Congress Hindus that would include a 'a common minimum programme'. Nair, *Changing Homelands*, p. 258.

85. Rashid, *Foreshadowing of Bangladesh*, p. 255.

86. Mohammad H.R. Talukdar (ed.), *Memoirs of H.S. Suhrawardy* (Dhaka: University Press Limited, 1987), p. 17.

87. Governor Burrows to Viceroy Wavell, 3 June, 1946, Home Political L/P & J/5/153, pp. 141–3.

88. Statements of Suhrawardy and Kiran Shankar Roy, *The Statesman*, 23 April 1946, pp. 3–4. As, much like Huq, Suhrawardy also often impersonified the distinct spirit of independence of the Bengal Provincial League, there is still room for a historical re-exploration of his political role and ideological conflicts.

89. *The Statesman*, 7 June 1946.

90. *The Statesman*, 8 July 1946.

91. N.N. Mitra, *Indian Annual Register, 1946*, vol. 2 (Calcutta: Annual Register Office, 1947), p. 178.

92. Waliullah, *Yuga-Bichitra*, p. 497.

93. Waliullah, *Yuga-Bichitra*, p. 497.

94. A.M. Ahmed, *Foreshadowing of Bangladesh*, p. 249.

95. A.M. Ahmed, *Foreshadowing of Bangladesh*, p. 250.

96. Waliullah, *Yuga-Bichitra*, p. 500.

97. A.M. Ahmed, *Foreshadowing of Bangladesh*, p. 288.

98. Ahmed, *Foreshadowing of Bangladesh*, p. 288.

99. Jibanananda Das, *1946–47*, translated by Clinton Seely in *A Poet Apart: A Literary Biography of the Bengali Poet Jibanananda Das* (Newark: University of Delaware Press, 1990), pp. 197–9. The original lines are as follows:

There's a rather indistinct human anxiety all around in the day's light:
On streets, in alleys, on tram line tracks and sidewalks ...
Thousands of Bengali villages, silent and powerless, sink into hopelessness and
lightlessness ...
They sleep on.
If I were to call, then from the river of blood as it
Billowed up, coming close by, he would say, 'I am Yasin,
Hanif Mahammad Makbul Karim Aziz—
And You?' placing a hand upon my chest and
Raising up those eyes from his dead face, he would
Ask—that blood river welling up would say,
'Gagan, Bipin, Sasi, of Pathuria Ghata;
Of Manik Tala, of Shyam Bazar, or Galif Street, of Entaly'
Who knew from where ...

100. Gautam Chattopadhyay describes the role of the police, 'a damning evidence about imperialist complicity in the riots', in *Bengal Legislature in India's Struggle for Freedom, 1876–1947* (Delhi: People's Publishing House, 1984), p. 208. Harun-Or-Rashid defends the Suhrawardy administration by passing the buck on to the Congress. 'The killings [perhaps] could have been averted had there been a Congress–League coalition in the province which Suhrawardy had tried to secure after the 1946 elections.' See *Foreshadowing of Bangladesh*, p. 261. He also thinks that the declaration of a closure of the government by Suhrawardy on the 16 August could not have worsened the situation, since there was enough instigation by the Mahasabha on the eve of the Great Calcutta Killings. Joya Chatterji points out that along with the highly pitched extremism of the Leaguers, long traditions of pseudo-military training of the bhadralok youths and active associations like Rashtriya Swayam Sevak Sangha, organizationally and politically related to Mahasabha, prepared the ground for the riot. See *Bengal Divided*, pp. 232–4.

101. According to Azad,

> The acceptance of Cabinet Mission Plan by both the Congress and the Muslim League was a glorious event in the history of the freedom movement in India. It meant that the difficult question of Indian freedom had been settled by negotiation and agreement and not by methods of violence and conflict. It also seemed that the communal difficulties had been finally left behind. Throughout the country there was a sense of jubilation and all the people were united in their demand for freedom.

> Maulana Abul Kalam Azad, *India Wins Freedom* (Delhi: Orient Blackswan, 2014), p. 158.

102. The Congress dilemma on provincial autonomy is discussed in the next section.

103. Sarat Chandra Bose, *I Warned My Countrymen* (Calcutta: Netaji Research Bureau, 1996), p. 154

104. *Amrita Bazar Patrika*, 16 April 1946.

105. Joya Chatterji's characterization of 'provincial bhadralok politics' raises questions in this context. Chatterji, *Bengal Divided*, p. 222.

106. Gordon, 'Divided Bengal', p. 167.

107. Suhrawardy claimed that bringing about a coalition government in Bengal was blocked by Patel. See Gordon, 'Divided Bengal', p. 154.

108. Gordon, 'Divided Bengal', p. 154. Gordon mentions that Sasanka Sanyal and Surendra Mohan Ghosh, two contemporary Congress leaders, later testified in the interviews with Gordon that Patel during this time controlled Bengal extra firmly in his desire to replace Sarat Bose with some more malleable leader.

109. Sarat Bose, Statement issued in Calcutta on 20 August 1946, *I Warned My Countrymen*, pp. 132–3.

110. In the proposal placed on 27 August, 1946, the following demands were made: (*a*) First, an All-Party Ministry was to be formed in Bengal; (*b*) The morale of the police force had to be restored; (*c*) Hindus and Muslims in towns and villages were to combine for the purpose of counteracting communal propaganda; and (*d*) People had to be made to realize that non-violence, not violence, was the remedy. See Bose, Statement issued in Calcutta on 20 August 1946, p. 134.

111. 'Banglar Mantri-sabhai Rad-badoler Sambhabona', *Anandabazar Patrika*, 30 August 1946.

112. 'Banglar Mantri-sabhai Rad-badoler Sambhabona'.

113. Mention may be made of one such article published exactly a month after the Calcutta Killings: 'The Best and Only Permanent Solution Seems to be a Congress–League Coalition Ministry in Bengal', *Anandabazar Patrika*, 16 September 1946.

114. For the impact of the riots on Bengali Hindus and the 'decisive' turn towards partitioning the province, see *Gordon*, 'Bengal Divided', pp. 153–4; Chatterji, *Bengal Divided*, pp. 232–5.

115. For example, hundreds of such imported goondas showed up in the crowds attending the Muslim League meeting before the Ochterlony Monument in Calcutta on the eve of the fateful rioting. 'The dispersion of this mass rally marked the beginning of Goonda violence in Central Calcutta; and from that time on, they were found engaged in all sorts of violence, including street fighting, looting, arson, and killing.' Nakazato, 'The Role of Colonial Administration, "Riot Systems", and Local Networks during the Calcutta Disturbances of August 1946', p. 291. Also see Suranjan Das, *Communal Riots in Bengal*, pp. 184–6; Suranjan Das, 'The *"Goondas"*: Towards a Reconstruction of the Calcutta Underworld through Police Records', *Economic and Political Weekly* 29, no. 44 (October, 1994): 2877–83; Suranjan Das and Jayanta K. Ray, *The 'Goondas': Towards a Reconstruction of the Calcutta Underworld* (Calcutta: Firma KLM, 1996).

116. Partha Chatterjee tells us about an autobiographical account of an urban observer of the riots. The observer talked about the 'rapidly unfolding political events, also seen as unreal'. Reading this, one might wonder if this sense of unrealness and unpreparedness for such calamitous events signifies the prior state of stability and the efforts to maintain a social balance in those trying times. See Partha Chatterjee, 'The Second Partition of Bengal', in *The Present History of West Bengal: Essays in Political Criticism* (New Delhi: Oxford University Press, 1997), p. 43. The author quoted by Chatterjee is Birendranath Chattopadhyay, a voluntary social worker, not tied to any political organization and his tract is named *Delirium* (*Sampratik Hangama*) (Alambazar: Databya Bibhag, 1947).

117. Sarat Bose, Report of a Press Conference held in Calcutta on 4 December 1946 after a tour of Noakhali and Tippera, *I Warned My Countrymen*, pp. 137–9.

118. Sarat Bose, Report of a Press Conference held in Calcutta on 4 December 1946, p. 141.

119. Chatterji, *Bengal Divided*, pp. 233–8. While the rise of the Swayam Sevak Sangha and the ultra-conservative volunteer organizations rapidly gained strength in these years, there is, however, room to reconsider the reliability of the intelligence reports and the actual strength and role of these 'private armies', as personal narratives and unofficial sources provide evidence of a contrary role played by similar local groups. For several such narratives, see Hiralal Dasgupta (ed.), *Swadhinata Sangram-e Barisal* (Calcutta: Sahitya Samsad, 1972), pp. 260–328.

120. Several reports in *Anandabazar Patrika*, 24–30 August 1946; Sripantha, 'Ekhono Shona jai Challish-er Garjan', in *Sat Dashak: Samakal O Anandabazar* (Calcutta: Ananda Publishers, 1992), p. 71.

121. Anisuzzaman's father, an accomplished doctor and a soft-spoken gentleman, rushed to save a Hindu milkman from the assaults of hooligans marauding in their locality. Anisuzzaman, 'Amra Pakistan-e Elam', in *Deshbhag: Binash O Binirman*, edited by Madhumoy Pal (Calcutta: Gangchil, 2011), pp. 43–7. Similar accounts are mentioned in Sripantha, 'Ekhono Shona jai Challish-er Garjan', p. 72. Some literary works also evoke the memory of tremendous goodwill and cooperation among the Hindus and Muslims of Bengal during the devastations of riots. Samaresh Basu's story *Adab*, and Rameshchandra Sen's *Sada Ghora* are just a few instances.

122. Anisuzzaman, 'Amra Pakistan-e Elam', p. 45.

123. The section on Pirojpur town and division in Barisal, in Dasgupta, *Swadhinata Sangram-e Barisal*, p. 265.

124. Hasan Ajijul Huq, 'Kromagato Atma-khandan', in Pal, *Deshbhag*, p. 131.

125. The wistful hope of the author mentioned in Chatterjee's article is significant. He thought, 'The clashes now taking place will soon lead to a

situation where people of both communities will get fed up with those who preach untouchability, communal hatred and religious hypocrisy. Perhaps then a new nation will arise in India.' Partha Chatterjee, 'The Second Partition of Bengal', p. 42. That the author could nurture this hope in such a trying situation tells us about the contemporary social climate, not wholly and hopelessly marked by a sense of irretrievable social harmony.

126. Bengal: Ministry and Political affairs including Calcutta Riots, August 1946 to August 1947, Coll 117/c66/E, IOL.

127. Governor Burrows' speech at the annual convocation of Dacca University, 21 November 1946, Burrows Papers, L/I/1/1328, IOL.

128. A recent study has also pointed out that the importance of the Calcutta Disturbances must be reassessed. It challenges the common view that the Indian political situation changed all of a sudden in August 1946 from a 'revolutionary situation' to 'a frenzy of communal passion'. 'The crucial months from the end of 1945 down to August 1947 may more usefully be looked upon and studied as a historical period in which a less spectacular and less discontinuous shifting of gears occurred.' See Nakazato, 'The Role of Colonial Administration, "Riot Systems", and Local Networks during the Calcutta Disturbances of August 1946', p. 316. However, I agree with Nakazato only partially. While there is a need to see this period in a 'less discontinuous' manner, it is difficult to be convinced of a pervasive 'civil war' situation in Calcutta. The official or government sources may provide such a depiction, but the unofficial or vernacular sources deal more with the attempts at normalization and mutual cooperation, thus throwing considerable doubt on such a wholly negative assessment.

129. According to Sarat Bose:

I confess that the resolution [on the Division of India, 15 March 1947] has surprised me not a little. By accepting religion as the sole basis of the distribution of Provinces, the Congress has cut itself away from its moorings and has almost undone the work it has been doing for the last sixty years. [It] was a violent departure of the traditions and principles of Congress.

See Sarat Bose, *I Warned My Countrymen*, p. 154.

130. An important study on these 'options' can be found in the work of Haimanti Roy, who also challenged the thesis of inevitability of Bengal partition and argued that it is 'belied by the existence of multiple discourses on the issue of the division'. Haimanti Roy, 'A Partition of Contingency? Public Discourse in Bengal 1946–47', *Modern Asian Studies* 43, no. 6 (2009): 1355–84.

131. Durga Das (ed.), *Sardar Patel's Correspondence, 1945–50*, vol. 2 (Ahmedabad: Navajivan Publishing Co., 1972), pp. 7–10.

132. Patel to Mountbatten, 25 February 1947, in *Constitutional Relations between Britain and India: The Transfer of Power, 1942–42* [henceforth *Transfer of Power*], edited by N. Mansergh, E.W.R. Lumby, and Penderel Moon (London: HMSO, 1977), vol. X, no. 252. Also cited in Chatterji, *Bengal Divided*, p. 235.

133. 'Banglar Dabi', *Anandabazar Patrika*, 15 January 1947.

134. Interview conducted on 20 August 1997 with Gopal Chandra Chakrabarty, a Congress worker of Krishnanagar, West Bengal, Gandhian in his social activism, and a follower of Kiran Shankar Roy in the late colonial days. Chakrabarty is now the head of a much acclaimed village-based ashrama in Birnagar, Nadia, with the objective of building up an alternative educational–vocational structure in the villages.

135. The essential political nature of the deliberations on the unity and Partition of the country has recently been emphasized by Sabyasachi Bhattacharya, *The Defining Moments in Bengal, 1920–1947* (New Delhi: Oxford University Press, 2014), pp. 315–18.

136. Congress Resolution, 8 March 1947, *The Transfer of Power*, vol. 10, p. 203.

137. Report on Suhrawardy, 'Banglar Samasya Bangalikei Samadhan Korite Haibe', *Millat*, September 1946 (3 Aswin 1353 BS).

138. Report on Suhrawardy, 'Banglar Samasya Bangalikei Samadhan Korite Haibe'.

139. Report on Suhrawardy, 'Banglar Samasya Bangalikei Samadhan Korite Haibe'.

140. Gordon, 'Divided Bengal', p. 158. Mountbatten commented that he did not want Balkanization of India and that if Bengal became independent, other regions might well follow suit. By this he appeared to have echoed Nehru's sentiments.

141. It is in this context that one might question the conclusion that 'the relevant decisions were made by members of the Bengal Assembly'. These 'decisions' appear to have been derived very differently if the pulls and pressures of all-India politics are considered. Partha Chatterjee, 'The Second Partition of Bengal', p. 37.

142. The details of this voting have been given in Gordon, 'Divided Bengal', p. 158.

143. Abu Mohammad Habibullah, 'Banglar Sanskritik Atma-Niyantran', *Millat*, September 1946 (19 *Ashwin* 1353 B.S.).

144. Abul Hashim's statement, *Millat*, 31 January 1947.

145. Hashim was accompanied by Shamsuddin Ahmed, one of his most trusted League companions, who had earlier been associated with the CPI as well. Thus, despite the CPI's non-involvement in the entire discussion, the news was published in its mouthpiece journal. This is mentioned in K. Ahmed, *Banglar Madhyabitter Atmabikash*, p. 84; and also Shila Sen, *Muslim Politics in Bengal*, p. 224.

146. 'Banglai Swatantra Rashtra', *Dhaka Prakash* 86, no. 46, 23 March 1947 (1353 BS).
147. *Amrita Bazar Patrika*, 16 March 1947.
148. *Amrita Bazar Patrika*, 16 March 1947.
149. Sarat Bose, *I Warned My Countrymen*, p. 170.
150. *Dainik Azad*, 9 June 1947.
151. 'Itihashe Sarbabhouma Bangla', *Millat*, June 1947 (29 Jaishthya 1354 BS).
152. 'Banglar Biruddhe Congress-er Satruta', *Millat*, July 1947 (19 Ashar 1354 BS).
153. Mustafa Nurul Islam in an interview conducted in Dhaka on 28 July 1997.
154. Waliullah, *Yuga-Bichitra*, p. 530.
155. *Dainik Azad*, 5 May 1947.
156. *Dainik Azad*, 5 May 1947.
157. Shila Sen, *Muslim Politics in Bengal*, p. 230.
158. *The Statesman*, 19 May 1947.
159. *The Statesman*, 24 May 1947.
160. Sarat Bose, *I Warned My Countrymen*, p. 176.
161. *The Statesman*, 16 May 1947.
162. Niharendu Dutt-Majumdar, *The Statesman*, 24 May 1947.
163. *Amrita Bazar Patrika*, 2 May 1947.
164. *Amrita Bazar Patrika*, 2 May 1947.
165. *Hindustan Standard*, 26 March 1947.
166. *Hindustan Standard*, 19 May 1947.
167. P.C. Ghosh's address at a public meeting at Comilla on 19 May 1947, *The Statesman*, 20 May 1947.
168. *Amrita Bazar Patrika*, 23 April 1947.
169. 'Bangala Bibhager Parikalpana', *Dhaka Prakash* 86, no. 45, 16 March 1947. Similar argument in 'Prithak Hindu Rashtra', *Dhaka Prakash* 86, no. 47, 30 March 1947; 'Bangali Hindur Swatantra Rashtra', *Dhaka Prakash* 86, no. 37, 19 January 1947.
170. 'Bangala Bibhager Parikalpana'.
171. 'Bangala Bibhager Parikalpana'.
172. Usually overlooked, this element of fluidity in Bengal politics in 1947 has been focused by Haimanti Roy. 'Bengali public opinion remained divided and marked with confusion when it came to the subject of the political future of the province.' See H. Roy, 'A Partition of Contingency?' p. 1360.
173. Sabyasachi Bhattacharya, *Defining Moments in Bengal*, p. 318.
174. Sabyasachi Bhattacharya, *Defining Moments in Bengal*, p. 318.
175. U.N. Pyarelal, *Mahatma Gandhi: The Last Phase* (Ahmedabad, 1958), p. 181.

176. According to Ayesha Jalal, in foregrounding a particular variety of communalism, South Asian history has long lumped under the rubric of religious communalism all those identities and ideologies which differed from the singular nationalism of colonial India. See her 'Exploding Communalism: The Politics of Identity in South Asia', in *Nationalism, Democracy and Development: State and Politics in India*, edited by Sugata Bose and Ayesha Jalal (New Delhi: Oxford University Press, 1997), pp. 76–103. This same argument can be found in the study of Punjab politics by Nair, *Changing Homelands*.

177. Shila Sen argues that Pakistan had never really been a Hindu demand, and implies by her own arguments that partition became a Hindu demand only by default, as a logical outcome of Muslim communal intransigence on the question of Pakistan. Sen, *Muslim Politics in Bengal*, p. 241. Chatterji, on the other hand, insists that the gradually heightening tenor of the Hindu bhadralok 'communalism' finally necessitated partition. Chatterji, *Divided Bengal*, p. 268.

178. By elaborating on how the Congress and Hindu Mahasbha organized the partition campaign in Bengal, Joya Chatterji wants to highlight how 'in the last months of 1946 and in early in 1947 these fears fuelled an organized and well-supported campaign among the Hindus for the partition of the province'. While there can be little doubt that the memories and fears around riots played a significant part in the discourse of partition, one wonders whether this campaign was potent enough to influence the Bengali public as well as the higher decision-making quarters in Delhi.

179. Partha Chatterjee suggests the same when he says, 'Reading through the political debates that took place in Bengal from August 1946 to August 1947, one cannot but sense that positions were being taken on the assumption that Pakistan was in the offing, that there was nothing left to be done to change that eventuality and that all that remained was to strike the best bargain for each sectional interest.' Partha Chatterjee, 'The Second Partition in Bengal', in *The Present History of West Bengal: Essays in Political Criticism* (Delhi: Oxford University Press, 1997), p. 38. That 'the decision to partition the province of Bengal did not involve the participation of masses' goes contrary to Joya Chatterji's assertions of popular communalism leading to Partition. However, the other part of this statement that 'the relevant decisions were made by members of the Bengal assembly, elected on the basis of a very limited sufferage' seems questionable if the political bargaining at Delhi is taken into consideration. Most of the 'relevant decisions' being directed from Delhi, there was little left for the Bengal assemblymen to decide. This latter argument has been put forward by Sabyasachi Bhattacharya also, in *Defining Moments of Bengal*, p. 318.

180. How such a 'new normal' state of affairs resurfaces after such violent riots is explained in a sociological study by Dipankar Gupta, *Justice before*

392 DIFFERENT NATIONALISMS

Reconciliation: Negotiating a 'New Normal' in Post-Riot Mumbai and Ahmedabad (New Delhi: Routledge, 2011).

181. *Satyabarta*, Chittagong, 10 September 1947. This was also confirmed by Mahbub Alam Chaudhury of Chittagong in an interview conducted on 28 February 1997.

182. *Satyabarta*, 10 September 1947.

183. Kamaluddin Ahmad Khan in an interview on 15 February 1997.

184. Dasgupta, *Swadhinata Sangram-e Barisal*, pp. 260–328.

185. Trailokyanath Chakrabarty, *Jail-e Trish Bachhor o Pak-Bharate-er Swadhinata Sangram* (Calcutta: Anushilan Bhavan Trust Board, 1981), pp. 356–7.

186. *Anandabazar Patrika*, 22–28 September 1946.

187. *Anandabazar Patrika*, 19 September 1946. An insightful observation was made by Krishna Bose about the beginning of a new year 1947 in the aftermath of the riots. 'I wonder if, at the beginning of 1947, we had any inkling of how the year would unfold for us. I do not think so. On 23 January, which was Netaji Subhas Chandra Bose's birthday, the tricolour flew over every house. In the morning, we awoke to the songs of the prabhat-pheri, the dawn rounds. In the afternoon, conch shells were blown in every household.... In the evening many homes were lit with lamps as well,... though compared to the previous year perhaps the romanticism had waned somewhat.' The change in the overall mood is nicely captured here: one of festive continuation, but in a restrained as well as apprehensive manner. One cannot but wonder how life in Bengal would have changed if it had a strong, inter-community provincial government with a focus on maintaining law and order during these months. Krishna Bose, *An Outsider in Politics* (Delhi: Penguin Books India, 2008), p. 11.

188. Penderel Moon (ed.), *Wavell: The Viceroy's Journal* (London: Oxford University Press, 1973), p. 427.

189. Sarat Chandra Bose to Sardar Patel, 27 May 1947, in *Sardar Patel's Correspondence*, edited by Durga Das, vol. 4 (Ahmedabad: Navajivan Publishing House, 1972), pp. 45–6. The same observation may be found in the autobiography of Trailokyanath Chakrabarty, who was, far from being a follower of Sarat Bose, a devout Gandhian and a social activist of Congress. See *Jail-e Trish*, p. 356.

190. Interview with Dr Anisuzzaman, 26 July 1997.

191. Anisuzzaman, '*Amra Pakistan-e Elam*', p. 52.

192. Anisuzzaman, '*Amra Pakistan-e Elam*', p. 52.

193. Interview conducted on 27 July 1997 with Jamil Chaudhuri, the Founder Manager of Bangladesh Television and a lexicographer working in Bangla Academy, Dhaka.

194. Jatin Sarkar, '*Pakistaner Janma-Mrityu Darshan*', p. 45.

195. Chakrabarty continued his task of Gandhian social reform in his locality and later became known as Trailokya 'Maharaj'. He wrote this autobiography at the age of 80. Trailokyanath Chakrabarty, *Jail-e Trish Bachhor*, p. 357.

196. Interview conducted on 24 January 1997 with Shaktibhuti Chaudhuri, a former Congress worker and a bookshop owner, Rajshahi.

197. A.M. Ahmed, *Amar Dekha Rajnitir Panchash Bachhor*, p. 269. The same reason behind Suhrawardy's choice of 'staying back' was of course given by Sheikh Mujibur Rahman, the most famous disciple of the former. He mentions in his autobiography that Suhrawardy wanted to be with the 'minority' Muslims in India in his mission to provide them as much moral and practical support as possible. Mujibur Rahman, *Asamapta Atmajibani* (Dhaka: The University Press, 2012), p. 82.

198. According to the 1951 Census of India, the first census of the independent country, the Muslims in West Bengal formed 19.85 per cent of the population as against 78.8 per cent Hindus.

199. In recent years, there has been a proliferation of Partition literature especially in the context of the Bengal border. To cite just a few: Haimanti Roy, *Partitioned Lives: Migrants, Refugees, Citizens in India and Pakistan, 1947–1965* (Delhi: Oxford University Press, 2012); Jayanti Basu, *Reconstructing the Bengal Partition: The Psyche under a Different Violence* (Calcutta: Stree Samya, 2013); Debjani Sengupta, *The Partition of Bengal: Fragile Borders and New Identities* (Cambridge: Cambridge University Press, 2016).

200. A.M. Ahmed, *Amar Dekha Rajnitir Panchash Bachhor*, p. 271.

201. Anisuzzaman, *'Amra Pakistan-e Elam'*, p. 54.

202. Mujibur Rahman, *Asamapta Atmajibani*, p. 79.

203. A.M. Ahmed, *Amar Dekha Rajnitir Panchash Bachhor*, p. 267.

204. A.M. Ahmed, *Amar Dekha Rajnitir Panchash Bachhor*, p. 267; Abul Kalam Shamsuddin, *Atit Diner Smriti*, p. 305.

205. A.K. Shamsuddin, *Atit Diner Smriti* (Dhaka: Naoroj Kitabistan, 1968), p. 306.

206. 'Nutan Rashtra Gathaner Dayitwo', *Millat*, June 1947 (12 Ashar 1354 BS). What appeared 'unthinkable' to the Bengali Muslims even in June 1947 became the reality in September 1947. The 'storm' nevertheless finally took place in less than a decade, in the form of the Language Movement of 1952.

207. Waliullah, *Yuga-Bichitra*, p. 530.

Conclusion

A brief comment on a few major characters of this book may be
helpful to indicate its central problematic. One among them is
Abul Kasem Fazlul Huq, arguably one of the most enigmatic
figures of colonial Bengal. He headed the Provincial Ministry of Bengal
twice, first time in an alliance with the Muslim League (1937–40), and
the next time in an alliance with the Hindu Mahasabha (1941–3). As
we know, these two parties were the most conservative faces of Muslim
and Hindu politics. However, Huq's real glory lay in his role of the chief
ideologue-cum-politician of a different party, a regional one—the KPP.
In the late 1930s, this party built itself around the praja movement,
championed the newly emerged Muslim middle-class interests, and
promoted popular politics rather successfully. It could not be dubbed
as conservative or 'communal', despite its reliance on religious–cultural
symbols of the Muslims in order to appeal to Bengal's peasant population, a major part of which happened to be Muslim.

Huq's strange political ventures indicate that although he was
by no means a Muslim hardliner, he had to undergo several trysts

with conservative politics during his political career. The question that naturally arises is: What lay behind his desperation to do so? We may also remember that when, in 1940, Mohammad Ali Jinnah selected him as the premier of the largest Muslim-majority province of India to present the first draft of the 'Pakistan' resolution at the Lahore session of the All India Muslim League, Huq (in)famously declared that he was a 'Muslim first and a Bengali afterwards'. Yet, this statement was immediately followed by his vocal demand for Bengal's provincial autonomy. This is again perplexing. Why should a Bengali Muslim leader, keen on presenting himself as Muslim, even think of being vocal on Bengal's autonomy in an all-India Muslim congregation, where being a part of the larger Muslim collective was supposedly the most cherished dream?

The answer perhaps lies here: Huq was torn forever between his twin loyalties, his Muslim-ness and Bengali-ness. But the social, cultural, and political realities around him made this internally split identity utterly questionable, even unfeasible. He was, therefore, constantly in search of a workable solution. That is why he never had an easy relationship with the AIML leadership, always suspecting that Bengal's interests were being neglected, even jeopardized by the League's activities. He also proved himself 'much too Bengali', hence, particularly untrustworthy in the eyes of the League High Command. At the same time, he never found it possible to make his position acceptable to the Hindu-dominated nationalist parties, who found him 'much too Muslim' for their all-inclusive, 'unitarian' nationalism. Consequently, he had to remain an outsider to either of the mainstream parties of the Hindus and the Muslims, both kept under the tight control of their all-India commands. All this was because he was looking for a 'different nation' where his Muslim self would be given a rightful place with his Bengali national self.

In the history of Bengali nationalism, Huq's story appears very important, and also, very representative. Here was a Bengali Muslim in a continuous quest for his own 'national' identity in an exceedingly challenging backdrop. Nationalism was an inevitable ideological abode for the anti-colonial quest of freedom and self-assertion. But, as a creed, it also bore deep strains of bondage and intolerance within itself. Its natural imperative to go beyond its internal differences had the danger of disrespecting such differences within itself. For many Bengali Muslims such as Huq, any idea or politics of 'nation' in colonial India inevitably meant an intense ideological and political struggle to do justice to his own self and priorities. They, however, never treaded along an identical line of political ideology, and had severe disagreements on the possible models of nation. But, significantly, for most of them, this struggle was perhaps easier on the regional plane than on the all-India plane, because their strong regional belongingness used to make them more 'Bengali Muslims' than 'Muslims'. Their views of a regional nation, as a result, often turned out to be an anathema to the larger uni-centric nations, either 'India', or the 'Pakistan' conceived by Jinnah. In the end, however, the 'different nationalisms' of the Bengali Muslims did not, and could not, find a headway in the politics of the subcontinent.

Were these 'different nationalisms' embraced only by the Bengali Muslims? The history of political ideology of Bengali Hindu nationalists would definitely suggest otherwise. Their thoughts and actions also provided divergent visions of nation, only to be ignored, marginalized, or submerged by the singular overarching version of nationalism in their course. Chittaranjan Das may be considered as a case in point. One of the most celebrated leaders of colonial Bengal, he envisaged a 'nation' which digressed fundamentally from that of his other contemporary and later colleagues. His 'nation' had an unabashedly 'Bengali' character, a regional core, which he thought would serve well as an immediate platform of belonging, as well as a stepping stone for any supra-regional identity. Moreover, his regional nation sought to accommodate the disparate interests of various communities and groups within the region through an unusual agenda of proportional representation of various communities as early as in the early 1920s. He displayed immense courage and conviction to stake his entire political capital, because this 'new' vision of nation, far from being unitary, served as a direct endorsement of the internal 'differences' within the nation. Only naturally, Das's project, the Bengal Pact, although reassuring to the Bengali Muslims, elicited most acrimonious criticism either for jeopardizing Bengali Hindu interests or for damaging the politics of a united and indivisible nation.

Das's Pact was born out of his acutely felt need of establishing 'unity' among the Bengali Hindus and Bengali Muslims on the basis of the principle of 'parity'. This objective, according to Das, was difficult to achieve through a nationalism which did not respect 'difference'. The same problematic surfaced in the writings and speeches of another towering ideologue of the time, Rabindranath Tagore. Like Das, Tagore also strongly believed that any alternative nationalist politics must foreground the task of local self-generation. However, Tagore would have a serious disagreement with Das on how to accommodate difference in approaching the national tasks so envisaged. A strong believer in universal humanism, Tagore used to value and preserve 'differences', but was never ready to give way to the smaller 'divisive' identities either in the political life or in the cultural expressions of the 'nation'. He not only refused to view the 'national' as an aggregation of communities/identities, but often even wished to downplay the need to highlight the markers of difference beyond a certain point. Having shared the same liberal respect for 'difference', Tagore's vision of nation was thus significantly different from Das's, and their divergences pointed to a fundamental crisis lying at the heart of the most liberal doctrine of the 'nation'. It is significant that this viewpoint of Tagore was to be partly shared by the later political stalwarts of Bengal, Subhas Chandra Bose and Sarat Chandra Bose, although both of them, in fact, used to consider themselves political disciples of Chittaranjan Das.

The contestations over 'nation' were not restricted to the realms of ideology alone. When Sarat Bose, as the leader of Bengal Congress and one of the most liberal 'Hindu' voices at that time, engaged in debates with Fazlul Huq in the Legislative Assembly over the real political issues of community representation and job reservation, it was proved that all those seemingly abstract notions discussed above imparted, in reality, a very deep and challenging political message in a Muslim-majority but Hindu-dominated province of India. Their sharp arguments and eventual Hindu–Muslim deals showed that the problem of difference was never exercised in ideological abstraction, but was a very real practical concern for a diverse regional reality.

It is in the context of this problem of difference that the regional version of 'Pakistan', formulated by leaders like Fazlul Huq, Abul Hashim, and H.S. Suhrawardy must be appraised. Little attention is usually directed to the contestations over the ideal of 'Pakistan', especially its regionally distinctive outlines in Bengal. But it was Huq who thought and wrote rather unswervingly that any conceivable 'Pakistan' could not be effected *solely* on the basis of religion, which might transform it into a mullah nation. In his imagination, such a perilous oversight could only be avoided if the cultural basis of 'Purba Pakistan' (East Pakistan, that is, in those days, Bengal) was taken as the abiding guideline. Abul Hashim, the Bengal Muslim League stalwart in the 1940s, asserted in no unambiguous terms, 'This is where Purba Pakistan has its own claims to nationhood. We are different from the Hindus, as well as from the Muslims of other regions.' With the most confident articulation of the Bengali Muslim 'nation', and the boldest refutation of Jinnah's 'two-nation theory', he was insistent on an autonomous Bengal where Bengali Muslims would rightfully form the majority. Suhrawardy, the premier of the Provincial Ministry after

Huq, was in complete agreement with Abul Hashim and lent himself to becoming the great defender of a 'united, sovereign' Bengal. The long history of championing the cause of provincial autonomy in a Muslim-majority province, starting from the pro-partition enthusiasts of 1905 to the upholders of the regional ideal of Pakistan in the 1940s, indeed contained robust visions of some 'different' nation, conceptualized in an unconventional and, more importantly, unacknowledged way.

The strong Bengali Muslim identity represented in these robust visions was, understandably, at tremendous odds with the totalitarian claims of the Muslim League led by Jinnah. Why the latter kept the idea of Pakistan so vague and under-explained might be partly comprehensible from this inherent contradiction between the Bengali Muslim interests and the pan-Indian Muslim interests, as espoused by Jinnah. It was clearly more important to mobilize a solid and unanimous 'Muslim' support behind the cause of Pakistan than to deal with its internal particularities. However much he insisted on the 'single Muslim identity' within India as constitutive of 'one whole nation', there was no such thing as that. At the same time, there could not be anything called 'Muslim communalism' all over the country, as opposed to 'Indian nationalism'. Muslim interests and Muslim voices were much too diverse and much too full of internal contestations than all-India leaders like Jinnah or Bengali ideologues like Maulana Akram Khan would have liked it to be. The story of Bengal Muslims, as traversed in this book, points towards this blatant reality of multiple strands within a community. It would therefore make a lot more sense if we seek to recover the internal texture of the Bengali Muslim voices, and assess their comparative strength vis-à-vis the all-India versions of 'Muslim nation' and the 'Indian nation' than to simply juxtapose a 'Muslim communalism' against an 'Indian nationalism'. This book has attempted to do so. It has marked out their deep, idiosyncratic 'Bengali-ness', even spontaneously reflected in their so-called 'Muslim' self-expressions and their readiness to forge a 'national' belonging shared with the Bengali Hindus if their interest and identity were given their due centrality. These Muslims, usually dismissed as 'communalists', indeed found identities to be multiple, layered, and co-existing, and their ideal nation a platform from where they would be able to address these multiple identities.

A similar dissection of the Bengali Hindu voices has also been mapped out in this book. Examples of Das and Tagore show how there could be no such overarching category as 'Hindu' or 'Bengali Hindu' nationalism. Not only among the leading figures, but across the broad spectrum of the emerging political and civil societies of colonial Bengal, debates, dialogues, and contestations were so frequent and extensive as well as so fundamentally political that they defy any such essentialization. While most of them failed to negotiate with the spirit of self-assertion of different communities like the Muslims or the low-castes, such failure cannot and must not be depicted as a brazenly chauvinist communalism of the Bengali Hindus. The crisis was much deeper, more structural, and therefore, in a way, more inescapable. The liberal nationalists like Tagore, the Boses, or many other thinkers or proponents of Bengali/Indian nationalism were the most liberal champions of an accommodative nation. Yet the true nature of the problem of difference in an age of incipient representative democracy and competitive politics often eluded their liberal principles. This was perhaps because they used to consider democracy to be meaningful only in its ability to represent the individual on a collective plane of the nation. Any middle ground between the individual and the nation was thought to be regressive in nature. On more than one occasion, such liberal predicaments came to be dangerously akin to majoritarian orthodoxy or intolerance, like in the case of Hindu reactions against the Bengal Pact, against the Communal Award, or against the regional creed of Pakistan. But it still remains an extremely important task to explode the allegedly singular category of Hindu communalism in order to recover these very different strands of thought, even when they were seemingly upholding the same cause of a unitary nation. Even while on certain occasions the Congress voices and the Hindu Mahasabha voices became appallingly close, it would be enormously misleading to brand Congress as just another quintessential keeper of Hindu communalism. Bengal's exploration of various nationalisms demonstrates that many liberals of this era were still in quandary on the question of finding a suitable compromise between their respect for 'differences' and their desperately felt need of transcending the same 'differences' for the sake of a 'nation'.

Integrally linked to this 'Bengal chapter' in the history of the nationalist thought was the centre–region dialectics of the nation. The very regionally and linguistically rooted Bengali Muslim nationalism was fundamentally incompatible with the unitary image of India or Pakistan; so it favoured an independent, unified subcontinent with a good measure of regional autonomy. With an emphatic rejection of the Congress claims of representing 'all' communities and classes in India, they believed that India needed, as Abul Hashim verbalized, 'majority-led provincial representative governments' rather than 'uni-centric Congress rule from Delhi'. Underlining the vacuousness of the dominating discourse of

Indian nationalism, a 'liberal nationalist' Bengali Muslim writer called S. Wajid Ali articulated the 'misfortune of Bengal' for being trapped in the unreasonableness of that dominant discourse. In the mid-1940s, it seemed to him that 'a Bengali nationalism would be far more acceptable to the people of this province than the vague ideal of Indian nationalism, the foundations of which are more or less mythical and, in the factual world, largely a creation of the administrative genius and Military efficiency of the British race.' Even on the eve of Partition, large numbers of Bengali Muslims and their leaders were willing to stay back and work together with Hindus if their legitimate concerns were met in a federal political structure. Of course, this idea of autonomous regions in a loose national federation was simply antithetical to the 'inclusive nationalism' of the Congress or the League. It is remarkable that this remained so even when many Bengali Hindu nationalists since the swadeshi days up to 1947 had consistently pointed out that a federal structure would be best-suited to India's interests as well as Bengal's realities. Chittaranjan Das and Bepinchandra Pal being the two most important protagonists of federal India, many other leaders and common advocates of nationalism believed in the exceptional relevance of federalist principles in this country. Pal verbalized this relevance in strong terms when he said, 'Federation is the way to democratic Swaraj,' and, 'Real democracy does not grow under unitary system of government. It is also against our spirit and traditions which have been essentially federal in character.' Significantly, no serious attention was paid to this idea of 'federal India' by the fervent believers in one strong and unified 'nation', rushing themselves to dismiss any alternative national claim by terming them either manifestly 'communal' or hopelessly 'provincial'.

All this asserts that, in colonial Bengal, 'being different' might have also signified a 'different belongingness' to the 'nation', as opposed to either dissociation from or antagonism against it. History has proved that an indifference or intolerance towards 'being different' has had to pay a high price. Instead of labelling 'differences' as a clash between the 'nation' and the 'anti-nation', they must be taken as a point of entry for the many possibilities of a nation. The variegated discourse of different anti-colonial nationalisms in Bengal, therefore, is strikingly poignant. It unveils an important message: the ultimate victory of a particular view of 'nation' must not reduce its 'other' visions into permanent footnotes of history.

Looking at postcolonial India, it is hard to miss the increasingly glaring dangers of an excessive focus on a prescribed 'Indian'-ness. The nation-state is still denying its citizens the much-needed space for other identities, and still seeks to impose an unwarranted singularity of identity on them. Historians, among others, have been urging a reconsideration of this perilous creed of 'oneness'. I hope, by explaining some of the tensions that beset nationalism in colonial Bengal, the arguments developed in this book underline why a greater accommodation of differences is an absolute priority in the subcontinental life.

Bibliography

Manuscript Sources

Official Records

General Miscellaneous Proceedings, 1905–7, Government of Bengal. West Bengal State Archives, Kolkata.

Home Political (Confidential) Files, including Fortnightly Reports from District Magistrates and Divisional Commissioners, Government of Bengal. West Bengal State Archives, Kolkata.

Home Political Files, Government of Bengal. West Bengal State Archives, Kolkata, and National Archives of Bangladesh, Dhaka.

Home Political Proceedings, Government of India. National Archives of India, New Delhi.

Home Public Proceedings, Government of India. National Archives of India, New Delhi.

Public and Judicial Proceedings, Government of India. India Office Records, British Library, London.

Private Papers

India Office Records, British Library

Governor Burrows Collection.
Governor Casey Collection.
Governor Herbert Collection.
Governor Lytton Collection.
Lord Curzon Collection.
Marquess of Zetland Collection.
Secretary of State Birkenhead Collection.

Printed Sources

Official Publications

Annual Report on Indian Papers.
Bengal and East Bengal and Assam District Gazetteers.
Bengal Legislative Assembly Proceedings.
Bengal Legislative Council Proceedings.
Census of India, 1911, 1921, 1931, and 1941; volumes on Bengal.
List of District Associations and Anjumans, 1907–37.
Report of the Indian Statutory Commission. London: His Majesty's Stationery
    Office (HMSO), 1930.
Report on Native Papers in Bengal.
Report on the Native-owned English Newspapers in Bengal.

Newspapers and Periodicals

Al Eslam
Amrita Bazar Patrika
Anandabazar Patrika
Atmashakti
Azad
Bande Mataram
Bangabani
Bangali
Bangashree
Bangiya Mussalman Sahitya Patrika
Barisal Hitaishi
Basana

Basumati
Bengalee
Bhandar
Bharati
Dhaka Prakash
Dinajpur Patrika
Islam Darshan
Ganavani
Hindustan Times
Kagoj
Krishak
Manashi O Marmabani
Millat
Moslem Chronicle
Moslem Pratibha
Muhammadi
Muslim Hitaishi
Nabanur
Nabya Bharat
Narayana
Nur Al Iman
Prabasi
Prachi
Sahitya
Sahitya Patra
Sammilan
Saogat
Satyabarta
Shikha
Soltan
Star of India
The Mussalman
The Statesman
Viswamitra

Select Oral Interviews: West Bengal and Bangladesh

Anisuzzaman, former professor of Bengali Literature, Dhaka University. Interview conducted on 26 July 1997.

Gopal Chandra Chakrabarty, former Congress member of Krishnanagar and a Gandhian social worker. Interview conducted on 20 August 1997.

Jamil Chaudhuri, founder-manager of Bangladesh Television and lexicographer in Bangla Academy, Dhaka. Interview conducted on 27 July 1997.

Jatin Sarkar, former professor at Mymensingh College. Interview conducted on 18 July 1997.

Kamaluddin Ahmed Khan, former Muslim League worker in Chittagong and former advocate at Bangladesh Supreme Court. Interview conducted on 15 February 1997.

Mahbub Alam Chaudhuri, former Communist Party worker in Chittagong and former lawyer in Dhaka. Interview conducted on 28 February 1997.

Mustafa Nurul Islam, former League activist of Calcutta and former professor of Bengali Literature, Dhaka University. Interview conducted on 28 July 1997.

Shaktibhuti Chaudhuri, former Congress worker and bookshop owner in Rajshahi, Bangladesh. Interview conducted on 24 January 1997.

Secondary Sources

Bengali: Books, Pamphlets, Speeches, Memoirs, and Tracts

Abdullah, Muhammad. *Nawab Salimullah: Jiban o Karma*. Dhaka: Islamic Foundation, 1986.

Ahmed, Abul Mansur. *Amar Dekha Rajnitir Panchas Bachhor*. Dhaka: Maola Brothers, 1970.

———. *Pak Banglar Culture*. Dhaka: Ahmad Publishing House, 1966.

Ahmed, Amanatulla. *Amar Desh*. Dhaka, 1920.

Ahmed, Basiruddin Mahmud. *Nehru Report o Bangiya Muslim Samaj*. Calcutta, 1928.

Ahmed, Kamruddin. *Bangali Madhyabitter Atmabikas*. Dhaka: Naoroj Kitabistan, 1975.

Ahmed, Muzaffar. *Amar Jiban o Bharater Communist Party*. Calcutta: National Book Agency, 1977.

———. *Prabandha Sankalana*. Calcutta: Saraswati Library, 1970.

Ahmed, Nur. *Bangiya Mussalman*. Calcutta, 1905. Vernacular Tracts, India Office Library.

Anisuzzaman. *Muslim Banglar Samayik Patra, 1831–1930*. Dhaka: Bangla Academy, 1969.

———. 'Amra Pakistan-e Elam'. In *Deshbhag: Binash o Binirman*, edited by Madhumoy Pal. Calcutta: Gangchil Publishers, 2011.

Anonymous. *Bangadeshiya Hindu Musalman*. Calcutta, 1911. Vernacular Tracts, India Office Library.

———. *Swadeshi Andolana*. Calcutta, 1906. Vernacular Tracts, India Office Library.

———. *Swaraj Pratishthar Bichitra Namunai Hatabhagya Mussalmaner Durgati*. Calcutta, 1923. Vernacular Tracts, India Office Library.

———. *League o Muslim Rajniti*. Dhaka, 1946. Preserved at the Dhaka University Library.

Ansari, Muhammad Shadat Ali. *Munshi Mohammad Mehraullah.* Jessore: Barandipara, 1983.

Bandyopadhyay, Brajendranath, ed. *Parishat Parichay.* Calcutta: Bangiya Sahitya Parishat, 1939.

Bandyopadhyay, C.R., ed. *Rabindra-Prasanga: Anandabazar Patrika,* vol. 2. Calcutta: Ananda Publishers, 1995.

Bandyopadhyay, Jogendranath. *Lanchhiter Samman.* Calcutta, 1905. Vernacular Tracts, India Office Library.

Bandyopadhyay, Kamakhyacharan. *Hindu Dubilo.* Calcutta, 1923.

Bandyopadhyay, Kshitishchandra. *Hak Katha.* Calcutta, 1921.

Basu, Arun Kumar. *Nazrul Jibani.* Calcutta: Pashchimbanga Bangla Academy, 2000.

Basu, Subhaschandra. *Netaji: Samagra Rachanabali,* 11 volumes. Calcutta: Ananda Publishers, 1992.

Bhadra, Gautam. 'Chintar Chalchitra: Bangiya Sahitya Parishat, 1300–1330 B.S.' In *Bangiya Sahitya Parishat Patrika,* edited by Satyajit Chaudhuri, pp. 39–68. Calcutta: Bangiya Sahitya Parishat, 1997.

Bhattacharya, Digindranarayan. *Hindur Nabajagaran.* Calcutta, 1931.

Bhowmik, Madanmohan. *Jater Name Bajjati.* Calcutta, 1924.

Biswas, Dilipkumar. 'Bangiya Sahitya Parishat: Uttar Swadhinata Parbo'. In *Sahitya Parishat Patrika,* centenary volume. Calcutta: Bangiya Sahitya Parishat, 2007.

Biswas, Raicharan. *Jatiya Jagaran.* Calcutta: Kuntaleen Press, 1921.

Biswas, Kalipada. *Yukta Banglar Shesh Adhyay.* Calcutta: Orient Company, 1966.

Biswas, Kashigopal. *Desher Abastha o Byabastha.* Calcutta, 1923.

Biswas, Raicharan. *Jatiya Jagaran.* Calcutta: Kuntaleen Press, 1921.

Chakrabarty, Trailokyanath. *Jail-e Trish Bachhor o Pak-Bharate-er Swadhinata Sangram.* Calcutta: Anushilan Bhavan Trust Board, 1981.

Chattopadhyay, Gita. *Bangla Swadeshi Gan.* Delhi: Delhi University Press, 1987.

Chattopadhyay, Sarat Chandra. *Sarat Rachanabali,* centenary edition, vol. 3. Calcutta: Sarat Samiti, 1976.

Chaudhuri, Kazi Motahar Hussain. *Sanskriti Katha.* Dhaka: Sarnakal Prakasani, 1958.

Das, Chittaranjan. 'Banglar Katha'. In *Deshbandhu Rachana-samagra,* edited by Manindra Datta and Haradhan Datta. Calcutta: Tuli Kalam, 1977.

———. *Desher Katha.* Calcutta, 1922.

———. Presidential Speech at the Bengal Provincial Conference. Faridpur, 2 May 1925.

Das, Naresh Chandra. *Namasudra Sampraday o Bangladesh.* Calcutta, 1961.

Dasgupta, Hiralal, ed. *Swadhinata Sangram-e Barisal.* Calcutta: Sahitya Samsad, 1972.

Dasgupta, Kedarnath, ed. *Shikshar Andolana.* Calcutta, 1905. Vernacular Tracts, India Office Library.

Dastidar, Purnendu. *Swadhinata Sangrame Chattagram.* Chittagong: Boi-ghar, 1970.

Datta, Aswinikumar. *Aswinikumar Rachanasambhar.* Calcutta: Adhyayan, 1969.

———. *Aswinikumar Rachana-Sangraha,* edited by Badiur Rahman. Calcutta: Jibananda Academy, 1992.

De, Amalendu. *Pakistan Prastab o Fazlul Huq.* Calcutta: Paschimbanga Rajya Pustak Parishad, 1989.

De, Sureshchandra. *Swadhinata Sangrame Nawabgunj.* Calcutta: Jijnasa, 1971.

Deushkar, Sakharam Ganesh. *Bangiya Hindu Jati Ki Dhwanshonmukha?* Calcutta, 1910. Vernacular Tracts, India Office Library.

Devi, Sarala. *Jibaner Jharapata.* Calcutta: Saraswati Press, 1957.

Dutta, Upendranath. *Desher Ahwan ba Ashahayog Andolane Narir Sthan o Kartabya.* Barisal, 1921. Vernacular Tracts, India Office Library.

Ghosh, Baridbaran, ed. *Rabindranath o Bepinchandra Pal.* Calcutta: Puthi Patra, 2010.

Ghosh, Nitapriya, ed. *Hindu–Mussalman Samparka: Rabindra-rachana Sangraha.* Calcutta: Mrittika, 2003.

Ghosh, Pratapchandra. *Bangadhip-Parajay,* vol. 2. Calcutta: published by Gopalchandra Ghosal, 1884; Pratibha Library centenary edition, edited by Shaktisadhan Mukhopadhyay, Calcutta: Sarsuna Association, 2006.

Ghosh, Sankha. *Bhinno Ruchir Adhikar.* Calcutta: Talpata Publishers, 2010.

Ghosh, Semanti, ed. *Deshbhag: Smriti Ar Stabdhata.* Calcutta: Gangchil Publishers, 2008.

———. *Swajati Swadesher Khonje.* Calcutta: Dey's Publications, 2012.

Gupta, Nalinikanta. *Bharate Hindu o Mussalman.* Calcutta, 1925.

Gupta, Sureshchandra. *Mahatma Aswinikumar.* Barisal, 1928; reprint, Calcutta: Seba Samiti, 1984.

Haldar, Mahananda. *Guruchand Charit.* Calcutta, 1943.

Hamid, Abdul. *Sashan Sanskare Gramya Mussalman.* Mymensingh, 1921.

Hamidi, Muhammad Mayezuddin. *Jatiya Kalyan.* Dhaka, 1924.

Hashim, Abul. *Draft Manifesto of the Bengal Muslim League, 1945.* Dhaka: Society for Pakistan Studies, 1970.

Hossain, Abul. *Abul Hossain-er Rachanabali,* edited by Abdul Kadir. Dhaka: Barnamichhil, 1968.

———. *Bangali Mussalmaner Shiksha Samasya.* Calcutta, 1928.

———. *Moslem Culture.* Calcutta, 1928.

Hossain, Mir Mosharraf. *Mussalmaner Bangala Shiksha.* Calcutta, 1903.

———. *Mussalmaner Bangala Shiksha,* edited by Abul Ahsan Chauduri. Dhaka: Suchipatra, 2006.

Hossain, Mohammad Golam. *Bangadeshiya Hindu Musalman.* Calcutta, 1911. Vernacular Tracts, India Office Library.

Huq, Mohammed Mozammel. *Jatiya Mangal.* Calcutta, 1910. Vernacular Tracts, India Office Library.

Hussain, Golam Gilani Nurul. *Moslem Jati-tattwa.* Calcutta, 1926.

Hussain, Mainuddin. *Khilafat Prasanga.* Calcutta: Saraswati Library, 1921.

Hussain, Maulana Abul. *Bangali Mussalmaner Shiksha Samasya.* Dhaka, 1928.

Ilias, Akhtaruzzaman. *Khoaab-nama.* Calcutta: Naya Udyog, 1996.

Iqbal, Bhuiyan, ed. *Selections from The Mussalman, 1906–1908.* Calcutta: Papyrus, 1994.

Islam, Mustafa Nurul. 'Munshi Jamiruddin'. *Bangla Academy Journal* 14, no. 4 (December 1968–April, 1969): 1–21.

———. *Samayikpatre Jiban o Janamat: 1901–1930.* Dhaka: Bangla Academy, 1977.

Islamabadi, Maniruzzaman. *Maniruzzaman Islamabadi Rachanabali.* Dhaka: Bangla Academy, 1986.

Jajabor [Binoy Mukhopadhyay]. *Drishtipat.* Calcutta: New Age, 1946.

Khan Yusufji, Naosher Ali. *Bangiya Mussalman.* Calcutta, 1315 BS. Vernacular Tracts, India Office Library.

Khan, Mujibur Rahman. *Pakistan.* Calcutta: Mohammadi Press, 1942.

Maiti, Upendranath. *Proceedings of Presidential Speech at Bengal Provincial Conference.* Calcutta, 1920.

Majumdar, Nepal. *Bharate Jatiyata, Antarjatikata ebong Rabindranath*, 5 volumes. Calcutta: Chatushkon Private Limited, 1971.

Majumdar, Satyendranath. *Gandhi o Chittaranjan*, Ashahayog Granthabali, Pustika 4. Calcutta: Saraswati Library, 1921.

Mostafa, Golam. *Pakistani Gan.* Dhaka, 1962.

Mukhopadhyay, Haridas and Uma Mukhopadhyay. *Upadhyay Brahmabandhab o Bharatiya Jatiyatabad.* Calcutta: Firma K.L. Mukhopadhyay, 1961.

Rahman, Habibur. *Swadhinatar Marmakatha.* Dhaka, 1926.

Rahman, Mujibur. *Asamapta Atmajibani.* Dhaka: The University Press, 2012.

Rashid, Muhammad Abdur. *Mussamander Arthasankat o Tar Protikar.* Calcutta, 1936.

Rasul, Golam. *Khilafat-nama.* Calcutta, 1921.

Ray, Debes. *Barishal-er Jogen Mandal.* Calcutta: Dey's Publication, 2010.

Ray, Matilal. *Hindu Jagaran.* Calcutta: Calcutta Burrabazar Hindu Sabha, 1935.

Ray, Saratkumar. *Mahatma Aswinikumar.* Calcutta, 1926.

Safi, M. *Swaraj-pathe Hindu-Mussalman.* Calcutta, 1921.

Sarkar, Jadunath. *Presidential Address, Uttarbanga Sahitya Sammilan*, session 4. Maldaha, 1911. Calcutta: India Press, 1912.

Sarkar, Jatin. 'Communist Party o Krishak Sabha'. *Pakistaner Janma Mrityu Darshan.* First published in *Kagaj*, Mymensingh, 1997. Reprint, Dhaka: Jatiya Sahitya Prakash, 2005.

Sarkar, Ramlal. *Nabya Bangalir Kartabya.* Calcutta: Nabya Bharat Press, 1906.

Seal, Narendrakumar, ed. *Swadeshi Sangeet.* Calcutta, 1907.

Sen, Asok. *Rajnitir Pathakrame Rabindranth.* Calcutta: Visva-Bharati, 2014.

Sen, Dineshchandra. *Mymensingh Gitika.* Calcutta: Calcutta University Publications, 1923.

Sen, Girishchandra. *Atma-jiban.* Calcutta, n.d.

Sensharma, Dakshinaranjan. *Ekata*. Calcutta, 1926.

Shamsuddin, Abu Zafar. *Atma-smriti*. Dhaka: Jatiya Sahitya Prakashani, 1989.

Shamsuddin, Abul Kalam. *Atit Diner Smriti*. Dhaka: Naoroj Kitabistan, 1968.

Shil, Kedarnath. *Swaraj-sadhanay Narasundar Samaj*. Sirajganj, 1925.

Siddiqi, Abu Bakr. *Khilafat Andolan Paddhati*. Barisal, 1921.

Singha, Dineshchandra. *Noakhalir Mati o Manush*. Calcutta: Gyan Prakashan, 1992.

Sobhan, Abdus. *Hindu Mussalman*. Dhaka, 1909.

Sripantha. 'Ekhono Shona jai Challish-er Garjan'. In *Sat Dashak: Samakal o Anandabazar*. Calcutta: Ananda Publishers, 1992.

Tagore, Rabindranath. *Bangla Sabda-tattwa*. Calcutta: Visva-Bharati, 1984.

———. 'Bhashar Katha'. *Bangla Sabda-tattwa*. Calcutta: Visva-Bharati, 1984.

———. *Rabindra Rachanabali*, Sulabh Sangskaran, 18 volumes. Calcutta: Visva-Bharati, 1986.

———. *Samajchinta*, edited by Satyendranath Ray. Calcutta: Granthalay Private Limited, 1984.

Thakur, Kshiticharan. *Tomra ar Amra*. Calcutta: Kuntalin Press, 1919.

Trivedi, Ramendra Sundar. *Ramendra Rachana Sangraha*. Calcutta: Bangiya Sahitya Parishat, 1964.

Umar, Badruddin. *Banga-bhanga o Samprodayik Rajniti*. Calcutta: Chirayata Publishers, 1987.

Wadud, Kazi Abdul. *Hindu Mussalmane Birodh*. Calcutta, 1936.

Waliullah, Mohammad. *Yuga-Bichitra*. Dhaka: Maola Brothers, 1967.

Yusufji, Naosher Ali Khan. *Bangiya Mussalman*. Calcutta, 1907. Vernacular Tracts, India Office Library.

English: Books and Articles

Adhikari, Gangadhar. *Pakistan and National Unity*. Mumbai: People's Publishing House, 1943.

———. 'Report to Central Committee of the CPI'. *Communist* 2, no. 9 (July 1940).

Adnan, Shapan. 'Fazlul Haq and the Bengali Muslim Leadership, 1937–43'. *Bangladesh Historical Studies* 1, no. 1 (1976): 1–18.

Ahmed, Abul Mansur. *End of a Betrayal and the Restoration of the Lahore Resolution*. Dhaka: Khosroz Kitab Mahal, 1975.

Ahmed Jamil-ud-din, ed. *Speeches and Writings of Mr. Jinnah*, vol. 2. Lahore: Shaikh Muhammad Ashraf, 1964.

Ahmed, Kamruddin. *A Social History of Bengal*. Dhaka: Pragati Publishers, 1970.

Ahmed, Rafiuddin. *The Bengali Muslims, 1871–1906*. Second edition, New York: Oxford University Press, 1988.

———, ed. *Understanding the Bengal Muslims: Interpretive Essays*. Delhi: Oxford University Press, 2001.

Ahmed, Sufia. *Muslim Community in Bengal, 1884–1912*. Dhaka: Oxford University Press, 1974.

Aiyar, Sana. 'Fazlul Huq, Region and Religion in Bengal: The Forgotten Alternative, 1940–43'. *Modern Asian Studies* 42, no. 6 (2008): 1213–49.

Alavi, Hamza. 'Peasants and Revolution'. In *Imperialism and Revolution in South Asia*, edited by Kathleen Gough and Hari P. Sharma. New York, 1973.

Ali, S. Wajid. 'A Talk on Tea'. In *Bengalees of Tomorrow*. Calcutta: Das Gupta and Co. Publishers, 1945.

Ambedkar, B.R. *Pakistan or the Partition of India*. Bombay: Thacker and Co., 1946.

Anderson, Benedict. *Imagined Communities: Reflections on the Origin and Spread of Nationalism*. London: Verso, 1983.

Anisuzzaman. *Creativity, Reality and Identity*. Dhaka: International Center for Bangladesh Studies, 1993.

Appadurai, Arjun. 'Disjuncture and Difference in the Global Cultural Economy'. In *Modernity at Large: Cultural Dimensions of Globalization*. Minneapolis: University of Minnesota Press, 1996.

Azad, Maulana Abul Kalam. *India Wins Freedom*. Delhi: Orient Blackswan, 2014.

Bandyopadhyay, Anirban. 'Orchestrating a Signal Victory: Ambedkar, Mandal and the 1946 Constituent Assembly Elections'. In *Invoking Ambedkar: Contributions, Receptions, Legacies*, edited by Biswamoy Pati. Delhi: Primus Books, 2014.

Bandyopadhyay, Sekhar. *Caste, Culture and Hegemony: Social Dominance in Colonial Bengal*. New Delhi: SAGE, 2004.

———. *Caste, Politics and the Raj: Bengal, 1872–1937*. Calcutta: K.P. Bagchi, 1990.

———. *Caste, Protest and Identity in Colonial India: The Namasudras of Bengal, 1872–1947*. London: Oxford University Press, 2011.

———. 'Rabindranath Tagore's Nation and Its Outcasts'. *Harvard Asia Quarterly* 15, no. 1 (2013): 28–33.

———, ed. *Bengal: Rethinking History: Essays in Historiography*. Delhi: Manohar, 2001.

Banerjea, Surendranath. *A Nation in Making: The Reminiscences of Fifty Years of Public Life*. 1925; reprint, Bombay: Oxford University Press, 1963.

Basu, Buddhadev. *An Acre of Green Grass*. 1948; new edition, Calcutta: Papyrus, 1982.

Bayly, C.A. *The Origins of Nationality in Modern South Asia*. Delhi: Oxford University Press, 1998.

Bengal Anti-Communal Award Movement—A Report. Calcutta: Secretaries Bengal Anti-Communal Award Committee, 1936.

Bhabha, Homi, ed. *Nation and Narration*. London: Routledge, 1990.

Bhattacharya, Sabyasachi. *The Defining Moments in Bengal, 1920–1947*. Delhi: Oxford University Press, 2014.

————, ed. *The Mahatma and the Poet: Letters and Debates between Gandhi and Tagore, 1915–1941*. Delhi: National Book Trust, 1997.

————. *Rabindranath Tagore: An Interpretation*. New Delhi: Penguin Books India, 2011.

Bose, Krishna. *An Outsider in Politics*. Delhi: Penguin Books India, 2008.

Bose, Neilesh. *Recasting the Region: Language, Culture and Islam in Colonial Bengal*. New Delhi: Oxford University Press, 2014.

————. 'Purba Pakistan Zindabad: Bengali Visions of Pakistan,1940–47'. *Modern Asian Studies* (March 2013): 1–36.

Bose, Sarat Chandra. *I Warned My Countrymen: Being the Collected Works (1945–1950) of Sarat Chandra Bose*. Calcutta: Netaji Research Bureau, 1996.

————. *Sarat Chandra Bose: Commemoration Volume*. Calcutta: Sarat Bose Academy, 1982.

Bose, Sisir Kumar, ed. *The Voice of Sarat Chandra Bose: Selected Speeches, 1927–41*. Calcutta: Netaji Research Bureau, 1979.

Bose, Subhas Chandra. *The Essential Writings of Netaji Subhas Chandra Bose*, edited by Sisir K. Bose and Sugata Bose. Delhi: Oxford University Press, 1997.

————. *Fundamental Questions of Indian Nationalism*. Calcutta: Netaji Research Bureau, 1970.

————. *The Mission of Life*. Calcutta, 1953.

————. *Netaji: Collected Works*, 12 volumes, edited by Sisir K. Bose and Sugata Bose. Calcutta: Netaji Research Bureau, 1985.

Bose, Sugata. *Agrarian Bengal: Economy, Social Structure and Politics, 1919–1947*. Cambridge: Cambridge University Press, 1986.

————. 'A Doubtful Inheritance: The Partition of Bengal in 1947'. In *The Political Inheritance of Pakistan*, edited by D.A. Low. London: Macmillan, 1991.

————. *His Majesty's Opponent: Subhas Chandra Bose and India's Struggle against Empire*. Cambridge: Harvard University Press, 2011.

————. 'Nation, Reason and Religion: India's Independence in International Perspective'. *Economic and Political Weekly* 33, no. 31 (1998): 2090–7.

————. 'The Spirit and the Form of an Ethical Polity: A Meditation on Aurobindo's Thought'. *Modern Intellectual History* 4, no. 1 (2007): 129–44.

Bose, Sugata, and Ayesha Jalal, eds. *Modern South Asia: History, Culture and Political Economy*. New Delhi: Oxford University Press, 1998.

————, eds. *Nationalism, Democracy and Development: State and Politics in India*. New Delhi: Oxford University Press, 1997.

Broomfield, J.H. *Elite Conflict in a Plural Society: Twentieth Century Bengal*. Berkeley: University of California Press, 1969.

————. 'The Forgotten Majority: The Bengal Muslims and September 1918'. In *Soundings in Modern South Asian History*, edited by D.A. Low. London: Weidenfield and Nicolson, 1968.

Chakrabarti, Asim Pada. *Muslim Identity and Community Consciousness: Bengal Legislative Politics, 1912–1936*. Calcutta: Minerva, 1995.

Chakrabarty, Bidyut. *The Partition of Bengal and Assam, 1932–1947*. London: Routledge, 2004.

Chakrabarty, Dipesh. *Habitaions of Modernity: Essays in the Wake of Subaltern Studies*. Chicago: University of Chicago Press, 2002.

———. *Provincializing Europe and the Postcolonial Thought and Historical Difference: Potential and Pitfalls of (Non-) Western Approaches to History*. Princeton: Princeton University Press, 2000.

Chandra, Bipan. *Communalism in Modern India*. New Delhi: Vikas Publishing House, 1984.

Chatterjee, Partha. 'Agrarian Relations and Communalism in Bengal, 1928–1935'. In *Subaltern Studies: Writings on South Asian History and Society*, vol. 1, edited by Ranajit Guha. Delhi: Oxford University Press, 1982.

———. *Bengal, 1920–1947: The Land Question*. Calcutta: K.P. Bagchi, 1984.

———. *Lineages of Political Society*. Delhi: Permanent Black, 2011.

———. *Nationalist Thought and the Colonial World: A Derivative Discourse?* London: Zed Publishers, 1986.

———. *The Nation and Its Fragments: Colonial and Post-colonial Histories*. Princeton: Princeton University Press, 1993.

———. 'The Second Partition of Bengal'. In *The Present History of West Bengal: Essays in Political Criticism*. Delhi: Oxford University Press, 1997.

Chatterjee, Srilata. *Congress Politics in Bengal, 1919–1939*. London: Anthem Press, 2002.

Chatterji, Joya. *Bengal Divided: Hindu Communalism and Partition, 1932–1947*. Cambridge: Cambridge University Press, 1994.

———. 'The Bengali Muslim: A Contradiction in Terms? An Overview of the Debate on Bengali Muslim Identity'. *Comparative Studies of South Asia, Africa and the Middle East* 16, no. 2 (1996): 16–24.

———. *Spoils of Partition: Bengal and India, 1947–1967*. Cambridge: Cambridge University Press, 2007.

Chattopadhyay, Gautam. 'The Almost Revolution: A Case Study of India in February 1946'. In *Essays in Honour of Prof. S. C. Sarkar*, edited by Barun De. Calcutta: People's Publishing House, 1976.

———. *Bengal Legislature in India's Struggle for Freedom, 1876–1947*. Delhi: People's Publishing House, 1984.

Chaudhuri, Keshab. *Calcutta: Story of Its Government*. Calcutta: Orient Longman, 1973.

Cohn, Bernard S. 'The Census, Social Structure, and Objectification in South Asia'. In *An Anthropologist among the Historians and Other Essays*. Delhi: Oxford University Press, 1987.

Collins, Michael. 'Rabindranath Tagore and Nationalism: An Interpretation'. Working Paper no. 42, *Heidelberg Papers in South Asian and Comparative Literature*. Heidelberg: South Asia Institute, University of Heidelberg, 2008.

Coupland, R. *Indian Politics, 1936–1942*. London: Oxford University Press, 1943.

Das, Durga, ed. *Sardar Patel's Correspondence, 1945–50*, vol 2. Ahmedabad: Navajivan Publishing Co., 1972.

Das, Suranjan. *Communal Riots in Bengal*. Delhi: Oxford University Press, 1991.

———. 'The "*Goondas*": Towards a Reconstruction of the Calcutta Underworld through Police Records'. *Economic and Political Weekly* 29, no. 44 (1994): 2877–83.

Das, Suranjan, and Jayanta K Ray. *The 'Goondas': Towards a Reconstruction of the Calcutta Underworld*. Calcutta: Firma KLM, 1996.

De, Amalendu. 'Fazlul Huq and his Reaction to the Two Nation Theory'. In *Islam in Modern India*, pp. 163–78. 2nd edition, Calcutta: Parul Prakashani, 2003.

———. 'The Social Thoughts and Consciousness of the Bengal Muslims in the Colonial Period'. *Social Scientist* 23, no. 4/6 (April–June 1995): 16–37.

Deshpande, Prachi. *Creative Pasts: Historical Memory and Identity in Western India, 1700–1960*. Delhi: Permanent Black, 2007.

Devji, Faisal. *Muslim Zion: Pakistan as a Political Idea*. London: Hurst & Company, 2013.

Dhulipala, Venkat. *Creating a New Medina: State Power, Islam, and the Quest for Pakistan in Late Colonial North India*. Cambridge: Cambridge University Press, 2015.

Faruqui, Ziya-ul-Hasan. *Deoband School and the Demand for Pakistan*. London: Ring House, 1963.

Freitag, Sandria. *Collective Action and Community: Public Arenas and the Emergence of Communalism in North India*. Berkeley: University of California Press, 1989.

Gallagher, John. 'Congress in Decline: Bengal 1930–39'. *Locality, Province and Nation: Essays on Indian Politics, 1870–1940*, edited by John Gallagher, Gordon Johnson, and Anil Seal. Cambridge: Cambridge University Press, 1973.

Gellner, Ernest. *Nations and Nationalism*. Oxford: Basil Blackwell, 1983.

Ghose, Aurobindo. 'More about Unity'. *Bande Mataram*, 7 September 1907.

———. 'The New Faith'. *Bande Mataram*, 1 December 1907.

———. *The Renaissance in India*. Chandernagore: Rameshwara and Co., 1927.

Ghosh, Shyamali. 'Fazlul Haq and Muslim Politics'. *International Studies* 13, no. 3 (July–September, 1974): 441–64.

Gilmartin, D. *Empire and Islam, Punjab and the Making of Pakistan*. Berkeley: University of California Press, 1988.

Gordon, Leonard A. *Bengal: The Nationalist Movement, 1876–1940*. New York: Columbia University Press, 1974.

———. *Brothers against the Raj: A Biography of Indian Nationalists, Sarat and Subhas Chandra Bose*. New York: Columbia University Press, 1990.

————. 'Divided Bengal: Problems of Nationalism and Identity in the 1947 Partition'. *Journal of Commonwealth and Comparative Politics* 16, no. 2 (1978): 136–68.

Goswami, Manu. *Producing India: From Colonial Economy to National Space.* Chicago: University of Chicago Press, 2004.

Greenough, Paul R. *Prosperity and Misery in Modern Bengal: The Famine of 1943–44.* New York: Oxford University Press, 1982.

Guha, Ranajit. 'On Some Aspects of the Historiography of Colonial India'. In *Subaltern Studies: Writings on South Asian History and Society,* vol. 1, edited by Ranajit Guha. Delhi: Oxford University Press, 1982.

Guhathakurta, P. *Bengali Drama: Its Origin and Development.* London: Kegan Paul & Co. Ltd, 1930.

Gupta, Dipankar. *Justice before Reconciliation: Negotiating a 'New Normal' in Post-Riot Mumbai and Ahmedabad.* New Delhi: Routledge, 2011.

Gupta, Swarupa. *Notions of Nationhood in Bengal: Perspectives on Samaj, c. 1867–1905.* Leiden: Brill, 2009.

Hasan, Mushirul. *A Nationalist Conscience: M.A. Ansari, the Congress and the Raj.* New Delhi: Manohar, 1987.

————, ed. *India's Partition: Process, Strategy and Mobilization.* Delhi: Oxford University Press, 1993.

Hashim, Abul. *In Retrospection.* Dhaka: Maola Brothers, 1998.

————. *Let Us Go To War.* 1945; reprint, Dhaka: Society for Pakistan Studies, 1970.

Hashmi, Taj-ul-Islam. *Pakistan as a Peasant Utopia: The Communalization of Class Politics in East Bengal, 1920–1947.* Boulder: Westview Press, 1992.

Hunter, W.W. *The Indian Mussalmans.* First edition 1871; reprint, Varanasi: Indological Book House, 1969.

Huq, A.K. Fazlul. *Memorable Speeches of Sher-e-Bangla,* edited by A.K. Zainul Abedin. Barisal: Al Helal, 1978.

Huq, Enamul. 'The Dream of Pakistan'. *Purba Pakistane Islam.* Rajshahi: Adil Brothers, 1948.

Jahir, Sajjad. 'Recent Muslim Politics in India and the Problems of National Unity'. *India and Contemporary Islam,* vol. 6. Simla: Indian Institute of Advanced Studies, 1971.

Jain, N.K. *Muslims in India: A Biographical Dictionary,* vol. 1. Delhi: Manohar Publications, 1983.

Jalal, Ayesha. 'Exploding Communalism: The Politics of Muslim Identity in South Asia'. In *Nationalism, Democracy and Development: State and Politics in India,* edited by Sugata Bose and Ayesha Jalal, pp. 76–103. Oxford: Oxford University Press, 1997.

————. 'Nation, Reason and Religion: The Punjab's Role in the Partition of India'. *Economic and Political Weekly* 33, no. 32 (1998): 2183–90.

————. 'Secularists, Subalterns and the Stigma of "Communalism"'. *Indian Economic and Social History Review* 33, no. 1 (1996): 93–103.

————. *Self and Sovereignty: Individual and Community in South Asian Islam Since 1850*. Delhi: Oxford University Press, 2000.

————. *The Sole Spokesman: Jinnah, The Muslim League and the Demand for Pakistan*. Cambridge: Cambridge University Press, 1994.

————. 'Striking a Just Balance: Maulana Azad as a Theorist of Trans-National Jihad'. *Modern Intellectual History* 4, no. 1 (2007): 95–107.

Jones, Reece. 'Whose Homeland? Territoriality and Religious Nationalism in Pre-Partition Bengal'. *South Asia Research* 26 no. 2 (2005): 115–31.

Kabir, Humayun. *Muslim Politics 1906–47 and Other Essays*. Calcutta: Firma K.L. Mukhopadhyay, 1969.

Kaviraj, Sudipta. 'The Imaginary Institution of India'. *Subaltern Studies: Writings on South Asian History and Society*, vol. 7, edited by Partha Chatterjee and Gyanendra Pandey. Delhi: Oxford University Press, 1993.

————. *The Invention of Private Life: Literature and Ideas*. New York: Columbia University Press, 2015.

Kripalani, Krishna. 'Bande Mataram and Indian Nationalism'. *Visva-Bharati News* 10, no. 4 (October 1937): 31.

Lelyveld, David. *Aligarh's First Generation: Muslim Solidarity in British India*. Princeton: Princeton University Press, 1978.

Majumdar, Sohini. 'A Different Calcutta: INA Trials and Hindu–Muslim Solidarity in 1945–46'. In *Calcutta: The Stormy Decades*, edited by Tanika Sarkar and Sekhar Bandyopadhyay. Delhi: Social Science Press, 2015.

Manjapra, Kris. 'Knowledgeable Internationalism and the Swadeshi Movement, 1903–21'. *Economic and Political Weekly* 47, no. 42, special issue (20 October 2012).

Minault, Gail. *The Khilafat Movement: Religious Symbolism and Political Mobilization in India*. New York: Columbia University Press, 1982.

Mitra, H.N., ed. *Indian Annual Register, 1940*, 2 vols. 1940; reprint, Delhi: Gyan Publishing House, 1990.

Mitra, N.N., ed. *Indian Annual Register, 1941*, 2 vols. Calcutta: Annual Register Office, 1941.

————, ed. *Indian Annual Register, 1943*, 2 vols. Calcutta: Annual Register Office, 1943.

————, ed. *Indian Annual Register, 1946*, 2 vols. Calcutta: Annual Register Office, 1947.

Momen, Humaira. *Muslim Politics in Bengal*. Dhaka: Sunny House, 1972.

Moon, Penderel, ed. *Wavell: The Viceroy's Journal*. London: Oxford University Press, 1973.

Mukherjee, Rudrangshu. *Nehru and Bose: Parallel Lives*. New Delhi: Penguin, 2014.

Mukherji, Haridas, and Uma Mukherji. *The Origins of National Education Movement*. Calcutta: National Council of Education, 1957.

Murshid, Tazeen. *The Sacred and the Secular: Bengal Muslim Discourses, 1871–1977*. Dhaka: University Press Limited, 1996.

Nair, Neeti. *Changing Homelands: Hindu Politics and the Partition of India.* Delhi: Permanent Black, 2011.

Nakazato, Nariaki. 'The Role of Colonial Administration, "Riot Systems", and Local Networks during the Calcutta Disturbances of August 1946'. In *Calcutta: The Stormy Decades*, edited by Tanika Sarkar and Sekhar Bandyopadhyay. Delhi: Social Science Press, 2015.

Nandy, Ashis. *The Illegitimacy of Nationalism: Rabindranath Tagore and the Politics of Self.* Delhi: Oxford University Press, 1994.

Overstreet, Gene, and Marshall Windmiller. *Communism in India.* Berkeley: University of California Press, 1959.

Pal, Bepinchandra. 'The Bedrock of Indian Nationalism II'. *Bande Mataram*, 12 June 1908.

———. *Character-Sketches.* Calcutta: Yugayatri, 1909.

———. *Nationality and Empire: A Running Study of Some Current Indian Problems.* Calcutta: Thacker, Spink and Co., 1917.

———. *The Presidential Address: Bengal Provincial Conference Session, Barisal.* Calcutta, 1921.

———. *Swadeshi and Swaraj: The Rise of New Patriotism.* Calcutta: Yugayatri, 1958.

———. *Swaraj, What Is It?* Calcutta: Vadhwani and Co., 1922.

Pandey, Gyanendra. *The Construction of Communalism in Colonial North India.* Delhi: Oxford University Press, 1990.

———. *Remembering Partition: Violence, Nationalism and History of India.* Cambridge: Cambridge University Press, 2001.

Philips, C.H., ed. *Evolution of India and Pakistan.* London: Oxford University Press, 1962.

Pirzada, S., ed. *Foundations of Pakistan*, vol. 1. Karachi: National Publishing House Ltd., 1970.

Pollock, Sheldon, ed. *Literary Cultures in History: Reconstructions from South Asia.* Berkeley: University of California Press, 2003.

Prabhu, R.K., and Ravindra Kelekar, eds. *Truth Called Them Differently: Tagore–Gandhi Controversy.* Ahmedabad: Navajivan Publishing House, 1961.

Rai, Mridu. *Hindu Rulers, Muslim Subjects: Islam, Rights, and the History of Kashmir.* Princeton: Princeton University Press, 2004.

Rashid, Harun-or. *The Foreshadowing of Bangladesh: Bengal Muslim League and Muslim Politics, 1936–47.* Dhaka: Asiatic Society of Bangladesh, 1987.

Ray, Rajat K. *The Felt Community: Commonality and Mentality before the Emergence of Indian Nationalism.* Delhi: Oxford University Press, 2003.

———. 'Masses in Politics: The Non-cooperation Movement in Bengal 1920–22'. *Indian Economic and Social History Review* 11, no. 4 (1974): 343–410.

———. *Nationalism, Modernity and Civil Society: The Subalternist Critique and After.* Presidential Address, Indian History Congress, Calicut, 2007. Visva-Bharati: School of Historical Studies, 2007.

————. *Social Conflict and Political Unrest in Bengal, 1875–1927*. Delhi: Oxford University Press, 1984.

Ray, Rajat K., and Ratnalekha Ray. 'Zamindars and Jotedars: A Study in Rural Politics in Bengal'. *Modern Asian Studies* 9, no. 1 (1975): 81–102.

Raychaudhri, Tapan. *Perceptions, Emotions, Sensibilities: Essays on India's Colonial and Post-Colonial Experiences*. Delhi: Oxford University Press, 1999.

Robinson, Francis. *Separatism among Indian Muslims: The Politics of the United Provinces' Muslims, 1860–1923*. Cambridge: Cambridge University Press, 1974.

Roy, Anwesha. 'Calcutta and Its Struggle for Peace: Anti-Communal Resistance, 1946–47'. In *Calcutta: The Stormy Decades*, edited by Tanika Sarkar and Sekhar Bandyopadhyay. Delhi: Social Science Press, 2015.

Roy, Asim, ed. *Islam in History and Politics: Perspectives from South Asia*. New York: Oxford University Press, 2008.

————. *The Islamic Syncretistic Tradition in Bengal*. Princeton: Princeton University Press, 1983.

Roy, Haimanti. 'A Partition of Contingency? Public Discourse in Bengal 1946–47'. *Modern Asian Studies* 43, no. 6 (2009): 1355–84.

————. *Partitioned Lives: Migrants, Refugees, Citizens in India and Pakistan, 1947–1965*. New Delhi: Oxford University Press, 2012.

Sarkar, Chandi Prasad. *The Bengali Muslims: A Study in Their Politicization, 1912–1929*. Calcutta: K.P. Bagchi, 1991.

Sarkar, Sumit. *Beyond Nationalist Frames: Post-modernism, Hindu Fundamentalism and History*. Bloomington: Indiana University Press, 2002.

————. *Modern India, 1885–1947*. Madras: Macmillan, 1983.

————. *The Swadeshi Movement in Bengal, 1903–8*. New edition, Delhi: Permanent Black, 2010.

————. *Writing Social History*. Delhi: Oxford University Press, 1997.

Sarkar, Tanika. *Bengal 1928–1934: The Politics of Protest*. Delhi: Oxford University Press, 1987.

Sartori, Andrew. 'Abul Mansur Ahmed and the Cultural Politics of Bengali Pakistanism'. In *From the Colonial to the Post-colonial, India and Pakistan in Transition*, edited by Dipesh Chakrabarty, Rochona Majumdar, and Andrew Sartori. New York: Oxford University Press, 2005.

Seely, Clinton. 'A Muslim Voice in Modern Bengali Literature: Mosharraf Hossain'. In *Understanding the Bengali Muslims: Interpretive Essays*, edited by Rafiuddin Ahmed. Dhaka: University Press Limited, 2001.

————. *A Poet Apart: A Literary Biography of the Bengali Poet Jibanananda Das*. Newark: University of Delaware Press, 1990.

Sen, Amartya. 'On Interpreting India's Past'. In *Nationalism, Democracy and Development: State and Politics in India*, edited by Sugata Bose and Ayesha Jalal. Delhi: Oxford University Press, 1997.

Sen, Dineshchandra. *Ramtanu Lahiri Fellowship Speech*, published as the Introduction in *Mymensingh Gitika*. Calcutta: Calcutta University, 1923.

Sen, Dwaipayan. "'No Matter How, Jogendranath Had to Be Defeated": Scheduled Caste Federation and the Making of Partition in Bengal, 1945–47'. *Indian Economic and Social History Review* 49, no. 3 (2012): 321–64.

————. 'Representation, Education, and Agrarian Reforms: Jogendranath Mandal and the Nature of Scheduled Caste Politics, 1937–1943'. *Modern Asian Studies* 48, no. 1 (2014): 77–109.

Sen, Shila. *Muslim Politics in Bengal, 1937–47*. Delhi: Impex India, 1976.

————. 'Some Aspects of Muslim Politics in Bengal, 1937–1946 and Fazlul Huq'. *Bangladesh Historical Studies* 1 (1976): 19–76.

Sen, Sunil. *Agrarian Struggle in Bengal, 1946–47*. Calcutta: People's Publishing House, 1972.

Sengupta, Debjani. *The Partition of Bengal: Fragile Borders and New Identities*. Cambridge: Cambridge University Press, 2016.

Shah, Muhammed. *In Search of an Identity: Bengali Muslims, 1880–1940*. Calcutta: K.P. Bagchi, 1996.

Sheikh, Farzana. *Community and Consensus in Islam: Muslim Representation in Colonial India, 1860–1947*. Cambridge: Cambridge University Press, 1989.

Sircar, N.N. *Bengal under Communal Award and Poona Pact*. Calcutta, 1936.

Tagore, Rabindranath. 'The Call of Truth'. In *English Writings of Rabindranath Tagore*, vol. 3: *A Miscellany*, pp. 412–25. New Delhi: Sahitya Akademi, 1921.

————. *Nationalism*. London: Macmillan, 1950.

Talbot, Ian. *Provincial Politics and the Pakistan Movement: The Growth of the Muslim League in North-West and North-East India, 1937–47*. Karachi: Oxford University Press, 1988.

Talukdar, Mohammad H.R., ed. *Memoirs of H.S. Suhrawardy*. Dhaka: University Press Limited, 1987.

Vajpeyi, Ananya. *Righteous Republic: The Political Foundations of Modern India*. Cambridge: Harvard University Press, 2012.

Veer, Peter Van der. *Religious Nationalisms: Hindus and Muslims in India*. Berkeley: University of California Press, 1994.

Wadud, Kazi Abdul. *Bengali Literature*. New Delhi: Sahitya Academy, 1959.

Washbrook, David. 'The Rhetoric of Democracy and Development in Late Colonial India'. In *Nationalism, Democracy and Development: State and Politics in India*, edited by Sugata Bose and Ayesha Jalal. Delhi: Oxford University Press, 1997.

Zutshi, Chitralekha. *Languages of Belonging: Islam, Regional Identity and the Making of Kashmir*. London: Hurst and Co., 2004.

Index

About the Author

Semanti Ghosh is Senior Assistant Editor at *Anandabazar Patrika*, Kolkata, India. She did her master's in modern history at the University of Calcutta, and earned her PhD in Modern South Asian History from Tufts University, Medford, Massachusetts, USA. Her interests range from history of nationalism and the Partition of India, literary and cultural history, and cultural theory to postcolonial history. She has edited and authored books on Partition and nationalism in Bengali.